BUSTED

A Whistleblower's Guide
to the War on Drugs

or

Drugs Are Legal In
America's Republics

by Kurt St. Angelo, J.D.[1]

BUSTED – A Whistleblower's Guide to the War on Drugs
Subtitled: Drugs Are Legal In America's Republics

To contact author Kurt St. Angelo, visit: http://www.drugsarelegal.com

Library of Congress Cataloging in Publication Data
St. Angelo, Kurt, 1955 -
        BUSTED – A Whistleblower's Guide to the War on Drugs; subtitled
Drugs Are Legal in America's Republics – Kurt St. Angelo
                p. cm.
        Includes bibliographical references and index
        ISBN: 9780692486788
                1. Law, natural and constitutional, 2. Law, controlled substances

ISBN 9780692486788
LCCN 2015911230

Back cover photo by Eric Barnes

I dedicate this book to my wonderful family,
but particularly to the memory of my parents
Beatrice and Gordon St. Angelo.

Table of Contents

continued...

Part 2:
Statutory law
arguments

Preface

This book is an exposé about the illegality of America's war on drugs. An exposé is a revelation about something discreditable, [3] which is a perfect adjective to describe the drug war.

This book will show that drug possession is both a natural and statutory right in most states, and that drug dealing is regulated – not criminally prohibited. I encourage all American attorneys to try to refute the above sentence or, for that matter, any sentence in this book.

The above sentence is true for one very simple reason: that within America's fifty states, the federal and state governments are to operate as republics. This means that if we can define America's special republican form of government – and we shall – then we will know how American governments are to treat not only most things, but also everyone within their borders. Although the book accomplishes this task also, it specifically serves to answer the legal question: How do America's republics properly treat drugs?

Given the nature of a republican form of government, which is promised to American states in the U.S. constitution, suffice here to say that a republic would not wage a war against some of its own citizens. Given that law exists in a republic to secure the near-equal rights of citizens, a war against disfavored ones would not be appropriate. Instead, as we shall see, such a war is either tortious (wrongful) or criminal.

What inspired (yet could have prevented the writing of) this book was a personal legal matter of mine, called *St. Angelo v. State of Indiana* (2012), [4] wherein I challenged the power of Indiana's judicial courts to adjudicate speeding infractions. I took my appeal all the way to the U.S. Supreme Court.

In that matter I argued 1) that administrative law courts of the Commissioner of the Indiana Bureau of Motor Vehicles have primary, subject matter jurisdiction over speeding infractions in Indiana, which is the power to adjudicate them, and 2) that trial courts in Indiana's judicial branch, to which I was falsely summoned and tried, do not have such power. This is similar to one of the main arguments in this book – that mere drug possession and dealing are not subject to U.S. or state judicial trial courts.

This argument is tantamount to saying that the state of Indiana has been falsely trying both traffic infractions and drug matters in the wrong courts, i.e., judicial courts. Such courts have no authority to try non-cases or regulatory matters, the latter which are subject to administrative law courts in Indiana's executive branch. The state's adjudications of traffic and drug matters in judicial courts are violations of such courts' subject matter jurisdiction over injury, violations of the separation of powers doctrine of Indiana's constitution, as well as substantive due process violations for all defendants.

The reason that my traffic infraction matter is relevant to this book is because it was to be a test case for a future challenge – by me or anyone else – against the illegality of the war on drugs. At least in Indiana, both traffic infractions and the drug war are falsely enforced in judicial courts.

A successful challenge to the enforcement of traffic infractions would have eventually doomed the use of judicial courts in Indiana to enforce the phony "misdemeanors" and "felonies" upon which the war on drugs is based. Consequently, challenging a speeding ticket was a perfect alternative to me getting busted with disfavored drugs in order to personally challenge the misuse of judicial courts in the illicit drug war.

I will spare you the details of this appeal until much later in this book. However, while I was involved in the appellate process, I did not realize that my challenge to judicial courts' subject matter jurisdiction over infractions was really a challenge to a *de facto* non-republic that has been falsely installed throughout the United States. [5]

In fact, subsequent to the appeal, and not until I was in the middle of writing this book, did I realize that my fight over jurisdiction was actually a fight to restore the republican form of government. [6] What I really seek to achieve with this book is to not only help end the war on drugs, but to get America's republics back on track.

As we shall see, America's judicially-waged war on drugs cannot operate under a republican form of government, and the drug war's mere existence – along with other evidence – is proof that Americans have lost their republics. As we shall also see, these republics can be regained if officials merely enforce laws, but particularly criminal laws, properly. This is because most statutes are written – however cryptically and deviously – to be constitutional. Thus, if officials can understand and follow these laws by staying within their delegated powers, then their actions will be republican.

But the fact is: Indiana and U.S. officials have not stayed within their granted powers and have acted extra-constitutionally. This is because they do not understand and follow the traffic and drug statutes, which are written to be republican. As this book shows, they follow a law that exists mostly in their minds – and based mostly on what they have been told to believe.

We know this to be true because, when pressed for answers – as I pressed officials for answers in my traffic infraction appeal – they have no real positive (written) law to show for their actions. Likewise, their drug war exists – not because of America's drug laws – but in spite of them.

I have known this fact for at least a dozen years. Thus, when I started writing this book on August 16, 2012, I had a vague idea about that which I was writing. I had read the Indiana Controlled Substances Act (CSA) and the Indiana Administrative Orders and Procedures Acts (AOPA) several times by then, and I knew that my U.S. Supreme Court argument, which was based on statutory and constitutional law, also applied to the false enforcement of drug laws.

However, I had no idea when I started to write this book 1) that I would find natural law to be the basis of statutory criminal law, which concept was not taught to me in law school, and 2) that lawyers' proper challenges to courts' subject matter jurisdiction over drugs and other *malum prohibita* could largely restore America's republican form of government. This book presents these concepts in aggregate, but the information (and the revelations about republican government) came to me quite randomly, the dates of which I luckily recorded in the endnotes.

Very ironically, I attribute all of these realizations to the authors of America's drug statutes. Their cryptic work made me think really hard and taught me how criminal and administrative law are to operate under America's republican form of government. This is information that no student should graduate from an American law school without knowing, but which nearly all likely do. As we shall see, the war on drugs would not exist if attorneys knew the proper separation of America's two police powers.

My teaching approach is to go from simple to complex, general to specific, and concrete to abstract. [7] I normally will introduce a concept with a brief statement and follow-up by describing it more thoroughly later.

I tried to write this legal book so that more than just attorneys can understand it. The book would be harder to read if it was not for my libertarian friend Cindy Kirkpatrick, who expertly edited about a third of it.

I try to make each sentence count, but there is no need to get bogged down with any single one of them. In fact, when sentences stop making sense, as they occasionally do even with me, this is a sign that your mind is getting tired, and that it is time to take a break. This book requires a lot of concentration and is best to read with a fresh mind.

If the law is "one" from all its sides, as I herein contend, then everything that I write about criminal and administrative law should be consistent and not contradicted. It should be in perfect harmony.

Although this may sound unbelievable, particularly to attorneys, I have read nothing substantive which contradicts any of the legal premises, citations or conclusions that I share in this book. As we shall see, the only things that seem to contradict this information are judicial exaggerations of legislative power, which we discuss – indeed refute – in chapter 10.

This means that there is literally nothing of value that I have found in the law of America's republics that accounts for the incarceration of people for merely possessing or selling drugs except 1) for the misrepresentations of law found in the CSAs themselves, which is a subject of chapters 17 – 23 and 26 – 29, and 2) for the act's improper enforcement by government officials, which is the topic of almost all of the book's other chapters.

For example, when I quote the Indiana and U.S. Supreme Courts as emphatically saying that one must allege an injury to invoke judicial authority, the reader will find nothing in the Indiana or U.S. constitutions, statutes and judicial case law that says anything otherwise. Nothing!

Yet the entire war on drugs inexplicably operates in contradiction of this and other seemingly incontrovertible rules of law and logic. As we shall see, this occurs because government officials do not know and follow the law – whether it be in the form of constitutions, case law or statutes.

It is impossible to see governments' improper enforcement of their drug laws without knowing how jurisdiction – or power – is to be distributed and exercised within the United States according to state and federal constitutions. The title of this book refers to drugs, but the book is really about legislative and subject matter jurisdiction – and the separation of powers (or jurisdictions) – among America's four varieties of sovereigns.

Briefly, these sovereign categories are 1) the states, 2) Congress legislating as a republic toward the states, 3) Congress legislating over the federal areas, and 4) individual sovereigns. All of America's Controlled Substances Acts (CSAs) are true to and cognizant of the separation of power between each of these four sovereigns.

As well, all criminal legislation applicable in America's republics is consistent with the idea that individuals grant government some of their power, including criminal power, but not all of their power. The nation's Founding Fathers reserved authority for individuals over the exercise of their natural rights, including self-defense, and built a law jurisdiction within the judicial branch to secure these rights for all people.

Thus, one cannot read any republican criminal legislation without acknowledging the role of each of the four sovereigns. Because this concept is not taught in law schools, government officials have been unable to properly read criminal and regulatory legislation, such as the state and U.S. CSAs, which acknowledge the authority of each relevant sovereign.

This lack of knowledge is at the core of the false enforcement of America's drug laws, of the law's misrepresentation to the public, of the false application of judicial jurisdiction, and of the breakdown in American jurisprudence, which is the science of law. Without this knowledge, everything we once believed about our drug laws and the righteousness of government with regard to drugs has been a fantasy, like believing in Santa Claus.

Far from violating people's rights to possess and use drugs, America's positive (written) law supports these rights. Otherwise the written laws would be unconstitutional. Thus, there is nothing real about the drug war except for its ignorance of law, its brute force and its hocus-poke us. The war on drugs is as if every government official and every attorney involved in it has signed a Santa clause – promising to believe the unbelievable.

Believing in the hoax of Santa Claus is just a dry run for believing in the war on drugs and the righteousness of a non-republican form of government. The natural process called logic that children use during grade school to determine that Santa does not pilot a sleigh behind flying reindeer is the same process that Americans can employ to discover the giant hoax called drug prohibition, which is a gross misrepresentation of American law that is not to be believed.

What is to be believed is this: that within America's republics, drugs are not criminally prohibited, drug commerce is regulated and individuals have natural rights to acquire and possess any kind of property.

In spite of this benign thesis, this book could be quite unpopular with government officials who have falsely been treating drug possession and commerce as crime. To these detractors, I have one initial response: Show us your law!

This book demonstrates that government officials have nothing to show on paper – in positive (written) law – and that their legal and moral authority for the judicially-waged war on drugs exists only in their heads, based mostly on what people have falsely told them.

Kurt St. Angelo
Indianapolis, Indiana
September, 2015
Revised April, 2017

Part 1:
Natural law and constitutional law arguments

Summary: America's republican form of government features two police powers: criminal prohibition and regulation. These two separate police powers operate in separate branches of government, in separate judicial jurisdictions, and over different kinds of persons and subject matter.

Prohibition operates criminally. Regulation operates administratively, or non-criminally. Prohibition is enforced exclusively in the judicial branch. Regulation is enforced primarily in the executive branch. Prohibition operates in the judicial jurisdiction called law. Regulation operates in equity.

Prohibition enforces the law of the natural sovereign. Regulation enforces the positive law of a legislative sovereign. Prohibition operates over natural persons. Regulation operates over artificial persons, such as commercial enterprises.

Prohibition has subject matter jurisdiction over injury or violations of natural right. Regulators adjudicate the legal right to engage the public in commerce. Prohibition offers such law remedies as compensation, fines and incarceration. Regulation offers equitable remedies such as forfeiture and injunction.

The Supreme Court in *Ohio v. Helvering* (1934) told us that the police power with regard to commerce is regulatory. All commerce, including disfavored drug dealing, is subject to regulation – not prohibition.

Criminal prohibition applies only to that which is *malum in se* (inherently wrong) or to that which is placed into the criminal law jurisdiction of judicial courts by constitutional amendments. Because this criminal jurisdiction excludes all commerce (except for slavery, which is *malum in se*), then the commerce in drugs is regulated in equity. While equity does not include the power to incarcerate drug dealers, it nonetheless includes the power to shut down and enjoin disfavored drug dealing.

1
"And to the republic..."

America's four types of sovereigns

Welcome to this unconventional law book. If you are an attorney, this book will give you a completely different view of American law than what we leaned in law school. If you are a U.S. citizen, this is likely the first book that you will read to explain the meaning of your citizenship under America's republican form of government.

Although this book focuses on America's drug war, it is really about restoring America to a republican form of government. Hopefully each page will show you how resplendent America's republican law really is. Almost every day of writing I would discover something new about it that tickled me as an art lover, for it is truly a work of art.

Unfortunately, it is a piece of art that has been woefully defaced and hidden away in the proverbial vaults of America's law libraries. [8] I will be taking it out, dusting it off, polishing it up, and showing you both its brilliance and relevance.

The premise of this book is that the law with regard to drugs in America is good and constitutional, and has never really changed, but that this good law is neither understood nor followed by government officials. These officials necessarily misunderstand, misrepresent and violate the controlling statutory law on drugs, which are the states' and federal Controlled Substances Acts (CSAs), because they have not read them properly or sufficiently. As well, they do not understand how American criminal law distributes power between four categories of American sovereigns.

A sovereign is that which has ultimate authority over a particular subject matter. *Black's Law Dictionary* defines a sovereign as "a person, body, or state in which independent and supreme authority is vested." [9]

The categories of American sovereigns are 1) state republics, 2) the U.S. congress legislating as a republic with regard to the fifty state republics, 3) the U.S. congress legislating over its federal areas and territories, and 4) individuals within the state republics. We will address and see the roles and powers of each of these sovereigns within the book's first nine chapters.

The power of these four sovereigns is called their jurisdiction. Jurisdiction means power. As the U.S. Supreme Court beautifully wrote in *Yick Wo v. Hopkins* (1886), "(L)aw is the definition and limitation of power." [10]

This book is about defining the law so that jurisdiction between each of America's four sovereigns, and their branches, is understood. These sovereigns' respective powers are carved out and secured in America's constitutions and reflected in America's constitutional statutes.

As we shall see, one must actually know *a priori* the legislative jurisdiction of each sovereign before being able to properly read and understand almost all legislation. For example, one must know the supreme law – i.e., state and U.S. constitutions – before being able to understand the federal and state Controlled Substances Acts (CSAs).

The CSAs include provisions for each of these sovereigns. Readers must know how and where the four sovereigns exercise their powers, which rules are defined by constitutions, in order to make sense of the CSAs.

For instance, state drug laws may list law enforcers' regulatory powers intermixed with their judicial powers. This fudges these two police powers. Thus, law enforcers and criminal defense attorneys must know the distinctions between administrative and judicial power in order to properly read the state drug laws and to carry out their jobs, which they have not.

Likewise, they need to know the distinctions between the law jurisdiction of judicial courts and their equity jurisdiction, which this book addresses in the next chapter. If law enforcers and defense attorneys do not know the differences between law and equity, then there is no way to prevent or defend against a state's improper enforcement of its CSA.

As well, the U.S. CSA does not tell readers that its administrative law provisions apply within the fifty states, and that its criminal law provisions apply only in the District of Columbia and in other federal areas. Thus, in order to read and understand the U.S. CSA properly, a reader must know *a priori* that Congress legislates over drugs in two sovereign capacities, and that these sovereigns operate in two separate territorial areas.

On one hand, Congress legislates over the fifty state republics as a republic would. Article IV, Section 4 of the U.S. constitution requires it to guarantee a republican form of government to the states. On the other hand, Congress legislates over the federal areas in its plenary authority granted at Article I, Section 8, Clause 17 and Article IV, Section 3, Clause 2

If the reader does not know this, which hardly anyone seems to, then there is no way to properly read the U.S. CSA and to properly react to its false enforcement. The national war on drugs exists because government officials and defense attorneys are not familiar with these distinctions – and with the proper distribution of power – in America's constitutions. Because of this, they have been unable to properly read the U.S. and states' CSAs.

Thus, because the separation of all of governments' powers is defined by state and U.S. constitutions, which are the supreme law in the United States, a reader must know *a priori* how constitutions distribute power to properly read and enforce either the federal or state drug laws. This is where the education and abilities of government officials and defense attorneys have broken down.

The first consideration in determining jurisdiction is to determine which sovereign is in charge. Although the separation of powers doctrine in state constitutions refers to separating power between the branches of government, the primary separation of powers is that between sovereigns.

The first rule of jurisdiction is that only one sovereign may legislate or adjudicate over any physical space or activity. There is room for only one sovereign on the head of a pin, so to speak. So if the pin prods or pricks, legally speaking, then these must be the acts of only one of the sovereign authorities within the U.S.

For example, state republics are sovereign over most crimes that occur within their land areas. Their legislatures prescribe crimes and their judicial courts adjudicate crimes that occur within the states' borders. A crime that occurs within Indiana, for example, is subject to the law of Indiana as the sovereign – not to the law of Ohio. Thus, there is generally only one legislative and adjudicative sovereign over any particular behavior in an American state or territory, and absent cases of concurrent federal-state jurisdiction, all criminal behavior that occurs within America falls under the rightful authority of only one of America's four sovereigns.

Understanding sovereignty and jurisdiction is like sorting mail, and is crucial to understanding America's drug laws. Conceptually, all behavior in America fits into the mail slot of one of these American sovereigns, each which has their own criminal jurisdiction. Knowing which sovereign is in charge is the key to understanding America's drug laws and how the drug war is waged unlawfully.

That there is only one sovereign authority over any particular subject matter raises the second rule of jurisdiction: that criminal jurisdiction is generally territorial (or spatial). (This is in contrast to state and federal regulatory jurisdiction over commerce and foreigners, which run concur-rently.) This means that judicial criminal power is generally exercised only within a specific area. "Criminal law is usually territorial," reads a report from the Congressional Research Service. Usually crime "is a matter of the law of the place where it occurs." [11]

The main exceptions to this are 1) that Congress may legislate over several crimes that occur within the states which relate to its enumerated powers in Article I of the U.S. constitution, 2) that Congress has criminal authority over offenses against the United States that occur within the states, and that the U.S. claims criminal authority over offenses against U.S. citizens that occur within foreign countries, [12] all three topics of which are discussed in chapter 9. Otherwise, all criminal jurisdiction in America is territorial (or spatial).

My path to conflict resolution

The true essence of the republican form of government is that it is orderly, harmonious and consistent. Statutory law is to be consistent and harmonious with our constitutions. Substantive and procedural rights walk hand-in-hand. Criminal law is to be consistent with natural law.

Thus, there is no reason for any criminal law to ever express disharmony with what comes naturally to people, which is that all people naturally pursue their own forms of happiness. Says the Declaration of Independence, all law is to serve our life, liberty and our natural pursuit of happiness.

The judicial branch of America's republics secures this harmony by enforcing the power that constitutions apportion among America's four sovereigns. There is disharmony and dissonance when the judicial branch does not properly do this job.

Likening disharmony to a bad odor, I am most sensitive to the disharmony between government propaganda and reality. Whether by fascination or neurosis, I am motivated to either resolve the anomalies that I see in the administration of law, and that I hear parroted by the American news media, or if not, to at least distill them to their least common dishonest or misguided denominators, as I do here with the stench of the war on drugs.

If America's republics follow the state and federal constitutions, which are based on natural law and the harmony of Nature, then within America's republics there is never any reason for the administration of criminal law to ever seem in disharmony with people's honest and peaceful state. When the criminal law appears to be at odds with honesty and peace, as is America's war on drugs, then something is likely afoul with the exercise of government.

Anomalies in the law are red flags that the powers of America's republics are being misused. They are telltale signs that the nation's harmonious criminal laws are being improperly enforced.

Thus, anomalies are my first smell test for the misuse of power that I call bad government. There are numerous anomalies and disharmonies in the administration of our drug laws – the malodorous effects of bad government so to speak. They have revealed the misuse of the People's power by government officials, and have put me on the path to understand our drug laws and to write this book.

The first anomaly that I can remember came to me back in 1971 when I was in high school, when the Controlled Substances Act was being superficially discussed in the media, and when many people were getting busted for marijuana (cannabis) possession under Indiana's prior law. I remember wondering out loud with friends why it took a constitutional amendment to outlaw alcohol, but that it took only a statute to outlaw marijuana.

A second anomaly occurred in the summer of '73 when a friend's car – with me and three others in it – was stopped by police officers, and all of us ignorantly consented to be searched for drugs. Unfortunately I had the only drugs in our possession – two hits of my favorite allergy medicine Chlor-trimeton.

At the time, I had terrible allergies which included asthma. I carried those drugs with me to prevent myself from suffocating. Suffice to say that I was threatened with arrest for not carrying my prescription container. (Indiana no longer requires a prescription to purchase Chlor-trimeton.)

It was then that I asked myself: What kind of government requires me to carry around its permission slips? And what kind of government can capriciously enslave me for doing what I do to get my needs met, or to stay alive? The answer to both questions is the same: a screwed-up, illegitimate government – the same one which most Americans blindly sanction with their votes instead of facing it with pitchforks.

Another anomaly presented itself when I attended college in California and took a wonderful botany class geared to plant classification. The California state flower happens to be in the Poppy Family. It looks like and is related to the poppy from which opiates are derived. At about the same time I learned from my botany textbook that marijuana is in the order of Rosales, which also includes roses, strawberries, raspberries, blackberries. apricots, almonds and figs.

This logically raised several odd anomalies in my mind, such as: How can the government outlaw one type of Rosales and one type of Poppy, but not others? And for that matter, how can government prohibit any type of rose or poppy? Would it not make more sense to prohibit poison ivy?

Another anomaly has been that home narcotics makers go to jail while officers of pharmaceutical companies that manufacture narcotics do not. If making and selling narcotics is a crime, how can the state grant permission to pharmaceutical companies to commit crimes?

In other words, if neither a home narcotics maker nor a pharmaceutical company officer is licensed to make the drug, would they both be criminal or neither be criminal for making and selling narcotics?

(The answer is neither. In America's republics, 1) only slave businesses are criminally prohibited, 2) other businesses are regulated, and 3) natural persons are not subject to incarceration except for their crimes or for contempt of court. Contempt powers are inherent in judicial power. They are the means by which judicial courts enforce their rightful orders.)

The above anomaly is like that of prosecuting people for non-crimes in judicial courts that require at least the commission of a tort or breach of contract for their subject matter jurisdiction. A tort is a private or civil wrong or injury. [13] If a tort or a breach of contract is the minimum criteria to get into a judicial court, how then do these same courts try people for drug "crimes" that do not amount to torts (or even breaches of contract)?

As well, Indiana Code 35-48-3-3(i) says that the Indiana Attorney General may use judicial courts to enjoin unwanted drug dealing. This means that a judicial court may order unwanted drug making and dealing to stop. Assuming that drug making and dealing were crimes, and that drug dealers are to be prosecuted for these crimes, why would the Indiana legislature grant authority to the Indiana Attorney General to seek to enjoin criminal activity? [14]

Would not the state just prosecute and jail the criminals instead of enjoining them? Is the Attorney General supposed to treat some drug dealers with injunctions and treat other drug dealers with criminal prosecutions? How does he or she determine which drug manufacturer, distributor or dispenser belongs in jail?

This anomaly led me to discover one of the first and most important pieces in the puzzle to understanding the Indiana Controlled Substances Act, i.e., that the state's ultimate power over unwanted drug dealing is to enjoin it, and not to criminally prosecute it. [15] Later this anomaly led me to realize that all commerce, including all drug commerce, is to be adjudicated in equity, not the criminal law jurisdiction. [16] Without this anomaly and the incongruities it suggested to me, I would not have been able to read the CSA properly and to reach this book's proper conclusions.

As well, one of the first things I learned in Constitutional Law class in law school was that all U.S. judicial courts – called Article III courts – require cases and controversies to invoke judicial authority. Article III,

Section 2 of the U.S. constitution says that judicial power shall extend to cases and controversies of various sorts, all which require an injury-in-fact.

This raises a major anomaly over the justiciability of most drug matters, which do not involve injury and do not even amount to cases or controversies. As such, strictly as a matter of law, these matters do not belong in the criminal law jurisdiction of any republican judicial court. That drug matters are tried in judicial courts reflects not only that judges do not know their courts' criminal jurisdiction, but also the loss of a republican form of government.

It was also an anomaly that led me to understand that law enforcers within republics have both judicial and regulatory functions, and that their arrest powers relate strictly to their judicial functions involving real crime or judicial contempt. [17] Such knowledge, which I did not learn in law school, and which I learned from reading statutes, is essential to correctly understand and enforce the CSA in every American territorial jurisdiction.

The above-referenced discovery is that law enforcers within republics may make arrests only for matters that are judicial. They can arrest people only for matters over which the judicial branch has criminal subject matter jurisdiction, i.e., injurious matters, or when people are in contempt of judicial orders.

Law enforcers may not make criminal arrests when they are solely enforcing regulations, such as busting up methamphetamine labs. Such commercial activity is subject to the equity jurisdiction of government, and it constitutes neither criminal nor judicial subject matter within a republic.

Such knowledge is essential to understanding the differences between judicial and executive authority, and to understanding when police officers may arrest people in possession of drugs and when they may not arrest people in possession of drugs. (Suffice to say that the proper exercise of police power is much simpler than knowing which drugs are favored and which are not.) In an American republic, where the right to property possession is unalienable for at least America's natural law citizens, and where the right not to be arrested except for crime is substantive, law enforcers must be certain to only arrest real criminals, regardless of what favored or disfavored drugs they possess.

This requires that law enforcers know what crime is – not to know the names and properties of drugs. The meaning of crime is particularly discussed in chapters 2 and 3. Says the 13th Amendment to the U.S. constitution and Article I, Section 37 of the Indiana constitution (1851), law enforcers are not allowed to arrest or incarcerate people for behavior that is not criminal. So, would it not be a big, big anomaly if law enforcers were putting non-criminals in jail? Indeed it would.

Conflicts such as weird anomalies in law enforcement can be greatly instrumental if they are channeled correctly, as I hope I have done with those that I have noticed. For example, all great movies – whether hero stories or tragedies – are full of conflict, and usually resolve the conflict by their endings. Or conflict can fester and cause negative consequences, such as cognitive dissonance in the form of political denial and the rationalization of evil, which has accompanied America's illicit war on drugs.

Of course these anomalies are not exclusive to my perception. They exist for everyone who uses their five senses and cognitive skills to see and recognize governments' actions for what they are. They are like the ashes from Auschwitz filling the skies over Krakow, Poland in the movie *Schindler's List* (1993) – telltale signs of bad government. Without their unsettling dissonance in Schindler's soul, he might not have sought a solution to German officials' breach of his personal morality.

Similarly, if my state and federal governments were being used correctly, there would be no anomalies for me to seek to understand or to resolve. Metaphorically, there would be no ashes falling from the sky due to the misuse of government power.

Metaphorically, as well, there would be no bad smell of government. Only criminals would be tried in criminal courts – not undesirables. There would be no disharmony between the actions of our governments and people's natural pursuit of happiness.

But in reality, there now is disharmony. I have just mentioned several obvious anomalies, with more to follow. The proverbial ashes are still falling from the sky, and the place still stinks! For the sake of the United States, I only wish that I had figured out and addressed the source of the ashes and the stench much sooner.

This book will address all these anomalies and smooth out all of our drug laws' seeming inconsistencies. It is my goal to resolve all the conflicts and to sing high praises for the law's consistent beauty and proper execution, though maybe not its current executioners.

What initially may surprise the reader is that all the seeming incongruities and anomalies in our drug policies will completely vanish overnight – not by changing the drug laws, but merely by understanding and enforcing them properly. This is because they are written to be constitutional, and harmonious with our human nature, although the opposite appears to be true because they have not been correctly enforced.

All the red flags of incongruity that dot the drug-law enforcement landscape are the result of the law's false enforcement. These red flags will completely disappear when our natural, constitutional and statutory law is understood and followed, which is the object of this book. [18]

My full disclosure

This book is written under the authority of the 1st Amendment to the U.S. constitution. It is strictly in opposition to the unnatural and subjective state religion – instead of law – that is being administered by American government officials with regard to controlled substances, where judicial subject matter jurisdiction – and thus justice – has become subjective.

I express opinions in this book both about the law and about its false enforcement by government officials. All of my opinions are just that: opinions, and none of my opinions amount to legal advice. I am not advising anyone to do anything, other than to follow the law.

But make no mistake. I believe so strongly in what I write that I will gladly take an oath upon it. I affirm that, as best as I can discern using my natural faculties, that which I tell you is true, the whole truth as best as I can understand and explain it, and nothing but the truth, so help me, God.

Yet not only is my analysis sincere, I seek to make every sentence in this book substantively correct. I encourage readers to note any sentences with which they disagree. Ultimately, I think that readers will be hard-pressed to either disagree with what I write or to find support for their disagreements. At least I have not.

Besides, anyone who thinks that I am wrong is welcome to write their own book, which will be full of inconsistencies and lies, I assure you. This is because government officials in the criminal justice system have nothing legal, moral or even objective upon which to justify the war on drugs within America's republics. As this book shows, the written law is very clear, its consistency is thick, and there is no justification, excuse or authority for government officials to not know it or to not follow it.

Nonetheless, no matter how convincing I am in my endeavor, remember that what I write here are just my opinions. I make no warranties or guarantees about the accuracy, completeness or adequacy of the information contained in this book, all of which is available to look up in law libraries. No one should rely on any of the information without assistance by a professional attorney. Although I believe what I tell you is true, full disclosure requires that I reveal two major caveats to my opinions' reliability.

First, my opinion that drugs are legal (and why) does not presently square with the opinions of most attorneys in the United States, if any of them. Most of the information in this book will be new to them. At the moment that I self-publish this book, I may be the only legally-trained person in America who believes what I do.

As well, this book may not convince anyone of my opinion. *Ergo,* after this book is published and bashed, I may still be the only person to believe as I do. Needless to say if this occurs, I would have reason to doubt the sanity of all of this book's readers.

That I am perhaps alone in my opinions (at the time this book is published) is unfortunate, but does not bother me in the least, except for the thought of the millions of innocent drug users, drug merchants and others (as collateral damage) who have been harmed by not knowing what I am here to reveal. It also means that I have a big job to convince others of my opinion – perhaps all others – starting with the nation's attorneys.

As bold as this sounds, I am trying to reach the entire American legal community with this book. This is because the community will enormously benefit from this book's information, and because the entire community will be needed to correct the parts of it which are terribly broken and acting falsely, i.e., those people who operate the criminal justice system. I appeal to all American attorneys – not only as people who swore to uphold the U.S. constitution, but also as fellow U.S. citizens – to join me in holding accountable those government officials involved in America's criminal justice system who have been enforcing criminal law falsely.

According to the Bureau of Labor Statistics, over three million Americans work within the criminal justice industry in the United States. This means that the three million Americans who are most necessary and responsible for securing America's republican governments – by operating a republican criminal justice system – have heretofore been misinformed about republics and incapable of fulfilling their essential republican roles. It is only the misguided opinions and faulty behavior of these people in America's criminal justice system that this book seeks to correct.

In this book you will learn about criminal law, administrative law, citizenship law and the republican form of government. To know these topics is to know the natural law meaning of crime and natural born citizenship. Given that these definitions literally secure America's republican form of government, current officials' justifications will be very thin to explain why they are using subjective and false definitions of crime and citizenship to uphold their state and federal non-republics.

The second caveat to the reliability of my opinion is that my state and federal governments have stealthily enforced their Controlled Substances Acts for over forty-five years in a manner grossly contrary to how they should have been enforced. If governments' enforcement was wrong, you might ask, how could government officials either 1) not know this or 2) act wrongly and not get caught for so long? In other words, why am I singularly correct about America's drug law, and why have millions of others gotten it wrong for nearly half a century?

This is a fair question, but it is essentially the same one that people have asked about other evil government programs, for which the answer is the same. Governments get away with bad things when their citizens or subjects let them. As we shall see, American officials get away with slavery and involuntary servitude on behalf of *de facto* non-republics that they falsely administer, instead of providing the *de jure* republics that are promised to U.S. citizens in America's constitutions and code books.

Bad, misused governments are really just degrees of misplaced public trust. In the case of controlled substances, our trust that government officials follow the drug laws has been sadly misplaced. This happens because both government officials and the American public have never learned the meaning of a republican form of government. Nor have they sufficiently read America's drug laws, which we will dissect beginning in chapter 16.

As we shall readily see, the war on drugs is a situation where the drug statutes adhere to the constitutional limitations of good government, but where the people running government do not follow the statutes and thus act outside the law. Because of this, if you share the same sense of incongruity and inconsistency about the war on drugs as I once had, then on an intuitive level you know that nothing about it can be trusted. This book serves to show that there is nothing honest or true or real about the war on drugs except its brute and brutal perversion of not only our constitutions, but statutory law as well.

This is a bold assertion, but government officials' wrongdoing is obvious and inexplicable. Thus, not noticing the fraud and the illegality of the war on drugs during most of our personal lives is like ignoring a knife in our backs as we labor to put together a large jigsaw puzzle. Heretofore, perhaps the knife wound has not been deep enough for us to notice. Or perhaps the puzzle has been too big and complicated to piece together. No longer.

2
The republican form of government

Common characteristics of America's republics

In the previous chapter I mentioned that there are four categories of sovereign authorities in the United States. These four types of sovereigns are 1) state republics, 2) Congress legislating as a republic with regard to the state republics, 3) sovereign individuals within the states, and 4) Congress legislating over the federal areas. We will address these sovereigns in the above order in this and the next seven chapters.

This and the next three chapters are about the first two of these four sovereigns: the fifty state republican governments and the U.S. republic. We will use the law of my home state Indiana to explain and demonstrate state law. Because Indiana uses the same Uniform Controlled Substances Act – promulgated by the Uniform Law Commission – as most other states, then discussion of Indiana's version of the act and of the U.S. CSA should be instructive of drug law throughout America. As well, state and federal constitutions will teach us about America's republican form of government.

Article IV, Section 4 of the U.S. constitution "guarantee(s) to every State in this Union a Republican Form of Government..." Likewise, no state may join the United States unless it is a republic. The Preamble to the Indiana constitution (1816) reads in pertinent part: "We the Representatives of the people of the Territory of Indiana... do ordain and establish the following constitution or form of Government..." "The form of government is to be guarantied," writes *Bouvier's Law Dictionary*, "which supposes a form already established, and this is the republican form of government the United States have undertaken to protect. See Story, Const. §1807." [19]

Black's Law Dictionary defines a republic as "a commonwealth; that form of government in which the administration of affairs is open to all the citizens." [20] "A government in the republican form" is "a government of the people;" reads *Bouvier's Law Dictionary*, "it is usually put in opposition to a monarchical or aristocratic government." [21] In general, citizens govern republics, and such monarchies govern their subjects.

Wikipedia succinctly defines the republican form of government as "one in which the powers of sovereignty are vested in the people and are exercised by the people, either directly, or through representatives chosen by the people, to whom those powers are specially delegated." [22] An American republic is where the People conduct their affairs for their own benefit rather than for the benefit of a ruler. They do this either directly – that is, personally – or indirectly, by means of delegating power to others.

Thus, under a republican form of government, both the People and their governments have power. The People delegate some of their personal power to government, but not all of it. The republican form of government works only if the powers of various sovereigns, but particularly the power of individual sovereigns, can be preserved and kept separate from the others.

Because Congress guarantees a republican form of government, it must legislate toward the state republics as would a republic, just as the states legislate over their own areas. Likewise, Article III of the U.S. constitution created republican judicial courts, called Article III courts, which share the same standards and criteria for liability as state republican judicial courts.

These fifty-one state and federal republics – and their court systems – share the meanings of cases and crimes, which words are used in state and U.S. constitutions to establish their judicial jurisdictions. All cases and crimes within republican courts involve injury. "The courts are open to those only who are injured," wrote the Indiana Supreme Court in *Gallup v. Schmidt* (1900). [23]

Sharing the same meaning of cases and crimes was a reasonable and necessary condition for the establishment of the U.S. republic. Otherwise, the federal courts might not recognize causes of actions by state citizens, or Congress might try to criminalize that which was lawful within the states.

Thus, one of the features that makes America's states and the U.S. government mutually republican is that they share the same definition of case and crime, both which include injury. All state and U.S. cases and crimes involve injury. Given this, and because mere drug possession and drug dealing do not cause injury, they are neither cases nor crimes within America's republics, and thus not primarily subject to judicial authority.

The war on drugs fundamentally violates America's republican form of government because it unnaturally treats natural rights as crimes, it criminalizes commercial activity, and it treats non-criminals as criminals. This is because the drug war is waged not only extra-constitutionally – that is, outside the power granted to the judicial system in U.S. and state consti- tutions – but also contrary to statutory law. In fact, if statutory law was followed, there would be no judicially-waged war on drugs and most of the features of republican government in America would properly operate instead of being dysfunctional.

In general, the legal features of America's republican form of government are:

1. that American republics have constitutions that are based on both natural (unwritten) law and positive (written) law,

2. that American republics have two judicial jurisdictions, i.e., law and equity, that respectively enforce natural and positive law,

3. that American republics have a judicial law jurisdiction based on natural law where the natural rights of natural persons are secured from legislatures by defining the jurisdiction of these courts to include only *malum in se* cases involving injury to natural persons or their property,

4. that American republics have an equity jurisdiction, which operates in both the executive and judicial branches, where commercial privileges are granted or withheld, where *malum prohibita* is enforced, and where commercial injuries to artificial persons are adjudicated,

5. that American republics do <u>not</u> have a plenary criminal jurisdiction (to be explained in chapters 8 and 9), which is inimical to a republican form of government,

6. that American republics define crime by natural law, not positive law, which is to say that crime is proscribed (prohibited) by Nature and only prescribed (written down) by legislatures,

7. that in America's republics, individual sovereigns – as potential crime victims – have primary, subject matter jurisdiction over crime, 24

8. that American republics' criminal justice is based upon an objective natural science, called jurisprudence, and not upon the supernatural subjectivity of religion, politics and nobility,

9. that in American republics commercial businesses are regulated in the non-criminal equity jurisdiction, and are not criminally prohibited in the law jurisdiction, where all crimes are adjudicated,

10. that American republics are made up of three separate, co-equal branches, i.e. the legislative branch, the executive branch and the judicial branch.

11. that American republics maintain not only a separation of powers between their legislative, executive and judicial branches, but also maintain a separation of powers between these branches and individual sovereigns,

12. that American republics' primary citizens, called natural born citizens, gain their political rights from their U.S. citizen fathers, and not from the positive law grant of government, from which naturalized citizens gain their political authority,

13. that consequently, natural born citizens do not naturally owe duties to the positive law of government, but instead only owe natural duties to other people, such as the duty to not harm them,

14. that consequently, only foreigners and naturalized U.S. citizens owe any political duties to the U.S. government, and

15. that American republics gain their moral authority from the natural delegation of authority from citizens, who do not delegate all their power to government, but who retain a jurisdiction over the exercise of their natural rights. To repeat Wikipedia (above), a republican form of government is where the People exercise power either directly (personally) or indirectly (by delegation).

The reservation of personal power – that we exercise as natural rights – was recognized by the Indiana Supreme Court in *Beebe v. State* (1855), which case declared unconstitutional the legislative criminalization of alcohol possession and sales. "Under our constitution, then," wrote the Court, "we all have some rights that have not been surrendered, which are consequently reserved, and which government can not deprive us of unless we shall first forfeit them by our crimes; and to secure to us the enjoyment of those rights is the great aim and end of the constitution itself." [25]

Law and equity

As mentioned in features 2 – 5 directly above, America's republics have two judicial jurisdictions, which are called law and equity. Article IV, Section 1 of the Indiana constitution (1816) reads:

> "The Judiciary power of this State, both as to matters of law and equity, shall be vested in one Supreme Court, in Circuit Courts, and in such other inferior Courts, as the General Assembly may from time to time, direct and establish."

This is part of the same jurisdiction that the People grant in the U.S. constitution to Article III courts. In pertinent part, its Article III, Section 2 reads:

> "The judicial Power shall extend to all Cases, in Law and Equity, arising under this Constitution, the Laws of the United States, and Treaties made, or which shall be made, under their Authority..."

Law is a republican judicial court's jurisdiction over natural persons. Equity is governments' authority over artificial persons. The law jurisdiction adjudicates violations of natural persons' natural rights, such as torts and crimes. Equity adjudicates contractual, commercial and legal rights of artificial persons.

Nature (and the nature of sovereign individuals) is sovereign over the law jurisdiction. Legislative positive (written) law is sovereign over equity.

The law jurisdiction is based on natural law. Equity is based solely on positive law.

The law jurisdiction is strictly judicial and, absent a constitutional amendment, is open only to injury. Equity both judicially adjudicates commercial disputes and administratively dispenses commercial privileges.

The law jurisdiction enforces only natural duties, such as the duty to not harm others. Equity enforces contractual, regulatory and other commercial duties.

Law originated and was installed here in the U.S. as judge-made law for the common man, called the common law. Equity springs strictly from positive law authority, for example the rules of a legislature.

Law's remedies include monetary compensation and restitution for torts, and incarceration and fines for crimes. Equity's commercial remedies include forfeiture of property, specific performance and injunction.

The law jurisdiction is an American republic's only criminal jurisdiction. It is mandatory upon all criminals. The equity jurisdiction has no criminal authority. One enters it with one's natural consent authority.

Cases and crimes are defined in the law jurisdiction by natural law always to include injury. Natural persons become subject to the law jurisdiction by negligently or intentionally violating the natural rights (including property) of other people. Artificial persons become subject to equity when they engage the public in commerce by selling goods or services.

Whereas the basis of equity is the positive law of a king or legislature, the basis of the law jurisdiction is Nature, which is outside and beyond kingly and legislative authority.

Whereas the legislature proscribes what is right and wrong (*malum prohibita*) in equity, Nature proscribes what is right and wrong (*malum in se*) at law. Regulation operates in equity. Criminal prohibitions, i.e., those which are either *malum in* se or that are placed into the law jurisdiction by constitutional amendment, operate at law.

In equity, legislatures legislate all legal "rights" (which are artificial privileges) and artificial duties. At law, legislatures merely prescribe or codify preexisting natural rights and duties. This is because republican legislatures are sovereign over equity, but not sovereign over law. Again, Nature and her laws are sovereign over the law jurisdiction.

The basis of the law jurisdiction is this: that in exchange for the reservation of the natural benefits of individual sovereignty, which is independent of and above the positive law of legislatures and other people, we naturally owe compensation to people we harm, and can be incarcerated or enslaved if we cannot properly and civilly exercise the sovereignty over which we are solely responsible. This is the basis, indeed moral authority, of American tort and criminal law.

In other words, the basis of the law jurisdiction is individual liberty and self-responsibility. Individuals remain free and sovereign over the natural law jurisdiction of republican constitutions, including its criminal jurisdiction, unless they negligently or intentionally harm others.

When their actions go beyond that which is allowed in the natural law jurisdiction, i.e., when they violate the equal natural rights of other natural persons, then the law jurisdiction of judicial courts gains authority over this natural law jurisdiction to adjudicate the injuries that they have caused to other people and their interests.

Thus, a natural person becomes subject to a judicial court's (natural, common, civil and / or criminal) law jurisdiction only when he or she harms another person negligently or intentionally. The law jurisdiction is our civil society's mandatory authority over injury caused by natural persons, which are torts and crimes that humans for millennia have naturally opposed. Individual sovereigns exercise primary jurisdiction over crime unless they exercise their right of self-defense irresponsibly, at which time the authority of the criminal law jurisdiction of judicial courts is invoked.

In contrast, artificial persons such as corporations, which exist solely by privilege of a legislature's positive law, do not have natural rights that are subject to adjudication in the law jurisdiction. Instead, they have positive law (legal) privileges and duties, to which they consent by voluntarily entering the equity jurisdiction.

"Equity is a body of jurisprudence, or field of jurisdiction, differing in its origin, theory, and methods from the common law;" writes *Black's Law Dictionary*, "though procedurally, in the federal courts and most state courts, equitable and legal rights and remedies are administered in the same court." [26]   Part of the Founding Fathers' brilliance was combining Britain's two historical systems of justice into state and federal judicial courts. These republican courts adjudicate cases in either law or equity based on the facts and parties of each case.

The law and equity jurisdictions of judicial trial courts are based respectively on individual and commercial injury. The equity jurisdiction is also exercised by administrative law courts in the executive branch. The decisions of these latter courts, which dole out commercial privileges, are subject to review or enforcement by judicial courts, acting in their appellate capacity. Only one of these jurisdictions has primary authority over any given subject matter, and only the law jurisdiction has criminal authority, which is the rightful power to throw a natural person in jail.

Equity lacks criminal jurisdiction ostensibly because governments cannot enslave artificial persons, such as corporations and other commercial enterprises. Instead, republican governments have equitable authority to shut down and enjoin such unwanted artificial persons.

Whether a case involves natural or artificial persons, involves natural duties or artificial duties, and involves natural or artificial rights will determine 1) whether law or equity has jurisdiction over the subject matter, and 2) whether the matter is subject to the criminal law jurisdiction. In America's republics, criminal law adjudicates only violations of natural duties by natural persons, who can be physically placed in jail. It does not adjudicate any duties imposed by positive law or by contract upon artificial persons and enterprises, which cannot be placed in jail.

Republican legislatures can legislate over commerce in equity, but 1) may not legislate over the duties of natural persons, and 2) may only prescribe and codify *malum in se* crimes that are already proscribed by Nature.

This translates into two important concepts: 1) that legislatures have no authority to define crime inconsistently with the natural and constitutional law definition of crime, and 2) that no commerce (except slavery) is subject to criminal law and criminal sanction within an American republic.

This means that states have no authority to treat as criminal any commercial activity, such as drug dealing, which is instead subject to its non-criminal equity jurisdiction. In other words, drug dealing cannot be criminal because, as a commercial activity, it operates under equity, which is not a criminal jurisdiction.

Consequently, statutes that define the equity jurisdiction in America's republics, such as state administrative procedures acts, neither have criminal provisions nor have any criminal force or effect upon natural persons. Such natural persons are subject to the law jurisdiction, where violations of natural rights, i.e., torts and crimes, are adjudicated.

For example, statutes that define how the state is to regulate drug commerce do not apply to natural persons who merely use drugs, and whose actions are not commercial, and are thus not subject to regulation. Conversely, equity was established to adjudicate the privileges granted by kings and legislatures to artificial entities that have no natural rights.

Thus, all the artificial duties and privileges that the Indiana legislature decrees for artificial persons have no recognition under the law jurisdiction – and thus, under the criminal law jurisdiction. This judicial jurisdiction serves only to adjudicate injury caused by natural persons – not to adjudicate violations of legislative decrees. Accordingly, all criminal authority in Indiana is against natural persons in the law jurisdiction, which we will see is not subject to legislation that is inconsistent with natural law.

The recognition of the natural duty of all people to refrain from harming others, and the principles of Justinian justice, were established by the Indiana constitution and under the common law of Indiana and Great Britain. This was long before Indiana's legislature codified this duty for the benefit of Hoosiers who could read. Justinian justice, Sir William Blackstone wrote, "reduced the whole doctrine of law" to three principles: "that we should live honestly, should hurt nobody, and should render to every one his due." [27] As we shall see, these precepts are the foundations for Indiana and U.S. judicial courts. They are a succinct summary of law courts' subject matter jurisdiction over individuals.

The above analysis means that neither the Indiana legislature nor Congress has ever created or imposed any legitimate criminal duties upon natural persons in America's republics. In their republican capacities, their positive law is sovereign only over equity within America's republics. As we shall see, Nature is sovereign in the law jurisdiction, and the legislature has authority only to consistently codify the duties that are naturally preexisting and that were already recognized by the common law of England before it was imported to the United States. [28]

As we shall also see, the Indiana legislature has misrepresented its lawmaking authority by prescribing statutory penalties in the Controlled Substances Act at IC 35-48-4 for duties that do not naturally exist in natural persons. For example, the trumped-up duty to not possess drugs is not a natural preexisting duty in any of us, and is therefore not enforceable at law or at criminal law. To say the least, such a duty would necessarily violate the "natural, inherent, and unalienable right... of acquiring, possessing, and protecting property," which is recognized in Article I, Section 1 of the Indiana constitution (1816).

In the United States, we all – including foreign kings and domestic Presidents – have a natural preexisting duty to not harm other people, which is enforceable in the law jurisdiction. Some of us, such as parents, also have a natural duty to care for children, which duty is codified. Others, such as able-bodied male citizens, may also have a natural duty to defend the homeland, which Congress may prescribe and codify.

As well, natural born citizens also have natural political duties to help adjudicate others' cases and crimes, either as jurors or witnesses, which legislatures may prescribe. These are the only natural duties (that I can think of) 1) which the law jurisdiction naturally imposes upon natural persons, 2) over which republican legislatures may not legislate, but merely write down, and 3) over which legislatures may only prescribe in a manner consistent with natural law.

However, we do not have a natural preexisting duty, for example, to not grow certain things in our gardens or to not carry certain things in our pockets. Such unnatural and artificial legislative prohibitions are called *malum prohibita*. This is in contrast with inherently wrongful behavior which is naturally prohibited, called *malum in se*. The former is the jurisdiction of Caesars. The latter is the jurisdiction of Nature.

"An act is said to be *malum in se*," says *Black's Law Dictionary*, "when it is inherently and essentially evil, that is, immoral in its nature and injurious in its consequences, without any regard to the fact of its being noticed or punished by the law of the state..." [29] Thus, *malum is se* is inherently immoral and injurious behavior that is "enforceable without the denouncement of a statute..." [30] because people naturally know that it is bad. *Malum in se* involving injury is the natural standard of criminal culpability under American law.

Republican governments may use their regulatory powers under equity to shut down or enjoin commercial enterprises that violate their *malum prohibita*, but republics are neither allowed to regulate nor criminally prohibit natural persons from doing what comes natural to them, such as gardening or possessing property. This is not only because *malum prohibita* and the equity jurisdiction do not apply to natural persons operating in their natural capacities, but because republican governments fundamentally may not legislate inconsistently with the exercise of people's natural rights, such as producing and possessing property.

This may sound like an overly broad statement of law, but as we shall see about statutory law – beginning with chapter 16 – this is exactly what the Controlled Substances Acts tell us. In Indiana, for example, people's natural right to produce natural sources of controlled substances is codified at IC 35-48-1-26 and their natural right to possess drugs for their own use is codified at IC 35-48-3-3(e)(3). These statutes reflect that statutory law secures people's natural rights, as is required of republican legislation.

Within the fifty state republics, the law does not grant any monarch, legislature or other artificial entity the authority to govern, try to govern or claim to govern Nature on behalf of others. This includes human nature. Because legislatures cannot legislate over Nature, and because Nature defines what is *malum in se*, then legislatures may not legislate cases or crimes inconsistently with their natural law definitions, which include injury.

Likewise, natural law defines republican governments criminal authority. Because in America's republics, individual sovereigns delegate some of their powers to these republics, but reserve others, governments have only such authority that individual sovereigns are capable of granting. For example, if individuals have no rightful authority to use violence to make their neighbors quit using drugs, then such individuals may not delegate their lack of natural authority to government to use violence to cause their neighbors to quit using drugs.

If you add up each of our individual authority to use violence to cause our neighbors to quit doing drugs, which sum would equal zero, then the government representing our moral authority would have zero moral authority to use violence to cause our neighbors to quit using drugs. "No law has any effect, of its own force, beyond the limits of the sovereignty from which its authority is derived," poignantly wrote the U.S. Supreme Court in *Hilton v. Guyot* (1895). [31]

This is based on the natural law of logic and reason. It is not based on illogical delusions 1) that kings or legislatures have divine authority to dictate Nature, or 2) that citizens can delegate moral authority to government that they do not personally have, or 3) that a person or body of people can claim authority over the natural rights of others, as kings and non-republican legislatures claim to do. These are the illogical and unnatural foundations for not only the illegal war on drugs, but for rotten, non-republican government.

Look at it this way: if my neighbor owes me no natural duty to quit using drugs, or to quit drinking beer, then the Indiana legislature cannot (and as we shall see, statutorily does not) impose such a duty upon my neighbor by means of legislation on my behalf. Such legislation would be unconstitutional because I cannot delegate moral authority to government to use violence against honest and nonviolent people to achieve my happiness.

Instead, the opposite is true. I owe a natural duty to my neighbors to <u>not</u> initiate violence against them in any manner, including to impose the criminal arm of government upon them. These are the sole moral reasons why the Controlled Substances Act does not impose such unnatural and unreasonable duties upon us or our neighbors. As well, it respects our natural rights to produce and possess things for our own individually perceived needs.

Using reason alone, we can see that the war on drugs is unjustified because there can be no moral or statutory justification for it. By extension, our governments have no more moral or legal authority than we do as individuals to force our our neighbors to stop using drugs.

As we shall see, America's republics have authority to use compulsory process against natural persons only based on injury to one's person, property or reputation. [32] Compulsory judicial process over natural persons in the law jurisdiction always begins with an injury.

Because the only mutual natural duty of natural persons is to refrain from harming the persons or property of other people, which duty is enforced in the law jurisdiction of judicial courts, then the only criminal statutes that apply to all natural persons are legislative codifications of the violation of this natural duty. Legislatures may codify only criminal law that is *malum in* se, which is inherently wrongful behavior that violates other persons' natural rights.

Because of the separation of powers doctrine in most state constitutions, then without a constitutional amendment, republican legislatures cannot expand the subject matter jurisdiction of judicial courts by expanding the meaning of crime to include *malum prohibita*. In America's republics, *malum prohibita* – such as driving too fast – operates in non-criminal equity and is enforceable only against artificial entities – such as automobile drivers – which are subject to the legislature and are regulated.

For example, speed limit prohibitions apply only to drivers who as a class are regulated. They do not apply to passengers, to people walking on the side of roads or to people watching television and eating potato chips.

Malum prohibita, for example not to drive too fast, applies only to regulated people involved in the regulated activity of driving. It is enforced in the equity jurisdiction, which has no criminal authority. The state's equitable remedies against drivers who drive too fast is to revoke their licenses and to enjoin their future driving. The state's remedies do not include incarcerating drivers for having lead feet.

In the Indiana Controlled Substances Act at IC 35-48-4, there are nine *malum in se* crimes that may be enforced in Indiana's judicial courts against real drug criminals. However, most other statutory provisions in the act are inapplicable to natural persons and the law jurisdiction. Most of the remaining provisions in the Indiana CSA apply only to artificial persons and to commercial activities that are subject to the state's regulatory mechanisms, which operate in equity.

Legislation such as the Indiana CSA, which predominantly defines the state's equity jurisdiction over drug commerce, neither creates nor imposes any duties upon natural persons that are not already established by the Indiana constitution and its judicial law jurisdiction. Thus, no one really needs the CSA to tell them what a drug crime is because real crimes are self-evident facts of Nature. For example, getting ripped off in a drug deal is inherently wrong and universally recognized as such.

This is because, under the law jurisdiction of judicial courts, natural persons are naturally duty-bound to not injure other people, which harmful behavior is *malum in se* whether a legislature writes it down or not. Needless to say, other than to pay its bills and to build its courtrooms, Indiana's judicial branch has never needed the legislative branch in any way to uphold natural duties and to punish torts and crimes, which standards were established by judges instead of legislatures.

Since 1851, when Indiana adopted a new republican constitution, the legislature has merely enacted and codified these procedural and substantive standards that the judicial branch had already established under Indiana's common law. This means that the Indiana legislature is not in charge of these standards, but is only in charge of writing them down.

For example, the legislature cannot invent crimes. Nor can it immunize people for committing them. To redefine the meaning of crime would be to change the subject matter jurisdiction of judicial courts, which was determined and granted by the Indiana constitution. The state legislature cannot legislate crimes, which are self-evident facts of Nature, but may only write down their elements and determine their punishment.

Likewise, no one needs the CSA to tell them that they have a natural right of drug possession. The Indiana CSA provides for this at IC 35-48-3-3(e)(3), but such provision is merely redundant of preexisting rights secured by the Indiana and U.S. constitutions.

Thus, if one sufficiently knows one's state and U.S. constitutions, then one already knows what is criminal in a republic and what is not. That current officials arrest and prosecute non-criminals for non-crimes is evidence that they are likely unaware of the meaning of crime in America's constitutions, which is a topic in chapters 4 and 5.

Statutes that define equity do not define the duties of natural persons. This is because a legislature's equity jurisdiction does not apply to natural persons and cannot create duties in them. This is all consistent with the concept that legislatures' positive law jurisdiction does not apply in, and cannot inconsistently invade, the natural law jurisdiction of our constitutions or the law jurisdiction of judicial courts, where natural law is enforced.

Nor can positive law grant artificial privileges to natural persons. An example of an artificial privilege is the privilege of unlimited life that the state bestows upon corporations. If the Indiana legislature had jurisdiction over natural persons – that is, if it could legislate over natural persons as it can over artificial persons – then it could bestow natural persons with unlimited life as it does corporations.

But of course it cannot grant unlimited life to natural persons. This is because the Indiana legislature cannot legislate over Nature, including how Nature defines crime, lawful possession, marriage, production, natural citizenship and our genetic potential.

Natural persons and their natural duties are in contrast with duties imposed upon artificial entities by the state of Indiana, which is the No. 1 artificial person in the state. Indiana's legislature divvies out artificial privileges to lesser artificial persons, such as corporations and other licensees. Its rules governing these privileges are enforced in the non-criminal equity jurisdiction of the executive branch – not in the criminal law jurisdiction of the judicial branch.

When the Declaration of Independence says that "all Men are created equal," it is only in the law jurisdiction of judicial courts, whose basis is in natural law, that this declaration is true. It is as Thomas Jefferson wrote: that the "best principles [of our republic] secure to all its citizens a perfect equality of rights." [33]

In contrast, equity – which is the jurisdiction of kings and legis-latures – does not treat all artificial persons equally. For example, it treats some drug manufacturers, distributors and dispensers better than others. According to the 14th Amendment to the U.S. constitution, it is required only to provide all drug dealers with due process and equal protection.

Equality before the law exists only in the law jurisdiction of judicial courts which administer natural equality as a substantive right. This equality cannot be alienated from any natural person within the authority of a law court. Such court is the only place in American government – and perhaps in all the world – where all natural persons are to be treated equally.

It is also the only place in America where a republican government can legitimately deprive a natural person of his or her liberty, based on violations of natural duty. The separation of the law and equity juris-dictions is what makes America's judicial courts republican.

Based on the distinctions between law and equity, I can truthfully say that I have never practiced law. (This is not a trick statement.) As a former appellate tax attorney, all of my "law" practice was in equity. Law is the judicial jurisdiction over natural persons. All of my tax practice was with artificial tax subjects. Only attorneys who practice tort and criminal law can claim to practice real law. However, as we shall see, they have to know law's natural basis to practice it correctly.

The role of the 13th, 18th and 21st Amendments

The separate roles of law and equity are demonstrated by the 13th, 18th and 21st Amendments to the U.S. constitution. The 13th Amendment prohibits slavery and indentured servitude except for the punishment of crime. The 18th Amendment prohibited the commerce in alcohol. The 21st Amendment repealed the 18th Amendment.

Prior to the 13th Amendment, slaves were regulated in equity, and were subject to taxation. This is because slaves were considered commercial property. The 13th Amendment took former slaves out of the equity juris-diction over commercial property and placed slavery into the law jurisdic-tion where it could be treated as a crime, instead of as a commercial privilege.

The effects of the 13th Amendment were to not only declare former slaves free, but to change the judicial jurisdiction in which they operated.

That is, the 13th Amendment essentially extended the substantive rights available to freemen in the law jurisdiction to former slaves.

Although it took the 14th Amendment to effectuate these rights within the southern states, the 13th Amendment theoretically granted former slaves all the substantive rights of free natural persons, to be secured in the law jurisdiction of all American republics. These substantive rights are discussed in the next chapter.

The law jurisdiction secures the right of liberty by not enslaving people who do others no harm. Law is the only criminal jurisdiction in America's republics, in that it is the only judicial jurisdiction with subject matter jurisdiction to enslave people. It is the law jurisdiction of judicial courts, as reflected in the 13th Amendment, that keeps U.S. citizens and former slaves free from wrongful enslavement, that secures all natural persons' natural physical rights, and that secures natural born citizens' natural political rights and duties.

Similar to the 13th Amendment, the 18th Amendment took the commerce of alcohol – its manufacture, sale and transportation – out of the equity jurisdiction where it had been previously regulated, and placed it into the law jurisdiction where it could be criminalized against natural persons by both the federal and state governments. Subsequently, the 21st Amendment took alcohol commerce out of the law jurisdiction and placed it back into equity where it is today regulated.

Similar to alcohol, the commerce of drugs is to be regulated in equity, and is subject to equitable remedies such as commercial confiscation and injunction – but not to criminal punishment. Only a handful of actual drug crimes, mostly that involve the fraudulent conveyance of drugs, are criminally punishable under the Indiana Controlled Substances Act.

However, these actual crimes exclude the non-crimes of drug possession or dealing. The latter only look illegal because, as I mentioned earlier, government officials do not follow the CSA, but instead wantonly violate it.

To sum up this chapter: within America's state republics, and under Congress' guarantee to provide the states "a Republican Form of Government...," [34] drug possession is a natural right of all natural people. As well, drug dealing is not a crime in such republics, but is instead a commercial privilege that is primarily subject to regulation by non-criminal administrative law courts in the executive branch. Federal and state statutes make these regulatory courts and administrators answer to republican judicial courts acting in their appellate capacity, which apply equitable remedies, such as forfeiture and injunction to unwanted drug dealing.

All substantive, natural and legal rights in America's republics are secured by the law and equity jurisdictions. Whereas the law jurisdiction of judicial courts is republican governments' authority over injury by natural persons, equity is republican governments' judicial jurisdiction over artificial persons, such as foreigners and commercial entities. In America's republics, legislatures are sovereign over commerce and the equity jurisdiction, whereas Nature and her laws are sovereign over the law – and thus, the criminal law – jurisdiction.

Within America's republics, people who are engaged in commerce, such as in drug commerce, are subject to non-criminal commercial regulation as defined by Congress as the U.S. republic and by the state legislative republics. People who are neither in commerce nor harming other people's interests are to be left alone, which is their substantive right.

As Article I, Section 8, Clause 3 of the U.S. constitution reads, Congress has authority "to regulate Commerce... among the states..." This power does not include the authority to criminally prohibit any kind of commerce among the states or to incarcerate people for such commercial activity. A constitutional amendment like the 18th Amendment is needed to do that.

Because "the Federal Government has no police powers except those specifically conferred by the Constitution, the 18th Amendment was necessary to confer upon the Federal Government police powers to prohibit the manufacture, transportation and sale of liquor within the several states..." wrote John F. Finerty in a *Notre Dame Law Review* article (1932). [35] Otherwise, he points out, the federal government already had "full powers" to regulate such activity under the Commerce clause at Article I, Section 8, Clause 3. [36]

Criminally prohibiting any kind of business within America's states is not a power granted to Congress in Article I, Section 8 of the U.S. constitution, where all of Congress' powers are granted. Thus, in order to be constitutional, we can be assured *ipso facto* that Congress' constitutional statutes do not criminalize drug possession or dealing anywhere within America's republics., or they would be adjudged unconstitutional.

The substantive rights discussed in the next chapter – such as to due process, to equal protection, to the separation of governmental powers, to the supremacy of republican constitutions, and to liberty and property – belong to all natural persons in America's republics. In the case of drugs, such substantive rights are secured not only by federal and state constitutions, but also by the various Controlled Substances Acts. Unfortunately these rights are not recognized in America's drug war because the CSAs are not properly understood and followed.

Combined, the facts 1) that judicial courts lack subject matter jurisdiction over non-injury, 2) that drug dealing is consensual activity which is not a violation to a natural right, 3) that drug dealing is commercial activity that is subject to regulation and administrative due process in equity, 4) that the law jurisdiction is the only criminal judicial jurisdiction in a republic, and 5) that equity has no criminal authority, each and all lead to the obvious conclusion that drug dealing – which is commercial behavior – is not subject to the law jurisdiction of judicial courts, and thus cannot be criminal.

Instead, drug dealing is primarily subject to non-criminal regulation in the executive branch of America's republics, and to the republics' equitable remedies of forfeiture and injunction. Because only the law jurisdiction has criminal authority, the state's equitable remedies are legislative admissions that neither drug possession nor dealing are crimes to be tried in the criminal law jurisdiction. As we shall see, individuals have jurisdiction over personal property, and all consensual commerce – even unwanted drug commerce – is regulated in equity and is not subject to criminal law.

3
Substantive and natural rights

Substantive rights in the law jurisdiction

The law jurisdiction of judicial courts exists to secure the natural rights of natural persons, or to compensate natural persons for violations to their rights. It does this by enforcing substantive rights.

Substantive rights are constitutionally inherent or expressed rights that are granted by republican constitutions to natural persons in the law jurisdiction and that are not subject to inconsistent legislation. These are rights which may not be taken away or denied by a republican legislature or a court. They are one's expressed or inherent rights as a natural person with regard to the republican form of government and what it guarantees.

Substantive rights are what makes all natural persons free from other people and their republican governments. They are rights enforced in the law jurisdiction that make our natural rights, such as to life, liberty and the pursuit of happiness, unassailable by kings or dictatorial legislatures. Substantive rights belong to all natural persons, regardless of citizenship, strictly because they are natural persons. They are rights that, if they are not recognized, then America's republics fail to exist.

These substantive rights are either enumerated (written down) in the U.S. or state constitutions, or they are inherent. The following is a list of these substantive rights, and where we can find them in the law.

- The right to seek a judicial remedy for harm done to one's person, property or reputation by someone else (Article I, Section 12 of the Indiana constitution (1851) and Article III, Section 2 of the U.S. constitution)
- The freedom of religion, speech, the press and assembly (Article 1, Sections 2 – 7, 9 and 31 of the Indiana constitution (1851) and the 1st Amendment to the U.S. constitution)
- The right to keep and bear arms (Article I, Section 34 of the Indiana constitution (1851) and the 2nd Amendment)
- The right in time of peace to not consent to the quartering of troops

in one's home (Article I, Section 34 of the Indiana constitution (1851) and the 3rd Amendment)

- The protection against unreasonable searches and seizures (Article I, Section 11 of the Indiana constitution (1851) and the 4th Amendment)
- The right to a presentment or indictment (5th Amendment)
- The protection against double jeopardy (Article I, Section 14 of the Indiana constitution (1851) and the 5th Amendment)
- The right not to be compelled to be a witness against oneself (the 5th Amendment)
- The right to due process of law (the 5th and 14th Amendments)
- The right to just compensation for property taken for public use (the 5th Amendment)
- The rights in a criminal prosecution to a speedy and public trial, to an impartial jury, to be informed of the nature and cause of the accusation, to be confronted by witnesses, to have compulsory process to present witnesses and to have assistance of counsel (Article I, Section 13 of the Indiana constitution (1851) and the 6th Amendment)
- The right to trial by jury in common law suits exceeding twenty dollars (Article I, Section 20 of the Indiana constitution (1851) and the 7th Amendment)
- The protection against excessive bail and fines, as well as cruel and unusual punishment (Article I, Section 16 of the Indiana constitution (1851) and the 8th Amendment)
- The reservation of natural rights (Article I, Sections 1 and 2 of the Indiana constitution (1816 and 1851) and the 9th Amendment)
- The right of U.S. citizen males to be the sole source of U.S. Presidents (Article II, Section 1 of the U.S. constitution)
- The right not to be enslaved or placed into involuntary servitude except as punishment for crime (Article I, Section 37 of the Indiana constitution (1851) and the 13th Amendment)
- The right of due process of law and equal protection for all persons (the 14th Amendment)
- The right to vote for citizens of the United States regardless of race, color or previous condition of servitude (Article II, Sections 1 and 2 of the Indiana constitution (1851) and the 15th Amendment)
- The right to vote for citizens of the United States regardless of sex or gender (the 19th Amendment)
- The right of citizens of the United States to vote for President, Vice

President and Members of Congress without being subject to a tax (the 24th Amendment)

- The right of 18-year old citizens of the United States to vote (the 26th Amendment)
- The right to rely on the U.S. and state constitutions as the supreme law (Article I, Section 25 of the Indiana constitution (1851) and Article VI, Paragraph 2 of the U.S. constitution)
- The right not to be regulated when operating in one's natural capacities (inherent, see *Brown v. Texas* (1979)) [37]
- The right to a separation of governmental powers (Article III Indiana constitution)

As we shall see more extensively later, the war on drugs violates several of the above essential guarantees. To lay some foundation, I will mention a few violations here.

The war violates due process of law by trying most drug defendants in judicial courts without subject matter jurisdiction, by denying drug dealers their rights to administrative due process in the executive branch, and by governments' failure to exhaust their administrative remedies.

Given that drug possession and dealing are not crimes (see chapters 4 and 5), the drug war's false arrests violate constitutional prohibitions against unreasonable searches and seizures.

The war also violates the separation of powers doctrine by trying drug matters in the wrong courts, in the wrong branch of government, without jurisdiction.

It also violates the equal protection clause by treating favored drug dealers in equity while treating disfavored ones to prison.

Most flagrantly, the drug war violates the 13th Amendment right not to be enslaved except for the commission of a crime. The 13th Amendment to the U.S. constitution reads: "Neither slavery nor involuntary servitude, except as a punishment for crime whereof the party shall have been duly convicted, shall exist with the United States, or any place subject to their jurisdiction."

Government officials violate the 13th Amendment by using legislatures' definitions of "crime," "offense," "felony" and "misdemeanor" which are inconsistent with the constitutional meaning of crime as used in the 13th Amendment. To put such statutory definitions above constitutional definitions is to also violate the Supremacy Clause of Article I, Section 25 of the Indiana constitution (1851) and of Article VI, Paragraph 2 of the U.S. constitution. The Supremacy Clause is also a substantive right because defendants have a substantive right to rely on the constitutional definition of crime before they are incarcerated.

> Note: Throughout the rest of this book, I place quotation marks around such words as "case," "civil case," "crime," "criminal case," "offense," "felony," and "misdemeanor" whenever the Indiana legislature or Congress use these words in statutes to connote or convey different meanings than the same words used in the Indiana and U.S. constitutions.
>
> I also refer to these strictly statutory "crimes," "criminal cases," "offenses," "felonies" and "misdemeanors" as false-, phony- or faux- "crimes" or non-crimes because such are not real *malum in se* crimes. This *malum prohibita* is fraudulent because it was intended to mis-represent the subject matter jurisdiction of judicial courts – which is over injury – to attorneys and to the public. All such phony "crimes" are *malum prohibita,* which are non-crimes without victims.

The constitutional definition of crime is *malum in se*. This is why crime is referred to several times in the U.S. constitution, and twice in the Indiana constitution (1851), but without the word being defined. Crime does not have to be defined because it has a meaning which is separate from and which predates the creation of written law. This is because crime is a fact of Nature – and not a creation of positive law.

This is to say that criminal defendants have an inherent substantive right to rely on the meaning of constitutional words, such as case, crime, offense, felony and misdemeanor. Otherwise, their substantive right not to be enslaved except for the commission of crime – as recognized by the 13th Amendment – can necessarily be violated. This is also to say that the drug war is fraudulent because it is based on fraudulently conveying the false meaning of certain co-opted constitutionally-secured words.

As I said, our substantive rights under our constitutions secure our natural rights, which are discussed below. These substantive rights apply to all natural persons within America's state republics, and are enforceable by natural persons in the republican law jurisdiction of America's state and federal judicial courts, which is only where natural rights are secured.

For example, only if we are availed the substantive right to seek a judicial remedy for harm done to us by other people are our natural rights to life, property and compensation, i.e., an eye-for-an-eye, secured. In such a case, we can seek a civil remedy in court for monetary damages and / or the state can prosecute the same action as a crime in the same judicial law jurisdiction.

Conversely, only if we are free from arrest or enslavement except for the commission of *malum in se* crime are our natural rights to life, liberty and the pursuit of happiness secured by the judicial branch. Otherwise the state can deprive us of our liberty for any 'ole reason, such as for property possession, which is a natural right, or for being in business, which is at most subject to regulation – not imprisonment.

The substantive right to seek a judicial remedy for a violation of a natural right and the substantive right to not be enslaved except for the commission of crime are the *raison d'etat* of the law jurisdiction of judicial courts. The law jurisdiction was created to fulfill the natural right of compensation and to secure the natural right of liberty.

Substantive rights apply equally to all natural persons within America's republics. Thus under republican constitutions and in republican court rooms, foreigners share the same rights of compensation, liberty and due process as Americans. Yet strangely, this substantive right is codified for foreigners at 28 USC 1251(b)(1), which says that they have a right to seek a judicial remedy in a U.S. court for torts against them.

I say this is strange because, given that other criteria is met, foreigners already have a constitutionally-secured substantive right to seek a judicial remedy in an Article III court for a tort. So, there is no need to have a statute that says the same thing. For example, there is no similar statute (that I can find) that says U.S. citizens may use U.S. courts to remedy interstate torts. (Of course they can. Getting compensated for others' injurious behavior is the main reason why the courts were established.)

This right to use courts to seek compensation for harm does not have to be repeated by statute because the right is constitutional and substantive, not legislative. With regard to natural persons, getting natural compensation – or some kind of moral equivalence for harm done – is the reason for the courts. This reason is embodied at Article III, Section 2 of the U.S. constitution and at Article I, Section 12 of the Indiana constitution (1851), both which say in their own ways that courts are open to remedy injury to one's person, property or reputation.

Thus, this statute regarding the right of foreigners to seek compensation codifies, and is merely redundant of, foreigners' preexisting substantive right to seek a judicial remedy, which is already recognized by the U.S. constitution. The statute likely exists to ensure that the U.S. constitution is not misunderstood by those who might otherwise misunderstand it, or who otherwise would not know that the law jurisdiction – by its very nature – treats all natural persons equally.

Equality under the law reflects the nature of Nature and its law jurisdiction, which enforces natural law and substantive rights upon all natural persons equally.   At 28 USC 1251(b)(1), with regard to foreigners, Congress was merely good enough to remind us of this.

Our natural rights

As I wrote above, substantive rights secure our natural rights, which are inherent and unalienable. Probably the very best example of a natural right is babies' right to poop, which is unalienable and undeniable. This right exists even though it is not mentioned in the U.S. or Indiana constitutions. It is one of those unenumerated natural rights that are recognized and secured by the 9th Amendment.

Whether exercising their rights thousands of years ago or in today's world of disposable diapers, babies exercise their natural right to poop without thinking at all about government or positive law. They do not ask government's permission to soil their diapers, and governments do not give them this right.

This right comes from Nature. Governments do not regulate anyone's pooping, which is governed by natural law. Instead, government regulates municipal corporations and utility companies that carry the stuff away.

Babies know little about government (except their parents' dictatorships), and because they cannot read, positive law is utterly meaningless to them. (Note: When adults do not or cannot read and comprehend positive law, as we shall see beginning in chapter 16, then it is meaningless to them as well.)

However, most Americans would agree that it is our governments' job to secure babies' right to poop, sleep, eat, breathe, drink and drool. Without these unwritten rights, babies could not live very long or pursue happiness. Thus, babies have a natural right to poop and a substantive right to not be arrested or regulated for pooping. The same goes for you and me.

These babies might grow up to learn about George Washington and the U.S. government in school, but this does not change their primary relationship with Nature and natural law. The right and need to poop is a universal expression of our nature. Short of death, starvation and temporary constipation, there is nothing that mankind (or other living things) can do to escape it or to stop it.

Humans do all sorts of other things by our nature besides just pooping, eating, sleeping, breathing and drinking. We trade our labor and our minds for things we want. We carry these things in our hands, in our pockets and in our motor vehicles. We go from here to there to get our needs met. We naturally acquire things and take dominion over them.

As well, we hook up with people with whom we are attracted. We naturally have children and try to keep them safe and healthy. We exert force to protect our families and property. We vomit and urinate, for example, without anyone's permission.

These are all things that we do naturally, and that bipeds have done for millions of years, with or without the operation or permission of government and its positive law. Exercising natural rights is what we do naturally, regardless if there is a government or regardless on which side of the bed our governments awake.

In addition to babies' natural physical right to poop, the following is a non-exhaustive list of natural persons' other natural rights, which we established government to help us secure, and certainly not to violate. These natural rights may be commonly named or described differently than how I name or describe them.

I did not consult anyone when making this list. Although I have thought about rights for many years, I am sure that my list is missing a few that I failed to include. With the exceptions of natural political rights regarding citizenship (below), which were pointed out by a friend of mine, [38] most of these rights came to me naturally, with little outside help.

> The natural right to life, which is mentioned in the Indiana constitution (1851) at Article I, Section 1, includes the rights to lawfully obtain and consume food and medicine, to urinate, to vomit, to defecate, to recuperate and to breathe (and inhale). It also includes the natural rights to reproduce life (in the form of children) and to end one's own life. It is bittersweet that we all have the natural right to jump off a cliff (if we can get there).

> The natural right to physical liberty, which is posited at Article I, Section 1 of the Indiana constitution (1851), is to have complete sovereignty over one's personal, non-commercial actions to the extent they do not violate the equal rights of others.
>
>> "(R)ightful liberty is unobstructed action according to our will within limits drawn around us by the equal rights of others," wrote Thomas Jefferson. [39]
>>
>> It is when the equal rights of others are violated that the law jurisdiction of republican judicial courts is invoked, which holds American republics' only rightful authority to

compel, incarcerate or enslave natural persons. The natural right of physical liberty is attainable only by using an objective basis for judicial criminal authority, i.e., injury.

The natural right to pursue happiness, which is recognized at Article I, Section 1 of the Indiana constitution (1851), includes all human behavior, except that which injures other people, which is tortious or criminal.

The natural right of possession (of property) is the right to acquire, possess, use and defend lawfully-acquired property, including drugs, to the exclusion of other people's rights to possess or use the same property. This right is recognized at Article I, Section 1 of the Indiana constitution (1816) and Article I, Section 21 of the Indiana constitution (1851).

> "So far, then, we find that the people have expressly reserved the right of property, and its enjoyment, in forming their constitution, from the unlimited power of the legislature;" wrote the Indiana Supreme Court in *Beebe v. State* (1855), "and further to guard the right, have ordained that it shall not be taken from them without just compensation, nor be injured without a remedy therefor by due course of law..." [40]

The natural right to communicate includes the natural rights to speak, write, sign, and otherwise use our body parts to convey meaning.

The natural right of travel is the right to use natural locomotion to go unimpeded from one place to another in order to pursue happiness or to get one's needs met.

The natural right of valuation is the right to exchange our labor and other property for things valuable to us.

The natural right of association is the right not to be forced to be with one's in-laws for very long. (Just kidding. I can joke about this because I am not married.)

The natural right of attraction is that feeling you get when you are with someone that you like. Legislatures have no real effect on this.

The natural right to barter is the right of two people to exchange one thing for another, based on their natural right of valuation.

The natural right of conscience is the right to believe in and worship whatever one wants, including nothing. This natural right is posited in the Indiana constitution (1851) at Article I, Section 2.

The natural right of self-defense is the right to use sufficient force to defend one's person or property, or the person or property of another.

The natural right of compensation is best known as "an eye-for-an-eye." It is this natural right to be compensated for injury by others upon which tort and criminal law is based.

The natural right to contract is part of the natural rights of barter, compensation and valuation. To contract is to agree to exchange future value.

The natural right of ingestion is the right to put into one's body anything that does not belong to other people. This natural right always comes with the natural responsibility to accept the consequences for one's actions.

The natural right of intoxication is the right to get high and pursue happiness through the ingestion of an artificial medium, or through such things as exercise.

The natural right of inaction is the right to do nothing, unless one has other natural duties, for example to raise one's children.

The natural right to keep one's mouth shut is also known as the positive law right to remain silent. Anyone with a natural right to keep one's mouth shut can exercise the 5th Amendment right not to be a witness against oneself.

The natural right of representation is our political right to have others speak, deliberate or vote on our behalves. For natural born citizens, this natural political right can only be fulfilled by having a natural born citizen as U.S. President.

The natural "Right of the People to alter or to abolish" "any Form of Government" that becomes destructive to the People's natural rights is recognized in the 2ⁿᵈ paragraph of the Declaration of Independence.

The natural right to be natural born (or to be a natural born citizen of a republic) is the natural political right to be born free of a monarchy or other non-republic, which is the right to be born free of the will of other people.

The above right is similar to the right to consent only to a natural political order which is based on facts that are discernible by the use of our five senses and our powers of reason alone, such as how crimes and natural born citizens are defined. This and the above right are opposite and opposed to the artificial non-consensual privilege to be born subject to a monarch, upon which there is no objective basis of authority – only subjective justice – and no natural right of liberty.

The natural right to convey natural born citizenship belongs solely to males, who have the natural political right to bestow citizenship under natural law. Because in Nature there are no witnesses to a male's fatherhood, Nature requires males to attest to their fatherhood and take responsibility for their children in order to create natural born citizens. This is accomplished under U.S. law either by marriage or legitimation, which is codified at 8 USC 1409(a). As we shall see, those children who are not claimed in one of these two ways by U.S. citizen fathers do not share in the natural political rights of natural born citizenship.

The natural right to determine the natural law citizenship of their children (by choosing with whom to marry and have children) is a natural political right exclusively belonging to women. Under the Political Laws of Nature, women may go from nation-to-nation and may create natural born citizens with the males of different nations. Rape is not only a violation of a woman's natural right of physical liberty, but it can also violate a woman's natural political right to choose the natural born citizenship of her children.

The natural right to marry is central to citizenship in America's republics. It is a means by which male U.S. citizens signify their fatherhood of their natural born citizen children and the means by which women, by selecting who to marry, choose the natural born citizen status of their children. According to 8 USC 1409(a), when a child is born outside of marriage, in a foreign country, with a foreign mother – that is, in the state of Nature – the U.S. male must take affirmative steps to claim and prove a child as his own in order to create a natural born citizen. Outside of marriage, a U.S. woman cannot guarantee her children's natural born citizenship, but instead qualifies her children for the naturalization statutes of her own country and / or of the place of each child's birth.

Consider as well the natural right to migrate. "Consult jurists, Grotius, Puffendorff, Burlamaqui, Vattel," wrote the U.S. Supreme Court in *McIlvaine v. Coxe's Lessee* (1804), "they are of opinion, that every man has a natural right to migrate, unless restrained by laws, and that these cannot restrain the right but under special circumstances, and to a limited degree." [41]

When our governments violate these natural rights, which are the natural basis to America's political order, we as natural people naturally defy our governments.

Civil disobedience is an expression of the natural right to disobey unlawful authority. Conversely, civil disobedience is not an expression of the natural right to disobey lawful authority. The Controlled Substances Act is lawful authority. However because government officials do not follow it, the war on drugs is based on unlawful governmental action and is subject to natural disobedience.

The natural right to disobey unlawful authority includes the right of inaction, which is the right to do nothing when told to do something by a positive law power. Given that we all have only one mutual natural duty, i.e., to refrain from harming the interests of one another, which is enforced solely in the law jurisdiction, then with few exceptions, all U.S. citizens have the right of inaction and the right to disobey all so-called civil or criminal duties imposed solely by American legislatures.

This is evident in U.S. draft registration laws, which do not apply to natural born citizens, who are born free of congressional authority, but instead apply to (naturalized) citizens of the United States, whose political rights and duties are granted by Congress.

50 USC App. 453 makes it "the duty of every male citizen of the United States" to register. 5 USC 3328 (a) enforces this artificial duty with a non-criminal regulatory sanction, i.e., to deny non-registrants with future government employment. This is of no relevance to natural born citizens when they operate in their natural political capacities.

The lack of artificially imposed duties upon natural persons is also evident from Good Samaritan cases under the common law, where individuals are held not to have a natural duty to save others from peril, although some heroically do. This is evident from the *Brown v. Texas* case (1979), [42] which held that people, who the police do not suspect of committing crimes or regulatory violations, have no duty to stop and answer police officers' questions. In *Illinois v. Wardlow* (2000), the Court wrote: "If they do not learn facts rising to the level of probable cause, an individual must be allowed to go on his way." [43]

To "go on his way" is a natural right. In other words, if the person is not suspected of being a criminal or is not suspected of a regulatory violation, then he is not subject to the positive law of government. "(T)he person approached, however, need not answer any questions put to him; indeed, he may decline to listen to the questions at all and may go on his way" wrote the Supreme Court in *Florida v. Royer* (1983). [44]

The republican points to remember are 1) that republican legislatures may not prescribe duties for natural persons in the criminal law jurisdiction when such duties have not already been naturally imposed, 2) that individuals are not subject to regulation unless they traverse into the commercial, regulatory jurisdiction of equity, and 3) that individuals are not subject to criminal arrest unless they commit a real crime, based on injury.

For example, crimes are defined in Nature and we naturally know what crimes are. They are facts of Nature. So when governments treat obviously non-criminal behavior as crimes, such as certain kinds of intoxication and commercial sex, then some natural persons naturally disobey their governments to get their perceived needs met.

This disobedience just comes naturally. It is natural to be born free of and to ignore wannabe kings, whose rule is not natural. Natural persons naturally know that their behavior is not criminal – and thus, not against natural law – when it is consensual and when it does not victimize anyone. In contrast, it is very unnatural to have kings or legislatures, which are artificial entities, try to establish people's personal standards of behavior.

4

Cases and crimes

In the previous chapters we learned that the republican form of government requires a law jurisdiction in the judicial branch which secures our natural rights, including the natural right of liberty. This right of liberty is conveniently defined for us by the 13th Amendment and by the Article I, Section 37 of the Indiana constitution (1851), which prohibit enslaving people except for the commission of crime. If the legislature can change the meaning of crime, then logic tells us that the substantive right of liberty can be arbitrarily violated.

The substantive right not to be enslaved except for crime and the natural right to a republican form of government are maintained only by judicially maintaining the meaning of case and crime, which the current judicial branch has failed to do. As we shall see in this and the following chapter, the words case, crime, offense, felony and misdemeanor have constitutional meanings that define the criminal subject matter jurisdiction of judicial courts, which legislatures may not contradict or exceed.

Because the substantive right of liberty depends on judicial courts using the proper definitions of case, crime, offense, felony and misdemeanor, then reliance upon the constitutional meanings of these words is also a substantive right. This right fulfills the Supremacy Clauses in the U.S. and Indiana constitutions, which say that such constitutions will be the supreme law of the land. Below we shall look at the constitutional meaning of each of these words and their substantive effect on justice.

Consistency in meaning secures jurisdiction and the republican form of government

Fundamental to the proper exercise of law in the United States is to recognize that the U.S. and state constitutions are the supreme law of the land. Article VI, Paragraph 2 of the U.S. constitution reads:

"This Constitution, and the Laws of the United States which shall be made in Pursuance thereof; and all Treaties made, or which shall be made, under the Authority of the United States, shall be the supreme Law of the Land, and the Judges in every State shall be bound thereby, any Thing in the Constitution of Laws of any State to the Contrary notwithstanding."

As well, Article I, Section 25 of the Indiana constitution (1851) reads:

"No law shall be passed, the taking effect of which shall be made to depend upon any authority, except as provided in this Constitution."

Similarly, Indiana Code 1-1-2-1 states that all Indiana legislation must be consistent with the Indiana and U.S. constitutions. Likewise, IC 33-28-1-5(2) says that judges will render all decisions consistently with the Indiana and U.S. constitutions.

This logically means that the meaning of words that are used by the Indiana legislature in statutes must be consistent with the meaning of the same words as used in the Indiana constitution. Words used in both constitutions and statutes must connote the same meaning.

The Indiana Supreme Court wrote in *In re Todd* (1935) that "the same rules of construction should be applied to constitutional provisions as to statutory provisions when, in relation to the same general subject, the same or equivalent words are used both in a constitution and a statute." [45]

Because constitutions predate and reign supreme over statutes, the meaning of words used in Indiana's criminal statutes, such as "case," "civil case," "crime," "criminal case," "offense," "felony," and "misdemeanor" must conform to the meaning of those same words as used in the Indiana and U.S. constitutions.

Thus, whenever the Indiana legislature refers to "felonies" and "misdemeanors" in legislation that are not real felonies and misdemeanors as defined by the Indiana and U.S. constitutions, then those statutes are invalid and are not to be given legal effect in judicial trial courts. This is because judges are presumed to know their courts' jurisdiction over injury and to know the meaning of words used in America's constitutions. For example, the Indiana General Assembly may call walking on one's hands a criminal "offense," but Indiana's judges are presumed to know the constitutional meaning of an offense.

Article VII, Section 8 of the Indiana constitution (1851) grants judicial courts "such civil and criminal jurisdiction as may be prescribed by law." The term "as may be prescribed by law" means for the legislature to authoritatively write something down which is subject to and consistent with the Indiana constitution. The Indiana legislature is not allowed to prescribe or define law that is inconsistent or contrary to the Indiana constitution, or that exceeds its or another branch's powers under the constitution. This is because the Indiana and U.S. constitutions, which are inherently consistent and compatible, are the supreme law within Indiana.

There are two main varieties of judicial trial courts in Indiana. There are Circuit Courts that were created by the Indiana constitution, and there are Superior Courts that are created by the Indiana legislature with constitutional permission. The following statutory provisions show that these courts have equal statutory power, and according to IC 33-29-1-4, that they have roughly the same overall power.

At IC 33-28-1-2 the Indiana legislature defines the power of Circuit Courts.

> "(a) All circuit courts have: (1) original and concurrent jurisdiction in all civil cases and in all criminal cases; (2) de novo appellate jurisdiction of appeals from city and town courts; and (3) in Marion County, de novo appellate jurisdiction of appeals from township small claims courts established under IC 33-34.
> (b) The circuit court also has the appellate jurisdiction that may be conferred by law upon it.

At IC 33-29-1-1.5 the legislature defines the power of Superior Courts.

> "All standard superior courts have: (1) original and concurrent jurisdiction in all civil cases and in all criminal cases; (2) de novo appellate jurisdiction of appeals from city and town courts; and (3) in Marion County, de novo appellate jurisdiction of appeals from township small claims courts established under IC 33-34."

These statutory provisions grant Circuit and Superior Courts almost equal judicial power. Both have "original" subject matter jurisdiction "in all civil cases and in all criminal cases," as well as appellate jurisdiction over appeals from city, town, small claims and administrative law courts. What is particularly relevant to our discussion is the Circuit and Superior Courts' "original" subject matter jurisdiction, i.e., their power to try or adjudicate subject matter, "in all civil cases and in all criminal cases." [46]

These statutory terms "in all civil cases" and "in all criminal cases" referred to in IC 33-28-1-2 and IC 33-29-1-1.5 are the same terms are used in

Article I, Section 5 of the Indiana constitution (1816) and in in Article I, Sections 19 and 20 of the Indiana constitution (1851).

> Article I, Section 19 of the Indiana constitution (1851) reads: "<u>In all criminal cases</u> whatever, the jury shall have the right to determine the law and the facts."

> Article I, Section 20 of the Indiana constitution (1851) reads: "<u>In all civil cases</u>, the right of trial by jury shall remain inviolate."

> Article I, Section 5 of the Indiana constitution (1816) reads: "That <u>in all civil cases</u>, when the value in controversy shall exceed the sum of twenty dollars, and in all criminal cases, except in petit misdemeanors which shall be punished by fine only, not exceeding three dollars, in such manner as the Legislature may prescribe by law; the right of trial by Jury shall remain inviolate."

Statutory "civil cases" and "criminal cases" that are mentioned in the Indiana Code are to have the same meaning as the civil cases and criminal cases referred to in the above provisions of the 1816 and 1851 constitutions, or be invalid and unenforceable. Courts may not adjudicate "cases" that are not real cases. This is because judicial courts have subject matter jurisdiction only over cases, not over all subject matter that the legislature calls "cases." Cases are self-evident. They all involve injury.

When the Indiana legislature grants judicial courts "original and concurrent jurisdiction in all civil cases and in all criminal cases" at IC 33-28-1-2 and IC 33-29-1-1.5, these "civil cases" and "criminal cases" are to carry their constitutional meaning. Thus, the courts' subject matter jurisdiction extends to all "civil cases" and "criminal cases" that are respectively civil cases and criminal cases referred to in the Indiana and U.S. constitutions, and to nothing more.

Drug possession and drug dealing are not cases or controversies

Similar to Indiana courts' subject matter jurisdiction over civil and criminal cases, the U.S. constitution grants judicial power to Article III courts over cases and controversies, which terms mean roughly the same thing. In pertinent part, Article III, Section 2 reads: "The judicial Power shall extend to all Cases, in Law and Equity..." Thus, to enter a judicial court in a republic and to invoke judicial subject matter jurisdiction requires a case or controversy in law or equity.

"(W)ithout the jurisdictional element of a case or controversy," wrote the Indiana Supreme Court in *Board of Trustees of the Town (Now City) of New Haven v. City of Fort Wayne* (1978), "any court is without power to render a decision." [47] "Indeed," wrote the Indiana Supreme Court in *Brewington v. Lowe* (1848), "absent a 'case or controversy,' we have no jurisdiction to proceed." [48]

This rule is unequivocal. It applies to all plaintiffs who seek a judicial remedy.

In conformity with the Indiana Constitution, the state's General Assembly grants "original and concurrent" subject matter jurisdiction to Circuit and Superior judicial courts "in all civil cases and in all criminal cases." [49] The common denominator of civil cases and criminal cases is that they are both cases that require an injury.

As well, because of the supremacy of constitutions over statutes, and the supremacy of constitutions over the legislature, the legislature's use of the word "case" must connote the same meaning as the word case as used in both the Indiana and U.S. constitutions. That is, the meaning of the statutory word "case" is confined to the constitutional meaning of the word case.

The requirement in Indiana that a case be based on an injury-in-fact comes from the Indiana constitution, which opens judicial courts only for cases of injury to one's person, property or reputation. Article I, Section 12 of the Indiana constitution (1851) reads: "All courts shall be open, and every person, for injury done to him in his person, property, or reputation, shall have remedy by due course of law."

Whether a prosecutor brings a criminal case or a private plaintiff brings a civil case, the requirement of injury is the same in all cases or controversies. In *Gallup v. Schmidt* (1900), the Indiana Supreme Court wrote: "The courts are open to those only who are injured." [50] In *Whitmore v. Arkansas* (1990) the U.S. Supreme Court wrote:

> "To establish an Art. III case or controversy, a litigant first must clearly demonstrate that he has suffered an 'injury in fact.' Further, the litigant must satisfy the 'causation' and 'redressability' prongs of the Art. III minima by showing that the injury 'fairly can be traced to the challenged action' and 'is likely to be redressed by a favorable decision." [51]

Similarly the U.S. Supreme Court in *Summers v. Earth Island Institute* (2009) wrote that "the requirement of injury in fact is the hard floor of Article III jurisdiction that cannot be removed by statute." [52] Thus, statutory "cases" that do not involve an injury are not real cases that are cognizable by judicial courts, and legislatures may not by statute remove the requirement of injury. Judicial subject matter jurisdiction extends only to real civil and criminal cases that involve injury, as referred to in the U.S. and Indiana constitutions.

Absent such a case, judicial courts have no constitutional authority to act. Unless a statutory "case" is also a real case, Indiana prosecutors have no authority under IC 33-28-1-2 and IC 33-29-1-1.5 to bring such "cases" to judicial courts. They only have authority to bring real cases and controversies to judicial courts, to which the above statutes actually refer.

Thus, all natural persons in the Indiana republic have a substantive right not to be subject to the law jurisdiction of judicial courts unless civil plaintiffs or criminal prosecutors have a case or controversy to assert against them. Case was defined in the law and equity jurisdictions of Great Britain long before the word was used in the U.S. or Indiana constitutions. Because defendants' 13th Amendment right would be emasculated if a legislature could define criminal cases arbitrarily, then defendants have a substantive right to rely on the constitutional meaning of the word case in order for the state to establish its criminal jurisdiction.

Without an injury, there is no constitutional authority for any party to seek a judicial remedy. Without an alleged injury to someone – that is to say a private wrong – then there is no case or controversy of any kind. In the parlance of today's Supreme Court, there is no civil action without being "adversely affected." [53] Likewise, without private harm, there is no criminal case and there is no crime committed within the meaning of America's constitutions.

This same conclusion can be gleaned from *Aetna Life Ins. Co. v. Haworth* (1937). There the U.S. Supreme Court wrote: "The term 'controversies,' if distinguishable at all from 'cases,' is so in that it is less comprehensive than the latter, and includes only suits of a civil nature.'" [54] This statement makes clear that the definition of cases comprehends all controversies, which at a minimum require injury to maintain "suits of a civil nature." [55] It also makes clear that case comprehends a criminal case. Thus, to bring a criminal case into a judicial court requires an injury.

At the very least, all criminal cases share the elements of the above referenced "suits of a civil nature," which require an injury or private wrong. Lacking the element of injury, the vast majority of drug possession and drug dealing matters brought before Indiana's judicial courts have not been cases or controversies. Indiana's judicial courts have subject matter jurisdiction only in civil and criminal cases. [56] The judiciary is presumed to know and use the constitutional meanings of case and crime, which define their courts' civil and criminal jurisdictions.

As we have seen above, the meaning of a case is determined by America's constitutions, not America's legislatures. Drug cases involve injury. Mere drug matters or "cases" do not. Thus, the false power exerted by judicial courts over statutory drug "cases" is negated and dethroned by the meaning given to the word case by American constitutions.

Besides co-opting the constitutional word case to give faux legitimacy to phony "cases," there is no historical, constitutional or even statutory authority to adjudicate most drug matters in judicial courts. Due to the lack of injury, most of these matters simply do not amount to cases or controversies which are required to invoke judicial jurisdiction.

Prosecutors have no judicial standing in drug matters

Closely related to the case or controversy requirement of judicial courts is a concept called standing, which requires plaintiffs to demonstrate the elements of injury-in-fact in order to enter a judicial court. Thus, what is said about the need for injury to establish a case is equally true to establish standing, and vice versa.

Because the state of Indiana must always have a case and / or a crime to enter a judicial court, by the same rules it must also always have standing. "Standing is a requirement that the plaintiffs have been injured or been threatened with injury...," reads *Black's Law Dictionary*, "and focuses on the question of whether the litigant is the proper party to fight the lawsuit." [57]

The U.S. Supreme Court in *Horne v. Flores* (2009) called standing "an essential and unchanging part of the case-or-controversy requirement." [58] This means that no matter what the Indiana General Assembly legislates, it cannot change the constitutional requirement that a party must have standing based on injury to enter a republican judicial court.

This judicial "requirement of actual or threatened injury amenable to judicial remedy... is not merely a troublesome hurdle to overcome..." wrote the U.S. Supreme Court in *Valley Forge Christian College v. Americans United for Separation of Church and State, Inc.* (1982). [59] "Absent this showing, complainants may not invoke the jurisdiction of the court," wrote the Indiana Supreme Court in *State ex rel. Cittadine v. Indiana Dep't of Transp.* (2003). [60]

To refute the above argument, Indiana officials might claim that the above judicial statements of law do not apply to the prosecution by governments of criminal cases, but instead only to civil cases. However, this would be a misrepresentation of law because both criminal cases and civil cases are cases. As cases, by definition, both civil cases and criminal cases involve injury to a right. Thus, there must at least be a private wrong to grant prosecutors standing to invoke criminal subject matter jurisdiction in matters involving drugs.

Drug matters lack justiciability

Drug possession and dealing also fail for want of justiciability, which is another prong in the state's judicial requirements. "Nonjusticiability" refers to "the inappropriateness of the subject matter for judicial consideration," wrote the U.S. Supreme Court in *Baker v. Carr* (1962). [61] A court's justiciability-inquiry is over "whether the duty asserted can be judicially identified and its breach judicially determined, and whether protection for the right asserted can be judicially molded." [62]

Because the only universal duty over which the law jurisdiction of judicial courts has civil and criminal jurisdiction is people's natural duty to refrain from harming other people, jurisdiction fails when there is no averment or element of injury. Justiciability is determined from the "merit in the averments." [63]

When no injury is alleged or existent, then the subject matter is inappropriate for judicial consideration. Any drug matter that does not cause injury and is not cognizable as a right of action under the common law is not a justiciable criminal matter in a judicial court of a republic.

To paraphrase *Baker v. Carr* (1962) above, neither the duty to not possess drugs nor the duty to not make or sell drugs can be judicially identified, their breach judicially determined or their remedies judicially molded. This is 1) because the only mutual duty of all persons that is recognized in the law jurisdiction of judicial courts is the natural duty to not harm others, 2) because neither drug possession and drug dealing is a breach of a duty to be judicially determined, and 3) because the law jurisdiction may mold a judicial remedy only for injury.

"A crime may be defined to be any act done in violation of those duties which an individual owes to the community, and for the breach of which the law has provided that the offender shall make satisfaction to the public," writes *Black's Law Dictionary*. [64] Because all individuals owe the community only one duty, i.e., to refrain from harming others, only a violation of this duty can be a universal crime.

One's duty to get a license to perform privileged commercial activity, such as drug dealing, is not a natural duty, but an artificial one. Thus it is not a criminal duty imposed in the law jurisdiction, but is instead a commercial duty imposed under equity.

As such it is not a duty "which an individual owes to the community," [65] such that the judicial branch can deprive him of his physical liberty for its breach. Instead, it is a duty that only an artificial and commercial person owes to Congress or a state legislature, and one which is in equity, and thus is not subject to criminal penalty.

Without adding the element of force, theft or fraud to a drug deal, there are no legal victims resulting from such consensual behavior. Legal victims result from unconsented behavior. This is consistent with the legal maxim *volenti non fit injuria. To the willing, no injury is done, Scienti et volenti non fit injuria* says another maxim: *An injury is not done to one who knows and wills it.*

The law is clear and consistent. One cannot volunteer to be injured to create a civil or criminal case. That is, one cannot claim to be a victim in a consensual drug deal where no actual crime occurs. For example, to voluntarily smoke pot is to consent to its euphoric effects. Excluding drug dealing to minors, drug deals would only be subject to criminal authority if the drugs were unlawful, e.g., stolen, or if the drugs were fraudulently mislabeled to cause injury.

Criminal prosecutions apply to injury caused by other people – not to the natural effects of one's personal choices. A judicial court may not fashion a remedy for the natural consequences of one's voluntary behavior.

To paraphrase *Baker v. Carr* (1962) [66] above: That a person smokes too much pot is not a violation of a judicially identified duty, is not a breach that can be judicially determined, nor can a remedy be judicially molded. In other words, judicial courts do not have jurisdiction over possession and use of intoxicants, but instead have authority over injury and endangerment caused after intoxicants' use. The consequences to oneself for one's own voluntary behavior are not justiciable.

Courts that have no subject matter jurisdiction are precluded, at all times, from acting. One cannot volunteer into subject matter jurisdiction that a court does not have and that it may not exercise. This is why subject matter jurisdiction may be challenged at any time.

IC 35-34-1-4(b)(2) of the Indiana Code reads: "A motion to dismiss based upon lack of jurisdiction over the subject matter may be made at any time." This is a codification of the common law right to demur to a false assertion of authority. Demurring to the false authority of America's drug war is what this book is all about.

Challenging subject matter jurisdiction at any time is appropriate because courts either have power, or they do not, as a matter of law. Jurisprudence, which is the science of law, is presumed to be capable of this determination in short order. Judicial jurisdiction depends on if there is an injured party. Whether or not there is an injured party is the threshold legal question that most sixth graders could answer in most drug matters.

"Although circuit courts are presumed to have subject-matter jurisdiction," wrote the Indiana Supreme Court in *State v. Sproles* (1996), "Indiana courts have only such jurisdiction as is granted to them by our Constitution and statutes." [67] In *Herman v. State* (1979) it wrote: "A court of general jurisdiction is presumed to have acted within its powers until a want of jurisdiction appears affirmatively on the record," with the burden on the accused to affirmatively show that the court has no jurisdiction. [68]

This book – which is based on natural law, constitutional law, case law and statutory law – carries the burden to show that republican judicial courts have no subject matter jurisdiction over non-injurious drug matters. Given that there is no constitutional amendment that places drug commerce into the law jurisdiction, as the 13th and 18th amendments did respectively with slavery and alcohol commerce, this book demonstrates that the law jurisdiction of Indiana's judicial courts, as created and empowered by the Indiana constitution, does not have criminal subject matter jurisdiction granted from any source over mere drug possession or drug commerce.

Vices are not crimes

Regardless whether artificial governments acknowledge the true difference between crime and lawful behavior, i.e., whether or not there is an injury to a natural right, and between natural and artificial duties, natural persons do on a very natural level. This is because artificial governments cannot fool the Mother Nature within each of us about what is and what is not natural, and what is and is not a real crime.

It is as natural for some people to pursue intoxication as it is natural for others to pursue gobs of money. Both pursuits are lawful so long as they do not violate the natural duty that we owe to other people, which is to not harm them. Thus, we naturally know 1) that neither getting intoxicated nor becoming enormously rich are crimes, 2) that neither the mere possession of intoxicants nor of stacks of money are crimes, and 3) that we are not subject to the criminal jurisdiction of judicial courts when we merely consume intoxicants or roll in money, even while mocking people who are sober or poor. (Because consuming intoxicants and rolling in money are not crimes, then mocking people who are sober or poor are not hate crimes.)

Regardless of whether we attend law school, we naturally know that crimes occur only when people and their interests get harmed. We naturally express this knowledge by calling for governments' help when someone is severely injured, either by accident or intentionally.

Unless we are unnaturally brainwashed by artificial stimuli, we do not naturally call the police for help when people are not harming other people. When someone intentionally injures someone else, we call the police. This is a natural response.

In a republic, this reflects the natural jurisdiction of judicial courts over injury. Injury or threat of injury by natural persons is not only the constitutional criteria, but also the natural and objective standard to invoke our judicial courts' civil and criminal jurisdictions.

This is as 19th century political philosopher Lysander Spooner long ago told us. "Crimes are those acts by which one man harms the person or property of another. Vices are those acts by which a man harms himself or his property." [69] Consequently, there is no reason to confuse the two, Spooner wrote. "Vices are not crimes." [70]

Underlying this natural fact is the realization that we pretty much already agree on what is good and bad, or between what is tolerable and what is *malum in se.* We do not tolerate people hurting other people. We naturally tolerate other people's vices, at least to a point, and even build great festivals and industries around some of them.

Likewise, teenagers do not naturally call the police to bust their own intoxication parties. Nor does anyone call the police to report people when they return home from Las Vegas. Calling our government to rat on people because of their vices is unnatural behavior. So is putting them in jail for these vices.

Each of us has a natural sense of crime. Thomas Jefferson wrote that we have "an innate sense of justice." [71] We naturally know not to call the police unless there is trouble. We do not generally call for the fire department's help unless there is a fire. Because the law jurisdiction of judicial courts enforces natural law, based on objective criteria, knowing the scope of the criminal law jurisdiction and the need for fire departments just comes naturally to most of us. We naturally know what fires and crimes are.

Given that hundreds of thousands of Hoosiers have been incarcerated for behavior for which only the brainwashed among us would call the police, it is apparent that many natural persons have a better feel for

Indiana's criminal law jurisdiction than the people running it. For prosecutors and judges in the law jurisdiction to claim that our vices are criminal is just not natural. It is a subjective opinion that is divorced from the objective natural reality of a republican law court, where crime is a fact of Nature defined by injury.

To claim that vices are crimes is for government officials to try to redefine facts of Nature, such as to call red "blue." It is to forget the proper jurisdiction of the courts over injury and to divorce judges' natural criminal authority from their own human nature.

To prosecute and punish people for their vices is to forget that not only defendants, but also prosecutors and judges have vices. It is to betray one's natural personage, as well as the (natural) law jurisdiction of judicial courts over injury.

To enslave such non-criminals is for officials to forget the natural and objective source of their authority in the law jurisdiction, and to mistake this natural authority for artificial and subjective positive law authority of legislatures. It is to rule on a supernatural and subjective basis rather than on a natural and objective one, upon which jurisprudence is to be based.

That crime is adjudged by natural standards is expressed in America's jury system. For example, Article 1, Section 19 of the Indiana constitution (1851) reads: "In all criminal cases whatever, the jury shall have the right to determine the law and the facts."

For the jury to determine the law in a criminal case is for it to determine what is and what is not criminal. This is a power greater than the legislature's. This is the power to trump the will of the legislature. Alas, one of juries' forgotten roles is to secure the natural law basis of criminal law from the positive law of legislatures.

This process assumes, however, that judges have already vetted whether there is probable cause to believe that the defendant has committed a crime based on injury. (Injury is what places a matter in jury.) This is the false and fatal presumption that most defendants and juries have been making in judicial courts that are engaged in the war on drugs.

If Nature does not require natural compensation ("an eye for an eye") for behavior such as drug possession or dealing, then neither does the law jurisdiction, which enforces natural law. This rule is completely unheard of by (and lost on) today's government officials who are involved with drug enforcement, and who do not know the natural law basis of republican criminal authority.

We naturally know that getting intoxicated is activity over which adult individuals are in charge until either 1) they harm or endanger other people, which subjects them to the law jurisdiction of judicial courts, or 2) they get behind the wheel of an automobile, which also subjects them to regulation by the executive branch. Otherwise, on a very natural and intuitive level, we know that God or Nature allows them to get intoxicated, as we also naturally know that God or Nature will force them to accept the compulsory consequences of their intoxication.

Consequently, the People gave power to republican government only 1) to arrest them for harming or endangering the public, 2) to civilly or criminally compensate victims of their intoxication, which is accomplished in the law jurisdiction of judicial courts, and 3) to regulate their licensed activity in the executive branch, such as to revoke their licenses for driving (or to enjoin their future driving) because of drinking. Government of any other kind or scope is non-republican because it is repulsive to our human nature.

Within its proper role and function, as outlined above, the state has legitimate authority to regulate our licensed driving. Because it can legitimately establish that a blood-alcohol content of 0.08 percent or below is required for us to legally drive, it can just as legally set the rate to 0.00 percent. For the same reason, i.e., that both licensed drivers and corporations are creatures of the state, it can tax 100 percent of corporations' profits.

The legislature cannot prohibit our natural behavior, such as drinking alcohol in private, but it absolutely can prohibit driving under any level of intoxication or "influence." That it chooses less than zero tolerance, and that it chooses to take less than 100 percent of corporations' profits, is for political and policy reasons only, not for legal reasons. The state can set standards for all that it regulates, and for all that exist because of its permission, which of course excludes natural persons – like you and me – acting in our natural capacities.

When not harming other people and when not engaged in activity that is subject to regulation, such as driving or performing surgery, natural persons within republics may be as intoxicated in private as Nature will allow in the natural law jurisdiction of America's constitutions. This is part of our natural right to make fools of ourselves, just so long as we do not hurt or endanger anyone else.

For the very same reason that the state of Indiana has authority to regulate and set standards for automobile drivers, it has similar regulatory authority over people who construct buildings, cut hair, midwife babies, practice law, teach, do body piercings, operate casinos, perform surgery, and make and sell drugs, for example. These persons are in commerce.

Conversely, the state does not regulate who may use drugs, who may gamble, who may copulate, who may represent themselves in court, who may self-learn, who may get tattoos, who may pitch a tent or who may cut or shave their own hair. These people are acting in their natural capacities.

To use intoxicants is a natural, inherent right, but to deal in intoxicants is not. Says West's *Indiana Law Encyclopedia*, "the right to manufacture, sell, transport, or deal in intoxicating liquors is not an inherent right and is subject to legislative regulation." [72]

Through the positive law of the state legislature and under the rule-making authority of state agencies, the legislative and executive branches can set the standards for all who participate in commerce. Those participants exclude natural persons, while exercising their natural rights.

Drug possession and drug dealing are not crimes or criminal cases

The U.S. constitution and both the 1816 and 1851 Indiana constitutions are replete with references to crime and criminal cases.

The Indiana constitution of 1851 refers to crime at Article I, Section 13 and Article I, Section 37, and to criminal cases at Article I, Section 13. The Indiana constitution of 1816 refers to criminal cases at Article I, Sections 12 and 13.

The U.S. constitution refers to crime and / or criminal cases at Article II, Section 4; Article III, Section 2; Article IV, Section 2; 5th Amendment; 6th Amendment; 13th Amendment and 14th Amendment. A good example of a reference to crime in the U.S. constitution is at Article III, Section 2, which is also a good statement about the territoriality of criminal jurisdiction. It reads:

> "The Trial of all Crimes, except in Cases of Impeachment; shall be by Jury; and such Trial shall be held in the State where the said Crimes shall have been committed; but when not committed within any State, the Trial shall be at such Place or Places as the Congress may by Law have directed."

Crime and criminal cases have the same meaning under both the United States and Indiana constitutions. The U.S. constitution's references to crime were to crime that was already defined, prior to the adoption of the U.S. constitution, under the constitutions of the thirteen states. These states would not have allowed the U.S. republic to use a different definition of crime in fear of having people "tried for pretended Offences" (mentioned in the Declaration of Independence) and arbitrarily enslaved by the federal government, as they had been by the King of England.

The most illustrative provisions of American constitutions that refer to crime are the 13th Amendment to the U.S. constitution and a similar provision in the Indiana constitution, both which prohibit slavery or indentured servitude except as punishment for the commission of crimes. We have already read the 13th Amendment. Here is Article I, Section 37 of the Indiana constitution (1851):

> "There shall be neither slavery, nor involuntary servitude, within the State, otherwise than for the punishment of crime, whereof the party shall have been duly convicted."

These provisions show that both the U.S. and Indiana constitutions prohibit enslaving people unless they commit crimes. This makes it imperative for judicial courts to use the correct definition of crime so that, pursuant to our constitutions, judicial judges do not enslave the wrong people, and thereby convert free people into slaves.

So, constitutionally speaking, what does a crime look like and how is it defined? Article I, Section 13 of the Indiana constitution (1851) tells us. It reads:

> "Victims of crime, as defined by law, shall have the right to be treated with fairness, dignity, and respect throughout the criminal justice process; and, as defined by law, to be informed of and present during public hearings and to confer with the prosecution, to the extent that exercising these rights does not infringe upon the constitutional rights of the accused."

This constitutional provision tells us about the relationship of injury to crime in Indiana. First, it says that crime is defined by law, which means by natural law or by the (natural, common) law jurisdiction – not by the Indiana legislature. As mentioned earlier, Nature proscribes crime (prohibits it) within a republic, while legislatures prescribe crime (write it down).

Second, it is axiomatic that "crime, as defined by law..." produces injured victims. This echoes the provision at Article I, Section 12 of the Indiana constitution (1851) which says that Indiana's judicial courts are "open to injury."

The judicial branch adjudicates injury. The criminal law jurisdiction serves criminal victims. Not ironically, if we put these constitutional phrases and concepts together, they explain criminal courts' subject matter jurisdiction. Indiana's criminal courts are literally "open to injury" [73] of "victims of crime as defined by law." [74]

"In all cases, the crime includes an injury;" Sir William Blackstone tells us in his *Commentaries on the Laws of England*, "every public offence is also a private wrong, and somewhat more; it affects the individual, and it likewise affects the community." [75]

This relationship between crime and injury was reiterated by the Indiana Supreme Court in *State ex rel. Johnson v. White Circuit Court* (1948), where a rape victim sought to mandate a particular judge (and outcome) in a juvenile proceeding against her rapist. There the Court wrote:

> "The distinction between torts and crimes is based upon the public nature of the criminal offense. 'Although the same act may constitute both a crime and a tort, the crime is an offense against the public pursued by the sovereign, while the tort is a private injury which is pursued by the injured party.' 14 Am. Jur. 755, § 3. The same distinction has been noted by another authority in the following language: 'Therefore, the real distinction between a tort and a crime is to be sought for, not in a difference between their tendencies, but in the difference between the methods by which the remedy for the wrong is pursued, a wrong for which the remedy is pursued by and at the discretion of the individual injured or his representative being a tort, and a wrong for which the wrongdoer is proceeded against by the sovereign or state for the purpose of punishment being a crime.' 16 C.J. § 3; 22 C.J.S., Criminal Law, § 4." [76]

In other words, wrote the Indiana Supreme Court, there is no "real distinction between a tort and a crime" except between "the public nature of the criminal offense" and "the methods by which the remedy for the wrong is pursued..." [77] Both torts and crimes are injurious "wrongs" [78] by natural persons, subject to the law jurisdiction of judicial courts. All crimes are torts.

American Jurisprudence 2nd says that a "crime is said to be an offense against the sovereign, a wrong which the government deems injurious not only to the victim but to the public at large..." [79] The phrase "not only to the victim" signifies that all crimes injure natural persons or their rights as a condition precedent before the public at large is injured.

In contrast, in other matters where there is no private or public victim, such as in consensual drug deals, then such behavior does not "affect the community," [80] and there is no crime or criminal case under these terms' constitutional and common law meanings. The "public" has "rights" only to the extent of the duty of all persons, natural or otherwise, to refrain from harming the natural political rights of others.

It goes without saying that one cannot be qualified as a criminal law judge in a republic if one does not know that all crimes are torts, i.e., violations of a victim's natural rights. Without knowing what a crime is, then there is no way for a court to discern what is not a crime, or what is a false "crime," or what is a false basis for the court's subject matter jurisdiction.

Without knowing the meaning of crime, one could not know the meaning of probable cause. Without objective natural standards, such as injury, this would leave only subjective standards to determine real crimes from counterfeit ones.

Only *malum in se* involving injury may be adjudicated in the law jurisdiction of republican judicial courts. Therefore, only legislatures' codifications of *malum in se* are enforceable as crimes against natural persons in the judicial courts of America's republics.

Legislatures' enactment of phony "crimes" and "offenses," such as the "crime" of drug possession, are called *malum prohibita*. *Malum prohibita* is what legislatures – and not Nature – prohibit.

This book shows 1) that *malum prohibita* is regulatory and operates in equity in America's republics, over that which republican legislatures may legislate, and 2) that *malum prohibita* is not enforceable against natural persons in the law jurisdiction of republican judicial courts. This law jurisdiction has a republic's exclusive criminal authority, which is only over *malum in se* involving a private wrong, caused by natural persons.

5
Felonies, misdemeanors and offenses

"Due process" for false "criminals"

As we have seen, there is no crime without an injury caused by a natural person. As well, regulatory violations of mere *malum prohibita* do not amount to crimes and are not triable against natural persons in the law jurisdiction of judicial courts. These principles were expressed by the United States Supreme Court in the following two cases.

District of Columbia v. Clawans (1937) was a case about a defendant's right to a jury trial when sanctioned for selling the unused portions of railway tickets without a license. Selling tickets without a license from the District of Columbia is analogous to selling drugs without a license from the state of Indiana.

As we recall from the previous chapter, Article III, Section 2 of the U.S. constitution says that "(t)he Trial of all Crimes, except in Cases of Impeachment; shall be by Jury..." Clawans claimed that he was entitled to a jury trial in a judicial court because his was a criminal trial. The trial court disagreed.

The Supreme Court upheld the denial of a jury trial after it determined that violating a licensing statute "was not a crime at common law" and is today "at most but an infringement of local police regulations..." [81]

So too, as we shall see beginning at chapter 16, the dealing of drugs is at most a violation of a licensing statute, i.e., a regulatory infringement, and does not amount to a crime within the plain wording of the Indiana constitution and under the common law, which is required for criminal subject matter jurisdiction in a republican judicial court.

Similarly, in *District of Columbia v. Colts* (1930), another case about the right to a jury trial, the U.S Supreme Court pointed out that mere regulatory violations, such as driving too fast, "do not rise to the degree of crimes within the meaning of Article III..." of the U.S. constitution. [82] This means that they also do not rise to the definition of crime under the Indiana constitution.

The Court said that without recklessness, which was an element found in the driving of defendant Colts, merely driving above a posted speed limit is *malum prohibita* which cannot be described as "a crime within the meaning of the third article of the Constitution." [83] In other words, *malum prohibita* is not crime, is not the same thing as crime, and is not to be treated as crime in a republican judicial court.

If behavior amounts to a regulatory violation (*malum prohibita)* and does not amount to *malum in se*, then it is not a crime within the meaning of America's republics. Thus, neither drug possession, which is not prohibited, nor drug commerce, which is at most regulated by the executive branch as *malum prohibita*, are crimes cognizable by U.S. or Indiana judicial courts and subject to jury trials. This means that judicial courts have no subject matter jurisdiction over *malum prohibita* that is called or disguised as "crime," and that jury trials are not to be awarded to accused regulatory violators.

Injury-in-fact is constitutionally-determinative of what branch of Indiana government, if any, has power to adjudicate a matter. In *Board of Trustees of New Haven* (1978) the Indiana Supreme Court wrote that injury was "determinative of the circuit court's having any jurisdiction to entertain any of the further issues in the cause." [84]

This judicial requirement of injury-in-fact "is built on a single basic idea – the idea of separation of powers," wrote the U.S. Supreme Court in *Allen v. Wright* (1984). [85] In other words, to maintain the proper separation of governmental powers, the judicial branch must adjudicate only cases or crimes involving injury.

By perverting the meaning of case and crime to include non-injury, the executive and judicial branches of state governments collude to violate the separation of powers doctrine and enslave or indenture non-criminals. This perversion also adds inconsistencies, anomalies and ironies to the administration of law that are readily apparent.

For example, by calling drug dealing "crimes," the criminal justice system of Indiana must falsely provide jury trials to people who are not entitled to them. The U.S. Supreme Court held in the above *Clawans* and *Colts* cases that mere regulatory violations, such as selling tickets, oleomargarine or drugs without a license, are not entitled to jury trials under the U.S. constitution because they are not common law crimes. As the Supreme Court clearly said: regulatory violations "do not rise to the degree of crimes within the meaning of Article III..." of the U.S. constitution. [86] They are not crimes in the judicial branch of America's republics.

Thus, regulatory violations – whether driving without a license from the Indiana Commissioner of the BMV or selling drugs without a "registration" from the Indiana State Board of Pharmacy – 1) are not crimes, 2) are not subject to arrest, 3) are not subject to criminal penalty, and 4) are not subject to adjudication by the judicial branch.

Likewise, regulatory violations are not deserving of jury trials because they are not crimes. Jury trials, as secured by Article I, Section 13 of the Indiana constitution (1851) and the 6th Amendment of the U.S. constitution, apply only to real crimes – not to regulatory violations. That is what the Supreme Court told us.

In the case of drugs, that both states and the U.S. government 1) try violators of regulatory *malum prohibita* as "criminals" and 2) give jury trials to these non-criminals, is the height of judicial absurdity. Not only are drug dealers tried in the wrong branch of government, and in the wrong type of courts, but they are criminally tried for violating legislative prohibitions which operate in equity. This false process results from smearing the lines between executive and judicial jurisdictions and from fudging the meaning of words used in American constitutions.

Most of Indiana's drug-related "felonies" and all drug-related "misdemeanors" are not real felonies or misdemeanors

As with the words "crime" and "case," the Indiana legislature's use of the words "felony" and "misdemeanor" must match the meaning of felony and misdemeanor used in the Indiana and U.S. constitutions.

Felony is referred to in the U.S. constitution at Article I, Section 6; Article I, Section 8, Clause 10; and at Article IV, Section 2. Misdemeanor is referred to in the U.S. constitution at Article II, Section 4. Misdemeanor was also referred to in Article I, Section 5 of of the Indiana constitution (1816), which reads:

> "That... in all criminal cases, except in petit misdemeanors which shall be punished by fine only, not exceeding three dollars, in such manner as the Legislature may prescribe by law; the right of trial by Jury shall remain inviolate."

This provision, which is not in the 1851 constitution, shows that petit misdemeanors were a category of crime under the common law of England

and Indiana, albeit ones not deserving of jury trials. This category included such common law misdemeanors as petit larceny and petit theft. These activities were in fact torts or minor crimes because they involved injuring other people or harming their property interests. That is, they were *malum in se*, not *malum prohibita*.

This is consistent with the meaning of misdemeanor as used in the U.S. constitution at Article II, Section 4 which refers to "high Crimes and Misdemeanors." This is also consistent with the meaning given to misdemeanors by Blackstone in his *Commentaries on the Laws of England* (1753):

> "A crime or misdemeanour is an act committed or omitted, in violation of a public law either forbidding or commanding it. This general definition comprehends both crimes and misdemeanours, which, properly speaking, are mere synonymous terms; though, in common usage, the word 'crimes' is made to denote such offences as are of a deeper and more atrocious dye; while smaller faults, and omissions of less consequence, are comprised under the gentler names of 'misdemeanours' only." [87]

If a) "in all cases," as Blackstone wrote, "the crime includes an injury," [88] and b) if crimes and misdemeanors "are mere synonymous terms," [89] and c) if felonies are really just misdemeanors but "of a deeper and more atrocious dye," [90] then all misdemeanors and felonies involve injury and are mere degrees of severity of crime. Without an injury, there is no misdemeanor, no felony, no crime, no offense, and even no case for a judicial court to discern the severity of harm.

Judicial courts do not have jurisdiction over felonies and misdemeanors merely because the legislature calls something a "felony" or a "misdemeanor." Courts have specific jurisdiction and their judges are required to know it.

That operating in commerce is not a real misdemeanor was affirmed by the U.S. Supreme Court in *Schick v. United States* (1904) where the defendants challenged being fined for the "petty offense" of purchasing unapproved oleomargarine for resale – a regulatory violation. There the Court recognized true misdemeanors as a "class or grade of offenses called petty offenses, which, according to the common law, may be proceeded against summarily in any tribunal legally constituted for that purpose..." However, the Court differentiated the "petty offense" of violating oleomargarine regulations from true misdemeanors, saying that nothing could "lift this one [unapproved oleomargarine commerce] to the dignity of a crime." [91]

Judicial courts are constituted for the purpose of adjudicating crimes, not fake "felonies," "misdemeanors," or phony "offenses" such as participating in margarine or drug commerce. Judicial courts have subject matter jurisdiction over real crimes and offenses such as felonies and petty misdemeanors.

Republican judicial courts do not exist to adjudicate *malum prohibita* such as driving too fast, making rock cocaine or selling margarine without a license. Such rules apply only to commercial, artificial persons who are subject to non-criminal regulation, and who the Supreme Court says are not entitled to judicial jury trials for regulatory violations.

Similarly, law enforcers are constituted for the purpose of making arrests for felonies, not fake "felonies." At IC 16-42-20-1(b)(3) the Indiana legislature authorizes the Indiana State Board of Pharmacy to designate certain employees as drug enforcers. These enforcers may "(m)ake arrests without warrant... if the officer or employee has probable cause to believe that the person to be arrested has committed or is committing a felony relating to controlled substances."

This mention of "a felony relating to controlled substances" refers to those felonies in the Controlled Substances Act at IC 35-48-4 that are *malum in se*. It does not refer to the numerous "felonies" at IC 35-48-4 for drug dealing, which is subject to regulation under equity, and are not subject to criminal law. This means that a pharmacy board officer or employee may make an arrest without a warrant only for a constitutional felony for which he has probable cause.

This also means that all arrests for phony "felonies" have been false. In America's republics, drug enforcers have no authority to arrest people for regulatory violations. They have authority to make arrests only for criminal violations to others' natural rights. As the Supreme Court wrote in *Schick v. United States* (1904) about Schick's participation in oleomargarine commerce: nothing could "lift this one to the dignity of a crime." [92] Likewise, nothing can lift mere drug dealing to a crime.

Most "offenses" relating to drugs are not offenses

Similar to the misuse of crime, case, felony and misdemeanor, the Indiana legislature has also improperly co-opted the word offense from its constitutional definition. A statutory "offense" is defined at IC 35-48-1-19, which reads: "'Offense' means a crime. The term does not include an infraction."

Prior to the enactment of the above statute, the meaning of the word offense had already been established by its constitutional use. Offenses are referred to in Article 1, Section 17 of the Indiana constitution, which reads:

> "Offenses, other than murder or treason, shall be bailable by sufficient sureties. Murder or treason shall not be bailable, when the proof is evident, or the presumption strong."

Offenses are also referred to in Article I, Section 8; Article II, Section 2; and the 5th Amendment of the U.S. constitution.

It is obvious from the constitutional use of offense that it is synonymous with the word crime. As Blackstone wrote, all crimes include an injury. Likewise, all offenses involve injury, and according to the Indiana legislature, they do not include infractions.

Because of the supremacy of constitutions over statutes and because IC 1-1-2-1 says that Indiana's statutes must be consistent with the U.S. and Indiana constitutions, state officials must give the same meaning to the statutory word "offense" as they do the constitutional word offense.

For example, IC 35-34-1-2 defines what is needed in an indictment or information to allege the commission of an "offense." The statute requires the indictment or information to "be a plain, concise, and definite written statement of the essential facts constituting the offense charged."

Because an "offense" is to have the meaning of an offense in the Indiana constitution, the effect of IC 35-34-1-2 is to require prosecutors to state a criminal offense that is cognizable under the Indiana constitution and the common law in order to invoke judicial authority. Such offense would necessarily involve the averment of an injury. Otherwise, the matter would not be justiciable.

Conversely, the Indiana constitution does not allow prosecutors to allege any "offense," which does not involve an injury, over which the court has no subject matter jurisdiction. Doing this would be to misrepresent both the authority of the prosecutor to bring a matter to the court and the authority of the court to hear the matter. If knowingly done by prosecutors, this would amount to fraud upon a court.

Likewise, IC 16-42-20-1(b) (3) authorizes the Indiana State Board of Pharmacy to designate officers and employees of the board to "(m)ake arrests without warrant for any offense relating to controlled substances committed in" their presence. Given that such "offense" means a real crime and not a phony one, and because the power to arrest is strictly judicial, and not administrative, then the statute means that a board officer or employee may make an arrest without a warrant only for a constitutional offense or crime committed in the person's presence.

This would exclude making arrests for the non-criminal exercises of natural rights such as drug possession or for regulatory violations such as drug dealing. It would include arrests, for example, for fraudulently conveying drugs to the officer or in the officer's presence. This distinction occurs because drug dealing is not a *malum in se* crime, but committing fraud clearly is.

Given the constitutional meaning of the word offense, drug enforcers have no arrest authority over mere drug possession and dealing, which are "offenses" but not offenses. Drug possession is a protected natural right. Drug dealing is a regulated activity which is subject to the appellate jurisdiction of republican courts, operating in equity. However, the latter is not behavior for which an "offender" may be criminally imprisoned or prosecuted in the law jurisdiction, which is a republic's sole criminal authority.

The executive branch's power to arrest real criminals is to compliment the judicial branch's power to adjudicate real crimes. As the above *Clawans*, *Colts* and *Schick* cases indicate, law enforcers have no arrest authority over matters, such as personal or consensual drug matters, that are at most regulatory violations and that are not judicial crimes.

As well, whether done knowingly or not, prosecutors have been entering Indiana judicial courts in most matters relating to drugs only by misrepresenting phony statutory "offenses," such as drug possession and dealing, as real constitutional offenses and crimes over which judicial courts have constitutional authority to adjudicate. Yet as we shall in chapter 22, only nine of the drug "offenses" listed in the Indiana Controlled Substances Act at IC 35-48-4 qualify as constitutional offenses, which can therefore support judicial courts' constitutional subject matter jurisdiction.

In summary, when a statute such as IC 35-48-4-6.1 says that it shall be a felony to possess methamphetamine, it means that it is a phony "felony," and not a real felony that is needed to support judicial subject matter jurisdiction. Likewise, when the legislature calls possession of less than 30 grams of marijuana a "misdemeanor" at IC 35-48-4-11, this is false because possession of any property is not a real misdemeanor under the U.S. or Indiana constitutions. As we have seen, the injurious nature of real misdemeanors is self-evident in the Indiana constitution (1816).

Statutes that call drug possession a "misdemeanor" or a "felony" contradict Article I, Section 1 of the Indiana constitution (1816) which calls property possession an unalienable natural right. Either the constitution is correct or the contrary statute is correct, but not both. Judges are presumed to know which is correct.

Likewise, drug dealing is a fake "felony" and a "crime," and not a real felony or crime. Otherwise, officers of pharmaceutical companies would have criminal records. Most do not because their drug dealing operates in equity, which has no criminal jurisdiction.

Because the Indiana legislature does not legislate over the criminal law jurisdiction of judicial courts, but only codifies crimes and prescribes their punishment, then the state may not license criminal activity and the legislature may not grant immunity to commit crimes. Natural law defines crime, not republican legislatures. Legislatures may merely prescribe or codify what is *malum in se*.

Therefore, due to the separation of powers doctrine, nothing subject to regulatory control – such as drug commerce – is criminal, and nothing criminal is subject to regulatory control. Crime is subject to its natural definition in the law jurisdiction. Regulation violations and other *malum prohibita* are defined in equity by legislatures and their regulatory agencies.

State legislatures may not license people to commit crimes because crime is strictly prohibited in a jurisdiction that is separate from, antecedent to, and superior to state legislatures' positive law authority. Because of the separation of powers doctrine, the facts that states license drug making and dealing, and that states' ultimate remedies are equitable, is evidence – indeed proof – that drug making and dealing are not real crimes, but instead are subject only to non-criminal equity.

It would be absurd and intolerable if the legislature created state agencies to license people, for example, to murder and steal. Yet we act as if the legislature has licensed some drug makers and dealers, i.e., the ones we call legitimate, to legally commit crimes, while subjecting less favored drug makers and dealers to criminal prosecution (and to jury trials to which the Supreme Court says they are not entitled). Such is the logical consequence of illogically treating fake "crimes" as real crimes, and of using subjective judicial standards and definitions to violate American constitutions, not to mention to totally deceive ourselves about the real law.

The legislature may not grant immunity to commit crime because that would diminish the criminal law jurisdiction of the judicial branch, whose juries are the ultimate authority over crime. Likewise, the legislature may not expand the meaning of crime – to include fake ones – without unconstitutionally expanding the judicial branch's power.

The legislature has no positive law authority, as granted in our constitutions, to invade the law jurisdiction of judicial courts. When it seeks to do this with legislation that exceeds those powers granted in republican constitutions, then judicial courts can strike such legislation down as unconstitutional. [93]

In *Beebe v. State* (1855) the Indiana Supreme Court struck down legislation that criminally prohibited the possession and sale of alcohol. This legislation exceeded both legislative and judicial authority to treat *malum prohibita* as criminal. As the *Beebe* court mentioned, only a successful constitutional amendment process may criminalize lawful commerce and thereby increase the criminal authority of the law jurisdiction. [94]

Thus, home narcotics makers are no more criminal than drug company officers for making and selling narcotics. Such phony "felonies" and "misdemeanors" have no justiciability in judicial trial courts. Business people can be regulated, but they are not to be thrown in jail just because American fascists, who do not care enough about American constitutions or statutes to enforce them correctly – let alone ever read them – do not like their businesses.

All of the phony "felonies" and fake "misdemeanors" that relate to drugs are listed in the Indiana Controlled Substances Act at IC 35-48-4. We will go over all of these "criminal" penalty provisions against drug possession, making and dealing in chapter 22.

However, suffice here to say that all of the statutory "misdemeanors" and most of the statutory "crimes," "offenses" and "felonies" that are listed at IC 35-48-4 do not constitute real crimes, offenses, felonies, misdemeanors or even cases under the U.S. or Indiana constitutions. As such, they are misrepresentations of law by the Indiana legislature, which were intended by the legislation's authors in the Department of Justice and the Uniform Law Commission to deceive state officers, attorneys and all natural persons within the state, and to defraud natural persons of their substantive rights.

Because most drug-related statutory "crimes," "criminal cases," "felonies," "offenses" and "misdemeanors" do not amount to their constitutional counterpart, then the use of a judicial court to punish people for such "crimes" is to place them in slavery or involuntary servitude, unduly convicted, and in plain violation of the 13th Amendment and Article I, Section 37 of the Indiana constitution.

Procedural and substantive due process

To fraudulently co-opt constitutional terms to give them false meaning, so that one is tried in a court without real subject matter jurisdiction, is also to violate the due process clause of the 5th and 14th Amendments, which apply respectively to actions by the federal and state governments. To be tried by a court without jurisdiction is *per se* a substantive due process violation.

Due process encompasses both the concepts of procedural due process and substantive due process. The central meaning of procedural due process is that parties whose rights are to be affected are entitled to be notified and heard. [95] The Indiana Administrative Orders and Procedures Act (AOPA) and Indiana's CSA, for example, define the procedural due process that the state of Indiana owes all makers and sellers of drugs through the administrative law courts of the Indiana pharmacy board.

In contrast, because of the separation of powers doctrine and because of the autonomy of the judicial branch, the Indiana legislature defers to the judicial branch to make its own rules. IC 34-8-2-1 states that "(t)he general assembly of the state of Indiana affirms the inherent power of the supreme court of Indiana to adopt, amend, and rescind rules of court affecting matters of procedure...," including trial and appellate rules. In any event, by these legislative- and judicially-defined processes, people are accorded procedural due process.

Due process also has a substantive aspect which secures natural persons' natural rights and artificial persons' legal rights. The essence of substantive due process is protection from arbitrary and unreasonable action. [96]

To keep all the respective jurisdictions separate is the first and most fundamental key to establishing substantive due process of law at the state level. Substantive due process is achieved when state officials keep their police powers separate, for example when they regulate drug commerce and prosecute drug crimes. This occurs when law enforcers keep their regulatory (administrative) subject matter jurisdiction separate from their judicial (or criminal) subject matter jurisdiction. Substantive due process can be guaranteed only by first properly determining whether a judicial or administrative court has subject matter jurisdiction.

In *Osborn v. Review Bd. of Indiana Employment Sec. Division* (1913), the Indiana Supreme Court wrote that due process depends on whether the applicable system of jurisprudence, "with its provisions for safeguarding the rights of litigants," is followed. [97] It is the courts' "duty to follow that law or rule (unless, of course, it be unconstitutional)," the Court wrote in *State ex rel. Benjamin v. Criminal Court of Marion County, Division No. III* (1976). [98] "If these [statutes] are followed by the courts as designed by the legislature the parties will have due process as provided for by the Federal Constitution," wrote the Court in *State ex rel. Hurd v. Davis* (1948). [99]

Likewise, when statutes are not "followed by the courts as designed by the legislature," [100] such as when legal rights under the Indiana CSA and AOPA are ignored by judicial courts in drug matters, or when natural persons face jail time for exercising natural rights, then defendants' substantive due process is violated.

I have contended from the start of this book that America's drug laws are constitutional and essentially good (because they accord people due process), but that government officials do not follow the laws. Not following rules "as designed by the legislature" [101] deprives individuals of their natural right to property possession and of their substantive right not to be enslaved except for the commission of a crime. It also wrongly imposes criminal sanctions upon disfavored drug dealers, depriving them of their various administrative rights under non-criminal equity.

At the state level, the first and fundamental substantive due process violation by republican courts has been to try drug possession matters in the criminal law jurisdiction, which has no subject matter jurisdiction over non-injury and which exists to secure the natural right of drug possession, not to violate it. As a natural right, drug possession is neither a crime nor is it subject to regulation. Therefore, it cannot be adjudicated in any lawful republican court, whether the court is judicial or administrative.

Because drug possession is a natural right, individuals have subject matter jurisdiction over it. Any and all government adjudications of drug possession, over which <u>no</u> courts have jurisdiction, are *per se* substantive due process violations.

A second form of substantive due process violation is for government officials to try drug-dealing matters in the wrong judicial jurisdiction, i.e., in the criminal law jurisdiction, instead of in non-criminal equity. Unlike drug possession which is not subject to any human court, and is subject to neither the law nor equity jurisdictions of judicial courts, drug dealing is primarily subject to regulatory courts in the executive branch.

When the state's equitable administrative remedies are exhausted, such as confiscation and administrative injunction, then drug dealing becomes subject to judicial equitable remedies, such as forfeiture and judicial injunction. Thus, the second form of substantive due process violation is to falsely criminalize drug dealing, which is merely a regulatory violation that is subject to the state's non-criminal remedies.

A third form of substantive due process violation occurs when the U.S. Attorney General applies the criminal statutes that Congress legislated for the federal areas to drug dealers within the states, who are instead subject to regulation in the equity jurisdiction, which has no criminal jurisdiction over drug dealing. As we shall see in chapters 8 and 9, achieving substantive due process is near-impossible without recognizing that Congress legislates in two capacities.

Blurring jurisdictions occurs precisely because the statutes, with their "provisions for safeguarding the rights of litigants," [102] are not "followed by the courts as designed by the legislature..." [103] To illegitimately prosecute drug dealing in a judicial court, whose law jurisdiction only has authority over injury, and to fail to use the legitimate equitable remedies against drug dealing that are provided by statute, is to violate the law and the substantive due process rights of defendants. As well, to falsely prosecute disfavored drug dealers in the criminal law jurisdiction, all-the-while regulating favored drug dealers in equity, is *per se* arbitrary and unreasonable.

Substantive due process does not get defined better or more fundamentally than by subject matter jurisdiction. One cannot get substantive due process in the wrong court, in the wrong jurisdiction of a judicial court, or in a court without jurisdiction, which essentially amount to the same thing, i.e., the wrongful exercise of judicial power.

According to statute, only artificial persons are subject to administrative due process. Substantive due process for natural persons is strictly judicial and operates only for them in the law jurisdiction of judicial courts, to which only natural persons are subject for their torts or crimes. To subject non-injurious behavior to the original jurisdiction of judicial courts is to fundamentally violate defendants' substantive due process.

Essentially, due process is achieved when the executive branch of government follows the legislature's constitutional rules. These rules designate which court in which branch of government, if any, is to adjudicate our natural and legal rights.

Procedural due process is to have one's day in court. Substantive due process is to have one's day in the correct court. Thus, substantive due process is jurisdictional. It is achievable only in the right court which exercises the right delegated power.

Substantive due process for commercial enterprises, such as drug dealing, is for their state privileges to be adjudicated in non-criminal equity. Substantive due process for criminal defendants is to be tried for *malum in se* cases in the law jurisdiction of judicial courts. Substantive due process for people peacefully exercising their natural rights, such as possessing drugs or making art, is for government to leave them alone.

Therefore, substantive due process is achieved by a vigilant separation of the jurisdictions of America's four categories of sovereigns. Using the mail-slot analogy from chapter 1, substantive due process is the proper sorting of power into the four sovereigns' mail slots (or sub-slots, such as branches, departments, agencies).

Anything contrary to the above paragraph is a violation of substantive due process. Misusing power is analogous to misdelivering the mail. Anytime a power is falsely allocated or improperly used, a violation occurs. For example, prosecuting drug possession in a judicial or in an administrative law court – neither which has subject matter jurisdiction over it – is a violation of substantive due process.

Likewise, a judicial court's criminalization of a commercial privilege is a violation of substantive due process. To adjudicate only real torts, crimes and breaches of contracts based on substance between natural persons is the law jurisdiction's sole function. Anything more or anything less is a substantive due process violation.

For Indiana's judicial courts to try "criminal cases" as real criminal cases – in other words *malum prohibita* as *malum in se* – is to violate the Indiana constitution and to do the work of the political branches. It is a perversion of the purposes for which judicial courts were instituted, and an assumption of functions that do not belong to them.

In conclusion, as this and the previous chapter have shown, the executive and judicial branches enslave innocent people under false color of law by co-opting constitutional terms and by giving them false and perverse statutory meaning. We have been taking government officials at their word and they have been misrepresenting the meaning of constitutionally determined terms.

By this point in the argument, there should be absolutely no grounds for legal disagreement over which definition of crime, offense, felony, misdemeanor or case is the legal standard and requires conformity by the other. As soon as enough legal professionals in this country agree that our constitutions are the supreme law, that their definitions rule those of statutes, and that they created the judicial branch and defined its subject matter jurisdiction over injury, then the criminal misuse of our judicial system will end with regard to controlled substances. Until then, attorneys using false definitions of constitutional terms will falsely rule the roost.

Our judicial system's saving grace is that all government officials and attorneys have taken oaths to uphold our constitutions. In Indiana, this requirement is at Article XV, Section 4 of the state constitution. This oath encompasses upholding the separation of powers doctrine and the definitions of crime, offense, felony, misdemeanor, and case in our constitutions. Judicial officers are beholden by oath to the constitutions, and not to legislatures' inconsistent misrepresentations.

That the Controlled Substances Act misrepresents the constitutional subject matter of judicial courts, and that the act is difficult to understand, does not make it ambiguous or unconstitutional. Judicial officers are presumed to be able to recognize and see through these misrepresentations, just as I have, so as to render certain provisions unenforceable.

For example, that the Indiana legislature calls marijuana possession a "misdemeanor" does not make the act unconstitutional. It merely makes it factually wrong, the product of fraud, and unenforceable. Judges are presumed to know the meaning of a misdemeanor (and their courts' jurisdiction) because they took an oath to treat misdemeanors criminally.

Co-opting constitutional terms to give them new meaning merely makes the Controlled Substance Act fraudulent. (Frauds carry on until they are discovered.) The CSA is constitutional because it does not criminalize drug possession or commerce in the American republics, but instead subjects drug commerce to regulation, as it should.

The Indiana Supreme Court has sustained the constitutionality of the Indiana CSA in *Hall v State of Indiana* (1980). [104] However the defendant / appellant in that matter did not raise the enforcement issues that – thanks to this book – can now be raised by people in his position.

I contend that the drug laws treat drug dealers properly within the limitations of the Indiana and U.S. constitutions, but that officials' false enforcement does not. First, it causes a substantive due process violation because the state is required to give drug defendants administrative due process in the executive branch, instead of subjecting them to criminal law trials. As well, false enforcement of the law causes an equal protection violation because the state must treat all manufacturers, distributors or dispensers of drugs – as a commercial class – the same. Equal protection is to regulate all of them, and not to criminally prosecute only some of them.

The power to regulate nonetheless grants the state great power to shut down drug businesses, confiscate contraband, and enjoin future drug dealing, at the risk of being jailed for contempt. It merely does not provide the state with power to incarcerate drug dealers as a primary response to their commercial activity.

The substantive right not to be enslaved except for the commission of a crime, as promised by the 13th Amendment, is dependent on judicial courts' use of the constitutional meaning of crime. Or I should say: that to depend on the constitutional meaning of crime is a substantive right. [105] Our natural rights of life, liberty and to pursue happiness, as well as the guarantee of a republican form of government, each and all depend on the natural and constitutional law meanings of case, crime, offense, felony and misdemeanor being used in American jurisprudence.

6
Individual sovereignty

Natural born citizens are not naturally subject to positive law

In the previous chapters we learned that American states and the U.S. republic are two of the four categories of sovereigns in the United States. We also learned the characteristics of the republican form of government, and the constitutional meanings of case, controversy, crime, offense, felony, and misdemeanor.

We learned that the republican form of government can be maintained only 1) by limiting the subject matter jurisdiction of the law jurisdiction of judicial courts to injury, 2) by keeping the subject matter jurisdiction of the three branches of government separate, and 3) by keeping the authority of these branches from breaching the rights of individuals (operating under natural law).

This chapter is about the third variety of sovereigns within the United States – individuals. It is respect for the sovereignty of individuals that sets America's republics apart from most if not all other governments in the world. As we shall see, this individual sovereignty includes legislative and judicial subject matter jurisdiction, just as the states and the U..S. Congress have such power to exercise.

The following quotation from *Yick Wo v. Hopkins* (1886) is how the U.S. Supreme Court beautifully described individual sovereignty.

"Sovereignty itself is, of course, not subject to law, for it is the author and source of law; but in our system, while sovereign powers are delegated to the agencies of government, sovereignty itself remains with the people, by whom and for whom all government exists and acts. And the law is the definition and limitation of power. It is indeed, quite true, that there must always be lodged somewhere, and in some person or body, the authority of final decision; and in many cases of mere administration the responsibility is purely political, no appeal except to the ultimate tribunal of the public judgement, exercised either in the pressure of opinion or by means of the suffrage. But the fundamental rights to life, liberty, and the pursuit of happiness, considered as individual possessions, are secured by those maxims of constitutional law which are the monuments showing the victorious progress of the race in securing to men the blessings of civilization under the reign of just and equal laws, so that, in the famous language of the Massachusetts Bill of Rights, the government of the commonwealth "may be a government of laws and not of men." For, the very idea that one man may be compelled to hold his life, or the means of living, or any material right essential to the enjoyment of life, at the mere will of another, seems to be intolerable in any country where freedom prevails, as being the essence of slavery itself." [106]

Rarely can one find such a marvelous, all encompassing statement of law as the above quotation from the U.S. Supreme Court. It says several things that are relevant and important to our discussion. (All of the un-referenced quotations below are from the above longer quotation.)

First, the Supreme Court says that sovereignty is the "authority of final decision" which "must always be lodged somewhere, and in some person or body." This is the perfect definition of sovereignty.

Law is about divvying up this "authority of final decision." In this book I define this sovereignty in terms of legislative and subject matter jurisdiction. I frame sovereignty in terms of who may legislate over and who may adjudicate various subject matter.

As we shall see, individual sovereigns have "authority of final decision" in all non-injurious personal matters. The judicial branch has "authority of final decision" over cases involving injury and in appellate matters. The legislative and executive branches, which are called the political branches, have "authority of final decision" over the rules and participants of commerce.

Each of these entities in America's republics, i.e., individuals and the three branches of government, are sovereign over separate subject matter assigned to them, or in the case of individual sovereigns, retained by them. This, of course, is because "sovereignty itself remains with the people" in an American republic. Sovereignty remains with the people because they delegate some but not all of their natural political authority to government.

Second, the Supreme Court says that the source of all sovereignty is the People, which necessarily implies that Congress occupies a subordinate status to the People's sovereignty. This is because individual sovereignty is unalienable, and is a check upon the power of positive law. Power that is not "delegated to the agencies of government" "remains with the people."

Third, the Supreme Court says that "law is the definition and limitation of power." The law defines power, which is another word for jurisdiction. Power not delegated by the People is a limitation on jurisdiction.

For example, power not granted to judicial courts over non-injury is a limitation on the courts' subject matter jurisdiction over drug possession and commerce. Good law first defines the "authority of final decision."

Fourth, the Supreme Court says that it is the people "by whom and for whom all government exists and acts." This expresses that the nation's founders created the positive law of government to serve the People, not to preside over them.

Fifth, the Supreme Court distinguishes "the fundamental rights to life, liberty, and the pursuit of happiness" from those cases that are "purely political" and subject only "to the ultimate tribunal of the public judgement..." This recognizes that natural rights are not subject to politics or legislation.

Sixth, the Supreme Court says that slavery occurs when "any material right essential to the enjoyment of life," such as the right of property possession or the right of liberty, is "at the mere will of another." This is "to be intolerable in any country where freedom prevails, as being the essence of slavery itself."

This is to say that when the executive and judicial branches deprive natural persons of their liberty based on "the mere will of" the legislature, then this is a condition of slavery. This is to say that "any material right essential to the enjoyment of life," such as property possession and use, is not subject to the "mere will of another." America's war on drugs intolerably violates this key republican principle.

The seventh and most important lesson in *Yick Wo v. Hopkins* (1886) is that individual sovereignty "is, of course, not subject to law, for it is the author and source of law."

Hmmmm, did you read the above quotation correctly? The Supreme Court plainly says that we sovereigns in America are "not subject to law." Can this be so? Here's the answer.

Without acknowledging the natural law jurisdiction in the U.S. constitution, wherein Nature is sovereign, the above Supreme Court statement is not really comprehensible. In fact, without understanding the role of natural law, the Controlled Substance Act is not really comprehensible. Without knowledge of natural law, which such knowledge the Court in *Yick*

Wo v. Hopkins (1886) exhibits, or without acknowledging the existence of a law other than positive law, one must take the statement literally, i.e., that our individual sovereignty is not subject to law.

But of course our sovereignty is subject to law. We are just not naturally and normally subject to the positive law of government. Regardless of government, we are naturally and normally subject to Nature, or to the laws of our human nature.

In fact, America's primary citizens – its adult natural born citizens – are not born subject to any artificial government, but are instead born subject only to their nature (and to the natural authority of their parents). Natural born citizens are born free of duty to the common government. They only owe natural duties to other people.

For example, babies are not born owing income taxes. They are not naturally born with a duty to get Social Security numbers. As babies grow up, they voluntarily enter the income tax and Social Security systems – which operate in non-criminal equity.

Being born free in Nature, in the natural law jurisdiction, their sovereignty is still subject to and cannot escape the Laws of Nature, which is that natural jurisdiction outside and superior to the artificial positive law that the Founding Fathers created. This means that the above Supreme Court statement is properly understood as:

> "Sovereignty itself is, of course, not subject to (positive) law,
> for it is the author and source of (positive) law."

Because "the law is the definition and limitation of power," the People created the positive law to define and limit the positive law authority of government. Republics are limited in power in that they may not legitimately encroach upon the natural law jurisdiction over which individuals are primarily sovereign – where individuals have primary subject matter jurisdiction over their own personal affairs, such as over property possession and intoxication.

These sovereign, self-government zones in the natural law jurisdiction are not law-free or government-free. Instead, individual sovereignty is only positive-law-free. While positive law may not rule in this jurisdiction, natural law certainly does. Nature has its own rules and sanctions, which are separate from those artificial ones of governments when they claim to rule people's nature.

For those readers who do not yet believe in the natural law jurisdiction, try sitting at home alone and drinking a lot of alcohol. As long as you do not leave the house, Nature will be the sole prosecutor, judge and jury in the jurisdiction where "the Laws of Nature and Nature's God" [107] rule.

One way or another, Nature or the (natural) law jurisdiction of judicial courts – both which enforce natural law – punish people who cannot self-govern themselves. Nature will punish anyone who drinks a lot of alcohol. America's (natural, common, civil, criminal) law jurisdiction punishes anyone who drinks too much alcohol and who harms or endangers other people.

When individual sovereigns self-govern well, for example where they moderate their consumption of alcohol and do not drive their automobiles under its detrimental influence, then the punitive roles for natural law and positive law are limited. Only when individuals self-govern badly will natural law – sometimes with the help of the positive law of government – make them pay.

If individuals self-govern badly and harm only themselves, they remain subject to natural law. Where individuals exercise their sovereignty badly and harm or endanger other people, then they enter the law jurisdiction of our judicial courts where civil torts and public crimes, which are breaches of natural duty, are prosecuted.

Thus ultimately, as long as we sovereign individuals stay within our own positive-law-free zones by not harming or commercially engaging other people, then we operate in Nature, and we are neither subject to the judicial branch nor to the positive law jurisdiction of republican legislatures, which is the world of equity.

For Hoosiers like me, knowing this is like being in the state of Nature within the state of Indiana. Governments are to stay out of our positive-law-free zones where individual sovereigns have subject matter jurisdiction and the "authority of final decision." [108]

These personal positive-law-free zones are perhaps best explained by Sir William Blackstone in his *Commentaries on the Laws of England* (1753). Blackstone tells us that Nature is in fact our king, not some artificial person or some artificial legislature, with their artificial standards.

Blackstone explains that the authority of British law was based on two foundations: the law of nature and the law of revelation, both which "leave a man at his own liberty, but which are found necessary, for the benefit of society, to be restrained within certain limits." [109]

It is the scope of rightful restraint that is at issue in this book.

According to Blackstone, the scope of lawful restraint was clear. "(H)uman laws are only declaratory of, and act in subordination to" natural law and divine law, he wrote, and "no human laws should be suffered to contradict these." In other words, all man-made positive laws regarding torts and crimes of natural persons derive and gain their legitimacy from natural law, which may not be contradicted.

Because "man is subject to the laws of his Creator" and the "will of his Maker is called the law of nature," Blackstone wrote, then God "has graciously reduced the rule of obedience to this one paternal precept, 'that man should pursue his own true and substantial happiness.'" [110] So, "if any human law should allow or enjoin us to commit it [the will of the Maker], we are bound to transgress that human law, or else we must offend both the natural and the divine." [111]

In other words, if humans' positive law violates natural law, then humans "are bound" by their nature "to transgress that human law...," or we offend our human nature.

Justinian justice, Blackstone wrote, "reduced the whole doctrine of law" to three principles: "that we should live honestly, should hurt nobody, and should render to every one his due." [112] These precepts are a succinct summary of law courts' subject matter jurisdiction over individual sovereigns.

This constitutional arrangement, which was centered around individual liberty and self-responsibility, made Americans the envy of the world. It provided all natural people within the states, including foreigners, with legally-protected positive-law-free zones where they did not have to deal with a king or an emperor. For enslaved people around the world, the United States was a refuge from tyranny.

In America the power of government under positive law operates in a separate jurisdiction than individual sovereigns under natural law. Government rules in its proper sphere. Individuals naturally self-govern in theirs.

Individuals' positive-law-free zones are the natural law jurisdiction where only the Laws of Nature (and "the will of God") reign supreme over the will of people. It is in these sovereign zones where man's nature trumps the artificiality of the state and its positive law. Perhaps only under American law is there such a separation of power between the government and individuals, over which the government's rightful power does not extend.

In monarchies and modern dictatorships, there is no separation of power between positive law and individuals, who are not sovereign, but who are instead born subject to government. In contrast, natural born citizens are legally born subject to Nature – not government. Republican government was created subject to them.

As we shall see more specifically in chapters 12 and 13, natural born citizens are created in the natural law jurisdiction, completely apart from the positive law authority of American government – that is, without any grant, authority or permission from government's positive law. *Yick Wo v. Hopkins* (1886) reiterates this principle, saying that sovereigns are not subject to the positive law because they are its authors. [113]

Unlike with monarchical subjects, no artificial king nor congress authored natural born citizens, so the latter are not subject to the former. This means that fictions such as kings or congresses may not involuntarily convert a natural born citizen into a subject, which would be to convert a naturally free entity into an artificially enslaved one. "The law of nature, abstractly considered, knows neither prince nor subject," wrote the U.S. Supreme Court in *McIlvaine v. Coxe's Lessee* (1805). [114]

No fiction – be it a legislative statute or an administrative regulation – can convert a natural born sovereign into someone who is subject to positive law. Natural born citizens subject themselves to the jurisdiction of other sovereigns, such as other people and such as government, only by their voluntary actions – and not by their nature. Their nature is to be free from being enslaved by the "mere will of another." [115]

As we shall see, U.S. citizens have primary, subject matter jurisdiction not only over natural law citizenship, but over crime. Their primary criminal jurisdiction is known as their natural right of self-defense. As with all other natural rights, if they fail to exercise this power responsibly, then they subject themselves to the law jurisdiction of judicial courts.

That is, they become subject to the law jurisdiction of judicial courts when they fail to exercise their natural rights responsibly, i.e., when they negligently or intentionally harm other people without cause. Likewise, they become subject to government's equity jurisdiction when they volunteer into governments' jurisdiction over commerce and naturalization.

They also become subject to the federal government's panoply of powers when they enter a federal area. Otherwise, by their nature, natural born citizens are born free of, and are free of obligation to, those domestic governments that operate outside of their sovereignty.

For example, U.S. citizens have no obligation to government to either consume drugs or to not consume drugs. Their only duties are under natural law, one of which is to accept all natural responsibility for taking drugs, recommended or not. This is strictly a jurisdictional issue over who is sovereign over their drug use and other personal choices. Unless other people are forcing drugs into their bodies, then users are self-responsible.

In a republic, if the legislature was sovereign over people's drug use, then it could require people to take drugs, just as its officials claim the power to prohibit their use. Instead, the sovereign over individuals' personal affairs is not the common government, but the individual, whose use of drugs is primarily subject to Nature. There are natural consequences of drug use.

This individual sovereignty is secured at Article IV, Section 4 in the U.S. constitution by its guarantee to each state of "a Republican Form of Government..." What separates a republic from a non-republic, such as a monarchy, is that a republic provides a judicial jurisdiction in which the natural rights of natural sovereigns are secured and where violations to natural persons are adjudicated and remedied.

On the other hand, monarchies or other non-republics recognize only the leader as sovereign, and therefore one's rights are not natural, but are only available to the extent that the monarch unnaturally bestows them or makes them available. The Indiana Supreme Court in *Beebe v. State* (1855) explained the theory of monarchies:

> "that they were paternal in character; that all power was in them by divine right, and they, hence, absolute; that the people of a country had no rights except what the government of that country graciously saw fit to confer upon them; and that it was its duty, like as a father towards his children, to command whatever it deemed expedient for the public good, without first, in any manner, consulting that public, or recognizing in its members any individual rights." [116]

The Founding Fathers created republics whose "powers of sovereignty are vested in the people" [117] by creating a law jurisdiction in judicial courts to which only violators of natural law are subject. In such a system, people are only subject to being deprived of their liberty for the violation of natural law which results in injury – and not for violating the edicts of kings or legislatures.

The Founders did this as a stark break from the sheer artificial positive law authority theretofore exercised by kings and popes, who had ruled everyone's personal lives (with fear and fraud) and defined everyone's so-called "rights." Kings in the past could do this because they (and their agents) were not fully subject to the criminal law jurisdiction of judicial courts, and indeed dictated the positive law to everyone else. Here in America's republics, all government officials – from the President on down – are subject to the law jurisdiction for personal harm that they do to others' natural physical and political rights.

It is monarchical tyranny which the U.S. and Indiana constitutions abolish on behalf of natural persons by defining torts, crimes and rights of citizenship according to the Laws of Nature. In contrast, regardless of what Blackstone wrote to the contrary, no one has natural rights and everyone is a subject under monarchical governments.

By definition, monarchies are composed of subjects, not citizens. The authority for monarchies springs not from pooling the natural authority of citizens, but from the divine-right claim of the monarch. People retain no natural political authority in a monarchy because monarchs do not grant or recognize it.

For example, the subjects of kings have no natural right to run for the office of King, as natural born citizens have a natural right to run for the office of U.S. President. Indeed, the right to run for President is a natural right exclusive to natural born citizens, who gain their U.S. citizenship naturally. As with other natural rights, this natural right to run for President is secured in the law jurisdiction of judicial courts by the substantive right to remedy a violation to a natural right.

People living under monarchies are called subjects, or citizen-subjects, but they are really subject-slaves. Their lives and liberties belong to a dictator. They are slaves because, just like former African slaves in the United States, they have no law jurisdiction in judicial courts on which they can rely to secure their natural rights from monarchs, dictators, captains or slave masters.

A king may be a benevolent slave master, but he is a slave master nonetheless. Subjects may be happy, but they are happy slaves. Thus, just because one is happy does not mean that one is not subject to a monarch or to a slave master. In fact, one might not know that he is a slave, or that he is subject to a dictator, if the dictator claims to be republican, as does the dictatorship class in the United States.

To prevent monarchy, and thus enslavement, the U.S. constitution expressly guarantees a republican government for the states, and prohibits both our state and federal governments from establishing Titles of Nobility to which the People must bow. These prohibitions are at Article I, Section 9, Clause 8 of the U.S. constitution and at Article I, Section 35 of the Indiana constitution (1851), the latter which reads: "The General Assembly shall not grant any title of nobility, nor confer hereditary distinctions."

As well, the 1st Amendment to the U.S. constitution prohibits the state and religion from combining into one, which is a characteristic of monarchies under the divine-right-of-kings doctrine. The nation's founders brilliantly fused natural law with these prohibitions against nobility and state religion to prevent the office of the U.S. President from being occupied by a natural born foreigner or foreign monarch.

Monarchies exist only in the absence of natural law. Conversely, adherence to natural law is the only check upon monarchists and other non-republicans who think they have moral authority to rule the personal lives of other natural persons.

Monarchs can imprison and kill their political opponents because they claim to be above natural law and the law jurisdiction which treats kings and commoners equally. Monarchs' claims of power exceed the natural rights of everyone else. Because republican criminal law is based on natural law, this means that monarchs claim to be above natural law. Their claims over other people's lives are supernatural.

Monarchs are allowed to do dictatorial things against fellow natural persons only where their positive law ignores or does not recognize the natural law authority of those others. Monarchs may commit crime against their subjects because they define the meaning of crime for their subjects.

In contrast, in the republican form of government, crimes are objectively defined by Nature to include injury. In the republican form of government, criminal law is not subject to the "mere will of another," [118] and people who claim to be kings are nonetheless subject to natural criminal standards. In the republican form of government, the "crimes" invented by wannabe kings are subject to Nature, which does not recognize their supernatural claims of legislative authority.

The two reasons for the U.S. government

American legal exceptionalism stems only from the sovereignty of individuals in the natural law jurisdiction, as secured by the law jurisdiction of republican judicial courts. This is a judicial jurisdiction that is not subject to inconsistent positive law. It is in the law jurisdiction where natural persons hold the positive criminal law of kings and legislatures in check.

George Washington wrote: "Government is not reason; it is not eloquent; it is force. Like fire, it is a dangerous servant and a fearful master." Well aware of this, he and the nation's other Founding Fathers created the positive law jurisdiction of the U.S. government for two reasons.

The first reason was to secure people's unalienable rights and sovereignty in the natural law jurisdiction, which is explained by the Declaration of Independence. It declares that to secure the natural rights of life, liberty and the pursuit of happiness, "Governments are instituted among Men..."

In other words, the Founders created the positive law jurisdiction of constitutions, statutes and regulations to secure our natural rights in the natural law jurisdiction and to make them unassailable by a king (or a legislature). They created the law jurisdiction of the judicial branch to secure our rights to "Life, Liberty, and the Pursuit of Happiness" from violations by positive law.

The Founders were true to this premise when they adopted the U.S. constitution in 1787. The founders of Indiana were also true to this premise when they adopted the Indiana constitution in 1816. Both constitutions, as the highest expressions of positive law, acknowledge and carve out a role for the exercise, protection and enforcement of natural law. As pointed out by Blackstone, this was to serve mankind's natural inclinations to pursue happiness.

Ironically, we need not look beyond the first three words in the U.S. constitution, "We the People," to see the natural law jurisdiction in the U.S. form of government. We the People refers to sovereign natural persons upon whose natural moral authority the U.S. and America's state governments were established, and to the sovereign natural persons who reserved a certain jurisdiction from government.

It is We the People (or "WE" as referred to in the Declaration of Independence) who granted our natural authority to establish governments of limited positive law powers. It is in this natural law jurisdiction that We established the law jurisdiction of judicial courts to secure our natural rights, and where only violations to our natural rights are to be adjudicated.

It is only in this law jurisdiction of judicial courts where, as the Declaration of Independence says, "all Men are created equal" and where natural persons of all places, genders, races and even creeds have the same aforementioned substantive rights. These substantive rights in the law jurisdiction exist for all people in America's republics, notwithstanding the limitations placed on the freedom of foreigners (see chapter 9).

In Indiana, the natural law jurisdiction is evident – not in the first three words of the Indiana constitution – but in its very first two sections.

Article 1, Section 1 of the Indiana constitution (1816) recognizes the natural unalienable right of acquiring, possessing, and defending property.

Article 1, Section 1 of the Indiana constitution (1851) incorporates and rephrases the statement of natural law, also from the Declaration of Independence, that "all people are created equal; that they are endowed by their CREATOR with certain inalienable rights; that among these are life, liberty, and the pursuit of happiness."

Natural law, which is the source of these natural rights, is also evident in Article 1, Section 2's protection of "the natural right to worship ALMIGHTY GOD, according to the dictates of their own consciences."

Because these unalienable natural rights to life, to liberty, to pursue happiness, to possess property and to worship God come from Nature and not from positive law, then the natural law jurisdiction is clearly and undeniably recognized by Indiana's highest positive law – its constitution.

The 9th Amendment to the U.S. constitution is further evidence of the existence of the natural law jurisdiction in U.S. law. This amendment reads: "The enumeration in the Constitution of certain rights shall not be construed to deny or disparage others retained by the people."

The 9th Amendment refers to the two types of rights that we have been discussing in this book, i.e., positive law rights and natural rights, although it does not mention them by name. Positive law rights are those "certain rights" that are enumerated, which means written down. They include the substantive rights that we discussed in chapter 3, almost all which are written down in American constitutions. This means that any rights that people have that are not enumerated in the U.S. constitution logically are not written down, and by definition are not positive law rights.

If rights are not positive law rights, are not written down, and are not from the positive law jurisdiction, then they must necessarily be rights subject to and secured under a separate and preexisting jurisdiction to positive law, where rights need not be written down. This would be the natural law jurisdiction where natural rights and duties are self-evident and exist without having to be enumerated. Babies know all about this jurisdiction, but are unable to explain it to adults who tend to overlook it.

Our natural rights and duties are those that are not generally enumerated, and which are outside, separate from and antecedent to the authority of positive law's enumerated rights. Natural rights and duties are those that need not be written down to exist and to be recognized in an American republic. As we have seen, the rights and duties are so elementary that babies and parents naturally exercise them.

Natural rights and duties predate positive law. They existed even before Hammurabi (1810 – 1750, B.C.) first codified law. We exercise these rights and duties everyday generally without thinking about government. We do not need positive law in order to recognize and exercise our natural rights and duties. We need positive law to secure them.

"It thus appears conceded that rights existed anterior to the constitution," wrote the Indiana Supreme Court in *Beebe v. State* (1855). "(T)hat we did not derive them from it, but established it to secure to us the enjoyment of them." [119] As we shall shortly see, the 9th Amendment serves to secure the natural physical rights of all natural persons in America's republics, as well as the natural political rights of natural born citizens.

The nation's Founding Fathers created the law jurisdiction to secure our enumerated and unenumerated natural rights from violations by other people, including Presidents and kings. This is accomplished by enforcing our substantive rights, by securing jurisdictional distinctions, and by maintaining the constitutional meaning of crime. Unlike in monarchies where kings or dictators exempt themselves and their agents from criminal prosecution, all government officials in America's republics are subject to the law jurisdiction for violations to other people's natural rights.

These violations are prosecuted as torts and crimes. In other words, no government officials within America's republics are to act like kings or their agents without having to pay for their actions.

It is the existence and correct operation of the law jurisdiction in judicial courts that secure the U.S. and state republics from being monarchies and which prevent legislatures from being dictatorial. The law jurisdiction achieves this goal by operating properly, which is to secure the separation of powers doctrine. It does this only by adjudicating its proper subject matter, which is injury to natural persons and their property.

The separation of natural law from positive law is why republican legislatures cannot legislate over the natural law jurisdiction of judicial courts, which define crime as *malum in se*, or over the substantive rights of natural persons, which are unassailable by legislation. All those rights are secured by the natural law jurisdiction of American constitutions and in the law jurisdiction of republican courts, impervious to the actions of Congress and state legislatures.

This is the nature of substantive rights. They are constitutionally secured rights that existed before and are independent of all legislative action. They belong to everyone, and exist to secure everyone's natural rights from the misuse of republican government.

If the law jurisdiction did not exist to secure the rights of natural persons, and if it was subject to positive law as is equity, then legislatures could do away with the substantive rights of everyone, and make anything a crime. As we shall see, because they are not allowed to do this, legislatures only make drug possession and dealing appear to be crimes.

Positive law has no authority to trump or define natural rights which are secured by our constitutions to not only U.S. citizens, but to visitors and immigrants from other countries. The Founding Fathers knew that if legislatures can disregard our natural rights, and impose their positive law jurisdiction into the law jurisdiction of judicial courts, then we would be right back to where we were as a society under a British monarchy – subject to a dictator's will, where we find ourselves today.

Recognition of our natural rights in a separate natural jurisdiction from equity puts each of us on equal footing with kings and legislatures, who are sovereign over equity. The natural law jurisdiction creates for individuals an autonomy or sovereignty over certain activities with which kings and congresses may not legislate. The jurisdiction allows us to worship, garden, inebriate, possess property and learn life at our own paces without worry that some king is going to punish us for doing it in our less-than-royal ways.

America's Founders knew that Nature sufficiently punishes people for doing most things wrongly without needing any help from government. As natural persons, we need the judicial branch's help in civil and criminal matters only when someone else violates our natural rights. As natural persons, we have a substantive right to get help from government when our natural or contractual rights are violated. Otherwise, we also have a substantive right to be left alone by government if we do not violate the rights of others or enter governments' equity jurisdictions.

Natural persons cannot be free when born into physical or political slavery, as in a monarchy. Protections from kings or slave masters are only possible through the establishment and respect for the natural law juris-diction, as enforced by the law jurisdiction of republican judicial courts. These courts treat all natural persons equally, and they do not recognize the legitimacy of titles of nobility or the unnatural will of slave masters.

Thus ironically, slavery is only possible under a non-republican form of government, which by definition is one that does not secure natural rights equally for all natural people. Under all monarchies, the sovereign is still a slave master who denies the protection of natural rights to some or all of his or her subjects.

In this sense, the U.S republic was essentially a (democratic) monarchy until the passage of the 13th and 14th Amendments, when former slaves were recognized as having the same and equal substantive rights as their former slave masters. In essence, as long as the natural law jurisdic-tion of the U.S. constitution was not extended to secure the natural rights of all natural persons, the U.S. remained a national non-republic by definition.

Until the passage of the 13th Amendment, the supreme positive law of the land granted certain natural persons unnatural physical privileges over other natural persons, which is the mark of a non-republic. Such a system is only possible under a government that is not founded upon natural law.

The 13th Amendment placed former slaves under the natural law jurisdiction of America's republican law courts, where their natural rights could be secured. When commercial slavery finally ended, one of the last vestiges of the British monarchy in America died with it. Unfortunately the spirit of monarchy did not die and lives-on in the war on drugs.

Liberty may not be achieved or maintained without the law juris-diction properly operating to secure all natural persons' natural rights. Without the securing of natural law by the law jurisdiction, neither physical liberty for all natural persons nor political liberty for U.S. citizens is possi-ble. This is because they would each be subject to a monarch, who claims to be above natural law.

The second reason the founders created the positive law jurisdiction of government was to provide privileges (and immunities) that do not exist in the natural law jurisdiction. They needed a jurisdiction that could secure the borders of the country, that could regulate interstate commercial activity and that could assess and collect taxes. Thus, they created the positive law jurisdiction to administer government, and those subject to it, but not to regulate the natural activities of natural people.

The People agreed, for example, that government could regulate the privilege of commerce in its positive law jurisdiction, but only as long as it did not impose its kingly positive law authority upon them as individual sovereigns. They agreed for the U.S. government to secure the nation's border, just so long as U.S. citizens had the right to freely escape this juris-diction. They also agreed for their republican governments to adjudicate commercial disputes in judicial courts, and to hold people accountable in the law jurisdiction for their torts and crimes.

This is to say that, as long as we sovereigns can act civilly and non-commercially, then we are in charge of the natural law jurisdiction of Amer-ica's republics. When we cannot properly govern ourselves and when our actions harm others, then the (natural, common, civil, criminal) law jurisdiction of judicial courts – based on injury – exercises its rightful au-thority over us. As well, when we enter commerce or the federal areas, where privileges instead of rights are exercised, then we consent to be governed by positive law. Only by knowing this separation of power can we be free.

In conclusion, the natural law jurisdiction of individuals (and of republican law courts) and positive law government are two separate sovereigns that co-exist and operate concurrently as distinct constitutional authorities in America's republics. These jurisdictions can co-exist, and America's constitutional governments can be maintained, as long as these governments do not try to invade the role of God or Nature and as long as these governments' positive law does not invade the natural law that governs human nature in the law jurisdiction.

Ironically, to keep the positive law of government from invading the role of Nature (or a natural God) is similar to keeping a supernatural God out of the role of government. For example, the limited constitutional authority of republican legislatures does not include using religion to dictate what types of commerce are criminally prohibited, such as drug commerce. The latter is the role of the authors and source of government, We the People, through the constitutional amendment process that our forefathers defined for us.

Without the natural law jurisdiction in America's constitutions, and respect for it, which is opposite and opposed to the positive law jurisdiction of government, then there would be nothing to stop the positive law of an artificial Congress, king or dictator from assuming artificial control over everything again. That is why keeping jurisdictional boundaries, such as the boundaries between natural and positive law, between law and equity in judicial courts, between administrative and judicial courts, and between natural born citizens and all others is absolutely necessary to secure America's republics. Republics are based on the separation of these powers. All other forms of government are not.

As we shall see, this separation is maintained at a state level only 1) by maintaining the separation of power between natural law and positive law, and thus the power of the individual from that of the state, 2) by maintaining separation between the three branches of government within the government's positive law authority, and 3) by maintaining the separation between the judicial jurisdictions of law and equity. This is accomplished by respecting each sovereign's subject matter jurisdiction, or its "authority of final decision." [120]

As long as the executive and judicial branches stay within their jurisdictions by respectively regulating commerce and by adjudicating injury, and as long as they do not subject natural persons and their human nature to the artificial prohibitions of equity, which do not apply to natural persons, then the natural People and the positive law of government can get along just fine.

America was great by design. Perhaps only in its republics are governments to serve the sovereign People, instead of the People serving them as subjects, serfs or slaves. Perhaps only in America's republics can citizens be free from government by not entering the government's judicial or administrative jurisdictions, and by keeping those jurisdictions separate from their own sovereignty. Perhaps only in America's republics are citizens to be sovereign over their own affairs, free from unnatural impositions by kings or by legislatures.

7

How America's republics are to work

A diagram of the republican form of government

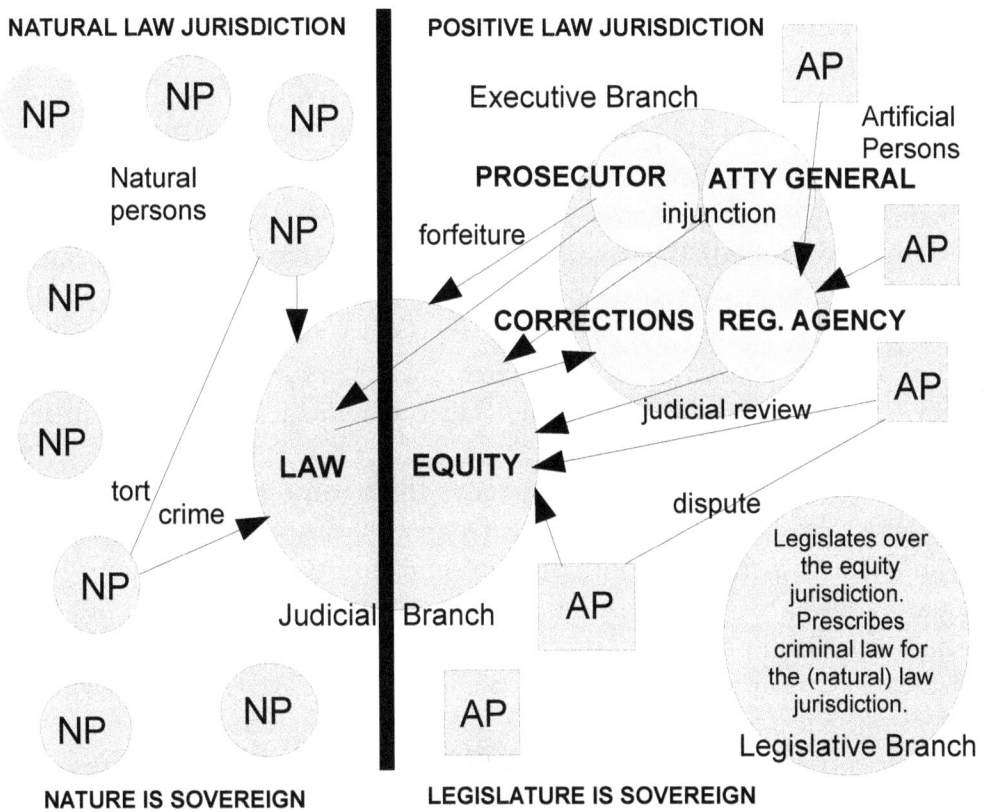

NATURAL LAW JURISDICTION

NP   NP   NP

Natural
persons

NP

NP

NP

tort
crime

NP

Judicial Branch

NP   NP

NATURE IS SOVEREIGN

POSITIVE LAW JURISDICTION

AP

Executive Branch

Artificial
Persons

PROSECUTOR   ATTY GENERAL

forfeiture   injunction

AP

CORRECTIONS   REG. AGENCY

AP

judicial review

LAW   EQUITY

dispute

AP

Legislates over
the equity
jurisdiction.
Prescribes
criminal law for
the (natural) law
jurisdiction.

AP

AP

Legislative Branch

LEGISLATURE IS SOVEREIGN

In the previous chapters we learned that individuals in America's republics are sovereign over the exercise of their natural rights, which are unassailable by republican legislatures and subject only to Nature as sovereign. Natural rights are secured by the enforcement of substantive rights.

We also learned that individuals are sovereign over the exercise of their natural rights 1) unless they engage the public in commerce or 2) unless they unreasonably exercise their natural rights and hurt someone, at which time the law jurisdiction of judicial courts gains subject matter jurisdiction over their torts or crimes.

With this in mind, the diagram on the previous page is meant to show how sovereignty is partitioned within America's republics. The Supreme Court in *Yick Wo v. Hopkins* (1886) called sovereignty the "authority of final decision" which "must always be lodged somewhere, and in some person or body." [121] The chart tries to show which sovereign has authority to adjudicate each activity in America's republics.

Central to the diagram is its thick vertical line that separates the two jurisdictions embodied in most if not all American constitutions, i.e., the natural law jurisdiction of sovereign individuals, which is distinct from the positive law jurisdictions of common government.

On the left side of the line, natural sovereign persons (represented as small circles) are separated from the three branches of common government (represented as larger circles on the right). Each of these sovereign entities, i.e., circles, have their own subject matter jurisdiction, i.e., their own authority to decide certain things.

As mentioned, the small individual sovereign circles have subject matter jurisdiction over their personal affairs, exercised as natural rights. The larger executive and legislative branch circles have subject matter jurisdiction over the regulation of commerce, foreigners and the administration of government. The circle representing the judicial branch has primary jurisdiction over injury.

The vertical line not only separates the natural law jurisdiction from the positive law jurisdiction of republican constitutions; it also segments the judicial branch circle into its law and equity jurisdictions. As the diagram shows, the law jurisdiction operates within the natural law jurisdiction of judicial power and on the basis of natural law. Its subject matter jurisdiction is over injury by natural persons, which are the small sovereign circles on the left.

In contrast, the equity jurisdiction of judicial courts operates solely under the positive law authority of American constitutions, on the right side of the vertical line. Equity is fulfilled both by judicially adjudicating commercial disputes of artificial persons, who are represented as small squares on the right side of the vertical line, and by providing judicial review and enforcement of administrative law decisions with regard to such artificial persons' commercial privileges, such as drug dealing.

With regard to drug control in Indiana, equity is ultimately fulfilled 1) by forfeiture proceedings carried out by county (district) prosecutors over property confiscated by drug regulators, and 2) by proceedings carried out by the state Attorney General to enjoin future unwanted drug dealing. These powers are also reflected on the diagram.

The vertical line on the diagram also denotes the separation of natural rights that individuals gain from Nature, which are listed in chapter 3, from the legal rights and privileges bestowed by the positive law of common governments. Violations to natural rights are adjudicated in the law jurisdiction of judicial courts, on the left side of the vertical line, which apply natural law and jurisprudence in their adjudications. In contrast, the legal (positive law) rights and privileges of artificial persons, and injuries to them, are adjudicated under positive law authority in equity, on the right side of the vertical line. Natural rights are adjudicated on the left. Artificial rights are adjudicated on the right.

The U.S. constitution not only recognizes the states and the United States as separate governments, but recognizes individual sovereigns to be separate governments as well. This is because individual natural persons have their own sovereignty over particular subject matter. They are self-governing in the natural law jurisdiction. This sovereignty means that the three branches of positive law republican government have no authority over the subject matter jurisdiction of individual sovereign self-governments.

As noted above, subject matter jurisdiction is the power to adjudicate, which means the power to settle, decide and decree. In a republican form of government, as defined by the U.S. and Indiana constitutions, individuals have the natural and inherent power to settle, decide and decree how they exercise their natural rights. For example, individuals in republics have the power to decide what property to acquire, possess and defend. This personal sovereignty is the main feature that separates American sovereigns from non-republican subjects.

American republics are to respect the inherent jurisdiction or sovereignty of individuals to exercise their natural rights. Monarchies or other non-republics by their nature do not. In America's republics, authority over the exercise of natural rights is the primary subject matter of individual sovereigns – not of the three branches of common government.

Conversely, individuals have no subject matter jurisdiction over the things that republican governments adjudicate, such as injury (in their judicial branch) and the privilege to engage in commerce (in their executive branch). Thus, the subject matter jurisdictions of individuals and of each of the three branches of republican government are mutually exclusive, and are to be mutually respected.

For example, when the natural need to sleep arises, car passengers inherently adjudicate this decision. They do not look to the three branches of common governments, or even to the automobile driver, but look within themselves to settle, decide and decree these important matters.

Therefore, it is within individuals' subject matter jurisdiction to decide when and how they will fulfill this need – not within the subject matter jurisdiction of common governments. In one's natural state, sleeping is among many wonderful powers that are within the sovereign authority of individuals, as regulated only by Nature.

In America's republics, all capable natural persons adjudicate their own personal matters, not just U.S. citizens. This is because in the law jurisdiction, the substantive rights of all natural persons are equal. They each have a right to seek a judicial remedy for harm done to them by others and each have a right in this jurisdiction to not be enslaved except for crime.

Because of these substantive rights, including the substantive right to rely on the U.S. constitution to be the supreme law, their natural right of sovereignty is secured. For example, they may not be enslaved for having property in their pockets that a king does not like.

Having subject matter jurisdiction – i.e., the power to settle, decide and decree within a certain physical sphere – is an attribute of sovereignty. The sovereignty of individuals is separate from the sovereignty of the three branches of republican government. Therefore, not only is the sovereignty of each of the three branches to be kept separate from each other, by the separation of powers doctrine in America's constitutions, but they are also to be kept separate from the subject matter jurisdiction of individual natural sovereigns.

As the diagram shows, all of the small sovereign circles in the natural law jurisdiction are separate from and outside of the positive law jurisdiction of the three branches of government, reflected as larger circles on the right side. The legislative branch legislates 1) over artificial persons, i.e., the squares on the right side of the main line, 2) over executive branch offices and agencies, and 3) over the privileges and procedures of equity.

However, it does not legislate over natural persons or the law jurisdiction of the judicial branch, which operate under natural law. It only prescribes (writes down) and codifies civil cases, crimes and judicial procedure from the common law. Therefore, individual liberty and the republican form of government require that the positive law authority of the three branches of government be kept separate from the subject matter jurisdiction of sovereign individuals and their law jurisdiction under natural law.

The U.S. and state constitutions are intended to keep each of these four powers separate in the U.S. and state republics. The war on drugs is essentially a breakdown in the line separating natural law from positive law, where the positive law authority of government has invaded the natural law jurisdiction of individuals and the law jurisdiction of the judicial branch. This has effectively done away with America's republican form of government.

In the natural law jurisdiction individuals self-govern. We determine when we go to bed, what we eat, with whom we make love, what we drink, and how we spend our money. We do not have formal legislative or judicial bodies in our heads, but we legislate, deliberate and adjudicate issues under our own sovereignty, just as the bigger sovereigns do.

Our individual sovereignty extends to the equal sovereignty of the other small circles in the diagram. Individuals can exercise their natural rights freely until their actions interfere with the rights other self-governments. As well, they cannot traverse into the realm of the larger circles either, or they become subject to their positive law authority.

When individual natural sovereigns are unable to live civilly, and instead violate the sovereignty of other individual sovereigns, i.e., by committing torts and crimes, they become subject to the law jurisdiction of judicial courts. This is illustrated on the diagram by the lines that extend between the small circles and the law jurisdiction of the judicial circle. The law jurisdiction serves to adjudicate only the torts and crimes, as well as breaches of contracts based on substance, of natural persons.

These lines reflect the only time (and the law jurisdiction of judicial courts is the only place) in American republics where any part of the compulsory positive law of government comes into contact with natural persons. With the exception of being in contempt of a judicial order, only when a natural person violates the sovereignty or interests of another natural person, or when a natural person violates a natural duty, such as the duty to defend the nation during attack, does the law jurisdiction of judicial courts gain authority over natural persons as parties, witnesses or jurors. Otherwise, legislatures may not act like kings or dictators by telling natural persons what to do with their time, talents and treasures.

Without an injury, an invasion or a commercial action, there are no compulsory lines (or connections) between natural persons and the positive law of American government. Without some injury, war or regulated activity, natural persons are essentially untethered from the positive law of common republican governments, and without duty to them. This is the essence of liberty, and what the diagram shows.

Thus, liberty from government is represented by the absence of lines between the small circles and the law jurisdiction of judicial courts, which is the sole jurisdiction of government that compulsorily applies to natural sovereigns. As long as these small circles of sovereignty do not encroach upon the rightful rule of other small circles, or enter the positive law jurisdiction of the larger circles, then these individual sovereigns are not subject to either the law jurisdiction of judicial courts, which secures the natural law, or to the jurisdiction of positive law government, which operates in equity within the states.

When big and small sovereigns exercise their jurisdictions correctly, without violating the sovereign space and subject matter jurisdiction of the other, then American legal systems operate properly. Conversely, when branches violate the sovereignty of other parts of government, or violate individual sovereign self-governments, as does the war on drugs, then constitutional conflicts occur.

The war on drugs exists because the positive law authority of America's artificial governments is violating both the natural law authority of our individual self-governments and the natural law authority of the law jurisdiction of judicial courts. This likely occurs because those operating the artificial governments do not know about the natural law jurisdiction over which natural persons are sovereign and which the law jurisdiction serves. Conflicts manifest when republican judicial courts, whose criminal law basis is in Nature (over *malum in se* crime), get misused to adjudicate non-crimes (*malum prohibita*), whose basis is in politics and religion.

By definition, the war on drugs is a constitutional conflict and a separation of powers issue because the positive law of government is encroaching upon the constitutional authority of natural law governments, i.e., individual sovereigns and their juries. (This is in addition to those separation of powers issues created when the judicial branch does the work of the regulatory branch.)

Under the proper constitutional scheme, as illustrated by the diagram, we as individual sovereign self-governments are to be naturally free from all other sovereign governments – both other individual natural self-governments and our artificial common governments. Being free to act in one's own space and being free from the will of other people are attributes of the natural rights of liberty and sovereignty.

That such individual sovereignty is secured from positive law is a crucial feature of America's republics. Only by securing our substantive rights in a judicial jurisdiction where our natural rights are protected can we be free from the criminal dictates of other people. As we have seen, the unalienable right of liberty is secured by the substantive right not to be arrested or enslaved except for the commission of real crime, as opposed to being jailed for violating a king's *malum prohibita*.

Maintaining the law jurisdiction of judicial courts to secure natural physical and political rights is the key, most salient attribute of all American republics. The United States cannot secure a republican form of government without respecting natural law and securing the law jurisdiction over injury.

Without understanding the role of natural law, then republican governance is next to impossible. State and federal governments become dictatorial – and are no longer republican – when their judicial courts fail to secure people's natural rights in the law jurisdiction from incursions by government agents who fail to follow constitutional and statutory law. The war on drugs is the nation's leading example of this.

However, once natural people – and particularly U.S. citizens – realize that they are sovereign over their own personal lives, such that they have subject matter jurisdiction over their own personal choices, and such that they may not be lawfully enslaved in the law jurisdiction of any state republic without injuring someone else, then they can stand up for the separation of government powers, which involves a separation of the positive law from their own natural law jurisdiction.

As well, only after individuals realize their sovereignty – which is represented in the diagram as small circles – can they then do what it takes to stay within these positive-law-free zones or bubbles, and to stay outside of the authority of all artificial governments and other natural self-governments. This takes three things:

First, sovereign individuals must refrain from entering a federal area that is under the exclusive authority of Congress, where Congress does not recognize their individual sovereignty. This is the subject of the next chapter.

Second, sovereign individuals must refrain from violating everyone's natural rights, contractual rights or positive law rights. Otherwise they become subject to the judicial branch of government. The judicial branch serves to provide remedies for wrongdoing. It exists to right wrongs, so to speak.

The third thing sovereign individuals must do to stay in their positive-law-free bubbles is to stay out of commerce. Once people derive gain from the sale of goods or services to the public, such as by drug dealing, then the executive branch of federal and state republics may rightfully regulate and tax their commercial behavior. This is justified because their commercial actions subject the public to heightened risk, whereas their individual actions normally do not.

As a political libertarian, I am not advocating regulation or taxation. In most ways I believe that commerce in America is over-regulated and overtaxed, and that it is not regulated in the proper manner. I am merely acknowledging republican governments' inherent authority to regulate commerce for the public's protection.

Congress' authority to regulate interstate commerce is in the U.S. constitution at Article I, Section 8, Clause 3 – called the Interstate Commerce Clause. Indiana's authority to regulate commerce within the state's borders is expressed at IC 1-1-2.5-2. Its Subsection (6) reads:

> "All: (A) goods grown, manufactured, or made in Indiana; and (B) services performed in Indiana; when the goods or services are sold, maintained, and retained in Indiana are not subject to the authority of the Congress of the United States under the constitutional power of Congress to regulate commerce among the several states."

Governments can cut the throats of all the things that they regulate with over-regulation, but such does not directly affect natural persons who are not subject to any regulation and who operate in a separate jurisdiction than regulated persons or activities. In America such artificial persons and regulated activities are subjects of and subject to legislatures operating in equity. However, all the statutes, all the regulations and all the enforcers of American positive law exist independently of U.S. citizens and other natural persons, who are not naturally subject to these statutes, regulations or bureaucrats.

For example, people are not naturally subject to the U.S. income tax system, which operates in equity. They may voluntarily join or enter this jurisdiction by making income. Until they do, they are not subject to it.

As we shall shortly see, if the Indiana legislature does not like a type of business, such as the business of drug-making in a residential neighborhood, its ministers in the executive branch can cut off the undesirable enterprise's head. Note however, that I said the enterprise's head – and not the head of the person making and selling drugs without the state's permission.

The state can cut off the head of privileged activity, e.g., the making and selling of nasty drugs, which it can do under its equity jurisdiction, but it cannot figuratively cut off the heads of natural persons who make and sell drugs. This is because criminal courts in American republics lack subject matter jurisdiction over natural persons who do not proximately cause injury to others, i.e., who do not commit torts or crimes. Only monarchies and other non-republics may legally enslave such non-criminals.

This is not to say that drug dealers who sell counterfeit or mislabeled drugs do not commit fraud, and are not criminals. Further, this is not to say that drug dealers who sell bad drugs are not responsible for the harm that they cause. Nor is this to say that drug-making is not an act of endangerment or a public nuisance for which there is some other legal remedy.

However, unlike the subjects of kings, U.S. citizens within state republics are not subject to the criminal law jurisdiction unless they harm others. Nor do they subject themselves to regulation unless they enter commerce, for example by manufacturing, distributing or dispensing drugs. Otherwise they are free from government.

In an American republic, whether one is a plumber getting licensed, a roofer getting a permit, or a drug dealer seeking permission from the Indiana State Board of Pharmacy to make and sell drugs, all such business persons are regulated because they are in commerce and subject to equity. Unlike the law jurisdiction where Nature is sovereign, equity serves the positive law of republican legislatures.

As the Declaration of Independence refers, one consents to be governed by this equity jurisdiction by entering commerce. Likewise, one mandatorily enters the law jurisdiction of judicial courts only by committing a tort or a more serious tort, called a crime. In a republic, equity is the jurisdiction over all commerce, except that which is tortious or criminal.

Regardless of the burden of regulations, or of the stupidity of legislatures to over-regulate, such servitude does not apply to U.S. citizens when not operating in commerce. As far as such natural persons are concerned, stupid legislatures may burden commerce all they wish because these burdens do not directly affect such natural persons, who are not subject to regulation.

For example, if Congress wishes to overtax and over-regulate business and industry, this is unfortunate, but it does not have any direct effect on natural persons who operate in a separate jurisdiction from business, industry and regulation. If a legislature wants to shoot businesses in the foot, that is its prerogative.

However, in their natural state, U.S. citizens are not subject to the positive law authority of either stupid or smart legislatures. In the realm where natural people govern themselves as sovereigns, they are kings and free from all other wannabe kings. In the words of the Supreme Court in *Yick Wo v. Hopkins* (1886): such sovereigns "are not subject to (positive) law" or to "the mere will of others." [122]

In our natural state, we as individual sovereigns are not subject to government's positive law, whether it is stupid or not. In the state of Nature, we are subject to our own natural stupidity, not to that of a king or legislature.

Nature – and not a king or legislature – defines what is right and wrong in the natural law jurisdiction of American republics, and in the criminal law jurisdiction of their judicial courts. To be free in one's own natural law jurisdiction and to be free from the positive law dictates of monarchs or legislatures is the meaning of liberty as used in the Declaration of Independence and in the Preamble of the U.S. constitution. Thank goodness that the 13th Amendment reiterates this fundamental right of liberty, such that it is undeniable by modern authoritarians.

In general, as the 13th Amendment tells us, liberty is the right not to be enslaved except for the commission of crime (or contempt of court). This includes the right not to be regulated when engaged in natural activities. [123] In a republic, only the law jurisdiction can rightly deprive natural persons of their right to physical liberty, and only when natural persons harm others through the commission of crimes.

When U.S. citizens are not injuring others, or are not engaged in commerce with the public, for example, then they are not subject to the positive law of America's constitutional governments. When citizens are acting outside of these legitimate artificial positive law jurisdictions, then they are naturally self-governing and positive-law-free.

For example, let's say we grow tomatoes and marijuana in our back yards. So long as we do not harm our neighbors with our gardening techniques, or by throwing rotten tomatoes at their houses, our neighbors and our republican governments have no grounds to invoke the civil or criminal jurisdiction of the judicial branch against us.

Likewise, so long as we do not sell (or distribute) our tomatoes or marijuana as commercials farmers, then the government has no grounds to regulate or tax our gardens. This is because we are not in commerce with the intent to profit. Our gardens are the products of our love and labor. They are our property. Our dominion over our gardens is not to be regulated by the executive branch unless we farm commercially.

Unlike our friends in Great Britain, we and our gardens are neither subjects of a king nor subject to a king. Our enumerated positive law rights and our unenumerated natural rights are recognized and secured by our constitutions against all kings in the world. In America, We the People are essentially the kings and queens in our own gardens. We are all-powerful monarchs over our own rightful subject matter jurisdiction.

Note however, given that ownership of real property in the U.S. is not (or is no longer) allodial – meaning "not holden of any lord or superior... the opposite of feudal" [124] – one could argue that private gardens are ruled in the equity jurisdiction of our republics. This suggests that the state of Indiana could regulate private gardens, just as it does the commercial privileges that it grants, and could confiscate people's tomatoes and marijuana.

However, because equity has no criminal jurisdiction, no one could be put in jail under equity for what one grows in one's garden, even if the gardens were subject to the positive law of legislatures. As we shall see beginning with chapter 18, under the rules of equity of American legislatures and upheld by the U.S. Supreme Court, republican governments can break up commercial marijuana farms for regulatory violations and can confiscate commercial produce. However, 1) they may not jail the growers (who are subject at most to regulation), and 2) they may not confiscate or destroy a garden intended solely for one's own personal use.

Enforcers of positive law have no authority in individual sovereigns' natural law jurisdiction, which extends to bathrooms, bedrooms, basements, kitchens and personal outdoor gardens. In America's republics, even foreigners have a natural right to garden, which is secured by the substantive right not to be arrested or enslaved except for the commission of real crime (or for being in contempt of a lawful court order).

Based on this substantive right, the nation's Founding Fathers put U.S. citizens on equal footing in their own natural law jurisdiction with kings. If a foreign king or U.S. President violates the jurisdiction of our self-governments, we can hold them accountable in the law jurisdiction of judicial courts, just as we can every other natural person who harms us.

Government officials' artificial positive law powers and immunities are strictly limited to the *de jure* powers granted to them, which do not include the power to violate a natural person's natural rights. Neither Presidents nor foreign kings are allowed to commit torts or crimes against people within America's republics without being civilly or criminally liable.

This may seem like an over simplification, but it is not. It is the essence of the greatest deal ever made for citizens, which deal is the envy of the world and embodied in likely every constitutional statute enacted by an American legislature (at least the ones that I have read). The only problem is that this sweet deal has made Americans fat and forgetful of what made it so special in the first place, and we have not been as vigilant to understand and protect our individual sovereignty as we should have been.

This thoughtlessness is why we never realized that our drug statutes are written to secure people's natural rights to possess and consume drugs, not to violate them. This thoughtlessness is why we never realized that all our statutes must be written to secure our natural rights, and to secure the operation of republican government as portrayed in the diagram, or they would not be constitutional.

The Controlled Substances Act is constitutional because it is faithful to the idea that we are endowed by our Creator with certain unalienable natural rights, and that it is a republic's role to secure these rights by staying out of our personal affairs. To the extent that this does not describe the behavior of our current government officials is the extent to which they do not follow the statutes that are to dictate their actions.

As well, the state CSAs and the republican provisions of the U.S. CSA are faithful to the idea that there are two jurisdictions in our constitutions – the natural law jurisdiction and the positive law jurisdiction – and that their powers never meet or clash. Because this separation of power is a precept of America's republics, it is also fully evident in America's drug statutes.

As we shall see beginning in chapter 16, which begins the statutory law portion of the book, not only does the CSA not regulate drug possession, which is not subject to commercial regulation, but it also statutorily exempts drug possession from regulatory and criminal liability. Under the Indiana Code, people have a statutory right to "lawfully possess" drugs for their own end use. [125] These provisions are acknowledgments of the natural law jurisdiction of the Indiana constitution, where natural persons have the "natural, inherent, and unalienable right... of acquiring, possessing, and protecting property." [126]

This raises one of the biggest ironies in the history of American law: that the positive law which has been used to punish drug users for nearly fifty years not only does not apply to drug users, but instead is completely compatible with and supportive of their natural rights to possess and use drugs. This sad irony is the result of the law not being read, not being read properly, and thus being arbitrarily disregarded.

The latter occurs because most Americans, their attorneys, their prosecutors and their judges do not currently know that the natural law jurisdiction of American constitutions exists. Thus, they know neither the scope of the criminal law jurisdiction of judicial courts nor how to secure one's substantive right not to be arrested, tried or enslaved without the commission of a crime. No one told them that crime is defined by natural law and that crime is not subject to a legislature's will or interpretation – only its codification.

Needless to say, it is difficult if not impossible to defend that which one does not know exists. For example, one cannot defend the right of drug possession if one does not know about the natural law jurisdiction of our constitutions and the law jurisdiction of judicial courts, where this right is recognized and secured.

Plus, one could prove that this natural unalienable right exists only if one has read Article I, Section 1 of the Indiana constitution (1816) (quoted above), which most Indiana criminal attorneys likely have not. (If they had, then they would have been fighting for this right of their clients, right?)

Both the natural law jurisdiction and the positive law jurisdiction walk hand-in-hand, each sovereign over their respective subject matter. American governments remain rightful as long as they keep their positive law jurisdiction out of the natural law jurisdiction, or as long as their codified criminal law remains consistent with natural law.

This is one of the limits of the "Consent of the Governed," which is a concept that is mentioned in the Declaration of Independence. In America's republics, where natural law duties are mandatory, then people consent to be governed only in their artificial capacities.

For example, people who enter commerce as well as foreigners are treated in America as artificial persons. In such capacities, each voluntarily consent to be governed by the commercial and foreign jurisdictions of state and U.S. governments. As well, with the exception of the President and Vice President, everyone who enter the federal areas, such as the District of Columbia, consent to be governed by Congress in a non-republican capacity.

But otherwise, within the states, we sovereign individuals have not consented to be governed by anyone. We do not consent to be enslaved for anything except crimes, as these crimes are referred to in the 13th Amendment. Nor do not naturally consent to use the power of the government to enslave others for anything but such real crimes.

Likewise, we have agreed to a compulsory judicial process to adjudicate our torts and crimes, and to have foreigners and commerce to be regulated in equity. However, we have not agreed or consented to having either people in commerce or foreigners within the states to be treated as criminals.

Without changing the U.S. constitution by amendment, we neither consent to the expansion of judicial power over things that are not crimes, nor to a judicial criminal jurisdiction that is foreign to common law. In the parlance of the Declaration of Independence, we do not consent to be transported "beyond Seas to be tried for pretended Offences."

Likewise, we do not consent for judges to be dependent on the will of legislatures alone, as is also denounced in the Declaration. We as natural persons consent only to judicial judges grounded in Nature, rendering law as an objective science instead of as a subjective religion.

In other words, We are entitled: 1) to the rights inherent under the dual jurisdiction of natural law and positive law and 2) to the separation of the legislative, executive, judicial and individual jurisdictions that make American constitutions so special.

To understand these separate jurisdictions, as enforced by the separation of powers doctrine, is to understand the limits of all positive law authority and the rightful reservation of individual sovereignty. The Controlled Substances Act is written – even if cryptically – to recognize the natural law jurisdiction of individuals by keeping positive law within its limits.

That is yet another reason why the CSA is constitutional. However, because officials in Indiana government do not follow the CSA, do not respect the boundaries that it codifies between natural and positive law, and likely do not even currently know that a natural law jurisdiction exists within America's constitutions, then their professional behavior necessarily falls constitutionally short.

Sex as an illustration of natural and positive law

As a youngster, one of my favorite cartoons in Playboy magazine was of a female hippy, during an antiwar parade outside, just after having had sex with a guy. Her "Free Love" sign sits on the bed. The hippy girl says to the guy: "The love was free, but the sex will cost you fifty bucks."

This poignant cartoon illustrates the difference between that which is subject to natural law and that which is subject to the positive law of legislatures. When sex is just in pursuit of happiness, as is non-commercial consensual sex, it is under the natural law jurisdiction. When sex is for monetary gain, it is subject to equity. Conversely rape, which is unconsented sex, is a crime because it is a violation of natural law, which requires consent.

In Nature, natural things get exchanged, such as body heat, passion, fluids and pathogens, and the consequences of natural law apply, including diseases and babies. As we shall see in chapters 12 and 13, another consequence of sex under the natural law jurisdiction of the U.S. constitution is the creation of natural born citizens, which can make sex a political act.

In contrast to having sex under the blanket of natural law, when sex is for hire it leaves the law jurisdiction and enters equity, which is ruled by positive law. Once people's body parts and cavities enter commerce, which subjects sex consumers to heightened risk, such commercial activity enters the realm of positive law and becomes subject to regulation in America's modern republics.

In other words, when sex leaves the natural law jurisdiction and becomes commercial, it becomes subject to regulation under equity. The only difference between a commercial and non-commercial activity is that the former is arguably for profit. In any event, having consensual sex is not a crime under Indiana law, whether it is for profit or not.

Republican legislatures cannot (and do not) define having consensual sex, which is a natural right, to be a crime. They only call it a "crime," and hope judges do not know their courts' subject matter jurisdiction.

Natural and positive law work the same way with regard to drugs. We will see throughout this book that acquiring and possessing property, such as buying or possessing drugs, is a natural right which republican legislatures cannot and do not regulate, prohibit or sanction. Just as positive law does not apply to our consensual non-commercial sex, which is the exercise of a natural right, America's republican drug laws explicitly exempt drug acquisition and possession from regulation and criminal liability because they are also natural rights. [127]

Within America's republics the drug laws apply only to two activities: 1) to *malum in se* crimes that involve drugs, which are defined and adjudicated in the state judicial branch, and 2) to the manufacture, distribution and dispensing of drugs within America's republics, which are subject to regulation by the executive branch as *malum prohibita*.

Because republican legislatures may not, without changing constitutions, make a crime out of that which comes naturally, even when it is practiced as a commercial activity, prostitution is no more a crime than drug possession or drug dealing. The commercial use of one's body parts is not subject to criminal prohibition in the law jurisdiction but only to commercial regulation, just as are the hands of surgeons and the eyes of automobile drivers.

Prostitution, drug commerce and professional surgery would be criminal only if America's republican constitutions were amended to place such activities into the criminal law jurisdiction of judicial courts. Until then, none of these commercial activities is criminally prohibited and each are merely regulated.

(Prostitutes are likely to be regulated by the Indiana Department of Health under authority of IC 16-19-3-4(b)(1), i.e., to regulate and make rules against "nuisances dangerous to public health." This is not to say that the state Department of Health does in fact regulate prostitution as it is likely supposed to. Again, this is true because prostitution has not been constitutionally prohibited as a form of commerce.)

So the rules for sex, drugs and alcohol are the roughly same in Indiana. If a person has sex, drinks alcohol or does drugs in the natural law jurisdiction, he answers only to Nature. But if one makes a living off of renting one's body, or brewing beer, or selling drugs, then the person is subject to the republic's taxation and regulation, which includes *malum prohibita*.

Additionally, those who offer sex, alcohol or drugs that harm others are subject to the civil or criminal subject matter jurisdiction of the judicial branch. For example, IC 16-41-7-1 and -9 call it a crime – because it is *malum in se* – for carriers of certain communicable diseases to not disclose their medical condition before sharing a needle or having sex with another person. Likewise, the Indiana legislature could make it criminal for prostitutes to knowingly pass diseases onto their customers. However, it may not make criminal merely having commercial sex with their customers, which operates in equity.

As if you have not already figured out the obvious, Hoosiers can do all the drugs, can drink all the alcohol and have all the consensual sex that they want, just so long as they do not hurt anyone in the process. Unless they are making money off the activity, it is their natural right to fiddle or diddle in private, alone or with consenting adults – of course, given relevant medical disclosures – in pursuit of happiness.

This is because the judicial branch of Indiana has no business or jurisdiction between consenting sovereign adults, unless some injury occurs. In terms of this chapter's diagram, there are no lines between two consenting adults and any branch of government unless there is injury or a commercial act. Only an illegitimate and perverted government would have any interest how people non-injuriously and non-commercially fiddle or diddle... or get intoxicated.

Natural rights are absolute to the extent that their exercise does not infringe on the equal natural rights of others, or enter regulation. The Indiana Supreme Court expressed this in *Beebe v. State* (1855):

> "And it should be here remarked that it is not said these rights are reserved to be used without restraint. Each individual being equally entitled to their exercise, the right of each operates as a check upon the right of every other, compelling mutual regard for those of each, and subjecting each to punishment by the juduciary, under legislative regulations, for violating the equal right of every other, and giving the injured in all cases redress by law." [128]

On the other hand, substantive rights are to be absolute as long as our constitutions do not change. For example, to rely on the natural and constitutional meaning of crime is a substantive right, or government can enslave non-criminals and can lapse into a non-republican form.

When our actions infringe on the equal rights of others, they invoke the law jurisdiction of judicial courts, which serves to provide civil and criminal remedies against people who are less than civil. But when we do not violate the rights of others, and merely do harm to ourselves, then the natural law jurisdiction makes us pay for our self-destruction. Harm to ourselves is not actionable in the law jurisdiction because we naturally cannot claim to be our own victims.

8
The U.S. non-republic

What is the form of government in the District of Columbia?

In the last six chapters we discussed the roles of three of America's four sovereigns: republican states, Congress as the U.S. republic legislating with regard to the states, and individuals. We learned that the state and U.S. republics maintain a law jurisdiction within their judicial branch where the sovereignty of individuals is secured by the enforcement of substantive rights. One of the main substantive rights at issue in the war on drugs is the right not to be enslaved except for the commission of crime. [129]

Central to securing this substantive right is to use the definition of crime according to the supreme law, which is America's republican constitutions. By use of the proper definition of crime, the law jurisdiction secures people's natural rights, such as the right to possess property. This in part secures the integrity of the republican form of government.

We also learned that equity is the jurisdiction over commerce and foreigners within America's republics, and that equity is under the exclusive authority of republican legislatures. For better or worse, legislatures determine who may visit the country and who may engage the public in commerce, and how such enterprises are regulated and taxed.

Of course, equity has no criminal jurisdiction because it cannot incarcerate artificial persons. Republican governments can only shut commercial persons down and enjoin them. That is why drug businesses are subject to regulation under equity, and not subject to criminal prohibition.

This chapter is about the fourth sovereign jurisdiction within the United States. In addition to Congress legislating toward the fifty states as a republic, it also legislates over its own physical area, as states also territorially do. Article I, Section 8, Clause 17 of the U.S. constitution grants Congress "exclusive Legislation in all Cases whatsoever" over the District of Columbia and other areas, which are referred to as the federal areas.

These federal areas, which are defined at 18 USC 7, include among other things the District of Columbia; the territories of the United States;

federal enclaves within the states; ships, planes and spaceships registered to the United States; all navigable waterways within the U.S.; the coastal waterways of the U.S., and acts by or against U.S. citizens in foreign countries. (We will discuss these areas more thoroughly later.)

This means that Congress has a territorial jurisdiction over which it exclusively legislates, just as do the states. This also means that Congress legislates in two capacities: 1) as a republic with regard to the fifty states, and 2) in a municipal or local capacity with regard to the federal areas, including over the nation's coastal and navigable waterways.

We have already seen how Congress legislates as a republic toward the states – where it respects people's natural rights and it regulates commerce and foreigners instead of prohibiting them. In the next chapter we will see that the U.S. republic also mostly defers to state criminal authority.

But the issue for us now is over what form of government that Congress operates in the federal areas. Does Congress operate as a republic there, as the states do within their borders, or is Congress free to be non-republican – or monarchical – in the federal areas?

So as to avoid confusion, I am going to tell you what I will argue in the balance of this chapter. I hope to show: 1) that there is no real, constitutionally-expressed or inherent reason for Congress to be given the power to act non-republican in the federal areas, 2) that a constitutional argument can be made that the Founders intended the form of government in the federal areas to be non-republican, 3) that – for right or wrong – the U.S. Supreme Court has interpreted Congress' power to be non-republican in the federal areas, 4) that because of this, criminal drug prohibition that is legislated by Congress for the federal areas is likely constitutional, 5) that this power is what accounts for the criminal penalty provisions in the U.S. Controlled Substances Act at 21 USC 841 – 844A, which otherwise violate republican law, 6) that these criminal provisions do not apply within the states where drug commerce is regulated and not criminally prohibited, and 7) that the enforcement of these criminal penalty provisions within the states is false and unlawful.

To make these arguments, let us first define the opposite of a republican form of government.

The characteristics of non-republics

This section asserts that there are really only two kinds of government: republics and non-republics. Almost all kinds of government with which the world is familiar, e.g., monarchies, dictatorships, social democracies, aristocracies, oligopolies, and totalitarian regimes, are forms of non-republics.

The moral authority for republics is that power resides in individual sovereigns, who delegate some of their authority to government so that it will fulfill certain essential functions. In contrast, non-republics are ruled by a single power, such as a monarch, a legislature or politburo, which does not answer to the People, and which is based upon artificial claims of authority over subjects, instead of upon the natural delegation of power from citizens.

Although many people may associate only monarchies with state religions, all non-republican rule is by force and opinion, whose moral authority is essentially subjective and religious. This is because their criminal adjudications are not based upon natural and objective criteria, such as injury, but instead upon subjective criteria, such as whatever the monarch or legislature says is criminal. The religious nature of non-republics is also evident by the faith that subjects place in their leaders as saviors.

Due to the religious basis of non-republics, the Founding Fathers established the U.S. republic to not be based upon religion. That is what the 1st Amendment is about. It says "Congress shall make no law respecting an establishment of religion, or prohibiting the free exercise thereof..." The Founders wanted government to secure their natural right to worship a natural God, with a natural basis of morality, i.e., to not harm one another, instead of being forced to worship an unnatural one that handpicked one man or a group of men to impose their morality upon others.

As we shall see, the legal characteristics of non-republics (below) are some of those same qualities that U.S. courts, including the U.S. Supreme Court, attribute to Congress' power within the federal areas.

1. that non-republics have supernatural power to subjectively define judicial cases and crimes without reference to objective natural law, which means that torts and crimes are *malum prohibita*, or whatever the monarch, dictator or legislature says they are,

2. that non-republics enforce their subjectivity with plenary power upon artificial persons, but their courts exercise no law jurisdiction, where natural law can be enforced and where natural people's natural rights can be secured from the will of others,

3. that a non-republic's subjects are born subject to a sovereign outside

of themselves, are without natural rights, and are not free of government as a result of being born in captivity, under claim. Such slaves' natural physical liberty – as natural persons – is achievable only by fleeing to a republic, which respects the natural rights of all natural persons,

4. that there exists no separation of power between branches of government in a non-republic, all of which serve the sole sovereign,

5. that all the physical and political "rights" are in fact privileges that the government's subjects are granted from the positive law authority of the government, and not from Nature, and

6. that the non-republic's artificial authority comes not from the natural delegation of power from citizens, but instead from the artificial claim of power by the despot, based on an unnatural fiction, and on its use of force to maintain this supernatural claim.

Before jumping into the following analysis, let me give you my personal opinion about the form of government in the federal areas. My personal opinion is that logically there is no reason for Congress to necessarily legislate in a non-republican fashion toward the federal areas.

For example, the law and equity jurisdictions of Article III of the U.S. constitution should both apply in the federal areas as they do in the state republics. Nothing in the U.S. constitution exempts the federal areas from the law jurisdiction, where people's natural rights are secured. This means that people's natural rights to possess drugs and commercial enterprises' rights to administrative due process could theoretically be applicable in both the states and the federal areas.

If natural rights were secured in both places, then drugs would be legal not only in America's republics, but in the federal areas as well. Congress would regulate drug commerce in the federal areas as it is to do within the fifty states. And if this was the case, then the criminal provisions in the U.S. Controlled Substances Act at 21 USC 841 – 844A would be ineffective or unconstitutional in not only the states, but in the federal areas as well.

In other words, if Congress was required to act republican toward the federal areas, as it is required to act toward the states, then drugs would be legal and drug commerce would be regulated throughout every inch of the United States – not just in America's republics. However, as we shall see below, the courts have largely interpreted Congress' power as non-republican in the federal areas, which justifies criminal drug prohibition there, instead of just commercial regulation.

This is not to say the courts have been correct in doing so, but that their rulings have been relatively clear and consistent. Ultimately a good argument can be made that the 18th Amendment's prohibition of the exportation and importation of alcohol demonstrates that without a constitutional amendment, Congress cannot legitimately use its plenary authority over the federal areas, which include the country's coastline and tariff jurisdiction, to criminalize the importation or exportation of drugs. That Congress uses its municipal (instead of republican) authority to prohibit the importation of disfavored drugs is yet another unlitigated anomaly of the drug war.

Before looking at how courts view the form of government that Congress legislates in the federal areas, we should see if there is anything in the U.S. constitution that requires or authorizes Congress to be non-republican there. My answer is that there are at least four things that suggest that Congress may legislate as a non-republic in the federal areas.

The first thing to note is that the U.S. constitution did not make the federal areas a state, to which the Guarantee Clause at Article IV, Section 4 applies. Article IV, Section 4 of the U.S. constitution guarantees "to every State in this Union a Republican Form of Government." Because the federal areas are not a state, then Congress is not explicitly required to guarantee a republican form of government to the federal areas.

This does not mean that Congress could not choose to adopt the republican form of government, and its basis in natural law, for its federal areas. But suffice to say that it has not.

A second argument is that the 13th Amendment's prohibition against slavery does not appear to apply in the federal areas. This would suggest that Congress can enslave people without the commission of real crime, such as in the cases of drug and gun commerce.

Arguably, the 13th Amendment does not apply to the federal areas because it prohibits slavery only "within the United States, or any place subject to their jurisdiction." As we learned in a prior chapter, commercial slavery can only exist in a non-republic 1) which does not respect natural law, and 2) which does not extend the law jurisdiction equally to all people, such as to drug dealers.

A third argument is that Article I, Section 8, Clause 17 of the U.S. constitution, which grants Congress "exclusive Legislation in all Cases whatsoever," means that Congress can legislate the meaning of "all Cases whatsoever" within the federal area. This would mean that it could legislate the meaning of criminal cases too, irrespective of how natural law defines case, crime and probable cause within America's republics.

A fourth argument is that Congress legislates over people within the federal areas as subjects, often called citizen-subjects, instead of toward them as citizens. This is the mark of a non-republic. Republics answer to their citizens, whereas subjects answer to non-republics.

The 14th Amendment refers to "(a)ll persons born or naturalized in the United States and <u>subject</u> to the jurisdiction thereof." This does not describe, and is in contrast to, natural born citizens 1) who gain their citizenship from their citizen fathers, 2) who need not be born or naturalized in the United States, and 3) who are not born subject to or subjects of the U.S. government, which are topics in chapters 12 and 13.

These are solid arguments that the Founding Fathers (and subsequent leaders) were less than strict about establishing a republican form of government within the federal areas. The 13th Amendment argument above suggests that Congress can define crime in the federal areas without regard to natural law, thereby violating people's rights to property possession or to administrative due process for engaging in drug commerce.

As well, because inhabitants of Washington, D.C. and other federal areas have a subject-status, it is hard to deny that they live under a non-republic. It is only under such a non-republican form of government that the criminal penalty provisions in the U.S. CSA at 21 USC 841 – 844A can be justified, which such provisions would apply only to the federal areas.

We know that these criminal penalty provisions for drugs do not apply within the fifty state republics because drug possession is lawful there, and because the U.S. Attorney General – using the Drug Enforcement Administration (DEA) – regulates drug commerce among the states.

In fact, whenever U.S. statutes use the word prohibition, as do the titles of the criminal penalty provisions at 21 USC 841 – 843, then we can be assured that they do not operate within the fifty state republics. This is because such states may not criminally prohibit the possession or commerce of any good or service without a relevant constitutional amendment.

Thus, if drugs are prohibited anywhere in the U.S., then they would only – and at most – be illegal within the federal areas where, based on the above four (or more) arguments, Congress may define what is a case or crime there, and therefore who may be enslaved, in defiance of natural law. These are the only constitutional justifications that I can discern for the existence of the criminal penalty provisions of the U.S. CSA, and for a non-republican form of government to operate in the federal areas.

Regardless whether the U.S. constitution establishes a non-republican form of government in the federal areas, the courts, including the U.S. Supreme Court, have interpreted Congress' power as characteristically non-republican there. In addition to the four arguments above, this is perhaps due to their misunderstanding of the word plenary, which the courts have used to describe Congress' power of exclusive Legislation over the federal areas.

Note that the U.S. constitution does not grant Congress plenary authority in the federal areas, but that only judges and justices have called such power plenary. As well, they have exaggerated the meaning of plenary.

To understand plenary, first note that it describes the power of each of the four categories of American sovereigns. Each American sovereign has its own plenary authority within its own legislative or subject matter jurisdiction. It is not a special power granted to Congress just over the federal areas. It is not a power that allows any of the sovereigns to violate the U.S. constitution. Plenary describes the full extent of each sovereign's authority under the constitution.

Black's Law Dictionary defines plenary as "full, entire, complete, absolute, perfect, unqualified." [130] Acceptance of this definition could easily persuade a judge that plenary power is unbridled and unlimited, or that this power attributed to Congress over the federal areas is a different kind of power than that which Congress exercises among the states, where such power is certainly not complete, absolute and unqualified..

However, this is a false understanding of plenary. Plenary power is always *a priori* limited by the legislative and subject matter jurisdiction of the sovereign. Plenary power is that "full, entire, complete, absolute, perfect, (and) unqualified" [131] power that each of the four sovereigns (and their branches) exercise within their legislative and subject matter jurisdiction.

Thus, one cannot understand a sovereign's plenary power without first understanding the scope of its legislative and subject matter jurisdiction. Each sovereign has absolute or plenary authority to exercise its delegated or reserved powers.

For example, Congress has plenary power to regulate interstate commerce in equity, but this does not include the power to criminally prohibit commerce at law, for which Congress has no legislative jurisdiction. Congress also has plenary authority to legislate over naturalization, but this power does not include any authority to legislate over natural born citizens, which is to say, over how Nature makes citizens or how citizens are made in Nature.

In addition, Congress has plenary authority over certain federal crimes, to be discussed in the next chapter, but otherwise the federal government has no criminal jurisdiction within the states. As well, judicial court's have plenary authority over cases and crimes, but no such authority over the regulation of commerce.

Instead, executive branch agencies have the "full, entire, complete, absolute, perfect, (and) unqualified" [132] power to regulate. However, this unqualified power to regulate does not include prohibition. This is because regulation in the executive branch is constitutionally held in check by the jurisdiction of the judicial branch, which holds the state's criminal power.

As we have seen, legislatures' legislative plenary authority is limited by the power granted to them in constitutions. Such plenary authority does not include the power to change or expand the criminal jurisdiction of judicial courts. As we also learned, state legislatures have plenary authority to legislate over equity, but they have no plenary authority to legislate crimes, which are instead subject to Nature's plenary authority.

With regard to individuals, for example, potential crime victims have plenary criminal jurisdiction in matter of self-defense, and U.S. citizen fathers have plenary jurisdiction over the creation of natural born citizens. Individuals also legislate over when they sleep, eat and use the restroom, for example. No other sovereigns have authority over this subject matter. Thus, individual sovereigns have "full, entire, complete, absolute, perfect, (and) unqualified" [133] authority over self-defense, over the creation of natural law citizens and over other exercises of natural rights.

Thus, as I wrote above, each American sovereign has plenary power over its own legislative and subject matter jurisdiction. Good government requires keeping these plenary powers separate. Good government also requires the exercise of all plenary powers to be within the jurisdictional limits imposed by constitutions.

Consequently, plenary power really means a sovereign's complete power to exercise that sovereign's rightful subject matter or legislative jurisdiction. This means that in order to define each sovereign's plenary power we must first consult republican constitutions, which grant certain powers to the state and federal sovereigns and which reserve certain power for individual sovereigns. Then all the plenary power of each and all of America's sovereigns can be properly understood and distributed.

How courts view Congress' plenary power over the federal areas

With regard to our fourth sovereign, i.e., the Congress that legislates over the federal areas, let us see what courts, including the U.S. Supreme Court, say about its plenary power granted over the federal areas under Article I, Section 8, Clause 17 and Article IV, Section 3, Clause 2 of the U.S. constitution. As mentioned above, and as we shall further see below, courts have interpreted Congress' power as quite non-republican in the federal areas. Hopefully, as the issues discussed in this book are raised by other attorneys, then courts will better define Congress' legislative authority within the federal areas.

As I asserted above, there are at least four constitutional justifications for thinking that Congress legislates over the federal areas as a non-republic. Either because of these reasons, or because the federal areas need a municipal court system just as the states do, or because of both reasons, the constitution allows and circumstances require Congress to establish its own court system for the federal areas and certain federal functions.

These courts are called Article I courts (or legislative courts) because they are created by Congress based on its legislative powers under Article I of the U.S. constitution. (These are contrasted with Article III judicial courts that are created by Article III of the U.S. constitution.) These Article I courts include territorial courts (as in the district of Guam, the U.S. Virgin Islands and the Northern Mariana Islands), the U.S. Court of Military Appeals, the U.S. Court of Veterans Appeals, the U.S. Court of Federal Claims and the U.S. Tax Court, for instance.

Whereas Article III courts adjudicate violations of natural rights, commercial conflicts, federal crimes and federal questions on behalf of the U.S. republic, Article I courts enforce Congress' plenary authority in the federal areas and over federal civil functions. They also adjudicate the "rights" and privileges that Congress grants to the people subject to its jurisdiction there. This makes Article I judges administrators for the federal areas and certain federal functions.

They are "not members of the independent judiciary which has been one of our proudest boasts, by reason of Art. III," wrote Justice Douglas of the U.S. Supreme Court in his dissent in *Palmore v. United States* (1973). [134] This is to say that they are not judicial officers who administer the law jurisdictions, where natural rights are secured.

The constitution "confers upon Congress the power to establish courts within the District of Columbia and to define the extent of the jurisdiction of such courts," wrote the Massachusetts District Court in *Ostrow v. Samuel Brilliant Co.* (1946). [135] This power includes the "authority to vest courts of the District of Columbia with a variety of jurisdiction," wrote the Court of Appeals for the District of Columbia in *Hill v. Dorsey* (1927). [136]

Congress "may, if it sees fit, unite legislative and judicial powers in a single hand," wrote the *Hill v. Dorsey* court [137] If this is true, then this would be to void the separation of powers doctrine needed to secure a republican form of government in the federal areas.

This plenary power to create Article I courts and to vest them with a variety of muddled power is in contrast with the lack of Congress' power to change the jurisdiction of Article III courts, whose jurisdiction is constitutionally fixed by the case or controversy requirement. In other words – suggests the above courts – the case or controversy requirement does not apply to Article I courts. As well, Article III courts respect the separation of powers between the executive. legislative and judicial branches of government – and unlike Article I courts, do not unite them "in a single hand." [138]

Note that what the above courts and the U.S. Supreme Court say about Congress' power over the District of Columbia is also applicable to Congress' power in the other federal areas. According to 18 USC 7, Congress exercises equal power in the District of Columbia that it does in rest of the federal areas.

Congress has "constitutional power to proscribe certain criminal conduct only in the District and to select the appropriate court, whether it is created by virtue of article III or article I, to hear and determine these particular criminal cases within the District," wrote the majority of the Supreme Court in *Palmore v. United States* (1973). [139] This is in contrast with Article III- and other republican courts for which Nature proscribes crime and legislatures merely prescribe it. The power of Congress to pick where crimes are adjudicated means that crimes in the federal areas are not always subject to the republican criteria of Article III courts, i.e., injury.

Article I courts "handle criminal cases only under statutes that are applicable to the District of Columbia alone," wrote the U.S. Supreme Court in *Palmore*. [140] As well, Article I courts adjudicate the subject status of those who voluntarily enter Congress plenary legislative jurisdiction, for example, foreigners and likely certain U.S. government employees.

"Congress has the entire control over the district for every purpose of government, and it is reasonable to suppose that in organizing a judicial department in this District, all the judicial power necessary for the purposes of government would be vested in the courts of justice," the U.S. Supreme Court wrote in *Kendall v. United States* (1838). [141] Congress may determine for itself when and how it shall delegate or distribute authority under its police powers, wrote the Court in *LaForest v. Board of Commissioner of*

District of Columbia (1937). [142]

This plenary power to create its own courts and to define the extent of their jurisdiction is an extraordinary power that Congress may not exercise over Article III courts. This is because such Article III courts owe their existence – not to Congress – but to the U.S. constitution.

This means that Congress controls the jurisdiction of Article I courts, but that it does not control the jurisdiction of Article III courts. With regard to the latter, it must legislate consistently with their republican jurisdiction, based on injury, as granted by the U.S. constitution.

Likewise, state judicial courts owe their existence to state constitutions, not to state legislatures. That is why constitutional amendments are required to change or expand the powers of state and federal judicial courts.

The power of Congress is plenary in the District of Columbia, wrote Justice Douglas in *Palmore v. United States* (1973), when it gives "Congress authority to establish the method by which the District of Columbia will be governed, and to alter from time to time the form of that government." [143] In that this book asserts that there are basically only two forms of government, i.e., republics and non-republics, thus to be able "to alter from time to time the form of that government" is extraordinary power not found in America's republics. For example, Article III courts do not have the power to act monarchical one moment and to act republican the next.

"In exercising this power, Congress is not subject to the same constitutional limitations, as when it is legislating for the United States..." wrote the U.S. Supreme Court in *Hooven & Allison Co. v. Evatt* (1945). [144] "And in general the guaranties of the Constitution, save as they are limitations upon the exercise of executive and legislative power when exerted for or over our insular possessions, extend to them only as Congress, in the exercise of its legislative power over territory belonging to the United States, has made those guaranties applicable." [145]

In other words, Congress has constitutional limitations when legislating as a republic for the union of state republics, where for example it regulates commerce and natural law defines crime. However, the guarantees of the U.S. constitution that extend to the federal areas or to the people in them are only as Congress makes those guarantees "applicable." [146]

Thus apparently, according to the U.S. Supreme Court, Congress has exclusive authority in the federal areas to determine what rights – both substantive and natural rights – apply. Apparently as well, both Congress and its Article I courts may disregard the natural law, the constitutional definition of crime and the guarantees of republican government, and may instead determine which rights apply.

The power to determine what rights are applicable is what makes governments non-republican. This is because non-republics do not recognize the law jurisdiction of republican judicial courts where crime is objectively defined by natural law to include injury and where natural rights are unalienable – thus secured from the subjective will of dictators.

The U.S. Supreme Court in *Palmore v. United States* (1973) echoed the sentiments of *Hooven*. "It is apparent," wrote the Court, "that the power of Congress under Clause 17 permits it to legislate for the District in a manner with respect to subjects that would exceed its powers, or at least would be very unusual, in the context of national legislation enacted under other powers delegated to it under Art. I, § 8." [147]

Given that Congress must legislate toward the states as a republic, this would make the "national legislation" referred to in the above quotation to mean: republican legislation. Thus the courts conclude that the plenary powers that Congress exercises in the federal areas exceed those that it may exercise as a democratic republic among the fifty states.

As well, as pointed out by the *Palmore* majority, such authority in the federal areas is exercised "with respects to subjects" [148] – meaning with respect to subjects of a non-republic – not with respect to republican citizens. A non-republic recognizes neither the natural physical nor natural political rights of citizens, but only the artificial "rights" that the leader bestows upon its subjects or citizen-subjects.

Non-republics have no basis in Nature. They and natural law are antithetical, incompatible and cannot operate in the same space. This is because non-republican leaders claim unnatural power, for example the power to rightly incarcerate people for *malum prohibita*.

Thus, as the above *Hooven* (1945) and *Palmore* (1973) cases tell us, the criminal and civil jurisdictions of Article I courts are as Congress determines, and their criminal jurisdiction may apparently be enlarged over that subject matter which Article III courts have authority to adjudicate, which is injury. This leads to the conclusion, which at least the Supreme Court seems to believe, that Congress' Article I courts may adjudicate "cases" and "crimes" that do not include injury, and that these courts are not subject to the case or controversy requirement to which U.S. courts created under Article III are subject, which we discussed in chapter 3.

If this is in fact the case, then Congress is adjudged a non-republic in the federal areas and it may criminally prohibit *malum prohibita* there, in Article I courts, as is exhibited by the criminal provisions in the U.S. CSA at 21 USC 841 – 844A. This is because Congress has authority to define both crime and probable cause for its artificial subjects within the federal areas.

This means that Congress, which the *Hooven* (1945) court said could determine which rights are applicable in the federal areas, may deny the right of property possession and may criminalize drug possession and dealing within its legislative Article I courts. Equally, as suggested by the *Palmore* (1973) court, Congress can try real crimes that occur within the federal areas in Article III courts and criminally prosecute its *malum prohibita* in Article I courts.

Congress has constitutional power, wrote the Court, "to proscribe certain criminal conduct only in the District and to select the appropriate court, whether it is created by virtue of article III or article I, to hear and determine these particular criminal cases within the District." [149] In other words, real *malum in se* crime that occurs in the federal areas can be adjudicated in Article III criminal courts, while not-so-criminal *malum prohibita* may be adjudicated as crime in Article I criminal courts.

As if learning that drugs are legal in America's republics was not significant enough, we now can surmise that the only basis for the criminal prohibitions in the U.S. CSA at 21 USC 841 – 844A is that courts, and particularly the Supreme Court, interpret Congress' plenary power over the federal areas to be non-republican.

The exercise of Congress is non-republican: 1) such that its Article I courts apparently do not have a case or controversy requirement for criminal prosecutions, 2) such that there is no separation of powers between branches of government (because the police powers serve Congress as the non-republic, not the People), 3) such that Congress can divvy-out rights as it chooses (as if it is above the constitution and Nature), 4) such that it can enslave people without the commission of crimes (because the 13th Amendment may not apply in the federal areas), and 5) such that federal inhabitants and naturalized citizens serve Congress as subjects.

Only Congress' non-republican form of government accounts for the criminal prohibitions in the U.S. CSA at 21 USC 841 - 844A, which can apply only in the federal areas. Given this, I will briefly demonstrate that these provisions do not apply against drug dealing within and between the states, which is instead regulated under equity.

Take any 'ole U.S. drug-dealing indictment. (I dissect a dozen criminal drug complaints and indictments in chapter 25.) A typical one will include a count, usually entitled *Possession of Controlled Substances With Intent to Distribute*, for violating 21 USC 841(a). Its subsection (1) makes it unlawful "to manufacture, distribute, or dispense, or possess with intent to manufacture, distribute, or dispense, a controlled substance." I contend that this criminal penalty provision applies only against drug dealing in the federal areas – not within the states where drug dealing is regulated.

Now we turn our attention to 21 USC 822(a). It is one of the regulatory provisions that apply to interstate drug commerce, which the U.S. Attorney General and the DEA regulate. It says that every person who manufactures, distributes or dispenses controlled substances, or proposes to do this, must "obtain annually a registration issued by the Attorney General in accordance with the rules and regulations promulgated by him..." [150]

So, do you see the conflict? 21 USC 841(a) criminalizes the manufacture, distribution or dispensing of controlled substances. In contrast, 21 USC 822(a) regulates the manufacture, distribution or dispensing of controlled substances, which regulation does not include incarceration. These two provisions treat the same behavior differently. They appear to be in direct and absolute conflict, which if true could jeopardize the constitutionality of the U.S. CSA.

However, there is no real conflict between these provisions. This is because these two contradictory provisions operate in different territorial jurisdictions. Within and among the state republics, interstate drug commerce is regulated by the Attorney General under 21 USC 822(a). Drug dealers are to be licensed ("registered") by the Attorney General. The office can enjoin those who are not.

In contrast, within the federal areas, where courts essentially claim that Congress legislates as a non-republic, drug commerce is criminally prohibited at 21 USC 841(a). Being *malum prohibita*, these actions are to be prosecuted by U.S. Attorneys in Article I courts, not in Article III courts. Article III courts have jurisdiction only over real crimes, and particularly those relating to federal enumerated powers – a topic in the next chapter.

As we shall see, only a few of the dozen drug indictments that I analyze in chapter 25 involve real drug crimes. While most drug defendants in these indictments are charged with violating 21 USC 841(a)(1), which is *malum prohibita* enforceable only in an Article I court of the federal areas, the U.S. CSA also include real drug crime. For example, 21 USC 841(a)(2) says that it is unlawful "to create, distribute, or dispense, or possess with intent to distribute or dispense, a counterfeit substance."

As a form of fraud, this is *malum in se*, which is naturally prohibited in every American law jurisdiction. Committing such a fraud in a federal area would be subject to Congress' codification of *malum in se*. As the Court in *Palmore v. Unites States* (1973) told us, Congress can direct causes of action in the federal areas to either Article I or Article III courts. [151]

Given the limited case law on the subject, it is difficult to discern the scope of criminal power between Article I and Article III courts in the federal areas. Alternatively, given that Congress can apparently define the criminal jurisdiction of Article I courts any way it wishes, it is difficult to discern the proper role and scope of Article III courts in the federal areas.

We shall see that the U.S. non-republic operates in its admiralty jurisdiction in U.S. navigable and coastal waterways, [152] but whether the U.S. operates exclusively in admiralty or also in equity within the other federal areas has not been fully vetted. Legal rights are ambiguous and tenuous where there is no rule of law, but only the law of the ruler.

The rule of law applies only in a republic which has a law jurisdiction that secures people's natural rights. Says Wikipedia, a republican form of government is one whose "leaders exercise power according to the rule of law." If a government need not respect people's natural rights, through the enforcement of substantive rights, then it is not an American republic.

Thus, the U.S. CSA's non-republican criminal drug prohibitions operate only in the federal areas, and as *malum prohibita* they are criminally enforceable only in Article I courts of Congress operating in a non-republican capacity. As we saw above, the U.S. CSA also contains real *malum in se* drug crimes which Congress can also grant Article I courts to adjudicate. [153]

The U.S. CSA's criminal drug prohibitions do not apply within the states where drug commerce is regulated, where it is not criminally prohibited, and where Article III courts have no jurisdiction over *malum prohibita*. Thus, the U.S. criminal enforcement of *malum prohibita* within the states is false and unlawful. Such subject matter is regulatory.

The above example is an excellent lesson in understanding the scope of U.S. criminal law. Because the U.S. CSA is legislation by Congress in both of its sovereign capacities – as both the U.S. republic and the U.S. non-republic – then a reader must know which sovereign legislated each provision to determine where the provision applies. In general, if not exclusively, the U.S. CSA's regulatory provisions apply within the fifty states. Its penal or criminal provisions apply only in the federal areas.

Knowing jurisdiction is a key to understanding the illegal national war on drugs. As we saw above, two seemingly contradictory provisions do not conflict because they operate in separate territorial jurisdictions.

The scope of the U.S. non-republic's power is territorial

As we saw above, Congress legislates territorially over the federal areas, as states legislate territorially over their areas. This essentially means that every square inch of the United States is under a territorial sovereign.

The U.S. Supreme Court expressed this principle of territoriality of criminal jurisdiction in *United States v. Bevans* (1818). There it upheld federal authority over murders on America's navigable waterways that, according to 8 USC 7, are federal areas under the exclusive jurisdiction of Congress. This case shows that "jurisdiction of a state is co-extensive with its territory; co-extensive with its legislative power," [154] and that federal criminal authority on such waterways operates under admiralty or maritime law, [155] which is different than the common law authority of state republics.

As we have seen, the U.S. constitution grants Congress its territorial jurisdiction at Article I, Section 8, Clause 17, which grants power:

> "To exercise exclusive Legislation in all Cases whatsoever, over such District (not exceeding ten Miles square) as may, by Cession of particular States, and the Acceptance of Congress, become the Seat of the Government of the United States, and to exercise like Authority over all Places purchased by the Consent of the Legislature of the State in which the Same shall be, for the Erection of Forts, Magazines, Arsenals, dock-Yards and other needful Buildings..."

Accompany this grant is Article IV, Section 3, Clause 2 which reads: "The Congress shall have Power to dispose of and make all needful Rules and Regulations respecting the Territory or other Property belonging to the United States..." Because of the principle of territorial jurisdiction, the Congress that legislate over the federal areas and each state legislature are separate sovereigns, and ordinarily one cannot enforce the laws of the other.

When Congress legislates for the federal areas, as states legislate over their own land areas, such legislation is local or municipal in scope and nature, rendering it foreign with respect to state sovereignty. In *National Bank v. County of Yankton* (1879) the U.S. Supreme Court explained: "All territory within the jurisdiction of the United States not included in any State must necessarily be governed by or under the authority of Congress." [156] This "authority of Congress" is its power to act in its plenary capacity over the federal areas.

An important 1956 report written by some of the U.S. government's finest and most conscientious attorneys, called *Jurisdiction Over Federal Areas Within The States, Report of the Interdepartmental Committee for the Study of Jurisdiction Over Federal Areas Within the States*, explains the nature and scope of Congress' legislative jurisdiction within the states.

I first read this two-volume government report during my first year of law school in 1983 – 1984. I have read it twice since then. It is the best publication that I have ever read on federal criminal jurisdiction. It should be mandatory reading for all American law students, criminal defense attorneys and government attorneys.

Essentially the *Report* on *Jurisdiction Over Federal Areas Within The States* says that – with the exception of several federal crimes related to Congress' enumerated powers (to be discussed in the next chapter) – then Congress has legislative (and thus, criminal) jurisdiction within states only 1) over land that it owns and 2) over land to which a state has ceded either partial or exclusive legislative (and thus, criminal) jurisdiction.

The *Report* shows that legislative jurisdiction within state republics is acquired by Congress through state consent statutes and cession laws. As Article I, Section 8, Clause 17 of the U.S. constitution (above) explains, U.S. legislative jurisdiction – and thus, U.S. criminal jurisdiction, extends to "all Places purchased by the Consent of the Legislature of the State in which the Same shall be..."

The degree of U.S. legislative jurisdiction depends on how much authority is acquired from state legislatures or reserved by Congress when a state is created. The *Report* classifies the legislative jurisdiction as 1) exclusive legislative jurisdiction, 2) concurrent legislative jurisdiction (shared with states), 3) partial legislative jurisdiction, and 4) proprietary interest only. [157]

All four of these degrees of U.S. legislative authority are based on federal ownership of land or buildings within the states. Thus, except by constitutional amendment, such as the 18th Amendment which granted Congress concurrent legislative (and criminal) jurisdiction with state legislatures over alcohol commerce, this shared or concurrent jurisdiction is always over land owned by the federal government and over land which the state has ceded only partial legislative authority.

In contrast, "(a)reas over which the Federal Government has acquired exclusive legislative jurisdiction are subject to the exclusive criminal jurisdiction of the United States," states the *Report*. [158] Congress exercises its exclusive plenary criminal jurisdiction in these areas defined by 18 USC 5 and 18 USC 7. "(T)he transfer to the United States of exclusive legislative jurisdiction over an area has the effect, speaking generally, of divesting the State and any governmental entities operating under its authority...," [159] reads the *Report*.

That the states can neither define nor make punishment for crimes in such federal areas is made clear in the case of *In re Ladd* (1896). There the federal court wrote: "the state certainly cannot claim jurisdiction criminally by reason of acts done at places beyond, or not within, its territorial jurisdiction." [160]

In other words, with only the exceptions of crimes relating to Congress' enumerated powers and of offenses against the United States, both topics to be discussed in the next chapter, criminal jurisdiction is strictly territorial. In areas under the authority of states, where states have not ceded legislative jurisdiction to the U.S. government, the U.S. government has very limited criminal jurisdiction· "The criminal jurisdiction of the Federal Government extends to private lands over which legislative jurisdiction has been vested in the Government, as well as to federally owned lands," [161] succinctly states the *Report*. Conversely, the *Report* reads:

> "It scarcely needs to be said that unless there has been a transfer of jurisdiction (1) pursuant to clause 17 by a Federal acquisition of land with State consent, or unless the Federal Government has reserved jurisdiction upon the admission of the State, the Federal Government possesses no legislative jurisdiction over any area within a State, such jurisdiction being for exercise entirely by the State, subject to the non-interference by the State with Federal functions, and subject to the free exercise by the Federal Government with respect to the use, protection, and disposition of its property." [162]

In other words, there is normally "(n)o Federal legislative jurisdiction without consent, cession or reservation" [163] of power over state property. Unless a state legislature or constitution sells land and cedes partial or complete legislative jurisdiction to Congress, pursuant to Article 1, Section 8, Clause 17, or unless a person's actions, such as counterfeiting or tax evasion, invoke a federal function as mentioned in the above quotation, then there is no exclusive or concurrent federal criminal jurisdiction within a state over the same subject matter. In *Caha v. United States* (1894) the U.S. Supreme Court wrote:

> "Generally speaking, within any state of this Union the preservation of the peace and the protection of person and property are the functions of the state government, and are not part of the primary duty, at least, of the nation. The laws of congress in respect to those matters do not extend into the territorial limits of the states, but have force only in the District of Columbia, and other places that are within the exclusive jurisdiction of the national government." [164]

"Those matters" referred to by the Court in *Caha v. United States* (1894) are regulatory and criminal matters that invoke the exercise of police powers. Congress has regulatory authority, which is a police power, within the states according to the Interstate Commerce Clause at Article I, Section 8, Clause 3 of the U.S. constitution. However, the laws of Congress in respect to criminal matters normally "do not extend into the territorial limits of the states," wrote the Court in *Caha*, "but have force only in the District of Columbia, and other places that are within the exclusive jurisdiction of the national government." [165] This includes most of the criminal provision in the U.S. Criminal Code (Title 18 USC) and all of the criminal prohibitions that are listed in the U.S. CSA at 21 USC 841 – 844A.

Whether Congress' legislation is non-republican and applies only to the federal areas, or whether it is republican and applies to the fifty states, is strictly a question of legislative jurisdiction. As the U.S. Supreme Court wrote in *Cohens v. Virginia* (1821): "Whether any particular law be designed to operate without the District or not, depends on the words of that law... In such cases the constitution and the law must be compared and construed. This is the exercise of jurisdiction. It is the only exercise of it which is allowed in such a case." [166]

Due to the territorial nature of legislative jurisdiction, and thus the territorial nature of criminal jurisdiction, unless defendants commit crimes in a federal area, including federal enclaves within states which have ceded criminal jurisdiction to Congress, then criminal jurisdiction is, with the few exceptions noted in the next chapter, the exclusive province of states. In other words, says the *Report*:

> "while the Federal Government has power under various provisions of the Constitution to define, and prohibit as criminal, certain acts or omissions occurring anywhere in the United States [i.e., crimes relating to federal functions, to be discussed in the next chapter], it has no power to punish for various other crimes, jurisdiction over which is retained by the States under our Federal-State system of government unless such crimes occur on areas as to which legislative jurisdiction has been vested in the Federal Government." [167]

That criminal jurisdiction is largely territorial is also evidenced by the U.S. criminal code, which is Title 18 of the United States Code. 18 USC 5 defines the United States in its "territorial sense," saying that its legislative jurisdiction "includes all places and waters, continental or insular, subject to the jurisdiction of the United States," excluding the Canal Zone.

This reference to the United States is a reference to the area under the authority of Congress in its plenary capacity. Further, the "special maritime and territorial jurisdiction of the United States," which is defined at 18 USC 7, explains where Congress may legislate as a non-republic.

More specifically, this jurisdiction includes, among other things, the territories and possessions of the United States. These territories and possessions include the District of Columbia, the Commonwealth of Puerto Rico, the Commonwealth of the Northern Mariana Islands, Guam, the Virgin Islands of the United States, American Samoa and federal enclaves within states. Federal criminal law applies in all of these places.

Such enclaves within the states, wherein the federal criminal law of the U.S. non-republic is applicable, are described at 18 USC 7 (3) to include "(a)ny lands reserved or acquired for the use of the United States, and under the exclusive or concurrent jurisdiction thereof, or any place purchased or otherwise acquired by the United States by consent of the legislature of the State in which the same shall be, for the erection of a fort, magazine, arsenal, dockyard, or other needful building."

The U.S. non-republic's legislative jurisdiction at 18 USC 7 also includes the coastal waters, the high seas, and the navigable waterways within the U.S.; ships, aircraft and spaceships that are registered under the laws of the United States; and places with respect to offenses against U.S. citizens, such as occurred against U.S. personnel on September 11, 2012 in Benghazi, Libya. That the U.S. non-republic has criminal jurisdiction, based on 18 USC 7, is why agents of the Federal Bureau of Investigation were sent to Benghazi to investigate the crimes that occurred there (albeit a month after the crimes were committed).

The territorial and non-republican nature of the federal criminal jurisdiction is also evident by 18 USC 23 which defines the Article I criminal courts of the United States to include the non-republic's colonial courts in Guam, the Northern Mariana Islands and the Virgin Islands, which by definition are Article I courts.

We can conclude from these references that the scope of the U.S. criminal code, except in the case of crimes relating to specific federal functions, does not include crimes committed within the fifty state republics, where natural law, as secured by the states' judicial law jurisdiction, defines most crimes committed within their state borders. This is because 1) the U.S. criminal code (Title 18 United States Code) largely operates upon the United States in its "territorial sense," i.e., within its federal areas; [168] 2) because the code does not specifically include the fifty state republics and their land areas to be within these federal areas, [169] and 3) because the states are not "subject to the jurisdiction of the United States," [170] i.e., Congress as a non-republic, in that they are separate territorial sovereigns.

This is all to say that, 1) with the exception of being in a federal area, 2) with the exception of being subject to the Congress as a non-republic, as are federal employees, and 3) with the exception of a handful of crimes that relate to Congress' enumerated powers, which do not include drug possession or dealing, most people within America's states are not subject to most of the U.S. criminal code, which operates mostly within the federal areas.

Wrote the U.S. Supreme Court in *United States v. Fox* (1877), it is a state crime when "an act committed in a state has no relation to the execution of a power of Congress or to any matter within the jurisdiction of the United States." [171] In other words, it is a state crime when the action is not related to a federal enumerated power, or if it is not committed "within the jurisdiction of the United States," [172] which refers to the territorial jurisdiction of Congress as defined at 18 USC 5 and 18 USC 7.

This principle is expressed in the U.S. Controlled Substances Act, which defers to state authority over crime. 21 USC 903 states that Congress seeks not to "occupy" "the same subject matter which would otherwise be within the authority of the State," such as crime. It reads:

> "No provision of this subchapter shall be construed as indicating an intent on the part of the Congress to occupy the field in which that provision operates, including criminal penalties, to the exclusion of any State law on the same subject matter which would otherwise be within the authority of the State, unless there is a positive conflict between that provision of this subchapter and that State law so that the two cannot consistently stand together."

Because there are no ostensible conflicts between the states' CSAs and the U.S. CSA, which were written at the same time by the same people, this is Congress' admission to having no criminal authority over drug possession or dealing within the states. This is to say that the criminal penalty provisions of 21 USC 841 – 844A, which apply exclusively in the federal areas, are not to "occupy" the criminal subject matter jurisdiction of states within their own borders.

Because under the Supremacy Clause of Article VI, Paragraph 2, and under the Interstate Commerce Clause at Article I, Section 8, Clause 3, Congress has supreme authority over interstate commerce, and consequently may preempt concurrent state regulation of the same subject matter. Given this, the above provision at 21 USC 903 is strictly a reference to criminal law and makes no actual reference to regulatory matters.

Thus, while Congress is sovereign over interstate commerce within the United States, most crimes committed within America are state crimes, subject to state prosecution, and there are very few federal crimes within the states to be adjudicated by Article III courts. That the few federal crimes to be enforced by the U.S. government within the states involve the execution of a power of Congress, or involve an actual offense against the U.S., is what the U.S. Supreme Court told us in *Bond v. United States* (2014):

> "In our federal system, the National Government possesses only limited powers; the States and the people retain the remainder. The States have broad authority to enact legislation for the public good- what we have often called a 'police power.' *United States v. Lopez*, 514 U.S. 549, 567 (1995). The Federal Government, by contrast, has no such authority and "can exercise only the powers granted to it," *McCulloch v. Maryland*, 4 Wheat. 316, 405 (1819), including the power to make 'all Laws which shall be necessary and proper for carrying into Execution' the enumerated powers, U.S. Const., Art. I, ¶ 8, cl. 18. For nearly two centuries it has been 'clear' that, lacking a police power, 'Congress cannot punish felonies generally.' *Cohens v. Virginia*, 6 Wheat. 264 (1821). A criminal act committed wholly within a State 'cannot be made an offence against the United States, unless it have some relation to the execution of a power of Congress, or to some matter within the jurisdiction of the United States.' *United States v. Fox*, 95 U.S. 670, 672 (1878)." [173]

To know this is to know that the U.S. criminal code at Title 18 USC and "the jurisdiction of the United States" operate almost exclusively in the federal areas, and that Congress legislates in two capacities – both as a republic for the states and as municipal legislature over the federal areas. It is to also surmise that Congress' legislation, such as the U.S. CSA, may (and in fact does) contain provisions separately applicable to both the U.S. republic and the U.S. non-republic.

This means that both the U.S. criminal code at Title 18 USC and the U.S. CSA in Title 21 contain provisions for both the U.S. republic and the U.S. non-republic. Although Title 18 is a criminal code, it does not contain all of the U.S. criminal provisions. Congress' drug crimes are written in Title 21, for example. As well, Titles 18 and 21 each contain both criminal and regulatory provisions – the latter which apply within the fifty states.

An example of the latter – about licensing gun and ammunition dealers – is at 18 USC 923. It reads: "No person shall engage in the business of importing, manufacturing, or dealing in firearms, or importing or manufacturing ammunition, until he has filed an application with and received a license to do so from the Attorney General."

The fact that the Attorney General licenses the commerce of guns within America's republics is proof that selling guns is not criminal there, but is instead a regulated activity that operates within the states – just like drug commerce. It is as the U.S. Supreme Court told us in *Ohio v. Helvering* (1934): that "the police power is and remains a governmental power, and applied to business activities is the power to regulate those activities..." [174]

Commerce and its regulations operate in equity, not law. Therefore, the criminal penalty provisions at 18 USC 922 for unlicensed gun dealing cannot logically operate where the Attorney General regulates gun dealing, which is within the fifty states. Therefore, 18 USC 922 operates only in the federal areas, subject to Article I courts, just as do the criminal penalty provisions of the U.S. CSA at 21 USC 841 – 844A that we discussed above.

This is not to forget that certain federal enumerated crimes such as counterfeiting and forgery (Title 18, Chapter 25) operate within the states, but most of the criminal provisions in Title 18 apply only within the federal areas. As well, any and all of Title 18's regulatory provisions, such as 18 USC 923 about selling guns (noted above), apply within the states. As with the commerce of drugs, the Attorney General regulates interstate gun commerce within the states, and the office has authority to criminally prosecute gun commerce only within the federal areas.

Thus, U.S. law treats the commerce of drugs and guns fundamentally the same. This is because both drugs and guns are forms of property, and the commerce of drugs and guns operate in equity – not under criminal law.

Thus, one must know *a priori* the respective powers of the U.S. republic and of the U.S. non-republic to discern where the provisions of Title 18 (the U.S. criminal code) and Title 21 (which includes the U.S. CSA) apply. One must know *a priori* the differences between Congress as the U.S. republic and Congress as a non-republic to properly read all the administrative and criminal provisions in the United States Code. The wars on drugs and guns is evidence that most American attorneys have not known the differences.

9
Commerce and
crimes within the states

Congress' power to regulate interstate commerce

In addition to Congress' territorial legislative jurisdiction over the federal areas, as we discussed in the previous chapter, the U.S. constitution grants Congress several interstate powers at Article I, Section 8 of the U.S. constitution, which are relevant to our discussion. These powers are what the *Report* on the *Jurisdiction Over Federal Areas Within The States* referred to as "Federal functions" when it said that jurisdiction for crime is normally exercised "entirely by the State, subject to the non-interference by the State with Federal functions..." [175] We can classify these exceptions to territorial jurisdiction – i.e., these Federal functions within the states – into two categories: non-criminal (regulatory) and criminal (judicial).

Congress' non-criminal powers are reflected in the Interstate Commerce Clause at Article I, Section 8, Clause 3, which grants Congress the power "(t)o regulate Commerce with foreign Nations, and amongst the several States, and with the Indian Tribes." This power is non-criminal in that regulation is to be carried out in administrative law courts of the executive branch, which operate in equity and which have no criminal authority.

The Interstate Commerce Clause does not grant the U.S. government power to criminally prohibit interstate commerce. Congress can regulate businesses but not criminalize them.

The Supreme Court decision in *United States v. Lopez* (1995) [176] describes the transformation of the Court's view on interstate commerce – from the role of negating the effects of state regulation upon interstate commerce to one of actively regulating intrastate trade, with greater powers to confiscate, to acquire by forfeiture and to enjoin.

"In 1887, Congress enacted the Interstate Commerce Act, 24 Stat. 379, and in 1890, Congress enacted the Sherman Antitrust Act, 26

Stat. 209, as amended, 15 U. S. C. § 1 *et seq.* These laws ushered in a new era of federal regulation under the commerce power... (W)here the interstate and intrastate aspects of commerce were so mingled together that full regulation of interstate commerce required incidental regulation of intrastate commerce, the Commerce Clause authorized such regulation. See, e. g., *Shreveport Rate Cases*, 234 U. S. 342 (1914)." [177]

Given that the regulation of commerce is accomplished in the equity jurisdiction of a republic, and given that Article IV, Section 4 of the U.S. constitution requires Congress to guarantee a republican form of government for the states, this means that Congress legislates over interstate commerce as a republic instead of as a non-republic. The U.S. republic must treat commerce just as state republics treat commerce, which is to regulate it in administrative law courts, not to criminalize it in judicial courts.

This is because republican legislatures have no authority to criminally prohibit anything except *malum in se* crimes that injure others. State republican legislatures and Congress as the U.S. republic may not declare any commercial activity to be criminal by legislating it as *malum prohibita* because such prohibitions operate upon unwanted commerce only in non-criminal equity.

As well, republican legislatures have no plenary criminal jurisdiction, as does Congress over its federal areas, where they can define what is criminal. This is because Congress' plenary criminal authority is incompatible with the republican form of government, which state legislatures and Congress owe to U.S. citizens outside of the federal areas.

When dealing with U.S. citizens within the states, Congress must always treat them as do the state republics. This means that the U.S. republic must always provide a law jurisdiction within its Article III judicial courts where the natural rights of U.S. citizens are secured from the laws of the U.S. non-republic.

As we have seen, acting republican with regard to crime is chiefly accomplished by courts' adherence to the constitutional and natural law meaning of case and crime to include injury. It is also accomplished by properly regulating commerce in equity – as opposed to prohibiting it as Congress does in the federal areas.

In republics such as Indiana and in the U.S. republic, which apply republican law to the union of fifty states, there is no plenary jurisdiction granted to these republics' legislatures over the natural law jurisdiction or over the exercise of natural rights by individuals. Congress' plenary power as a non-republic to confer extraordinary authority onto its Article I courts in the federal areas does not allow Congress as the U.S. republic to enlarge the criminal jurisdiction of Article III judicial courts operating within the republics. [178]

Thus to guarantee to the states a republican form of government, Congress must – among other things – guarantee the maintenance of a law jurisdiction in its Article III courts where the natural rights of natural people are secured. This would preclude, as a matter of law, criminal prosecutions by the U.S. government of any business activity, such as drug dealing, within the state republics.

Liberty is a natural unalienable right of U.S. citizens in all of America's republics. In such places, a U.S. citizen may be alienated from his or her liberty and other natural rights, and be subjected to the law jurisdiction of judicial courts, only for the commission of a real tort or crime that includes injury. That is the meaning of liberty under a republican form of government.

In contrast, in a non-republic, a subject may be incarcerated or subject to compulsory process for any reason. He has no natural rights of liberty, sovereignty or property possession from which to be alienated. He has only the political rights extended to him by the non-republican sovereign.

A non-republic's justice is what the sovereign says it is, no matter how republican-looking that the justice system seems to appear. In a non-republic, there is no law jurisdiction where a person's natural rights are secured from someone with more power than him or her.

Therefore, in general, when Congress legislates general law that is applicable to the states, it must act as a republic. It acts republican by respecting people's natural rights, such as to drug possession, and by regulating interstate commerce, instead of prohibiting it. That is, the United States acts republican – and is true to the U.S. CSA – when its agents regulate drug commerce within the states, instead of falsely criminalizing it.

Crimes relating to federal enumerated powers

In addition to the non-criminal power of Congress to regulate interstate drug commerce, Congress has exclusive authority to define and enforce certain federal crimes both within and outside the states. This criminal authority within the states implicates, as best as I can tell, only about seven of Congress' powers that are enumerated at Article I, Section 8.

These powers were referred to as "Federal functions" in a prior quotation from the *Report* on the *Jurisdiction Over Federal Areas Within The States*. In addition to Congress' territorial jurisdiction, the *Report* mentions that "the Federal Government has power under various provisions of the Constitution to define, and prohibit as criminal, certain acts or omissions occurring anywhere in the United States." [179] These criminal powers "under various provisions of the Constitution" [180] related to:

Congress' power to tax at Article I, Section 8, Clause 1

Congress' power "(t)o provide for the Punishment of counterfeiting the Securities and current Coin of the United States" at Article I, Section 8, Clause 6;

Congress' power "(t)o establish Post Offices and Post roads" at Article I, Section 8, Clause 7;

Congress' power "(t)o define and punish Piracies and Felonies committed on the high Seas, and Offences against the Law of Nations" at Article I, Section 8, Clause 10;

Congress' power "(t)o declare War, grant Letters of Marque and Reprisal, and make Rules concerning Captures on Land and Water" at Article I, Section 8, Clause 11, called its war powers; and

Congress' power to do what is "necessary and proper for carrying into Execution the foregoing Powers..." at Article I, Section 8, Clause 18; and

The above provisions involve real *malum in se* crimes that injure others or actual offenses against the United States. They involve the crimes of tax frauds, counterfeiters (who commit a form of fraud), pirates, felons on the high seas, disloyal U.S. employees, offenders against the Law of Nations, and criminals who use the U.S. postal system to defraud, threaten or physically harm others.

Thus, the U.S. constitution grants the United States authority to legislate over, investigate, seize and prosecute these real criminals within the fifty states. Congress, who has non-republican authority over the high seas, coastal waterways and navigable waters, may also arrest counterfeiters, pirates and such felons when found in these federals areas.

Otherwise, as the U.S. Supreme Court told us in *U.S. v. Fox* (1877), all other crimes committed within the state republics – outside of federal enclaves within the states – are subject to state criminal law. It is a state crime, wrote the Supreme Court, when "an act committed in a state has no relation to the execution of a power of Congress, or to some matter within the jurisdiction of the United States." [181]

Congress regulates foreigners as it does commerce

The regulation of visitors and immigrants to the United States works in much the same manner as the regulation of commerce, where Congress has supreme regulatory authority within the states. Its authority over immigration and naturalization are enumerated at Article I, Section 8, Clause 4 of the U.S. constitution, which grants Congress power "(t)o establish an uniform Rule of Naturalization..."

However, compared with the regulation of commerce, 1) states play a much smaller role in regulating immigrants than the federal government does, and 2) both state judicial and Article III courts' law jurisdictions are required to treat all foreigners – both documented and undocumented – as natural persons, with substantive rights in the law jurisdiction.

This means that foreigners are to be treated by the law jurisdiction of the judicial system as natural persons who cannot be arrested – just like other natural persons – except for the commission of *malum in se* crime. Nonetheless they are subject to non-criminal regulation under equity for being foreign, just as business people are subject to regulation for being in commerce.

Thus foreigners are accorded the Bill of Rights to secure their natural rights as natural persons in the law jurisdiction – just like Americans – but are nonetheless subject to regulation for having expressly or tacitly consented to the jurisdiction of Congress as immigrants or visitors. This is analogous to a U.S. citizen being owed the protections of the law jurisdiction, but yet being owed only administrative due process when acting as an artificial person, such as a licensed driver or regulated businessperson.

In *Wong Wing v. United States* (1896) the Supreme Court ruled that: "The Fourteenth Amendment to the Constitution is not confined to the protection of citizens." [182] The 14th Amendment explicitly requires due process of law and equal protection by states for both natural persons and artificial persons, such as foreign persons.

For foreigners as natural persons, the 14th Amendment redundantly secures due process of law in the law jurisdiction of state republican courts, where the natural rights of foreigners can be secured. Similarly, Congress also recognizes foreigners' standing as natural persons in federal tort claims which are based on injury. [183]

However, unlike U.S. citizens, foreigners do not have a right to be within the United States, but instead exercise a privilege that is grantable by Congress. As such, they exist within the United States as artificial persons, with artificial rights, subject to Congress.

Thus, foreigners within the United States have natural rights that are secured in the law jurisdiction of the judicial branch, all the while having artificial duties that they owe to Congress – just as do all interstate commercial persons. The requirement that all people who manufacture, distribute and dispense controlled substances must register with the D.E.A. [184] is analogous to the requirement that all foreigners over fourteen years of age must register with the Department of Homeland Security.

Registration is an artificial duty owed only in equity. Nature does not require anyone to register for anything.

Consequently, all drug dealers and foreigners over fourteen years old who do not respectively register with the D.E.A. or the D.H.S. are *malum prohibita*. They are outlawed in equity, but not at law.

This is because they are not *malum in se* – evil by their nature, which is to be *unlawful* and subject to the law jurisdiction of state or U.S. courts. Instead they are *illegal* according to the legislative sovereign, which determines what is legal under equity, but not what is lawful under law. What is legal and what is lawful have separate sovereigns and operate in separate judicial jurisdictions.

For example, the law jurisdiction has no authority over foreigners unless they commit torts or crimes. Thus, foreigners by their honest and nonviolent nature may be lawful, which term refers to behavior that is not *malum in se* in the natural law jurisdiction. However, these same foreigners may be illegal (which correct term refers to their lack of artificial rights to be within the United States), which privileges operate under equity.

So, undocumented immigrants may be both lawful and yet illegal. On one hand they may be peaceful and honest, and thus compliant with natural law. On the other hand they may be unregistered and in violation of positive law, i.e., *malum prohibita*.

This works the same way for business people in publicly disfavored commerce, for instance prostitution. Prostitution is lawful – and not criminal – in that it is voluntary and consensual. However it may be illegal, i.e., *malum prohibita*, by a health department. As consensual and commercial activity, it is behavior that can be enjoined, but which is not criminal.

People's lawfulness is defined by natural law in the law jurisdiction.

Their legality is defined by their compliance with duties imposed under equity by an artificial sovereign, which do not apply to natural persons.

Foreigners have the same rights under Nature and its law jurisdiction as U.S. citizens do. However they are duty bound under equity because their status in the United States is privileged and not of natural right.

Whether for documented or undocumented visitors, removal proceedings are conducted in U.S. immigration courts, which are administrative law courts, whose adjudications may be appealed to the Board of Immigration Appeal in the Executive Office for Immigration Review (EOIR). [185]

Deportation orders by these U.S. immigration courts are in the nature of equitable orders of specific performance. They are based on visitors implied consent to obtain Congress' permission to be within the United States.

Many current deportation orders grant deportees time before being deported. Those aliens who fail to comply with such orders, by not showing up for their transportation home, are deemed to be fugitives. Being in contempt of court, they are subject to being physically seized and deported.

Thus, these non-criminal equitable orders against foreigners are enforced by the exercise of contempt authority by U.S. courts, just like injunctions are enforced against unwanted drug dealers. Neither drug dealers nor immigrants are criminals under the law jurisdiction, which adjudicates *malum in se*. Instead both are subject to regulatory agencies that ultimately and respectively can use courts to throw them in jail or out of the country for being in contempt of court.

Relevant to foreigners is the scope of state regulatory authority. As with states' regulation of commerce, states' regulation of foreigners is subject to congressional preemption based on the Supremacy Clause.

A case in point was Arizona's challenged immigration law, the so-called Arizona Senate Bill 1070. Among other things, this act 1) required all foreigners over fourteen years old in Arizona to register with the state, just as they are to register under federal law, 2) instituted immigration status checks during law enforcement stops, and 3) criminalized foreigners for not carrying proof of registration.

In the case of *Arizona v. United States* (2012) the U.S. Supreme Court upheld the state provision that required status checks during law enforcement stops, but struck down the other provisions as violations of the Supremacy Clause. One of these provisions was the state's criminalization of foreigners who failed to carry registration papers.

This particular provision is relevant to our discussion because readers now know 1) that Nature defines crimes within state republics, not legislatures, 2) that foreigners are subject to the equity jurisdiction, which is non-criminal, and 3) that within a republic, no individual may be arrested for a regulatory violation (because regulation and prohibition operate in separate judicial jurisdictions).

Thus, this state criminal provision constitutionally failed not merely because the U.S. Supremacy Clause preempted it, but because the provision violates the republican form of government. Republics can only arrest criminals, not regulation violators – not even if they are foreign.

In the republican form of government, all crimes are defined by Nature, and such definition is applied to all natural persons equally. All foreigners and citizens – as natural persons – are owed due process of law and the other Bill of Rights in the law jurisdiction. Redundantly, some of these rights are secured for foreigners and positive law citizens by the 14th Amendment.

Because of the Separation of Powers Doctrine, republics are not allowed to criminalize violations of regulatory duties, such as the duty of a foreigner to register or to carry papers. Foreigners, like citizens, can be arrested for crimes only when they violate others' rights.

In any event, both commerce and foreigners are regulated in the United States. Congress has supreme regulatory power over both. Unlike natural born citizens, both commercial activity and foreigners exist in the United States by permission of the legislative sovereign, and are therefore subject to it.

This is all to say that Congress may declare unwanted commerce and unwanted foreigners as *malum prohibita,* and subject them to equitable remedies such as injunction and specific performance. However, neither Congress nor state legislatures may declare them to be unlawful or criminal. This is because Nature – and not republican legislatures – determines what is lawful and unlawful in a republic.

Equally relevant is what we learned in the previous chapter – that Congress may criminally prohibit *malum prohibita* only in the federal areas. However within the states, *malum prohibita* is subject only to regulation in equity. This means that 8 USC 1304(e), which is the federal provision that makes it a misdemeanor for foreigners to not carry their papers, can apply only in the federal areas, where Congress determines what is criminal.

As mentioned above, foreigners are not *malum in se* – bad by their nature. However, unwanted foreigners and their unwanted residency may be made *malum prohibita,* and subject to government's equitable powers of deportation.

Given that foreigners are regulated, Congress' rules over visitation could include drug prohibition, if Congress so chose. That is, Congress in fact could prohibit drug possession and dealing as a condition for foreigners to remain in the United States.

Any foreigner caught possessing or dealing disfavored drugs within the states could not be arrested, because property possession is not a crime within a republic, but instead could face deportation for this *malum prohibita*. This is only to say that Congress legally could subject foreigners to such a condition because – unlike U.S. citizens – they are regulated in equity.

Foreigners are subject to Congress because they must seek Congress' permission to enter the United States. These foreigners owe their visitation privileges strictly to Congress and its agents. Says 8 USC 1201(i), their visitation and immigration are subject to the discretion of the consular officer or the Secretary of State.

This special power of the consular officer and the Secretary of State to revoke a foreigner's visitation rights "at any time, in his discretion" [186] is the ball and chain that accompanies all foreigners whenever they are in the U.S. Their presence is always conditional. If a war breaks out, they may be sent home.

However, while within the state republics, these foreigners have the same substantive rights in the law jurisdiction – including the Bill of Rights – as do U.S. citizens. This is because the law jurisdiction secures the natural political equality of all natural people, from wherever they come.

For example, foreigners have the right to a seek a judicial remedy for harm done to them and the right not be enslaved except for the commission of crime. These substantive rights apply to all natural persons in state republics, regardless if such persons are foreign, and regardless if they are unauthorized to be in the United States by the U.S. government. However, the republican law jurisdiction cannot protect them from the plenary power of regulators under Congress' power over naturalization.

With regard to the topic of this book, this is all to say that Congress does not need a war on drugs – waged against U.S. citizens – in order to deport foreign drug users or dealers. Nor must it meet the criminal law jurisdiction's extraordinary burdens of proof, i.e., beyond a reasonable doubt. Given Congress' plenary authority over U.S. coastal and border areas, and given Congress' power to regulate foreigners, then Congress does not need a domestic war on drugs to secure the nation from the importation of unwanted contraband from foreign sources.

This is also to say that drug prohibition may be an unpopular policy for people who support free trade, but it is likely wholly legal over people and places under Congress' authority, such as foreigners and all people within the federal areas. However, the U.S. government remains legitimate only as long as it exercises its police powers in areas and over people subject to it.

Thus, this book in no way challenges Congress's policy or power to interdict foreign-made drugs from being imported into the U.S., and to criminalize such drug dealing in the federal areas, such as the coastal seaways and other border zones. Nor do I challenge Congress' equitable authority over its foreign subjects.

The main point of this book is merely that, absent a constitutional amendment, drug possession and drug dealing are not crimes within America's fifty state republics. The former is a natural right. The latter is a regulated activity that is subject to governments' non-criminal powers.

Within the state republics, except for crimes relating to federal functions, the nation's Founding Fathers literally exempted all U.S. citizens from the U.S. criminal jurisdiction. Within America's republics, U.S. citizens are subject only to U.S. crimes relating to Congress' enumerated powers, including offenses against the United States.

Being free of the United States is the nature of U.S. citizens unless they voluntarily enter the jurisdiction of the U.S. government: 1) by committing a crime against the United States or related to a federal enumerated power, 2) by entering commerce to be regulated by either a state republic or the U.S. republic, 3) by entering into a federal area to be subject to the U.S. non-republic, 4) by agreeing to be criminally bound under the U.S. non-republics rules, as do some U.S. employees, or 5) by agreeing to be civilly bound under Congress' rules, as for example do welfare recipients, to whom states may deny benefits for drug use. [187]

As the Declaration of Independence says: free natural born citizens enter these artificial, positive law jurisdictions only voluntarily – that is, by consent. This is because U.S. citizens are the source of Congress' authority, not its subjects. As *Yick Wo v. Hopkins* (1886) told us, Congress exists on account of these citizens, not in spite of them or independently of them.

Thus, in its legislative capacity for the U.S. republic, Congress owes duties to U.S. citizens – not the other way around. Two of these duties are 1) to make certain that its role for the U.S. non-republic is kept separate from its role for the U.S. republic, and 2) to make certain that the U.S. republic serves to secure the physical and political rights of U.S. citizens from the false exercise of power by the U.S. non-republic, both tasks which it has failed to do.

Tying-up some loose ends

We can now see that the subtitle of this book *Drugs Are Legal In America's Republics* tells only one part of a three-part story.

Part one is based on Article IV, Section 4 of the U.S. constitution, which "guarantee(s) to every State in this Union a Republican Form of Government..." Because of this, Congress must legislate toward the state republics as a republic, just as the states legislate over their own areas.

Thus, there are currently fifty state republics and one U.S. republic within the United States 1) where drug possession is an exercise of a natural right and 2) where drug commerce is subject to regulation. These are republics a) where drug possession is lawful for all individuals, b) where drug dealing is legal for manufacturers and distributors which are approved by drug regulators, and c) where drug dealing is illegal – but not criminal – for unapproved drug manufacturers and distributors.

Drugs are lawful for natural persons when they operate under republican legislative sovereigns – outside of the physical authority of the U.S. non-republic. By definition, individuals may not lawfully be arrested or incarcerated for the possession of any lawfully acquired personal property or for operating any business – except slavery – within an American republic.

A second part of the story is that drugs are always lawful for U.S. citizens within the fifty-one republics, but that they are not necessarily legal for foreigners, who are subject to a regulatory jurisdiction that U.S. citizens are not. All foreigners exist within the U.S. by permission (or in defiance) of Congress. Given administrative due process, foreigners are essentially always subject to being deported <u>as</u> *malum prohibita*, particularly those who involve themselves <u>in</u> commercial *malum prohibita*.

The U.S. constitution secures foreigners' natural and substantive rights within America's republics, but their privilege to be within the U.S. is within Congress' and its agents' discretion. Based on the differences between law and equity, foreigners may be lawful yet may be made illegal.

The third part of the story is that drugs <u>are</u> criminally prohibited in certain specific areas of the U.S. – called the federal areas – which are under Congress' exclusive control, but that these areas exclude the states. At 18 USC 7, Congress calls these federal areas under its exclusive authority the "special maritime and territorial jurisdiction of the United States."

In these federal areas, according to Article I, Section 8, Clause 17 of the U.S. constitution, Congress exercises "exclusive Legislation in all Cases whatsoever...," This includes the plenary power to define what is a crime and who belongs in jail, including unauthorized drug dealers.

10
What proscribes crime?

The limits of legislative power

Indiana's original constitution from 1816 contains an inherent conflict. It both assigns judicial courts with power to adjudicate civil cases and crimes based on the common law, and it empowers the Indiana legislature to prescribe the law, which means to write it down.

This means that it gave common law judges the power to use common law precedents to determine one's culpability and punishment for crimes, but it also gave the legislature the power to prescribe what the elements and punishment for crime should be. Thus, two branches of government had power to write down criminal law, which powers were inherently conflicting.

The Indiana constitution (1851) corrected this issue by assigning power to prescribe the elements of, punishment for and procedures for torts, crimes and breaches of contract solely to the Indiana legislature. This effectively ended common law jurisprudence in Indiana, where judges used precedents from previous-like cases to determine a defendant's culpability and punishment. Since 1851 the Indiana legislature has had the sole power and public duty to write down the elements of and punishments for crimes.

However, this assignment of power to the legislature did not change the jurisdiction of the judicial branch. Judicial courts still had original, subject matter jurisdiction over civil cases and criminal cases – based on injury – which were the same cases referred to in both the U.S. constitution and the Indiana constitution (1816). However, given the removal of the reference to "common law" in the new 1851 constitution, the legislature solidified its position to prescribe the law for all to read.

As part of this transformation from common law to statutory law, the Indiana legislature enacted IC 1-1-2-2 in 1852. IC 1-1-2-2 reads: "Crimes shall be defined and punishment therefor fixed by statutes of this state and not otherwise." Thus, according to this statute and the new constitution, no longer were the elements and punishments for crimes to be based on the precedents of common law judges. They were to be written down by the legislature.

The Indiana Supreme Court has reiterated this theme many times. In *State ex rel. Camden v. Gibson Circuit Court* (1994) it wrote: "(T)he subject matter jurisdiction of the circuit courts is entirely a creature of the legislature." [188] In *Utley v. State* (1972) it wrote: "The legislature has the sole power to define crimes..." [189]

However, taken literally – which no doubt misguided attorneys do – the above two judicial statements overstate the power of the legislature. In reality, if the subject matter jurisdiction of judicial courts was "entirely a creature of the legislature," [190] then the legislature could either criminalize any kind of lawful behavior or immunize any kind of criminal, such as a murderer or thief. If the legislature has "the sole power to define crimes," [191] as the Indiana Supreme Court exaggerates, then logically the legislature can make the judicial branch adjudicate false "cases," "crimes" and even infractions, even though the constitution authorizes courts to adjudicate only real cases and crimes. [192]

Only a judiciary that does not recognize our judicial courts' primary jurisdiction over injury, and only a judiciary that thinks subject matter jurisdiction of judicial courts over crime is not of constitutional origin, would allow drug matters to be adjudicated in Indiana's judicial courts. Such judicial reliance is the logical consequence of the Indiana Supreme Court's misused or overly broad use of the words "entirely" and "sole," which mean to the exclusion of others.

The phrases "entirely a creature of the legislature" [193] and "the legislature has sole power" [194] logically mean to not be created by or subject to anything else, which is a false and wanton description of Indiana's statutory and constitutional law. Being false, they are misrepresentations of law, whether meant to be false or not by their overzealous authors.

It is a logical imperative that these statements are misrepresentations of law because they are illogical and because jurisprudence is a science based on the Laws of Nature, for example logic. Logically, if the Indiana legislature could legislate crime as the Indiana Supreme Courts suggests, then Indiana would by definition be a non-republic, which would inherently contradict the republican form of government secured by the Indiana constitution.

If the statements are true, then legislatures could imprison people, just as monarchs claim authority to do. Thus, the implications of these statements cannot be true, or they would violate the Indiana constitution.

It is the belief in misrepresentations of law such as the phrases above that have misled all Indiana officials into believing that the legislature defines the meaning of crime and that it can dictate judicial courts' criminal subject matter jurisdiction. Instead, as we have seen, the criteria for cases and crimes are determined by a higher authority – i.e., the Laws of Nature, as set in stone by the U.S. and Indiana constitutions.

Maintaining the meaning of cases and crimes is an essential way by which the judiciary is to secure people's natural right of liberty. Securing these definitions and that of natural born citizen is only means to secure Americans' natural right to a republican form of government. Therefore, using these definition is the preeminent duty of American judicial officers.

Whether the legislature can or cannot turn false "cases" into real cases or false "crimes" into real crimes, and whether it can subject them to the criminal jurisdiction of judicial trial courts, is the threshold issue of this chapter. It is the answer to this question upon which the legitimacy of Indiana's drug war depends.

As we shall see, the Indiana legislature does not have – and never has had – constitutional authority to define or redefine the word crime to include non-injurious false "crimes." To do so would be to exceed its *de jure* authority and to convert the state from a republic to a non-republic. Thus, we can be assured that America's constitutional statutes do not do this, but being the product of devious minds, only feign doing it.

All crimes are based on injury, which in a republic is the only subject matter legitimately able to invoke judicial courts' criminal or civil law jurisdiction. Any subject matter that amounts to less than injury, such as an infraction, provides illegitimate authority for judicial sanction. To state otherwise is to misrepresent the law of America's republics, which are maintained by strict adherence to judicial subject matter jurisdiction over injury and to various separations of power.

Criminal law 101

As we discussed in chapters 4 and 5, "crime" is defined by Indiana statute at IC 35-48-1-6, which reads: "'Crime' means a felony or a misdemeanor." As well, IC 35-48-1-19 reads: "'Offense' means a crime. The term does not include an infraction." Thus, statutory "crimes" and "offenses" mean the same thing, and they are not infractions.

The Indiana legislature classifies drug possession and drug dealing as "crimes" and "offenses" by designating them as "misdemeanors" and "felonies" in the Controlled Substances Act at IC 35-48-4. As a logical consequence, judicial trial courts falsely adjudicate drug possession and commerce as "crimes" because they believe their subject matter jurisdiction is "entirely a creature of the legislature," [195] which it is not.

They adjudicate drug "crimes" because they exaggerate the meaning of the legislature's "sole power to define crimes...," [196] which does not mean to invent them. In any event, the first duty of all judicial judges is to know their court's subject matter jurisdiction over injury.

In reality, both the state legislature and state courts answer to the Indiana and U.S. constitutions. The Indiana constitution created both the legislature and the courts, and they answer to the U.S. constitution as the supreme law. Because of this, crime is not at all a creature of legislation.

The existence, meaning and prohibition of crime predates all American legislatures. Its meaning was known and agreed upon before the U.S. and Indiana constitutions were adopted, and before the Indiana legislature ever met. Crimes are violations of natural rights. These rights are secured by a (natural) law jurisdiction that is unassailable by inconsistent positive law.

This is the reason that the words crime and offense are not defined by these constitutions. Everyone (figuratively speaking) had already agreed to what crimes and offenses were before American constitutions were adopted and before American legislatures convened.

That legislatures can determine what is criminal is a misguided premise, and is contrary to what the U.S. Supreme Court has repeatedly written. In *Payne v. Tennessee* (1991) the U.S. Supreme Court wrote, "The state laws respecting crimes, punishments, and criminal procedures are, of course, subject to the overriding provisions of the United States Constitution." [197]

This is reiterated at IC 33-28-1-5(2) which mandates Circuit Courts to act "in conformity with Indiana laws and Constitution of the State of Indiana." Moreover, this is confirmed by IC 1-1-2-1, entitled "Hierarchy of law," which says that the hierarchy of law puts our constitutions at the top, and that all statutes must be consistent with these constitutions. I have referred to IC 1-1-2-1 several times by now. So here it finally is in the flesh:

> "The law governing this state is declared to be:
> First. The Constitution of the United States and of this state.
> Second. All statutes of the general assembly of the state in force, and not inconsistent with such constitutions.
> Third. All statutes of the United States in force, and relating to subjects over which congress has power to legislate for the states, and not inconsistent with the Constitution of the United States.

> Fourth. The common law of England, and statutes of the British Parliament made in aid thereof prior to the fourth year of the reign of James the First (except the second section of the sixth chapter of forty-third Elizabeth, the eighth chapter of thirteenth Elizabeth, and the ninth chapter of thirty-seventh Henry the Eighth,) and which are of a general nature, not local to that kingdom, and not inconsistent with the first, second and third specifications of this section."

This statute and IC 1-1-2-2 (noted above) were both enacted together in 1852 – shortly after Indiana's 1851 constitution was ratified. They sit side-by-side at the very beginning of the Indiana Code. IC 1-1-2-2 says that the legislature defines crime. IC 1-1-2-1 states that its legislative definitions must be consistent with the U.S. and Indiana constitutions. Taken together this means that the powers to prescribe (write down) crime granted to the legislature at IC 1-1-2-2 must be read to conform to the U.S. and Indiana constitutions, not the other way around.

Further, IC 1-1-2-1 signifies the given role of the common law in Indiana jurisprudence, which has been whitewashed by the drug war. Far from being eliminated from Indiana law by the term's removal from the state's 1851 constitution, IC 1-1-2-1 (which was enacted in 1852) says that the common law is alive and well in Indiana. This is because, even though the Indiana legislature now prescribes and defines crime, the criminal jurisdiction of Indiana's courts is still over common law offenses.

"It is well settled by our decisions," wrote the Indiana Supreme Court in *Millers Nat. Ins. Co. v. American State Bank of East Chicago* (1939), "that the Constitution of Indiana must be interpreted in the light of the common law of England." [198] Crimes that are cognizable in Indiana's judicial courts are essentially common law crimes from Great Britain that have been enacted into the Indiana Code. Drug prohibition is not one of them.

Read along with IC 1-1-2-2 above, IC 1-1-2-1 says that the power of the legislature at IC 1-1-2-2 to "define crimes" must be consistent with the definition of crime used by our constitutions. Thus IC 1-1-2-1 and IC 1-1-2-2 read together say that the legislature may prescribe (write down) crimes and their punishments, but that these statutory crimes must be consistent with the meaning of crime and offense (and the scope of punishment) not only in our federal and state constitutions, but under the common law of England and Indiana.

This analysis rests on logic and reason, which operate under natural law. That "the subject matter jurisdiction of the circuit courts is entirely a creature of the legislature" [199] is illogical because the subject matter jurisdiction of Indiana's judicial courts comes from the state constitution.

Likewise, that "(t)he legislature has the sole power to define crimes..." [200] is illogical because crime is already defined by natural law, and it is only prescribed or codified by the legislature. These judicial exaggerations misrepresent Indiana's criminal law.

Regardless of the intent behind these false statements, i.e., that a king or legislature can define crime in defiance of Nature, we now know better. We now know 1) that republican legislatures only prescribe crimes that Nature has already proscribed, 2) that crime operates in a completely different and preexisting jurisdiction than the edicts of wannabe kings, i.e., their *malum prohibita*, and 3) that natural persons, while operating in their non-commercial, non-criminal and non-foreign capacities, have substantive rights to be left alone in America's republics.

These conclusions are self-evident from reading and thinking about the Declaration of Independence, the U.S. constitution and the Indiana constitution, for example, which note the preexisting natural law jurisdiction in the 9th Amendment, the preexisting nature of crime, the preexisting natural right to create natural born citizens, the preexisting natural right to worship God, and the preexisting natural rights to life, liberty, property and the pursuit of happiness. Thus, logically, there is a preexisting natural law basis to the U.S. and Indiana constitutions that cannot be denied by government officials.

Because crime in an American republic is defined by natural law and because the positive law of the legislature is subject to and may not encroach upon courts' (natural) law jurisdiction, which has authority only over injury by natural persons, then criminal laws must be held in strict conformity with the natural law jurisdiction of American constitutions.

The words crime, criminal, case, and offense are referred to multiple times in the Indiana and United States constitutions. The words misdemeanor, felony, injury and victim are referred to in one or the other of the constitutions. These words used in these constitutions have specific meaning. The legislature cannot expand the words' meanings without exceeding legislative authority and without violating the subject matter jurisdiction of judicial courts, both which would violate the separation of powers doctrine of the Indiana constitution.

Thus, criminal subject matter jurisdiction is entirely NOT "a creature of the legislature." [201] It is a creature of the Indiana constitution. The legislature may prescribe and define crime, but may not proscribe or legislate crime inconsistently with its constitutional meaning.

Crime is already defined by natural law to be an injury to a natural right. Crimes may not be redefined by the legislature to include non-injury without violating republican constitutions and judicial subject matter jurisdiction, whose rules go hand-in-hand.

As we have seen, the legislature can prescribe all sorts of offensive and unfavorable human behavior as "crime," but its use of the words "case," "crime," "criminal," "felony," and "misdemeanor" in statutes must be consistent with the words' constitutional meaning, which define the subject matter jurisdiction of judicial courts. Otherwise, the legislature would be above the constitution and could change the separation of powers at will without a constitutional amendment, which the rule of law forbids.

Take, for example, the growing of tomatoes. The legislature cannot define the growing of tomatoes to be a crime, and to subject tomato growing to the criminal law jurisdiction of judicial courts, without expanding the power of the judicial branch to include false "crimes" in violation of the separation of powers doctrine.

Any reader who understands this also understands why America's republics may not prohibit the growing of any plant for one's own use. If legislatures had such power over natural things, then they could not only prohibit disfavored fruits and vegetables, but could also deem when they are ready to pick. If republican legislatures had such power – to apply their equitable powers to Nature – then they could grant unlimited life to our Ruby Reds, as they do America's corporations.

But all plants grow subject to natural law, not according to the positive law of legislatures. Republican legislatures cannot prohibit or regulate Nature. They do not make plants grow. America's republics may only regulate the commerce of produce and eradicate unwanted wild plants. [202]

As we learned in previous chapters, growing anything for one's own use operates in a different jurisdiction than the positive law of America's republics, whose authority is over equitable subject matter, civil cases and criminal cases. Growing anything for one's own use is outside the power of the three branches of government, and is subject only to one's self-government, i.e., individual sovereignty.

As we have seen, our republican constitutions define the civil and criminal subject matter jurisdiction of judicial courts to be over injury, and not over plant matter. This is in stark and emphatic contradiction of what the Indiana Supreme Court tells us, i.e., that subject matter jurisdiction is "entirely" a creature of the legislature. Such use of the word "entirely" is entirely an exaggeration, which is inherently subject to misinterpretation.

The legislature has no constitutional power to unilaterally change or expand the meaning of cases or crimes, or the courts' primary jurisdiction over injury. All the references to case, crime, offense, felony and misdemeanor in American constitutions inherently refer to injury because no human behavior creates a case, crime, offense, felony or misdemeanor that is cognizable in a republican court without it.

Each branch's powers are confined to how they are defined constitutionally. The legislature may not legislate inconsistently with the constitution, and the executive and judicial branches may not adjudicate subject matter over which the constitution has granted them no authority.

As constitutional history and the separation of powers doctrine show us, there is nothing that a republican legislature can legitimately do to criminalize the possession or commerce of anything, and to place such possession or commerce within the criminal subject matter jurisdiction of judicial courts, short of completing a constitutional amendment process. The legislature can call all sorts of things "crimes," but they are not crimes which are subject to the criminal jurisdiction of republican judicial courts unless they are crimes as referred to in our constitutions, over which the People established the governments' judicial power.

As well, the legislature can call all sorts of things "crimes," but judicial judges are presumed to know the meaning of crime and the criminal jurisdiction of their courts. Crimes are facts of Nature. Actions are not crimes unless Mother Nature says they are crimes, and we can't fool Mother Nature.

The Supremacy Clause at Article VI, Paragraph 2 of the U.S. constitution means that no republican legislature in America may define a case or crime differently than or inconsistently with the U.S. constitution. Consequently, it means that the Indiana legislature may write down crimes only in a manner consistent with natural law, as secured in the law jurisdiction of the state and federal republics.

Because American judges operate under false premises, e.g., 1) that legislatures are sovereign over crime, 2) that statutes can enlarge the criminal jurisdiction of judicial courts, and 3) that statutory terms have greater import than constitutional ones, then they are putting themselves and their courts above state and federal constitutions, not to mention natural law. This makes them agents of a non-republic, which is based solely on a lack of respect for natural, republican law. Logically and ethically, one cannot act non-republican and yet claim to be republican.

As a person trained in a similar law school as likely all American lawyers and judges, I can only look upon this judicial misrepresentation of legislative power with disdain and contempt. It is this misconception of law which is likely most responsible for the judicial branch's false assertion of subject matter jurisdiction over non-crimes, such as drug possession and dealing.

Not only is it ignorant of statutory law, such as the Controlled Substances Act (which regulates drug commerce and exempts drug possession from legal liability), and not only does it violate the Indiana constitution (which grants judicial courts no subject matter jurisdiction over non-injury and which secures the right of property possession), but it violates logic. As long as government officials define crime subjectively, i.e., that there is no objective basis in crime's definition, and as long as they claim that legislatures are above constitutions, then logic, jurisprudence and the republican form of government will necessarily fail.

Under the criminal law of the Indiana republic, positive law can criminally prescribe what is already proscribed in the criminal law juris-diction, and nothing more. The legislature has no authority to invent new crimes because our constitutions long ago determined what our courts may adjudicate, i.e., cases and crimes involving injury.

IC 1-1-2-1 says that all criminal statutes must be consistent with the common law and our constitutions. Those that are not consistent with the common law, such as the numerous phony drug "crimes" legislated in the Indiana CSA at IC 35-48-4, are not to be enforced.

The Indiana legislature may not define crime because crime is already defined by the Laws of Nature as secured by the Indiana constitution (1851). Its Article I, Section 13(b) mentions "victims of crime as defined by law."

In swearing to uphold Indiana's constitution, all state officials have taken oaths – perhaps unwittingly – that all crimes are defined by (natural) law and that by definition, all crimes include victims. For Indiana judges to enforce phony "crimes" without victims is to exceed judicial authority, is to overlook the Indiana constitution and is to violate their oaths of office.

America's state legislatures neither legislate over natural persons nor in the natural law jurisdiction. Because crimes are facts of Nature, legisla-tures may merely prescribe the elements of these facts, and attribute appro-priate penalties.

As we have seen, crime as referred to in the Indiana constitution is the same as that referred to in the U.S. constitution. All crimes are torts. A tort is a "private or civil wrong or injury, other than breach of contract, for which the court will provide a remedy in the form of an action for damages." [203] To commit a crime (a public injury) within an American republic, one must at least commit a tort (a private injury to one's person or property).

As we have also seen, crimes are torts in which the state claims that the public has been damaged as well as the actual victim. Thus, to prosecute a crime is to prosecute a tort. Such criminal prosecution requires a proportionally higher degree of proof than a civil one because of the greater severity of a criminal sanction.

Nonetheless, a judicial court's law jurisdiction is the same for a crime as it is for a tort. This is because both torts and crimes involve natural persons and injury. Without a natural person, there is no tort. Without a tort, there is no crime and no criminal law jurisdiction within a republic.

Whether crime is codified by a legislature, such as the British Parliament or the Indiana General Assembly, or whether crime is merely recognized as evil in Nature by a common law judge, the criminal jurisdiction of Indiana's judicial courts, which is at law, is over injury-in-fact. This is behavior that harms other people. It is this subject matter, and not the mere will of the legislature, upon which the judicial systems of American republics are based.

Perhaps a majority of Americans, even a super-majority of Americans, think that drug use is bad, wrong or evil. However, unless one's drug use harms, threatens or endangers other people – in violation of their natural right not to be harmed, threatened or unduly endangered – then drug use is not injurious or *malum in se,* and neither the civil nor criminal jurisdictions of republican judicial courts may be invoked against it.

Since Indiana became a sovereign state in 1816, the criminal jurisdiction of all judicial courts in Indiana has always been at law, where natural rights are enforced over *malum in se* that involve real injury committed by natural persons. The civil and criminal jurisdiction of judicial courts is the same now as back then because the constitutional requirement of injury has not been removed by an amendment to the Indiana or U.S. constitutions. Nor has there been a constitutional amendment prohibiting controlled substances and placing their commerce into the criminal law jurisdiction, as there once was with alcohol.

That prosecutors invoke judicial authority in drug matters without private or public injury, which is to say over behavior which is not *malum in se* or even justiciable, occurs only because defense attorneys and judges do not challenge them. Without *de jure* authority over non-injury, Indiana courts asserts *de facto* authority over false "crimes." *De facto* judicial authority over drug possession and drug commerce is a perversion of judicial courts' *de jure* jurisdiction over injury, which judges are responsible to defend.

False enforcement of drug laws results from government officials' false allegiance to the legislature's phony words instead of their allegiance to the real meaning of the same words used in our constitutions. It is a mis-representation of American law – not to mention a usurpation of constitutional power – to suggest that republican legislatures can define crime inconsistently with crime referred to in America's constitutions.

11
The subject matter jurisdiction of judicial courts

Why do you think they call it dope?

Books and books have been written about how stupid the drug war is as a public policy. (This book is probably the first one to show it to be illegal.) The drug war consumes half of our judicial resources, promotes a police state with a prison-industrial complex, diminishes our civil liberties, does horrible collateral damage in our urban neighborhoods and neighboring countries, is enforced with a racial and class bias, and destroys the natural dynamic between individual liberty and self-responsibility, which is the lifeblood of the American society.

Worse, the drug war has not worked at all to diminish drug use and instead has probably promoted it. Millions of people are hooked on prescription drugs made by governments' favored drug dealers. And thanks to the U.S. and state governments' fraudulent drug prohibition, the potency of marijuana is now staggering. So, as public policies go, busting drug users and dealers is truly one of the most destructive public policies ever conceived, next to slavery, war and human extermination.

But the real stupid thing about the drug war is how long the executive branch of our various governments has illegally waged it, how feebly the drug-defense bar has responded to it, and how most officials in the judicial and executive branches do not really understand the separation of government's powers that each swore to uphold.

As this book demonstrates, the law is very clear and it exists for all to read and to understand. However, the people in charge of enforcing and upholding the law have either not read it or have not understood it. This is giving officials the benefit of the doubt that some are not willfully enforcing the drug laws in a false manner to support their authoritarian tendencies and special interests.

It is for want of reading the drug laws properly, for want of defending the principles of a limited republican government (including the separation of powers doctrine), for want of knowing about the natural law jurisdiction, and for want of believing in and defending people's unalienable rights to life, liberty, property and the pursuit of happiness that the drug war exists. It is for officials' want of acknowledging and knowing how natural law operates in the U.S. constitutions that our judicial system has been so grossly misused to wage the drug war, which can only exist in the absence of natural law and of the republican form of government.

In the previous chapters of this book, we discovered the natural law basis of the law jurisdiction of judicial courts in which torts and crimes are adjudicated. We learned that all torts and crimes are violations of natural rights, and that the law jurisdiction of judicial courts exists to adjudicate these violations – not violations of legislative edicts.

This means that no crimes are created by the legislature. All statutes against real crimes are mere codifications of *malum in se* that are already recognized as crime under natural law and America's republican constitutions. Because positive law is subservient to natural law in the law jurisdiction, legislatures may not make-up or invent crimes.

For this reason alone, the war on drugs is not compatible with natural or criminal law in an American republic. In the balance of this chapter we shall see that the war on drugs also does not comply with the U.S. and Indiana constitutions.

Judicial subject matter jurisdiction

Our discussion now focuses on judicial subject matter jurisdiction, which is the power of a judicial court to try or adjudicate a particular matter.

The subject matter jurisdiction of courts in Indiana's judicial branch is granted and determined by the Indiana constitution, which created Indiana's judicial courts. In contrast, the subject matter jurisdiction of administrative law courts in the executive branch is determined by the state legislature, which created these courts. Short of the passage of a constitutional amendment, it is not within the Indiana legislature's prerogative to expand the subject matter jurisdiction of the state's judicial courts, which it did not create.

As readers will soon see, there is absolutely no constitutional justification for using Indiana's judicial system to try ordinary matters of drug possession or commerce, or even traffic citations for that matter. The courts' constitutional power to adjudicate is strictly confined to legal injury, and this has not changed since Indiana gained statehood. Anyone who refutes this needs only to demonstrate how Indiana's constitution has changed so that judicial courts may now adjudicate matters that are not civil cases or criminal cases, over which they have primary jurisdiction. [204]

Since high school, when several of my friends were busted for marijuana possession, I have seen drug offenders processed like cattle in Indiana's judicial system. As a clerk with the local prosecutor's office in the summer of 1984, and as good Centurion, I even participated in wrongly prosecuting drug offenders in judicial courts.

I was like Paul in the New Testament of the Bible, who persecuted Christians before becoming one. Like him, I did not know any better at the time. Nor did I then have a way to refute the ubiquitous false regime.

In the history of my legal education and experience, using judicial courts to prosecute drug offenders is something that the legal profession has routinely just done, and that Indiana's judicial courts have routinely allowed. It is what all Indiana attorneys who are involved in controlled substance matters, including all judges, are apprenticed in.

Thus, no attorney or judge that I have ever known gives the use of our judicial system to adjudicate drug matters a second thought. In their religiosity, there is no question that judicial courts have subject matter jurisdiction over drug possession and dealing. In my mind, however, there are no positive law grounds to claim such jurisdiction, which most attorneys have never questioned.

As I pointed out in chapter 1, I have had fundamental questions about the propriety and legality of the war on drugs ever since it started in the late 1960s, which were my middle school years. Even then, the war was full of legal anomalies and inconsistencies which gave pause and cause to ponder its legitimacy.

Chief in heretofore-unmentioned anomalies is how the law seemingly treats alcohol, tobacco and recreational drugs differently. From a logical or natural law perspective, there is little reason for this disparate treatment.

This is because people consume alcohol, tobacco and recreational drugs for the same reasons. Some use these substances to alter their consciousness to emotionally feel better. Others use them to deaden or lessen physical pain. Others are psychologically or physically addicted to them.

Because of this similarity, the power and use of the government toward these intoxicants theoretically should be the same or similar. *De similibus ad similia eadem ratione procedendum est,* says a legal maxim. *From similars to similars, we are to proceed by the same rule.* This is similar to Euclid's first notion, as mentioned in the film *Lincoln* (2012), that things that are equal to the same thing are equal to each other.

Treating alcohol, tobacco and drugs differently violates logic and reason, which are operations of natural law. Nature says that alcohol, tobacco and drugs should be legally treated the same. Said alternatively: by their nature as intoxicants, these substances should be treated the same.

The same thing can be said about subsets of intoxicants, such as wine, brandy, beer, gin and whiskey, or such as peyote, amphetamine, cocaine and pot. While all these substances are different, they share the common power to intoxicate.

A friend of mine applies a similar natural law argument to the disparate treatment of alcohol, tobacco, pharmaceutical narcotics and marijuana. He points out that alcohol kills countless Americans each year, encourages domestic violence, and is horribly addictive. Tobacco is so deadly that entire hospital wards are dedicated to its consequences. Pharmaceutical companies are by far the biggest source of drug addiction in America.

Yet authoritarians in American society have tried to ban marijuana even though not a single person has died from a marijuana overdose, even though it sedates people instead of making them violent, and even though it is minimally-toxic and -physically addictive. If Plato's philosopher king or an enlightened legislature should pick intoxicants which to favor, they should clearly favor marijuana use over alcohol, tobacco and pharmaceutical drug use.

Yet the war on drugs has in fact targeted marijuana, which policy violates the above logic. (It does not violate the logic that large and politically powerful pharmaceutical companies have wanted marijuana banned because of its extraordinary natural medicinal properties.)

However, because our constitutional and statutory criminal law is compatible with and based on natural law, Indiana's positive law <u>does</u>, in fact, treat intoxicants roughly the same. The possession of alcohol, tobacco, pharmaceutical drugs and marijuana is similarly lawful, and the state similarly has the legal power to regulate the manufacture, distribution and dispensing of all these intoxicants, whether it chooses to or not.

Hmmmmm. So if the law on alcohol, tobacco and drugs is roughly the same, and the law does not prohibit or criminalize drugs, just as it does not prohibit or criminalize alcohol and tobacco, then under what authority does Indiana as a republic treat drugs differently than alcohol? Why does the state use its judicial system to put drug users and dealers in jail, yet it accommodates the possession, sale and use of alcohol and tobacco?

The simple answer is that the executive and judicial branches do not follow the laws on drugs as well as they probably do the laws on alcohol and tobacco. If they did, they would regulate the making and selling of drugs similarly to how they regulate the making and selling of alcohol and tobacco.

If state officials followed their drug laws, they would administratively shut down disfavored drug dealers as they administratively shut down moonshiners. Without a constitutional amendment that places drug commerce into the law jurisdiction, as the 18th Amendment did with alcohol commerce, then the making and selling of drugs is to be strictly regulated under equity, just as the commerce of alcohol and tobacco is today.

Thus, the Indiana pharmacy board is to treat unwanted makers and sellers of drugs the same as Indiana's regulators do unwanted makers and sellers of alcohol and tobacco. In a perfect world – I mean, under a functioning republican government that followed its own statutes – they would treat methamphetamine and crack cocaine makers the same as moonshiners, and provide both kinds of disfavored merchants with administrative due process.

The more complex answer to the above question is that, with the exception of national Alcohol Prohibition, the positive law with regard to alcohol, tobacco and drugs has never really changed since the beginning of Indiana, but that the people who run the state government subjectively believe otherwise, without any objective basis for their beliefs. This is what I mean about their running a religious government, or about their running of government religiously. There is no objective basis for their belief that drugs are unlawful. At most, they are legally regulated.

That the government for which they work has greater power over drug commerce than over alcohol or tomato commerce is as unprovable as the religious belief that there is a supernatural God who handpicks kings and legislatures to rule over natural law and lesser natural people. Nothing in the law, i.e., the Indiana constitution or the state's statutes, allows them to prosecute the possession or commerce in drugs as crime. Upon nothing but unprovable misrepresentations of law do Indiana officials stand.

The first thing Indiana's officials should realize is that alcohol, tobacco and drug possession has always been lawful in Indiana (and in areas regulated by the U.S. republic). The 18th Amendment prohibited the commerce of alcohol, but not its possession. Thus even during Alcohol Prohibition, possession and consumption of alcohol, tobacco and drugs were not criminally prohibited.

Only the commerce of alcohol was placed into the criminal law jurisdiction by the 18th Amendment. Because drugs are not alcohol, neither they nor their commerce has ever been criminally prohibited, as they are not now within America's republics.

This means that, except during Alcohol Prohibition, the criminal subject matter jurisdiction of Indiana's judicial courts and of Article III U.S. couts has always been the same toward possession of alcohol, tobacco and drugs. Only the commerce of alcohol was placed by the 18th Amendment into the law jurisdiction of these courts to be criminally sanctioned – and not the commerce of tobacco or drugs (or their possession).

Conversely, other than during Alcohol Prohibition, the Indiana legislature has always had authority to regulate alcohol, tobacco and drug commerce, as it does today. It did not have authority to regulate the commerce of alcohol during Prohibition (because it was criminalized).

Such commerce was subject – not to equity – but to the criminal law jurisdiction of the judicial branch of America's republics. In this regard, the 13th, 18th and 21st Amendments all stand for the proposition that the separation of powers between the branches, or their subject matter jurisdictions, may only be changed by constitutional amendment.

The law is clear about the judicial and regulatory processes, and about the subject matter jurisdiction of their respective courts. The executive and judicial branches adjudicate two separate subject matters, i.e., respectively commerce and injury. Because most officials in the Indiana executive and judicial branches do not know this, and have allowed the co-mingling of these powers, they have violated the separation of powers doctrine in our constitutions, and have exceeded both constitutional and statutory authority in their enforcement of our drug laws.

Because there is no constitutional amendment that makes drug possession or commerce crimes, and that places such activity into the criminal law jurisdiction of judicial courts, as there was with slavery under the 13th Amendment and with alcohol under the 18th Amendment, thus the state of Indiana has usurped this power by executive and judicial fiat.

We know this to be true because the supreme positive laws of the land, i.e., the Indiana and U.S. constitutions, have not changed. Only statutes and officers of the state have changed.

As we shall see, there are neither constitutional grounds nor constitutional amendments that allow republican judicial courts to adjudicate any matters against natural persons that do not cause an injury, or to incarcerate non-criminals for phony "crimes" that are invented by a legislature.

How does Indiana justify prosecuting infractions in judicial courts?

As readers shall begin seeing in chapter 16, statutes delegate most drug matters to the executive branch of Indiana government, and not to the judicial branch. The commercial privileges of drug dealers – big and small, rich and poor, corporate or individual, licensed or unlicensed alike – are to be determined by administrative law courts of either the Indiana State Board of Pharmacy or of the DEA (under authority of the U.S. Attorney General), both which work in their respective executive branch.

This occurs because the Indiana and U.S. constitutions grant judicial courts subject matter jurisdiction only over injury, which is not an element in most drug possession and drug dealing matters. Thus, judicial courts may not regulate commercial activity. To follow the constitution, the Indiana legislature assigns regulatory power over the privilege of making and selling drugs, which are neither cases nor crimes, to administrative law courts of the Indiana pharmacy board.

However, because the legislature in the Controlled Substances Act prescribes penalties for particular behavior, such as jail time for drug possession or drug dealing at IC 35-48-4, this begs the question: On what statutory authority does the state of Indiana justify entering judicial courts to try and to punish non-injurious drug matters, particularly when drug commerce is only regulated? This is the question addressed in the balance of this chapter.

As we have seen, the right to enter a judicial court begins with the Indiana constitution, which creates Indiana's Circuit Courts. The Indiana constitution also allows the Indiana legislature to create Superior Courts, which exercise similar judicial power as the Circuit Courts. Article VII, Section 1 reads:

> "The judicial power of the State shall be vested in one Supreme Court, one Court of Appeals, Circuit Courts, and such other courts as the General Assembly may establish."

Later at Article VII, Section 8, the Indiana constitution tells us about the power of "Circuit Courts, and such other courts as the General Assembly may establish." [205]

> "The Circuit Courts shall have such civil and criminal jurisdiction as may be prescribed by law."

The term "prescribed by law" means for the legislature "to lay down authoritatively as a guide, direction, or rule..." [206] As we have briefly seen, legislatures prescribe or "lay down" law in two manners. They 1) legislate and they 2) codify natural civil and criminal law.

They legislate over things that they create and that are under their equity authority, such as corporations. "The sovereignty of a State extends to every thing which exists by its own authority, or is introduced by its permission;...," wrote the U.S. Supreme Court in *McCulloch v. Maryland* (1819) [207]

In contrast to this, republican legislatures also codify law, such as crimes and judicial procedures, which Nature and the common law have already defined.

In other words, legislatures 1) legislate positive law that applies to artificial persons in equity within America's republics, and they 2) write down the natural law (and procedures of jurisprudence) that apply to natural persons in the law jurisdiction of America's republics. As we have seen, republican legislatures legislate over neither natural law nor constitutional law, both laws of which are beyond their authority.

The Supremacy Clause of the U.S. constitution at Article VI, Paragraph 2, the Supremacy Clause of the Indiana constitution (1851) at Article I, Section 25, and IC 1-1-2-1 all require that the Indiana legislature prescribe law that is consistent with the U.S. and Indiana constitutions. Thus, the jurisdiction that the legislature prescribes for judicial courts must be consistent with the jurisdiction granted by the Indiana constitution. Likewise, IC 33-28-1-5(2) insists that Indiana's judicial courts rule in conformity with the Indiana constitution, which is redundant of the Supremacy Clause and judges' oaths of office.

In particular, the Indiana legislature's criminal prohibitions have to be consistent with the constitutional meaning of crime, which includes injury. Those that are not consistent are *malum prohibita*. *Malum prohibita* is that which only the legislature proscribes, and not Nature.

Such prohibitions embody no objective criminal criteria, create no legal duties in natural persons, and are not enforceable against natural persons in the law jurisdiction of republican judicial courts. Instead, *malum prohibita* are enforceable only against foreigners and commercial entities or endeavors in equity over which, according to *McCulloch v. Maryland* (1819) above, [208] legislatures may regulate within America's republics.

This is essentially because the legislature and its positive law are not sovereign in the natural law jurisdiction of republican constitutions, as secured by the law jurisdiction of republican courts. It is in the law jurisdiction where Nature is sovereign and where the People are free from inconsistent and subjective positive law from legislatures.

That is why the legislature has limited power to prescribe law in the law jurisdiction. The Indiana legislature can only define crime, due process and equal protection in the law jurisdiction consistently with the Indiana and U.S. constitutions and with prior judicial adjudications, such as by codifying real crimes and judicial procedure.

To allow the legislature to legislate contrary to the constitution and the common law would be to defy the reason to have a constitution and a judicial branch. Only the legislature's positive criminal law, which is consistent with natural law, the common law and the constitutional jurisdiction of judicial courts, applies in criminal cases in the law jurisdiction of America's republics.

In *Hook v State* (2002) the Indiana Court of Appeals wrote that "(s)tatutes that are criminal or penal in nature must be strictly construed." [209] This is ultimately because the positive law of the Indiana legislature is not sovereign in the law jurisdiction of judicial courts. Only those criminal provisions under positive law that are strictly consistent with the natural law jurisdiction of our constitutions, with the law jurisdiction of judicial courts over injury, and with the common law may legitimately be enforced. This precludes phony "crimes" from being enforced as real crimes.

Consistent with the Indiana constitution, the state legislature prescribes the Circuit Courts' jurisdiction at IC 33-28-1-2 and the Superior Courts' jurisdiction at IC 33-29-1-1.5. These are the only statutes in which the legislature confers original, subject matter jurisdiction upon Indiana's judicial courts. Both statutes confer the following powers upon the respective courts.

"(1) original and concurrent jurisdiction in all civil cases and in all criminal cases;
(2) de novo appellate jurisdiction of appeals from city and town courts; and
(3) in Marion County, de novo appellate jurisdiction of appeals from township small claims courts established under IC 33-34."

Merely by reading the above statute(s) we can see that the power of Indiana's judicial courts essentially includes only two kinds of power: 1) "original and concurrent jurisdiction in all civil cases and in all criminal cases," which we know as subject matter jurisdiction, and 2) appellate jurisdiction. The courts' appellate jurisdiction includes that power conferred by the Administrative Orders and Procedures Act at IC 4-21.5-5 over administrative law decisions, which is a topic in chapter 16.

As we can plainly see, the courts' subject matter jurisdiction does not expressly include infractions, which are not cases. Instead, infractions are *malum prohibita* that is created by the legislature and that is to be adjudicated in the executive branch against artificial persons, such as licensed automobile drivers, doctors, engineers, etc.

It is the first of the above powers, i.e., subject matter jurisdiction, that is particularly at issue in our challenge to the judicial miscarriage called the war on drugs. Original jurisdiction, as mentioned in the above statute, is another term for subject matter jurisdiction. *Black's Law Dictionary* says that it is the power to take cognizance of a cause at its inception, to adjudicate it, and to pass judgment upon the law and facts. [210]

Thus, according to the Indiana constitution and the Indiana Code, the state's two kinds of judicial courts, i.e. Circuit and Superior Courts, have subject matter jurisdiction over all civil cases and criminal cases (or crimes). These courts would have jurisdiction over infractions only if infractions are cases or crimes, which they are not.

We have seen that "crime" is defined in the Indiana Code at IC 35-48-1-6, which reads: "'Crime' means a felony or a misdemeanor." As well, IC 35-48-1-19 reads: "'Offense' means a crime. The term does not include an infraction." As well, IC 33-28-3-8(a) distinguishes infractions from felonies and misdemeanors, so we know the terms are not synonymous.

From a reading of these three provisions alone we know 1) that "crimes" are "offenses" and 2) that infractions are neither "misdemeanors," "felonies," "crimes" nor "offenses." Thus, according solely to the Indiana legislature, and based on the logic of these statutes alone, we know that the subject matter jurisdiction of Indiana's judicial courts – i.e., that which is prescribed for judicial courts by the state legislature – extends, at most, to "crimes" and "offenses," but not to infractions, which are neither cases, "crimes" nor "offenses."

Thus, the civil and criminal jurisdiction of judicial courts does not include infractions, such as getting ticketed for driving too fast (IC 9-21-5-2) or for not heeding traffic and pedestrian control signals (IC 9-21-17-1). These infractions are assigned to courts under authority of the Commissioner of the BMV in the executive branch, but have heretofore been adjudicated – in violation of the separation of powers doctrine – in Indiana's judicial trial courts.

This means that the judicial courts have no statutory (or constitutional) jurisdiction over infractions because they are not even statutory "crimes" or "offenses," let alone real constitutional crimes or offenses. Likewise, because the Indiana constitution assigns jurisdiction to courts only over cases that involve injury, there is no constitutional subject matter jurisdiction for infractions either.

In fact, there is neither natural, constitutional nor statutory authority to try infractions in Indiana's judicial courts. Even without looking to the Indiana constitution, a reading alone of IC 35-48-1-6, IC 35-48-1-19 and IC 33-28-3-8(a) (cited above) leads to this inexplicable conclusion. Besides, all infractions apply to artificial persons, such as automobile drivers, whose behavior is regulated in the executive branch, not criminally prohibited in the judicial branch.

Indiana's judicial courts justify taking subject matter jurisdiction over infractions under IC 33-33-51-1(b), IC 33-28-3-2(b) and IC 33-28-3-8(a). [211] However, none of these statutes confer subject matter jurisdiction because none of them even mention primary, original or subject matter jurisdiction. And again, the only statutes that confer subject matter jurisdiction to Indiana judicial courts are IC 33-28-1-2 and IC 33-29-1-1.5 (cited above), which do not mention infractions and only mention civil and criminal cases, which infractions are not.

Whereas cases and crimes are facts of Nature, infractions are strictly the creations of Indiana's legislature. As such, they are not mentioned in the Indiana or U.S. constitutions.

As legislative creations, they can be adjudicated in courts created only by the legislature – not in republican courts created by express authority of the state and U.S. constitutions. Constitutionally-created judicial courts have civil and criminal subject matter jurisdiction over injury, which infractions do not include. As well, they have civil and criminal jurisdiction only over civil and criminal cases, which infractions are not.

Thus, infractions are not subject to adjudication by Indiana's constitutionally-created judicial courts and can only be tried in courts that are strictly the creation of legislatures, which are administrative law courts in the executive branch. Infractions based on *malum prohibita*, and over actions that cause no injury, apply only to regulated artificial persons and do not rise to the level of a case or crime needed to invoke judicial authority over natural persons. Plus, they do not even amount to the legislature's definition of "crimes" or "offenses" – whether real or phony.

This is to say that natural persons are subject to judicial process neither for infractions nor phony "misdemeanors" and phony "felonies," which are not defined by natural law and all of which are creations of a legislature. Instead, natural persons are subject to arrest for real misdemeanors, felonies, crimes and offenses, which cause injury, which are criminally prohibited by the unwritten natural law and by common law, and which legislatures have the power and duty only to write down.

This information is relevant to the drug war because there are several infractions sanctioned in the penalty provisions of the Indiana Controlled Substances Act at IC 35-48-4. IC 35-48-4-8.1 makes it an infraction to manufacture drug paraphernalia. IC 35-48-4-8.3 calls it an infraction to possess paraphernalia. IC 35-48-4-8.5 says that it is an infraction to deal in paraphernalia.

The above discussion leads to the conclusion that these three infractions are not enforceable in Indiana's judicial courts, which have no subject matter jurisdiction over infractions. As we have seen, possession of drug paraphernalia is a natural right in Indiana, [212] secured by the substantive right not to be incarcerated except for the commission of crime, [213] and its prohibition is not enforceable in any Indiana court, in any branch of government, for jurisdictional reasons alone.

Plus, the commerce in drug paraphernalia, such as bong pipes, falls under the authority of the Indiana State Board of Pharmacy. Clearly, Indiana's judicial courts have no subject matter jurisdiction over bong pipes, or one's commerce in bong pipes. Anyone who thinks otherwise has been hitting-on propaganda-bong pipes way, way too long.

It is because the legislature's Controlled Substances Act at IC 35-48-4 declares drug possession and drug dealing to be "misdemeanors" or "felonies" that Indiana's judicial courts claim subject matter jurisdiction over these so-called "crimes" or "offenses." However, because judicial courts have failed to use the true definition of crime and offense, which is defined by the natural law jurisdiction of the U.S. and Indiana constitutions, of which they have not been cognizant, they have religiously applied their judicial authority to non-criminal behavior to which it does not apply.

How the State justifies arresting drug users and dealers

In the absence of a constitutional amendment that changes the subject matter jurisdiction of Indiana's judicial courts to include drug commerce or possession, the state of Indiana justifies busting and arresting drug users, and trying non-injurious drug matters in Indiana's judicial courts, based on the following erroneous premise: that the Indiana constitution grants the Indiana legislature power to define or dictate the criminal subject matter jurisdiction of the judicial branch by redefining the essence of crime to be something other than injurious behavior.

This premise is faulty because the subject matter jurisdiction of Indiana's judicial courts is determined by the Indiana constitution – not by the Indiana legislature. It is the constitution by which the People created Indiana's judicial courts and the legislative branch, and by which the People empowered their courts with jurisdiction over civil and criminal cases. Therefore, behavior that does not constitute a civil case or a criminal case, based on injury, as the words case, crime and injury are referred to in the Indiana and U.S. constitutions, does not provide sufficient subject matter to invoke original judicial jurisdiction.

As we have seen, the constitution's separation of powers doctrine is secured only by the proper exercise of judicial subject matter jurisdiction and the proper adherence to the constitutional meanings of case and crime. The judicial branch is in charge of real torts and crimes, which are violations of natural law. Among other things, the executive branch is in charge of regulating commerce under equity.

In addition to these judicial and executive authorities, natural persons are in charge of exercising their own natural rights. Subject only to Nature, such persons are sovereign over this natural law jurisdiction unless or until they violate the natural rights of others, at which time they become subject to the law jurisdiction of the judicial branch.

In contrast to the above statement of law, the state of Indiana's faulty reasoning to justify using judicial courts to try non-injurious drug matters is as follows:

> That the Indiana constitution grants subject matter jurisdiction to judicial courts over crimes and offenses;

> That the legislature defines drug and paraphernalia making, distribution, dispensing and possession to be "crimes" or "offenses" (and infractions);

> That judicial trial courts have subject matter jurisdiction over all "crimes" and "offenses" (and infractions) as defined by the legislature, regardless if these "crimes" or "offenses" (and infractions) match the definition of the crimes and offenses referred to in the Indiana constitution (where infractions are not mentioned); and

> Thus, that the legislature may legislate in the criminal law jurisdiction inconsistently with the U.S. and Indiana constitutions.

The above statement is the state's entire justification and rationalization to wage its war on drugs using Indiana's Circuit and Superior Courts. The essence of its argument is 1) that judicial courts have criminal subject matter jurisdiction over anything that the state legislature says that they have, and 2) that grants of criminal authority by the state legislature to the judicial branch are not restrained by constitutional limitations placed upon either the legislature or the judicial courts.

This is another way of saying: a) that legislatures may prohibit whatever they want to prohibit, b) that they can criminalize whatever and whoever they wish to criminalize; and c) that it is the judicial system's function to enforce the legislature's will, regardless of the limitations imposed on the law jurisdiction of judicial courts by American constitutions. These are misrepresentations of law espoused by people who do not support America's republican form of government.

This raises an essential issue for our judicial branch: To what does it answer? Do Indiana's judicial courts ultimately answer to the state's constitution or to the state's legislature? Do judicial courts define their criminal jurisdiction according to how Nature and the Indiana constitution consistently define crime, or how the legislature inconsistently defines "crime"?

The current premise used in Indiana's judicial courts is that the judiciary answers to the legislature, not to the Indiana constitution. The war on drugs is based on the false concept that Indiana's legislature can expand the subject matter jurisdiction of judicial courts to encompass non-crimes (including drug-paraphernalia infractions) that are not injurious.

The false prosecution of drug possession and dealing as legitimate crimes is based on the faulty concept that legislatures can define "civil case," "crime," "criminal case," "offense," "felony," and "misdemeanor" to mean anything they want without reference to the same terms' constitutional meanings. This claimed power is that of a monarch or dictator. This claimed power amounts to the same plenary power as exercised by Congress in the federal areas, which is non-republican. Thus, to claim and enforce such illegitimate power is to convert a republic into a *de facto* non-republic.

That is, Indiana's judicial courts operate upon the false premise that the Indiana legislature can make anything a crime or offense, in order to invoke the courts' criminal jurisdiction, just by calling the behavior a "crime" or "offense." This is to say that the Indiana legislature can take the possession of property, which is an unalienable natural right recognized in Article I, Section 1 of the Indiana constitution (1816), and can convert it into a crime merely by calling it a "crime."

In all seriousness and quite literally, this premise is the only thread upon which the legitimacy of the war on drugs hangs within America's republics. As we shall see, not only does this premise violate statutory and constitutional law, both which recognize the natural right of drug possession and both which put the authority of American constitutions above legislatures, but it also violates one of the Laws of Nature, i.e., logic. As such, it is an embarrassment to anyone who respects the real law, which is rational and verifiable.

It is not logical or rational that a legislature stands above a constitution which created it. It is not logical that a legislature can legislate and criminalize something as fundamental as our right to possess property without violating the fundamental rules of the game. It is completely irrational that the judiciary would view the criminalization of property possession in Indiana as anything but unconstitutional.

For example, if the legislature made it a "crime" to do jumping-jacks, the Indiana's judiciary would know that this is unconstitutional, even though there is no such natural right to do jumping jacks that is mentioned in the Indiana constitution. However, if the legislature made it a "crime" to acquire, possess and defend certain property, as the war on drugs suggests, then the judiciary becomes oblivious to the natural right of property possession, even though it is actually enumerated in the Indiana constitution (1816). To overlook an enumerated right makes no sense.

Further, it would be illogical to argue that this natural right of property possession disappeared when it was not mentioned in the 1851 constitution. This would be a misstatement and misrepresentation of law 1) because natural law is anterior to positive law, 2) because natural rights are ubiquitous and timeless, and 3) because natural rights do not just go away upon the closing of our eyes to them, or by erasing them from a page.

That is, we cannot just ignore the elephants in the room. As the 9th Amendment to the U.S. constitution says, just because the nation's supreme positive law lists certain natural rights to be secured, this list is not meant to deny or disparage the numerous natural rights that are not acknowledged.

I mentioned some red-flag anomalies regarding the war on drugs in chapter 1, and a few others along the way, but not this one. The idea that the government can take our natural unalienable right "of acquiring, possessing and protecting property" [214] and can convert it into crime just by calling it a crime is far more whack than any of them.

Government officials would automatically see the warpedness of criminalizing jumping jacks, but cannot see the inherent violation of a natural right that criminalizing drug possession and dealing amount to, even though property possession is a right written in state constitutions. Again, this is irrational behavior.

Given the nearly fifty years of nonsense called the war on drugs, this realization comes by means of a slow boat to Cairo on the river of denial. In order to justify the war on drugs, government officials would either 1) have to deny the natural right of property possession that is enumerated in the Indiana constitution (1816), or 2) to deny that drugs are personal property.

Thus, to justify the war on drugs, officials would have 1) to deny the existence and viability of a constitutional provision which is contrary to their war on drugs, or 2) to deny the reality that drugs are defined as property within a constitutional republic. Mind you, to deny natural reality is a form of insanity. The war on drugs can be justified only by adopting insane, religious attitudes about natural criteria, such as the meaning of crime, natural production and lawful possession.

How does a state legislature criminalize a right? And how did the state convert our rights into "crimes" right under the noses of all the state's legal experts?

The war on drugs is the result of not reading drug statutes sufficiently to understand them. It reflects a justice system that does not even approximate the checks and balances of legislative, executive and judicial power that are embodied in the laws themselves. It also reflects a professional incompetency in attorneys that has been no match over time for the constitutional vandalism by non-republicans. [215]

The ultimate answer to how the state converted our rights into "crimes" is 1) that the legislature did not criminalize the right of drug possession or the privilege of drug dealing, which would be unconstitutional, but 2) that officials in the executive and judicial branches only think and act as if it did. The Indiana legislature merely calls drug possession and dealing "misdemeanors" and "felonies," and the executive and judicial branches – without any state standing or subject matter jurisdiction whatsoever – falsely treat this *malum prohibita* as real crimes and offenses.

This false enforcement is not the fault of the Indiana legislature. It is due to the false and artificial standards used by prosecutors and judges who do not understand judicial courts' jurisdiction over cases involving injury.

Indiana prosecutors and judges are presumed to know what crimes and offenses are because they took an oath to the Indiana and U.S. constitutions, which include and refer to those actual words. But to not know what crimes and offenses are, or to not know that natural law defines these words, is to have a subjective view of crime, is to not know the authority of governments' branches, and is to make a false and vacuous oath to the constitutions. One cannot take an oath to fight crime without knowing the meaning of crime.

To not know the meaning of crimes and offenses in constitutions to which one takes an oath is to literally not be qualified to take the oath – particularly as a criminal judge. Then, for prosecutors and judges to judicially enforce *malum prohibita* as crime is to violate these false and vacuous oaths, along with the substantive rights of natural persons.

Pitifully, the entire war on drug users is solely based upon the above false premise about legislative superiority, upon faulty logic and upon fraudulent word use, and upon little else. That the legislature's "crimes" and "offenses" are constitutional crimes and offenses is the state's only argument – and a false, frivolous and fraudulent one at that – to support its illegitimate use of the judicial branch with regard to drug possession and dealing.

There is nothing in either the Indiana or U.S. constitutions, or in judicial case law, that supports what the state's executive and judicial officials have been doing with regard to drugs. Again, the drug laws are good, but these officials do not follow the drug laws.

Likewise, there is nothing in Indiana's republican constitution or case law which says that judicial courts have anything but criminal subject matter jurisdiction over injury, or which says that the legislature can change this requirement without a constitutional amendment. Given that the executive and judicial branches operate contrary to this premise, everything about their war on drugs – from top to bottom, start to finish – is false and illegitimate.

Why the prosecution of drug matters in judicial courts is wrong

The following is a summary of the premises and reasoning of this chapter's argument that judicial courts do not have subject matter jurisdiction over matters of drug possession and dealing:

That the Indiana and U.S. constitutions are the supreme law in the territorial area known as the state of Indiana;

That the Indiana constitution grants subject matter jurisdiction to Indiana's judicial trial courts only over civil or criminal cases involving injury to one's person, property or reputation.

That the constitution – and not the state legislature – determines the meaning of the constitutional terms case, civil case, criminal case, crime, offense, felony and misdemeanor to include injury, over which judicial courts have subject matter jurisdiction;

That all the statutory "misdemeanors" and most of the "felonies" relating to controlled substances that are described in the Indiana Controlled Substances Act at IC 35-48-4, do not legally constitute a case, civil case, criminal case, crime, offense, felony or misdemeanor under the Indiana or U.S. constitutions;

That state prosecutors falsely represent and prosecute infractions, "cases," "crimes," "offense," "felonies" and "misdemeanors" in judicial courts as cases, criminal cases, crimes, offenses, felonies and misdemeanors, as if the former were entitled to the courts' jurisdiction.

That judicial courts have no subject matter jurisdiction over the above-mentioned false "crimes" and "offenses" (and infractions) that do not amount to a case, civil case, criminal case, crime, offense, felony or misdemeanor under the Indiana or U.S. constitutions;

That the state legislature does not have authority to redefine case, civil case, criminal case, crime, offense, felony or misdemeanor in a manner inconsistent with the Indiana or U.S. constitutions, Indiana's common law and the law of Great Britain, which had already used and given meaning to these terms.

Thus, that Indiana's judicial courts have no power to enforce all the infractions and statutory "misdemeanors" as well as most of the "felonies" relating to controlled substances that are described in the Controlled Substance Act at IC 35-48-4, most of which are false "crimes" and "offenses."

Indiana's judicial courts have subject matter jurisdiction only over nine statutory crimes relating to controlled substances described at IC 35-48-4 because they constitute *malum in se*, as crime is referred to in the Indiana constitution, the United States constitution and by the common law of Great Britain.

Given the 13th Amendment to the United States constitution and Article 1, Section 37 of the Indiana constitution (1851), both which prohibit slavery and involuntary servitude except for the punishment of crime, this reference to crime does not include the false "misdemeanors," "felonies" and infractions described by the Indiana legislature at IC 35-48-4.

The state of Indiana and the state's judicial courts have rightful authority to enslave or impose involuntary servitude upon natural persons only for real crimes, but not for any of the false and phony "crimes" described by the Indiana legislature at IC 35-48-4.

Therefore, the state of Indiana and the state's judicial courts have falsely enslaved or imposed involuntary servitude upon almost every single drug defendant for their commission of false "crimes" relating to controlled substances, over which the judicial branch has had no constitutional or statutory subject matter jurisdiction.

This includes the state's law enforcement officers who have falsely arrested drug defendants without proper judicial power and the state's prosecutors who have falsely prosecuted them without express statutory authority, without judicial standing and without justiciable cases in judicial courts that are without subject matter jurisdiction.

As well, the Indiana State Board of Pharmacy has shirked its duty to regulate drug dealing by means of administrative due process.

This amounts to mass violations of the rights of due process and equal protection, as well as slavery and indentured servitude, for exceeding executive and judicial authority under our constitutions and, as we shall see, for not even understanding and following the state's statutory drug laws.

Ultimately, statutes cannot enlarge the powers granted to the judicial branch by our constitutions. Statutes may not enlarge the criminal subject matter jurisdiction of judicial courts because the legislative branch is not the source of judicial power and may not legislate inconsistently with the judicial branch's (natural, common, criminal) law jurisdiction.

Judicial courts answer directly to constitutions because the constitutions created them. This precludes them from adopting statutory definitions of crime that are dissimilar in essence to the definitions of crime in constitutions, to which judicial officers take oaths.

Statutes are not written to change or expand our constitutions, but to be accountable to them. Otherwise they are to be declared unconstitutional or invalid.

As we have seen, the only statutes in the Indiana Code that apply to natural persons are ones: 1) that define the elements and punishment for torts and real crimes, 2) that define the rights, responsibilities and judicial process for natural persons as judicial parties, witness and jurors, 3) that reserve natural rights, and 4) that define arrest powers over natural persons.

Because these are codifications of natural law, and were established by the common law of Great Britain, these standards existed prior to American positive law. The rights existed both prior to and after Indiana became a state. They exist now. The law has not changed.

Natural law has always said that drugs and other property are lawful in America's republics. There is no monarch to say otherwise. Adopting this principle, the positive law of America's republics says that drugs are lawful and that drug commerce may be regulated. This law about property possession and commerce was well established before the Indiana legislature adopted the CSA, which did not (because it could not) change any of the state's separation of powers.

Thus the law exists, and has always existed since Indiana became a state republic, to protect individuals' natural rights to possess property and to get intoxicated, if they so choose. In effect, the law jurisdiction serves to secure the state of Nature for individuals within state republics. The coercive and violent nature of the war on drugs is to not only violate the drug laws, but to primitively substitute the law of the jungle – where fraud and might make right – for the republican rule of law based on the objective criminal standards of Nature.

Plus, as a way for a society to deal with unwanted behavior, criminal prohibition is a very primitive political tool. As the war on drugs demonstrates, little good can be achieved with such Neanderthal policies as clubbing people over the head for their own good.

America's republics may regulate the commerce of drugs, but without amending their constitutions, they may not impose a blanket criminal prohibition on their commerce, possession or use. Ultimately their courts' law jurisdiction over civil and criminal injury does not extend to non-injurious activity such as mere drug possession or dealing, which amount to neither cases nor crimes.

12
The natural law basis of citizenship

As we learned in chapter 3, it is natural persons' substantive rights, particularly from the Bill of Rights, that make them free in America and that make their natural rights unassailable by kings or dictatorial legislatures. A substantive right is a right expressly or inherently granted by a constitution and one which may not be taken away or denied by a republican legislature. It is strictly and solely through these substantive rights that all natural persons' natural rights to life, liberty, property, religion and the pursuit of happiness are enforced within America's republican states.

For example, only if we are availed a judicial remedy for harm done to us by other people are our natural rights to life, property and compensation secured. In such a case, we can seek a civil remedy in court for monetary damages and / or, if an action is of a particular nature or severity, the state can prosecute it in the same judicial law jurisdiction as a crime.

Conversely, only if we are free from arrest or enslavement except for the commission of *malum in se* crime are our natural rights to life, liberty and the pursuit of happiness secured by the judicial branch. Otherwise the state can deprive us of our liberty for any 'ole reason, such as for unpopular property possession (which is to be treated as a natural right) or for being in a disfavored business enterprise (which is to be subject to regulation in the republics, not imprisonment).

Thus, all of our natural rights are secured by our substantive rights, which operate in the natural law jurisdiction of American constitutions, as enforced in the law jurisdiction of judicial courts. As we have seen, these substantive rights apply to all natural persons within America's republics, including foreigners.

With regard to drug users and dealers, the 13th Amendment's substantive right not to be enslaved except for the commission of real crime is paramount. As well, the 14th Amendment guarantees that all manufacturers and distributors of drugs will be given administrative due process and equal protection. Because the commerce of all controlled substances is regulated in equity and is not prohibited at law, this prevents disfavored drug dealers from being subject to the the criminal law jurisdiction.

Natural law defines America's primary citizens

As briefly mentioned previously, the natural law jurisdiction of the U.S. constitution not only defines crime in America's republics, it also defines citizenship. Americans cannot understand crime, U.S. citizenship or the lawful role of marriage, for instance, without understanding natural law. As we shall also see in the next chapter, only the proper application of citizenship defines the competence and legitimacy of the United States of America as a representative republic.

As odd as this sounds, as will be shown, only if government officials know the meaning of citizenship can they operate within the law. Plus, only if one understands citizenship can one understand why we have birth and marriage records.

Marriage and birth certificates, as state institutions, exists to secure the political rights of children. But for children, state recognition of marriage would be unnecessary. But for marriage, male U.S. citizens would literally have to formally claim their children, as if they were in the state of Nature, in order to secure their children's natural political rights within the political society.

As there are two opposite and opposed jurisdictions in our constitutions, i.e., one based on natural law and the other based on positive law, there are also two types of U.S. citizens: i.e., one based on natural law and the other based on positive law.

Americans who inherit their citizenship by natural law, as a political inheritance from their U.S. citizen fathers, are called natural born citizens. In contrast, adopted or naturalized U.S. citizens, who gain their citizenship by positive law grant from Congress, are referred to as citizens of the United States.

Whether citizen is capitalized or not, and whether used in the U.S. constitution or in a statute based on the constitution, the terms Citizens of the United States (as used at Article I, Section 2 of the U.S. constitution) and citizens of the United States (as used in the 14th Amendment) always refer to naturalized U.S. citizens, who owe their political rights to Congress. Thus, their political rights are not natural, but are artificial or man-made.

Likewise, whether or not the word Citizen is capitalized (as it is in the U.S. constitution), the term natural born citizen refers to a citizen who gains his or her citizenship in a tribe or nation based on the affirmative acts of his or her citizen father, where marriage is such an affirmative act. A natural born citizen is a citizen of either gender who is born into their father's tribe or nation.

The reason that an affirmative act – such as the act of marriage – by the citizen father is necessary to create natural born citizens from any country is that no one can be a witness to the parenthood of the father, as they can the mother. This means that under natural law, in the state of Nature, the father must in fact claim a child as his own to grant natural political rights. This will be discussed more thoroughly below.

In contrast, if a male does not claim the child as a natural born citizen, then the republican nation might adopt the child as a naturalized citizen, based on the child's place of birth or on the nationality or citizenship of the mother. That is up to a nation's positive law.

"As the society can not maintain and perpetuate itself except by the children of its citizens," wrote Swiss legal philosopher Emmerich de Vattel in *The Law of Nations* (1758), "these citizens naturally take on the status of their fathers and enter upon all the latter's rights." [216] These political rights are "given to him (a child) by nature..." [217] Thus, one becomes a natural born citizen of any republic "by nature..." [218] – and not by a positive law grant from its legislature.

In contrast to a natural born citizen, a naturalized U.S. citizen is a natural born citizen or citizen-subject of a country that is foreign to the United States, and one who gains his or her U.S. citizenship by positive law grant from the U.S. government. Vattel explains: "A Nation, or the sovereign who represents it, may confer citizenship upon an alien and admit him into the body politic. This act is called naturalization." [219]

Bouvier's Dictionary (1856) defines naturalization as "(t)he act by which an alien is made a citizen of the United States of America." [220] Again note the specific term given to naturalized U.S. citizens, i.e., citizen of the United States.

A citizen of the United States is essentially the legal opposite of a natural born citizen, at least originally. By definition, a naturalized U.S. citizen is a citizen or subject of a foreign country, i.e., an alien, who has been adopted by the positive law of the U.S. He or she is not a natural born citizen, who is claimed into the body politic by the natural authority of a U.S. citizen father. Bouvier defined a naturalized citizen as: "One who, being born an alien, has lawfully become a citizen of the United States under the constitution and laws." [221]

Almost everyone born within the United States or to a U.S. citizen mother is a U.S. citizen, but not everyone born within the United States is a natural born citizen. Only children born to U.S. citizen fathers can be natural born citizens. Under U.S. law a child born in America to a foreign citizen father is a citizen or citizen-subject of that father's country, as well as a naturalized U.S. citizen.

Within America's republics, U.S. law universally respects the natural political rights of all natural persons to secure citizenship through the males of their nations. This is how the Laws of Nature work with regard to the Law of Nations, wrote Vattel. The full title of his book was *The Law of Nations or Principles of the Law of Nature Applied to the Conduct and Affairs of Nations and Sovereigns.*

Based on the above criteria, everyone in America and throughout the world has one of three different relationships with the U.S. government. Each of us are either 1) natural born citizens, 2) (naturalized) citizens of the United States, or 3) people who are foreign to and un-adopted by the positive law jurisdictions in the United States.

The original citizens of the United States, who are noted in Article II, Section 1 of the U.S. constitution (see directly below)), such as George Washington and Thomas Jefferson, were necessarily naturalized U.S. citizens. This is because they originally were British subjects. As well, before the U.S. constitution naturalized them as citizens of the United States, they were citizens of states that were foreign to the U.S. All of the Founding Fathers (and Mothers) had to be naturalized because they were naturally alien to the United States.

This status, and the separate status of natural born citizens, is made evident by Article II, Section 1 of the U.S. constitution which states:

> "No Person except a natural born citizen, or a Citizen of the United States, at the time of the Adoption of the Constitution, shall be eligible to the Office of the President, neither shall any Person be eligible to that Office who shall not have attained to the Age of thirty five Years, and been fourteen Years a Resident within the United States."

These original and naturalized "Citizens of the United States, at the time of the Adoption of the Constitution" were grandfathered-in by the U.S. constitution to be eligible for President. They are the only U.S.-adopted, naturalized citizens that have ever been eligible to be U.S. President.

Without them, according to the above provision, the United States would not have had a President for its first thirty-five years. After all of these original citizens of the United States passed away, all other U.S. Presidents have been required to be natural born citizens.

Similar to being the first baby born in a given year, I wonder who the first natural born citizen was. Similar to being honored as the last veteran of a war to die, I wonder who the last original citizen of the United States was.

Starting on the day that the U.S. constitution took effect, natural born citizens were the children born to the original citizens of the United States. These were the first of "our Posterity" referred to in the constitution's Preamble, which says that the constitution is created to "secure the Blessings of Liberty to ourselves and our Posterity..."

The creation of natural born citizens did not require any act by Congress. The original U.S. citizens were naturally creating natural born citizens long before Congress ever met. Natural born citizens are born into a constitutional jurisdiction – i.e., the natural law jurisdiction – that is separate from Congress' positive law authority. They are creations and citizens under natural law, not positive law. They are not born subject to Congress, and Congress may not legislate contrary to their natural political jurisdiction.

That America's primary citizens are defined by natural law is analogous to crime being defined by natural law. Natural law also defines marriage. This means that crime, natural law citizenship and marriage in America's republics are naturally defined outside of artificial positive law authority. As well, without amending constitutions, legislatures and courts may not propagate written law that is inconsistent with these natural definitions.

More on natural born citizens v. naturalized U.S. citizens

The distinction between natural and naturalized citizens was recognized by the U.S. Supreme Court in the case of *Minor v. Happersett* (1887). [222] This is the seminal case where the Court denied Mrs. Virginia Minor, who was a natural born citizen from Missouri, the right to vote in federal elections. It was this case that necessitated the passage of the 19th Amendment, which is the positive law that grants women the right to vote.

Minor sued under the equal protection clause of the 14th Amendment for the right to vote in the presidential election. (The 14th Amendment applies to "(a)ll persons born or naturalized in the United States, and subject to the jurisdiction thereof.") Thus, she sued as a citizen of the United States, which means as a naturalized citizen. However, Minor was born in the U.S. to married U.S. citizen parents. Thus, the Court said that her rights "do not depend upon the amendment" because she was already a citizen "before its adoption." [223]

In other words, Virginia Minor was a natural born citizen. The Court, which for reasons described below inaccurately refers to her as a "citizen of the United States," did however accurately write that a person may become a citizen in two ways:

> "first, by birth, and second, by naturalization. This is apparent from the Constitution itself, for it provides that 'No person except a natural-born citizen or a citizen of the United States at the time of the adoption of the Constitution shall be eligible to the office of President,' and that Congress shall have power 'to establish a uniform rule of naturalization.' Thus, new citizens may be born or they may be created by naturalization." [224]

"The Constitution does not in words say who shall be natural-born citizens...," the Court added. (This is because – like crime and marriage – a natural born citizen is defined by Nature, which is a jurisdiction that predates the U.S. Constitution, where crimes, natural born citizens and marriages are facts of Nature.)

"These were natives or natural-born citizens, as distinguished from aliens or foreigners," [225] wrote the Court. Thus, the Supreme Court acknowledges that there are two kinds of citizens: 1) natural born citizens who are "born" and who inherit their citizenship "by birth," i.e., by being naturally born, and 2) naturalized U.S. citizens who are naturally foreign and who become citizens by grant of Congress.

At Article I, Section 8, Clause 4, the U.S. constitution empowers Congress to "establish an uniform Rule of Naturalization..." However, the constitution does not grant Congress power to define or to create natural born citizens, which are creations in Nature, defined by natural law and outside of legislative authority. Their rights are secured and established by U.S. citizen fathers under the natural law authority of the U.S. constitution, not by the legislative authority of Congress.

This is evident from the Court's use of the term "by birth" in the above quotation. "By birth" should be contrasted with the term "at birth," the latter which means at the same time as one's birth. Inheriting citizenship "by birth" is by natural law. Gaining citizenship at birth – by operation of positive law at the time of birth – is naturalization.

U.S. males confer natural born citizenship "by birth" either through marriage, or as we shall see in the next cited case, through other affirmative acts – called legitimation – when a child is born outside of marriage and in a country that is foreign to the U.S. Neither of these acts of establishing fatherhood – and thus, passing-on the rights of natural citizenship – are required to occur at birth. For example, an unwed father may not be present at the birth to begin establishing the child's natural political status.

In contrast, naturalization may occur by operation of positive law at birth. For example, according to 8 USC 1409(c), children born to foreign fathers and eligible U.S. mothers are U.S. citizens at birth, regardless where the children are born. So are children born on U.S. soil to foreign mothers and foreign fathers.

Both of these types of children gain naturalized U.S. citizenship by operation of statute at birth, yet because of the foreign nationalities of their fathers, they are foreign children "by birth." These children 1) become eligible to be natural born citizens or citizen-subjects of their fathers' nations, as well as 2) to become naturalized U.S. citizens at birth by operation of statutory U.S. law.

Thus under U.S. law, a child born to a foreign father and a U.S. mother may become both a natural born citizen or citizen-subject of a foreign country by birth, which status operates under natural law and the Law of Nations, and become a naturalized U.S. citizen at birth, which status operates under U.S. positive law. For example, I have a Swedish friend named Anita who is a naturalized U.S. citizen because of her birth in the U.S., but who is also a subject of the Swedish crown due to her parents being Swedish subjects. According to *Bouvier's Law Dictionary* (1856), as a (naturalized) citizen of the United States, my friend "has all the rights of a natural born citizen except that of being eligible as president or vice-president of the United States." [226]

Because under U.S. statutory law and under natural law, U.S. females have no authority to confer natural born citizenship upon their children made with foreign males, the U.S. Congress extends naturalized citizenship both to children of U.S. mothers born to foreign males and to children born on U.S. soil to foreign parents. Those who qualify to be citizens of the United States are described at 8 USC 1401 and 1409. Whereas natural law bases one's natural born citizenship on the actions of the citizen father, the positive law confers naturalized citizenship based on criteria that natural law does not use, i.e., the citizenship of the mother, the place of birth or upon an alien's application.

Again, that natural born citizenship naturally follows the citizenship of the father, according to natural law, is explained by Emmerich de Vattel's *The Law of Nations, or The Principles of the Law of Nature applied to Nations and Sovereigns:*

"As the society cannot exist and perpetuate itself otherwise than by the children of the citizens, those children naturally follow the conditions of their fathers, and succeed to all their rights...The country of the fathers is therefore that of the children; and these become true citizens merely by their tacit consent. We shall soon see, whether, on their coming to the years of discretion, they may renounce their right, and what they owe to the society in which they were born. I say that, in order to be of the country, it is necessary that a person be born of a father who is a citizen, for if he is born there of a foreigner, it will be only the place of his birth, and not his country." [227]

Thus, one can be born in the United States to non-U.S. parents or to non-U.S. fathers, but "it will be only the place of his birth, and not his country." [228] One's place of birth is where one is born, not where one is politically from. Under the natural law jurisdiction of the U.S. constitution, a child's country is essentially that to which his father is loyal.

In contrast, the child's naturalized country would be that which adopts this foreign child based on the government's soil jurisdiction (*jus soil*) or on the citizenship of the mother (*jus sanguinis*). In the U.S., such a child would be naturally foreign to the U.S. by birth, yet a naturalized U.S. citizen at birth, just like my Swedish friend.

If the positive law of the country respects natural law, as does the United States' constitution, then such child will have dual citizenship: one bestowed by the father under natural law and the Law of Nations, and one established for (on behalf of) the mother under the country's positive law authority. The latter occurs by operation of positive law – not based on the natural acts of marriage or legitimation by citizen fathers.

This difference how natural born citizens and naturalized U.S. citizens are created is seen in 8 USC 1409. 8 USC 1409(a) states what a U.S. citizen father must do to secure the U.S. citizenship of his child born out of wedlock on foreign soil to a foreign mate – in the so-called state of Nature. The father 1) must establish a blood relationship with the child by clear and convincing evidence, 2) must establish the father's U.S. nationality at the time of the child's birth, 3) must agree in writing to provide support for the child until the age of eighteen and 4) must legitimate the child or establish his paternity during the child's minority. [229]

In contrast, the general requirements for acquiring U.S. citizenship for children born abroad to unwed foreign fathers and U.S. citizen mothers are much simpler, more direct and automatic. According to 8 USC 1409(c), the child gains U.S. citizenship if the nationality of his mother is of the United States and if the mother had previous physical presence within the U.S. for a continuous period of a year. No marriage, no claiming of the child, no taking of responsibility, and no legitimation of the child by the U.S.-citizen mother is necessary, as it is with U.S. citizen fathers, to secure a child's U.S. citizenship. But why the difference?

Under natural political law, both U.S. citizen males and females are naturally and equally empowered to secure the natural political rights of their off-spring. This is most obviously achieved by both genders through the act of marriage.

Marriage signifies the parenthood of the father, and thus the political status of his children. Marriage to a U.S. male is a woman's means of choosing the natural born citizen-status of her children. Outside of marriage, or in marriages to foreign males, female U.S. citizens (meeting a minor U.S. residency requirement) automatically establish naturalized U.S. citizenship for their children, anywhere that they have them.

So, U.S. citizen mothers can create naturalized U.S. citizens anywhere in the world with foreign mates, married or unmarried. However, these mothers do not create natural born citizens with foreign males.

This is because in the state of Nature – that is, outside of marriage, in a foreign country, to a foreign mate – U.S. male and female citizens confer political rights upon their offspring differently. As we saw above, 8 USC 1409(a) and 1409(c) treat male and female U.S. citizens quite differently.

As we shall see below, this disparate legal treatment has been properly upheld by the U.S. Supreme Court as consistent with the equal protection clause of the U.S. constitution, based on inherent biological differences between men and women. The Court did not go into details, but I will describe these differences and their legal implications directly below.

The first difference is that females do not naturally rely upon their own testimony in order to secure political rights for their offspring. Instead, females in all societies naturally rely only upon the witness testimony of others in order to secure such political rights.

For example, friends and neighbors witness a woman's pregnancy for nine months. A doctor or midwife witnesses the delivery of the child. The mother naturally feeds and cares for the child during its infancy.

Naturally, there is no reasonable doubt that the mother is the mother. Her role in creating the child is also witnessed on the birth certificate. Such woman is the authentic mother, based on eye-witness testimony. In the state of Nature, the U.S. government bestows U.S. citizenship – which is naturalized citizenship – upon the children of U.S.

mothers based on the eye-witness testimony of others.

On the other hand, there are no witnesses in the state of Nature to the father's fatherhood. He may have bragged about having sex with the mother nine months before a child's birth, or someone may have witnessed the sex act through a window, or the father may have even been present at the child's birth. However, no one can say for sure – in the state of Nature – that he is the father. As 8 USC 1409(a) says, if his child is born out of wedlock in a foreign country to a foreign mate, the U.S. father will have to step forward and prove his fatherhood – that is, genetically.

Outside of marriage, the natural circumstance of being unmarried requires the father to step forth and claim the child as his own, just as 8 USC 1409(a) says. Outside of marriage and in a foreign country, only in this manner does a U.S. male secure the natural political rights of his offspring as natural born citizens. These acts are required by natural law, as codified by Congress at at 8 USC 1409(a).

The second political difference between the genders is that U.S. men may confer only natural political rights upon their children, i.e., natural born citizenship, whereas U.S. women may chose the type of U.S. citizenship that they want for their children. They do this by choosing with whom they bear children. U.S. females 1) may secure natural political rights for their offspring by marrying and bearing children of U.S. males, or 2) may secure positive law U.S. citizenship for their children by bearing children with foreign males. Thus, except in cases of rape, U.S. mothers exclusively control the type of U.S. citizenship that their children receive.

Marriage, which is a natural right as defined in the natural law jurisdiction, is an essential component of U.S. citizenship. Marriage is the natural way for females to signify – regardless of their country's natural-ization laws – that they wish their children to have the natural citizenship status of the father. Likewise, marriage is the natural way for males to express the exclusivity of their contributions in creating their offspring. Outside of marriage U.S. males must attest to this relationship because it is not presumed, or witnessed as in the case with mothers.

Marriage is the manner by which U.S. citizens of both genders primarily establish the citizenship status of their offspring. It is also the preferred means by which males accept responsibility for their children. Thus, marriage is recognized in America's republics primarily to secure the political status of and responsibility for males' offspring.

While marriage may serve other purposes in an American republic, it fundamentally serves to secure the political rights of children. In particular, it determines whether children have natural political rights that are inherited from their U.S. fathers, or instead that children have artificial citizenship rights that are bestowed by Congress on account of their U.S. mother or place of birth. This determines whether they may serve as U.S. President.

Outside of marriage within the U.S., particularly when the name of the father is absent on a child's birth certificate, only the presumption of naturalized citizenship is created, and a child's status as a natural born citizen is rather tenuous. This is important only to natural parents who aspire or dream for their children to one day be the U.S. President. As mentioned before, this is because natural born citizens have one right, which is a natural political right, that citizens of the United States do not have – that of being eligible to be President or Vice President.

This process of certifying citizenship is analogous to why the Roman republic instituted birth registration. Rome forbade the registration of illegitimate children, i.e., children who were unclaimed by Roman fathers, to differentiate Rome's second class citizens from its natural born ones. [230] By definition, republics are to be representative of their natural law citizens.

In the state of Nature – outside of marriage – it is the responsibility of the U.S. citizen father to take affirmative steps if he wishes that the natural political rights of his offspring are secured. This is also to ensure that such rights are not instead legal privileges of naturalized citizenship, bestowed by a government by operation of law, according to the mother's citizenship or the place of birth.

Thus, it is the male U.S. citizen father only – by his actions alone – who secures the natural born citizen-status of his offspring in the state of Nature. In the absence of affirmative acts by the father, nations usually then confer naturalized citizenship based on the mother's nationality or place of birth. This is exemplified by 8 USC 1409, where Congress legislates naturalized citizenship at 8 USC 1409(c) under its positive law authority, and where it codifies the natural born citizenship requirements of natural law at 8 USC 1409(a), over which it may not legislate.

This analysis is compatible with the discussion of natural rights in chapter 3. There we acknowledged that men have the natural right to confer natural born citizenship upon their children, while women have the right to choose both their children's nationality and the type of citizenship. Thus, both parents may guarantee the natural born citizenship of their children, but because of their biological differences, they do this in different ways.

This reflects the political laws of Nature, the natural order, and the natural biological capabilities between the genders. We naturally have this legal arrangement because – in the state of Nature – women are naturally capable of proving their parenthood at birth by witness testimony, but men are not. This is a natural fact upon which U.S. citizenship law is based. This fact is analogous to the natural fact – of injury – upon which republican criminal law is based.

U.S. citizen males have plenary jurisdiction over citizenship

Natural law silently operated and was completely overlooked by the U.S. Supreme Court in the case of *Nguyen v. Immigration and Naturalization Service* (2001). [231] This was a case about the citizenship of Tuan Anh Nguyen who was born out of wedlock in Vietnam to a Vietnamese mother and to a U.S. citizen father, and who was then raised in the United States by his biological father.

At age 22 Nguyen pleaded guilty in a Texas state court to two counts of sexual assault on a child. Based on these felonies involving moral turpitude, the INS initiated deportation proceedings against him as an alien. The INS adjudged him an alien because his father had not fulfilled the requirements of 8 USC 1409(a) (see above), by failing to legitimate his son.

Nguyen and his natural father argued that 8 USC 1409, which determines Nguyen's citizenship, violates the equal protection clause of the U.S. constitution by having different rules for attainment of citizenship of children born abroad to U.S. males and to U.S. females. (Note: the father Joseph Boulais was a party in the case. However, neither he nor the justices on the Supreme Court realized that it was his right to confer citizenship that was at issue.)

As we saw above, U.S. naturalization law does not require any burdensome affirmative actions or reporting requirements for the U.S. mother to make a U.S. citizen, as is required of the U.S. father. (This is because of the self-proving attributes of motherhood and because the types of citizenship that U.S. males and females secure are different.)

A short residency requirement and a foreign birth certificate is all that is required for an unwed U.S. mother to secure naturalized U.S. citizenship for her offspring under 8 USC 1409(c). However, according to the 8 USC 1409(a), an unwed father's name on a Vietnamese birth certificate is lawfully insufficient for him to confer U.S. citizenship. As the Supreme Court noted: "Section 1409(a) thus imposes a set of requirements on the children of citizen fathers born abroad and out of wedlock to non-citizen mother(s) that are not imposed under like circumstances when the citizen parent is the mother." [232]

This is because 8 USC 1409(a) is a codification of natural law, under which Nature imposes the requirements upon the father – not Congress. Congress does not legislate over, but instead merely codifies, that which Nature dictates to Congress in the natural law jurisdiction.

In spite of the differences in how 8 USC 1409 treats U.S. men and women, which differences are based solely on gender, the Supreme Court upheld the "discriminatory means employed" by Congress as "consistent with the constitutional guarantee of equal protection." [233] In other words, the Court properly decided that this disparate legal arrangement did not violate U.S. male fathers' rights to equal protection.

The Court reasoned that Congress treats men differently because the father's relationship to the child is not as inherent, or as easily verified and documented as the mother's. [234] "To fail to acknowledge even our most basic biological differences," wrote the Court, "such as the fact that a mother must be present at birth but the father need not be—risks making the guarantee of equal protection superficial, and so disserving it." [235] This assertion is an unrecognized reference to natural law which says that women must always be present at their children's births – a natural fact.

These "most basic biological differences," [236] as discussed by the Court, are the natural law basis of citizenship. Under natural law, as codified at 8 USC 1409(a), U.S. males create natural born citizens by siring them, by establishing their paternal relationship with the children, and by promising to provide for their support during their minority, just as they would on a tribal level.

Because under natural law, U.S. females cannot create natural born citizens except by the will of males who impregnate them, then Congress' naturalization laws provide the means by which U.S. females may none-theless secure U.S. citizenship both out of wedlock and of their children from foreign fathers. This points out that U.S. females may create natu-ralized U.S. citizens throughout the world, but without the help of male U.S. citizen fathers, they cannot create natural born U.S. citizens anywhere.

Thus, what citizenship law reflects, but which the Nguyen Court does not acknowledge, is that the provisions of 1409(a), which relate to U.S. citizen males, explain how natural born citizens are created <u>by birth</u> in the state of Nature. In contrast, the provisions of 1409(c), which relate to U.S. citizen females, define how naturalized U.S. citizens are nonetheless creat-ed <u>at birth</u> under like circumstances – i.e., out of wedlock to a foreign mate.

8 USC 1409(a) codifies the natural process in the natural law jurisdiction by which male U.S. citizens naturally secure the natural born citizen-status of their children. In contrast, 1409(c) does not codify, but instead legislates the process of naturalization, which Congress was granted

power to establish at Article I, Section 8, Clause 4 of the U.S. constitution.

Even though Section 1409(a) is included in the Immigration and Naturalization Act of 1952, the provision is not at all about immigration or naturalization. Instead, it codifies what it takes for a U.S. father to secure a natural born citizen under natural law, absent the legal presumptions given to children born worldwide within marriages.

Because natural born citizens are created in the natural law jurisdiction and under the natural authority of male U.S. citizens (in contrast to naturalized citizens who are created by positive law), Congress cannot establish requirements for the creation of natural born citizens under 1409(a) that are inconsistent with the meaning of natural born citizen under law decreed by the natural sovereign.

In other words, as with the constitutionally-used words crime, offense, felony and misdemeanor, the citizenship of section 1409(a)-natural born citizens is not really subject to Congress at all. As we established above, this is because natural born citizens are born free of the U.S. government, in a separate and superior jurisdiction than positive law, regardless where they are born.

They are not subject to U.S. positive law because, as the Supreme Court in *Yick Wo v. Hopkins* (1886) told us, they are not the creations of positive law, as are naturalized citizens, but are instead the authors and source of positive law. [237] This is why Congress cannot legislate over them (and as far as I can tell, does not). However, Congress does occasionally legislate over citizens of the United States, who owe their U.S. citizenship and their political rights to Congress.

Section 1409(a) literally shows that for a child born outside of the U.S. and out of wedlock, Congress defers to the U.S. citizen father to determine the child's citizenship during the child's entire minority. This is because U.S. citizen fathers have plenary subject matter jurisdiction – the power to decide – over the citizenship status of their biological children, not the U.S. Congress.

That the 2001 members of the U.S. Supreme Court did not understand this, and were unaware of the natural law basis of citizenship, is evident in the oral arguments of *Nguyen v. INS* (2001), available online at Oyez / Scholars. [238] There the justices groped for justifications why Congress places greater requirements upon men to establish U.S. citizenship for their children than it requires of citizen mothers, which only knowledge of the meaning of natural born citizens and of the existence of the natural law jurisdiction in the

U.S. constitution explain.

I highly recommend that readers listen to these oral arguments. What you will find are brilliant, brilliant attorneys who lack an education in the natural law, and who are without understanding of the basis of natural born citizenship and 8 USC 1409(a). This means that it is their educations – and not their brilliant minds – that fail their analysis.

What these attorneys fail to realize is that citizenship is a subject matter jurisdiction issue within America's republics, and that U.S. citizen fathers are sovereign over the granting of natural born citizenship. In fact, Congress defers to the natural right of U.S. fathers to make citizens during the entire minority of their children's lives because U.S. fathers have primary jurisdiction over the citizenship of their children. When this substantive political right to confer natural born citizenship lapses at the age of majority, the positive law of Congress gains plenary subject matter jurisdiction to decide citizenship under its powers of naturalization.

By analogy, republican criminal courts defer to the subject matter jurisdiction of potential crime victims to exercise their natural right of self-defense in a responsible fashion before gaining jurisdiction over crime. Only if this natural right is exercised irresponsibly, or if an innocent person is victimized, is the criminal jurisdiction under natural law then conferred to a republic's judicial branch.

In America's republics, individual sovereigns have primary, subject matter jurisdiction over crime, just as U.S. citizen fathers have primary subject matter jurisdiction over the citizenship of their offspring. These facts of Nature are unknowable without recognition of natural law's role in criminal and citizenship law.

In the state of Nature, in their natural sovereignty, U.S. citizen fathers owe the U.S. government no duties and are not subject to legislative definitions. The U.S. constitution grants Congress the power to create laws regarding naturalization, but it does not grant Congress power to legislate over either the duty to create natural born citizens or how to create them, both issues of which are defined by natural law.

The U.S. male perhaps has a moral duty to make his children natural born citizens, i.e., to secure the greatest political rights in the world for them. Arguably also, because to be a natural born citizen is a natural right, U.S. fathers owe their children the legal duty to secure their natural born citizen-status. However, under no circumstance do U.S. fathers owe the U.S. government a positive law duty to secure such citizenship. This is because

U.S. citizen fathers have plenary subject matter jurisdiction over their children's citizenship and because Congress may not – and does not – legislate inconsistently with fathers' natural political authority.

At 8 USC 1409(a) Congress merely wrote down or codified the proximate criteria that natural law had already established for fathers to naturally secure their children's citizenship in their tribes or nations. This is another example that the natural and positive law jurisdictions are separate, opposite and opposed in America's constitutions, and that the positive law has no real force and effect within the subject matter jurisdiction of natural law, including how it defines crime and primary U.S. citizens.

Thus, the natural process of creating natural born citizens is defined by Nature and exists independently of America's republican legislatures. This is analogous to crime, which is proscribed by Nature and only pre-scribed by republican legislatures. Nonetheless, Congress was thoughtful enough to write down the process how to create citizens in Nature for attorneys, jurists and citizens who otherwise would not know this, or who would not recognize the grand political laws of Nature which operate with-in the U.S. constitution under one obscure, under-read, ignored, misunder-stood, seemingly inconsequential, and spit-on clause that mentions two kinds of U.S. citizens. [239]

8 USC 1409(a) reflects, in the state of Nature, outside the presumptions of positive law, that the natural political rights of natural born citizens are not necessarily created at birth, but instead at the point that U.S. fathers acknowledge and take responsibility for their offspring prior to their age of majority. The statute defines criteria how fathers establish paternity and accept responsibility for the U.S. citizens that they create with foreign women, out of wedlock in foreign countries.

U.S. males always create natural born citizens by their affirmative acts – because Nature requires it – which such natural process is codified for the state of Nature at 8 USC 1409(a). In contrast, naturalized citizenship is acquired through the U.S. mother (or from U.S. soil jurisdiction) at birth strictly as a matter of positive law, which is established by Congress in Section 1409(c) and 1401.

In contrast to the affirmative acts required by males to secure natural citizenship out of wedlock and outside of the U.S. under 8 USC 1409(a), a birth certificate which identifies the U.S. mother and / or a U.S. place of birth are sufficient to grant naturalized U.S. citizenship to a child under Congress' naturalization authority. A certificate is available from the United States government to authenticate this artificial citizenship. [240]

In contrast, a certificate is not available to authenticate one's natural born citizen status. Only a U.S. father's marriage to a child's mother or the fulfillment of requirements at 8 USC 1409(a) can authenticate such status. That is, only the law jurisdiction of an Article III court – which enforces natural law – can authenticate one's natural born citizen status.

Given all of this, one who argues that his U.S. citizenship is based on his mother's nationality or on his place of birth is making an argument as a (naturalized) citizen of the United States – not as a natural born citizen. Likewise, to argue that one's place of birth or one's mother are the exclusive reasons why one is eligible to be U.S. President is to make the argument that one is not eligible to be U.S. President.

It is understandable that a naturalized (naturally foreign) citizen would not know the attributes of natural born citizens, but it defies logic that natural born citizens would not know. (As a natural born citizen, I admit to not knowing this information until around 2013, when it was taught to me by Paul Guthrie.) [241] The reasons that citizens have not known this information is 1) because few people presently know it, and 2) because it does not serve the non-republic that runs the United States to teach this to us, or to even Supreme Court justices. Or maybe especially such justices.

Non-republics by definition are antithetical to natural law. By their nature, they treat everyone as subjects by defining their political rights. But natural born citizens are not born subject to a political sovereign, but instead are born free of owing political duties to Congress. However, they must wake up to this realization, or risk thinking of themselves as naturalized citizens, whose rights are defined by Congress.

That 8 USC 1409(a) codifies the natural process of creating natural born citizens is evidenced by the fact that natural born citizens were created under the natural law jurisdiction of the U.S. constitution immediately after the constitution went into effect. U.S. citizen fathers constitutionally did not require an act by Congress, such as the 1802 and 1952 immigration and naturalization acts, to establish the means of granting natural born citizenship.

The means of passing-on citizenship were already established by Nature, as secured by the U.S. constitution, before Congress or any U.S. court had ever convened. In other words, 8 USC 1409(a) does not confer any rights or impose any duties that U.S. fathers did not already naturally have to secure the political rights of their children.

This would be analogous to the substantive rights of a hypothetical French fur trader in Indiana who was victimized by another inhabitant on the day after the state's constitution was ratified in 1816. This foreigner would have had a substantive right to his day in court even though the

Indiana legislature had not yet met to effectuate this right, e.g. to create the courts and pay for their operation. Therefore, the Indiana legislature did not create the foreigner's cause of action; the Indiana constitution did.

Similarly, just as the natural rights of life, liberty and the pursuit of happiness are secured at Article I, Section 1 of the Indiana constitution (1851), then the U.S. constitution at Article II, Section 1 – and not the act of Congress at 8 USC 1409(a) – secures the substantive right of U.S. males to create natural born citizens. This right comes from Nature, and is secured by the U.S. constitution. This right has been codified at 8 USC 1409(a), and is not subject to inconsistent legislation by the state or U.S. republics.

In other words, these means of creating natural law citizens (and of securing justice for the French fur trader) were already established by the natural law jurisdiction of the U.S. (and Indiana) constitutions prior to all acts of Congress and of the Indiana legislature, neither which have power to legislate inconsistently with Nature, the latter which defines citizenship, marriage, torts, crimes and injury as a basis for judicial jurisdiction. Just as crimes are merely prescribed by republican legislatures, and are not the creations of republican legislatures, the means of creating natural citizens were merely prescribed at 8 USC 1409(a), and are not creations of Congress.

Congress was granted constitutional power to establish rules for adopting or naturalizing foreign citizens, but not the power to legislate in any way over natural born citizens, including their definition and how they are created. (This is likely why I have never seen duties imposed upon natural born citizens by a U.S. statute.)

Natural born citizens are those citizens created in Nature – not under the positive law of government. They are both natural persons and natural citizens whose political rights are defined by Nature, are adjudicated in the law jurisdiction, and are not subject to positive law that is inconsistent with natural political law.

In fact, if Congress gets its codification process wrong, such as by defining a completely wrong procedure to create a natural born citizen that is inconsistent with natural law, or by codifying a "crime" that is not a crime under natural law, or by enacting a statute that says that foreigners may be excluded from U.S. courts for torts done to them, then the judiciary is presumed to know the U.S. constitution sufficiently enough to prevent these types of legislative overreaching. All of the above government actions would be violations of natural persons' substantive rights, which would violate America's constitutions.

This is to say that if judges knew the U.S. constitution, its natural law jurisdiction and substantive rights well enough, they would not need statutes to codify crimes, or to codify how to make natural born citizens under 8 USC 1409(a), or to codify the right of foreign citizens to a judicial remedy for harm done to them while in the U.S., as under 28 USC 1251(b)(1).

These substantive rights are each attributes of natural law as secured by America's constitutions. They are each secured by American constitutions – not American legislatures. They each existed prior to any of Congress' enactments and codifications, and are each subject matter over which Congress has no real authority to legislate – only to write down.

Because the rights of foreigners to a judicial remedy for a tort is codified at 28 USC 1251(b)(1), federal judges need not know that such right of action for injured foreigners is a substantive right at law based on their natural personage. Because of this statute, judges need not know that the power of the law jurisdiction applies only to natural persons and to all natural persons equally, and that all torts are violations of natural law.

As well, judges need not know that the natural law jurisdiction exists in the U.S. constitution, that natural rights are adjudicated in the law jurisdiction, or that foreigners have natural rights not to be harmed, just as do Americans. This is because the redundant statute sufficiently tells federal judges all they need to know, i.e., that a foreigner has standing in a judicial court for physical harm done by another person.

Thus, it is not required of judges to know the natural law basis of the U.S. constitution, or to go through the analysis that I did in order to learn it, or to know that certain rights of foreigners are on equal footing with those of U.S. citizens, but others are not, or that citizens and aliens operate under separate sovereigns, etc., in order to adjudicate a tort case initiated by a foreigner. Instead, federal judges can merely read the above statute, which tells them about foreigners' right at law and the courts' authority to adjudicate it.

No understanding of the U.S. constitution is required to fulfill the statute or to adjudicate such torts. Torts and crimes were adjudicated long before the U.S. constitution was ever even conceived. Knowledge of the former does not necessarily require knowledge of the latter.

Likewise, it was not necessary for U.S. judges to realize that 8 USC 1409(a), which defines what U.S. fathers must do to secure their children's U.S. citizenship out of wedlock to foreign mothers in foreign countries, codifies the creation of natural born citizens. A judge can determine whether a U.S. citizen father meets the criteria of 8 USC 1409(a) while being totally oblivious to natural law, as was the Supreme Court in *Nguyen v. INS* (2001) when it correctly upheld the constitutionality of the statute.

Thus, to adjudicate a tort involving a foreigner or to determine whether someone born outside the U.S. is a U.S. citizen according to statute, judges need not know much if anything about the U.S. constitution, about its natural law basis or about natural citizenship. They need not consider natural law in any manner. They can merely follow statutes, such as those discussed above, and can even believe (albeit incorrectly) that all their authority over torts and citizenship derive from these statutes.

We now know better: to wit that these statutes merely codify what is already substantive law as dictated by Nature in the natural law jurisdiction, over which Congress and state legislatures may not inconsistently legislate.

In contrast, it is not so easy for judges to adjudicate crimes or the eligibility requirements for Presidents because judges must actually know the natural law basis of the U.S. constitution and the meaning of crime and natural born citizen under natural law to correctly do their jobs. This is 1) because our constitutions do not expressly define the terms crime or natural born citizen, 2) because Congress has not definitively codified the meaning of crime or natural born citizen (or scarcely ever mentioned natural born citizens, over which Congress may not legislate), and 3) because, as we will extensively see in part 2 of this book, Congress and state legislatures cannot be relied upon – indeed trusted – to prescribe and codify crime and natural born citizen openly, forthrightly and consistently with their meanings under natural law and in the U.S. constitution. Heretofore, it would be difficult for Congress to do the latter, given that its members do not yet know or recognize that natural law is the basis of crime and natural born citizenship, as those terms are referred to in the U.S. Constitution.

This is to say that, unless the terms crime and natural born citizen are also codified consistently with their substantive constitutional meanings under natural law, then judges <u>must</u> know the inherent natural meanings of crime and natural born citizen in order to both 1) secure their own *de jure* relationship to the People, and 2) to provide substantive justice, which in most drug matters and in all natural born citizen matters they have not.

Because legislatures do not always act consistently with constitutions, then judges and adversarial parties must know applicable constitutions well enough to know the legitimacy of each statute. For example, if Congress defined 1409(a)-citizens inconsistently with natural law, which it did not, then a competent judge who is knowledgeable of natural law would see this inconsistency and act to prevent the provision's enforcement.

Or, for example, if the Indiana legislature misrepresents false "crimes" as real crimes, as it does in many sections of the Indiana Controlled Substances Act at IC 35-48-4, then competent Indiana defense attorneys and judges would recognize this, and stop the false enforcement of the phony

"criminal" provisions in these sections, over which the courts have no jurisdiction.

Thus, in at least all criminal cases and in all presidential eligibility
cases, judges must know the natural law basis and definitions of crime and
natural born citizen in order to render proper jurisprudence, which is the
science of law. In other words, judges must know the correct <u>natural</u>
definition and authority for crimes and natural born citizens to render
proper natural science in the law jurisdiction. Science cannot be rendered
using false and artificial definitions of natural things, such as crimes,
marriage and natural born citizens.

> The U.S. Supreme Court's validation of gay "marriage" in *Obergefell
> v. Hodges* (2015) [242] does not change U.S. citizenship law. For
> purposes of bestowing natural born citizen-status, 1) a child has only
> one biological father and 2) only such real father can be the source of
> the child's natural political status and rights. Without such a
> certified-biological U.S. citizen father, a child in a gay "marriage" can
> be at most a (naturalized) citizen of the United States. Thus without
> changing the U.S. constitution, neither a non-biological father nor
> two women in a "marriage" can secure their children's natural
> political right to run for U.S. President. Based on the Court's false
> decision, Congress must act to secure the natural rights of biological
> U.S. citizen fathers in or with regard to gay "marriages."

Whether one commits a crime, whether one is married or whether
one is a natural born citizen are facts of Nature to be adjudicated using
natural science. Judges are to apply rules for crimes, marriage and natural
born citizens according to what Nature dictates – and not what American
legislators and other non-republicans make up subjectively.

"Jurisprudence" that is not based on natural law is not a science, but
instead a religion. That the U.S. legal system now renders religion instead
of jurisprudence is the reason America suffers under not only a national
non-republic, due to its waging of the illegal war on drugs, but between
2009 and 2017, suffered under a naturally foreign non-republic.

Thus, it is essential for the judiciary to know the natural law basis of
the law jurisdiction in order to render substantial justice in all criminal,
marriage and presidential eligibility cases. Without such knowledge, judges
cannot know what separates real crimes from fake "crimes" or what
distinguishes natural born citizens from naturalized ones. Nor would they
know what a republic is, or how to secure it from being a foreign non-repub-

lic. At least, they haven't so far.

Without using objective definitions and criteria from Nature, judges could put non-criminals in jail for phony "crimes" and marry the un-marriable. Likewise, Supreme Court justices could swear-in naturalized U.S. citizens to be phony "Presidents."

Thus, to adequately adjudicate crime, marriage and citizenship matters, and to properly render oaths to all persons, judges must know what crimes, citizens, marriage and republics are under natural law. In contrast, if they do not know that natural law prevents America's republics from succumbing to non-republican rule, then logically they cannot give or take oaths to uphold the federal and state republics.

As we have seen, in the state of Nature – that is, out of wedlock, outside of the U.S., and with a foreign mother – Congress at 8 USC 1409(a) acknowledges a U.S. citizen-father's superior natural jurisdiction to create U.S. citizens, compared with its own. Congress literally waits eighteen years for U.S. fathers to exercise their substantive right to make natural born citizens before the right lapses, as happened with the authority of the father in *Nguyen v. INS* (2001). When the father does not sufficiently secure this status by his actions, then the Court looks to positive law to determine naturalized citizenship.

Because Nguyen was born to a Vietnamese mother under the soil jurisdiction of South Vietnam, then U.S. naturalization laws, which apply to U.S. mothers and to births on U.S. soil, did not apply to him. He was ordered to be deported as an alien because he was adjudicated as neither a U.S. citizen under 8 USC 1409(a), which is a natural born citizen, or as a naturalized U.S. citizen under 8 USC 1409(c) and 1401.

This is not to say that the Supreme Court in *Nguyen* (2001) recognized that the citizenship described at 8 USC 1409(a) is that of natural born citizens. As best as I can tell, Supreme Courts since the *Minor v. Happersett* (1875) decision have been unaware of the natural law basis of both the U.S. constitution and the term natural born citizen. Given this, in the case of Barack Obama, the justices on the U.S. Supreme Court were unable to discern an artificial fiction from a natural fact... an interloper from a real President. This stems from their lack of understanding of the meaning and natural origins of natural born citizens, and of the differences between such citizens and (adopted) citizens of the United States.

If the law be known to them, there are basically four key differences between these two types of citizens, whose discussion below summarizes some of this chapter's important information. These differences make them two separate classes of U.S. citizens. This means that the U.S. constitution establishes a political class system based on citizenship. In the next chapter we will discover why the nation's founders made it this way.

The first difference between natural born and naturalized citizens, which has been previously mentioned, regards the source or origin of their political rights. Natural born citizens gain their political rights under natural law from their U.S. citizen fathers. Naturalized U.S. citizens gain their political rights from positive law by grants from Congress.

The second difference is that natural born citizens exercise their political rights as natural rights. Natural born citizens have a natural right 1) to be in the United States, 2) to vote, 3) to run for the office of President, and 4) to have a natural born U.S. President. Male U.S. citizens also have the right to be the exclusive source U.S. Presidents.

Because these are natural rights, they cannot be alienated. For example, a natural born citizen may not be deported because he or she naturally belongs, and has a natural right to be, within the United States.

In contrast, naturalized U.S. citizens exercise legal rights established by positive law. They have enforceable positive law rights to live in this country, to vote and to have a natural born citizen President. These positive law rights are not derived naturally from their biological fathers, who are alien to the United States, but are instead artificially granted by the positive law authority of Congress. If naturalized citizenship is acquired by fraud, it may be revoked. Unlike natural born citizenship, it not unalienable.

Thus, naturalized U.S. citizens have no constitutionally-secured natural rights to be in this country, to vote, or to have a natural born U.S. President, as do natural born citizens. Their rights are nearly equal to those of natural born citizens, but theirs are legal rights that come from Congress, granted to them as artificial citizens. This is why they may not represent as President the natural political rights of natural born citizens.

The third difference is that only natural born citizens are eligible to be U.S. President. This is the main topic of the next chapter.

The fourth difference is a real shocker in its conceptual simplicity. [243] All natural born citizens have the DNA (deoxyribonucleic acid) of U.S. citizen fathers. All (naturalized) citizens of the United States have the DNA of foreign fathers.

Given that jurisprudence is the science of law, DNA is the law's best evidence of one's natural or naturalized citizen status. It makes one's citizenship objective and verifiable – based on natural science – just as criminal justice, with its basis in injury, is designed to be.

13
Why a natural born citizen clause?

The natural born citizen clause

By beautiful design, only natural born citizens may be U.S. President. To repeat, Article II, Section 1 of the U.S. constitution reads:

> "No Person except a natural born citizen, or a Citizen of the United States, at the time of the Adoption of the Constitution, shall be eligible to the Office of the President; neither shall any person be eligible to that Office who shall not have attained to the Age of thirty five Years, and been fourteen Years a Resident within the United States."

Other than the original adopted citizens of the United States such as George Washington and Benjamin Franklin, only U.S. citizens who gain their U.S. citizenship through natural law may become the U.S. President. As this chapter will show, this natural born citizen provision was made to ensure that the U.S. President is a natural law citizen of one of the United States, to ensure that the President is representative of natural citizens, and to avoid the imposition upon U.S. citizens of a government led by a person of foreign origin or of non-republican loyalties.

On its face, the natural born citizen provision (above) does not require a natural born citizen to be born "within the United States," but only to reside there at least fourteen years before becoming President. Thus, the irrelevancy of one's place of birth in creating a natural born citizen is self-evident from the U.S. constitution itself. A natural born citizen may be born outside of the United States, as was the 2008 presidential candidate John McCain, who was born to married U.S. citizen parents in Panama.

One's place of birth is irrelevant to whether one is a natural born citizen. (As we learned in the previous chapter, one's place of birth to an eligible U.S. citizen mother is irrelevant to naturalized citizenship.) "By the law of nature alone, children follow the condition of their fathers, and enter into all their rights (§ 212);" wrote Emmerich de Vattel. "The place of birth produces no change in this particular, and cannot, of itself, furnish any reason for taking from a child what nature has given him." [244]

Only natural born citizens who derive their citizenship naturally from U.S. citizen fathers, under the natural law jurisdiction of the U.S. constitution, which is applicable to U.S. citizen fathers everywhere on Earth, are entitled to occupy the office of U.S. President. To be eligible for the office of U.S. President is what singularly distinguishes natural born citizens from all other citizens and people in the entire world – foreign or domestic, commoners and kings alike. People around the world may become naturalized U.S. citizens, and they may gain the rights to vote and to have a natural born citizen President, but they may never be natural born citizens and eligible to be U.S. President.

This entitlement to pursue the leadership of the nation's government is a natural political right belonging only to natural born citizens, and is inherited only from U.S. citizen fathers. For natural born citizens, to have a natural born citizen President is also a natural political right.

As well, U.S. citizen fathers with children over thirty-five years of age have a natural right to be the sole source of U.S. Presidents. Violations to these natural political rights are enforceable in the law jurisdiction of judicial courts, just as are violations to one's other natural rights.

Because the U.S. constitution requires only natural born citizens to be President, it excludes from the office everyone who is foreign by nature and who is merely naturalized or adopted by the naturalization rules of Congress. Thus, the U.S. constitution serves to protect some inequality between natural and naturalized citizens.

Political inequalities were built into the U.S. constitution to prevent foreign monarchs from siring children to U.S. females or from having their children born in the United States so that these children may run for President. If foreigners, such as foreign monarchs, could create natural born citizens (of the United States) merely by causing their babies to be born within U.S. boundaries, then these monarchies could officially take over the U.S. republic, instead of just unofficially.

By defining the qualification of the office of President to be under natural law, under which citizenship is passed to sons and daughters from their citizen fathers, the founders of this country made use of a brilliant system to prevent foreign citizens and monarchies – the latter which claim to be above natural law – from infiltrating our republican form of government and from occupying the People's house.

Thus, to install a naturalized citizen as "President" 1) is to violate the natural political rights of all natural born citizens to have a representative government, 2) is to violate the natural right of U.S. citizen males (with children over thirty-five years of age) to be the sole source of U.S. Presidents, and 3) is to grant an unauthorized artificial privilege, or title of nobility, for a naturalized citizen to occupy the office.

This artificial privilege, which lacks objective natural criteria – such as DNA from a U.S. citizen father – and is itself an artificial claim – renders the government to be a non-republic – just as does one whose judicial system treats a subjective "crime" as a crime. That is, America's republics fail when their jurisprudence lapses into religion, and when it fails to enforce natural law – and its natural criteria – with regard to crime, citizenship and natural political representation.

Using natural criteria, the U.S. non-republic that operates in the federal areas can always be held in check by a natural representative of state citizens. In this manner, foreign artificial kings would always be required to look eye-to-eye with a true representative of the world's natural, most powerful and preeminent sovereign citizens.

Thus, that natural born citizens are allowed to be President – to the exclusion of citizens and subjects of foreign countries who have been naturalized – is to ensure the natural law authority of America's constitutions and the absence of a monarchy. It also ensures the natural political order, i.e., that the authority for government is passed from one natural citizen of the nation to another, and that America's republics will be representative of the country's natural sovereign citizens.

This protection from a foreign authority running the U.S. government would not be possible without basing the eligibility requirements for President on natural law, which emasculates the artificial positive law claims of monarchs that operate in defiance of Nature. Congress' granting of artificial positive law citizenship, i.e., naturalized citizenship, does not change the constitutional principle of defining one's eligibility to be President under natural law, over which Congress and Article III courts have no authority to be inconsistent.

Congress may regulate foreigners in equity, but must define cases, crimes, marriage and natural born citizenship according to natural law. Likewise, Congress has plenary authority over naturalization, but must bow to the natural law authority of U.S. citizen fathers, who have plenary authority over the making of natural born citizens and all U.S. Presidents.

As we have seen, Congress legislates consistently with the true meaning of natural born citizens. However, either out of ignorance, arrogance or cowardice, both Congress and the courts have refused to enforce the U.S. constitution against the nation's past phony "President."

To allow a naturalized citizen the authority to lead a nation of natural born citizens is to defy natural law; is to violate the natural born citizen provision, [245] the Title of Nobility clause [246] and the 1st Amendment of the U.S. constitution; and is to undermine the natural law basis of the U.S. constitution. It is to install a government whose natural political authority is foreign to the government of natural citizens. This and the war on drugs can only occur in a government that fails or refuses to acknowledge the role of natural law, which makes it non-republican.

The making of monarchs and the war on drugs

Whereas the authority to be a natural born citizen and to be a U.S. President is based on Nature, and is naturally verifiable, the authority for a monarch is based on his or her artificial claim of a divine right to lead, which claim is not verifiable. Whereas the authority for the U.S. constitution is natural, i.e., derived from the collective natural delegated authority of sovereign individuals, and whereas the authority to be the U.S. President comes naturally from one's U.S. citizen father, a divine right claim of a monarch is a title of nobility based on that which is supernatural, i.e., that a supernatural God ordained one man, woman or legislature to rule others in defiance of natural law. To authenticate this claim of divine right, monarchies are frequently accompanied by state religion.

State religion is prohibited by the 1st Amendment to the U.S. constitution in order to prevent such a supernatural basis for the government, and to secure the law's natural basis. America's republican governments are based on Nature. Their justice is based on natural science. Republics are not based on a supernatural god that hand picked one person or handfuls of people to rule over the natural sovereignty of others.

Thus, America's republican governments are not based on divine authority, as are monarchies. As we have seen, American governments are based on the natural moral authority that the People collectively delegate to government, based on what they naturally have or do not have to delegate as individuals. Only a king or dictator would claim to have such power that natural people cannot delegate, such as the power to violate other people's unalienable natural rights. Ironically, this is really the only right or power that U.S. citizens do not morally have and thus cannot delegate.

Because it is not natural for one person to rule others, it is only a subjective belief in the supernatural upon which the legitimacy of a monarchy or non-republic is based. Only a monarchy that gains its authority from the will of a supernatural god could claim such false and perverse authority to violate natural law. Monarchies' basis in supernatural gods is antithetical to the republican form of government based on natural law.

A government based on natural authority cannot and would not violate natural law. As we will see, that Indiana and the U.S. officials routinely violate natural law is primarily due to their not knowing that most American constitutions are based on the People's natural moral and political authority.

Likewise, because it is not natural for one person to rule others, the *malum prohibita* of a king or legislature is ineffectual and unenforceable in the criminal law jurisdiction of republican judicial courts, where only natural duties are imposed. This law jurisdiction was established to apply a natural, objective and scientific process to discern truth and render justice. It was not created to be a pawn to political legislatures or kings.

The jurisprudence of the law jurisdiction is to be a science. As a science it is to ascertain principles upon which legal rules are based and to apply them to relevant circumstances. "Jurisprudence is more a formal than a material science," says *Black's Law Dictionary*. [247] *Jurisprudentia legis communis anglae est scientia socialis et copiosa*, says a common law maxim. *The jurisprudence of the common law of England is a science social and comprehensive.*

As a science, jurisprudence operates upon the objectivity of Nature, not the subjectivity of man or upon artificial criteria. As a science, "(i)t has no direct concern with questions of moral and political policy, for they fall under the province of ethics and legislation..." [248]

Thus, if judicial determinations are not based on Nature, such as the *Obergefell* (2015) decision on gay "marriage," [249] then they cannot be called jurisprudence. If they are not based on objective and natural criteria, then their basis is the supernatural.

Trying to treat drug dealing as a crime is a case in point. To think such matters are judicial is to not understand the criminal subject matter jurisdiction of republican judicial courts, which is over injury. It is for a judge to religiously view his or her delegated power as super human, and to view subject matter jurisdiction subjectively – not objectively.

Likewise, the claim of a naturalized U.S. citizen to be "President" is, by definition, supernatural and subjective. Such a citizen would have no natural – indeed verifiable – claim to the office of President, as would a natural born citizen. To make such an adopted U.S. citizen the U.S. President is to create a *supernatural born citizen*, which is a monarch or a messiah.

The substantive political rights of natural born citizens

Just as all torts and crimes in the law jurisdiction involve violations of natural rights, the occupation of the office of the President by a naturalized U.S. citizen would be a violation of natural born citizens' natural political right to be led by a natural born citizen President. It is to also rob natural born citizens of a republican form of government, which we saw in chapter 3 is a natural right.

To occupy the White House as a naturalized citizen is to exercise a *de facto* privilege, and to not exercise a *de jure* natural right of natural born citizens. Such a privilege is a title of nobility that is prohibited by the U.S. and state constitutions. [250]

This usurpation would amount to an injury 1) to the natural political right of natural born citizen candidates – as a class – to be President, 2) to the natural political right of all natural born citizens – as a class – to have a fellow natural born President, 3) to the positive law political right of all naturalized citizens – as a class – to have a natural born President, and 4) to the natural political right of all U.S. male citizens with children older than thirty-five years of age – as a class – to be the sole source and authority for U.S. Presidents within the nation. In other words, having a naturalized "President" violates – in one way or another – the natural and positive law political rights of ALL U.S. citizens, for which each citizen has a cause or causes of action.

For a foreigner to seek a judicial remedy for injury to his person and property, and for a natural born citizen to seek a judicial remedy for injury to his natural political rights, are both examples of exercising the substantive judicial right to be compensated for injury to a natural right, as guaranteed by the U.S. and Indiana constitutions in the law jurisdiction of judicial courts. The law jurisdiction adjudicates injury to natural rights, including natural born citizens' natural political rights. As well, the law jurisdiction serves to secure U.S. citizen fathers' substantive right to be the sole source of all U.S. Presidents.

If the above civil injuries are severe enough, a republican government steps in and prosecutes the action as a crime. This is because crime in the law jurisdiction of America's republics is always a violation of someone's natural rights, including their natural political rights.

For example, the occupation of the office of President by a naturalized U.S. citizen would be not only a private civil wrong to the rights of U.S. citizens, which is actionable in a judicial court. The false occupation might also amount to several real crimes, such as fraud and sedition that, as public wrongs, are to be criminally enforced in a republic's law jurisdiction. In any event, both in its civil and criminal capacities, the law jurisdiction has authority only to adjudicate violations of natural rights, including the natural political rights of natural born citizens and U.S. citizen fathers.

Only if we secure the natural authority of the U.S. constitution in the law jurisdiction of judicial courts can we secure people's rights from arbitrary rule, whether this arbitrariness is the installation of a naturalized citizen "President" or the false use of the judicial branch to enforce phony drug "crimes."

In chapter 5 we learned that arbitrariness is the mark of a substantive due process violation. It was arbitrary and an affront to the rights of natural born citizens to have installed a unrepresentative "President" who is not natural born.

If America's judiciary did its fundamental job to secure the natural law basis of the law jurisdiction, then the U.S. could not entertain either an illicit war on drugs or a false occupation of the White House. The failure of America's judiciary to know the law, with its natural law basis, and to do its job is the cause-in-fact of America's illegal non-republic. The bloodied head of the republic lies at the judiciary's feet.

The only check upon the power of false positive law authority is the natural law jurisdiction, as secured in the law jurisdiction of our courts. Only the enforcement of natural law and the protection of our natural rights in the law jurisdiction separate America's governments from their monarchical predecessors. Only with knowledge of natural law can the nation's republics be secured. In the absence of such knowledge, the principles of America's republics have been forgotten and suspended.

If monarchies respected people's natural rights and upheld natural law, there would be nothing unnatural or dictatorial about them. They would not be monarchs because they would operate only upon those entities subject to positive law, which would exclude natural persons. They would share power, or design useful political systems to share power, as the nation's Founding Fathers did.

However, America's current state and federal *de facto* non-republics do not respect natural rights nor uphold natural law, but instead depend on the People not knowing what crimes and natural born citizens are. America's *de facto* non-republics depend on the People not knowing natural law and their natural selves sufficiently enough to secure their natural political rights. To be divorced from our natural rights is to be divorced from our human nature. It is inherently neurotic because it is to ignore that which is natural and self-evident.

We know that the natural law jurisdiction of America's constitutions and the law jurisdiction of judicial courts still exist because American constitutions have not relevantly been changed to eliminate them and, as we shall see in part 2 of this book, because statutory law reflects and secures the natural law. However, the role and function of the Laws of Nature in judicial jurisprudence have been nearly, if not completely, wiped out. Because no one of authority (except statute writers) have known the natural law basis of the U.S. constitution, let alone of jurisprudence, then no one has been able to secure the nation from an unnatural, foreign non-republic.

Natural law, and its meanings of crime and natural born citizens, define the U.S. republic and judges' authority under it. Without a natural born citizen President, Congress ceases to be capable of legislating because no one is authorized to sign its acts into law. Without a natural born citizen President, there are no presidential appointments, and there are no Supreme Court majorities upholding Obamacare and gay "marriage."

During the Obama administration, these courts lacked natural authority delegated from natural born citizens, who consent only to a natural political order where a natural born citizen leads the nation. This means that "Article III" courts were operating without U.S. citizens' consent authority, which means outside of the U.S. constitution.

This knowledge presents a marvelous opportunity for criminal defense attorneys to move to dismiss all faux "criminal" cases in faux "republican" courts between January, 2009 and January, 2017, based on their lack of subject matter jurisdiction and *de jure* authority. Without a natural born citizen President, and without the existence of the U.S. republic, so-called Article III courts have had no source of republican authority. They have had no authority to render judgments until the republic was restored.

At least, that is what Article II, Section 1 of the U.S. constitution stands for. It says that the U.S. President must be a natural born citizen. It is unequivocal. The clause means that the U.S. republic, which exists for all U.S. citizens, ceases to exist without a natural born citizen President. This means that the union of the several states was constitutionally suspended and that the United States had unwittingly been in a major constitutional crisis.

Of course, one would not know this without recognition of the natural law basis of the U.S. constitution and without knowing the meaning of a natural born citizen which, given that officials have taken oaths to America's constitutions, they have a duty to know. Thus, the crisis is not necessarily that officials installed a non-President into the office of President, but that they are blind to and operate outside the limitations imposed upon them by natural law. Their phony "President," their man-made "marriages," and their war on non-crimes are just symptoms of their fall into the worship of Man's artificial, subjective and arbitrary authority.

The nation is also in an identity crisis. Neither U.S. citizens nor their officials, including their judicial officers and their "Presidents," know what citizens are. Needless to say, the union was already in peril when its leading officials forgot the natural law basis of crime, and started jailing merely disfavored people instead of real criminals.

That the U.S. republic ceased to exist under the leadership of a natural born foreign "President" is a logical imperative whose only defense is religious fanaticism. As I wrote earlier, attorneys in the criminal justice system either practice law, which uses science to adjudicate rights, or they practice religion, which is subjective and assumes the supernatural.

Criminal law and citizenship law in the republican form of government have a natural objective basis, respectively based on injury and the existence of certain DNA. Religious zealousness does not.

Only by restoring natural law and jurisprudence to the judicial branch, which would include restoring the U.S. presidency forever to natural born citizens, can we restore the U.S. government and state governments to their proper republican form. It is the avoidance of natural law in judicial courts today that defines our federal and state governments as foreign to natural born citizens in both form and substance.

In most of the nation's fifty-plus years of prosecuting phony drug "crimes" as crimes, the courts in the U.S. have been *de jure* courts that have acted illegally. In the case of having an alien "President," the courts not only still acted illegally in drug matters, but were themselves unlawful. Because they were representative of the natural authority of foreign fathers – instead of U.S. fathers who were to be the source of all U.S. Presidents – they were not *de jure* courts of U.S. fathers' government.

Without a natural born citizen President, the United States is not a government of the People, i.e., natural born citizens, but a government of and by naturally foreign people. Without a natural born citizen President, the U.S. government places the artificial legal rights of artificial positive law citizens above the natural political rights of natural born citizens. This is to stab natural born citizens in the back on the steps of their courthouses.

This puts positive law above natural law, the latter which is the People's only check upon positive law. Such obscene violations can happen only in a government that is void and ignorant of natural law, that is operating outside of the U.S. constitution, that has lost nearly all historical perspective, that lied through its broad smile, and that could no longer be, by definition, the U.S. republic. The U.S. government was a sham of its former greatness. It has been a fraud to all U.S. citizens and to the world.

But whether the courts in the U.S. <u>were</u> illegal (as in the case of a naturalized "President") or just <u>act</u> illegally (as in the case of the war on drugs), they work for a *de facto* non-republic for the very same simple reason. This reason is that America's judges do not recognize the natural law jurisdiction of our constitutions (because it was not taught to them), and thus do not understand the natural source and meaning of either crimes or natural born citizens.

Without use of objective and natural standards for crime and natural citizenship, the courts are incapable of jurisprudence and of securing our natural rights. These include our natural right to a republican form of government, which is the same thing as the natural right not to be born subject to someone else's arbitrariness, as Americans have been.

Only a constitutional amendment would change the intended *de jure* relationship between natural born citizens and their natural birthright to a representative government led by a fellow natural born President. Likewise, only a constitutional amendment could change the meaning of crime as used in the U.S. and Indiana constitutions to include non-torts and non-crimes. That neither such constitutional amendments exists shows that the U.S. government has been acting outside its *de jure* republican authority.

To legitimately remove the natural law jurisdiction of our constitutions by amendment would be to leave only the positive law of a non-republican legislature. However, to forget or to ignore that this natural law jurisdiction exists produces the same kind of rotten and intolerable government, i.e., a *de facto* non-republic that burdens Americans today.

Thus, only judges' knowledge of and respect for natural law and its law jurisdiction in judicial courts secures Americans from a rotten government. Judges' ignorance of and lack of respect for natural law, as well as the natural subject matter jurisdiction of their republican judicial courts over injury, is the proximate cause of the war on drugs as well as the former illegal occupation of the U.S. government.

America had not only a *de facto* non-republic that is running its show, including its despicable war on drugs, but was an actual foreign one to boot. By forgetting the natural law basis of crime and citizenship, America's prosecutors, judges and defense attorneys have not only lost their way, but have lost natural born citizens' unique and precious republican form of representative government.

I am not saying that these people (and other attorneys like me) are to blame, but we are certainly responsible. That this book puts all attorneys on notice of our oversights now requires us to conform our practices to republican standards, to which we have all taken oaths.

In the United States the only legitimate governments that remain in tact are our own self-governments in the natural law jurisdiction. However, even these sovereigns are unstable because very few of us know the scope of our own constitutional authority.

For example, very few Americans know what natural born citizens are. Those that do, or those that at least have a hunch, get outvoted by authoritarians who do not. Because such authoritarians do not even know what their citizenship means, then they can hardly be qualified to vote (let alone be "President").

As long as the law jurisdiction of judicial courts has been invaded and usurped by non-republicans, as long as the courts are used to punish political opponents, and when the government is unrepresentative of natural citizens, then there exists no actual judicial jurisdiction to secure the natural rights of sovereign natural persons, as well as the natural political rights of natural born citizens. Without a natural born citizen President, people's rights under the suspended U.S. republic did not exist. The rule of law had been overtaken by the law of the rulers. Article III courts lawlessly exercised the same non-republican power as Article I courts.

Historically, the income tax, the creation of the Federal Reserve, the direct election of U.S. Senators, and the nation's going off the gold standard have diluted the strength of America's republican form of government. However the drug war and the former naturalized U.S. "President" are the most salient examples that America's republics have become *de facto* non-republics. Few things define the American non-republics quite as well as 1) their fraudulent misuse of republican power to incarcerate disfavored citizens by converting them into subjects, and 2) the title of nobility bestowed upon an artificial, positive law citizen to occupy an office strictly reserved for natural U.S. citizens.

In the first instance, non-republicans have overtaken the judicial branch of America's republics. On the other hand, the occupation of the White House by a naturalized "President" suspended the operation of the U.S. republic. To have allowed the war on drugs for nearly fifty years (and the war on other vice for even longer), and to allow a natural born alien to occupy the U.S. presidency, is for the judiciary to not understand the natural law meaning of crime, of natural born citizens and of a republican form of government upon which their entire legitimacy as judges is based.

It is a crime for a naturalized U.S. citizen to occupy the office of the

U.S. President, as it is a crime to misuse the criminal authority of the judicial branch in the war against drugs. The latter is to create a non-republic and to commit crime by denying natural law in the criminal law jurisdiction. The former is to void the republican government of the People during its foreign occupation.

For criminal defense attorneys, particularly defense attorneys in U.S. courts between 2009 and 2017, grounds for motions to dismiss are ripe. These grounds are: 1) that neither state republican nor Article III courts have subject matter jurisdiction over drug possession and commerce, the latter which is subject to regulation, and 2) that such republican courts did not actually exist under a non-republican form of government, as led by a naturalized citizen. Legitimate American governments that had been suspended during this period could not sustain legitimate trials of any kind.

However, the irony of all this is that – with or without a natural born citizen President – Article III courts and state judicial courts have never had subject matter jurisdiction over drug commerce, which is instead subject to U.S. and state regulators in equity. As well, they have criminal authority only over respective federal-enumerated and state crimes, which do not include drug commerce.

Thus, that the U.S. republic was suspended for eight years because of a false presidency does not affect the illegality of using Article III and state judicial courts to wage America's drug war during the prior forty. Both constitutional perversions are grounds for dismissal of all drug "cases" in Article III and state judicial courts, based on the lack of *de jure* power.

Educational malpractice

Particularly in the previous chapter, we saw that children born in the United States to foreign parents become (naturalized) citizens of the United States at birth. Because these children's fathers are foreign, the children are naturally foreign by birth.

By birth, these children are natural born citizens or citizen-subjects of their fathers' countries. Because their fathers are foreign, the children are not natural born citizens (of the United States). As we have seen, the constitutional term citizen of the United States always denotes an offspring of an alien or non-citizen father. This is objectively verifiable through DNA.

Given this, the falsity of the following information posted by the Legal Information Institute of Cornell University Law School is readily apparent. This information – which is posted on two different webpages – was found after doing a search on the website for natural born citizen. This false information is typical of the bad information provided by American law schools on a variety of subjects. Perhaps the Cornell law school should rename its organization: the Legal Mis-Information Institute.

At http://www.law.cornell.edu/wex/example/%5Bfield_short_title-raw%5D_27, the Institute provides a fallacious example of a natural born citizen.

> "Natural born citizen example
>
> Bob's parents are British citizens. Bob is born in Hawaii and is subject to the jurisdiction of that state.
>
> Under 8 USC 1401(a) (2008), Bob acquires U.S. citizenship at birth. Therefore, Bob is a 'natural born citizen' of the United States."

Then at http://www.law.cornell.edu/wex/natural_born_citizen, the Institute writes:

> "Some debate exists as to the meaning of this phrase. Consensus exists that anyone born on U.S. soil is a "natural born citizen." One may also be a "natural born citizen" if, despite a birth on foreign soil, U.S. citizenship immediately passes from the person's parents."

This information will likely be removed as soon as someone at Cornell reads this book because the information is false, if not also fraudulent, i.e. intended to prop-up an illegitimate regime to the harm of the political rights of U.S. citizens. As the reader can see, the information is biased to justify the "presidency" of Barack Obama. Could the politicized nature of the Institute's presentation of law be any more obvious?

The above information is blatantly false. It only serves to diminish the natural political rights of natural born citizens, which is likely most of this book's readers. It does this by completely confusing and equating natural born citizens with citizens of the United States, and by claiming that two foreign parents can create natural born citizens "at birth" by having their children born on U.S. soil. It is this type of false information that reflects both a breakdown in logic and an ignorance of the law jurisdiction, both facts which secure America's *de facto* non-republics.

Cornell's false information reflects that the publisher 1) does not distinguish citizens of republics from subjects of monarchies, 2) does not know the differences between natural born citizens and (adopted) citizens of the United States, 3) does not recognize the two jurisdictions from which citizens arise, i.e., natural law and positive law, 4) does not recognize the role of the father in determining the political status of his offspring, and 5) does not realize that natural born citizens are defined and created in Nature – and verifiable by science – and thus not subject to "consensus" or religious opinion.

The information reflects that the teachers and products of American law schools do not know the meaning of their own citizenship, which I did not until 2013. [251] The information also suggests that teachers and students believe the sublimely ridiculous, i.e., that the nation's Founding Fathers secured the right of the King of England to have his children born on the soil of the United States so that they could grow up to be both a U.S. President and the King or Queen of England.

That is the logical (or illogical) consequence of these fairy tales put out by Cornell's law school, i.e., that foreign fathers can create natural born citizens by having their children born in Hawaii. Cornell's false statements about fundamental law accurately reflect the low state of legal education, of the criminal law practice and of jurisprudence in the United States, which are mostly the result of blindly ignoring the role of natural law in our republican form of government.

It also reflects the inadequacy of President George W. Bush who, as a natural born citizen, failed to vet his successor and to pass the torch to another natural born citizen. It is a pathetically sad day in a republic when its own President – and everyone being paid in the U.S. government – either does not even know what a natural born citizen is, or won't go to bat to secure the blessing of liberty for themselves and their Posterity.

So as to correct all false impressions that Cornell's two web pages now convey, they should be revised to read:

(Naturalized) citizen of the United States vs. natural born citizen example

Bob's parents are British subjects, also referred to as citizen-subjects. Bob, who was born in Hawaii and who has a Hawaiian birth certificate, acquired naturalized U.S. citizenship at birth under 8 USC 1401. Children born on U.S. soil to foreign parents, as was Bob, and children born to U.S. citizen mothers without U.S. citizen fathers, are naturalized at birth by the positive law authority of Congress. See 8 USC 1401 and 1409(c).

Therefore, Bob is a (naturalized) citizen of the United States, and is not a natural born citizen. The former denotes the offspring of alien, non-citizen fathers. The latter denotes the offspring of U.S. citizen fathers. Because the actions of U.S. citizen fathers are what secure the natural political rights of their offspring, and because the political rights of offspring follow those of the father, the citizenship of a person's mother or a person's place of birth are irrelevant to the person's natural born citizen status. The mother's nationality and the place of the child's birth are relevant only to naturalized citizenship.

This analysis that natural born citizens are the products of citizen fathers is supported by *Steinkauler's Case* (circa 1875), [252] cited by the U.S. Supreme Court in *Perkins v. Elg* (1939). [253] In *Steinkauler 's Case* before U.S. Attorney General Pierrepont, "Steinkauler, a Prussian subject by birth, emigrated to the United States in 1848, was naturalized in 1854, and in the following year had a son who was born in St. Louis." [254] Four years later the elder Steinkauler returned to Germany with his son and resumed his former allegiance to Weisbaden. Upon the age of majority, the son sought to secure his U.S. citizenship, which was upheld by the U.S. Attorney General. The Attorney General wrote:

> "Young Steinkauler is a native-born American citizen. There is no law of the United States under which his father or any other person can deprive him of his birthright. He can return to America at the age of twenty-one, and in due time, if the people elect, he can become President of the United States." [255]

In other words, because his father was a U.S. citizen, young Steinkauler was a natural born citizen. This inherited status is a birthright that is not subject to any "law of the United States." He could not only return to the U.S. to live, but also had an unalienable birthright to run for President.

"(N)o law of the United States... can deprive him of this birthright," wrote the Attorney General. This is 1) because natural born citizen status occurs by operation of natural law, which is not subject to inconsistent positive law, and 2) because, as we learned earlier, the bestowing of natural citizenship is within the plenary power of the citizen father, which in the *Steinkauler's Case* the father exercised as a naturalized U.S. citizen.

Further, the Attorney General explained what the last two chapters have sought to show, to wit that there are two kinds of U.S. citizenship – one that is acquired by positive law and the other that is "natural" and secured by U.S. citizen fathers as a birthright. As Attorney General Pierrepont explained:

> "Under the treaty, and in harmony with the American doctrine, it is clear that Steinkauler, the father, abandoned his naturalization in America and became a German subject (his son being yet a minor) and that, by virtue of German laws, the son acquired German nationality. It is equally clear that the son, by birth, has American nationality, and hence he has two nationalities, one natural, the other acquired." [256]

The son's "natural" nationality – his natural born citizen status – was that inherited from his naturalized U.S. citizen father "by birth," which is to say by Nature. The son's "acquired" nationality was that of naturalized German citizenship, which was granted by the German government, which is to say by positive law.

Thus, the son attained his natural born citizen status irrespective of U.S. or German legislation, which has no authority over natural law and the creation of natural law citizens. As 8 USC 1409(a) shows, Congress does not legislate over, but merely codifies what natural law requires fathers to do to secure their children's natural citizenship in the proverbial state of Nature, and respects U.S fathers' plenary authority to create natural citizens.

Because natural law defines all natural rights, and because to be a natural born citizen in a republic is a natural right, such citizenship is a fact of Nature. (This is analogous to Congress calling the right not to be enslaved by another person a "fact." [257] It is a fact of our human nature to not wish to be enslaved.) All natural born citizens, by Nature, share the DNA of their U.S. citizen fathers. All (naturalized) citizens of the United States, by Nature, share the DNA of their foreign fathers. These are verifiable facts of Nature.

This is analogous to crime as a fact of Nature. Crime is not a subjective concept in a republic, but is to be based on objective natural criteria, i.e., injury. To deny this fact, which America's judiciary does routinely, is to say that all rights are subjective, based upon an unprovable religion, i.e. that legislatures and courts can make anyone a criminal (or a President) by calling him or her a "criminal" (or "Mr. President"), irrespective of certain natural facts.

In conclusion, during these first dozen or so chapters, we have seen that both crimes and natural born citizens are not statutory constructs that are subject to legislative or judicial subjectivity, but are facts of Nature that are based on natural criteria. Whether one is a natural born citizen of an American republic or whether one commits a crime within an American republic are discernible, objective and verifiable natural facts, and are thus not subject to anyone's subjective or supernatural claims or to consensus.

In America's republics, both crime and one's natural born citizen status are defined by natural law, which is superior to any opposite, opposed or inconsistent positive law. Equally true is that *malum prohibita* is inapplicable to people's natural political rights in republics, as naturalization is inapplicable to the natural political rights of natural born citizens.

Both the right of all people within America's republics to not be enslaved except for the commission of *malum in se* crime, as well as the birthright of natural born citizens, are natural and unalienable. One cannot adequately adjudicate crime or the fact of natural born citizen status without consideration of natural law.

14

The strange unnatural concepts of slavery and Alcohol Prohibition

As we saw in previous chapters, mere drug possession and dealing do not amount to constitutional crimes, offenses, felonies, misdemeanors or even simple cases or controversies that are required to invoke the subject matter jurisdiction of judicial courts. Instead, drug possession and dealing are false representations of crime, which lack the required element of injury that is needed for standing and justiciability.

Since 1865 three main events have affected the criminal subject matter jurisdiction of judicial courts in America's republics that are relevant to our topic. The first event was the passage of the 13th Amendment to the U.S. constitution in 1865, which prohibited commercial slavery and indentured servitude throughout the U.S.

The second event was the passage of the 18th Amendment in 1919, which prohibited the commerce of alcohol, including its import and export into or out of the United States. The third main event was the enactment of the 21st Amendment, which repealed Alcohol Prohibition that was established under the 18th Amendment.

As we first mentioned in chapter 2, the 13th and 18th Amendments respectively removed the commerce of slaves and of alcohol from the equity jurisdiction of judicial courts and from the regulatory jurisdiction of executive agencies, and placed them into the criminal law jurisdiction of republican judicial courts. Conversely, the 21st Amendment removed the commerce of alcohol from the law jurisdiction and replaced it back under equity regulation.

We will address the prohibition of slavery and alcohol commerce in this chapter, and will compare the 18th Amendment with the Controlled Substances Act in the next.

Slavery and the 13th Amendment

The 13th Amendment abolished commercial slavery in the United

States and criminalized its practice. It was adopted as of December 6, 1865 after Georgia's ratification brought the number of ratifying states to 27 of 36 states. The 13th Amendment reads:

> "Section 1. Neither slavery nor involuntary servitude, except as a punishment for crime whereof the party shall have been duly convicted, shall exist within the United States, or any place subject to their jurisdiction.
>
> Section 2. Congress shall have power to enforce this article by appropriate legislation."

Regardless of the 13th Amendment, slavery had already been prohibited within Indiana's borders since the Northwest Territory of the United States was established. Section 1 of the 13th Amendment (above) is similar to Article 1, Section 37 of the Indiana constitution (1851), which reads:

> "There shall be neither slavery, nor involuntary servitude, within the State, otherwise than for the punishment of crimes, whereof the party shall have been duly convicted."

This provision reiterated what had already been the law in Indiana, as stated twice in the 1816 Indiana constitution. Its Article XI, Section 7 reads:

> "There shall be neither slavery nor involuntary servitude in this state, otherwise than for the punishment of crimes, whereof the party shall have been duly convicted. Nor shall any indenture of any negro or mulatto hereafter made, and executed out of the bounds of this state be of any validity within the state."

Thus, from the beginning of the state of Indiana, to enslave or indenture natural persons was a recognized crime that was subject to the criminal law jurisdiction of the state's judicial courts. It is their violation of natural law that makes slavery and indentured servitude crimes in Indiana, and therefore subject to the law jurisdiction.

The timelessness of Nature's prohibition against slavery, i.e., that people are not naturally born to be slaves, is reflected in Article VIII of the 1816 Indiana constitution. This provision emphatically says that the state's positive law could never be changed to allow such a natural abomination. It reads:

> "But, as the holding any part of the human Creation in slavery, or involuntary servitude, can only originate in usurpation and tyranny, no alteration of this constitution shall ever take place so as to introduce slavery or involuntary servitude in this State, otherwise than for the punishment of crimes, whereof the party shall have been duly convicted."

Conversely, it is because Southern state constitutions regulated slavery in equity and exempted slavery from the law jurisdiction of judicial courts that slavery was legal in the South. Because positive law denied natural law to slaves, slavery was taxed and regulated as commerce, and the rights to slaves were adjudicated in equity.

As we have steadily seen, equity is the jurisdiction of kingly privileges that have no natural basis. Only in the equity jurisdiction of southern states, or under Congress' plenary jurisdiction in the federal areas, could one's positive law privilege to violate natural law, for example to own other natural people, be recognized and secured.

The 13th Amendment was an amendment to the highest U.S. positive law, which effectively declared slavery and involuntary servitude to be *malum in se* under natural law, and expanded the criminal subject matter jurisdiction of judicial courts to include these true crimes against humanity.

The amendment also took slavery and indentured servitude out of judicial courts' equity jurisdiction, where disputes over commercial subject matter were adjudicated, and placed them into the courts' law jurisdiction, which is the jurisdiction over natural rights of natural persons. In the preamble to 22 USC 7101 where Congress bans human trafficking, Congress states "The right to be free from slavery and involuntary servitude is among those unalienable rights."

Because the 13th Amendment outlawed slavery in the equity jurisdiction where it once had been authorized, the amendment recognized slavery for what it naturally was, i.e., a crime. Because all crimes are also civil wrongs by or against natural persons, and because the 13th Amendment effectively acknowledged the natural personage in former slaves, the amendment also granted to former slaves all the substantive rights that belong to all natural people within the states.

Thus, the amendment placed former slaves under natural law, on par with other natural persons, and gave their natural rights substantive protection in the law jurisdiction. All of the substantive rights listed in chapter 2 were theoretically extended to them because they were free natural persons.

Of course the conquered southern states came to this requirement reluctantly, and did not readily extend the rights of natural persons or the political rights of state citizenship to former slaves. This necessitated the 14th Amendment. Consistent with the discussion about citizenship in the two previous chapters, the 14th Amendment naturalized former slaves as citizens of the United States. As newly created (naturalized) citizens of the United States, this granted black males the means to create natural born citizens under natural law.

> Given the significance of this to the concept of equality, it is historically unfortunate that the first black "President" was not a natural born descendant of an original 14th Amendment citizen. Instead, he is a descendant of men and women who never suffered the effects of American slavery, and of whom the 13th and 14th Amendment likely meant little. Shared history is one of the attributes of most natural born citizens, in which naturalized citizens do not necessarily share.

Knowing the above, it is now obvious that one cannot truly understand the legal nature of slavery and involuntary servitude without recognizing 1) the duality of natural and positive law, 2) the transition of former slaves from equity to law, and 3) the acquisition of political rights by former male slaves to create natural born citizens... or as the Preamble to the U.S. constitution says, to "secure the Blessings of Liberty" for themselves and their Posterity. As well, as we have seen, one cannot understand the meaning of crime without comprehending the law jurisdiction's relationship with natural law.

Congress' codification of the crime of human trafficking at 22 U.S.C. 7101 reflects this duality. As opposed to making up "crimes" or criminalizing false ones, this statute embodies the exact function of how legislatures are to exercise their limited criminal authority, i.e. to recognize and codify that which is already inherently evil and criminal.

As we previously discussed, this reflects the true meaning of the terms "prescribed by law," which essentially means to enact legislation that is consistent with a constitution. It is the job of American legislatures – not to make up "crimes" – but instead to codify and apportion punishment for *malum in se* that is already recognized in the law jurisdiction, such as is slavery and human trafficking. Republican legislatures cannot prohibit or make anything unlawful in the law jurisdiction, for which they codify crime.

The meaning of the 13th Amendment

With the above in mind, I would like to address several other aspects of the 13th Amendment and of Indiana's constitutional prohibitions against slavery and involuntary servitude that are relevant to our discussion. Each observation is based on the amendment's prohibition of slavery, "except as a punishment for crime whereof the party shall have been duly convicted..." [258]

First, what the above clause means is that the United States has <u>not</u> done away with slavery or made it completely illegal. There is both lawful slavery and unlawful slavery in the United States today. Unlawful slavery is that which we normally think of as commercial slavery, i.e., the use and sale of slaves, which violates natural law.

In contrast, lawful slavery is that which is performed by governments as punishment for crime (or for whatever Congress says is criminal in the federal areas). In America's republics, slavery is prohibited by the U.S. and state constitutions "except as a punishment for crime..." [259]

So, slavery is still lawful and still lawfully exists in the United States, but it is the exclusive province of America's governments. Slavery is rightful and righteous (as in the "right use" of republican governments) when it is in response to crime. Thus, slavery was not done away with by the 13th Amendment, but is merely monopolized by fifty-two rightful slavers. These are 1) the fifty states, 2) the U.S. republic which has criminal jurisdiction over crimes involving Congress' enumerated powers, and 3) the U.S. non-republic which has plenary criminal jurisdiction over the federal areas. Within America's republics the power to enslave is no longer a privilege accorded to artificial persons by the political sovereigns.

Second, as slavery is the exclusive province of government, the 13th Amendment makes the law jurisdiction of America's judicial systems the exclusive jurisdiction over slavery. Not only is the law jurisdiction that which secures the rights of freed natural persons by providing them civil remedies for others' wrongdoing, and by enforcing slavery as a crime, but it is the only jurisdiction where the state may rightfully enslave natural persons. The state may not rightfully enslave such persons in equity because equity has no jurisdiction over natural persons or their crimes.

The law jurisdiction, which has authority only over natural persons, has all of the courts' criminal jurisdiction and none of their commercial jurisdiction. This logically means that if one is merely operating in commerce, for example selling drugs to satisfied customers, one cannot be committing a crime that is subject to the law jurisdiction. At most, one can be violating a commercial duty, e.g., the duty to get a license to sell drugs, over which judicial courts have no power to primarily adjudicate.

Natural persons have only one mutual natural criminal duty, which is to not violate the equal rights of others. That is the main duty enforced in the law jurisdiction. Thus, criminal law courts may not impose commercial duties upon natural persons. State-imposed commercial duties do not apply to natural persons, who have few natural duties that the law jurisdiction may criminally enforce.

Third, given that readers now know what the meaning of crime is, the 13th Amendment stands for the truth that Indiana officials commit illegal slavery, i.e., commercial slavery that is a crime, when they enslave people who do not commit real crimes. This is logically undeniable.

Slavery is permitted by the People's government only in the law jurisdiction and only after it proves the commission of a crime, based on injury. Slavery and indentured servitude are legitimate and appropriate for people who commit real crimes and who are duly convicted.

Conversely, slavery and indentured servitude are illegitimate and inappropriate for people who do not commit real crimes, such as people who commit phony "crimes." Such *malum prohibita* applies only to commercial and foreign entities that government legitimately regulates, and is to be enforced by means of the executive branch of government, not criminally in the judicial branch.

If natural persons were criminally subject to *malum prohibita*, state officials could convert all of our natural rights into phony "crimes," misuse the law jurisdiction at will, and put people in jail for anything they want (which is what government officials have been doing to drug users for at least the past fifty years). This is also logically undeniable.

As we shall see in part 2 of this book, the Controlled Substances Act is skillfully written to be constitutional, yet to misrepresent the law to those who enforce it. Being fooled is the only legitimate reason (if there is one) why prosecutors have been bringing false "crimes," "offenses," "felonies," "misdemeanors," "cases" and infractions without standing into judicial courts, which have subject matter jurisdiction only over real cases.

Being fooled is the only legitimate reason why government officials have participated in the practice of illegal slavery, which accurately describes their war on drug users and distributors. Government officials may enslave people for real crimes, but they are no better than commercial slavers when they enslave people for something less.

Putting innocent people in jail for false "crimes" is a particularly obscene form of slavery in which Indiana's judicial system daily participates. It is uniquely obscene because legal professionals and officers of the courts do not even realize that putting non-criminals in jail is a perversion of U.S. law. This situation is truly intolerable given that the meaning of crime is fixed by the U.S. constitution and is comprehensible, and given that government officials have a duty to know it.

If the government can legally enslave people only for crime, and we all know now how America's constitutions secure crime's natural definition, then American constitutions – and not legislatures – define the limit of government's power to enslave people. That state officials incarcerate innocent people out of ignorance of how constitutions define crime, and in the name of righteousness, does nothing to change their character as unlawful slave masters (read: tortfeasors or criminals). Officials' immunity for their torts and crimes ends today, as officials become aware of the real law.

As we have seen, the executive and judicial branches enslave innocent people under false color of law by co-opting constitutional terms and by giving them false statutory meaning. This means that we have been taking government officials at their word and that they have been misrepresenting the meaning of constitutionally determined words in order to enslave the undesirable. Logically, the executive and judicial branches cannot participate in the perversion of false "crimes" without falsely enslaving or indenturing non-criminals.

By extending executive and judicial power to phony "crimes" of state legislatures, executive and judicial officials are acting outside the scope of their authority and operating as private slavers. This misuse of our judicial system amounts to a slavery racket for private gain, based on nothing but the color of the law that officials figuratively wear.

When the legislature tries to expand the constitutional conditions or terms under which people may be enslaved by misrepresenting false "crimes" as real crimes, and when the executive branch enforces criminal statutes as if the legislature did in fact expand the meaning of crime, which it may not, and when the judicial branch does not realize that its own subject matter jurisdiction under law is confined to personal or property injury, then anything including illegal slavery and a prison-industrial complex is not only possible but likely to happen in America's so-called free society, which the people in these branches singularly have perverted.

The final point that I would like to make about the 13th Amendment is that it does not appear to apply in the federal areas. Not only are the federal areas under the authority of Congress as a non-republic, which apparently can enslave anyone without the commission of real crime, but the 13th Amendment expressly applies only to the states. The amendment prohibits slavery "within the United States, or any place subject to their jurisdiction," where the United States refers specifically to the union of republican states. (Thus, one cannot properly read even the 13th Amendment without knowing about the U.S. republic and the U.S. non-republic.)

In summary, the 13th Amendment was essentially a judicial amendment that placed slavery into the criminal law jurisdiction of all republican judicial courts, where slavery belongs. It also placed former slaves into the law jurisdiction of southern states, where their rights were to be secured. It stands for the proposition that all of mankind is created equal and that there is a rightful place within government, called the law jurisdiction of judicial courts, where everyone's natural rights are to be honored, free from the positive law and prejudice of others.

Before the 13th Amendment, slavery operated in equity in the southern states merely as a regulated positive law privilege, just like selling other things. The amendment is an acknowledgment that natural law exists as an opposite and opposed jurisdiction to positive law, in that it extended to freed slaves the equal substantive rights and remedies that were already available to all other natural persons – domestic or foreign – in the law jurisdiction of America's judicial courts.

The 18th Amendment and Alcohol Prohibition

Whereas the 13th Amendment made criminal under positive law that which was already *malum in se* and against natural law, the 18th Amendment criminalized a commercial, regulated freedom – the commerce of alcohol. The 18th Amendment reads:

> "Section 1. After one year from the ratification of this article the manufacture, sale, or transportation of intoxicating liquors within, the importation thereof into, or the exportation thereof from the United States and all territory subject to the jurisdiction thereof for beverage purposes is hereby prohibited.
>
> Section 2. The Congress and the several states shall have concurrent power to enforce this article by appropriate legislation.
>
> Section 3. This article shall be inoperative unless it shall have been ratified as an amendment to the Constitution by the legislatures of the several states, as provided in the Constitution, within seven years from the date of the submission hereof to the states by the Congress."

The 18th Amendment took the manufacture, transportation and sale of alcohol, which had been legal and regulated by the executive branch of the federal and most state governments, and placed these activities into the law jurisdiction of state and U.S. judicial courts, which could operate concurrently.

Whereas slavery violates natural law and is *malum in se*, the making and selling of alcohol to consensual buyers creates no cognizable injury, does not violate natural law, and is only *malum prohibita*. Thus, because *malum prohibita* against alcohol commerce did not naturally belong in the criminal law jurisdiction, a constitutional amendment to the supreme positive law was needed to place it there.

This is evidenced by the Indiana legislature's failed attempt in 1855 to criminalize the sale and possession of alcohol using legislation alone, without fulfilling an amendment process. The Indiana Historical Society tells us the background for this legislation.

> "With the support of the Know-Nothings and Republicans, Indiana temperance groups were able to secure the passage of a statewide prohibition law in 1855. The Indiana law, modeled after an 1851 Maine temperance law, prohibited the manufacture and sale of spirits, including beer, wine, cider, and other fermented beverages. The inclusion of beer in this law was an expansion of earlier attempts at legislating against the manufacture and sale of alcohol. Previously, the focus had been mainly on hard liquor. Indiana's 1855 law permitted alcohol sales only for medicinal, chemical, mechanical and religious purposes and allowed the sale of 'cider, wines, etc in quantities of more than three gallons.' Bootleggers were punished with a $100 fine and thirty days in jail, while those who purchased illegal liquor could be fined $10 and sent to jail until the fine was paid. It remained legal to import and export liquor, since this activity was governed by Congress through the U.S. Constitution's Interstate Commerce Clause. Celebrations for the passage of Indiana's statewide prohibition law were short lived. In 1858 (sic), just three years after it went into effect, the Indiana Supreme Court declared the law unconstitutional." [260]

Actually, the Liquor Law of 1855 was declared unconstitutional in 1855 by the Indiana Supreme Court in *Beebe v. State*, [261] which spells out the natural law basis of Indiana's constitution. The Liquor Law was voided by the Indiana Supreme Court 1) for criminally prohibiting "the trade and business of manufacturing" liquors, [262] 2) for criminally prohibiting the production and use of alcohol, and 3) for monopolizing the manufacture and sale of alcohol within the state by state corporate agents "for medical, chemical and mechanical uses only..." [263]

To declare the act unconstitutional – that is, "to annul the act of legislative usurpation" of individuals' rights, [264] the majority invoked the doctrine of judicial review, as introduced by chief Justice Marshall in *Maybury v. Madison* (1803), [265] Consistent with this holding, the Court later dismissed a series of other criminal cases based on the same Liquor Law of 1855, including *O'Daily v. State* (1857) [266] and *Connell v. State* (1858). [267]

With regard to the last issue above, i.e., the monopolization of the state over the manufacturing and selling of alcohol for medical, chemical, mechanical and religious uses, the majority in *Beebe v. State* (1855) said that it was not the function of government to do this. "(I)t is not competent for the government to take the business from the people and monopolize it," wrote the Court.

"The government can not turn druggist and become the sole dealer in medicine in the state..." wrote the Supreme Court. [268] "(F)or the government now to seize upon those pursuits is subversive of the very object for which it was created, and is inconsistent with the right of private property in, and pursuits by, the citizen." [269]

With regard to whether the state could criminally prohibit the personal production, possession or use of personal property such as alcohol, the court held that the legislature overstepped its authority "and invaded the constitutional right of the citizen" to produce and use property. [270] Quoting *Andrews v. Russell* (1845), [271] it wrote, "There are certain absolute rights, and the right of property is among them, which, in all free governments, must of necessity be protected from legislative interference, irrespective of constitutional checks and guards." [272]

Referring as well to the natural right "of acquiring, possessing and defending property" at Article I, Section 1 of the Indiana constitution (1816), the *Beebe* court wrote "that the people have expressly reserved the right of property, and its enjoyment, in forming their constitution, from the unlimited power of the legislature..." [273] If the legislature can steal even one natural right and "one of the recognized pursuits of the citizens, [then] it can [steal] all," wrote the Court. [274] Furthermore,

> "the legislature has no more right to violate the constitution, under the guise of a regulation of commerce, than by a statute literally in conflict with it. And if, as in the above instanced cases, the express provisions of the constitution secure to the citizen his property and

its reasonable use, the legislature can not take away the right by any legerdemain of legislation." [275]

The above paragraph makes one of the main points in this book. Because republican legislatures cannot deny people's substantive and natural rights by enacting legislation, the Controlled Substances Act is constitutional because it does not deny anyone their rights. Instead, within America's republics, CSAs secure the natural right of drug possession for drug users, and they secure the legal right of administrative due process for all drug merchants.

Thus, the CSAs are not like the Liquor Law of 1855, which tried to criminally prohibit the sale and use of alcohol. In contrast, the provisions of the CSAs only regulate the commerce of drugs within the states. Thus, the CSAs are not unconstitutional as was Indiana's 1855 liquor law. Plus, the criminal provisions of the U.S. CSA which prohibit drug dealing are likely not unconstitutional because they operate only within the federal areas.

With regard to whether the state could criminally prohibit the manufacture and sale of alcohol (in addition to stealing an industry from its citizens), the Court properly differentiated regulation from criminal prohibition, as this book also repeatedly does. As we have seen, criminal prohibition is accomplished in the law jurisdiction of judicial courts, which has subject matter jurisdiction over injury. On the other hand, regulation 1) operates under equity in the executive branch, 2) has no criminal authority, and 3) features the power to confiscate and enjoin, but not the power to incarcerate.

The majority in *Beebe v. State* (1855) knew this. The issue in the case was over the propriety and constitutionality of legislative prohibition, not regulation. [276] Thus, the Court wrote, "When a case shall arise calling for a decision as to the extent of the power of the legislature to regulate, without prohibiting, we shall be prepared to make that decision according to the best of our judgment." [277]

It should be noted what the elements of the state's arguments were in *Beebe v. State* (1855). First, the state denied the existence of any natural rights in Indiana. Astonished, the Court answered that "the constitution above quoted has settled the point here" and that the legislature "is estopped by its solemn declaration to deny the existence of the natural rights there asserted. That assertion, while it remains, is binding within the territory of Indiana." [278]

Second, the state argued that the legislature was competent to treat "any property and pursuit deemed injurious to the public..." as criminally prohibited. The Court denied this position, writing: "We deny that the legislature can enlarge its power over property or pursuits by declaring them nuisances, or by enacting a definition of a nuisance that will cover them." [279] This is analogous to the argument in this book that the legislature cannot enlarge the law jurisdiction of judicial courts by co-opting law words, such as nuisance and crime, and by misrepresenting their meaning.

Third, state attorneys as well as Justice Gookins in his dissent argued against the doctrine of judicial review in *Marbury v. Madison* (1803). [280] They claimed that the Indiana legislature has discretion over the criminal prohibition of property and commerce, "and that the determination of that body is not subject to review in this tribunal." [281] This is analogous to the state's fourth main claim that "the legislature has unlimited power over the commerce of the state," [282] including the power to incarcerate people for possessing goods or being in business.

The state's fifth obscene and meritless argument was that the purchase of alcohol by consumers is a commercial transaction. As we have seen, the acquisition of anything by a natural person is the exercise of a natural right. It is the manufacture, distribution or dispensing of goods and services to the public for gain that is commercial behavior, and therefore subject to regulation. Thus, this argument by the state is either very misinformed or disingenuous, as were its others above.

According to the *Cyclopaedia of Temperance and Prohibition*, published in 1891: 'The law of 1855, having been pronounced unconstitutional, was promptly wiped out by the Republicans in 1858, and no attempt was made to enact new Prohibitory legislation. A license law (placing the fee at $50) was substituted for it.' " [283] This is to point out that after alcohol's statutory criminalization was declared unconstitutional, the state reverted to regulation of alcohol commerce through licensing, just as it is currently required to do with the commerce of alcohol, drugs and guns.

It was not until the 'Blind Tiger' Law of 1907, which allowed for the search and seizure of suspected illegal speakeasies (blind tigers), that the Indiana legislature again attempted to criminalize alcohol commerce using legislation alone, as it had unsuccessfully first tried in 1855. If convicted of operating a blind tiger, a defendant would receive a mandatory jail sentence, "making this one of the strictest laws in the country." [284]

The argument in this book demonstrates that this "Blind Tiger" Law was "one of the strictest laws in the country" [285] because – like the Liquor Law of 1855 – it was unconstitutional. Similar to the illegal operation of today's war on drugs, commercial saloon owners were falsely incarcerated for violating a licensing statute. That is what the *Beebe v. State* (1855) Court told the Indiana legislature fifty-two years earlier, to wit: that it "must regulate within the restrictions of the constitution," [286] and that regulation does not mean prohibition.

As the reader may recall from the *Schick* (1904) [287], *Colts* (1930) [288] and *Clawens* (1937) [289] cases discussed in chapter 5, the U.S. Supreme Court holds that violating licensing statutes is not a crime, but is instead a regulatory violation, and thus jury trials are not required for them. Therefore, operating a blind tiger was a regulatory offense, subject to Indiana's executive branch. It was not a criminal offense, subject to the judicial branch and to criminal incarceration.

This means that the U.S. Supreme Court's holdings in *Clawens*, *Colts* and *Schick* were consistent with the Indiana Supreme Court in *Beebe v. State* (1855), to wit that operating in any commercial capacity and in any regulated industry is not criminal. As pointed out by the Indiana Court of Appeals in *Morrison v. Sadler* (2005), [290] *Beebe v. State* (1855) was overruled only during the era of Alcohol Prohibition.

Within America's republics, the police power of regulation operates in a different jurisdiction than criminal enforcement. Whereas the state's judicial courts had jurisdiction only over *malum in se*, the state misused the criminal law jurisdiction of the courts to enslave owners of blind tigers for the legislature's commercial *malum prohibita*. This is what *Beebe v. State* (1855) held to be unconstitutional. This is exactly analogous to what the state of Indiana is illegally doing with drug users and dealers today.

This constitutional infringement against blind tigers became moot after the 18th Amendment overwhelmingly passed Congress on December 18, 1917; after Indiana went completely dry on April 2, 1918; after the 18th Amendment was ratified on January 16, 1919; and after the passage of the Volstead Act on October 17, 1919. These acts took the commerce of alcohol out of equity and subjected it to the law jurisdiction of America's republics.

Thus, Indiana's unconstitutional 1855 legislation that attempted to prohibit the commerce and possession of alcohol, as well as the "blind tiger" law of 1907 which meted out criminal sanctions for licensing violations, would finally be made constitutional by the 18th Amendment that criminalized alcohol commerce. Because of the lack of a similar constitutional amendment with regard to controlled substances, the commerce in controlled substances is regulated among the states like alcohol commerce was before 1920 and after 1933, and is not criminally prohibited.

Unlike the acts of 1855 and 1907, the Indiana Controlled Substances Act is constitutional because, as we will see in part 2 of this book, it does not prohibit or criminalize drugs in any manner. Instead it leaves drug possession alone and only regulates drug making and selling in non-criminal equity. Only the U.S. CSA criminalizes drug commerce, and this prohibition occurs only under Congress' plenary power in the federal areas.

The Indiana CSA merely regulates drug commerce, just as the alcohol licensing statutes did prior to and after Alcohol Prohibition. Because non-injurious drug matters are still outside the criminal jurisdiction of judicial courts, the CSA cannot impose criminal penalties for non-injurious drug "crimes," which have no grounds to be judicially enforced.

The only reason that drugs are treated differently than alcohol is because today's government officials do not follow statutory law and fail to recognize defendants' two republican rights: 1) the right of individuals of property possession and 2) the right of business people to administrative due process. Without a constitutional amendment that criminalizes drugs, the commerce of drugs is outside the criminal jurisdiction of republican judicial courts and is to be regulated, and only regulated, by the executive branch of government, just like the commerce of nearly everything else. Again, this is what *Beebe v. State* (1855) and Indiana's CSA tell us.

This means that there is no lawful basis to put people in jail for drug use or dealing, just as there was none for dealing in alcohol before the 18th Amendment. The war on drugs violates natural, constitutional, statutory and case law. A comparison of the 18th Amendment and the operative provisions of the CSA will shed light on these violations.

15

The making of
political prisoners

Comparing the 18ᵗʰ Amendment to the Controlled Substances Act

In the last chapter we looked at the legal characteristics of criminally prohibiting slavery and alcohol commerce. In this chapter we will compare the 18ᵗʰ Amendment with the U.S. Controlled Substances Act, and we will compare criminal prohibition in the judicial branch with regulation in the executive branch. In the process we shall see that non-criminals who judges incarcerate are their political prisoners.

The first thing to note between the 18ᵗʰ Amendment and the U.S. Controlled Substances Act is that they both relate to commerce. The 18ᵗʰ Amendment criminally prohibits the manufacture, sale and transportation of alcohol. The U.S. CSA both 1) licenses the manufacture, distribution and dispensing of controlled substances within the interstate regulatory capacity of the U.S. republic, as well as 2) criminally prohibits the commerce of drugs within the federal areas, under Congress' non-republican authority. Neither the amendment nor the CSA try to control or license all commerce – just two specific kinds of commerce.

Given this, we should also note that the 18ᵗʰ Amendment did not prohibit the possession or consumption of alcohol, only its manufacture, sale and transportation. Thus, as I write about the legality of the possession of drugs under current law, the possession of alcohol was also not illegal during Alcohol Prohibition. Some states made themselves dry, but the 18ᵗʰ Amendment did not criminalize alcohol possession or consumption.

"Prohibition said nothing about purchase, possession, or consumption of alcoholic beverages," wrote historian Ian Frazier in his chronicle called *Family* (1994). [291] "You could make apple cider, leave it in your garage to harden, and get drunk on it in your parlor without breaking any law." (This is the historian's reference to what I have been calling the natural law jurisdiction.)

As well, the 18th Amendment prohibited the commerce of alcohol under the government's positive law jurisdiction, but not the fermentation process which operates under natural law. "No law could do anything about what happened chemically to fruit juices if left to sit," wrote Frazier. "Of course, putting additives in the juice or otherwise treating it would constitute manufacture, a crime." [292]

Likewise, no positive law can do anything about what happens to seeds when they come into contact with soil, water and light. Plants and other living things grow according to natural law, not according to the dictates of legislatures.

In Indiana, pursuant to the drug statutes that we will begin to discuss in the next chapter, positive law regulation does not extend to the cultivation of plants but only 1) to the extraction of controlled substances from plants (which constitutes manufacture); 2) to the sale of plants (which constitutes distribution); and 3) to the eradication of wild plants from which controlled substances can be extracted. [293]

The 18th Amendment is significant because it tells us that the manufacture, distribution and sale of anything is to be regulated by the executive branch, and that it takes a constitutional amendment to make the commerce in anything a real crime. In order to make certain business people criminals, such as alcohol distributors, and to subject them to a criminal jurisdiction in the judicial branch, American governments were required to constitutionally convert their regulated business activities into crimes via the amendment process, which subjected bootleggers personally to the criminal law jurisdiction of the republics' judicial branches.

The 18th Amendment demonstrates that in the absence of a constitutional amendment that criminalizes certain activity, then merely the acts of possessing anything or being in business, such as selling crack cocaine, alcohol or oleomargarine, is never a crime. This is because commerce is not within the criminal subject matter jurisdiction of judicial courts, but instead operates in equity.

Only by amending constitutions may artificial persons who are engaged in free enterprise be made criminals and be subjected to the criminal jurisdiction of republican courts. Otherwise, businesses and business people that operate in equity can only be regulated by the executive branch, and are subject only to the judicial branch for individual crimes, for commercial disputes or for appeals over their commercial privileges.

So the real significance of Alcohol Prohibition to us is that it shows that the judicial branch has criminal subject matter jurisdiction only over behavior that is either *malum in se* or that has been placed into the law jurisdiction by a constitutional amendment. Conversely, judicial courts have no subject matter jurisdiction over commercial behavior that is mere *malum prohibita,* such as unwanted drug dealing, and that has not been placed into the law jurisdiction by a constitutional amendment, which describes the false and fraudulent "crimes" involving drug possession and commerce in America today.

The absence of a constitutional amendment that criminalizes drug possession or drug commerce proves that such activity has not been properly criminalized, and therefore neither activity is subject to adjudication by the law jurisdiction of the judicial branch, which currently has jurisdiction only over real cases and crimes to which America's constitutions refer.

Matters of drug possession and commerce would only be subject to criminal prohibition 1) in the federal areas under Congress' plenary authority, 2) if the Indiana or U.S. constitutions were amended to make drug possession and / or drug commerce crimes, or 3) if drugs were involved in the commission of real crime.

In any event, the 18th Amendment had no effect on any other type of commerce, such as drug or tomato commerce, which has always been and continues to be lawful, and which is still subject only to regulation, not criminal prohibition. Neither the U.S. nor Indiana constitution has ever changed with regard to tomato growing or drug dealing.

Tomato growing is a natural right. Drug and tomato dealing are subject to regulation, including injunction. Other than the criminal prohibition of slavery, the law on property possession and commerce in America has never really changed. Yet officials act as if it has.

Possession of property and free enterprise (except in slaves) are not crimes under America's current republican constitutions, and therefore they are not subject to the criminal subject matter jurisdiction of our republics' judicial branch. All commerce (except in slaves) operates under equity, not law. The equity jurisdiction has no criminal authority. Therefore, simply stated and as I've said all along, the war on drugs fails the republican litmus test for want of criminal jurisdiction.

Given this, it is almost unbelievable that our judicial branch has tried millions of people for drug "crimes" over the past fifty years. In part 2 of this book, I will try to explain how this incredible scam came to be.

It took a constitutional amendment to criminalize the commerce of alcohol because in an American republic, commerce is regulated, not prohibited. This means that if drugs appear to be prohibited, then in the absence of an amendment, America's *de jure* republics are not operating.

Republican legislatures may not criminally prohibit voluntary and consensual adult behavior which is both natural and outside the law jurisdictions of judicial trial courts. Because neither drug possession nor drug commerce are crimes, the adjudication of drug matters in the judicial branch is without lawful and moral authority.

Without a constitutional amendment, the commerce in anything (except in slaves) is not a crime and not subject to judicial trial courts in America's republics. Therefore, adjudicating drug matters in the judicial branch, without first making drug possession or commerce real crimes via the constitutional amendment process, exceeds the subject matter jurisdiction of judicial courts, which have authority only over civil and criminal cases that involve injury.

The differences between prohibition and regulation

As we will see in the part 2 of this book, which is about statutory law, the commerce of drugs within America's republics is regulated, and is not criminally prohibited. The Indiana State Board of Pharmacy that administers the CSA in Indiana has no authority or means to criminally prosecute regulatory violations. And nowhere does the act say that commerce in drugs is unlawful or prohibited, as the 18th Amendment expresses about the commerce of alcohol.

The word prohibit is not used in the Indiana CSA because prohibition of any business requires a constitutional amendment in a republic. The word prohibit is used in the headings of the U.S. CSA at 21 USC 841 – 843 because drug dealing is criminally prohibited in the non-republican federal areas, where those provisions apply.

As with the words case, crime, offense, felony, misdemeanor and injury, whose statutory meanings derive from our constitutions, so too do the meanings of prohibit and regulate. The 18th Amendment says the commerce in alcohol "is hereby prohibited." Article I, Section 8, Clause 3 says that Congress has power to regulate interstate commerce.

Thus, the words prohibit and regulate have constitutional meanings, and their meanings are *prima facie* different. Regulation applies to commerce. Prohibition applies 1) to *malum in se* that is prohibited by natural law in the law jurisdiction of republican courts, 2) to *malum prohibita* and *malum in se* in the federal areas, and 3) to *malum prohibita* that has been placed by constitutional amendments into the law jurisdiction of federal and / or state republics to be treated as crime, as was once the commerce of alcohol.

Because drug commerce has not been constitutionally placed into either the state or U.S. republic's limited criminal law jurisdiction, then interstate drug commerce is not prohibited, but is at most only regulated under Congress' interstate commerce authority. There are several important differences between regulation and prohibition.

Prohibition is both a judicial function performed in the law jurisdiction of America's republics, and it is a plenary criminal jurisdiction of Congress in the federal areas. To prohibit means to criminalize a particular activity, which is to subject that activity to the courts' criminal sanctions. As we have seen, prohibition occurs in republics by means of legislative codifications against *malum in se* and by means of constitutional amendments that place certain *malum prohibita* into the criminal law jurisdiction of republican courts.

Regulation is a bird of another feather. It is primarily an executive branch function. As part 2 of this book will show, it is a process by which the executive branch of government divvies out, sanctions and adjudicates commercial privileges, such as the privilege to make and sell drugs. It is not a process that involves or includes criminal sanctions.

As we will also see in part 2, the regulation of drugs in Indiana involves the investigation, inspection, confiscation and enjoining of unwanted commercial drug activity. Because drug commerce is not a crime, the state's regulatory power does not include the power to arrest or incarcerate those involved in unwanted drug dealing, who are not subject to the criminal law jurisdiction of Indiana's judicial courts. However, this unwanted commercial activity is nonetheless subject to the state's equitable remedies, such as forfeiture and injunction, which are enforceable by judicial courts when acting in their appellate capacity.

Proper regulation involves giving all drug dealers their day in administrative (non-judicial) court, whether they are home meth lab owners or reputable pharmaceutical company presidents. This administrative due process is defined in Indiana by the CSA and the Administrative Orders and Procedures Act (AOPA). It is administered by the administrative law courts of the Indiana State Board of Pharmacy, with oversight by Indiana's judicial courts. This due process is owed to all interstate drug dealers.

Because the pharmacy board's administrative courts may not adjudicate injury, they instead determine whether drug dealers may or may not exercise the privilege of making and selling drugs. These courts either grant permission to make and sell drugs (called a "registration"), or they do not grant such permission. They may not order unwanted drug dealers to jail, and their armed enforcement officers may not arrest anyone except for their commission of real crime, such as a fraudulent drug transaction.

If Indiana drug dealers do not meet the standards of the Indiana pharmacy board its regulatory capacity (or if interstate drug dealers do not meet the standards of the DEA), then they are not awarded permission to make or sell drugs. Those drug dealers who defy this lack of permission are subject to being enjoined at the state and federal administrative level. [294]

If this does not stop their unwanted drug activity, then the administrative injunctions may be enforced by state judicial and U.S. Article III courts, which may send unwanted drug dealers to jail for contempt of their judicial orders. [295]

Thus, regulation can involve the thwarting of drug commerce on a case-by-case basis by administrative law courts of the Indiana pharmacy board or of the DEA, and it can involve drug dealers being incarcerated for being in contempt of judicial enforcement orders. However, jail time for honest and nonviolent drug dealers in republics can only be ordered by judicial courts under their equitable appellate powers, as a sanction for judicial contempt, and not under their criminal subject matter jurisdiction, which requires cases involving injury.

This means that drug dealers in Indiana are not subject to jail unless they commit real crimes or unless they violate orders from judicial courts which enforce administrative injunctions against their unwanted drug activity. This also means that making or selling drugs within Indiana are not crimes and that the state and federal CSAs do not treat them as crimes.

Only officials in the executive and judicial branches of the Indiana and U.S. governments, who have not sufficiently read the CSAs, falsely treat the making or selling of drugs as crimes within America's republics. In doing so, they arbitrarily favor some drug "criminals," i.e., those wearing ties or white lab coats, more than others.

The 18th and 21st Amendments regarding commerce in alcohol were enacted to change the separation of powers between government's branches. Prior to the 18th amendment, commerce in alcohol was merely subject to regulation under equity by state and federal licensing regime in the executive branch, just as drugs are today.

The 18th Amendment changed this by making commerce in alcohol a crime, subject to the law jurisdiction of republican courts. Commerce in alcohol became the only true crime in the history of America's law jurisdiction that did not require an injury or victim.

Otherwise the criminal jurisdiction of the courts throughout U.S. history has remained the same. The 18th Amendment gave judicial courts criminal jurisdiction over alcohol commerce, but admittedly no criminal jurisdiction over any other type of commerce or over alcohol possession.

In other words, other than with the 13th, 18th and 21st Amendments (and similar state constitutional amendments), the criminal law jurisdiction of America's republics has not changed. Only those administering the law have changed, and they likely do not realize either 1) that criminal jurisdiction has not changed in America's republics, or 2) that republican drug laws secure natural persons' natural right of drug possession and artificial, commercial persons' legal right to administrative due process.

Political law is not criminal law. Political prisoners are slaves.

Due process is a republic's process that is due to people when it seeks to deprive them of their rights and privileges, including their natural rights and commercial privileges. As we have seen, the substantive due process of incarcerating any natural person is judicial and based on injury. As we shall see, the administrative due process of adjudicating artificial rights and duties is regulatory, done by the executive branch.

Due process is for the executive and judicial branches to follow the state's statutory and constitutional rules of play. With regard to drugs in Indiana, substantive due process is achieved by adjudicating the privilege of drug dealing in administrative law courts of the Indiana State Board of Pharmacy. Procedural due process is achieved by these courts when they follow the procedural rules written in the Administrative Orders and Procedures Act (AOPA) and the Indiana CSA.

Under these rules, the Indiana pharmacy board may enjoin those drug dealers who do not meet the board's manufacturing and distribution standards, and judicial courts may enforce these administrative injunctions under threat of incarceration for contempt. This is the process that is due to all drug dealers in Indiana before the state incarcerates them.

Other than in matters of contempt of court, or in matters involving real crime, the due process of addressing unwanted drug dealers does not rightfully involve the judicial system or the exercise of judicial authority to physically enslave people. As we have seen, only judicial courts may deprive people of their physical liberty, and only for crime or contempt.

Because drug possession and commerce do not invoke the criminal law jurisdiction of judicial courts in republics, and because the regulation of drugs is the job of the political branches, then the adjudication of drug matters by judicial courts is for them to act politically, and to not act judicially. To act politically, i.e., to enforce political law in the form of *malum prohibita*, is for judicial courts to do the job of the executive branch and to violate the separation of powers doctrine.

When a judicial trial court does not act judicially, i.e., when it does not act in its judicial capacity to adjudicate injury or to hear appeals, then it is acting politically and illegally. When people are enslaved for behavior which is not criminal, but which is merely politically incorrect, then they are the courts' political prisoners.

Political prisoners are non-criminals who are incarcerated by a non-republican "judicial" court using criteria that is foreign to republican adjudication, which requires injury. These prisoners wear scarlet letters wrongly attached to them by "judicial" officers who have acted politically under color of law outside of their republican judicial capacities.

Political law is the law of the political branches, such as *malum prohibita*, that does not apply to natural persons, that is not enforceable in the law jurisdiction, and that applies only to that which is subject to executive branch regulation in equity. Judicial trial courts are not to make political decisions, but are to confine themselves to that which is judicial, i.e., adjudicating that which is justiciable and deciding appeals over commerce.

Law judges are to engage in jurisprudence, which is the science of law. They are not to engage in politics, which is the "science of government; the art or practice of administering public affairs." [296] "Jurisprudence is more a formal than a material science. It has no direct concern with questions of moral or political policy, for they fall under the province of ethics and legislation...," [297] writes *Black's Law Dictionary*.

For judicial courts to adjudicate political law is a perversion of the primary role that the judicial branch is to fulfill. Enforcing *malum prohibita* with criminal penalties against natural persons places the judicial branch clearly in bed with the political branches. This extra-constitutional lovefest is responsible for their factory-like propagation of political prisoners and for America's gulags.

At the state level, the war on drugs is the result solely of judicial courts falsely doing the dirty work of Indiana's political branches. At the federal level, it results from Article III judges exercising the power delegated to Article I courts.

The drug war exists ultimately because the state and federal judiciary has been thinking religiously and acting politically, in violation of the 1st Amendment and of the separation of powers doctrine. Judicial courts of America's republics cannot criminally enforce political law without violating their law jurisdiction over injury. The war on drugs is the collusion of executive and judicial officers – likely each acting together without awareness of their lack of constitutional and statutory authority.

For a former attorney like me, who took an oath to uphold the separation of powers doctrine and the rest of the Indiana and U.S. constitutions, there is nothing as grotesque than to watch America's sacrosanct courts be misused and defiled for unconstitutional purposes. Executive and judicial officers could not enforce our drug laws more lawlessly than if they were on bad drug trips. The war on drugs is like watching the misuse of baseball bats at Little League Baseball games.

Courts and baseball bats are good as long as they are used properly. When they are not, they can very destructive to the lives of innocent people.

This book serves to give notice to government officials, at least in Indiana, that they have not been properly following the Controlled Substances Act and that they have been enforcing drug laws outside of their constitutional capacities, in the wrong manner, in the wrong courts, and using the wrong branch of government. As we have thoroughly seen, judicial courts have subject matter jurisdiction only over cases and crimes, neither of which most personal or commercial drug matters amount to.

Politically the legislative branch can prohibit all kinds of behavior, called *malum prohibita*. However in America's republics, these prohibitions apply only to entities and activities over which the legislature may legislate and over that which the executive branch can regulate. This does not include natural persons acting in their natural capacities.

It is as the U.S. Supreme Court told us in *McCulloch v. Maryland* (1819), that: "The sovereignty of a State extends to every thing which exists by its own authority, or is introduced by its permission..." [298] But such authority does not extend over individual sovereigns, who are born free of positive law. *Malum prohibita* has no force and effect in the law jurisdiction of America's republics, where the natural rights of all natural persons – which rights Congress calls a fact [299] – are secured from positive law.

The Supreme Court expressed this in *Yick Wo v. Hopkins* (1886):

"For, the very idea that one man may be compelled to hold his life, or the means of living, or any material right essential to the enjoyment of life, at the mere will of another, seems to be intolerable in any country where freedom prevails, as being the essence of slavery itself." [300]

Indeed, being subject to "the mere will of another" is "the essence of slavery itself." [301] Such political law of the political branches does not apply to natural persons, but instead to commercial persons and "the organization and administration of government." [302]

The political branches operate out of equity, not law. Again, legislatures legislate the rules of equity for artificial persons – not natural persons – and they codify the Laws of Nature that operate upon natural persons within the law jurisdiction of judicial courts.

All American officials are presumed to know this. Why? Because it is the fundamental law of America's republics. That they currently do not know this shows just how fundamentally inadequate their (and my) legal education has been, and how flawed the American judicial system has become. It is so flawed that it does not even know its true natural self.

As long as Indiana's prosecutors and judges apply political law from equity to natural persons, then they violate republican constitutions and they manufacture political prisoners. This occurs because of their lack of discernment between the law and equity jurisdictions – i.e., one which applies to natural persons and one which applies to artificial persons. This also occurs because of their reliance upon the subjective and supernatural criminal criteria of non-republics, instead of upon their fidelity to the natural and objective criminal criteria to be used by republican governments.

Part 2:
Statutory law
arguments

Summary: America's Controlled Substances Acts (CSAs) are falsely enforced because their authors intentionally misrepresented the law to government officials and to the public so as to deny equal protection and due process to disfavored drug users and dealers. Despite their fraudulent intent, they wrote the CSAs to be republican, and therefore constitutional.

The state CSAs are constitutional 1) because they statutorily secure the natural right of drug possession for ultimate (or end) users of drugs within the states, and 2) because they regulate all drug commerce, instead of prohibiting some of it.

The U.S. CSA is constitutional 1) because it legalizes drug possession within the federal areas, 2) because it treats drug possession within the state republics just as do the states, i.e., as a natural right, 3) because it treats interstate drug commerce just as do the state republics, i.e., by regulating it under its Interstate Commerce power at Article I, Section 8, Clause 3 of the U.S. constitution, and 4) because it prohibits drug dealing only in the federal areas, which is subject to Congress' plenary authority at Article I, Section 8, Clause 17.

Outside the federal areas and among the states, the U.S. constitution grants Congress with power to regulate interstate drug commerce, but with no power to criminally prohibit it. Thus, the U.S. CSA's regulatory provisions apply within the states, while its criminal drug provisions apply only in the federal areas.

The Supreme Court in *Gonzales v. Raich* (2005), which upheld the DEA's regulatory authority within the states, told us that Congress is to regulate all manufacturers and distributors of drugs as a class. This interstate regulatory authority includes the powers to inspect commercial premises, to confiscate contraband, to get such property forfeited and to enjoin future drug dealing.

16
Administrative due process

The limitations of judicial power

As we have seen, government officials' misuse of judicial courts to criminally prohibit drugs as *malum prohibita* violates – among other republican principles – the natural law basis of criminal law, the courts' constitutional subject matter jurisdiction over injury, the separation of powers doctrine, and defendants' substantive rights. Judicial courts have inherent limitations to adjudicate only injury in criminal law cases, which is a constitutional condition that is unassailable by positive law statutes.

Because of this, both the Indiana legislature and Congress as the U.S. republic have created a separate administrative process to be carried out in their respective executive branches to regulate commercial enterprises that are subject to these legislatures' equitable authority.

This administrative process applies to people who operate motor vehicles, who work in dangerous occupations, and who run businesses under various safety, environmental and fire-prevention regulations. Anytime we seek a license, a permit or a specific status from a government to do anything, we are seeking permission to do it as a privilege.

As babies teach us, we do not need to seek governments' permission to exercise our natural rights. We get licensed only to exercise artificial privileges that involve the health, safety and welfare of the public.

For example, when we fix food at home or brew beer for our own households, then the statutes about the privilege of serving food and selling beer to the public do not apply to us. Likewise, when we grow tomatoes in our backyards for ourselves and our families, farming regulations do not apply to us. As well, when we possess drugs in our natural capacities, and we do not sell them for profit or otherwise distribute them, then the republican portions of all Controlled Substances Acts – which are mostly apply to the privilege of making and selling drugs – do not apply to us.

In other words, we fix food, we garden and we possess property as natural rights under natural law, without need of anyone's permission and without any statutes applying to us. In contrast, we drive our cars and sell food and drugs as privileges under the state's positive law authority.

Government is to leave us alone in the natural law jurisdiction and may regulate our activities in the equity jurisdiction. Needless to say, that these jurisdictions be kept separate is fundamental to the concepts of sovereignty, liberty and the republican form of government.

Unfortunately, with regard to controlled substances, the distinctions in the Controlled Substances Acts (CSA) between law and equity are so obvious as to be overlooked by government officials for the past fifty years. This has occurred with no rational basis other than for attorneys 1) to not know the differences between the law and equity jurisdictions, 2) to not read and comprehend America's constitutions and drug statutes, and 3) to rely on false authority figures telling them what the law says.

We have seen how the war on drugs violates natural law and our constitutions. This is the first of several chapters about how it also violates statutory law. In most states, statutory drug laws take the form of two legislative acts that work in tandem to address the public issue of drugs.

One of these is the state uniform version of the CSA, written by the Uniform Law Commission. It defines 1) the right of individual drug possession, 2) the right of administrative due process for drug makers and dealers, 3) the power of the state to regulate drug dealing, and 4) the power of the state to incarcerate people for a handful of real crimes that involve drugs, for example the fraudulent conveyance of drugs. This act implicates both the equity and criminal law jurisdictions within state republics.

The other state legislative act is called the Administrative Procedures Act (APA) in most states. In Indiana the APA was replaced by the Administrative Orders and Procedures Act (AOPA). Throughout the United States, the APA or the AOPA work in conjunction with the state CSAs, and the CSAs incorporate the APAs or AOPAs by reference.

These acts define the administrative process that is due to all artificial persons, such as commercial enterprises and foreigners, in order to adjudicate their artificial privileges and duties, such as the privilege to make and sell drugs. The APA and the AOPA have no criminal provisions. They operate solely in equity both upon government agencies and offices, and upon artificial persons seeking to adjudicate their artificial rights.

On the federal level, the republican provisions of the U.S. CSA at 21 USC 824(c) incorporate by reference the U.S. Administrative Procedures Act (U.S. APA), i.e., 5 USC, Chapter 5. Together these acts define the regulatory procedures that the DEA and the U.S. Attorney General must use to deny or revoke the privilege to manufacture and distribute drugs interstate. Article III courts serve as appellate courts for the administrative adjudications by the DEA, under authority of the Attorney General.

Ultimately only Article I courts have criminal subject matter jurisdiction over drug dealing, and only in the federal areas. Article III courts have no original jurisdiction over drug possession and only appellate jurisdiction over drug commerce – the latter only after the U.S. Attorney General has exhausted his offices' administrative remedies within the DEA against unwanted drug dealers.

In context of controlled substances within America's republics, state APAs, the Indiana AOPA and the U.S. APA do not apply to natural persons or to natural rights under the law jurisdiction, such as to the right of drug possession. These acts apply only to government agencies and to artificial persons operating in equity that republican governments can regulate. In conjunction with the state and U.S. CSAs, the states' APAs, the Indiana AOPA and the U.S. APA tell regulators – for example those of the Indiana State Board of Pharmacy and in the DEA – how they are to adjudicate the commercial privileges of all drug makers, distributors or dispensers throughout the United States, licensed or otherwise.

This is to say that the Indiana AOPA is completely and thoroughly administrative law under equity, whereas the Indiana CSA, which contains about a dozen criminal law provisions that apply to natural persons, contains both law and equity provisions. Together these acts define all natural persons' natural right to possess drugs and all commercial drug defendants' minimum procedural rights to adjudicate the privilege of being in drug commerce. We know these minimum commercial rights and the state's minimum procedural duties as administrative due process.

Similarly, the U.S. APA is wholly administrative law, but the U.S. CSA is both 1) administrative law to be applied to commerce among the states and 2) civil and criminal law to be applied within the federal areas. Together the U.S. and state CSAs a) define the rights of natural persons in America's republics, b) define the administrative due process rights of commercial drug enterprises in America's republics, as well as c) mandate duties upon Congress' subjects in the federal areas to not deal drugs there.

Administrative due process is the executive branch process that all American republics owe to people when they seek to adjudicate their commercial privileges. At IC 4-21.5-2-1, the Indiana AOPA reads: "This article creates minimum procedural rights and imposes minimum procedural duties."

The AOPA basically says that when a state agency seeks to sanction or revoke a privilege, such as the privilege to make and sell drugs, that it must give the artificial person who is subject to its regulation a fair hearing, whose outcome can then be appealed to or enforced by a judicial court. IC 4-21.5-3-8(a) reads: "An agency may issue a sanction or terminate a legal right, duty, privilege, immunity, or other legal interest… only after conducting a proceeding under this chapter."

Because the only mutual duties that natural persons have are under the law jurisdiction, for example the duty to not harm others, which are not subject to regulation but instead only to judicial process, the "duties" mentioned in the above statute are not duties owed by natural persons.

Likewise, the "rights" mentioned are not natural rights, but legal rights that the state legislature's positive law bestows upon those seeking to gain or retain commercial privileges provided by the state. Because these commercial privileges are bestowed by republican legislatures, which are artificial sovereigns over equity, then there is nothing natural about them.

In Indiana, the AOPA and the CSA apply together and equally to the commercial privileges of giant pharmaceutical companies as to those of home methamphetamine makers. Together the acts essentially say that whenever the Indiana pharmacy board wants to sanction or terminate a drug dealer's privilege to make and distribute drugs, that it must give this drug maker or dealer a fair hearing and a chance to appeal its decision.

The AOPA guarantees the "minimum procedural rights" of those who are regulated, as it also imposes the "minimum procedural duties" upon the state toward those it regulates. Again, these legislated minimum procedural rights and duties are called administrative due process.

Thus, while it is a state-regulated <u>privilege</u> to manufacture, distribute and dispense drugs in Indiana, the CSA and AOPA guarantee all people who are involved in such drug commerce within the state with a statutory legal <u>right</u> to adjudicate this privilege before the pharmacy board. The AOPA defines the duties of the pharmacy board with regard to such regulated persons. Because the adjudication of such state privileges is a legal right, says IC 4-21.5-2-2, the act "does not permit the waiver of any procedural duty imposed by the article" upon the state.

In other words, these procedures are mandatory upon the state of Indiana, and they are owed to all drug dealers. The state may not avoid these procedures that it owes to all commercial drug enterprises, and it may not use judicial courts without subject matter jurisdiction to achieve the same results. As we have seen, to do so violates the separation of powers doctrine, the subject matter of judicial courts and the administrative due process of disfavored drug dealers, who are instead to be regulated with the following positive law rights under equity from Indiana's AOPA:

- Right to notice of and service of process in administrative proceedings IC 4-21.5-3-1
- Right to notice of orders IC 4-21.5-3-3
- Right to a quorum to make orders IC 4-21.5-3-3(b)
- Right to notice of a grant or denial of a license IC 4-21.5-3-4
- Right to notice of a tax due, grant of property or service IC 4-21.5-3-5
- Right to notice of a sanction or termination of a legal right, privilege, immunity or other legal interest IC 4-21.5-3-6
- Right to review of a personal action
- Right to a proceeding to sanction or terminate a privilege, and right to notice IC 4-21.5-3-8
- Right to petition to disqualify an administrative law judge IC 4-21.5-3-9
- Right against *ex parte* communication IC 4-21.5-3-11
- Right to a judge not involved in pre-adjudicative stages of a proceeding IC 4-21.5-3-13
- Right to a record of a proceeding and to assert affirmative defenses IC 4-21.5-3-14
- Right to participate or have a representative IC 4-21.5-3-15
- Right to an interpreter IC 4-21.5-3-16
- Right to file pleadings, motions and objections and submit offers of settlement IC 4-21.5-3-17
- Right to notice of a prehearing IC 4-21.5-3-18
- Right to notice of a hearing IC 4-21.5-3-20
- Right to petition to intervene in a proceeding IC 4-21.5-3-21
- Right to move for subpoenas, discovery orders and protective orders IC 4-21.5-3-22
- Right to move for a summary judgment IC 4-21.5-3-23
- Right to a default judgment IC 4-21.5-3-24
- Right to an orderly proceeding, recorded IC 4-21.5-3-25
- Right to receive notice of material evidence IC 4-21.5-3-26
- Right to findings of fact and conclusions of law IC 4-21.5-3-27
- Right to an appealable order IC 4-21.5-3-28
- Right to object to a final order IC 4-21.5-3-29
- Right of review by a separate agency IC 4-21.5-3-30
- Right to move for stay of effectiveness of final order and for rehearing IC 4-21.5-3-31
- Right of public to inspect final orders IC 4-21.5-3-32

- Right to public maintenance of records IC 4-21.5-3-33
- Right not to settle a matter using informal procedures IC 4-21.5-3-34

The above are all legal rights granted to artificial persons or enterprises subject to regulation, such as all drug dealers. These rights are granted by the Indiana legislature, and not by the state constitution, because they are the procedures that the Indiana legislature established in equity for the administrative law courts that it created under its power to regulate commerce. Such regulatory courts and rules are necessary to adjudicate commercial privileges, over which judicial courts have no subject matter jurisdiction.

The above legal rights that are prescribed in the AOPA, in conjunction with similar legal rights in the Indiana CSA, define commercial drug defendants' procedural due process in the executive branch. The two acts operate symbiotically with regard to intrastate drug commerce, if not also redundantly. The U.S. CSA and the U.S. APA work the same way with regard to regulating interstate drug commerce.

With this in mind, both the Indiana CSA and AOPA and the U.S. CSA and U.S. APA will be a part of the following statutory discussion.

The scope of statutory law

The first thing we should know about statutes is that they have specific application. Most statutes in the Indiana Code apply only to governmental agencies that the legislature created, or to entities that are subject to regulation and that operate by government's permission, which excludes natural persons.

In fact, few of the pages and little of the ink in our state and U.S. code books apply directly to natural persons who operate in the law jurisdiction. For example, the aforementioned Indiana AOPA and the U.S. APA, which apply to commercial persons within the fifty states, do not apply at all to natural persons in their natural capacities. This means that these act about administrative law are enforced entirely in equity – not in the law jurisdiction – and are without criminal sanction.

Thus, the non-criminal procedures that are due all drug dealers in equity precludes all authority of the criminal law jurisdiction over the same activity or subject matter, i.e., their drug dealing. As we learned in chapter 2, due to the separation of powers doctrine, generally only one jurisdiction has authority over any given subject matter within America's republics. In other words, the law jurisdiction over natural persons and the equity jurisdiction over artificial persons are mutually exclusive and do not operate upon the same subject matter.

The war on drugs stands for the false proposition that the equity jurisdiction, which regulates all drug makers, distributors and dispensers, can share disfavored drug makers, distributors and dispensers with the law jurisdiction, where the latter can be criminally prosecuted. Instead, all drug dealing – indeed, all commerce but slavery – operates in equity, which makes it subject only to the state's equitable remedies of confiscation, forfeiture and injunction – not to criminal prosecution. Instead, only *malum in se* involving drugs, such as the use of fraud or violence in a drug deal, can be criminally sanctioned, and most *malum in se* in America is subject to state criminal authority, not federal criminal authority.

As we shall specifically see, only about a dozen provisions in the Indiana CSA are enforceable in or applicable to the criminal law jurisdiction and to natural persons. Otherwise, its provisions exclusively regulate drug commerce by artificial persons, and these provisions operate in equity. (Similarly, because the U.S. government has criminal jurisdiction within the states only over crimes relating to Congress' functions, which we discussed in chapter 9, and because Article I, Section 8, Clause 3 grants Congress power to regulate but not criminally prohibit interstate commerce, then the U.S. CSA only regulates businesses involved in interstate drug commerce.)

Ultimately, the only statutes in the entire 36-volume Indiana Code that apply to natural persons are those statutes that codify elements, remedies and judicial procedures for torts and crimes, all of which involve natural persons and are adjudicated in the law jurisdiction of judicial courts. Said differently, all statutes that apply to natural persons in their non-commercial capacities are enforced in the law jurisdiction.

Thus, most of the Indiana Code deals in equity and does not apply at all to natural persons. The only parts of the Indiana Code that apply to natural persons are the code provisions that are enforced in the law jurisdiction, such as torts, crimes, criminal defenses and civil and criminal procedures. All of these cases, crimes, defenses and procedures were established by the judicial branch – as prescribed by common law jurisprudence– and are merely codified by Indiana's legislature, which did not create these torts, crimes, defenses or procedures.

Thus, most of the Indiana Code applies to artificial persons and most of this code has only indirect effect on natural persons. For example, statutes that directly apply to alcohol distributors only indirectly affect how consumers purchase alcohol. Statutes that directly apply to hospitals only indirectly affect how patients are treated. Statutes that apply to automobile drivers only indirectly affect the comfort and safety of passengers and pedestrians.

To put this into perspective, consider a family from Dayton, Ohio, who travels to Indianapolis during summer break to visit the Children's Museum. If the Indiana Code really meant anything to them, they would stop at the first law library in Richmond, Indiana to read a copy, or they would read the Indiana Motor Vehicle Code on their cell phones.

If they did, it would likely take many years of thinking (as it did with me) to discover that the driver of the family vehicle, let's say the father, is the only one directly subject to a change in statutory (positive) law when his family crossed the state border. As a licensed driver, he became subject to Title 9 of the Indiana Code (called the Motor Vehicle Code) and to the administrative law courts of the Commissioner of the BMV as soon as he drove the licensed vehicle into Indiana.

In contrast, the rights and responsibilities of his passengers – his wife and children – were unaffected when they rolled into the state. His wife and children are not licensed passengers. They sit in their passenger seats as unregulated natural persons. They are not subject to any duties imposed by positive law 1) because their only mutual duty – from natural law – is to not harm others, and 2) because as natural persons – particularly natural born citizens – they are not naturally subject to positive law, only to codifications of natural law.

After all, in this example, they are just sitting. As weird as it sounds, sitting is an exercise of a natural right, just as is having something in one's pocket. Neither is subject to the police powers of prohibition or regulation. In this example, Ohio and Indiana only regulate the father's driving.

As passengers exercising their natural rights of sitting and traveling (as opposed to the licensed father who is exercising a driving privilege), the mother and children have no natural duties upon them to fasten their seat belts. (There are no seat belts or safety nets in Nature.) Instead, the state imposes the duty upon the driver to make certain that his passengers are buckled-up because only the driver is subject to regulation. He is also responsible for insuring them.

When an Indiana law enforcer stops the family for not wearing seat belts, only the driver is ticketed. It is a licensee's responsibility to know the positive law that applies to him as a licensee, but his passengers are not responsible to know driving statutes that do not directly apply to them as natural persons, who are not regulated. Besides, the kids are too young to read motor vehicle statutes that – quite frankly – even Indiana officials cannot seem to read or to understand. See chapter 30.

As natural persons, their only mutual duty is to not harm other people. They have this same duty in Indiana as in Ohio. Other than the big "Welcome to Indiana" sign on Interstate 70, and the quality of the highways, no one in the family can tell the difference between Indiana and Ohio.

The mother and children did not become subject to Indiana positive law when they crossed the state line. As natural persons, they are never really subject to it unless they violate the state legislature's codification of natural law, by committing a tort or a crime.

Because cases and crimes referred to in the Indiana and Ohio constitutions are the same as the cases and crimes referred to in the U.S. constitution, then civil and criminal liability does not really change when one crosses a border between two state republics. Only the elements of torts and crime slightly change, as well as the legislatures' sanctions.

Fundamentally because all crimes are torts, then torts and crimes in Ohio are like torts and crimes in Indiana. No one may redefine the meaning of torts and crimes, which would change judicial jurisdiction, without a constitutional amendment. Their definitions are given to us by Nature. They were defined before the United States was even created. People carry these definitions wherever they are in America's republics.

This is all to say – or to repeat – that the vast, vast majority of the Indiana Code does not apply to natural persons, whether from Indiana or Ohio. Almost all of it applies only to government agencies that the Indiana legislature created. or to the artificial privileges that these agencies regulate, including the father's driving. The only statutes that apply to natural persons are legislative codifications of common law jurisprudence regarding torts, crimes and breaches of contract based on substance which are applicable in the law jurisdiction of judicial courts.

Natural law is the only law to which the wife and children are subject, as codified by the Ohio and Indiana legislatures. As citizens, they are not subject to positive law, but are its authors. In this hypothetical, only the father is currently subject to republican governance, and only in his capacity as a regulated driver.

This is also to say that as natural persons, we do not really need an external code book to tell us how to act. As the prophet Jesus told us, it is our nature – the Father within – that tells us right from wrong. Plus, our upbringing largely shows us that there are consequences for our destructive behavior.

Ultimately we know that our *malum in se* subjects us to either natural punishment (such as from our parents), or to retribution (from victims), or to the civil and criminal law jurisdiction of our judicial courts.

When we violate natural law, then we naturally must pay for these violations, whether we get caught or not. People who subscribe to metaphysics would recognize this as a universal principle.

Conversely, we do not need to read any of our states' code books to stay out of trouble or out of court. The code books are almost entirely for those artificial persons that governments regulate, or for natural people who lack a strict internal code.

The few civil and criminal code provisions that apply to natural persons say very little about that which we do not already naturally know. For example, we know it is wrong to murder. We merely do not know – without looking in the code books – how long Indiana or Ohio will imprison us for murdering.

Thus, the family from Ohio does not have to stop at a law library when they enter Indiana because the only relevant law that really changed as they entered the state was the commercial law regulating the father's driving. In the state of Nature, the rest of the family is not regulated at all, and they are not subject to the judicial courts of Indiana unless they violate Nature by committing torts or crimes while within the state.

This process comes so naturally to everyone that no one in the family even thinks about it. It comes so naturally that even America's attorneys overlook it.

Because positive law is subservient to natural law in the law jurisdiction, the family is just as free in the Indiana republic as they were in the Ohio republic. The 13th Amendment says that in an American republic people may be enslaved only for the commission of crime. Because their constitutions share the same definition of crime, criminal law is basically the same in Indiana and Ohio.

Injury still suffices to define the civil and criminal jurisdiction of Indiana's and Ohio's judicial courts for all the family members. Indiana's criminal code, which is a codification of crime, only tells them how long they will sit in jail when they commit acts in Indiana that they already naturally know not to do in Ohio.

As long as the family members do not murder, rape, steal and do other nasty things to hurt other people and their interests, and do not engage in commerce to become subject to commercial regulation, like the father, then they are essentially in the state of Nature and above positive law, whether in Ohio or Indiana. This is because natural law is the basis of the law – that is, constitutional law – in Indiana and Ohio.

Of course we know that the family is not above natural law. There is no arguing with Nature that they must occasionally stop to use the restroom, to eat, and to fill up the gas tank. There is nothing that positive law can do to change these and other laws of Nature.

In their natural individual sovereign authority, the family members are not above natural law, but are merely above the positive law of Indiana, Ohio and the U.S. government. Within the scope of their natural sovereignty, positive law is irrelevant to most of them. For example, the name of the Indiana governor on the "Welcome to Indiana" billboard means almost nothing to the kids in the back seat, particularly when they are antsy to get to the Children's Museum.

Likewise, how government regulates doctors, alcohol distributors and automobile drivers is largely irrelevant to a natural person walking to a liquor store to buy an intoxicant or to one sitting in the back seat of a moving car. Natural persons have little reason to think about positive law as they wake up each morning, use the toilet, brush their teeth, take out the dogs or sit as a passenger in a bus. Artificial governments are almost completely irrelevant and out-of-mind when doing what comes naturally.

Thus most natural persons, but particularly U.S. citizens, are not subject to the U.S. or Indiana governments unless they harm other people or unless they are regulated, such as the father. The positive law of governments is largely irrelevant to natural persons, exercising their natural rights, such as the passengers in the family vehicle.

These people operate in their positive-law-free bubbles, floating above the positive law, stopping only to acknowledge their duties to Nature. Thus, the bookshelves that hold the Indiana Code are not the temple to which they must kneel and pray, or even stop to read, when they travel into the state. As natural sovereigns within reciprocal republics, they are not subject to positive law because they are its natural source.

As natural sovereigns, they are naturally beholden only to the natural rights and property of other natural sovereigns. Government code books only codify the few, but important duties that they naturally owe to other people.

So, if we do not have to read the Indiana constitution and the Indiana Code to determine if we do our jobs as natural persons correctly, why should we read them?

We read the positive law, not because it applies to us, but to make sure that those to whom it applies follow it correctly. Given the history of governments throughout the world, and throughout world history, we can pretty well trust that officials will scheme around the rules. If we do not know what the positive law says, then we can neither hold republican governments accountable to their inherent limitations nor secure our rights in the natural law jurisdiction, which is above and superior to positive law.

Conversely, we read the positive law to make sure that it does not get incorrectly applied to us as individuals. For example, the Controlled Substances Acts exempt individual drug users from the acts. [303] Of course we would not know this if we did not read, study and understand the CSAs.

However, even without reading these acts we know that something is afoul because of all the anomalies and contradictions in law enforcement, which is supposed to be harmonious. Eventually we are forced to read and understand the law on drugs because we realize that honest and nonviolent people have been incarcerated for possessing and using their own property, which America's constitutions say is their right.

Using the *Schindler's List* (1993) metaphor from chapter 1, even without stopping at law libraries and without combing through statute books that mostly do not apply to us as natural persons, we naturally know the signs of bad, misused government from the stench in the air and from the snowflakes that fall from the summer sky.

17

Cracking the drug code(s)

Drug statutes define the power of America's four sovereigns

In previous chapters we defined the four categories of criminal territorial sovereigns within the United States: i.e., the states, the U.S. republic, the U.S. non-republic and individual sovereigns. We learned that each of these sovereigns have their own territorial or spatial – and thus criminal – subject matter jurisdiction. Because each of these sovereigns have their own legislative and subject matter jurisdictions, each are recognized in the Controlled Substances Acts.

The state CSAs are 100 percent republican. They recognize and respect the distinctions 1) between the natural law jurisdiction where the individual is sovereign and the positive law jurisdictions where the government is sovereign, 2) between the republics' judicial jurisdiction of law over natural persons and the equity jurisdiction over artificial persons, and 3) between the executive and judicial branches' exercise of their equity powers. The state CSAs' provisions operate in either law or equity, but not both.

In contrast with the state CSAs, the U.S. CSA is both republican and non-republican. Its provisions that are legislated by Congress in its republican capacity, which apply among the states, are regulatory in nature. They are based on Congress' authority to regulate interstate commerce at Article I, Section 8, Clause 3 of the U.S. constitution. Being republican, these provisions recognize and respect the above three state jurisdictional distinctions.

However, Congress' provisions in the act that operate over the federal areas are non-republican in nature, as suggested by the Supreme Court in the *Hooven* (1945) and *Palmore* (1973) cases. [304] In the federal areas, Congress likely can decide who is and who is not criminal, which it cannot do within the states. Thus, the substantive and natural rights of individual sovereigns are not respected in the federal areas. This is because, using the words of *Yick Wo v. Hopkins* (1886), Congress is "the author and source of the law" [305] in the federal areas. Congress is the sovereign there – instead of the People.

To read the state and U.S. CSAs properly one must know about America's four sovereigns and know that the drug laws partition power among them. There are provisions in the state acts which relate to the three sovereigns that operate in America's republics: state republics, the U.S. republic and individual sovereigns. State republican CSAs separate power between the equity jurisdiction, the law jurisdiction of judicial courts, and the law jurisdiction of individual sovereigns, the latter who (as potential victims) have primary subject matter jurisdiction over criminal law.

Likewise, the U.S. CSA has provisions that operate for the U.S. republic among the states and others that operate for the U.S. non-republic in the federal areas. As we shall see, its republican provisions 1) regulate commerce within the states, 2) respect individuals' natural right of drug possession, and 3) defer to the states to fight real crime within their borders, over which Congress has very limited legislative jurisdiction.

The U.S. CSA's criminal provisions against drug dealing apply only in the federal areas. Only armed with this knowledge can one properly read and understand the state and federal CSAs.

The state CSAs, which are the products of the Uniform Law Commission (see chapter 27), are good and constitutional because they acknowledge and respect both the law and equity jurisdictions of the judicial branch. They do this by respecting the natural right of drug possession in the (natural) law jurisdiction, and by regulating drug commerce in equity.

The U.S. Controlled Substances Act is constitutional and good 1) because it acknowledges and respects Congress' power to legislate separately as a non-republic in the federal areas and as a republic over the states, and 2) because it sufficiently separates regulatory provisions that are applicable within the states from its criminal provisions that are applicable in the federal areas.

The war on drugs has been waged for nearly fifty years based upon the false enforcement of the CSAs by government officials, and upon defense attorneys who have been unaware of these distinctions. This reflects a breakdown 1) in understanding the differences between the law and equity jurisdictions, 2) in understanding the differences between regulatory and criminal law, and 3) in understanding the separation of governmental powers a) between the executive and judicial branches of government, b) between the law and equity jurisdictions within the judicial branch, c) between the original (subject matter) jurisdiction and appellate jurisdictions of judicial courts, and d) between the powers of the U.S.

republic and the U.S. non-republic. America's drug laws may be properly read, understood and enforced only after 1) the roles of the four sovereigns and 2) these distinctions in jurisdiction are *a priori* understood, which they have not been.

The Controlled Substances Act

With the exception of recent marijuana reform statutes, referendums and state constitutional amendments, the drug laws throughout the United States are relatively uniform. The Indiana General Assembly and the legislatures of most of the states have adopted similar versions of the Uniform CSA, as promulgated by the National Conference of Commissioners on Uniform State Laws (referred herein as the Uniform Law Commission). Most state medical and recreational marijuana statutes are mere amendments to the Uniform CSA.

At the federal level, the U.S. CSA was legislated by Congress as Title II of the Comprehensive Drug Abuse Prevention and Control Act of 1970. The Indiana General Assembly enacted the Uniform CSA in 1976. Both the federal CSA and the Uniform CSA used by the states were written by attorneys in the United States Department of Justice (with help from attorneys in the pharmaceutical industry, for which the acts were written).

The U.S. CSA established the U.S. Drug Enforcement Administration (DEA) and placed the enforcement of drug laws under the U.S. Attorney General. (Previously, drug regulation was under the authority of the Secretary of the Treasury.) Indiana's CSA assigns power to the Indiana State Board of Pharmacy to enforce most of the state's drug laws.

Under the U.S. CSA, the U.S. Attorney General serves two functions. On one hand, the Attorney General acts in his role for the U.S. republic as a regulator of interstate drug commerce. On the other hand, his U.S. District Attorneys act as prosecutors of crime on behalf of the U.S. non-republic, whose criminal drug jurisdiction is confined to the federal areas. As we previously discussed, this is in addition to U.S. District Attorneys' role to prosecute crimes throughout the United States that relate to federal powers and offenses against the U.S. Absent the use of the U.S. postal service to distribute drugs – such federal crimes do not include drug dealing.

The Indiana State Board of Pharmacy serves the same republican regulatory function in Indiana as the DEA (on behalf of the U.S. Attorney General) does in its regulatory capacity over interstate drug commerce. As with the administrative law courts of the DEA in its role as an interstate drug regulator, the administrative law courts of the pharmacy board determine who may and may not make and sell drugs intrastate in Indiana. In contrast, the role of prosecuting real crimes that involve drugs is assigned to Indiana's district (county) prosecutors.

Law enforcement agents of the Indiana pharmacy board serve the same function, and have similar powers within Indiana as agents of the DEA, who serve the U.S. Attorney General. Similar to the powers of the U.S. Attorney General, the authority of federal and state drug enforcers is both regulatory and judicial. Properly enforcing the CSAs requires that these enforcers keep their regulatory and judicial powers separate, and to apply them to separate subject matter, respectively to commerce and crime.

Given this background, there are two preliminary points that I would like to make about the CSAs. First, the federal CSA serves to not only regulate interstate drug commerce, but also serves to criminalize drug commerce within the federal areas. Thus, the U.S. Attorney General and DEA both 1) regulate interstate drug commerce and 2) criminally prosecutes intra-territorial drug commerce.

Second, the state CSAs and the republican portions of the U.S. CSA contain both regulatory and judicial provisions. Together their provisions serve to say 1) that the U.S. and Indiana republics are to regulate drug commerce using their respective executive branches, 2) that states are to prosecute real crimes involving drugs in their judicial branch, 3) that the U.S. Attorney General may, under his authority for the U.S. non-republic, criminally prosecute drug "violations" [306] in federal areas, and 4) that individuals within both the states and the federal areas may lawfully possess drugs for their own use. [307]

In America's republics the separation of authority between the executive and judicial branches is reflected in law enforcers' dual authority to regulate some drug activities and criminally fight other drug activities. All republican law enforcers are both regulators in one capacity and crime fighters in another, which powers they exercise for separate branches of government and over separate subject matter, i.e., commerce and crime.

In contrast, under the U.S. non-republic in the federal areas, there is little if any distinction between the regulatory and the criminal processes because Congress regulates or prohibits whatever it wants there. As a ruler over the federal areas, Congress can dole out justice any way it wishes, and can determine its courts' jurisdictions. Even slavery may be legal there because Congress can enslave whoever it wants and because the 13th Amendment literally does not expressly apply to Congress legislating for the federal areas.

Thus, the U.S. Attorney General and the office's agents, e.g., U.S.

District Attorneys and DEA agents, are bestowed with three powers: 1) the power to regulate interstate drug commerce in the executive branch, 2) the power to prosecute "crimes" in the federal areas in Article I courts, and 3) the power to prosecute federal enumerated crimes and offenses against the U.S. in Article III courts. None of these powers include the power to criminally prosecute false drug "crimes" and other *malum prohibita* in Article III courts.

Article III courts require injury to establish standing, to meet the case or controversy requirement, and to substantiate justiciability. The Attorney General's judicial authority does not apply to any commercial enterprises among the fifty state republics, including drug enterprises, which he instead is to regulate in his role for the U.S. republic.

Drug-law enforcers' dual regulatory and judicial powers serve these same functions. They inspect, investigate, ticket, confiscate and help to enjoin regulatory violators. They have authority to arrest real *malum in se* drug criminals.

These regulatory and criminal powers are exercised on behalf of not only two different branches of government. In fact, the judicial powers of law and equity are exercised on behalf of two separate sovereigns, i.e., respectively Nature and the positive law authority.

Having various types of power is fine so long as Attorneys General and drug enforcers can keep their regulatory and criminal functions separate, which they have not been able to do. As we have seen, proper enforcement within America's republics is possible 1) only if officials can keep Congress' two sovereign capacities separate and 2) only if they know the republican meaning of crime. Otherwise they wrongly arrest and prosecute mere regulation violators as criminals and prosecute them in the wrong courts.

That law enforcers do not know the meaning of crime is evidenced by criminal prosecutions of *malum prohibita* within the state republics. Plus, that they have been clueless about the application of the U.S. CSA's criminal provisions only in the federal areas evidences their misunderstanding of legislative – and thus criminal – jurisdiction.

As well, making Congress a non-republic in the federal areas is also fine so long as the U.S. Attorney General and the Department of Justice do not act non-republican outside of these areas, which they have been doing. Contrary to law, U.S. Attorneys General have been simultaneously 1) regulating favored interstate drug dealers in the equity jurisdiction of the U.S. republic, 2) wrongly prosecuting disfavored interstate drug dealers in Article III courts, all-the-while 3) using criminal provisions and sanctions, e.g., at 21 USC 841 – 844A, in Article III courts, but which apply only in the federal areas and in Article I courts.

In any event, the Attorney General is to prosecute drug violations that occur within the federal areas and to regulate interstate drug commerce among the states. Under his regulatory authority, he may bust up, confiscate and enjoin interstate drug commerce, but he may not enslave people.

In this paradigm, the only drug people who go to jail are 1) real criminals in all American jurisdictions who commit real crimes involving drugs, 2) artificial persons who violate Congress' non-republican edicts in federal areas, and 3) drug dealers who violate judicial injunctions or deportation orders.

With this background in mind, we will analyze the Indiana CSA (and ancillary state drug statutes) in the following pages, and in the process make a few comparisons to the republican portions of the substantially similar U.S. CSA. The summary of our Indiana analysis is as follows:

> Indiana's drug statutes grant primary jurisdiction over all drug commerce within the state to the Indiana State Board of Pharmacy, which is a regulatory agency in the executive branch of state government. IC 16-42-20-1(a) makes the agency "primarily responsible for the enforcement of all statutes and rules of Indiana relating to controlled substances." In other words, Indiana's prosecutors and judicial courts are not primarily responsible for the enforcement of Indiana's drug laws.
>
> The CSA grants the pharmacy board power to regulate the manufacture, distribution and dispensing of drugs, which does not include the power to regulate the mere possession of drugs. IC 35-48-3-3
>
> The law says that the state's law enforcement officers, a term which includes prosecuting attorneys, may work together against drug trafficking, eradication and addiction, which excludes jurisdiction over mere drug possession. IC 16-42-20-4
>
> More importantly, at IC 35-48-3-3(e)(3), i.e., called the ultimate user provision, the CSA in fact waives legal liability and acknowledges the natural right to possess and use controlled substances for one's own personal use and the use of people and animals in one's household.

Because IC 35-48-3-3(e)(3) admits that drug possession is lawful and because judicial courts lack subject matter jurisdiction over drug offenses that do not involve a tort or a crime, only nine of the penal provisions of IC 35-48-4 are real *malum in se* drug crimes over which Indiana's republican judicial courts have criminal jurisdiction.

This limited criminal jurisdiction defines the state's power to arrest and prosecute people over matters involving controlled substances. The arrest and prosecution of drug defendants for mere drug possession and dealing exceeds the state's criminal authority, which is defined by the constitutional meaning of crime.

The Indiana CSA grants the Indiana State Board of Pharmacy with powers to investigate and inspect premises, to deny licenses to manufacture and distribute controlled substances, to confiscate contraband from unlicensed activity, and to administratively enjoin unlicensed activity. These are the pharmacy board's and the state of Indiana's main administrative remedies against unwanted drug making and dealing. To support these administrative powers, IC 34-24-1-3(a) grants Indiana prosecutors authority to institute judicial forfeiture proceedings against property properly seized.

Likewise, IC 16-42-20-3 says that pharmacy board courts have "jurisdiction to restrain or enjoin violations of laws relating to controlled substances." If such administrative injunctions are ineffective to stop unwanted drug making and dealing, then IC 35-48-3-3(i) grants the Indiana Attorney General authority to enter a judicial court to judicially enjoin the drug dealing. (This is similar to the U.S. Attorney General's injunctive powers at 21 USC 882, which are enforceable only in his republican role. The Attorney General does not need the power to enjoin drug dealing in the federal areas, where the office can instead prosecute drug dealers as criminals.)

The above summary of Indiana's drug laws does not even remotely match the state's administration and enforcement of those same laws. The state of Indiana routinely busts people for drug possession and dealing, and hauls them into judicial courts which, as we have seen, have no subject matter jurisdiction over mere drug possession or dealing.

Because the drug laws are clear, this abusive process by the state could not be more constitutionally or statutorily bankrupt. The state has never had statutory or constitutional power to compel, arrest or prosecute people for non-torts and non-crimes. People who work in the judicial branch are presumed to know this.

For them to not know this is for Hoosiers to be forced to deal with two kinds of addicts: people addicted to drugs and people addicted to power. One of these groups is composed strictly of tortfeasors or criminals; the other is not.

For the past fifty years nearly all of the state's arrest and prosecutions for drugs have been false – under false color of law. It is for this kind of highway robbery by government officials that 42 USC 1983 was enacted. Lacking natural and constitutional authority to arrest, prosecute and jail drug "offenders," the only authority that these officials have had are their kingly delusions about laws they have never read or understood.

If you will oblige me another movie metaphor – these officials have turned the criminal law jurisdiction into a human glue factory. Their insane and unreal drug war is their *Fight Club* (1999). The first rule of *Fight Club* is to never admit that there is a fight club, or a glue factory.

It helps to know what we are looking for

Our discussion of the relevant portions of Indiana's drug laws means that we will not be discussing the portions that are irrelevant or not-so-relevant to our discussion, which is much of the whole. It also means that we won't necessarily be discussing the readers' local drug laws.

Because of this, I recommend that you find and read the controlling drug laws in your own area. This and the next several chapters will help you understand them. The U.S. CSA and the CSAs of the states are available online. The U.S. and Indiana acts are both organized and presented in a relatively straight-forward and logical manner. It has been my experience that other states' drug laws will not be as easy to find or to piece together, especially California's.

Indiana's drug laws are codified in titles 16, 25, 34 and 35 of the Indiana Code. They work in conjunction with Indiana's Administrative Orders and Procedures Act (AOPA) at IC 4-21.5. You can find the U.S. Controlled Substances Act at 21 USC 801 – 971, and the U.S. Administrative Procedures Act (APA) at 5 USC 500 *et seq*.

Reading these statutes correctly is the key to understanding what actual power either Congress or state legislatures delegate to drug regulators and prosecutors, and over what and who they regulate and prosecute. This means that reading and thoroughly understanding statutes is essential to understanding the law. Fundamentally, the failure to read and then to also understand the CSAs is most likely why they everywhere are so falsely enforced.

When first reading a CSA we are naturally looking for the governmental entity or office to which the legislature grants authority over drugs and drug matters. Once we discover this, we will seek to learn the scope of power granted to this entity or office.

The answers that we seek are what legislative drafting manuals call the "principal operative provisions" of a statute. Says the *Texas Legislative Council Drafting Manual* (2014), these are the "administrative provisions, which relate to the creation, organization, powers, and procedures of the governmental units that enforce or adjudicate the law" and the "substantive provisions, which give to or impose on a class of persons rights, duties, powers, and privileges." [308]

An important concept in this book is that either constitutions or legislatures create, organize and empower a governmental unit "to enforce or adjudicate the law." [309] As we have seen, this power to adjudicate the law is called subject matter jurisdiction. One of the main issues in this book is which state governmental unit – an administrative law court or a judicial court – has subject matter jurisdiction to enforce and adjudicate our drug laws. On the federal level, the main issue is over which U.S. sovereign has subject matter jurisdiction over controlled substances, and where.

The proper answer that we have seen is: It depends. As this and the next chapters show, whether a court has subject matter jurisdiction over controlled substances depends entirely on the facts of each case or drug matter.

Republican judicial courts have subject matter jurisdiction over cases or crimes, which involve injury, including drug cases or crimes. Administrative law courts have subject matter jurisdiction over the commercial privilege of making and selling drugs. Article I courts that operate in the federal areas have criminal jurisdiction over whatever Congress says they do. The U.S. CSA embodies each of these jurisdictions and, I might add, stealthily camouflages and fudges their distinctions.

However, we can see through this intentional smearing because we know *a priori* where the lines are drawn. Thus, we can read each and all provisions of the CSAs and, using a metaphor from chapter 2, sort them into the proper mail slot of each of the four types of sovereigns.

For example, the power over drug possession in a republic belongs to individual sovereigns. The power over drug commerce belongs to the equity jurisdiction of legislatures and their regulators. The power over drug prohibition belongs solely to the U.S. non-republic in the federal areas. Only first knowing these facts are we then able to read the various CSAs properly.

Nonetheless, the proper statutory scheme is discerned by our reading of the CSAs' principal operative provisions. [310] They will answer what governmental unit is in charge of drugs, the nature and scope of this unit's power, and the procedures and safeguards required to exercise this power.

The separation of powers doctrine in republics ensures that regulatory powers granted to the executive branch will be consistent and compatible with the separate authority of the judicial branch 1) to adjudicate cases and crimes involving injury and 2) to serve as appellate courts for lesser judicial and regulatory courts.

Statutory decryption through dissection

I liken the reading of statutes to air-traffic control. When reading statutes you have to see the big picture, keep a lot of things in mind at the same time, and focus on the right elements at the right times. Although statutory reading does not normally involve issues of life and death, as does the work of air-traffic controllers, reading statutes properly may be even more important than air-traffic control.

This is because a false reading of legislation can adversely affect the lives of millions of people, not just hundreds. Over a million people in the United States are arrested or ticketed for drug "crimes" every year. This book's proper analysis of drug statutes is important because it can secure the freedom and choices of millions of Americans, all the while cutting off the criminal hand of odorous rotten government.

It is no accident (pun intended) that the CSAs, which I outlined above, have been misunderstood by most attorneys and the public since their debut in the U.S. Department of Justice under Attorney General John Mitchell. Even after I used the correct reading premises and even though I knew what I was looking for, i.e., the act's principal operative provisions, [311] it still took me several weeks of reading, re-reading and thinking about the Indiana CSA to mostly understand it. [312]

As these statutory chapters show, I read statutes quite well, so it should not take me or anyone else several weeks to fully understand a relatively short piece of legislation. Truly something is wrong with written positive law when it takes a specialist so long to fully grasp a statutory outline.

As we shall see more particularly in chapters 23 – 27, many statutes are hard to understand because they are essentially encrypted. By this I do not mean that we need a computer algorithm to unlock or decipher statutes, although that might help. I mean that unless we read statutes from a particular angle – in the right light so-to-speak – with different presumptions and premises than we normally apply to our other readings, and with a lot more effort, concentration and scrutiny, we are bound to make statutory mistakes. These have been fatal to the proper enforcement of drug laws.

The proper premise

I have a few personal rules about reading statutory law.

The first rule is to find all the relevant statutes. Indiana's drug laws are not only cryptically written, but are strewn over at least five separate titles (parts) of the Indiana Code: Titles 4, 16, 25, 34 and 35. I found all these provisions only by first reading the table of contents of each of Indiana's thirty-six separate titles.

For example, I found IC 1-1-2-1, which is at the very beginning of the Indiana Code and which requires statutes to be consistent in meaning with our constitutions, only by opening Title 1 and reading its relevant contents. I did not know that IC 1-1-2-1 existed or that it was relevant until I read it.

Generally, to find other relevant statutes, one must essentially pour over one's entire state code. While this is a very tedious and labor intensive process, though one made much easier by the Internet, it is nonetheless beneficial because it is likely the best way to see how the law is made up of many interrelated parts, and how all these pieces fit together.

Or I could say, maybe it's the only way. Only by reading and pondering the Indiana Code did I realize, for example, that law enforcers exercise two police powers, i.e., regulation and prohibition, in two separate jurisdictions, i.e., equity and law, and that whether they exercise authority for one jurisdiction or the other is a separation of powers issue, of which they must always be cognizant.

As well, only by reading and pondering the Code did I realize that the only portions of it that apply to natural persons are those few codifications of real crimes and judicial procedure that operate in the law jurisdiction of judicial courts. [313] For an attorney, these are huge revelations that I acquired only by really thinking hard about the Indiana Code, as opposed to hardly thinking about it.

As an aside, I was the leading legal research student in my law school class. I got the highest grade on the first year's legal research exam, which tested our ability to use law libraries. Although libraries offer various indexing and cross-referencing tools to find statutory law, there is no substitute for combing through and thinking about all of it.

As well, although much of the Indiana Code is cross-referenced by the Code's two independent publishers, i.e., West and Burns, these companies' indexing and cross-referencing tools are often inadequate. For example, only once in Title 7.1 regarding alcohol and tobacco could I find any reference to *Beebe v. State* (1855), [314] which is the quintessential case that we discussed in part 1 of the book about how Indiana treats alcohol.

> Based on *Beebe*'s importance to Indiana criminal law, the case should be copiously referenced by West and Burns both in Title 7.1 of the Indiana Code (regarding alcohol and tobacco) and at IC 35-48 about controlled substances. *Beebe* is the leading Indiana case 1) that upholds the natural rights of property possession and liberty, 2) that recognizes the differences between regulation and criminal prohibition, 3) that requires a constitutional amendment to criminalize natural rights and commercial privileges 4) that exposes the current illegality of criminal drug prohibition, and 5) that quite literally describes the role of natural law in the adjudication of rights.
>
> Given this, why is this important case so poorly referenced in Indiana's annotated codes? (I discovered the unnamed case – not in a legal book – but in a history article.) Is this omission due to neglect or willfulness? What role does the legal publishing industry play in misrepresenting the law to support the illegal war on drugs?
>
> That the case is scarcely referenced in Title 7.1 and not referenced in the annotated Indiana CSAs leads one to question both the competence and integrity of the legal publishing industry.

Second, to understand the CSAs and other drug laws, you have to read and understand ALL of the drug statutes – not just a provision here and there.

The violation of this rule of statutory reading is probably most responsible for the false enforcement of the CSAs throughout the United States. The myopia of government officials and defense attorneys alike is that they focus on the act's penalty provisions, for example at IC 35-48-4 and 21 USC 841 – 844A, instead of reading these penalty provisions in context of the rest of the CSA, and in context of subject matter jurisdiction, as laid out by the state and federal constitutions, with which the CSAs are consistent.

However, without reading or understanding the CSAs' other various components, which define how drug commerce is to be regulated and which show that drug dealing operates under equity and not at law, then it is easy to be distracted – indeed transfixed – by the devil of drug penalty provisions that predominate IC 35-48-4 and 21 USC 841 – 844A, most of which in America's republics are irrelevant and unenforceable.

For example, as mentioned in part 1 of this book, there are only nine real drug crimes at IC 35-48-4 that are enforceable in the law jurisdiction of Indiana's judicial courts. As well, all the criminal penalty provisions in the U.S. CSA at 21 USC 841 – 844A are enforceable only in the federal areas.

The third biggest key to understanding statutes (and constitutions) is to read them from the correct premise. The only correct premise is that governmental entities start with no power, and only have such power as is granted by constitutions or statutes, and nothing more. That is, if the legislature grants powers A and B to a governmental unit, these powers do not include powers C through Z or AA through ZZ.

For example, both the 1816 and 1851 Indiana constitutions say that the state's judicial courts will be open to injury. [315] Conversely, these provisions do not say that the courts are open to non-injury. Thus, one cannot argue that courts are open to non-injury without violating a rule of statutory reading, or without being dishonest.

As well, IC 33-28-1-2 grants subject matter jurisdiction to Indiana's Circuit Courts over civil cases and criminals cases, where case is defined by America's constitutions. However, this power does not extend to infractions which are non-injurious, which do not qualify as cases, which are not listed in the statute, and which are creations of American legislatures.

This strict construction of constitutional powers and criminal statutes, and only this construction, guarantees the separation of governmental powers, the protection of natural rights and the security of the republican form of government. That is why judges are required to strictly construe criminal statutes. [316] They are not allowed to fine or incarcerate non-criminals by loosely construing governments' police powers... but they do.

When the Indiana judiciary thinks their criminal courts are open to non-injury, because they do not construe constitutional grants of power strictly, then they are bound to necessarily exceed their constitutionally-granted judicial powers. In doing so, they fabricate *de facto* judicial power which is not granted by the *de jure* law.

Whether by a constitutional convention or by a legislative act, all grants of governmental power are always limited to their express powers. Otherwise, there would be no objective standard or rule of law attached to the meaning of statutory or constitutional words. Otherwise, the separation of powers between sovereigns (including the separation between their branches) cannot be understood or enforced.

If government is not limited by objective grants of power, and by the permanence and objectivity of the meaning of words, then there is no check upon the subjective exercise of power by those in government, which in fact has been the case. Again, the subjective exercise of power is inherently non-republican because it is not based on objective criteria or reasoning.

Such irrationality is reflected in officials' inability to properly read statutes. This reflects their inability to follow statutes' principal operative provisions, which limit governmental power by defining this power. It also reflects a breakdown in officials' ability or will to properly compartment-alize subject matter among America's four categories of sovereigns.

As the reader will see, finding a limited government of enumerated powers within the confusing CSAs is not an easy task. However, I assure you – and we will see – that such legitimate, limited governments can be found within the CSAs, or that the acts would not be constitutional.

Given the confusion in the operation of law that reading the CSAs has produced, I have done my best to organize, caption and explain Indiana's provisions in the next chapter so that you can finally understand them. The act is actually quite easy to understand and follow once we have the proper outline or framework in mind, as this book provides.

As well, because Indiana's and forty-five other states' CSAs are derived from the same Uniform Law Commission's Uniform CSA, then what I say about Indiana's CSA mostly likely applies to the other states' acts as well.

With this background, we turn to the principle operative provisions of the Indiana CSA, along with a few comparisons to the U.S. CSA.

18

How drug regulation works

Drug-law enforcement

IC 35-48 of the Indiana Code is Indiana's version of the Uniform Controlled Substances Act. As we have seen, it is to be primarily enforced by the Indiana State Board of Pharmacy, including the board's armed enforcers. This board serves the same regulatory function with regard to drugs as the Texas Director of Public Safety, the Kansas Board of Pharmacy, the Mississippi Department of Public Safety, the Wyoming State Board of Pharmacy, and the DEA on behalf of the U.S. Attorney General, for example.

The Indiana pharmacy board is an agency which operates in the executive branch of Indiana government. IC 25-26-13-3 says its seven members are appointments of the Governor for terms of four years. [317]

At IC 35-48-2-1(a) the act reads, "The board shall administer this article..." As well, IC 16-42-20-1(a), which is from the Indiana pharmacy act, reads: "Each member of the Indiana board of pharmacy, designated employees of the Indiana board of pharmacy, and all law enforcement officers of Indiana are primarily responsible for the enforcement of all statutes and rules of Indiana relating to controlled substances."

In other words, each member of the pharmacy board primarily administers and enforces "all statutes and rules of Indiana relating to controlled substances," not just some of them, and all other law enforcers in the state, including agents of the DEA, local police officers, prosecutors and the state Attorney General exist to assist them in their primary enforcement of drug laws.

As well, this enforcement is primarily regulatory – not criminally prohibitory. Most drug-law enforcement occurs in equity, not at law.

Similarly, the U.S. Attorney General regulates "every person who manufactures or distributes any controlled substance or list I chemical, or who proposes to engage in the manufacture or distribution of any controlled substance or list I chemical" and "every person who dispenses, or who proposes to dispense, any controlled substance." [318] He does this, with the help of the DEA, in his republican capacity among the states.

If one does not intend to manufacture, distribute or dispense controlled substances, then one need not apply to the U.S. Attorney General or the Indiana pharmacy board for permission to do this. These regulatory offices have no application mandate, process or form devoted to anyone merely for possessing drugs. In America's republics, officials may not regulate, and may not prosecute as crime, the possession of any drugs or the exercise of any of our other natural rights.

As we have seen, this is because neither Indiana's legislature nor Congress can legislate positive law duties within America's republics that would violate the exercise of natural rights, which are secured in the law jurisdiction of our judicial courts. Nor can these legislatures impose artificial duties upon any natural born citizens. Thus, the right of drug possession is subject to neither the regulatory nor judicial branches of America's good, legitimate governments.

This means that neither prosecutors nor the Indiana pharmacy-board enforcers have any authority over drug possession. In that the law enforcement powers of DEA agents and regular law enforcement officers are similar and analogous to those of the Indiana pharmacy board enforcers, none of these officers have any authority over drug possession either. This will be made clearer in the next chapter's discussion of law enforcers' arrest powers.

Indiana's law enforcement officers are defined at IC 35-31.5-2-185. Such officers include prosecuting attorneys, the Indiana securities commissioner and the inspector general, for example.

The powers of these offices with regard to controlled substances, if any, are specifically granted in separate statutes. For example, Indiana prosecutors have specific statutory power at IC 34-24-1-3(a) to institute judicial forfeiture proceedings for property that is lawfully confiscated by law enforcers in their administrative roles. As well, the Indiana Attorney General has express power to institute injunction proceedings against drug dealers at IC 35-48-3-3(i).

Conversely, Indiana prosecutors lack specific statutory grants of authority to prosecute drug possession and dealing matters in judicial courts. As well, the Indiana Attorney General lacks power to do anything but to seek injunctions against unwanted drug dealing. Thus, neither Indiana prosecutors nor the Attorney General have express power to criminally prosecute in judicial courts either natural persons (whose natural right of drug possession is not subject to positive law) or commercial persons (whose drug dealing is to be regulated).

Drug prosecutions violate one of the first rules we discussed in the previous chapter about how to read statutes – to wit, that the power of all government offices must be granted. However, neither state prosecutors nor Indiana's Attorney General have been granted power to prosecute drug users and business people in Indiana's judicial courts.

This lack of granted power is because such grants would violate the Indiana constitution's requirement of an injury to one's person, property or reputation that is needed to seek a judicial remedy in the law jurisdiction. As well, this is because drug commerce operates in equity, which is without criminal power. This means that the scope of the state's police power over drug commerce is limited to getting commercial property forfeited and to enjoining unwanted drug dealers, which does not include prosecuting them for crime. [319]

Again, because the actual grant of jurisdiction over false "cases" and "crimes" would render the Indiana CSA unconstitutional, in that it would assign subject matter to judicial courts that is outside their constitutional jurisdiction over injury, the legislation does not grant such power to Indiana's prosecutors or Attorneys General. Instead, the provisions at IC 35-48-4 merely call drug possession and dealing "misdemeanors" and "felonies," but without granting state officials with any power to prosecute this behavior as criminal. This is because the state legislature cannot grant power that it does not have to grant, and the state judicial branch cannot adjudicate subject matter over which it has no jurisdiction.

Judicial courts have inherent jurisdiction over *malum in se*. Such courts inherently require no legislation to prosecute crime. Law enforcers inherently require no legislation to arrest and prosecute real criminals. This is because crimes are self-evident facts of Nature.

Prosecutors and judges know torts and crimes when they see them. The former have no statutory authority to prosecute drug users and dealers when they do not commit crimes. Only the phony penalty provisions at IC 35-48-4 exist to encourage prosecutors to misuse Indiana's courts as they do.

Otherwise, as we have seen, Indiana prosecutors have judicial authority only over civil and criminal cases, [320] which are defined to include injury, and over which they can prove standing, a case or controversy, and justiciability. Likewise, because the U.S. Attorney General's criminal authority is limited 1) to his work for the U.S. non-republic, whose criminal code operates within the federal areas, and 2) to a handful of crimes that relate to Article III powers (that do not implicate drugs), then he has no express authority to prosecute any drug "crimes" within the fifty state republics.

Said differently, because of the territoriality of the U.S. non-republic's criminal jurisdiction, and because the U.S. republic's criminal authority is limited to a handful of crimes based on federal enumerated powers, which do not include drug possession or dealing, the U.S. Attorney General has authority to regulate drug commerce among America's republics, but no authority to prosecute it as crime there.

The power to regulate commerce is granted to his client – the U.S. republic – at Article I, Section 8, Clause 3 of the U.S. constitution. The power to criminally prohibit commerce is granted to his client – the U.S. non-republic – at Article I, Section 8, Clause 17, but this power only applies within the federal areas   So, these two powers of Congress are separate and operate over two separate land masses. Regulation of commerce happens throughout the fifty states. Criminal prohibition of drug commerce operates in the federal areas.

As with the power of Indiana prosecutors to seek forfeiture of property that is seized by state regulators, the U.S. Attorney General – acting in his republican capacity – also has such power to institute civil forfeiture proceedings of property seized within the state republics because of interstate regulatory violations. [321] This power is co-existent with his power on behalf of the U.S. non-republic both to prosecute violators of drug laws in the federal areas [322] and to seize their contraband, for example in America's coastal waterways. [323]

Thus, the regulatory powers of the Indiana State Board of Pharmacy and the U.S. Attorney General are similar and analogous, and both the state sovereign and the U.S. non-republic have criminal jurisdiction over the area under their respective territorial authority. Likewise, the powers of the pharmacy board's armed drug enforcers are similar and analogous to those of DEA agents within the Indiana republic. There they have administrative power over regulatory violations and judicial authority over real state crimes involving drugs.

Within Indiana, the pharmacy board and the DEA in its republican capacity exercise roughly the same regulatory powers and responsibilities, with state intrastate authority subject to federal interstate preemption. Whereas criminal jurisdiction is largely territorial, state and federal regulatory powers run concurrently. When in conflict, federal regulatory law generally preempts state law based on the aforementioned Supremacy Clause at Article VI, Clause 2 of the U.S. constitution.

Only under Congress' non-republican authority over the federal areas may it create special Article I courts to enforce its draconian penalties against drug dealing. Only in the federal areas is the separation of powers doctrine suspended and inoperative because Congress as a non-republic rules its Article I judges. This is in contrast to the operation of government in America's republics, where the separation of powers doctrine is maintained in the law jurisdiction of state judicial and Article III courts only by strict compliance with the rules of judicial subject matter jurisdiction over injury.

What are the Indiana State Board of Pharmacy's functions and duties?

The functions, powers, duties and procedures of the Indiana State Board of Pharmacy are defined in at least five Indiana Code titles, i.e., 4, 16, 25, 34 and 35, some provisions of which are cross-referenced.

In Title 25 at IC 25-26-13 the Indiana legislature defines the board's regulation of pharmacists and pharmacies which dispense controlled substances. In Title 35 at IC 35-48, which is the Indiana Controlled Substances Act, the legislature defines the board's authority over the manufacture, distribution and dispensing of controlled substances.

In Title 16 at IC 16-42-20 the legislature defines the board's enforcement powers and procedures over controlled substance registrants, applicants and non-applicants referred to at IC 16-42-20-2(c)(3). Title 34 at IC 34-24-1 contains the state's forfeiture powers. Title 4 contains the Indiana Administrative Orders and Procedures Act (AOPA) at IC 4-21.5.

Other powers of the Indiana State Board of Pharmacy and the U.S. Attorney General which are not particularly relevant to our discussion include: 1) the power to reclassify or recommend the reclassification of drugs (*see* 21 USC 811 and 814, and IC 35-48-2-1(a), and 2) the power to promulgate rules relating to the registration and control of the manufacture, distribution and dispensing of controlled substances (called rule-making power) (*see* IC 35-48-3-1, IC 25-26-13-4 and 21 USC 821).

At IC 16-42-20-1(b) the Indiana General Assembly authorizes the Indiana State Board of Pharmacy to designate officers or employees of the board to:

"(1) Carry firearms in the performance of the officer's or employee's official duties.

(2) Execute and serve search warrants, arrest warrants, administrative inspection warrants, subpoenas, and summonses

issued under the authority of this state.

(3) Make arrests without warrant for any offense relating to controlled substances committed in the officer's or employee's presence or if the officer or employee has probable cause to believe that the person to be arrested has committed or is committing a felony relating to controlled substances.

(4) Make seizures of property under this chapter.

(5) Perform other law enforcement duties that the Indiana board of pharmacy designates."

The federal counterpart is 21 USC 878 which grants similar powers to DEA agents, under authority of the U.S. Attorney General.

I point out the above enforcement powers because they become relevant to our discussion both below and in the next chapter. As we shall see, some of the above police powers at IC 16-42-20-1(b) are exercised on behalf of the judicial branch, while others are performed strictly under the pharmacy board's regulatory authority.

As well, some of the law enforcement powers of 21 USC 878 are exercised on behalf of the U.S. republic, while others pertain to the U.S. non-republic in the federal areas. Knowing which powers operate where is essential to enforcing the Indiana and U.S. CSAs properly. Arresting non-criminal regulatory violators always *per se* amounts to false arrest.

The board of pharmacy's regulatory authority

The Indiana General Assembly grants to the Indiana State Board of Pharmacy its sovereign authority to regulate the manufacture, distribution and dispensing of controlled substances within the border of Indiana.

IC 35-48-3-3(a) reads: "Every person who manufactures or distributes any controlled substance within this state or who proposes to engage in the manufacture or distribution of any controlled substance within this state must obtain biennially a registration issued by the board in accordance with its rules."

IC 35-48-3-3(b) reads: "Every person who dispenses or proposes to dispense any controlled substance within Indiana must have a registration issued by the board in accordance with its rules."

IC 25-26-13-4(a)(4) reads "The board may... regulate the sale of drugs and devices in the state of Indiana."

These are roughly the same regulatory powers granted to the U.S. Attorney General at 21 USC 822 in his enforcement of the regulatory provisions of the U.S. Controlled Substance Act. Essentially both the DEA and the Indiana pharmacy board have primary authority only to either 1) "register" (i.e., license) artificial persons to manufacture, distribute and dispense controlled substances within their respective jurisdictions, or 2) to not "register" (i.e., not license) them.

In other words, based on statutory and professional criteria, the pharmacy board and the DEA (on behalf of the Attorney General) either grant or withhold licenses to various artificial persons to manufacture and distribute controlled substances. Neither the pharmacy board nor the DEA has any authority to deal with any natural person, such as a natural born citizen, operating in his or her natural capacity. (Natural persons are not naturally subject to administrative agencies of republican governments, whose jurisdiction is over artificial persons.)

Indiana Code 35-48-2-1(g) calls this power to grant permission to make and sell drugs the pharmacy board's "authority to control" controlled substances. The statute reads: "Authority to control under this section does not extend to distilled spirits, wine, or malt beverages, as those terms are defined or used in IC 7.1, or to tobacco."

In other words, the pharmacy board's "authority to control" is limited to drugs. A separate state executive agency, called the Indiana Alcoholic and Tobacco Commission, has authority to control the licensing of manufacturers and distributors of alcohol and tobacco. The manufacture and distribution of drugs, alcohol and tobacco are regulated by these two agencies, but are not criminally prohibited.

> Parenthetically, allow me to use the above-cited IC 35-48-2-1(g) as an example of Indiana's low legislative standards. This provision is an unnecessary, redundant and superfluous statement of the law because the pharmacy board is not granted any authority over alcohol or tobacco in any other Indiana statute. The provision is a quantum waste of ink and a quantum waste of time to read and think about.
>
> If IC 35-48-2-1(g) was necessary, the Indiana legislature would have to exclude the authority of the pharmacy board to control everything else in the world that is regulated by other executive agencies. If IC 35-48-2-1(g) was necessary, then other code sections

would be needed to exclude the board's authority over other regulated things, such as drivers licenses, professional licenses, construction permits, environmental permits, health and safety standards, invasive medical procedures, etc.

So, just because the legislature does not exclude the pharmacy board from granting fishing licenses, nuclear regulatory permits or tax abatements, for example, we are not to assume that the pharmacy board has the power to do these things. Instead, we are to exercise the presumption – and to rely on the presumption – that government entities have only the power that is granted to them by either constitutions or statutes, and nothing more.

To assume or practice otherwise would be to make all positive law unreadable, unreliable and untenable. It would be to render law completely subjective.

Back to the point: The Indiana State Board of Pharmacy is granted authority to control the manufacture, distribution and dispensing of drugs, and to fight real crime, and nothing more. Whether a person is a pharmaceutical company or an LSD-lab owner or a corner drug dealer or a pharmacist in white, ALL manufacturers, distributors and dispensers of controlled substances within Indiana are to obtain "registration" with the pharmacy board and the DEA.

This is achieved at the state level either directly from the pharmacy board or indirectly through a professional licensing board. To obtain registration, either directly or indirectly, is to receive permission from the pharmacy board to manufacture, distribute or dispense controlled substances.

As was pointed out in chapters 2 – 4 about use of constitutional definitions, drug making and distribution cannot logically be real crimes because the state of Indiana does not have authority to license criminal behavior, which would be to permit crime. The state can only license (and therefore regulate) non-injurious, non-tortious and non-criminal commercial activity.

This is because real, injurious criminal behavior is subject to the criminal law jurisdiction of the judicial branch, which is outside of legislative authority. Nature proscribes crimes. Republican legislatures write them down. Judicial courts adjudicate them.

Each of America's four sovereigns (and their branches) have authority over particular subject matter, which excludes authority over all other. Whatever the behavior in America, it is subject to only one of these four sovereign jurisdictions, each which are recognized in the CSAs.

The pharmacy board regulates manufacturing, not all production

As stated in IC 35-48-3-3, the Indiana State Board of Pharmacy regulates the manufacture of controlled substances. The term manufacture means the same under Indiana law at IC 35-48-1-18 as under federal law at 21 USC Section 802(15). Manufacture means "the production, preparation, propagation, compounding, conversion, or processing of a controlled substance, either directly or indirectly by extraction from substances of natural origin ..."

Thus, to manufacture means to produce or process a controlled substance "from substances of natural origin." To regulate manufacturing does not mean to regulate the "substance of natural origin," such as a poppy or marijuana plant, but instead that which derives "from" such "substance of natural origin."

This is a statutory admission that the positive law of the Indiana legislature and Congress cannot prohibit or regulate Nature, which is sovereign over the natural law jurisdiction of our constitutions and which operates outside of positive law. America's republics cannot criminally prohibit any natural things, and can only regulate their commerce.

In contrast to the term manufacture, IC 35-48-1-26 and 21 USC Section 802 (22) say that "(t)he term 'production' includes the manufacture, planting, cultivation, growing, or harvesting of a controlled substance."

Because production includes manufacture which is defined at IC 35-48-1-18 (and 21 USC Section 802(15)) to involve the extraction of controlled substances from natural sources, and because the rest of the definition of production at IC 35-48-1-26 (and 21 USC Section 802 (22)) involves the mere cultivation of plants, thus manufacture at IC 35-48-1-18 (and 21 USC Section 802(15)) and production at IC 35-48-1-26 (and 21 USC Section 802 (22)) refer to two separate processes.

Production at IC 35-48-1-26 means to produce natural plants and other sources of controlled substances. To manufacture at IC 35-48-1-18 means to produce controlled substances from those natural sources produced under IC 35-48-1-26.

The regulation of the Indiana State Board of Pharmacy extends to the manufacture of controlled substances. However, because production is defined by statute to be different than manufacture, the pharmacy board's regulatory authority does not extend over all production. Regulation extends only to that production which is also manufacturing, as well as to all production (or "produce") that is distributed to the public.

Therefore, not all production is regulated. Between production and manufacturing, only all manufacturing is specifically regulated.

Thus, the board's authority extends only over production either 1) that amounts to manufacturing, such as converting marijuana to hashish or turning chemicals into LSD, or 2) to that production or "produce", for example of marijuana, that gets entered into commerce.

If marijuana production enters commerce by amounting to manufacture due to the extraction of controlled substances, or if production enters commerce due to plants being distributed to the public, then the Indiana pharmacy board can regulate such production. Otherwise production is not subject to the board's regulation.

This is because non-commercial production operates in the natural law jurisdiction of the Indiana constitution, not in the positive law jurisdiction. Mere production is subject only to the Laws of Nature, not to the Indiana legislature, which has authority over the manufacture, distribution and dispensing of goods and services.

Thus, manufacture excludes the mere cultivation of plants, and as we will see in chapter 21, particularly the cultivation of plants for one's own personal use. Only manufacturers, distributors, and dispensers of controlled substances are to be regulated, not all producers.

Likewise, the state regulates "narcotic drugs" as substances derived from Nature, "whether produced directly or indirectly by extraction from substances of vegetable origin, or independently by means of chemical synthesis, or by a combination of extraction and chemical synthesis." [324]

As with marijuana, neither the Indiana legislature nor Congress regulates the production or cultivation of poppy, coca, psilocybin, peyote, or kat, for example, but instead only the extraction of narcotics and other controlled substances from these natural sources, as well as to the distribution of these substances in commerce. If one enters commerce with these natural substances – either by manufacturing them or distributing them – then they become subject to regulation, which includes property forfeiture and commercial injunction.

That different natural sources produce inherently different effects, as a psilocybin mushroom does from a Portobella mushroom, does not change the rule or law that only the manufacture, distribution or dispensing of all kinds of mushrooms are subject to regulation, and that the commerce in any type of mushroom is not criminal (outside of the federal areas).

One mushroom sold into commerce may be subject to different regulations and to different regulators. For example, commerce in French

Horn mushrooms may be regulated by the Food and Drug Administration, while commerce in psilocybin mushrooms may be regulated by the U.S. Attorney General and the DEA under the Controlled Substances Act. However, nothing in current law makes possession or commerce of one type of mushroom criminal, and others not.

As well, the commerce of these items among the states is subject to regulation, but not criminal prosecution. This means that drug regulators can confiscate legislatively disfavored mushrooms, poppies and *Rosales*, and can shut down and enjoin these drug businesses, but they cannot arrest manufacturers, distributors or dispensers merely for being in business.

That which is both natural and intuitive, i.e., that natural people can grow what they consume without government interference, is both constitutional and codified. Republican governments regulate the manu-facture of drugs but not the production of the "sources of natural origin" [325] of drugs. As we shall also see, drug users have not only a natural, but also a statutory right to "lawfully possess" drugs. [326]

In other words, the statutory law of the government that America's Founding Fathers created out of natural law and to which the People granted positive law powers actually does respect our natural rights to pro-duce, as opposed to manufacture. This includes statutorily distinguishing production (i.e., the creation or cultivation of natural sources of controlled substances) from the manufacture of controlled substances, which involves extraction or chemical synthesis.

This distinction proves that the authors of the CSAs absolutely knew about the natural law jurisdiction, where natural persons are sovereign over production. The seemingly irrelevant distinction between production and manufacture reflects the important distinction between the natural and positive law jurisdictions in the U.S. and state constitutions, which the CSAs absolutely uphold.

The terms production and manufacture are statutorily distinguished so as to keep the positive law jurisdiction over manufacturing separate from the natural law jurisdiction over production, and so that the executive branch regulates only the proper things, i.e., those things that are manufactured, distributed or dispensed, not all things that are grown or produced.

We produce and consume things as a natural right. In contrast, we manufacture and distribute things as commercial privileges. In the law jurisdiction, where gardening is a protected natural right, natural persons are not required to ask permission of any positive law authority to produce anything or to exercise what comes naturally.

The states' CSAs reflect that natural persons produce plants as a statutorily-secured natural right, and that people are required to get state permission only to extract controlled substances from natural sources and to distribute natural resources or their extractions in commerce. This means that in Indiana, for this reason alone, growing pot or producing mushrooms for one's own use has always been legal.

State control of drug manufacturing includes control over extractions such as hashish and hash oil, but excludes control over the production of pot for one's personal use. It equally excludes the non-commercial canning of vegetables and fruits, including the fruit of marijuana plants, which does not involve extraction. This will become clearer in the chapter 21.

That plant cultivation is different than that which the Indiana State Board of Pharmacy regulates, i.e., manufacturing, is also seen from IC 35-48-4-11, which declares the cultivation of marijuana to be possession of marijuana. It reads in pertinent part: "A person who:...(2) knowingly or intentionally grows or cultivates marijuana ... commits possession of marijuana ... a Class A misdemeanor..."

Because property possession is a constitutionally-secured natural right, [327] then so is cultivation. Thus, the above provisions place cultivation, production and property possession within the natural law jurisdiction where they should be placed, over which the above statutory positive law regarding manufacturing, by its own above admissions, has no effect.

This regulatory scheme is not only constitutional but makes complete sense given that positive law has no constitutional or statutory authority over that which we produce for ourselves, and given that it cannot trump or displace natural law by trying to criminalize Nature and the natural products of our human nature and effort.

The positive law of America's republics may only and does only regulate commerce, including the commerce of all things natural such as marijuana and other garden produce. Because manufacturing is the extraction of controlled substances from Nature, and because it does not include the mere production of plants, then growing pot, mushrooms and other things for one's own use is not only legal and non-criminal, as a form of possession, but is also not subject to regulation by the Indiana pharmacy board as a form of manufacture or distribution.

Do you see how consistently the real law secures our natural rights to possess, produce and intoxicate? And do you see how the war on drugs comes from not knowing and from misrepresenting this real law? The real law secures people's rights, and does not violate them. Only government officials, who do not know the law, violate people's rights.

As long as a home grower of marijuana or Porta Bella mushrooms stays out of commerce, he and his produce are not subject to regulation by the Indiana pharmacy board. Plus, as long as he does not hurt others, the grower is not subject to a judicial trial court. These are conclusions gleaned merely from properly reading the CSAs, which secure the natural law jurisdiction of individuals from commercial regulation and criminal prohibition.

Seeking permission to make and sell drugs

As we saw earlier, the Indiana Controlled Substances Act at IC 35-48-3-3 says that anyone who enters or intends to enter into the manufacture, distribution or dispensing of drugs in Indiana must apply for a "registration" from the Indiana State Board of Pharmacy. This mandate applies to, for example, all marijuana growers in Indiana who sell marijuana to the public and all crack cocaine manufacturers. Because the Indiana legislature is sovereign over intrastate commerce, this provision is mandatory upon all drug dealers or artificial people who intend to manufacture, distribute or dispense drugs in Indiana.

For example, IC 35-48-3-3(b) states that: "Any person who dispenses or proposes to dispense any controlled substance within Indiana must have a registration issued by the board in accordance with the board's rules." These regulatory provisions are similar to those in the U.S. CSA which makes the U.S. republic sovereign over interstate drug commerce and all interstate drug enterprises.

An application for registration from a drug manufacturer or distributor grants the Indiana pharmacy board statutory authority to inspect the applicant's premises. IC 35-48-3-3(g) reads: "The board may inspect the establishment of a registrant or applicant for registration in accordance with the board's rules."

After the opportunity for inspection, and based on the pharmacy board's statutory and professional criteria, the board either 1) grants to the applicant a registration (or renewal) or 2) denies the applicant its requested registration (or renewal).

If the pharmacy board approves a registration, the enterprise is then approved to make, distribute and / or dispense drugs in accordance with the grant. However, for those enterprises who are denied registration, their privileges to make and sell drugs are owed administrative due process according to the Indiana Administrative Orders and Procedures Act and the CSA, both which require an administrative hearing to adjudicate the applicant's denial of privileges.

IC 35-48-3-6(a) of the CSA reads: "Before recommending a denial, suspension, or revocation of a registration, or before refusing a renewal of registration, the board shall serve upon the applicant or registrant an order to show cause why registration should not be denied, revoked, or suspended, or why the renewal should not be denied."

Such "show cause" orders give applicants or registrants the opportunity to appear before an administrative law "court of record" of the pharmacy board to make their cases why their registrations should be approved. This means that the board must provide a hearing on the record to adjudicate the applicant's privilege to manufacture or distribute controlled substances. Thus, marijuana growers and crack makers who wish to sell marijuana or cocaine to the public are to apply for registration from the pharmacy board, and if denied, are to be given a show cause hearing why the privilege to be in drug commerce was denied.

> In reality, if a commercial marijuana grower or crack maker applied to the pharmacy board for a registration, pharmacy board enforcers would have authority to enter and inspect the premises under IC 35-48-3-3(g), and would likely confiscate the contraband before denying the applicant a license.

The CSA at IC 35-48-3-6 says that "(t)hese proceedings shall be conducted in accordance with IC 4-21.5," which is the AOPA. These procedures are mandatory upon the pharmacy board because, according to IC 4-21.5-2-2, the procedures may not be waived by the state.

Then, says IC 35-48-3-6, applicants who are dissatisfied with the board's final determinations, i.e., the board's denial of permission to make or sell drugs, may seek judicial review of the decision in accordance with the AOPA at IC 4-21.5. This administrative structure and registration process is similar to that of the federal government under the regulatory authority of the U.S. Attorney General at 21 USC 822 – 824, which is subject to judicial review at 21 USC 877.

Powers to inspect and confiscate

Once an applicant obtains a registration from the Indiana pharmacy board, i.e. a license to enter drug commerce, the applicant's "controlled premises" [328] become subject to additional administrative inspections. The CSA grants the pharmacy board power to make "accountability audits of the supply and inventory of controlled substances." [329]

It also grants designated board officers or employees the authority to seek "administrative inspection warrants" to inspect "controlled premises" and to seize contraband. [330] Indiana Code 16-42-20-2 defines the procedure that an employee or officer of the pharmacy board would use to obtain an "administrative inspection warrant" from a pharmacy board administrative law judge.

IC 16-42-20-2(b)(3) reads: "If the judge is satisfied that grounds for the application exist or that there is probable cause to believe the grounds exist, the judge shall issue a warrant identifying the area, premises, building, or conveyance to be inspected, the purpose of the inspection, and, if appropriate, the type of property to be inspected."

The probable cause mentioned above is "a reasonable ground for belief" [331] that a regulatory – not a criminal – violation has occurred. The pharmacy board's administrative law court has no authority to issue a criminal warrant, which authority is strictly judicial. Likewise, because judicial courts have no subject matter jurisdiction over regulatory matters, they may not issue search or arrest warrants for non-crimes such as drug possession, dealing or other regulatory violations. They can issue search and arrest warrants regarding actual drug crimes, such as obtaining drugs through fraud or such as selling counterfeit controlled substances.

As well, IC 16-42-20-2(b)(1) recognizes that a "judge of a court of record within the judge's jurisdiction may, upon proper oath or affirmation showing probable cause, issue warrants for the purpose of conducting administrative inspections authorized by this chapter and seizures of property appropriate to the inspections."

These provisions are directed at disfavored drug dealers, i.e., people in drug commerce who have not applied for registration with the pharmacy board, and over which the pharmacy board does not have consent authority to inspect their "controlled premises." [332] Pharmacy board enforcers may routinely inspect the premises of registrants, but their authority is more limited with regard to drug makers or dealers who have not applied for registration. Such a warrant is based on probable cause that the drug dealer is violating the state's regulatory – non judicial – authority.

IC 16-42-20-2 (b)(4) says that an administrative inspection "warrant must do the following:

(A) State the grounds for the warrant's issuance and the name of each person whose affidavit has been taken in support of the warrant.
(B) Be directed to a person authorized by section 1 of this chapter to

execute the warrant.

(C) Command the person to whom the warrant is directed to inspect the area, premises, building, or conveyance identified for the purpose specified and, if appropriate, direct the seizure of the property specified.

(D) Identify the item or types of property to be seized, if any.

(E) Direct that the warrant may be served during normal business hours and designate the judge to whom the warrant shall be returned."

Says IC 16-42-20-2(c)(3), this procedure "does not prevent an inspection without a warrant of books and records under an administrative subpoena issued in accordance with IC 4-21.5-3 [the AOPA] or prevent entries and administrative inspections, including seizures of property, without a warrant if any of the following conditions exist:

(A) The owner, operator, or agent in charge of the controlled premises consents.

(B) A situation presents imminent danger to health or safety.

(C) A situation involves the inspection of conveyances if there is reasonable cause to believe that the mobility of the conveyance makes it impracticable to obtain a warrant.

(D) An exceptional or emergency circumstance where time or opportunity to apply for a warrant is lacking.

(E) A situation in which a warrant is not constitutionally required."

Thus, an officer of the Indiana pharmacy board may obtain an inspection warrant from an administrative law judge of the board, or if any of the five above immediate reasons are available, he may inspect and seize property without an administrative law warrant. These provisions for obtaining administrative inspection warrants, for performing administrative inspections and for seizing commercial contraband in Indiana are similar to the federal provisions at 21 USC 879 and 880.

The above state provisions are rather significant because they essentially are statutory admissions that unauthorized drug making is not a crime. If, for example, a methamphetamine maker was committing a crime, the Indiana legislature would have granted pharmacy board enforcers power to seek a judicial search warrant. Because making drugs is not a crime, but instead only a potential regulatory violation, drug enforcers may only seek administrative warrants.

Thus, Indiana's drug statutes respect the jurisdictional distinctions between the executive and judicial branches, but government officials have not.

Seeing how the pieces fit

Let's say that an Indiana pharmacy board enforcer gets a tip that someone is making methamphetamine in a residential area. The enforcer goes out and does some investigating. He secures affidavits from two eye-witnesses who have seen the drug lab. Based on this probable cause, he obtains an inspection warrant from a pharmacy board court of record.

When pharmacy board enforcers exercise the administrative warrant, they are not exercising criminal or judicial authority, but instead regulatory or administrative authority. As the above statute says, such warrants must be "served during normal business hours." [333]

Compare this to a federal criminal search warrant issued by a U.S. magistrate judge, under authority of 21 USC 879 of the U.S. CSA, that "may be served at any time of the day or night..." This power belongs to law enforcers working for the U.S. non-republic in the federal areas, which is only where Congress may criminally prohibit drugs. (Apparently, enforcing regulations does not have the same immediacy as fighting crime.)

This power to issue criminal search warrants regarding mere drug commerce does not exist for Article III courts or for state courts. This is because drug possession and dealing are not crimes in America's republics. Because most crimes are state crimes, thus only state courts have criminal jurisdiction over actual crimes involving drugs, such as drug counterfeiting and fraud. However, they and Article III courts have no criminal authority over mere regulatory violators.

With regard to the latter, inspection warrants afford drug regulators (and other law enforcers) authority to inspect premises and confiscate property used in making and dealing controlled substances. However, they do not empower law enforcers to arrest people for the non-crime of drug making or for being in any business (except slavery). The statutory provisions for administrative inspection warrants are admissions of this.

IC 16-42-20-5 says that controlled substances seized by the board of pharmacy enforcers or other law enforcement officers during inspections are "considered to be in the custody of the Indiana board of pharmacy subject only to the orders and decrees of the court having jurisdiction over the forfeiture proceedings."

(*See* also IC 34-24-1-2(b)(3) which allows law enforcement agencies to "require another agency authorized by law to take custody of the property and remove it to an appropriate location." In the case of controlled substances, the pharmacy board is the state agency charged with custody and destruction of the contraband.)

Without the commission of a crime, the district prosecutor is to involve himself in this matter only to get the property that was seized from drug dealers by drug enforcers legally forfeited to the state. This judicial process begins only 1) after a pharmacy board officer or employee inventories the seized property, [334] 2) after the employee provides a copy of this inventory to the property owner, [335] and 3) after an administrative law judge files the list of confiscated property with the clerk of a judicial court, [336] which step initiates a forfeiture proceeding.

This is not a criminal process in the law jurisdiction, but instead a civil process in equity. That this process operates in equity is a legislative admission that drug dealing does not operate under criminal law.

In addition to the above powers, the prosecuting attorney may seek reimbursement for the costs of enforcement and forfeiture. IC 34-24-1-3(a) says that prosecuting attorneys may "cause an action for reimbursement of law enforcement costs and forfeiture to be brought by filing a complaint in the circuit or superior court in the jurisdiction where the seizure occurred." This procedure is also in non-criminal equity.

As previously noted, the state prosecutor has no similar expressed statutory authority to prosecute the unauthorized drug maker for a crime. This is 1) because judicial courts lack subject matter jurisdiction over drug making and selling, 2) because in an American republic it is not a crime to be in any business, except the slave business, and 3) because all non-slave businesses are subject to non-criminal equity.

Absent the commission of a real case or crime, Indiana prosecutors only have authority to get the seized property legally forfeited and to seek reimbursement for the costs of the state's actions. Confiscation, forfeiture and reimbursement are three of the state's equitable remedies, which are legislative admissions that drug control operates in equity, and not under criminal law.

Along with these legislative admissions, executive branch confessions should also be forthcoming. For decades law enforcers have taken advantage of their asset forfeiture powers to line their own pockets. Thus, not only has the judicial branch been misused to jail non-criminals in the war on drugs, but regulatory powers have been abused as well. Abusing power is the nature of all governments. Such abuse can only be justified in non-republican ones, which are loyal to kings instead of to the rule of law.

19

More on equitable remedies

The power of injunction

In addition to the above-described state's powers to inspect, shut down and confiscate the property of unregistered manufacturers, distributors and dispensers of controlled substances, IC 16-42-20-3 says that "(a)ny court of record has jurisdiction to restrain or enjoin violations of laws relating to controlled substances." This means that, given evidence of regulatory violations, an administrative court of record of the Indiana pharmacy board has authority to issue administrative injunctions against non-criminal regulation violators, such as unwanted drug dealers.

Under the Indiana AOPA, according to the administrative due process rights described in chapter 16, these persons are entitled to notice of the board's dispositions [337] and a right to review. [338] This right to review is the right to get the board to reconsider its injunction. If 1) a drug dealer's arguments do not result in the release of an administrative injunction and in his registration by the board, and if 2) a drug dealer does not stop his unwanted drug dealing, then the Indiana Attorney General may seek a judicial injunction against this person's continued unwanted behavior. [339]

These judicial injunctions are enforceable in equity under courts' judicial contempt authority. This is consistent with the the U.S. Attorney General's similar injunctive powers at 21 USC 882, which he is to exercise among the states in his regulatory capacity.

It is this power to enjoin which led me to realize that the state of Indiana and the U.S. republic are to regulate all drug commerce. The realization came after I asked the logical question: If "violations of laws relating to controlled substances" are statutory crimes, as the penalty provisions at IC 35-48-4 suggest, then why would the state have the power to enjoin them?

That is, if violations of drug laws, such as drug making and dealing, were crimes, then why not just arrest and prosecute the offenders instead of enjoining their unlawful behavior. Then the light bulb went off.

Here's the answer: 1) because the manufacture and distribution of controlled substances are not crimes subject to the Indiana judicial branch, 2) because the administrative law courts of the pharmacy board do not have jurisdiction to criminally sanction statutory violations, and 3) because only one jurisdiction – i.e., either equity or law, but not both – has authority over drug commerce, then the delegated power to enjoin the manufacture and distribution of controlled substances, which is an equitable power, both expresses a) that drug commerce operates in non-criminal equity – not law, and b) that the state's ultimate remedy against such unwanted commercial drug activity is to enjoin it – not to criminally prosecute it. [340]

In that the state lacks criminal authority over drug commerce (because such commerce has not been placed into the law jurisdiction by a constitutional amendment), the state's only other powers and remedies against unwanted drug commerce include investigation, inspection, confiscation, judicial forfeiture, reimbursement of costs, and judicial injunctions, which are non-criminal powers under equity.

Because of the separation of powers doctrine, subject matter may fit within the subject matter jurisdiction of either the judicial branch or the executive branch, but not both. Likewise, subject matter is either under equity or law, and law has the only criminal authority. If drug making and dealing were real crimes, then the state's remedy would be to arrest and prosecute the criminals at law – not to enjoin them. If drug dealing was a real crime, then the pharmacy board could not license it.

Thus, the state's forfeiture and injunctive powers are significant statutory admissions that unlicensed drug dealing is not criminal, but is merely a regulatory infraction under equity – not law. To enjoin unlicensed drug making and dealing is the full extent of the power that the Indiana legislature grants to Indiana's executive branch, which power may be invoked only after the Indiana State Board of Pharmacy has exhausted its own remedies to administratively shut down and enjoin unwanted commercial drug activity.

Republican legislatures lack authority to license criminal behavior. For an activity to be licensed, such as the making and selling of drugs, is to mean that it is not criminal behavior. Because licensing operates under equity, to license something in a republic is the government's admission that the activity is commercial and operates in a non-criminal jurisdiction.

Because the criminal law jurisdiction applies equally to all natural persons, then if one drug maker is criminal, then all drug makers are criminals. If one drug dealer is subject to arrest, then so are the others. As we shall see more extensively later, the U.S. Supreme Court in *Gonzales v. Raich*

(2005) told us that as a class, all enterprises that manufacture, distribute and dispense drugs are to be treated the same. [341]

This is the principle of equal protection under the 14th Amendment. As well, under the due process clause of the 5th and 14th Amendments, all drug merchants have legal rights to administrative due process under the CSAs and APAs (or Indiana's AOPA).

In Indiana, for example, both a meth maker and a licensed manufacturer of methamphetamine are entitled to have their privileges to make and sell drugs adjudicated by either the DEA (as the regulator of interstate drug commerce) or by the Indiana pharmacy board (as the regulator of intrastate drug commerce) before being subjected to the judicial branch. In Indiana, due process requires the state pharmacy board and the DEA to exhaust their administrative remedies before seeking judicial help to enforce their administrative decisions.

Judicial review (under IC 4-21.5-5 and IC 16-42-20-7) and judicial enforcement (under IC 34-24-1 and IC 35-48-3-3(i)) are not available to any litigant until after all administrative remedies by state regulators and defenses are exhausted. To exhaust one's administrative remedies allows one to invoke the appellate jurisdiction of Indiana's Circuit and Superior Courts respectively under IC 33-28-1-2 and IC 33-29-1-1.5. In contrast, "Failure to exhaust administrative remedies deprives the trial court of subject matter jurisdiction," wrote the Indiana Court of Appeals in *LHT Capital, LLC v. Indiana Horse Racing Comm'n* (2008). [342]

"Indiana views the failure to exhaust administrative remedies as a matter of subject matter jurisdiction [*cases omitted* [343]], wrote the Indiana Supreme Court in *Austin Lakes Joint Venture v. Avon Utilities, Inc.* (1995). "Stated otherwise, where an administrative remedy is available, such remedy must be pursued before the claimant is allowed access to the courts. [344] Thus, a party's failure to exhaust its administrative remedies creates a jurisdictional defect and makes a motion to dismiss for lack of subject matter jurisdiction appropriate." [345]

"The exhaustion rule assumes an available statutory remedy at the time the challenged judicial relief is sought," wrote the Indiana Court of Appeals in *Title Service, LLC v. Womacks* (2006). [346] In the case of drug commerce, the state's available statutory remedy is for the Indiana pharmacy board to enjoin unwanted drug dealing. This remedy is not only readily available, but it is the state's ultimate administrative remedy.

The exclusivity of administrative remedies "is typically expressed in either of two forms:" wrote the Indiana Court of Appeals in *Title Service, LLC v. Womacks* (2006). Either "the statute states that its provisions constitute the exclusive remedy for such actions, or the statute provided judicial review is available only after the administrative remedies provided in the statute are exhausted." [347]

In the case of drugs, not only does the AOPA define the state's "minimum procedural duties," [348] which are unique duties and which the state may not waive, [349] but it also allows parties access to judicial review "only after exhausting all administrative remedies available within the agency..." [350]

Given that the state of Indiana has unique, exclusive and non-waivable "minimum procedural duties" to fulfill in the executive branch, [351] its failure to use and exhaust these procedures in the pharmacy board "deprives the trial court of subject matter jurisdiction." [352] "When the legislature has provided a statutory scheme with an exclusive administrative remedy," wrote the Court of Appeals in *Title Service, LLC v. Womacks* (2006), "our courts lack jurisdiction to hear the matter until the administrative procedures have been exhausted or a request for relief has been denied." [353]

This administrative process works similarly at the federal level as at the state level. The U.S. Attorney General – as chief drug regulator – must always first exhaust his administrative remedies that are available under the U.S. Administrative Procedures Act at 5 USC Chapter 5, which is incorporated by reference into the U.S. CSA at 21 USC 875. That is, he would exhaust his administrative remedies using administrative law courts in the DEA before bringing regulatory interstate drug matters to Article III U.S. courts for injunctive relief under 21 USC 882.

The U.S. Controlled Substances Acts at 21 USC 824(c) says that "(s)uch proceedings shall be independent of, and not in lieu of, criminal prosecutions or other proceedings under this subchapter or any other law of the United States." This legislative admission obviously reflects that the interstate regulation of drugs, for example under 21 USC 875, 877, 880 and 882, is a separate process to be performed in a separate branch of government, and on behalf of a separate sovereign, from prosecuting crimes relating to drugs in the federal areas, to which 21 USC 824(c) refers. Indeed, the criminal prosecution of drug defendants in the federal areas is independent of the US. Attorney General's regulation of drug commerce within the states.

As well, because judicial enforcement of administrative injunctions may involve incarceration of violators within the U.S. republic, 21 USC 882 makes available jury trials for alleged violators of U.S. injunctions or restraining orders. It reads: "In case of an alleged violation of an injunction or restraining order issued under this section, trial shall, upon demand of the accused, be by a jury in accordance with the Federal Rules of Civil Procedure."

This right to a jury trial exists because 21 USC 882 is a provision in the U.S. CSA that relates to defendants' legal rights within America's republics, not the federal areas. Likely in the U.S. republic, according to the 6th Amendment to its constitution, a right to a jury trial is available when the government seeks to deprive a defendant of his or her liberty, as in a judicial contempt hearing.

Note as well that the administrative process is not compulsory on drug defendants. Administrative due process requires that they be given notice that their privilege to make and sell drugs is being adjudicated, but they are not in criminal contempt for not showing up at these non-criminal "show cause" hearings, or for not obeying administrative orders.

The administrative process is that which the state owes to them before it shuts down their *malum prohibita* – not what drug defendants owe to the state. Drug dealers owe governments only one general duty, i.e., to register their drug enterprises with state drug regulators and / or with the U.S. Attorney General,. [354] which to violate is not criminal within the states.

One cannot be held in contempt of court for not attending an administrative court proceeding because administrative law courts in the executive branch have neither criminal nor contempt authority. They only adjudicate state privileges or functions. Government agents have no authority to jail anyone for any reason, except for the commission of real crime or for judicial contempt of an order, such as an injunction against drug dealing.

The Indiana Attorney General and the U.S. Attorney General (in his capacity for the U.S. republic) may use judicial courts only to enjoin parties from making or distributing drugs. Within an American republic, no honest and nonviolent person is subject to arrest or prosecution for engaging in any drug business until a judicial officer says so, and this is to happen only after administrative due process for this person's drug business has been exhausted and fulfilled.

The war on drugs is supported only by misrepresentations and misunderstandings of law

We have seen that drug possession is not subject to any judicial or regulatory court within a republic. We have also seen that drug commerce is subject to regulation in equity, which means that it is not subject to criminal arrest and prosecution in the law jurisdiction. As well, we learned that the equitable remedies of forfeiture and injunction are the states' and the U.S. republic's ultimate remedies against unwanted drug dealing.

With this background in mind, consider a 2012 Congressional Research Service's report on medical marijuana which discusses the constitutional doctrine of federal preemption. Says the report, this doctrine "generally prevents states from enacting laws that are inconsistent with federal law. Under the Supremacy Clause, state laws that conflict with federal law are generally preempted and therefore void." [355]

The Indiana Controlled Substances Act reflects this. IC 35-48-3-5(e) reads:

> "If the Drug Enforcement Administration terminates, denies, suspends, or revokes a federal registration for the manufacture, distribution, or dispensing of controlled substances, a registration issued by the board under this chapter is automatically suspended."

However, that was then and this is now, suggests the report. "Courts, however, have not viewed the relationship between state and federal marijuana laws in such a manner." The report continues:

> "nor did Congress intend that the CSA displace all state laws associated with controlled substances. Instead, the relationship between the federal ban on marijuana and state medical marijuana exemptions must be considered in the context of two distinct sovereigns, each enacting separate and independent criminal regimes with separate and independent enforcement mechanisms, in which certain conduct may be prohibited under one sovereign and not the other." [356]

I included this quotation to point out how it is both correct and incorrect. It is correct in that medical- and recreational-marijuana states are sovereigns. As well, state sovereigns are no doubt clashing with the U.S. republic as a sovereign. As we well know by now, only one of these sovereigns is sovereign over marijuana commerce within these states.

Based on the Interstate Commerce Clause at Article I, Section 8, Clause 3, the U.S. republic is granted authority to regulate marijuana commerce among the state republics. Under the Supremacy Clause at Article VI, Clause 2 of the U.S. constitution, states' concurrent authority to regulate marijuana commerce is generally preempted by federal authority.

However, this federal authority is only the power to regulate marijuana commerce, and it does not include the power to criminally prohibit commerce. Only Congress as the U.S. non-republic, within its territorial jurisdiction defined at 18 USC 7, has authority to prohibit any type of commerce. However, Congress as the U.S. republic does not have such authority within the states. There Congress as the U.S. republic regulates drug commerce and enforces a handful of federal crimes based on its enumerated powers, which do not include drug trafficking.

This raises what is incorrect about the above quotation and the CRS report in general. Indeed, as the report says, "two distinct sovereigns" [357] are clashing. However, it is not the "criminal regimes" [358] of these sovereigns that are clashing, but instead their regulatory non-criminal regimes. It is not their separate law jurisdictions over crime that are clashing. It is instead their concurrent equity jurisdictions over commerce that are in conflict.

Both Congress and the states legislate as republics. As American republics, 1) their laws agree on the meaning of crime, 2) their laws agree on which sovereign has authority over crime, i.e., the states have such authority except over crimes relating to Congress' enumerated powers, 3) their laws agree that drug commerce is not within the subject matter jurisdiction of state judicial or Article III courts, but is regulated by state or U.S. administrative law courts, and 4) their laws agree that Congress' authority to regulate interstate commerce is supreme over that of the states. That is what Congress and the state legislatures agree upon, which principles are reflected in their constitutional statutes, such their CSAs, which they do not follow.

Whereas the federal regulatory regime seeks to break up all marijuana commerce by means of confiscation and injunction, which is within that regime's rightful authority, the regulatory regimes of the reform states allow marijuana to be commercially grown, sold and taxed. These two regulatory sovereigns that are clashing have nothing to do with criminal law. This is because drugs are legal in America's republics and because drug commerce is regulated – not criminally prohibited.

Criminal law is not implicated because no crime is committed – or ever has been committed – by merely growing, selling or possessing marijuana in a republic. Criminal law is not implicated because America's republics regulate commerce. Thus, if one hears a loud crash, it is not from the clashing of state and federal criminal jurisdictions but instead from the concurrent state and federal regulatory regimes.

Because of the principle of federal preemption, and based on the U.S. Supreme Court decision in *Gonzales v. Raich* (2005) [359] – to be soon discussed – federal regulators have superior authority over state regulators.

This means that they likely can legitimately 1) shut down marijuana businesses in reform states, 2) confiscate marijuana business property, 3) gain judicial forfeiture of seized property and 4) judicially enjoin the future operation of marijuana businesses in all the fifty states, regardless of state constitutional or statutory law. This would be due to the supremacy of the U.S. regulatory power over concurrent state regulatory power.

As a political libertarian, while I do not believe that it is good public policy for the U.S. Attorney General to regulate marijuana in the above heavy-handed manner, I fully recognize the office's lawful authority under *Gonzales v. Raich* (2005) to do this. I wish however that the Attorney General would instead exercise the office's authority to reclassify marijuana so that the U.S. republic would instead respect state marijuana reforms.

The CRS report makes another mistake common to drug literature, claiming that "federal law prohibits the cultivation, distribution, and possession of marijuana." [360] Indeed, federal law <u>does</u> criminally prohibit marijuana commerce, but only in the federal areas, which important fact the report omits (because its author does not realize this). As we shall also see, federal law does not prohibit the possession of marijuana anywhere.

Because of the territoriality of criminal jurisdiction, the federal law does not criminally prohibit growing or selling marijuana within any of the state republics, as the CRS report falsely suggests. Congress may regulate commerce within the states, but it has no authority to criminally prohibit it.

Within America's republics, possession of property (including marijuana) is a natural right secured by the substantive right to not be enslaved except for the commission of crime. This right is to be recognized in state and in Article III republican courts.

Within America's republics, the *malum prohibita* of the U.S. non-republic is inapplicable and unenforceable in all criminal law courts. Congress' *malum prohibita* against drugs is criminally enforceable only in the federal areas. Within the states, Congress' *malum prohibita* against drugs is subject only to regulation, including forfeiture and injunction.

The above CRS' misstatement of law is similar to its claiming that "individuals who use medical marijuana in compliance with state law are still in violation of federal law and subject to prosecution by federal authorities at any time..." This statement is false because in republics, individuals have the natural right to possess and use marijuana – medical marijuana or otherwise – and also have state and federal statutory rights to possess drugs as ultimate users, to be discussed in chapter 21. [361]

As well, federal criminal law applies only to people who commit crimes relating to Congress' powers within the states and to those who violate Congress' criminal prohibitions within the federal areas. In other words, the above statement is false because federal law does not apply at all to drug users within the states. As we established in part 1 of this book, Congress does not generally legislate over U.S. citizens who are not engaged in commerce. As we shall see in chapter 21, drug users have a statutory right to lawfully possess drugs for their own use and for those in their household.

Another point I would like to make about the CRS report is that it completely misses the mark by not acknowledging how Congress deals with all commerce in its republican capacity, i.e., by regulating it. This is obvious by the report's frequent loose use of the word *prohibition*, which we know is strictly a judicial, non-regulatory term that, within an American republic, operates in the law jurisdiction. By confusing Congress' power to prohibit within the federal areas with its power to regulate within the states, the CRS report exemplifies the misunderstandings and misrepresentations of law that sadly yet necessarily exist to support the illegal war on drugs.

This lack of understanding between the words regulate and prohibit, and their misrepresentations, are evident at the highest levels of U.S. government attorneys. Witness the opening argument by U.S. Solicitor General Paul D. Clement in *Gonzales v. Raich* (2005), in which the U.S. Supreme Court upheld the power of the DEA to regulate interstate marijuana commerce:

> "Justice Stevens, and may it please the Court: Through the Controlled Substances Act, Congress has comprehensively <u>regulated</u> the national market in drugs with potential for abuse. And with respect to Schedule I substances, like marijuana, that have both a high potential for abuse and no currently accepted medical use in treatment, Congress <u>categorically prohibits</u> interstate trafficking outside the narrow and carefully controlled confines of federally approved research programs." [362]

As we have seen, the words regulate and prohibit do not mean the same thing. Regulation operates in equity upon artificial persons in America's republics. Prohibition operates 1) in the federal areas over that which Congress has plenary power, 2) in the law jurisdiction where Nature is sovereign and proscribes crime, and 3) in the law jurisdiction after a constitutional amendment places *malum prohibita* into the criminal law jurisdiction. Republican legislatures legislate over equity. Absent a constitutional amendment, they cannot legislate criminal prohibitions within the republican criminal law jurisdiction.

Thus, contrary to what Mr. Clement told the Supreme Court in his opening statement, Congress does not "categorically prohibit" [363] any kind of interstate trafficking or commerce. Its criminal prohibitions at 21 USC 841 – 844A operate only in the federal areas under Congress' non-republican power. Otherwise, it <u>categorically regulates</u> all commerce among the states.

That is what the Interstate Commerce Clause at Article I, Section 8, Clause 3 of the U.S. Constitution stands for. That is what the Supreme Court wrote in *Ohio v. Helvering* (1934): "Nevertheless, the police power is and remains a governmental power, and, applied to business activities, is the power to regulate those activities..." [364]

In other words, contrary to what Mr. Clement told the Supreme Court, the police power as applied to drug commerce is to not criminally prohibit it, but to categorically regulate it. (The opening two paragraphs of Justice Paul Stevens' opinion in *Gonzales v. Raich*, where he uses the words regulate and prohibit almost interchangeably, also show this confusion.)

Mr. Clement's misunderstandings and misrepresentations derive from his reliance on *Champion v. Ames (the Lottery Case)* (1903), [365] which he cited in his oral argument. This was a case where, in a 5-to-4 decision, the U.S. Supreme Court affirmed the denial of a writ of habeas corpus for a man arrested and detained for conspiring to transport lottery tickets from one state to another, in contravention of the U.S. code. Conceding that the federal government could criminalize the interstate mailing of lottery tickets, the issue before the Court was over the power of the federal government to prohibit the transporting of lottery tickets via a common carrier.

The Court held that lottery tickets were "subjects of traffic, and therefore are subjects of commerce," [366] and that independent carriers may be regulated under the Commerce Clause. The majority noted the broad discretion that Congress enjoys in regulating commerce, saying that this power "is plenary, is complete in itself, and is subject to no limitations except such as may be found in the Constitution." [367]

One limitation of regulation "found in the Constitution" is that it is not criminal prohibition, which separate and distinct term is also found in the constitution. What is relevant about the *Lottery Case* (1903) for purposes of this book is that the Court upheld the petitioner's criminal confinement for trafficking in lottery tickets between states, and held that Congress' "regulation may take the form of prohibition." [368]

Given this, the majority opinion in the *Lottery Case* (1903) is the basis of likely the U.S. government's only constitutional argument that it may criminally prosecute interstate drug trafficking. This argument would be in spite of the existence of the statutory scheme to instead regulate drug commerce in the DEA's administrative law courts.

As we shall see shortly below, the *Lottery Case* (1903) presents about as frivolous of an argument to violate the U.S. constitution, and to violate its distribution of powers between America's four categories of sovereigns, as should ever be tolerated in a U.S. court room. It is on par with the frivolity and disingenuousness of the state of Indiana's argument in *Beebe v. State* (1855), where state attorneys argued that the Indiana constitution did not recognize people's natural rights to possess and use their own property, in spite that the Indiana constitution (1816) expressly did. [369]

Like the state of Indiana's ridiculous arguments in that case, the majority's decision in the *Lottery Case* (1903) is a misrepresentation of law. This is because regulation is not prohibition. The U.S. government has authority to regulate interstate commerce – but not to criminally prohibit it.

To argue for the merit and application of the *Lottery Case* (1903) to justify federal criminal drug prohibition would be equally as smarmy. The argument's objectionable basis is that the power to regulate commerce means the power to criminally prosecute people who are involved in commerce. This is similar to the misrepresentations of law that phony state drug "crimes" and "offenses – which legislatures fabricate – are real crimes and offenses that are subject to judicial jurisdiction.

This is to emphasize how the justification for the war on drugs can only be achieved through misrepresentation of law and exaggerations of legitimate government power. Both the *Lottery Case* (1903) itself and Mr. Clement's citing of the case to justify interstate drug prohibition – which was not even at issue in the *Gonzales* case – are examples on point. As we shall see below, the majority's opinion in the *Lottery Case* (1903), i.e., that regulation involves criminal prohibition, is not only inherently faulty, it is also inapplicable to trafficking in drugs.

To make my point, let us take a look at Congress' criminal authority over state borders. This issue is relevant because the majority in the *Lottery Case* (1903) claimed that a person could be arrested and criminally confined for transporting lottery tickets (intended for resale) across state borders.

From my jurisdictional perspective, there are two kinds of state borders. There are 1) natural borders, such as the Ohio River between Indiana and Kentucky, and there are 2) artificial borders, such as the line drawn between Indiana and Ohio.

Recall that Congress as the U.S. non-republic has criminal jurisdiction on the Ohio River. Its territorial jurisdiction defined at 18 USC 7 includes all navigable waterways and coastal waterways of the nation. Thus, if one transports drugs for resale by boat from Indiana to Kentucky, one is violating a criminal prohibition of the U.S. non-republic at 21 USC 841 – 843, and such person faces draconian penalties for drug dealing. (I do not know about the U.S. non-republic's jurisdiction over bridges which span its criminal jurisdiction on the rivers, although I imagine that the United States has criminal jurisdiction on such bridges, also.)

Now, contrast the Ohio River, where the U.S. non-republic exercises its plenary criminal jurisdiction, with the imaginary line between Indiana and Ohio. The issue in the *Lottery Case* (1903) and in the war on drugs is this: excluding crimes relating to federal functions, what is the criminal jurisdiction of the U.S. republic over the artificial lines between states?

Note, I referred to the U.S. republic – not to the U.S. non-republic. We know that this line is not subject to the U.S. non-republic because 1) its jurisdiction is territorial and 2) because its stated jurisdiction at 18 USC 7 does not include the land areas belonging to the states or the lines between the states. Thus, the issue is strictly about the criminal jurisdiction of the U.S. republic. Can Congress as the U.S. republic criminally prohibit trafficking in drugs or lottery tickets over these imaginary lines?

To answer this, consider first that the U.S. republic has the same judicial standards as the state republics. In cases involving natural persons, the U.S republic's Article III courts share the same requirements for injury to invoke their criminal jurisdiction as do state republican courts.

As well, they share the same definitions of case, crime, offense, felony, misdemeanor and slavery that the state courts are to use. Thus, if Congress had general authority to legislate interstate crimes, which it does not, then its crimes would be real, *malum in se* crimes, which is the standard for all crime within and between America's republics.

This is to say that, if Congress imagined or claimed that it had authority to criminally prohibit drug commerce between the states, which it does not, then Article III courts would still not have subject matter jurisdiction over these phony drug "cases." Therefore, Congress might think that it has such power, but the Article III case or controversy requirement would say otherwise.

Second, consider that we have already defined the criminal jurisdiction of Congress as the U.S. republic. When it operates within the states, Congress has criminal jurisdiction only over a handful of crimes relating to its federal functions. These include counterfeiting, offenses against the laws of nations, piracy, felonies on the High Seas, fraud upon the U.S., and misuse of the postal system. As well, Congress has plenary authority to adjudicate the rights of foreigners. These enumerated federal powers

within and between the states do not include the power to criminally prohibit commerce, whether in drugs, oleo margarine [370] or lottery tickets. [371]

Third, except for the above federal enumerated powers, states have
criminal jurisdiction over what occurs within their borders. The U.S.
Supreme Court told us in *United States v. Fox* (1877) that "(a) criminal act
committed wholly within a State 'cannot be made an offence against the
United States, unless it have some relation to the execution of a power of
Congress, or to some matter within the jurisdiction of the United States.'" [372]

In other words, a U.S. crime relates 1) to either Congress' enumerated
powers within the states, or to matters within the federal areas, where
Congress has criminal authority. However, Congress' enumerated power
with regard to all interstate commerce is to regulate it. [373]

The fourth and most central point is that the U.S. republic, indeed,
has legislative jurisdiction over the artificial line between Indiana and Ohio,
but that this jurisdiction 1) is criminally limited to federal enumerated
powers, and 2) is otherwise regulatory, such that it operates strictly in equity
and not at law. Thus, Congress has plenary jurisdiction over the lines
between the states. However, this power is limited to a handful of crimes,
and is otherwise regulatory, operating in non-criminal equity.

Therefore, the majority opinion in the *Lottery Case* (1903) was
indisputably incorrect, as the dissenting opinion pointed out. Congress'
power to regulate interstate commerce operates in equity, which has no
criminal jurisdiction. Thus regulation may <u>not</u> "take the form of prohibition," [374] as the majority opinion claimed.

Criminal law operates in a separate judicial jurisdiction than does
commerce and regulation. Article III courts' criminal jurisdiction is limited
to crimes relating to federal functions within the states and likely to some if
not all real *malum in se* crimes within the federal areas.

In line with the second and third arguments above, the four-justice
dissent in the *Lottery Case* (1903) correctly argued that the power "to
impose restraints and burdens on persons and property in conservation and
promotion of the public health, good order, and prosperity is a power
originally and always belonging to the states... [375] This would be compatible
with the holding in *United States v. Fox* (1877).

The "power to suppress lotteries" ... "belongs to the states, and not to
Congress," correctly wrote the dissent in the *Lottery Case* (1903). "To hold
that Congress has general police power would be to hold that it may
accomplish objects not entrusted to the general government, and to defeat
the operation of the Tenth Amendment, declaring that 'the powers not
delegated to the United States by the Constitution, nor prohibited by it to

the states, are reserved to the states respectively, or to the people.'" [376]

The dissent quoted Justice Catron in the *License Cases* (1847), who succinctly wrote: "that which does not belong to commerce is within the jurisdiction of the police power of the state, and that which does belong to commerce is within the jurisdiction of the United States." [377] Further, it quoted itself in *United States v. E. C. Knight Company* (1894), [378] saying that:

> "It is vital that the independence of the commercial power and of the police power, and the delimitation between them, however sometimes perplexing, should always be recognized and observed, for while the one furnishes the strongest bond of union, the other is essential to the preservation of the autonomy of the states as required by our dual form of government..." [379]

The "one" referred to above is Congress power to regulate interstate commerce. The "other" refers to states' power over crimes committed within their borders. Keeping "one" from the "other" is how to maintain the republican form of government and the system of checks and balances called federalism. Federalism fails when U.S. Attorneys General and Solicitors General assert criminal authority within the states that the federal government does not have, and when they faultily fail to regulate commerce, as their offices are required to do.

Having shown that neither the U.S. republic nor the U.S. non-republic has criminal jurisdiction over drug commerce among the states, i.e., over the artificial lines between the states, I would like to point out several other things relevant to the lack of merit and applicability of the *Lottery Case* (1903) to interstate drug prohibition.

First, the legislation that operated in the *Lottery Case* (1903), which was called "*An Act for the Suppression of Lottery Traffic through National and Interstate Commerce and the Postal Service, Subject to the Jurisdiction and Laws of the United States,*" was different than the U.S. Controlled Substances Act. Section 1 of the former called for criminal punishment for carrying lottery tickets from "from one state to another in the United States..." In contrast, the U.S. CSA does not contain any such interstate language.

The reason for this difference is that the *Act for the Suppression of Lottery Traffic* is an actual attempt by Congress to criminalize certain commerce between the states, where it was to legislate as a republic. In contrast, the U.S. CSA does not use such wording because it criminalizes drug dealing only in the federal areas.

In the U.S. CSA, Congress does not assert any interstate criminal authority, as it did in its lottery act. This is: 1) because Congress has no such interstate criminal authority over drugs, 2) because Congress has interstate criminal authority only with regard to federal enumerated powers, and 3) because Congress regulates interstate commerce, including drug commerce.

By design, the U.S. CSA's criminal prohibitions do not operate over the artificial lines between the states, as did the lottery act's. Instead, its criminal prohibitions operate only in the federal areas. In fact, each and all of America's CSAs legislate crime territorially.

Unlike the lottery act, there is no criminal authority asserted by Congress within the U.S. CSA over drug commerce among the states. Because Congress asserts no such power, the majority's holding in the *Lottery Case* (1903) is not only faulty, but is also irrelevant to the legality of the national war on drugs, which operates outside the written law.

The second point that I would like to make about the *Lottery Case* (1903) is that its criminal defendant was arrested on a warrant for an indictment "either to commit any offense against the United States, or to defraud the United States in any manner or for any purpose..." [380] If this indictment was for fraud upon the United States, then the defendant was not solely committing a regulatory violation, but also a *malum in se* crime.

Thus, theoretically he could be held for trial under the auspices of the law jurisdiction, and his petition for a writ of habeas corpus was rightfully rejected by the Supreme Court. However, I would argue that this fraud would have been a state crime, over which neither the U.S. republic nor the U.S. non-republic would have had jurisdiction.

The third point I would like to mention is that the 18th Amendment (1919) drove a fatal spike into the false concept of the *Lottery Case* (1903) that "regulation may take the form of prohibition," [381] i.e., criminal prohibition. The 18th Amendment leaves no doubt that Congress' power to regulate interstate commerce 1) is different than the power to criminally prohibit commerce in America's republics, which takes a constitutional amendment to effectuate, and 2) is different than Congress' plenary power to prohibit commerce within the federal areas.

Ultimately Congress, through the office of the U.S. Attorney General, has the authority to regulate drug commerce between states, which includes the power to shut down unauthorized drug dealing. However, the office has authority neither to prosecute interstate drug dealers for "crimes" (because their trafficking is subject to equity) nor to confiscate what drug users produce for their own personal consumption (which operates as a natural right under law – not equity).

Because Congress must legislate as a republic toward the states, 1) Congress may only regulate drug commerce among the states under its Interstate Commerce powers, just as the states regulate their own commerce, and 2) the U.S. Attorney General may only prosecute drug violations occurring in the federal areas, where Congress rules as a non-republic. This is a far cry from how U.S. Attorneys General and the legions of U.S. District Attorneys treat disfavored interstate drug dealers today.

Drug dealers' commercial "crimes" within America's republics are false 1) because only the U.S. non-republic may criminally prohibit drugs, and only in the federal areas, 2) because the U.S. republic has criminal jurisdiction within the states, but only over a handful of crimes relating to federal enumerated powers, which crimes do not involve drugs, 3) because the U.S. republic through the U.S. Attorney General regulates interstate commerce in the equity jurisdiction, 4) because no commerce except slavery is subject to the criminal law jurisdiction within America's republics, and 5) because otherwise all crimes within the U.S. republic are state crimes, subject to state judicial courts.

Consequently, Congress may not criminally prohibit interstate drug commerce without a constitutional amendment, similar to the 18th Amendment, 1) which places drug commerce into the law jurisdiction where it can be tried as a crime, and 2) which grants the United States concurrent criminal jurisdiction over drug commerce within the states. Otherwise, Congress – in either of its sovereign capacities – has no criminal jurisdiction over drug commerce within or between the states.

In a republic, Congress must guarantee that the liberty of ALL business owners may not be deprived of them unless they commit real crimes or are contemptuous of judicial authority. This is especially true of U.S. citizens whose right to liberty is unalienable, except for the commission of crime, which is the meaning of the 13th Amendment.

Thus, only in the federal areas may the U.S. Attorney General prosecute drug dealing as if these violations of congressional edicts were real crimes. At most, only on behalf of Congress as a non-republic over the federal areas may the Attorney General criminally prosecute the non-republic's *malum prohibita.*

Within the states, all crimes except those relating to Congress' enumerated powers are to be adjudicated by the state republican sovereigns – based on injury. In America's republics, all *malum prohibita* is enforced in non-criminal equity against artificial persons who are subject to regulation.

In other words, Congress can make crimes out of non-crimes (*malum prohbita*) only under its plenary authority in the federal areas.

However, throughout the fifty states, where Congress regulates interstate commerce as a republic, where it has no concurrent criminal jurisdiction (outside of federal enclaves within the states), and where it is not allowed to criminalize any interstate commerce without a constitutional amendment, then the Attorney General is only to regulate drug commerce with licensing, investigation, confiscation and injunction. When the office and its U.S. District Attorneys falsely prosecute mere business people within America's republics as criminals, these attorneys are in fact the real criminals.

These hats that the U.S. Attorney General wears not only express the duality between administrative and criminal law (to which the above CRS' report and Mr. Clement appear blind), but also the duality between positive and natural law, to which the entire criminal justice system is currently blind. These hats also express the duality of Congress' legislative authority – i.e., that between its role as a republican legislature and its role as a non-republic over the federal areas. This situation mandates that litigants know each of the Attorney General's functions and jurisdictions, which heretofore they (and even U.S. Solicitors General) apparently have not.

Assuming that the U.S. Attorneys General have known the powers and multiple capacities of their office as herein described, and given that they have had a duty to know, then can we assume that they have knowingly prosecuted the drug war in a fraudulent fashion? Or, because Attorney Generals are political appointments based more on political loyalty than legal merit, is it more likely that they are in the dark about the false drug war like everyone else?

Either way – whether the war on drugs is the result of deceit or ignorance of the law – this mal- or misfeasance has been practiced by generation-upon-generation of officials at all levels of the criminal justice system. Regardless if U.S. Attorneys General are informed or not about the two U.S. sovereigns that they represent, the war on drugs is waged because politically appointed U.S. District Attorneys and federal drug defense attorneys likely have not known about Congress' two sovereign legislative capacities.

They likely do not know that the U.S. CSA is written by Congress in both of these legislative capacities, and that each substantive provision in the act applies in one but not both of the two physical areas over which Congress legislates, i.e., over the fifty states as the U.S. republic or over the federal areas as the U.S. non-republic.

The judicially-waged drug war has also occurred because defense attorneys have not exercised their clients' 6th Amendment right "to be informed of the nature and cause of the accusation" against them, or to discover who the real party of action is. The issue of such inquiry would be:

Is plaintiff in this drug matter the United States that operates with plenary power over the federal areas under Article I, Section 8, Clause 17, or is plaintiff the United States that operates as a republic under Article IV, Section 4 and Article I, Section 8, Clause 3, the latter which may only regulate interstate drug commerce and which has no criminal jurisdiction over drugs?

Whether U.S. District Attorneys conceive of their prosecutions as occurring in Article I courts or in Article III courts is likewise also relevant. The U.S. District Attorneys' answers to these questions define everything about the nature and legality of their drug prosecutions within America's republics.

If their client is the U.S. republic, then they should not be prosecuting drug-possession or -dealing matters within the states. This is 1) because the U.S. republic has no criminal jurisdiction within the states except over a handful of crimes relating to Congress' enumerated powers, which exclude drug possession and dealing, 2) because if the U.S. republic did have jurisdiction over crime within the states, it would define crime just as the state republics do, i.e., to include injury, and 3) because the only U.S. jurisdiction over interstate commerce is regulatory, which operates in non-criminal equity.

If instead the U.S. District Attorneys' client is the U.S. non-republic, then its criminal jurisdiction is territorial and its criminal provisions are inapplicable in Article III courts against drug dealers within the states.

Either way, the U.S. District Attorneys have no criminal authority over mere drug dealing within the union of the states that, as a class of commercial activity, is to be regulated.

20

More evidence that drug possession is a natural right

What's missing from the Controlled Substances Act?

In the previous two chapters we discovered how the Indiana State Board of Pharmacy and the U.S. Attorney General (in his republican capacity) regulate the manufacture, distribution and dispensing of controlled substances in Indiana through licensing. Dispensing and adjudicating commercial privileges is not a function of judicial trial courts, whose law jurisdiction has constitutional subject matter jurisdiction only over civil cases and crimes that involve injury. The judicial courts of Indiana and the judicial Article III courts of the U.S. republic also have statutory appellate jurisdiction over adjudications by the administrative law courts respectively of the Indiana pharmacy board or the U.S. Attorney General. [382]

The above sums up how the making and selling of controlled substances are to be treated at least in Indiana by both the state and federal governments. Granting commercial privileges over drug commerce in Indiana is the jurisdiction of the state pharmacy board and the DEA (under the U.S. Attorney General's authority). Enforcing regulators' determinations and injunctions against unwanted drug commerce is a legitimate role of republican judicial courts. In contrast, it is baseless to use the judicial courts of America's fifty-one republics to adjudicate drug crimes that are anything but real crimes involving drugs.

The above description is accurate, but it is not complete. As particularly as we combed through the Controlled Substances Act in the previous chapters, did you notice anything in particular that was missing from our analysis? Sometimes a legislature's failure or disability to grant power is even more apparent than the grants of power themselves. Below are two examples where the Indiana legislature failed to grant power to the executive or judicial branches because to do so would have violated the state and federal constitutions.

However, as we shall see, despite this lack of delegated authority, government officials carry-on as if the legislature actually had granted the power. I have already mentioned these omissions, but this is a good time to look at them more closely.

Omission No. 1. The first notable omission in the Indiana Controlled Substances Act is that the Indiana General Assembly grants no criminal jurisdiction to the Indiana State Board of Pharmacy over manufacturing, distribution or dispensing drugs. Although the pharmacy board is granted primary authority to enforce the law, it has no power to sanction anyone for crime. Thus, the agency that is exclusively granted with authority to enforce all the state's drug laws cannot enforce any of them criminally.

In other words, the Indiana legislature has granted no criminal jurisdiction to the administrative law courts of the Indiana pharmacy board, which have primary, subject matter jurisdiction over drug commerce within the state. This is because the Indiana constitution assigns all criminal power to the law jurisdiction of Indiana's judicial courts, which have criminal subject matter jurisdiction only over cases involving injury to people and their property.

The Indiana pharmacy board's courts are to administer and enforce the drug laws, but the legislature gave these courts no power or means to criminally sanction anyone in any drug business. Thus, armed pharmacy board enforcers (and their DEA counterparts) have no arrest authority over mere drug commerce. They have arrest authority only over real crimes, which are to be adjudicated in judicial courts.

Except in the federal areas, to arrest any business person merely for being in a particular business would be to violate the Indiana and U.S. constitutions' separation of powers doctrine. This is 1) because in republics, all criminal authority granted to the judicial branch is over cases involving injury, and 2) because the privilege of engaging in commerce is subject only to regulation in equity. Thus, America's republics have no criminal power over American businesses – only over business people as natural persons.

The power to sanction people for crime is strictly a judicial power. Likewise, the power to arrest is strictly incident to the judicial power over crime or contempt. Enforcers of the Indiana pharmacy board as well as other law enforcers have no authority to arrest anyone for mere regulatory violations, such as dealing drugs without the pharmacy board's permission.

Under the 13th Amendment to the U.S. constitution and Article 1, Section 37 of the Indiana constitution (1851), only judicial courts (and law enforcement officers acting in their judicial capacities) can enslave or indenture people. This enslavement can only occur as punishment for the commission of crimes involving injury, or for being in contempt of a judicial court order.

Likewise, the legislature that created the Indiana State Board of Pharmacy also limited its regulatory authority by statute. It gave the pharmacy board power to shut down unwanted drug commerce, to confiscate contraband, to gain legal title to property and to destroy it. It gave the board power to administratively enjoin violators' future unlicensed manufacture, distribution and dispensing of controlled substances, which such injunction can be judicially enforced.

However, it did not grant the pharmacy board authority to prosecute drug commerce as crime, or to participate in treating drug commerce as crime. Nor is the pharmacy board authorized to abdicate its regulatory role and to ignore the "minimum procedural duties" [383] that it owes to all drug dealers regarding the adjudication of their commercial privileges.

As the reader can see, because the judicial branch has no criminal subject matter jurisdiction over drug dealing, it serves essentially to support the pharmacy board's non-criminal enforcement of the drug laws. It does this in three main ways.

First, at IC 16-42-20 prosecuting attorneys are authorized to invoke judicial power to gain forfeiture of property seized by pharmacy board enforcers. Second, at IC 35-48-3-3(i) the Indiana Attorney General is authorized to seek injunctions against unlicensed drug dealers. Third, at IC 4-21.5-5, IC 4-21.5-6, IC 16-42-20-7, IC 33-28-1-2 and IC 33-29-1-1.5, for example, judicial courts are empowered to provide judicial review or enforcement of administrative decisions.

This means that neither the judicial branch nor the executive branch, for their own separate reasons, may criminally prosecute mere matters of drug possession or commerce. Judicial courts cannot criminally adjudicate such drug matters because they have no constitutional subject matter jurisdiction over non-cases and non-injury. Likewise, administrative courts of the pharmacy board cannot prosecute drug cases as crimes because the legislature did not grant (and constitutionally could not grant) their courts with criminal jurisdiction, which belongs only in the law jurisdiction of Indiana's judicial courts, whose standards are constitutionally-based.

This analysis is in conformity with the separation of powers doctrine in the Indiana constitution. Under the doctrine, the judicial branch is not allowed to do the regulatory work of the executive branch, and the executive branch is not allowed to do the criminal work of the judicial branch.

As well, the executive branch is required to exhaust its administrative remedies before seeking judicial enforcement or review under IC 4-21.5-5, IC 4-21.5-6 and IC 16-42-20-7. Thus, both statutorily and constitutionally, the use of the judicial system to adjudicate matters of drug commerce could not be more legally bankrupt than it is. There is no American court with competent jurisdiction outside of the federal areas to impose criminal penalties upon those merely engaged in drug possession or commerce.

Omission No. 2. The Indiana Controlled Substances Act's most notable omission, and its most relevant omission with regard to the subtitle of this book, is that neither the Indiana legislature nor Congress grants power respectively to the Indiana State Board of Pharmacy or the U.S. Attorney General over individual possession of controlled substances. Thus Indiana and the U.S. republic have or claim no authority over drug possession. This is because property possession is a natural right, which operates under the subject matter jurisdiction of sovereign individuals.

We earlier noted the irony of this fact, i.e., that neither the Indiana legislature nor Congress claims any jurisdiction over drug possession. Over a million people in America are arrested or ticketed each year for drug possession, yet American legislatures claim no authority over it. Drug possession is proscribed neither by natural law nor by the nation's constitutions – nor even by its statutes. This is because drug possession is not a crime. It is not a crime because it does not violate anyone else's natural rights.

At IC 35-48-3-3 and 21 USC 822 the CSAs require all manufacturers, distributors and dispensers of controlled substances to be registered with the Indiana pharmacy board and / or the U.S. Attorney General. However, they require nothing from individual possessors and users of controlled substances, who are not regulated within the state republics. This means that the sole state and federal offices with authority to administer and enforce the nation's drug laws within America's republics were granted zero authority over the controlled substances in people's pockets and purses for their own personal use.

As first pointed out in chapter 3, the right of property possession is in the natural law jurisdiction of the Indiana and U.S. constitutions. Article I, Section 1 of the Indiana constitution (1816) recognizes the natural and unalienable right of acquiring, possessing, and defending property. Because of this, the positive law jurisdiction may not impose duties upon this right – and in fact does not.

American legislatures cannot impose duties upon anything outside their positive law jurisdiction over artificial entities. Because natural persons are subject only to the natural law and the law jurisdiction of our judicial courts, which are not subject to inconsistent positive law, then they have no mutual civil or criminal duty beyond not harming other people.

Consistent with this, state and U.S. Controlled Substances Acts do not impose any positive law duties upon drug users. Drug use occurs within the natural law jurisdiction when users neither cause others legal harm nor enter into the commerce of drugs. The CSAs respect this by not requiring drug users to register with either the Indiana pharmacy board or with the U.S. Attorney General, and by recognizing that drug users – called ultimate users – may lawfully possess drugs for their own use and the use of their households. (We discuss ultimate users in the next chapter).

The distinction between 1) an ultimate (or end) user of drugs, who is not regulated and is not required to register with the pharmacy board or the U.S. Attorney General, and 2) someone who is regulated is that those who are regulated make, distribute and / or dispense drugs. Says a *DEA Update on Regulations and Enforcement:* "Ultimate users are not permitted to distribute controlled substances without being separately registered." [384]

This is based on the separation of the natural law jurisdiction from the positive law jurisdiction of American constitutions. Drug users in America's republics may exercise their right of drug acquisition and possession, but this does not <u>ever</u> include a right to distribute drugs.

In other words, one has a right to possess and take drugs, but no right to sell them. People who sell drugs within America's republics are subject to regulation and injunction. People who distribute drugs in the federal areas, without the Attorney General's approval, are subject to prison.

In this regard, the CSAs are constitutional because they do not interfere with the jurisdiction of natural persons within America's republics and because they expressly confine the executive branch to do what it is constitutionally empowered and supposed to do, i.e. to regulate drug commerce. The CSAs do not claim governmental authority over individual sovereigns, except in the federal areas where individuals are not sovereign, or where they lose their sovereignty to Congress.

To further keep these jurisdictions separate, the above cited *DEA Update* notes that because of drug dealers' "registration requirement, it is unlawful for ultimate users to give their controlled substances to pharmacies, reverse distributors, etc., for destruction." [385]

This is an odd and interesting admission: that drug users have a right to lawfully possess drugs, but that this does not include the right to dispense drugs TO ANYONE without being regulated – even to drug experts for the purpose of disposing of drugs. In other words, people have a right to possess and use drugs, but no right to sell or to dispense them to others (outside of their own households), including giving them to real drug experts for disposal.

Thus, the judicial branch of America's republics has no constitutional authority over the non-injurious behavior of natural persons, such as drug possession, and the executive branch has no statutory authority over the non-commercial behavior of natural persons. Thus no branch of government has authority over the non-injurious and non-commercial behavior of natural persons, such as their drug possession and use. This necessarily leads to the same conclusion that I have asserted all along: that drugs are lawful within America's republics, outside of the federal areas.

The duty to not possess drugs

Another way of seeing the legality of drug possession is by defining what the state makes dutiful. The state of Indiana and Congress require manufacturers, distributors and dispensers of controlled substances to register respectively with the pharmacy board and the U.S. Attorney General, but they impose no such duty upon people in possession of controlled substances for their own personal use.

Likewise, no one has a common law duty to not possess drugs, to not use drugs, or to register their possession with the Indiana pharmacy board or U.S. Attorney General. Failing to fulfill (or omitting) a duty to the pharmacy board cannot be made a crime. IC 35-41-2-1 says that one can commit a criminal omission "only if he has a statutory, common law, or contractual duty to perform the act."

However, contrary to what IC 35-41-2-1 says, there are and can be no statutes that create any criminal duties in natural persons. This is because Indiana's criminal courts may only adjudicate duties imposed by Nature and consistent with the common law, which the legislature has codified under IC 1-1-2-2. Thus, there is no statute that imposes a duty upon natural persons to not possess drugs.

This is ultimately because positive law does not apply to natural persons (or to their natural law jurisdiction), and only applies to artificial persons, such as foreigners or businesses. As we have seen, natural born citizens are not born subject to any American legislature. They are born subject to Nature and to only Nature's prohibitions and imposed duties.

Because IC 1-1-2-1 says that criminal statutes must be consistent with the Indiana constitution, the U.S. constitution and the common law, then criminal statutes may not create duties in natural persons beyond those already established by the Indiana common law. The common law subjected people to judicial jurisdiction and to criminal penalty only for harming other people. Because criminal statutes answer to constitutions, to natural law and to common law, they cannot create any duties in natural persons that do not already naturally exist.

As well, it goes without saying that the above legislative provision about basing one's criminality on a "contractual duty" is also completely erroneous and misleading. One cannot contract into the criminal law jurisdiction of a republic, regardless what the Indiana legislature claims in the above statute. One can only contract one's way 1) into the equity jurisdiction of judicial courts, which has only contempt authority, and 2) into the criminal jurisdiction of the U.S. non-republic, which U.S. employees essentially do. Thus, one may contract oneself into the criminal jurisdiction of a non-republic, but not into that of a republic.

As well, all people compromise their sovereignty when they visit a federal area, which is similar to contracting into a criminal jurisdiction. This is because the federal areas are non-republican, and thus do not respect the unalienable rights of individuals under natural law.

One of these unalienable rights is the right to physical liberty. Says the 13th Amendment and Article I, Section 37 of the Indiana constitution (1851), liberty can be alienated from individuals in America's republics only for the commission of crime. It cannot be indentured by an agreement that is enforceable in the law jurisdiction, where indentured servitude is a crime.

As we have discussed since chapter 1, the criminal law jurisdiction of judicial courts is fixed by American constitutions. In America's republics, the criminal law jurisdiction is over injury to one's person or property, [386] not over the violation of one's contractual duties or of statutory edicts. One creates a criminal case by injuring someone else, or one does not.

Thus, there are no such things as contractual or statutory duties that can subject natural persons to the criminal law jurisdiction of republics. Such criminal jurisdiction is not subject to contracts or statutes that are inconsistent with our constitutions, the common law, or natural law. Statutes and contracts cannot establish criminal liability, i.e., enslavement, for failing to fulfill these contracts or artificial duties.

Having eliminated the false concepts 1) that natural born citizens and other natural persons in America's republics are subject to positive criminal law that is inconsistent with natural law and common law, and 2) that natural persons can contract themselves into the criminal jurisdiction of republican judicial courts, the above-referenced statute can only be properly read as follows:

> "However, a person who omits to perform an act commits an offense only if he has a common law duty to perform the act."

This statement, and not that of the state legislature (above), is the proper statement of <u>criminal</u> law. Instead, the legislature's statement (above) is a correct statement about committing <u>civil</u> omissions. Civil – but not criminal – cases may try omissions of contractual and statutory duties.

Thus, it is a misrepresentation of republican criminal law to say that legislatures and contracts may create criminal duties in people. Only Nature creates criminal duties in natural people in America's republics. People rely on America's criminal defense attorneys, prosecutors, judges and legislators to know this, which they have not.

America's defense attorneys have failed their duty to know that neither legislatures nor contracts can impose criminal liability onto non-criminals for their non-crimes. To allow the imposition of criminal sanctions based solely on positive law or contract, as is done today, is to fail to understand the meaning of unalienable rights, which cannot be contracted or legislated away in a republic. It is to also fail to understand the role of the law jurisdiction in securing these rights.

The Indiana legislature can only criminally codify that which the state constitution imposes as duties. If there is one law, and its basis is our constitutions, then the above statutory references to criminalizing *malum prohibita* and contractual duties is either surplusage or garbage. In any event, such references do not belong in the Indiana criminal code because they are not factually correct and they tend only to confuse those who do not understand the law jurisdiction of judicial courts.

As we discussed in chapters 2 and 3, people in America's republics really only have two inherent duties. The first duty, which is adjudicated in the judicial branch, is to refrain from violating other people's natural, contractual and statutory rights. If we violate these rights, we subject ourselves to civil and / or criminal sanctions through the state's judicial apparatus. If we respect other people's natural, contractual and positive law rights, we are to remain free of the judicial branch.

The only other main duty that Americans have under our constitutions is to submit to the reasonable regulation of our commercial activities. People consent to be regulated by the legislative branch when they enter commerce, which is that branch's exclusive jurisdiction.

All licenses that we have, whether professional licenses or drivers licenses, are the result of governments' power over our commerce. According to the separation of powers doctrine, commercial regulation is to be performed in non-criminal equity by the executive branch.

Ultimately, sovereign natural persons in America's republics exist in their positive-law-free bubbles and submit to the government only by entering the above two governmental jurisdictions. They become subject to the judicial branch's compulsory jurisdiction by violating the natural or contractual rights of others, including their natural political rights. With few exceptions, they consent to the executive branch's regulatory jurisdiction by being foreign and by engaging the public in commerce.

What makes these jurisdictions constitutional is that U.S. citizens, but particularly natural born citizens, must affirmatively do something either artificial or injurious to become subject to them. They must consent to these jurisdictions by their actions. Otherwise, natural born citizens are not subject to government, which condition makes them free.

They are not subject to government when born. They are not subject to government while, for example, growing tomatoes, eating breakfast or taking showers. They are subject to republican government only when they enter government's two positive law jurisdictions over injury and legal rights. Without constitutional amendments, they need not consent to government in their gardens, kitchens, bathrooms and bedrooms.

America's republican form of government is not allowed to impose its positive law authority on peoples' natural activities. No citizens subject themselves to our republican governments, or their criminal law jurisdiction, just by pursuing happiness. Government can exist in its rightful place, and individual sovereigns can live peacefully and privately in theirs. That is the whole idea embodied in the U.S. constitution, if you don't already know.

Thus, if we do not want to be regulated by the Indiana State Board of Pharmacy, and if we do not wish to register with it, then we do not have to manufacture, distribute or dispense controlled substances. If we do not want to be regulated by the Bureau of Motor Vehicles, then we do not have to drive.

If we do not want the Alcoholic and Tobacco Commission on our backs, we do not have to deal in those products. If we do not want to be taxed by the Internal Revenue Service, we do not have to earn income. If we do not want to pay sales taxes, we do not have to shop.

You see, if public servants would merely follow the law, the law would set Americans free. All natural persons are naturally free of government unless they harm others or enter legislative authority. They are also essentially free of taxation – just like babies – unless they affirmatively enter a taxing authority. Unfortunately, this simple truth has been lost in translation during American republics' lapse into *de facto* non-republics.

Republican governments do not impose duties upon us to make drugs, drive cars, distribute alcohol, earn income or shop. If consumers, for example, were subject to positive law instead of natural law – that is, if they were beholden to government instead to their nature and financial means – then the legislature could require them to shop and work and drink beer. That we all agree that republican legislatures may not make natural persons shop, work or drink beer, this is our mutual acknowledgment of a sovereign jurisdiction over which no congress may legislate.

Americans become subject to government regulation only when we perform commercial activities that are regulated, like dispensing drugs or practicing the privilege of medicine. Otherwise, we are free from government regulation, are unregulated and are not directly affected by regulation.

Statutes such as the Controlled Substances Act are constitutional as long as they keep us free and impose duties only upon those who are subject to regulation or criminal law, which it does. We know this is true because we can read the statutes and constitutions with our own eyes. The Indiana CSA properly regulates drug commerce, codifies drug crimes and leaves individuals alone.

This being said, the Indiana State Board of Pharmacy is primarily responsible for the enforcement of Indiana's drug laws. Because the legislature grants it no authority over drug possession, other law enforcers whose enforcement of drug laws is ancillary to that of the pharmacy board's enforcers also have no authority over drug possession.

Indiana Code 16-42-20-4 limits the pharmacy board's cooperation with federal and other state agencies to "discharging the board's responsibilities concerning traffic in controlled substances and in suppressing the abuse of controlled substances..." Combating the trafficking and abuse of drugs does not encompass fighting drug possession. As well, "the board's responsibilities concerning traffic in controlled substances" are regulatory, and not criminal or judicial.

Likewise, 21 USC 873(a) limits the U.S. Attorney General's cooperation with local, state, tribal and federal agencies to "traffic in controlled substances and in suppressing the abuse of controlled substances." This also does not grant the Attorney General, his DEA agents or his U.S. District Attorneys authority over drug possession within America's republics. The pharmacy board and the Attorney General have authority to deal with the interstate "traffic in controlled substances" [387] by regulating it.

Thus, neither the DEA nor the Indiana State Board of Pharmacy has independent authority to regulate drug possession because their respective Controlled Substances Acts do not grant them such jurisdiction. This also means that they have no joint or mutual jurisdiction over individual drug possession either. This is because the Indiana and U.S. CSAs respect the natural law basis of crime and the natural rights of natural persons within

America's republics. Only government officials do not.

With regard to marijuana growing, IC 16-42-20-4(a)(4) grants drug enforcers at most joint powers to "(c)onduct programs of eradication aimed at destroying wild or illicit growth of plant species from which controlled substances may be extracted," i.e., manufactured. The statute supports regulators' authority to shut down commercial growing operations, but does not grant them authority to destroy anyone's domesticated, un-wild and legal (and lawful) plants that are cultivated for one's own use.

The above provision is yet another statutory admission that the government claims no authority over marijuana plants on someone's real property except over the plants' commercial role or value. The DEA and state pharmacy board can regulate both trafficking in marijuana and manufacturing by extraction of hashish and hash oil, but not someone's personal possession of a living or harvested plant which is not intended for commerce.

In other words, the enforcement agencies can regulate commercial farming, but not one's personal gardening. Commercial farming is within governments' positive law jurisdiction. Personal gardening is not.

To sum things up, the state and federal agencies that have primary power over all drugs in their respective republics have no statutory authority over drug possession, either jointly or independently. Consequently, state law enforcement officers with ancillary power over drugs, such as local and state police and elected prosecuting attorneys, also have no statutory authority over drug possession.

Neither the Indiana General Assembly nor Congress regulates or prohibits in any manner the possession of controlled substances by individuals and their households within America's republics. This is apparent because neither the Indiana legislature nor Congress grants regulatory power over drug possession to the sole Indiana and federal offices respectively charged with the authority to control drugs.

This means that, without any further evidence of the state's treatment of drugs, the legislature assigns absolutely no jurisdiction over drug possession to an executive branch office, be that a prosecutor or the pharmacy board. The legislature cannot claim such power over property possession in the law jurisdiction because that would violate the natural law jurisdiction of the Indiana constitutions, to which the legislature's positive law is subservient.

Likewise, the legislature does not delegate such power over property possession to the executive branch because fundamentally it does not have any such power to delegate. As explained by the Indiana Supreme Court in

Beebe v. State (1855), [388] the right and power of property possession resides in the sovereign individuals, subject only to a constitutional amendment.

Thus, neither the Indiana pharmacy board's enforcers nor other state law enforcement officers, including prosecutors, are granted statutory jurisdiction over drug possession. The same can be said about the DEA and federal prosecutors. This means that ALL the arrests, prosecutions and criminal sentencing of people for drug possession over the past fifty years have been false and under false color of law within at least Indiana, but likely within all other American republics and, as we shall see, in the federal areas as well.

According to the states' and federal CSAs, drug possession is neither a regulated nor a criminal matter. Absent a constitutional amendment that places the possession or commerce of personal property into the criminal law jurisdiction, Indiana's and Congress' only republican powers are regulatory, i.e., to break up and enjoin unwanted drug manufacturing, distribution and dispensing.

21

The ultimate user defense

The ultimate user provision

For those of you who do not yet believe that the absence of granted power confers no power, think of it this way: that the Controlled Substance Act did not confer to the Indiana State Board of Pharmacy the power to sell lottery tickets or to mow the medians of interstate highways or to issue state bonds. Likewise it did not confer power to the pharmacy board over the mere possession of controlled substances by individuals.

The pharmacy board's authority is that which the legislature has granted. Thus – by legislative admission – the state agency with primary authority over drugs is granted no power over individual drug possession.

If the legislature had granted such power, we would have found such grant within its legislation. However, the Indiana CSA only grants the pharmacy board power to regulate the manufacture, distribution and dispensing of drugs, including unwanted drug dealing, and to fight real drug crimes.

As well, the legislature grants Indiana's prosecutors with statutory authority to instigate forfeiture proceedings in order to acquire title to confiscated drug contraband. It also grants the Indiana Attorney General authority to seek to enjoin unwanted drug dealing. However, it does not grant authority to prosecutors to prosecute business people who are to be regulated, or for the Attorney General to defend such wrongful actions.

The absence of authority granted over drug possession means that the pharmacy board, its gun-toting enforcers, and its ancillary state and federal enforcers have no authority over individuals' drug possession. The state legislature exclusively conferred upon its administrative agency in the executive branch only the powers 1) to fight real drug crimes and 2) to regulate the commerce of controlled substances, and nothing more.

However, if you need more proof that it is lawful to possess drugs in Indiana, then merely read the ultimate user provisions at IC 35-48-3-3(e)(3) of the Indiana CSA, as defined by IC 35-48-1-27. As we shall see in the next section, these provisions are similar to the ultimate user provisions at 21 USC 822(c), 21 USC 844(a) and 21 USC 802(27) of the U.S. CSA. Quite simply, the Indiana and U.S. statutes together say the following:

> That everyone who manufactures, distributes or dispenses controlled substances within the borders of Indiana must apply for "registration" (a license or permit) from the pharmacy board and the DEA, but that this requirement does not apply to "ultimate users" in possession of drugs for their own personal use, or the use of their households, who may "lawfully possess" those drugs.

Specifically, IC 35-48-3-3(a) reads: "Every person who manufactures or distributes any controlled substance within this state or who proposes to engage in the manufacture or distribution of any controlled substance within this state, must obtain biennially a registration issued by the board in accordance with its rules."

Similarly, IC 35-48-3-3(b) reads: "Every person who dispenses or proposes to dispense any controlled substance within Indiana must have a registration issued by the board in accordance with its rules."

Then IC 35-48-3-3(e) states that this requirement does not apply to the following persons who "need not register and may lawfully possess controlled substances under this article:

(1) An agent or employee of any registered manufacturer, distributor, or dispenser of any controlled substance if he is acting in the usual course of his business or employment.
(2) A common or contract carrier or warehouseman, or an employee thereof, whose possession of any controlled substance is in the usual course of business or employment.
(3) An ultimate user or a person in possession of any controlled substance under a lawful order of a practitioner or in lawful possession of a schedule V substance." *(emphasis added)*

It is the third to last exemption of an "ultimate user" that is pertinent to our discussion of whether the state of Indiana (or Congress acting within Indiana) can regulate or criminally prohibit drug possession of ordinary drug users.

The first thing we should note is that such ultimate user in IC 35-48-3-3(e)(3) of the Indiana act is a separate lawful person from the other two persons mentioned in subsections 3(e)(1) and 3(e)(2). An ultimate user is distinguished from an agent or employee of a commercial drug maker or of a drug warehouseman. These persons referred to in 3(e)(1) and 3(e)(2) are artificial persons engaged in drug commerce. In contrast, the persons referred to in 3(e)(3), including ultimate users, are natural persons acting in their natural capacity to lawfully acquire, possess and use property.

As well, it is apparent that such ultimate user in section 3(e)(3) is a separate person from the other two persons mentioned in 3(e)(3). This is because such persons are separated by the conjunction "or." Thus, section 3(e)(3) waives the registration requirement for three separate natural persons, each who exercise a natural right to lawfully possess property.

Thus, merely within IC 35-48-3-3 we can see both the law and equity jurisdictions in action. The natural right of drug possession, which is secured by the ultimate user provision, operates at law under the natural law jurisdiction. In such capacity, ultimate users are not regulated, and are subject to the law jurisdiction only if they violate other people's rights. On the other hand, agents or employees of commercial drug makers or warehousemen, who are mentioned in subsections 3(e)(1) and 3(e)(2), operate in equity and are subject to regulation.

IC 35-48-3-3(e)(3) states that neither 1) an ultimate user of controlled substances nor 2) a "person in possession of any controlled substance under a lawful order of a practitioner" nor 3) a person "in lawful possession of a schedule V substance" needs to register their drug possession with the pharmacy board, and that all such persons may "lawfully possess" drugs.

In other words, because an ultimate user at 3(e)(3) is distinguished from a "person in possession of any controlled substance under a lawful order of a practitioner," then an "ultimate user" need not have a lawful order of a practitioner to lawfully possess controlled substances. Likewise, an ultimate user need not possess "a schedule V substance" to be lawful. He or she may possess any substance for his or her own use and still be lawful.

The Indiana General Assembly at IC 35-48-1-27 defines an ultimate user as "a person who lawfully possesses a controlled substance for the person's own use, for the use of a member of the person's household, or for administering to an animal owned by the person or by a member of the person's household." In other words, an ultimate user is an end user of drugs.

Because the term "lawfully possess" is not defined by the legislature, we are to apply a statutory rule of construction to it. IC 1-1-4-1(1) says that statutory "(w)ords and phrases shall be taken in their plain, or ordinary and usual, sense. Technical words and phrases having a peculiar and appropriate meaning in law shall be understood according to their technical technical import."

However, both the ordinary and technical meanings of the term "lawfully possess" are the same. To lawfully possess any property is to voluntarily acquire the property by finding it, producing it, growing it, buying it, bartering for it, or receiving it as a gift. In contrast, it is not lawful to acquire property by force, theft or fraud, or to acquire property knowing that it was acquired that way.

Those within the state republics who lawfully acquire drugs through barter, purchase, gift, or self-production are not criminals, but are merely exercising a natural right. Article I, Section 13 of the Indiana constitution (1851) tells us that "crime as defined by law" always involves a victim. We know that mere drug users are not criminals because their behavior does not meet the definition of crime in our constitutions, which is needed to invoke the subject matter jurisdiction of criminal courts.

As with crime and natural born citizens, lawful possession of personal property operates and is defined in the natural law jurisdiction of the Indiana and U.S. constitutions, and it is adjudicated at law. Neither a republican legislature nor a republican judiciary may redefine lawful possession of any property inconsistently with what the law jurisdiction long ago established. Otherwise, if the legislative and judicial branches had such power, then logically they could declare theft to be legal.

Republican legislatures may not make crime lawful or make lawful possession criminal because they do not define crime or lawful possession. As Nature proscribes crime, it also defines lawful possession. As crime is a self-evident fact of Nature, so too is lawful possession. Legislatures only codify real crime and lawful possession according to natural law, as exemplified by the ultimate user provisions.

Legislatures – other than perhaps Congress in the federal areas – may not define lawful possession in America's republics to be different than how natural law defines it. This is supported by Article I, Section 1 of the Indiana constitution (1816) which recognizes the unalienable natural right to acquire, possess and defend property. This natural right predates all legislatures and remains inviolable to all republican legislative acts.

The Indiana Supreme Court recognized the natural right to acquire and possess property in *Beebe v. State* (1855), which declared the criminal prohibition of alcohol by the state legislature to be unconstitutional. It quoted an Illinois Circuit Court, which mused: "A freeman may buy and sell at his pleasure. This right is not of society, but from nature. He never gave it up. It would be amusing to see a man hunting through our law books for authority to buy or sell or make a bargain." [389]

Such a man would not likely find such written authority because, as the Illinois court entertains, the right and authority to trade exists ante-cedent to all positive law and does not have to be written down in a judicial system that respects natural law. Such authority to acquire property "is not of society, but from nature." [390] It is not a right granted from a legislature, and as the courts point out, it does not necessarily have to be written down to be recognized.

As we learned in chapter 3, a baby's right to poop is not going to be denied. Nor would legislative prohibitions against it have any effect. Like-wise, governments cannot stop how individuals pursue happiness, for example by prohibiting certain kinds of property in their pockets.

The natural right of property possession operates at law. That is why the ultimate user provision says that end drug users may "lawfully possess" drugs for their own use. That is why drug possession is also authorized for those "under a lawful order of a practitioner" and with those "in lawful possession of a schedule V substance." [391] It is in the law jurisdiction where natural persons lawfully possess property. In equity, artificial persons legal-ly possess property, by permission of the state.

That drugs are lawful in America's republics would have been a more accurate subtitle to this book than that they are legal. Drugs are lawful in the natural law jurisdiction of individual sovereigns, where individuals have a natural right to possess property.

In contrast, the word legal refers to artificial rights and duties that are provided for by positive law. Illegal means prohibited under equity, but not at law. Drug commerce is legal only for drug companies that are approved by regulators. The illegality of unapproved drug enterprises is dealt with by non-criminal equitable powers.

Our natural, constitutional and statutory rights exist only for those who know that they have these rights, only for those who can find them in the law books and show their operation, and only for those who will defend them. I call such persons: republicans [with a small "r"].

Of course, one's republican right to lawfully acquire drugs from unlicensed people does not exist in a world where defendants, defense attorneys and government officials do not know or follow the republican law. Obviously, the statutory ultimate user defense in the Indiana and U.S. CSAs, which secures drug users' natural and legal rights to "lawfully possess" drugs, is not meant to be easily found, understood or acted upon. The Indiana legislature could have been more forthright by saying that drug possession is a natural right that is secured by the substantive right not to be enslaved except for the commission of a crime, but instead chose to be snarky with the ultimate user provision.

The ultimate user in the U.S. Controlled Substances Act

The U.S. CSA treats ultimate users in two different manners. These manners reflect the two sovereign capacities in which Congress governs, i.e., as the U.S. republic with regard to the states and as the U.S. non-republic with regard to the federal areas.

In its republican capacity, Congress treats ultimate users exactly the same way as state republics like Indiana do. 21 USC 822(c) and 21 USC 802(27) say the same thing that IC 35-48-3-3(e) and IC 35-48-1-27 say. They say that ultimate drug users in American republics need not register with the U.S. Attorney General and may lawfully possess drugs for themselves and their households.

Thus, Congress as the U.S. republic recognizes natural persons' natural right to possess drugs, which is secured in the republic's Article III courts. According to Congress as the U.S. republic, drug possession is lawful throughout America's republics. Thus, national republican law is compatible and consistent with state republican law.

On the other hand, 21 U.S.C. 844 of the U.S. CSA – which appears to criminally prohibit drug possession – is legislated by Congress as the U.S. non-republic and applies in the federal areas only. 21 U.S.C. 844(a) reads:

> "It shall be unlawful for any person knowingly or intentionally to possess a controlled substance unless such substance was obtained directly, or pursuant to a valid prescription or order, from a practitioner, while acting in the course of his professional practice, or except as otherwise authorized by this subchapter or subchapter II of this chapter."

Based on a superficial reading of this provision, it appears that it is unlawful to possess drugs in a federal area unless they are obtained from medical practitioners. (This conclusion would be silly given that people can buy drugs in Washington, D.C. supermarkets and drugstores.) However, the final two clauses of 21 USC 844(a), i.e., "or except as otherwise authorized by this subchapter or subchapter II of this chapter," indicate that obtaining controlled substances from a medical practitioner is not the exclusive manner to lawfully obtain them in the federal areas.

That is, according to 21 USC 844(a), there are at least two lawful ways to acquire and possess drugs in the federal areas: i.e., either 1) from a medical practitioner or 2) from another means "otherwise authorized by this subchapter or subchapter II of this chapter." "This subchapter" refers to sections 801 through 904 of the U.S. CSA. "(S)ubchapter II of this chapter" refers to sections 951 through 971 of the act.

Within these groups of statutes, drug possession is "otherwise authorized by this subchapter" at 21 USC 822(c), which is the ultimate user provision, as defined by 21 USC 802(27). As we have seen, 21 USC 822(c) exempts ultimate users from registering with the Attorney General, and says that they may "lawfully possess" controlled substances "for a purpose specified in section 802(27)." The purposes specified in 21 USC 802(27) are "for his own use or for the use of a member of his household or for an animal owned by him or by a member of his household."

Thus under 21 USC 844(a) – even in the federal areas – a person is an ultimate drug user, is exempt from registration with the U.S. Attorney General, and may lawfully possess controlled substances if they are "for his own use or for the use of a member of his household or for an animal owned by him or by a member of his household." This is the case regardless if he obtains the controlled substance from a medical practitioner. This is the same standard for an ultimate drug user within America's republics.

Therefore it appears as if the ultimate user provision is not only a criminal defense for natural persons within Article III courts of the U.S. republic, which operate among the states, but is also a defense for federal subjects within Article I courts of the U.S. non-republic in the federal areas. Whereas 21 USC 822(c) codifies the natural right of property possession in a republic, 21 USC 844(a) is legislation by Congress which grants its subjects in the federal areas the legal right to possess drugs. Said differently, the latter is a legal right granted by Congress as the U.S. non-republic – and is not a natural law right codified by Congress as the U.S. republic.

According to the Supreme Court in *Hooven & Allison Co. v. Evatt* (1945), all constitutional guarantees extend to people in the federal areas "only as Congress, in the exercise of its legislative power over territory belonging to the United States, has made those guaranties applicable." [392] Based on this authority, Congress has made applicable the legal right of drug possession in the federal areas at 21 USC 844(a). This legal right extends to artificial persons within the federal areas, which describes all people who are subjects of and subject to the U.S. non-republic.

This legal right to possess drugs in the federal areas, which is a right granted by Congress, is in contrast to the natural law right of drug possession within America's republics, which is secured both by American constitutions and by the codification of this natural right – embodied in the ultimate user provision. Thus, whether as the exercise of a codified natural right within America's republics or as the exercise of a legislated legal right (privilege of Congress) within the federal areas, drug possession is apparently lawful and legal everywhere throughout the United States, not just in America's republics. [393]

However, that Congress makes applicable the right of drug possession in the federal areas does not necessarily answer the bigger question for the U.S. Supreme Court: i.e., whether the U.S. constitution requires it to, as the constitution requires of states and the U.S. republic. This bigger question is essentially the same question as the following three questions: 1) whether Congress must define crime in the federal areas as do America's republics, based on crime's meaning in state and U.S. constitutions, or whether it can define non-crimes to be crimes, 2) whether the 13th Amendment applies to Congress in the federal areas, or whether Congress can enslave people for non-crimes in those areas, and 3) whether Congress must regulate drug commerce in the federal areas as it does commerce within the states, or whether it may criminally prohibit drug commerce there?

In other words, is Congress a republic or a non-republic in the federal areas, and if the latter, can it deprive its subjects of certain substantive rights that we discussed in chapter 2? If so, which rights?

That the majority of the Supreme Court in *Palmore v. United States* (1973) defined the federal areas as non-republican is why Justice Douglas' dissented. Quoting the Court in *O'Donoghue v. United States* (1933), he wrote that Article I courts may not be used "to destroy the operative effect of the judicial clause within the District." [394] In other words, he was saying, just because Congress can create its own Article I courts for the federal areas or functions does not mean that Congress or its courts are above the constitution and may violate people's substantive rights.

(Recall that in the *Schick v. United States* (1904), [395] *District of Columbia v. Colts* (1930) [396] and *District of Columbia v. Clawans* (1937) [397] cases which we discussed in chapters 4 and 5, the Supreme Court upheld the substantive right to a jury trial for crimes committed within the federal areas. However, because some of the defendants were mere regulation violators, instead of real criminals, they were denied jury trials.)

As exemplified by Douglas' dissent, the scope of Congress' plenary legislative power over commerce within the federal areas has not been sufficiently addressed. For example, in *Gonzales v. Raich* (2005) the Supreme Court upheld only the constitutionality of Congress' interstate regulation of drugs, but not its power to criminally prohibit the commerce of drugs.

In fact, during the forty-five years of the CSAs' existence, the Court has not directly addressed the constitutionality of the U.S. CSA's criminal penalty provisions, nor has it defined where these provisions are applicable.

(I argue that Congress' criminal drug prohibitions might be constitutional and applicable in the federal areas, but that they are inapplicable – and unconstitutionally applied – within the state republics.)

The reason that we do not know these answers is likely because no one has brought the issues to the Supreme Court's attention. This is most likely because so few attorneys realize that Congress legislates as two sovereigns in the U.S. CSA, in two capacities, over two territorial jurisdictions. This is likely also because most criminal attorneys do not know that the U.S. criminal code, i.e., Title 18 of the USC, is mostly municipal legislation, which therefore mostly operates territorially – only within the federal areas.

The nature and scope of Congress' criminal power over the federal areas is very important in a constitutional sense. This is because Congress has been using municipal legislation over the federal areas, which include America's coastal waterways, to establish a national importation and exportation barrier for controlled substances.

This raises the issue whether Congress may use municipal legislation over the federal areas to criminalize certain commerce for the entire country. The 18th Amendment, whose ban on alcohol commerce included its importation and exportation, suggests that a constitutional amendment is instead required to criminalize the importation and exportation of drugs.

Nonetheless and more significantly, Congress does not need to criminalize drug commerce in the federal areas to fight it there. Given that Congress' power to regulate commerce includes the power to confiscate, as upheld by the U.S. Supreme Court in *Gonzales v. Raich* (2005), Congress therefore already has authority – even if required to act as a republic over the federal areas – to prevent the unauthorized importation or exportation of drugs by confiscating them.

Thus, Congress needs no criminal authority at all to wage its war on drugs. It can more than sufficiently wage its war on drug importing and exporting solely by using the regulatory police powers of the U.S. republic.

The U.S. requires criminal authority only to wage its criminal war against real people. However, this book shows that – at least in an American republic – it has no constitutional authority to do this.

Congress' regulatory powers alone – i.e. its powers to investigate, confiscate and enjoin – are more than sufficient to fulfill its public policy of banning the importation and domestic commerce of unwanted drugs. The U.S. does not need the criminal justice system to accomplish this goal. Its regulatory system is more than adequate.

This is to say that Congress and state legislatures as republics have abundant power to wage their war on drug commerce. These sovereigns merely do not have any authority to wage a war against Americans and other natural people. Unless Congress truly is a non-republic in the federal areas, as the Supreme Court suggests, then it is required to regulate the importation of unwanted drugs, just as it regulates that of desired drugs.

To know this is to know the proper operation of government's two police powers – one being regulatory over commerce, the other being judicial over real criminals. People importing drugs are not criminals, except perhaps in the federal areas where Congress appears to legally operate as a non-republic.

The U.S. CSA is lawful and constitutional because, as we have just seen after a careful reading, it does in fact acknowledge and authorize ways to lawfully acquire drugs other than through medical practitioners, even in the federal areas where Congress' criminal prohibitions may apply. But one would only learn this if one reads the U.S. CSA very, very thoroughly, and thinks about it really, really hard, plus in context of knowing about the multiple jurisdictions operating within the act. Otherwise, fat chance of really understanding the U.S. CSA, of understanding its ultimate user provision, and of knowing under which U.S. sovereign either the criminal provisions or the regulatory provisions in the act operate.

Only attorneys who know the relationship between the natural law and positive law jurisdictions of our constitutions could write a legislative act, such as the Controlled Substances Act, to deliberately give the wrong impression to other attorneys who do not know about this relationship, or who superficially read statutes with a subjective, religious perspective, i.e., that some supernatural god picked the legislature to rule over the natural law jurisdiction of individuals.

As well, only attorneys who knew the relationship between the U.S. republic and the U.S. non-republic could have written the act to camouflage their differences. Since its enactment throughout the country, the CSAs' encrypted misrepresentations of law have deliberately fooled professional attorneys about our governments' proper separation of powers. As we shall see in chapters 26 – 29, this was the authors' intention.

To conclude this section: the plain, ordinary and technical meaning of the term ultimate user under both federal and Indiana law is someone who voluntarily acquires controlled substances by chance, gift, purchase, self-production or exchange, with reasonable certainty that the property is not stolen, for one's own use or the use of one's household.

Ultimate means end. The ordinary and technical meaning of an ultimate user of controlled substances is an end user of drugs. The statute means exactly what it says: that end users of drugs need not apply for registration with the Indiana pharmacy board or the U.S. Attorney General, and may lawfully acquire and possess drugs for their own use and that of their household, without anyone's permission. This is a natural right at law within America's republics, and a legal right within the federal areas.

Believe your own eyes

If this book has any negative impact on the drug war, then we have a Johnny Appleseed to thank. Metaphorically, a Johnny Appleseed is one who plants seeds that grow into towering or useful trees. A Johnny Appleseed is the cause-in-fact of this book.

Maybe about ten years ago, an email was forwarded to me from a guy in Pennsylvania, noting his state CSA's ultimate user provision. His email essentially said, "Hey, look at this! Pennsylvania law says I may lawfully possess drugs for my own use."

As an attorney, when I read the Pennsylvania ultimate user provision for the first time, I said three things to myself. First I said: "Shazam, this guy is right! He is correct to read the statute as he does. There is nothing ambiguous about the statute. It means what it says: that ultimate drug users may lawfully possess drugs for their own use."

Second, I immediately recognized the provision as a Rule 8 defense, to be discussed in the next section. Rule 8 is a rule from federal and state rules of court, which refers to affirmative defenses.

Third, I literally said to myself dumbfounded: "Wow. The statutory law actually does secure our natural rights, just as the Declaration of Independence says it will!"

It was then that I realized or affirmed to myself: 1) that statutory law must secure our substantive rights, or else it constitutionally fails, and 2) that the CSA is consistent with the state constitution in that it secures the right of drug users to possess drugs. However, despite the act's constitutionality, I realized that it was not being properly enforced.

Thus, I realized the thesis of this book from that email, and at that very moment. Little did I know that I would have to write a book to make my argument to other attorneys. At the time, I incorrectly thought that I could challenge the improper enforcement of Indiana's drug laws by using Indiana's judicial courts. Chapter 30 shows why that was not possible.

I wrote this book for two basic reasons. First, I cannot stand being lied to. Chapters 26 – 30 are all about misrepresentations of law and of fraud by government officials. The second reason is to show other attorneys that the constitutional limitations placed on republican governments are not only real, but in fact embodied in statutes.

For example, the ultimate user provision acknowledges, respects and secures the natural right of property possession under republican constitutions' natural law jurisdiction. It negates the conflicting legislative misrepresentations at IC 35-48-4 which falsely call drug possession either a misdemeanor or a felony.

The clear meaning of IC 35-48-3-3 is that it not only fails to grant government power over drug possession, but it also specifically exempts drug possession from government regulation and criminal prosecution, calling it lawful. Possession of lawfully acquired drugs has never been criminal because it has always been exempt from judicial authority, regardless that the ultimate user provision codifies and confirms this.

As we have seen, drug possession is a right defined by Nature, which is secured by the substantive right of all natural persons not to be arrested or enslaved except for the commission of crime, as the 13th Amendment says. This natural right is also secured by statute for those who are not aware of the natural law jurisdiction of the U.S. and Indiana constitutions, and who are not aware of the 13th Amendment or its meaning under law.

Thus, the ultimate user provision is not a loophole, but a statutory failsafe provision against those who do not really comprehend criminal law under the U.S. and Indiana constitutions. It is a portal to the natural law jurisdiction where our rights can be invoked and are to be adjudicated. The government tramples all over our rights unless we know them, unless we can spot these rights in statutes, and unless we can properly invoke our rights over the objections of those who violate the law in the most fundamental of ways.

Because the ultimate user provision is an accurate reflection of republican law (and because most of the penalty provisions at IC 35-48-4 are not), its presence in the CSAs is likely the only reason that the acts are constitutional. That is, all the nation's CSAs are constitutional only because the ultimate user provision provides a means for natural persons to secure their substantive rights in the law jurisdiction by means of a Rule 8-defense under the trial rules (to be discussed below).

Otherwise, the CSAs would completely misrepresent the law – even more than they already do. Otherwise, one would have to know the Indiana constitution very, very well to know the law, i.e., that drug possession is lawful, that drug commerce is regulated, and that neither are criminal.

Otherwise, in order to challenge judicial subject matter jurisdiction, one would have to know and assert all the consistent arguments in this book, which took me years to discover, to process and then to convey.

For those readers who really do not yet believe that American state and federal constitutions are based on natural law, this is yet another statute that confirms it. Readers can either believe that American constitutions secure their natural rights in their natural law jurisdictions, as I know to be true. Or, if they still think the natural law concept is fallacious, that Congress and state legislatures are kings, and that their positive law is the alpha and omega of law, then they can just read and rely on the ultimate user provision in their kings' code books.

The ultimate user provision is equally an expression of natural law as are American legislatures' codifications of crimes, their codifications of courts' procedural rules, their codifications of how natural born citizens are created, their codifications of the differences between production and manufacture, and their codifications of lawful property possession. All of these provisions reflect the natural law jurisdiction operating within America's republics, to which almost all government officials have heretofore been blind.

As with crime and the creation of natural citizens, the ultimate user provision is redundant and unnecessary for people who already know the law, i.e., that there exists a law jurisdiction in the judicial branch that secures natural persons' unalienable rights, for example the right to possess property. These people already know, from reading the U.S. constitution: 1) that foreigners as natural persons have rights of judicial action for torts done to them (because it is the nature of the law jurisdiction to treat all natural persons equally and to enforce the natural law of compensation), and 2) that drugs are legal in America for U.S. citizens, at least outside of federal areas, merely because Article IV, Section 4 of the U.S. constitution guarantees them a republican government, with a law jurisdiction, which secures their natural rights to possess and use property.

For people (like me) 1) who have read the Indiana constitution and who know about people's enumerated natural right to property possession, 2) who have read the Indiana constitution and recognize the law jurisdiction as that which secures people's natural rights, 3) who have read the Indiana constitution and know about the subject matter jurisdiction of judicial courts over injury, 4) who have read the Indiana constitution and who know the definition of crime to include victims, 5) who have read the Controlled Substances Act and know that drug commerce is regulated, not criminally prohibited, and 6) who know the differences between the law and equity jurisdictions, then the ultimate user provision merely acknowledges what the rest of the law already tells them (and me).

Drugs are lawful because it is the nature of America's republics to make all personal property and all commerce lawful, unless constitutionally prohibited. To not know this is to not know the meaning of an American republic, is to not know the difference between a republic and non-republic, and is to not realize that Americans today live under a *de facto* non-republic that grossly violates the *de jure* republic to which U.S. citizens are entitled.

The ultimate user provision exists for lawyers and jurists who do not recognize the natural law jurisdiction of American constitutions, and who mistakenly believe that legislatures determine what is and is not criminal in a republic. It exists so that these people can read for themselves what republican legislatures say about their own power over drug possession.

The ultimate user provision exists so that judicial judges can still render justice in drug matters without ever needing to read or understand the Indiana or U.S. constitutions, or state and U.S. CSAs. It is a failsafe provision to protect defendants from those who do not understand the role and power of America's four types of sovereigns.

For example, Indiana's judges can recognize the ultimate user provision as a criminal defense to drug possession without knowing anything else in this book. It is through this trapdoor that the CSA's authors provided the uninformed a means to find the constitutional guarantee of a republic.

As a formerly misinformed attorney, it was exclusively through this gateway – introduced to me by that Johnny Appleseed in Pennsylvania – that I ultimately found the Indiana and U.S. republics. Without the seeds planted by that stranger, I would not have discovered the meaning of America's republican form of government. Given that this is one of my greatest personal realizations, I thank you, Johnny, for planting its seed. (My thanks also go out to RJ, who forwarded Johnny's important email, which got me to thinkin'.)

Similar to the federal statute at 28 USC 1251(b)(1), which guarantees a foreigner's right of action for torts, the ultimate user provision is redundant of natural persons' substantive rights under the U.S. and Indiana constitutions. It is redundant of the right of liberty expressed in the 13th Amendment and in Article 1, Section 37 of the Indiana Constitution (1851).

It is redundant of the right to acquire, possess and protect property at Article 1, Section 1 of the Indiana constitution (1816). It is also redundant of the constitutional requirement of injury to enter a judicial law court at Article 1, Section 12 of the Indiana constitution (1851).

Consistency breeds redundancy. Because criminal statutes are consistent with our constitutions, with natural law and with the common law, knowing one is like knowing the other. Because law is to be consistent, it leads to the same results and conclusions, regardless of the source of law – natural or artificial, constitutional or statutory. All law with regard to drugs leads to the same conclusion: that drugs are lawful in America's republics (and that drug possession is legal in America's non-republic).

As we saw earlier, IC 1-1-2-1 and the Supremacy Clause say that all various types of Indiana law must be consistent with the state and federal constitutions. Because governments' rightful positive law jurisdiction is both compatible and consistent with the natural law jurisdiction, never does governments' rightful criminal authority overlap or interfere with either its regulatory jurisdiction or our personal positive-law-free jurisdictions. Thus, most statutory law is rightful and constitutional. When justice fails, it is normally because this rightful law is falsely known and enforced.

The ultimate user provision in the Indiana and U.S. codes exists because of (and also confirms) the natural law jurisdiction where we have natural rights to property possession and to intoxicate. Largely because of defense attorneys' lack of vigilance and knowledge of subject matter jurisdiction, and of the natural law basis of most American constitutions, government officials have walked all over these statutory and constitutionally-secured rights. As we shall see, although this false process may be carried on by people ignorant of the law, it was initiated years ago by people in the U.S. Department of Justice with great knowledge of the law, as well as the will to pervert it.

In conclusion, if you have a natural right to breathe and a natural right to garden and a natural right to make fire, would you not have a natural right to smoke the fruit that you grew in your back yard? Of course you would, and that is what the ultimate user provision says.

It says that end users in America's republics may lawfully possess controlled substances for their own use. In Indiana, because IC 35-48-4-11 states that cultivation of marijuana is possession, and because production of plants is different from commerce in plants, ultimate users may lawfully cultivate plants for their own use as well.

Thus one may lawfully cultivate and / or possess the natural sources of controlled substances for one's own use, not only because the natural law jurisdiction of the constitution says so, but because the positive law of the legislature also says so. Whether from natural law or positive law, the law is the same from either source.

This is because the law is the law is the law, in spite that the law is not read, understood or followed. Drugs are lawful for U.S. citizens in America's republics under natural law, constitutional law, statutory law and judicial case law   It does not matter upon which law attorneys rely.   It matters only that they properly read know and follow the law.

The ultimate user provision likely had to be included in the CSAs to carve out the natural law jurisdiction where phony "criminal" defendants could escape the act's intended improper enforcement. The provision is a key to invoking the law jurisdiction where rights are secured. It is "criminal" defendants' obvious but overlooked escape hatch to due process.

The demurrer and the defense

This section is about challenging a court's jurisdiction in a drug possession matter by a demurrer and by an affirmative defense. According to Indiana's trial rules, a challenge is made to subject matter jurisdiction with a motion to dismiss under Trial Rule 12(b)(1). The essence of the motion is that the defendant moves to dismiss an action because the court lacks jurisdiction over the subject matter. This motion applies to both civil and criminal cases.

In context of America's drug laws, the motion would specifically mean: Defendant moves to dismiss this "criminal" action because this judicial court lacks jurisdiction over controlled substances and has criminal jurisdiction only over crimes or other violations of right involving controlled substances. To argue for such a motion to dismiss, it would help for one to know every single argument in this book, which are all consistent.

However, in addition to this motion to dismiss drug matters based on courts' lack of subject matter jurisdiction under Trial Rule 12, which must be affirmatively pleaded and proven, the ultimate user provision of IC 35-48-3-3(e) also provides an affirmative defense under Trial Rule 8.

In the case of controlled substances, an affirmative defense would essentially say: Even if this court has subject matter jurisdiction over controlled substances, the defendant nonetheless has a statutory (legal) right to lawfully possess them. This court may have jurisdiction over drugs, but IC 35-48-3-3(e)(3) waives defendant's liability in this court and exempts him from prosecution for his possession of drugs for his own use.

Unlike a motion to dismiss for want of subject matter jurisdiction, which may be raised at any time in or even after a proceeding, an affirmative defense must be made in the defendant's response or it is likely waived. Rule 8(D) of the Trial Rules states: "Averments in a pleading to which a responsive pleading is required, except those pertaining to amount of damages, are admitted when not denied in the responsive pleading."

Under both a Rule 12(b)(1) motion and a timely Rule 8 response taken together, even if a court had subject matter jurisdiction over drugs, the defendant would still have an affirmative defense in that his drug possession as an ultimate user is statutorily exempt from prosecution.

Nonetheless, both the motion or response should have the same effect, i.e., to cause the false drug prosecution to be dismissed. Not only have judicial courts no authority over non-crimes involving no injury, to which a Rule 12(b)(1) motion applies, but even in a sham trial in a "judicial" court without jurisdiction, drug possession has a statutory affirmative defense to be timely asserted under Rule 8.

The ultimate user provisions of IC 35-48-3-3(e) and 21 USC 822(c) respectively are the Indiana General Assembly's and Congress' subtle, obscured and overlooked way of admitting that no branch or agency of republican government has any kind of jurisdiction – original or appellate – over drug possession. It is the legislature's muddled way of admitting that its positive law has no authority over natural persons in the natural law jurisdiction, which guarantees people a substantive right not to be arrested except for the commission of real crime. The provision is the legislature's admission that drug possession is not a real crime, or even a case.

From the law of the Northwest Territories... to the statehood of Indiana... to the enactment of the Indiana Controlled Substances Act, the law regarding possession and intoxication has never really changed in Indiana. We now know this lesson constitutionally and statutorily. The state of Indiana has been falsely enforcing the CSA in gross error against lawful end users of drugs.

Ultimately, the laws of Indiana do not prohibit lawfully obtaining or possessing any personal property. There is no judicial mechanism to treat drug possession as a crime, and there is no legitimate criminal *malum pro-hibita* in Indiana's statutes or constitution that apply to natural persons. Instead, as we have seen, people in Indiana have a natural right to acquire, possess and protect their property, [398] and there is an overlooked but irrefutable statutory defense for drug possession under state and federal law, called the ultimate user provision. [399]

The ultimate user provision was apparently not argued or invoked by the plaintiffs in the U.S. Supreme Court case of *Gonzales v. Raich* (2005). [400] This is the government's leading case in the war on drugs, which upheld the DEA's power to confiscate contraband involved in unwanted commerce.

There the DEA confiscated Diane Monson's six marijuana plants because she was sharing marijuana with Angel Raich – as medical marijuana patients. The Court held that this arrangement was subject to Congress' power to regulate commerce because of its negative effect on Raich's local marijuana purchases. Justice Stevens for the majority wrote:

"Our case law firmly establishes Congress' power to regulate purely local activities that are part of an economic 'class of activities' that have a substantial effect on interstate commerce. [401] As we stated in *Wickard*, 'even if appellee's activity be local and though it may not be regarded as commerce, it may still, whatever its nature, be reached by Congress if it exerts a substantial economic effect on interstate commerce' [402] ... When Congress decides that the 'total incidence' of a practice poses a threat to a national market, it may regulate the entire class." [403]

Because Diane Monson plainly was in commerce, she clearly was subject to regulation. The Court held that despite her *de minimis* effect on interstate commerce, she was nonetheless subject to the DEA instead of just California regulators. That a small marijuana grower was subject to federal instead of state drug regulators was the controversial aspect of the ruling.

However, other things that Justice Stevens wrote on behalf of the Court's majority should be refuted or clarified. Take for example his statement that "Congress devised a closed regulatory system making it unlawful to manufacture, distribute, dispense, or possess any controlled substance except as authorized by the CSA. 21 U.S.C. §§ 841(a)(1), 844(a)."

This is false in at least three regards. First, neither drug possession nor drug commerce is "unlawful" in California. Instead, as Justice Stevens tells us (above), drug dealing is regulated, which means it is lawful.

Second, regulators who operate in equity cannot regulate unlawful things, which are adjudicated at law. As we learned, unlawful things and regulatory things are ultimately adjudged in separate judicial jurisdictions. To be regulated and to be subject to law are mutually exclusive statuses.

Third, drug dealing is only "unlawful" in the federal areas where the statutes that Justice Stevens cites, i.e., 21 USC 841(a) and 844(a), apply. That Diane Monson was instead subject to 21 USC 822(a), which regulates her drug dealing in California, demonstrates that not only Justice Stevens, but surprisingly all others on the Court were (are) unaware that the U.S. CSA is legislation from Congress in both of its sovereign capacities.

Another false sentence in the opinion is:: "Marijuana is classified as a Schedule I substance... This classification renders the manufacture, distribution, or possession of marijuana a criminal offense. §§ 841(a)(1), 844(a)."

This statement is incorrect 1) because 21 USC 841(a) and 844(a), which apply in the federal areas, are irrelevant to the DEA's subject matter in California, 2) because marijuana commerce is regulated by the DEA in

California, and 3) because possession of marijuana as an ultimate user is both a) a codified natural right in California under 21 USC 822(c), as well as b) a legal right granted by Congress in the federal areas under 21 USC 844(a), which does not apply in California, but which Justice Stevens falsely cites in support of his statement.

Thus, because ultimate users have a statutory right to lawfully possess drugs everywhere in the United States, his calling marijuana possession "a criminal offense" is false. Such a false statement could only result 1) from the Court's use of definitions for crime and offense that are different than those from the U.S. constitution, and 2) from the Court's not knowing about the ultimate user provision, which at least partially exempted Monson's plants from Congress' commerce power.

For example, had Monson's natural and statutory rights as an ultimate user under 21 USC 822(c) and 802(27) been properly asserted, she could have claimed that at least three of her plants were for her own ultimate use, and not subject to confiscation. Thus, the case offered a missed opportunity to show the role of the ultimate user provision and the operation of natural law in the U.S. CSA. To have seized the opportunity would have required a more thorough reading and understanding of the U.S. CSA., which was not shown by either of the parties or by the Court.

Likewise, if Raich and Monson had lived in the same household, then they would have both been ultimate users, who could both have lawfully possessed drugs for their own use and the use of their household under 21 USC 822(c) and 21 USC 802(27). (The ultimate user provision at 21 USC 844(a), which such irrelevant criminal statute Justice Stevens falsely cites in his opinion about regulation, did not apply to Monson or Raich because they were in California.)

22
Drug crimes and
real grounds for arrest

Most drug-penalty provisions are meaninglessness, unenforceable and fraudulent

When asked what makes drugs illegal, most Indiana defense attorneys point to the criminal penalty provisions at IC 35-48-4, which lists and describes the various statutory criminal "offenses" that relate to controlled substances.

For purposes of our discussion, these offenses in IC 35-48-4 can be broken down into four categories:

1. invalid and ineffectual statutes of *malum prohibita* that appear to criminalize drug possession, over which the state has no judicial or regulatory authority,

2. invalid and ineffectual statutes of *malum prohibita* that appear to criminalize drug commerce, which the state instead regulates using the executive branch, and over which the judicial branch has only equitable appellate authority,

3. invalid and ineffectual statutes of *malum prohibita* that appear to criminalize regulatory omissions owed to the pharmacy board, and

4. valid, effectual and legitimate codifications of *malum in se* crimes involving drugs over which the criminal law jurisdiction of the judicial branch has subject matter jurisdiction.

The first thing to note about these categories is that there are two types of penalty provisions in the Indiana CSA: valid ones and invalid ones. The valid penalty provisions of category 4 are those that sanction real crime. These provisions belong in the criminal code and are the subject matter of judicial courts. The invalid ones of categories 1, 2 and 3 are those that seek to judicially sanction phony "crimes" and *malum prohibita*, over which judicial courts have no subject matter jurisdiction.

Again, the latter penalty provisions are invalid and ineffectual 1) because judicial courts have no constitutional subject matter jurisdiction to try drug "offenses" that do not involve real cases or crimes, and 2) because the administrative law courts of the pharmacy board, which are empowered to administer and enforce the drug laws in Indiana, have no criminal authority.

In other words, no branch of republican government has criminal jurisdiction over the possession or commerce of drugs. The provisions of categories 1, 2 and 3 are bogus and indeed fraudulent because 1) they are not enforceable in republican judicial courts, and 2) they were placed in the CSA only with the intent to misrepresent the law. Other conflicting provisions in the CSA that we have read show that drug possession is not subject to positive law, and that drug commerce is the subject of equity, not criminal law.

As we shall see below, the same can be said about the federal CSA. It grants no criminal jurisdiction over drug commerce within the states 1) because Congress has legislative jurisdiction only over crimes relating to its enumerated powers within the states and 2) because Congress regulates drug commerce within the states, and does not criminally prohibit it there. Thus, all the criminal sanctions in the U.S. CSA, including those for both *malum prohibita* and *malum in se,* apply only in the federal areas.

Category 1. The false criminalization of drug possession

With regard to the first category of statutory provisions, i.e., the Indiana legislature's attempt to criminalize drug possession, it should be obvious by now that drug possession is not a crime in an American republic and that a republican legislature, without amending the constitution, cannot criminalize it. Not only can drug possession not be used to invoke the criminal subject matter jurisdiction of judicial courts, which requires injury, but as we just extensively examined, it is statutorily exempted from regulatory control and criminal liability in likely most states and the federal areas by the ultimate user provisions at IC 35-48-3-3(e), 21 USC 822(c), and 21 USC 844(a), with definitions at IC 35-48-1-27 and 21 USC 802[27]

This is because drug possession, as with the possession of any property, is a natural right in the natural law jurisdiction of the Indiana and U.S. constitutions over which positive law has no authority to be inconsistent. Article I, Section 1 of the Indiana constitution (1816) recognizes the natural unalienable right "of acquiring, possessing and protecting property." That is why neither Congress nor the Indiana General Assembly claims any explicit authority in the CSAs over drug possession, but in fact exempts it from liability.

This means that all the sections in the Indiana Code that appear to prohibit drug possession and to place criminal penalties on such behavior are without judicial and regulatory effect. They exist in print, but are ineffectual because there is no judicial or administrative mechanism to enforce them.

These provisions are ineffectual and not unconstitutional because they do not prohibit anything, which word has constitutional meaning. Nor do they declare anything to be un<u>law</u>ful, as does the U.S. CSA. They merely apply inaccurate labels and ineffectual penalties to lawful natural and commercial behavior. Judges are presumed to know that these provisions are ineffectual because they are presumed to know their courts' jurisdiction.

These provisions includes section 6 for possession of cocaine or narcotic drug; section 6.1 for possession of methamphetamine; section 7 for possession and obtainment of a controlled substance in a school zone; section 8.3 for possession of paraphernalia; section 11 for possession of marijuana, hash oil, hashish, salvia or a synthetic cannabinoid; and section 13 for visiting or maintaining a common nuisance "to unlawfully use a controlled substance."

As an aside, because I do not know a better place to mention this, please note the above penalties 1) for unlawful "obtainment of a controlled substance in a school zone," and 2) for visiting or maintaining a common nuisance "to unlawfully use a controlled substance" at IC 35-48-4-13. Similar to the misleading provision in the U.S. CSA which suggests that people can lawfully acquire drugs only through medical practitioners, the phrases "obtainment of a controlled substance" and "to unlawfully use a controlled substance" are meant to make readers also believe that drug use is illegal without permission of a government-licensed practitioner.

Because we know that it is lawful for ultimate users to acquire, possess and use controlled substances in any manner that does not injure others, which the separation of powers doctrine in our constitutions is intended to secure, the above reference to unlawful use is a misrepresentation of law because it is not a crime to honestly and non-violently use any property, including drugs.

Under the Indiana constitution the only unlawful obtainment of property is to use force, theft or fraud to acquire it, and the only unlawful use of any property is to harm someone with it or to steal it from them. Thus the phrases about unlawful acquisition or use of controlled substances do not refer to anyone's ultimate use of drugs, which is constitutionally and statutorily secured. Instead, it refers to the use of unlawfully acquired drugs or the use of drugs to unlawfully harm someone else. Otherwise in Indiana, drug acquisition, possession and use are lawful.

Category 2. The false criminalization of drug commerce

As drug possession is not a crime, neither is drug commerce. We saw previously that within America's republics it takes a constitutional amendment to turn commercial activity into a crime over which a judicial court would have constitutional criminal subject matter jurisdiction. That is the lesson of Alcohol Prohibition.

Neither the U.S. nor the Indiana constitution has been changed to eliminate this requirement. Criminal prohibition of commerce without a constitutional amendment is a attribute of America's *de facto* monarchy, not its *de jure* law.

Not only does the criminal jurisdiction of republican judicial courts not extend to artificial commercial entities, which operate in the non-criminal equity jurisdiction, but such courts do not exist to regulate commerce. Instead they adjudicate commercial wrongs using their equity powers. This means that they have no subject matter jurisdiction over drug commerce that does not otherwise involve a civil or criminal injury. Instead, state judicial courts and Article III courts deal with the privilege of being in commerce in their appellate capacity under equity.

Drug dealing may be a statutory "crime" but is not a real crime in a republic because, like any other commerce, it is based on voluntary and consensual behavior without injury. Given this, and given that the executive branch has power to regulate drug commerce but no authority to criminally prosecute it, the legislature's "criminal" sanctions for dealing drugs at IC 35-48-4 are also completely unenforceable.

These provisions include: section 1 for dealing in cocaine or narcotic drugs; section 1.1 for dealing in methamphetamine; section 2 for dealing in a schedule I, II, or II controlled substance; section 3 for dealing in a schedule IV controlled substance; section 4 for dealing in a schedule V controlled substance; section 8.1 for the manufacture of paraphernalia; section 8.5 for dealing in paraphernalia; and section 10 for dealing in marijuana.

As well, this second category of unenforceable criminal provisions also includes the criminal penalties for drug paraphernalia at 8.1 (manufacture of paraphernalia) and 8.5 (dealing in paraphernalia), which are designated as infractions.

I bring this up again to mention not only that making and selling smoking apparati are obviously not crimes (because you and I can naturally make pipes from metal cans), but to point out again that judicial courts have no criminal jurisdiction over infractions. In that infractions do not involve injury, and according to IC 35-31.5-2-215 do not amount to even statutory "crimes" or "offenses," they cannot be tried in judicial courts as crimes or criminal cases, or even as fake "crimes" or "offenses."

Unlike the words "crime," "criminal case," "offense," "felony" and "misdemeanor," whose meaning the Indiana legislature attempts to fraudulently co-opt from the Indiana and U.S. constitutions, infractions are not mentioned in the constitutions. They are strictly creations of the legislature and have no basis to be recognized by constitutionally-created judicial courts, as do crimes and misdemeanors involving injury that are mentioned in the constitutions.

Because IC 35-48-4-8.1 (manufacture of paraphernalia) and -8.5 (dealing in paraphernalia) are commercial activities, they may be legitimately regulated by the executive branch. However, absent an injury, this commerce cannot be adjudicated by the judicial branch as a crime or as a case.

Suffice to say that if the state's "misdemeanors" and "felonies" for possession and commerce of drugs do not qualify as real misdemeanors and felonies for purposes of the criminal law jurisdiction, then certainly infractions regarding smoking paraphernalia do not qualify either. Thus, Indiana's judicial courts have no criminal subject matter jurisdiction over infractions, and violate defendants' substantive due process by trying them.

Category 3. The criminalization of regulatory omissions

Of all the illegitimate misrepresentation of law in the Indiana CSA, this category is the most devious. At IC 35-48-4-14(a) the Indiana legislature attempts to criminalize the failure of drug makers – both those licensed by the pharmacy board and those unlicensed – to keep records of their drug transactions and to allow the regulatory agency access to their premises for inspection. Of course, this provision is intended to snare into the criminal justice system unwanted drug dealers who do not keep records.

With regard to these provisions, I would point out three things. First, regardless of this phony "criminal" penalty provision, the board of pharmacy already has an administrative remedy against a drug maker or distributor that does not keep records or does not allow it access for inspection. Its remedies are to take away the license to make and sell drugs, or to enjoin the drug making and dealing. The pharmacy board must exhaust these remedies before it can seek judicial help.

Second, the legislature cannot criminalize *malum prohibita* such as drug making or dealing. Without a constitutional amendment to the republican form of government, it cannot place *malum prohibita* into the criminal subject matter jurisdiction of judicial courts. As we have seen, *malum prohibita* does not apply to natural persons and is not enforceable in the criminal law jurisdiction.

In America's republics *malum prohibita* operates only upon artificial persons in equity. For example, prohibitions against driving too fast apply only to regulated drivers. They do not apply to natural persons exercising natural rights. *Malum prohibita* applies only to artificial persons who exercise state privileges, and thus their sanctions apply in non-criminal equity.

The Indiana legislature created the Indiana pharmacy board to both regulate desirable drug manufactures and distributors and to enforce the legislature's *malum prohibita* against unwanted drug makers and dealers. Once unwanted drug litigants are given their day in court, where the board either denies their registration or enjoins their unlicensed drug making and dealing, the board's determinations may be enforced by the judicial branch.

Thus, the state of Indiana can use its authority to eliminate unwanted drug activity, but it must use the administrative due process of the regulatory system to enforce its *malum prohibita* against disfavored drug dealing. As well, it may not use the criminal jurisdiction of judicial courts to criminally punish activity that is subject only to regulation, such as book keeping.

The criminal law jurisdiction of America's republics sanctions real crime, based on violations of natural duty. As we recall from chapter 20, criminal penalties cannot spring from artificial duties, such as the statutory duty to keep records.

Third, as was previously explained, the Indiana legislature cannot impose criminal duties upon natural persons, but can only codify that which Nature already imposes. For example the legislature can define and codify crimes, but it cannot impose criminal penalties for regulatory duties, such as bookkeeping, that it imposes on commercial activity.

Failing to fulfill a regulatory duty is not a criminal – thus a judicial –

issue. A violation of a regulatory duty is not subject to a judicial court until administrative remedies are exhausted. Judicial courts are powerless to provide remedies for regulatory violations, such as criminal sanctions for not keeping records. The ultimate remedy against unwanted drug dealing and bad record keeping, i.e., injunction, is already provided to the executive branch by the legislature. The remedy exists in equity, and not at law.

Criminalizing the failure to keep records for the pharmacy board is akin to criminalizing one's failure to use turn signals while driving. Under no circumstance are such violations of regulatory duties to be treated as real crimes over which our judicial system has cognizance. These faux "criminal" provisions against regulatory violations can only exist out of legislators' ignorance of law or their deliberate legislative malfeasance.

Under both of these hypothetical examples, governments' ultimate solution is to use the regulatory process to revoke the licenses to drive and to make drugs, and to enjoin their future operation. The state's remedy is not to put unwanted drivers and undesirable drug makers in jail through the criminal process, but to halt their driving and drug making primarily with its regulatory powers and processes.

In a republic, violating licensing statutes cannot in any way be criminal, as IC 35-48-4-14(a) falsely suggests. Licensing statutes apply only in equity, and do not apply to natural persons, who are subject only to the (natural, common, criminal) law jurisdiction over injury. In America's republics, regulatory omissions such as the failure to keep records operate in a completely separate jurisdiction than criminal law. Alas, they are not subject to criminal sanction.

The subject matter jurisdiction of judicial courts dictates that the legislature cannot impose criminal penalties for anything but *malum in se* crimes, which are violations of natural duty. Blackstone explains that the natural and common law, which define judicial courts' criminal jurisdiction, recognize only three duties: to be honest, to do no harm to others, and to render everyone his due. [404] Neither legislatures nor judicial courts have constitutional authority to impose additional duties, such as bookkeeping, upon natural persons in the criminal law jurisdiction.

Absent a constitutional amendment, commercial activities are not crimes subject to the law jurisdiction. All the state's remedies for unwanted drug dealing (as well as for disfavored drug dealers' horrendous bookkeeping practices) are primarily administrative. These equitable remedies must be exhausted before the executive branch may seek any help from the judicial branch for bad bookkeeping.

To conclude these first three sections about unenforceable drug penalty provisions, we have established that the penalty provisions for drug possession, for drug and paraphernalia dealing, and for failing to fulfill regulatory duties are without legal effect and cannot lawfully be enforced. That they exist in the Indiana Code is solely because of legislative incompetence or criminal fraud. However, this does not render the Controlled Substances Act unconstitutional.

Instead, these provisions are irrelevant in the law jurisdiction because they have no legal effect there and are mere legislative surplus intended to distract us from the real law, which is to regulate commerce and penalize real drug crimes. Indeed, we can see through these legislative misrepresentations, and judges are to pay them no heed.

However, as misrepresentations of law, the Indiana legislature has a duty to remove them from its CSA. Otherwise, the legislation will continue to misrepresent the law, and perhaps the state's judiciary will continue to rely on these misrepresentations as they have for the past forty years.

Within America's republics the real law says 1) that judicial courts lack subject matter jurisdiction over non-cases and non-crimes, 2) that drug users have a Rule 8 defense and a Rule 12 demurrer for mere drug possession, and 3) that drug commerce is to be regulated by an administrative agency, not adjudicated by the judicial branch.

This is the true law. It is available for anyone to discover, read and comprehend. This real law says that there are nine real crimes in Indiana relating to controlled substances (see below), but that these real crimes exclude the phony "crimes" for which the executive and judicial branches of Indiana government routinely and illegally enslave people.

Within America's republics, regulatory violations do not rise to the level of a crime, let alone a judicial case, both which require injury. The U.S. and Indiana Supreme Courts have told us that judicial jurisdiction requires injury-in-fact. In *Schick v. United States* (1904), [405] *District of Columbia v. Colts* (1930) [406] and *District of Columbia v. Clawans* (1937) [407] the U.S. Supreme Court told us that regulatory violations are not crimes. In America's republics, exercises of natural rights and violations of commercial duties are not to be criminally sanctioned.

Category 4: Real, *malum in se* drug crimes

As we saw above, the criminalization of drug possession, of drug commerce and of regulatory violations is invalid and unenforceable because these are false "crimes" over which judicial courts have no subject matter jurisdiction. However, so as to not throw the baby out with the bath water –

that is, good law with bad – I have the pleasure of pointing out up-to nine real crimes relating to controlled substances that the Indiana legislature has properly codified as criminal in the Controlled Substances Act.

I say *up-to-nine real crimes* because I am not certain about the first and the last ones that I list below. They may codify mere regulatory violations or they may amount to torts or crimes, depending on circumstance. Notwithstanding this factor, these nine actual crimes and offenses in the Indiana CSA relating to controlled substances include:

- Dumping of controlled substance waste at IC 35-48-4-4.1
- Dealing in a substance represented to be a controlled substance at IC 35-48-4-4.5
- Unlawful manufacture, distribution, or possession of counterfeit substance at IC 35-48-4-4.6(a)
- Dealing in a counterfeit substance at IC 35-48-4-5
- Fraud in an application or report submitted to the board of pharmacy at IC 35-48-4-14(a)
- Counterfeiting drugs with a stamp or die at IC 35-48-4-14(b)
- Knowingly and intentionally acquiring a controlled substance by misrepresentation, fraud, forgery, deception, subterfuge, alteration of a prescription order, concealment of a material fact, or use of a false name or false address at IC 35-48-4-14(c)
- Affixing a false or forged label on controlled substance package at IC 35-48-4-14(d), and
- Duplicating or printing prescription pads without prior written approval of a practitioner at IC 35-48-4-14(e).

These are analogous to the real, *malum in se* crimes in the U.S. Controlled Substances Act at 21 USC 843(a)(2), (3), (4) and (5), which are sandwiched between violations of Congress' *malum prohibita* at 21 USC 843(a)(1) and (6) – (9), 843 (b) and 843 (c)(1) and (2). Again, other than the handful of crimes relating to Congress' enumerated powers within the states, then all criminal provisions of the U.S. CSA and of the U.S. criminal code at 18 USC – both those against *malum in se* and *malum prohibita* – are criminally enforceable by the U.S. government only in the federal areas.

With regard to Indiana law, whether the first and last activities listed above are real crimes depends on the situation. For example, it is not *per se* a tort or a crime to dump chemicals onto one's own property, although it may amount to a regulatory violation. As well, it is not *per se* a tort or a crime to print prescription pads without a state agent's permission, although it may under the circumstances amount to such.

Although a case could be made that duplicating someone else's property is criminal conversion instead of just a regulatory violation, it is indisputable that to acquire controlled substances with a false prescription would be a crime. This is because that would amount to "knowingly and intentionally acquiring a controlled substance by misrepresentation, fraud, forgery, deception," etc., which criminal prohibition is codified at IC 35-48-4-14(c) above.

The point I am making here is that at least seven of the above nine criminal penalty provisions relate to real crimes that are subject to the criminal jurisdiction of Indiana's judicial courts. At least seven, and arguably all, of these "offenses" are real crimes and offenses under the law jurisdiction, as crimes and offenses are referred to in the Indiana and U.S. constitutions.

In that all of these "offenses" are designated as "felonies," this means that at least seven of them amount to real felonies, as the word felony is used in the U.S. constitution. The legislature can treat behavior as a felony if it really is *malum in se* under the common law and our constitutions, such as defrauding a pharmacy with a false prescription.

Of all the penalty provisions at IC 35-48-4, the ones above are the only statutory drug "crimes," "offenses" or "felonies" that arguably constitute valid codifications of *malum in se* crimes, offenses and felonies under the words' constitutional meanings, and that are legitimately justiciable by Indiana's judicial courts. To prosecute these real drug crimes and to review or enforce administrative law decisions about drug commerce are the only legitimate uses of Indiana's Circuit and Superior Courts with regard to drugs.

Other than the nine-or-so criminal provisions listed above, all the rest of the Indiana "crimes" described at IC 35-48-4 are at most regulatory violations which are subject neither to Indiana's judicial trial courts nor to criminal penalty. I say *at most* because drug possession is not subject to any regulation in a republic, and unwanted drug commerce is subject at most to being enjoined.

The names have changed, but the story is the same with regard to the federal CSA. 21 USC 843 (a) of the federal CSA includes actual crimes at (a) (2), (3), (4), (5). Because Congress has criminal authority within the states only over a handful of federal crimes, which do not include drug prohibition, then these federal provisions against *malum in se* are only enforceable in the federal areas. In pertinent part 21 USC 843 (a) reads:

"It shall be unlawful for any person knowingly or intentionally—

(2) to use in the course of the manufacture, distribution, or dispensing of a controlled substance, or to use for the purpose of acquiring or obtaining a controlled substance, a registration number which is fictitious, revoked, suspended, expired, or issued to another person;

(3) to acquire or obtain possession of a controlled substance by misrepresentation, fraud, forgery, deception, or subterfuge;

(4)(A) to furnish false or fraudulent material information in, or omit any material information from, any application, report, record, or other document required to be made, kept, or filed under this subchapter or subchapter II of this chapter, or (B) to present false or fraudulent identification where the person is receiving or purchasing a listed chemical and the person is required to present identification under section 830(a) of this title;

(5) to make, distribute, or possess any punch, die, plate, stone, or other thing designed to print, imprint, or reproduce the trademark, trade name, or other identifying mark, imprint, or device of another or any likeness of any of the foregoing upon any drug or container or labeling thereof so as to render such drug a counterfeit substance;"

These are actual *malum in se* crimes of misrepresentation, fraud, forgery, deception, subterfuge and counterfeiting. Each of these actions involving controlled substances creates a victim due to injury. However, because the states have criminal jurisdiction over such crimes within their own borders, these *malum in se* federal crimes are only enforceable by the U.S. Attorney General (through U.S. District Attorneys) within the federal areas.

As the U.S. Supreme Court has told us, Congress can assign real crimes committed in the federal areas to Article III courts. Congress has "constitutional power to proscribe certain criminal conduct only in the District and to select the appropriate court, whether it is created by virtue of article III or article I, to hear and determine these particular criminal cases within the District," wrote the majority of the Supreme Court in *Palmore v. United States* (1973). [408] These Article III courts have authority to exercise actual judicial power over real cases and crimes.

Crime and contempt, the basis of arrest

We learned immediately above that there are, at most, only nine statutory drug crimes in Indiana, and that these crimes do not include drug possession or drug dealing, which are judicially-unenforceable "crimes." We know these nine codifications are the only drug crimes because, according to IC 1-1-2-1, they are the only activities that relate to controlled substances which are potentially recognized as crimes by all three types of Indiana law: the common law, our constitutional law and the legislature's statutory law, which all must be consistent.

That is, these are the only statutory drug crimes that are consistent with the natural, constitutional and common law meaning of crime. These are crimes today because only these are consistent with crimes of the past.

In this section I will show that these nine-or-so drug crimes and defendants' contempts of court are the only actions upon which the enforcers of the Indiana State Pharmacy Board, DEA agents, and other state law enforcers may base legitimate drug arrests and prosecutions in Indiana. As previously mentioned, the enforcers of the Indiana State Board of Pharmacy (and all the other state law enforcers who may help them to enforce drug laws) exercise two different authorities, or police powers.

Most of law enforcers' police powers with regard to controlled substances are exercised under the regulatory authority of the pharmacy board. The Supreme Court in *Ohio v. Helvering* (1939) [409] told us that the police power with regard to commerce is regulatory.

The other police power is that over crime, which is judicial. These judicial and regulatory police powers are exclusive, but they may be exercised simultaneously, over separate subject matter.

The power to arrest is a power or function that law enforcement officers exercise strictly with regard to the judicial branch, not the executive branch. The power to arrest is based solely on the judicial branch's subject matter jurisdiction over crime involving injury and on its inherent power to enforce its decisions with contempt orders.

That Indiana drug enforcers and other law enforcers have both regulatory and judicial functions is apparent from IC 16-42-20-1(b) which describes the powers granted to the Indiana pharmacy board's enforcers. The enforcers' judicial arrest powers are specifically described at IC 16-42-20-1(b)(1), (2) and (3) below. Their regulatory functions for the executive branch are described at IC 16-42-20-1(b)(1), (2), (4) and (5) below. IC 16-42-20-1(b) reads:

"(b) An officer or employee of the Indiana board of pharmacy designated by the board may do any of the following:

(1) Carry firearms in the performance of the officer's or employee's official duties.

(2) Execute and serve search warrants, arrest warrants, administrative inspection warrants, subpoenas, and summonses issued under the authority of this state.

(3) Make arrests without warrant for any offense relating to controlled substances committed in the officer's or employee's presence or if the officer or employee has probable cause to believe that the person to be arrested has committed or is committing a felony relating to controlled substances.

(4) Make seizures of property under this chapter.

(5) Perform other law enforcement duties that the Indiana board of pharmacy designates."

Thus, pharmacy board enforcers perform both judicial and regulatory functions. They serve warrants and subpoenas and make arrests for the judicial branch. They serve administrative inspection warrants and make seizures of property in their regulatory roles.

The above statute does not differentiate these functions, or the separate jurisdictions in which they operate. It relies on readers to know the differences between law enforcers' powers under law and equity. I contend that millions of people have been illegally arrested in America for drug possession and dealing because they, their attorneys, law enforcers and judges have not known the differences between the law enforcers' regulatory powers under equity and their judicial powers under law.

The overriding difference is that regulatory power derives strictly from the positive law jurisdiction of legislatures, while criminal authority over natural persons derives strictly from the People's grant of their sovereign natural authority (and primary jurisdiction) over crime to the law jurisdiction of judicial courts. Criminal actions are on behalf of (and are extensions of) the People's own sovereign criminal jurisdiction. Regulatory actions are on behalf of republican legislatures, and are over artificial persons that they create or recognize.

It is easy not to know the difference between these regulatory and judicial powers when one has not been taught to know the difference (as I was not), and when the statute fudges the distinction between administrative functions and judicial powers by combining them in one sentence. For example, 16-42-20-1(b)(2) says that pharmacy board enforcers may "(e)xecute and serve search warrants, arrest warrants, administrative inspection warrants, subpoenas, and summonses issued under the authority of this state."

Serving search warrants and arrest warrants is a judicial function. Serving administrative inspection warrants is regulatory. No one can read and enforce the above statute properly without realizing that it is describing separate powers over different subject matter to be exercised by law enforcers on behalf of separate branches of government. Thus, the separation of powers begins with law enforcers knowing which of their powers that they are exercising, which the statute's authors purposely co-mingle.

To perform their work properly, law enforcers must know the distinction between their police powers (judicial and administrative powers), as well as the distinction between crimes (*malum in se*) and false "crimes" / regulatory violations (*malum prohibita*). Otherwise, they will assume that they can make arrests for regulatory violations and other false "crimes." As we will discuss further, the drug statutes blur these distinctions so that law enforcers, including prosecutors, will both misunderstand the meaning of crime and will misrepresent it to courts.

The proper breakdown of law enforcers' powers is as follows: Where a judicial court has no criminal subject matter jurisdiction over the exercise of natural rights, such as drug possession, or over otherwise regulated activities, such as drug commerce, then enforcers for the Indiana pharmacy board lack judicial authority to make arrests in such circumstances.

However, they still have authority under their regulatory powers to investigate, inspect and shut down unlicensed drug manufacturing and dealing. IC 16-42-20-2(c)(3)(A) says that they do not need inspection warrants if they can gain voluntary entry into a suspected regulation violator's premises. As well, IC 16-42-20-1(b)(3) says that they also have authority to make arrests for real crimes committed in their presence, and for real felonies relating to controlled substances which they have probable cause to believe have been committed.

Drug crimes committed in their presence and these felonies relating to controlled substances are those offenses and felonies listed in category 4 (above) which are *malum in se*. As we have previously discussed, because statutes are to be read consistently with the Indiana constitution, the words "offense" and "felony" that are used in the above statute connote their constitutional meanings, which are limited to *malum in se* crimes.

Thus, IC 16-42-20-1(b)(3) fundamentally says that enforcers may arrest people only for drug crimes involving injury, not for those phony drug "offenses" and "felonies" described at IC 35-48-4 which are based on voluntary and consensual activity. This means that law enforcers' arrest powers are strictly limited to real crimes relating to controlled substances, listed in category 4 above, over which judicial trial courts have subject matter jurisdiction. The legislature cannot grant power to law enforcers to arrest and prosecute people for non-criminal activity.

Ultimately, except perhaps in the federal areas, law enforcers have the rightful authority to arrest people for drug crimes, but these crimes do not include phony "crimes" of *malum prohibita*. Given that the nine offenses (above) relating to controlled substances are codifications of actual *malum in se* crimes, law enforcers would absolutely have authority under IC 16-42-20-1(b)(3) to arrest persons who commit those offenses in Indiana.

Otherwise, any drug "offenses" that are not also real crimes or offenses cannot substantiate arrest or prosecution within a republic. Thus, it is these nine-or-so *malum in se* offenses relating to controlled substances over which the Indiana pharmacy board enforcers and other law enforcement officers exclusively have criminal arrest authority.

Intuitively and in fact inherently, because crime is defined by the natural law jurisdiction of the Indiana constitution, the power of law enforcers to arrest people comes from the Indiana constitution, not from the legislature. For example, a sheriff in early Indiana did not need a statute to grant him power to arrest a criminal because his arrest authority (over crime) was defined by the constitution. As well, crimes were self-evident.

Equally today, law enforcers have inherent authority to arrest real criminals. Perhaps that is why no specific statutory power is granted to law enforcers to arrest the real criminals referred to in category 4 above.

The irony gets thick

To this point in the book I have contended that the Indiana Controlled Substances Act is constitutional because it secures the right of drug possession and because it properly regulates drug commerce by adjudicating commercial privileges in administrative law courts in the executive branch. However, I would also contend here that a separate Indiana drug statute, from the Indiana pharmacy act, which is used to falsely enforce the CSA, is unconstitutional in Indiana, and should be challenged as such.

As we just saw, the Indiana Code at IC 16-42-20-1(b)(3) grants pharmacy board enforcers authority to arrest people for any real "offense relating to controlled substances" committed in the enforcer's presence and for a felony based on probable cause. An "offense relating to controlled substances" is defined at IC 35-31.5-2-217, which says:

"Offense relating to controlled substances" means the following:
    (1) Dealing in or manufacturing cocaine or narcotic drug (IC 35-48-4-1)
    (2) Dealing in methamphetamine (IC 35-48-4-1.1).
    (3) Dealing in a schedule I, II, or III controlled substance (IC 35-48-4-2)
    (4) Dealing in a schedule IV controlled substance (IC 35-48-4-3).
    (5) Dealing in a schedule V controlled substance (IC 35-48-4-4).
    (6) Possession of cocaine or a narcotic drug (IC 35-48-4-6).
    (7) Possession of methamphetamine (IC 35-48-4-6.1).
    (8) Possession of a controlled substance (IC 35-48-4-7).
    (9) Possession of paraphernalia (IC 35-48-4-8.3).
    (10) Dealing in paraphernalia (IC 35-48-4-8.5).
    (11) Offenses relating to registration (IC 35-48-4-14)."

    The constitutional problem with the above statute is that the Indiana legislature grants law enforcers authority to arrest people for the above non-crimes over which the judicial branch does not have subject matter jurisdiction. More startling, the statute does not grant authority to law enforcers to arrest people for the nine real drug crimes that we identified in category 4 above, which ironically are not mentioned in this statute.

    Thus, IC 16-42-20-1(b)(3) and IC 35-31.5-2-217 as read together say that law enforcers may enslave people for non-crimes, but not for the nine-or-so real crimes that we identified in IC 35-48-4. This statutory arrangement is unconstitutional and should be eliminated from the Indiana Code because it says the exact opposite of the 13th Amendment and of Article I, Section 37 of the Indiana constitution (1851), both which say that people may be enslaved only for real crime.

    IC 16-42-20-1(b)(3) and IC 35-31.5-2-217 read together violate the 13th Amendment and Article I, Section 37 of the Indiana constitution (1851) by authorizing law enforcers to exceed their constitutional powers. The Indiana legislature may no more empower law enforcers to arrest people for non-crimes, such as regulatory violations, than it may empower a judicial court to adjudicate non-cases and non-crimes. Both the power to arrest and the power to adjudicate crimes are powers exercised on behalf of the judicial branch, whose authority is determined by constitutions over which legislatures may not inconsistently legislate.

    Thus, the statutory authority that is granted to law enforcers to arrest people for non-crimes is unconstitutional, and it obviously exceeds their statutory authority to arrest people for real drug crimes, which are strangely not mentioned as "offenses relating to controlled substances." [410] In spite of this anomaly, IC 16-42-20-1(b)(3) grants drug-law enforcers all the authority they need to fight real crime, as discussed in category 4 above.

It says that drug enforcers may make lawful arrests for any "offense relating to controlled substances" committed in the enforcer's presence and or for a "felony" based on probable cause. We now know that such an "offense" or "felony" is an actual offense or felony as referred to in America's constitutions, and does not apply to the non-crimes listed at IC 35-31.5-2-217. We also now know that probable cause in criminal cases is based on the real meaning of crime.

> Note to Indiana defense attorneys: Although this book is about how the drug laws are not properly enforced, the drug war can also be halted by attacking the constitutionality of IC 16-42-20-1(b)(3), as read in conjunction with IC 35-31.5-2-217. Given the constitutional definition of crime, these statutes read together are obvious violations of Article I, Section 37 of the Indiana constitution and the 13th Amendment to the U.S. constitutions, which prohibit enslaving people except for their commission of real crime.
>
> The fact that real drug crimes are not listed at IC 35-31.5-2-217 is evidence that the drug war is a scam perpetrated by its authors, as assisted by state legislative services agencies. The authors knew that law enforcers have inherent authority to arrest real criminals, but no real authority to arrest regulatory violators and other fake "criminals." That is why the legislature listed the non-crimes as being subject to false arrest.
>
> If Indiana attorneys can successfully challenge the constitutionality of law enforcers' arrest powers under IC 16-42-20-1(b)(3) and IC 35-31.5-2-217, then there will be no phony drug "crimes" to adjudicate and the drug war in Indiana will be effectively over. Thus, there are three grounds to challenge Indiana's drug war: 1) using the jurisdictional arguments in this book, 2) using the ultimate user defense and 3) challenging the constitutionality of law enforcers' arrest authority with regard to controlled substances. All of these arguments lead to the same conclusion: that drugs are legal in the Indiana republic, that drug users and dealers are not subject to arrest, and that drug commerce is subject to non-criminal regulation.

23

Quack criminal law

The constitutionality of the U.S. Controlled Substances Act

Given the limited criminal jurisdiction of the U.S. government within the fifty states, under what constitutional authority do the U.S. Attorneys General, U.S. District Attorneys, and DEA agents arrest and prosecute U.S. citizens and others within the states as criminals for their drug businesses?

In *Gonzales v. Raich* (2005), [411] as we first learned a couple chapters ago, the U.S. Supreme Court upheld the regulatory authority of the DEA to confiscate six medical marijuana plants from a California resident named Diane Monson, who was supplying medical marijuana to herself and Angel Raich. Given this, then Monson was clearly in the commerce of drugs and thus subject to regulation by either the California Republic or the U.S. republic. The Supreme Court held for the regulatory U.S. republic.

One of the powers of drug regulators, held the Court, is to confiscate contraband that is not licensed, but which is nonetheless subject to their regulations. [412] This is what the DEA did in Monson's case. They took her six plants and otherwise left her alone. (Absent contrary facts outside of the courts' record, neither she nor Raich were arrested or prosecuted for crime.)

Now, what if DEA agents had caught Monson with a thousand hits of LSD or jarfuls of Oxycontin intended for resale? Would agents have confiscated the drugs under their regulatory authority in equity, as they did to Monson's marijuana plants? Or would they have arrested Monson for being a drug dealer, which clearly Monson was also for conveying marijuana to Raich?

If the latter, what would give DEA agents authority to treat Monson more favorably as a dealer of marijuana than a dealer of LSD and Oxycontin, particularly given that (as of the publication of this book) marijuana is classified as a Schedule 1 drug – a dangerous drug with no medical value? Would it be because the California legislature treats marijuana more leniently than other recreational drugs, and that the DEA now follows California law when regulating interstate commerce there?

Or is the non-criminal regulation of unlicensed marijuana commerce in California, including the confiscation of marijuana from unlicensed dealers, the model of how unlicensed LSD and Oxycontin dealers are also to be treated by the DEA when its agents follow federal law?

I think by now we all know what the answer is. *Gonzales v. Raich* (2005) gave us the model how U.S. Attorneys General are to treat all drug commerce. They are to regulate it.

Because under the Supremacy Clause at Article VI of the U.S. constitution the U.S. republic is sovereign over interstate commerce, it does not matter what California law says about marijuana or its commerce. Because federal law is supreme over concurrent state law with regard to interstate commerce, the California law with regard to medical marijuana was at the time (and still is) irrelevant to the enforcement of federal law in equity.

The federal law on marijuana and other drugs did not change when California first regulated medical marijuana in 1996. As we have seen, federal law criminally prohibits marijuana dealing in the federal areas, but regulates drug dealing among the states. California's medical marijuana law did not change this fact.

Thus, how the DEA treated Monson – by confiscating her six plants and shutting down her unlicensed marijuana-growing operation – is how the DEA (working for the U.S. Attorney General) is to treat all unlicensed interstate drug dealers, even those selling LSD and Oxycontin.

The power to regulate interstate commerce was the only federal power that the Supreme Court upheld in the *Gonzales v. Raich* (2005) case. Although the Court cited criminal statutes that are applicable only in the federal areas and that were irrelevant to the case, i.e., 21 USC 841(a) and 844(a), it did not uphold any U.S. criminal powers over drugs in California.

The decision was a tacit admission that regulation is the extent of the DEA's authority over interstate drug commerce. (Of course, one would not consider this possibility if one is married to the propaganda put out by state and U.S. Attorneys General.) Confiscating Monson's plants was the scope of federal authority that the Supreme Court upheld in *Gonzales*.

What is also particularly relevant about the *Gonzales* decision is that the Supreme Court said that Congress "may regulate the entire class" [413] of activities posing a threat to a national market. Would not this "entire class" encompass all makers and distributors of drugs, who are to be regulated?

Would this not also include either Monson as a commercial marijuana dealer or Monson as a commercial LSD and Oxycontin dealer? Are not drug dealers within the states – as a class – to be regulated, as the *Gonzales* Court said? We will answer this question in the next few pages.

In the meantime, allow me to first briefly discuss the constitutionality of the U.S. Controlled Substances Act. Ironically, over forty-five years since its passage, there is no good, definitive Supreme Court case which says that the criminal portions of the act – which I contend are enforceable at most within the federal areas – may be constitutionally applied within the state republics. As mentioned previously, this is likely because defense attorneys – who are generally unaware that Congress legislates in two capacities – have never raised this issue.

The *Gonzales* Court held that the federal confiscation of Monson's marijuana plants within California was constitutional under the Interstate Commerce Clause. The decision cited *Wickard v. Filburn* (1942) which held that interstate regulation "extends to those activities intrastate which so affect interstate commerce, or the exertion of the power of Congress over it, as to make regulation of them appropriate means to the attainment of a legitimate end, the effective execution of the granted power to regulate interstate commerce." [414]

To repeat, the Court held that Monson's sharing of her six medical marijuana plants with Raich amounted to interstate commerce because of its negative effect on Raich's marijuana purchases. In other words, Monson's sharing of marijuana caused Raich to purchase less marijuana elsewhere, which negatively affected interstate commerce. More significantly, the Court upheld the DEA's power to confiscate unauthorized commercial contraband.

As important as these rulings are, the case is only relevant to the DEA's authority to regulate the interstate commerce of drugs. The case is not about criminal law, but solely about the scope of regulatory law.

It did not address, for example, whether U.S. District Attorneys may prosecute interstate drugs dealers (such as Monson) in Article III courts, which is done routinely. The decision okay'd only the DEA's authority to confiscate Monson's property and shut down her unlicensed drug dealing.

Nor did the Court discuss whether the U.S. Attorney General, as both chief drug regulator within the states and as chief prosecutor in the federal areas, may exercise regulatory equity jurisdiction over favored interstate drug dealers, such as pharmaceutical companies, and simultaneously exercise criminal jurisdiction over disfavored members of the same class of business people, so called drug traffickers. This would raise an issue over equal protection.

Nor did the Court decide whether U.S. citizens within the states are subject to federal penal provisions for drug possession and dealing. Instead, *Gonzales v. Raich* (2005) was carefully chosen by the U.S. Justice Department (and the U.S. Supreme Court) to be dispositive only about the regulatory power of the U.S. Attorney General and his DEA agents under federal law.

Their non-criminal regulatory power of confiscation was all that the DEA agents exercised against the marijuana grower Monson. The legitimacy of their authority to shut down her operation and confiscate her six marijuana plants, which the government contended were in interstate commerce, was the only real issue in the case.

Consequently the Supreme Court has never addressed the legality of U.S. Attorney General's practice to mix and match his representative capacity for the U.S. non-republic with his representative capacity for the U.S. republic, and to treat favored and disfavored drug dealers disparately.

As well, the Court has never addressed the applicability of the U.S. CSA's criminal provisions to U.S. citizens within the states. I claim such criminal provisions are applicable at most in the federal areas, such that the draconian penalty provisions at 21 USC 841 – 843 for drug dealing do not apply to U.S. citizens within the states, but only at most to those people who deal drugs in a federal area.

Thus, the provisions at 21 USC 841 – 843 would likely be constitutional within the federal areas where they apply, and the U.S. CSA's criminal provisions could be declared constitutional, but the provisions' existence would not raise a constitutional question for the states because the criminal provisions do not apply within the states. Because of the territoriality of legislative – and thus criminal – jurisdiction, the act itself would not raise a constitutional conflict between the powers of state and federal governments.

On the other hand, the criminal provision's false <u>enforcement</u> within the states, using Article III courts, raises civil rights issues. After all, the criminal provisions of the U.S. CSA apply only in the federal areas, they are to be enforced by Article I courts, and the U.S. Attorney General is to regulate drug commerce within the states.

This means that a party or an attorney would have to know that the provisions at 21 USC 841 – 843 do not apply to U.S. citizens within the states to make a correct defense, or to move for a proper remedy for the false enforcement of the law. A court's remedy is to dismiss the action based on lack of subject matter jurisdiction.

To not know that such draconian penalty provisions do not apply to U.S. citizens within the states would render one's alternative defenses, if any, nearly useless. To move to dismiss such a matter for want of judicial jurisdiction is the only proper defense.

The Supreme Court has never addressed this issue, nor the legitimate constitutional issues regarding the criminal powers granted in the Controlled Substances Act that I raised in the above paragraphs. Courts would address these issues only if defense attorneys would raise them.

This has been precluded 1) by attorneys not knowing the scope of federal criminal jurisdiction which is mostly territorial and limited to the federal areas, 2) by their not knowing which United States is prosecuting their clients, 3) by their not knowing that the U.S. republic operates exclusively within the states and may only regulate but not prohibit commerce there, 4) by their not knowing that a republican form of government is due all U.S. citizens and their businesses, 5) by their not knowing the meaning of a republican form of government that they swore to uphold, 6) by their not knowing the meaning of crime in a republic, and 7) by their not knowing the role of the law jurisdiction in the judicial branch to uphold defendants' substantive judicial right (as enumerated in the 13th Amendment) not to be prosecuted and enslaved in an American republic except for the commission of real crime.

In spite of the facts that the constitutionality and territorial scope of the criminal provisions in the U.S. CSA have not been adequately addressed, I believe them to be constitutional because 1) they respect the natural right of drug possession by individuals in America's republics, 2) they grant and respect the legal right of drug possession by individuals in the federal areas, 3) they properly regulate the intrastate and interstate drug commerce within and among the state republics, providing administrative due process for defendants, and 4) they criminally penalize *malum in se* drug crimes and perhaps rightly criminalize *malum prohibita* within the federal areas.

Gonzales v. Raich (2005) addressed and upheld only point #3 above: that Monson was in interstate drug commerce, subject to the DEA's regulatory powers, and that administrative due process was fulfilled by the DEA's confiscation of her six plants. No case, however, has adjudicated the authority of the U.S. Attorney General 1) to simultaneously represent two separate U.S. sovereigns over the same subject matter, 2) to prosecute drug "crimes" in Article III courts, outside of the federal areas and 3) to treat favored and disfavored drug dealers unequally – one criminally, the other by regulation.

If the U.S. Department of Justice does not agree with the conclusions in this book, e.g., that Article III courts lack subject matter jurisdiction over mere drug commerce, I look forward to watching attorneys litigate the above issues on behalf of their clients.

The U.S. CSA's constitutionality is not dependent on treaty

As mentioned, in *Gonzales v. Raich* (2005) the U.S. Supreme Court upheld the DEA's authority to shut down the commerce of a small marijuana grower under Congress' constitutional authority to regulate interstate commerce. [415] The question addressed in this section is whether Congress could enter a treaty, or has entered a treaty, with a foreign sovereign which would allow it to criminally prohibit drug commerce within the state republics.

The answer to the second question is that Congress has not entered any treaty that allows it to criminally prohibit drugs within the states, as it does in the federal areas. Currently Congress has entered at least two kinds of international treaties that relate to controlled substances, neither of which imposes any criminal authority within the state republics.

One treaty is the Convention on Psychotropic Substances, signed at Vienna, Austria, on February 21, 1971, which is designed to establish suitable controls over the manufacture, distribution, transfer, and use of certain psychotropic substances. Another treaty is in conjunction with the Maritime Drug Law Enforcement Act (MDLEA), which provides the basis for drug interdiction by the Coast Guard in the Caribbean Sea and in the Pacific Ocean off the coast of Central and South America.

Acting as the U.S. non-republic, Congress outlaws the manufacture, distribution, or possession (with intent to distribute) of controlled substances aboard U.S. vessels within the federal areas. (Under 18 USC 5 and 7, the U.S. non-republic has plenary jurisdiction over not only U.S. coastal waterways, but also over vessels registered to the United States.) Thus under the MDLEA, the Coast Guard may thwart drug smuggling using Congress' plenary jurisdiction, but only in areas outside the territorial legislative jurisdiction of the states.

Consequently, MDLEA does not violate state sovereignty or the natural rights of natural persons within the fifty state republics because it operates outside of these areas. It applies to ships that are registered to foreign nations which consent by treaty to the application of Congress' plenary jurisdiction on those vessels. Thus, it in no way extends power to Congress over U.S. citizens for their drug commerce within the states.

The real issue for purposes of this brief analysis is whether Congress may enter into an international treaty that allows it to criminally prohibit the commerce of anything by U.S. citizens within the state republics, without first enacting and ratifying a constitutional amendment. This is essentially the same question as whether Congress may criminally impose *malum prohibita* within the states against U.S. citizens on any basis, let alone a treaty. Absent a constitutional amendment, the answer is no.

As the reader will recall, the U.S. constitution at Article IV, Section 4 guarantees a republican U.S. government for the states. This means that Congress may not violate the natural rights of U.S. citizens there, for example the right of liberty and the right of compensation for injury. Thus, to criminally enforce *malum prohibita* in Article III courts against U.S. citizens who are engaged in drug commerce within the states would necessarily violate this guarantee.

The Supreme Court in *Geofroy v. Riggs* (1890) noted that Congress' treaty power would not "authorize what the Constitution forbids, or a change in the character of the government, or in that of one of the states, or a cession of any portion of the territory of the latter, without its consent." [416] Thus, the constitution forbids Congress from entering a treaty to invade the states with its plenary criminal jurisdiction because that would be "a change in the character of the government," [417] i.e., a change into a non-republic, which would violate the guarantee of a republican government.

Likewise, the Court in *Holden v. Joy* (1872) made the same distinction when it stated that the treaty power "extend(s) to all those objects which in the intercourse of nations had usually been regarded as the proper subject of negotiation and treaty, if not inconsistent with the nature of our government and the relation between the State and the United States." [418] For Congress to conspire with a foreign country to enforce its non-republican authority within the states would not be a "proper subject of negotiation and treaty" and would be "inconsistent with the nature of our government and the [republican] relation between the State and the United States." [419]

This analysis is consistent with the Court in *Mayor of New Orleans v. United States* (1836) which succinctly wrote that "federal jurisdiction" may not "be enlarged under the treaty-making power..." [420] Given this, we can conclude that treaties do not authorize Congress to enforce criminal drug prohibition against U.S. citizens within the state republics. U.S. citizens are entitled to be tried for real crime in the law jurisdiction of America's republics, or are entitled – based on their statutory right to administrative due process – to have their drug businesses regulated instead of criminally prohibited.

The witting masquerade or the unwitting flub-up

Given that U.S. citizens are entitled to be tried only for real *malum in se* crime in America's republics, and entitled to have their businesses regulated there instead of prohibited, then to treat business people within the states as criminals is a major transgression of law by government officials.

Take, for example, two business people: 1) a president of a registered pharmaceutical company that makes narcotics and 2) an unregistered home maker of narcotics. Under today's regime, home narcotics makers go to jail only because U.S. attorneys treat them differently than presidents of pharmaceutical companies, which make a lot more narcotics and are responsible for more drug addiction.

Gonzales v. Raich (2005) recognizes "Congress' power to regulate purely local activities that are part of an economic 'class of activities' that have a substantial effect on interstate commerce..." [421] This would include the power to regulate all makers of narcotics because they are in the same class. If "a practice poses a threat to a national market, it [i.e., Congress in its republican capacity] may regulate the entire class," [422] the Court wrote.

This means that Congress legislates over all interstate narcotics makers and distributors as a class. The constitutional words regulate and prohibit have separate, mutually exclusive constitutional meanings. Thus to regulate narcotics commerce does not mean to criminally prohibit it.

In an American republic the only way to criminally prohibit any businesses of U.S. citizens is to amend the republic's constitution. Criminal law courts in republics have no criminal subject matter jurisdiction over personal or commercial *malum prohibita*.

Because of this, the U.S. republic may only administratively regulate drug commerce, and may not criminalize it within an American republic. Regulation nonetheless involves substantial authority because regulators may break up, confiscate and enjoin all unauthorized and unwanted drug businesses.

However, what U.S. Attorneys General have done for nearly the past fifty years is to regulate favored drug dealers under the U.S. republic's equity jurisdiction, and to have simultaneously caused their U.S. District Attorneys to prosecute disfavored drug dealers in Article III courts. As we have extensively seen, these judicial courts have subject matter jurisdiction only over injury to a right. As well, their criminal jurisdiction within the states is limited to federal crimes that relate to Congress' enumerated powers.

To disparately and unequally treat members of a single class of activity is contrary to the Supreme Court's ruling in *Gonzales* (2005) and to the principle of equal protection as guaranteed by the U.S. constitution. The U.S. Supreme Court in *Truax v. Corrigan* (1921) wrote that equal protection "means that no person or class of persons shall be denied the same protection of the laws which is enjoyed by other persons or other classes in the same place and under like circumstances." [423]

Generally, writes *Corpus Juris Secundum,* legislation that requires the licensing of a particular trade, occupation or business does not violate the guarantee of equal protection where classifications established by the legislation are not arbitrary and unreasonable, and operate equally on all persons similarly situated and subjects embraced in the same class. [424]

In the case of the war on drugs at the federal level, favored drug dealers within the states get treated by the U.S. republic to non-criminal regulation in equity, while the disfavored ones face criminal prosecutions in Article III courts – based on legislation applicable only in Article I courts in the federal areas. This is "arbitrary and unreasonable" and it operates un-"equally on all persons similarly situated and subjects embraced in the same class," [425] in contradiction to *Gonzales* (2005).

This also violates at least the substantive due process right of disfavored drug dealers within states, whose businesses are not subject to the criminal jurisdiction of either the U.S. republic or the U.S. non-republic, but are subject at most to regulation by the U.S. republic under federal equity. U.S. citizens cannot get substantive due process in a wrong court, or in a court without subject matter jurisdiction to which they are not subject.

But what is far more unprofessional – and if willful, then indeed criminal – is for U.S. Attorneys General to not only misapply the U.S. CSA's criminal prohibitions instead of administrative regulation to disfavored and unregistered interstate drug businesses, but also to apply the law of their two separate sovereign clients to the same subject matter. This is clearly a violation of the separation of powers doctrine that all U.S. Attorneys General have taken oaths to uphold. Without knowing that Attorneys General represent two sovereigns, defense attorneys (and likely also Attorneys General) have failed to identify this misrepresentation.

This is all to say that neither 1) the criminal law of the U.S. non-republic (for example, at Titles 18 and 21 United States Code), which applies mostly in the federal areas, nor 2) the criminal law of the U.S. republic over crimes relating to enumerated powers, nor 3) the law of the U.S. republic, which can regulate but not prohibit interstate commerce, legitimately applies federal criminal sanctions against anyone who manufactures, distributes or dispenses controlled substances within America's republics.

The U.S. republic has no criminal jurisdiction over drug commerce because its interstate power is to regulate all commerce in equity – not to prohibit some of it under law. This is also because its criminal jurisdiction among the states is limited to crimes related to Congress' delegated powers.

With regard to commerce, the police power of the United States is regulatory. The police power "applied to business activities, is the power to regulate those activities..." [426] the Supreme Court told us in *Ohio v. Helvering* (1934). In other words, the police power as applied to drug commerce is to not criminally prohibit it, but to regulate it.

As well, the Supreme Court in *Bond v. United States* (2014) told us that crimes 1) that do not involve Congress' enumerated powers, or 2) that do not occur within the jurisdiction of the United States are state crimes. [427]

Because the U.S. Attorney General is to regulate interstate drug commerce, then the criminal prosecutions of drug dealing by U.S. District Attorneys necessarily require their misrepresentation to U.S. District Courts of the authority of both of the Attorney General's clients – the U.S. republic and the U.S. non-republic – over drug dealing within the states. In essence, U.S. District Attorneys misrepresent the criminal authority of the U.S. non-republic, which is to operate in Article I courts exclusively in the federal areas or upon federal subjects, as being the authority of the U.S. republic, which has criminal authority in Article III courts only over crimes relating to Congress' enumerated powers.

Likely most U.S. District Attorneys do not know this dynamic, as they equally do not know the meaning of crime and natural born citizen. As well, they likely do not know that they operate as criminal attorneys in (at least) two possible capacities, either a) that they represent the U.S. non-republic under Titles 18 and 21 United States Code, whose criminal jurisdiction is confined to the federal areas, or b) that they represent the U.S. republic, which has criminal authority only over crimes within the states that relate to Congress' enumerated powers, which crimes have nothing to do with drug dealing.

In other words, not knowing that Congress legislates in two sovereign capacities, they likely think that they represent the U.S. republic at all times, which has no actual criminal power over drug commerce within the states, yet they falsely exercise the U.S. non-republic's criminal power, which is not to operate upon U.S. citizens within the states.

As we discuss later, I do not attribute any malice toward the U.S. constitution by present-day U.S. attorneys. In fact, I imagine that few of them are cognizant of the jurisdictional information contained in this book, which is needed to properly enforce U.S. drug laws and to do their jobs. (If any are aware of the information, then they are criminals.) Certainly none of them seem to know or care about the suspension of the U.S. republic under the false "presidency" of a (naturalized) citizen of the United States, which fact should be grounds to sanction them all either for their incompetence as citizens or for violating their superficial oaths to the U.S. constitution.

This confusion all serves to show that the national war on drugs is based on quack criminal law, engineered at the government's highest levels. It is a level of government malpractice on par with quack medicine.

It is waged illegally by U.S. District Attorneys who likely do not know 1) that there are two United States sovereigns, one which is a republic and the other a non-republic, 2) that the U.S. republic has authority over inter-state drug commerce and foreigners, 3) that the U.S. republic's proper response to commerce and foreigners is to regulate them, 4) that with only a few constitutional exceptions involving Congress' enumerated powers, Congress' criminal jurisdiction is territorial and confined to the federal areas, 5) that the U.S. republic has no interstate criminal jurisdiction over drugs because it operates as a drug regulator among the states, which have their own territorial legislative and criminal jurisdictions, 6) that Congress is granted the power to regulate interstate drug commerce but no delegated power to criminally prohibit it, and 7) that in interstate drug prosecutions they falsely represent either a) the U.S. non-republic which has no relevant legislative criminal authority over U.S. citizens within the states, or b) the U.S. republic which – short of a constitutional amendment – has no authority to criminally enforce *malum prohibita* within the states, which instead is enforced under regulation in equity.

All U.S. District Attorneys must necessarily know these things. To stay within the U.S. constitution – including its separation of powers doctrine – U.S. Attorneys General and U.S. District Attorneys must keep the jurisdictions of their clients separate. They cannot represent both U.S. sovereigns over the same space, class of persons or subject matter, as they routinely attempt to. Nor may they apply the law that Congress legislated as one sovereign to the land and people under authority or protection by the other. That they do so is perhaps understandable, but is still shameful, whether on a professional or moral level.

What is important for all U.S. government attorneys to note is 1) that the United States Congress legislates as two sovereigns with separate subject matter, 2) that depending on their role in the justice system, these attorneys represent one sovereign or the other, and 3) that they must know which law from which sovereign is applicable in any given land area or over any parti-cular subject matter to do their jobs properly.

Otherwise they are susceptible to being manipulated by better informed people. Equally, they must know the natural law meaning of crime and natural born citizen, or admit to not living up to the standards of

U.S. Attorneys – let alone as citizens of a republic – who swore (perhaps unwittingly) to uphold the natural meaning of those constitutional terms.

The law is knowable, or I would not be able to consistently explain it. These attorneys have a duty to know the law, which I do not, and which duty they have failed, and which duty I have not.

Violating not only the sovereignty of U.S. citizens, but also the sovereignty of all American republics is what the national war on drugs by the U.S. Department of Justice is (and has always been) all about. For the past fifty years, U.S. Attorneys General have not only treated interstate drug merchants disparately, which is not allowed under the equal protection and due process clauses of the U.S. constitution. [428] Furthermore in drug matters, they have falsely applied the law not only of two separate criminal jurisdictions, but also of two separate U.S. sovereigns, when ironically the criminal law of only state sovereigns applies.

This is either the most egregious example of officials' legal incompetence in American history or the best example of officials' malice toward the U.S. constitution. This makes the drug war the result of either legal malpractice, based on mistakes of law, or of sedition upon the People.

We could not have discovered this two-faced fraud or misfeasance of U.S. Attorneys General and U.S. District Attorneys without understanding 1) that Congress operates in two capacities, 2) that one operates as a republic, respectful of the natural rights of U.S. citizens, 3) that the other is a non-republic, which grants its subjects their rights, and 4) that U.S. attorneys have predominantly failed to keep the roles of these sovereigns separate.

One of the great beauties of the U.S. constitution is that it granted the federal government with criminal and contempt power which is limited 1) to the federal areas, 2) to the aforementioned foreigners, and 3) to Congress' other enumerated functions. However, the constitution bound this government down with natural law within the state republics, which are republican solely because their criminal and political standards are based on natural law and because they secure the natural rights of at least U.S. citizens.

Enslaving natural persons for any type of commerce is *per se* anti-republican. Only someone who knows what an American republic is would know this fact. This literally means that Attorneys General have either knowingly violated their oaths to secure the republics from Congress' non-republic, or more likely, that most of them really have not known what a republican form of government is to which they took oaths to secure. (It is an obvious and undeniable fact that they have not known the meaning of crime and natural born citizen.)

Likely most went through law school, as I did, without learning how American republics function and for whom, i.e., their sovereign citizens. Likely none were taught or realized that there are four sovereigns which American constitutions respect, and that the powers of these sovereigns are explicitly acknowledged in state and U.S. statutes – but particularly the state and U.S. CSAs.

This means that, prior to the publication of this book, scarcely anyone in America's entire legal community has been capable of defining crime and the criminal law jurisdiction of courts to secure America's republican form of government. Likewise, essentially every attorney in America has shown themselves incapable of either defining and defending natural born citizens, or to understanding their own personal rights of citizenship, at least sufficiently to secure the U.S. republic from a naturalized citizen "President."

These are serious failings in judicial stewardship by the industry of attorneys who, as this book serves to show, have an undeserved monopoly over America's criminal justice system. These failings have been nearly fatal to America's republican form of government.

24
Some examples

It is no crime to sell "da kine"

One of my close friends when I lived in Hawaii was a wild cowboy-type from Texas and New Mexico named Clifford Deaton, who died in 1986 or '87 from diabetes. One of my many funny stories about Clifford intertwine and sum-up several of the lessons of this book about the lawful possession of drugs, the proper role of the executive branch, and the proper role of the judicial branch.

In 1981 along Kalakaua Avenue in the heart of the Waikiki Beach tourist area, Clifford found a vacuum-sealed bag of marijuana in a trash can. (We later speculated that it had been stashed there by a marijuana dealer.) Clifford stuck the abandoned bag into his shorts and brought it to my apartment in Kahala.

I was thrilled with Clifford's fortune. I had lived on Oahu for a month by then, and his find was the prettiest *pakalolo* that I had ever seen. The buds were large, hard, seedless and multi-colored.

Through the plastic wrap, it looked like what locals call(ed) "da kine" bud, which is Hawaiian-pigeon for "the real good kind." It was worth around $300 back then, maybe $600 now. I couldn't find my scissors fast enough.

Ironically at the time, particularly on the mainland, some people still referred to marijuana as "grass." So when Clifford cut open the sealed package and we got a whiff of someone's newly cut front lawn, we were surprised to find not "grass" but real grass.

The faux marijuana buds were actual lawn clippings that had been manicured and tied in such a fashion so as to look like "da kine" bud – to be sold to unsuspecting tourists. This fraud was a work of art. Despite our disappointment, we got a good laugh over this gross "grass" misrepresentation.

This story is relevant to this book because it demonstrates the rights and responsibilities of Clifford and the Hawaiian state government, assuming that its Controlled Substances Act still works the same as Indiana's.

First, this story is an example of lawful possession. Clifford lawfully acquired the abandoned bag from a trash can. According to the ultimate user provision of Hawaii's Controlled Substances Act at Title 19, Chapter 329-32(c)(3), Clifford could "lawfully possess" the marijuana for his own use.

Second, because the presumed local drug dealer was in commerce, his commercial activity was to be regulated by the executive branch of the state of Hawaii. Using this branch's regulatory powers, the state could investigate his drug dealing, confiscate his *pakalolo* and enjoin the guy from selling it to tourists. This injunction could be judicially enforced.

Third, what was actually happening was an honest-to-goodness crime – not a faux or phony drug "crime" like drug dealing. The person who likely stashed his bag of grass in the trash can was ripping-off tourists by misrepresenting lawn clippings as "da kine" bud.

His commercial behavior was not only subject to regulation by the Hawaiian executive branch under its commercial equity jurisdiction. His behavior was also criminal, and thus subject to the judicial branch, because he was stealing money through deliberate misrepresentations, i.e. fraud.

Note, however, that ripped-off tourists likely did not report these crimes to law enforcers because they thought that buying marijuana was a crime, which it never has been, and that the criminal justice system did not really exist to serve them as crime victims. This is yet another anomaly produced by the false enforcement of drug laws. These two completely false American concepts are the products of one of the most warped and criminal American ideas of the 20th century, i.e., the war on drugs.

Although I could not find a codified crime in Hawaii's Uniform Controlled Substances Act regarding the fraudulent conveyance of counterfeit drugs, the act of selling counterfeit marijuana is criminally sanctioned in Indiana at IC 35-48-4-14, which says that it is a felony to misrepresent controlled substances. This is one of Indiana's nine real drug crimes, listed at IC 35-48-4, that we discussed in chapter 22.

The dealer's deliberate misrepresentations of grass clippings as marijuana would clearly be a real drug felony in Indiana. (Even in Hawaii, where the dealer's behavior is not specifically prohibited in the Hawaiian code books, the dealer would nonetheless be subject to criminal arrest because his behavior was *malum in se* fraud.)

The prosecution of fraud in the conveyance of controlled substances fulfills the proper role of the criminal justice system. However, prosecuting people who sell real "da kine" bud to eager and appreciative tourists, who rarely get to smoke such good, naturally grown marijuana, does not invoke any legitimate judicial criminal authority in any American republic.

Selling marijuana – particularly really good marijuana – is never a crime in America's republics. It does not invoke the criminal jurisdiction of the judicial branch, but merely the regulatory branch of government. In America's republics, only if the commerce in controlled substances was prohibited by a constitutional amendment, instead of being regulated by statute, could any person who honestly and non-fraudulently deals drugs be subject to criminal penalty.

Otherwise, as business people who are involved in fulfilling people's needs and desires, drug dealers are merely subject to having their contraband confiscated and forfeited, and to having administrative injunctions judicially enforced, including jail time for being contemptuous of judicial orders. That is the scope of republican power over their drug commerce that fulfills consumers' pursuits of happiness.

Ironically, as I was leaving Hawaii for law school in 1983, three things were occurring in the Hawaiian marijuana market. First, people were beginning to collect and trade seeds. I laughed at this until (years later) I realized that it was locals' way to preserve the genetic integrity of Hawaiian marijuana from confiscation by the Reagan administration. Second, people were beginning to grow marijuana indoors. This was in spite of Hawaii's perfect outdoor growing environment.

This aberrant behavior was naturally caused by the unnatural threat of black helicopters which the feds were using to destroy mountainside marijuana fields. It was not until I wrote this book that I realized that such confiscation was likely a legitimate – albeit unfortunate – exercise of the U.S. government's regulatory power over drug commerce.

I say unfortunate because, given marijuana's profound medical benefits, the U.S. Attorney General and the members of Congress should change their attitude toward marijuana commerce, and sincerely regulate it for adults as they do alcohol, tobacco and firearms.

Trafficking in drugs or guns

Consider now another example – that of a U.S. citizen in Indiana who while digging a pond on his newly purchased property, finds a cache of guns in a wooden box or finds bails of marijuana buried on his property. Having called ahead, he takes these legally-acquired guns or drugs to a dealer that he knows in Illinois, where he is promptly arrested by the BATFE or the

DEA for interstate gun or drug trafficking.

This book serves to say that such an arrest is illegal, and that regardless whether this hypothetical person found a cache of guns or drugs, his transporting of any lawfully acquired property across a state line is never a crime in the law jurisdiction of any of America's republics, all of which must use the same constitutional definition of crime.

Plus, the last time he checked, the U.S. Attorney General licenses people to sell guns at 18 USC 923 and to sell drugs at 21 USC 822. Given that in America's republics the Attorney General cannot license people to commit real crime, and because commerce in guns and drugs is regulated, this means that selling guns or drugs are not real crimes that are subject to a republican criminal law jurisdiction.

Congress may not legislate over the artificial lines between states except in a republican fashion. In a republic, invoking the subject matter jurisdiction of the law jurisdiction of judicial courts requires an injury. Thus, having not injured or endangered anyone, this hypothetical person should not be subject to arrest by Congress' police – be they the DEA or BATFE – when he gets to Illinois to sell his drugs or guns.

As well, he is not subject to any prohibitions of property by the states of Indiana or Illinois, which treat property possession as a natural right. Because the federal and state governments must treat him in their republican capacity, his commerce in drugs or guns is only subject to their regulation in equity.

He is not subject to any criminal prohibitions operating either under state law and under U.S. republican law. Drugs and guns may be illegal under the law of the U.S. non-republic, but he has not entered a federal area where such prohibitions are operable.

Under the state and federal republics, his transporting of guns or drugs with intent to sell them is an activity subject to regulation by the executive branch – not to criminal prohibition in the judicial branch. He may not commercially sell drugs or guns in either Indiana or Illinois without state permission. He also needs prior approval from the U.S. Attorney General (who licenses both drug and gun dealing) to sell his drugs or guns, or to carry them across state lines with that intent.

Thus everywhere in America's republics, this person's unlicensed transporting of legally-acquired guns or drugs, with the intent to sell them, is a regulatory violation. Having crossed state lines with the intent to sell drugs or guns, he is subject to Congress' interstate authority to regulate gun and drug commerce. As a U.S. citizen he is not subject to any criminal prohibitions of guns or drugs under the U.S. non-republic's plenary jurisdiction because he is outside of that authority.

I have not thoroughly read U.S. gun laws, but with regard to drugs, the above response is called for by the U.S. Controlled Substances Act. If this person wants to engage in the interstate commerce in drugs, he needs to first get a "registration" from the U.S. Attorney General. [429] That people sell guns and drugs legally is proof that selling guns or drugs is not a crime in the law jurisdiction. Within Indiana or Illinois, this U.S. citizen must solely answer 1) to natural standards for crime and 2) to the artificial non-criminal standards of regulators.

So, we can assume that this hypothetical person absolutely committed a regulatory violation over which the DEA or BATFE would have authority to address in their regulatory capacities. Thus, it is no wonder that he was faced by the DEA or the BATFE when he reached his destination.

However, because he has not committed a crime (because it is not a crime for U.S. citizens to possess lawfully-acquired property in Indiana or Illinois, and to transport lawfully-acquired property across state lines), and because these agents have no arrest authority over regulatory violations, then these agents are not allowed to arrest him, or likely even unnecessarily point their guns at him. Instead, they may only sanction him for his federal regulatory violations, i.e., for crossing state lines to sell drugs or guns without the Attorney General's permission.

Congress may not declare carrying lawfully-acquired drugs and guns across state lines to be a crime 1) because Congress' criminal jurisdictions are limited to the federal areas and to crimes relating to its enumerated powers, and 2) because as a legislative body for a republic, Congress must follow the natural law meaning of crime. This legislative imperative is secured by the case or controversy requirement of the U.S republic's Article III courts.

This means that Congress may regulate businesses within the states, but not criminally prohibit them. This rule applies even to disfavored drug and gun businesses.

Thus, Congress rightfully regulates interstate commerce of lawfully acquired drugs and guns of U.S. citizens, such that regulation by the DEA or BATFE would be proper. As *Gonzales v. Raich* (2005) showed us, the constitutional power to regulate includes the power to confiscate contraband.

Thus, the cache of drugs or guns brought to Illinois would be properly seized by the DEA or the BATFE, but our hypothetical guy would not be arrested. Under 21 USC 880(d)(3) of the U.S. Controlled Substances Act, he would be receipted for the drugs that the DEA takes from him.

However, if our hypothetical guy was knowingly carrying or selling stolen drugs or guns, he would be subject to arrest as a criminal by the DEA, by the BATFE and by Illinois and Indiana law enforcers under their criminal (judicial) authority. It is unlawful to knowingly possess or sell stolen property in Indiana and Illinois, because that is a natural wrong. However, it is not unlawful to possess lawfully-acquired property, which is a natural right.

Federal law enforcers exercise criminal authority 1) over offenses against the United States involving Congress' enumerated powers within the states, 2) over actions that are prohibited by Congress which occur within the federal areas, and 3) likely over real crimes within the states that they witness. For example, if they see a real felony committed in Indiana or Illinois, they can make an arrest to assist the state in its fight against crime. Otherwise, as we have seen, the U.S. government has very limited criminal authority within the states, which does not include the power to criminally prohibit any kind of commerce there.

The case of an immigrant marijuana smoker

Consider a foreign immigrant living in Denver who, when emptying his pockets at a security checkpoint in a federal building, reveals that he has been carrying marijuana. Alerted by the building's security guards before the immigrant is able to get his belt back on, DEA agents storm out of an office to arrest the man for possession of marijuana in a federal building. They say that marijuana possession is a federal crime under 21 USC 844 and 844A.

> This is only hypothetical. This is not to say that this is how DEA agents treat marijuana possession in federal buildings in Colorado. I do not know the DEA's policies and practices, only their powers.

The issue in this scenario is under which law the Colorado immigrant falls. This is an issue of subject matter jurisdiction. Does the immigrant fall under Colorado law that respects his rights to recreate with marijuana, or is he subject to the U.S. government's prohibitions at 21 USC 844 and 844A?

Depending on the answer, this immigrant may have really screwed up. Under the law of the U.S. non-republic, if it applies, he could be arrested, jailed, fined, deported and denied U.S. citizenship – just because the U.S. non-republic does not like his pot smoking. (We know that he has a Rule 8 affirmative defense as an ultimate drug user under 21 USC 844(a), 21 USC 822(c) and 21 USC 802(27), but likely his attorney does not yet know.)

However, if legislative jurisdiction and criminal law jurisdiction are territorial – as 18 USC 5, the U.S. Supreme Court, and the U.S. government's report on *Federal Jurisdiction Within the States* say they are – then Colorado law defines the person's criminal rights. This is the case, says the *Report*, unless the U.S. government owns the property upon which the federal building sits and unless the state has ceded such criminal law authority to Congress over this land. [430] Assuming that Colorado has not ceded such legislative authority to the U.S. non-republic, then Colorado would have criminal jurisdiction over the immigrant's marijuana possession.

However, because the man is not a U.S. citizen, his rights to be in the United States is defined by an additional jurisdiction – by Congress' plenary power over immigration. For example, assume that Congress makes a law that says marijuana possession by a foreigner in a federal building is a violation of immigration law, and requires deportation.

In this case, the immigrant would not be subject to arrest under Colorado law that respects his natural right of drug possession, or by the DEA who may not interfere with Colorado's enforcement of its state criminal laws. However, he might be subject to arrest under the U.S. non-republic's plenary jurisdiction over immigration violations. Knowing this, the DEA detains the guy just long enough for agents of the U.S. Immigration and Customs Enforcement (ICE) to serve him with papers to appear at an immigration hearing.

Thus, a lot depends on the facts of each case and which jurisdiction is asserting its authority over whom and what, and why. Be rest assured, however, U.S. citizens are free from the DEA and ICE, and because of the ultimate user provision at 21 USC 822(c), 21 USC 802(27) and 21 USC 844(a), may not rightfully be incarcerated by U.S. officials for drug possession in federal buildings. Those buildings within the states are generally subject to the states criminal codes – not to the municipal law of the U.S. non-republic.

As we have seen, other than arresting people who commit drug crimes within the federal areas, DEA agents operate within the states only in their regulatory capacity, and may assist state drug officials only 1) in their law enforcement against real criminals, 2) in their regulatory actions against drug commerce and 3) in the eradication of natural substances from which controlled substances may be derived. [431]

A Hoosier heroin user's brush with the DEA

Consider the scenario of a native born Hoosier who gets caught with a gram of heroin in a federal building in Indianapolis. The prior example shows that Indiana courts have jurisdiction over crime within the state unless the state legislature has ceded criminal authority over the property to the U.S. non-republic. As a natural born citizen, this Hoosier is not subject to any immigration laws. Thus, the man will go to jail only if heroin possession is illegal under Indiana law.

As we have seen, heroin possession is lawful, legal and unregulated in Indiana because it is a natural right. This natural right is codified as the ultimate user provisions in the Indiana and U.S. CSAs, respectively at IC 35-48-3-3(e) and 21 USC 822(c).

Thus, when DEA agents show up to arrest this native Hoosier, as he is retrieving his personal belongings from a tray, he demurs to both their federal regulatory jurisdiction (because he is not in commerce) and to their criminal jurisdictions (because he is neither in a federal area nor committing a *malum in se* crime). As well, he asserts his statutory defense (under both state and federal ultimate user provisions) that he may lawfully possess the heroin for his own use.

Because DEA agents only have immunity within their delegated powers, then they are not immune from civil or criminal liability for arresting him. Therefore, he is allowed to retrieve his heroin from the tray and to go on his way. This is because no one has any probable cause to believe that he has committed either a crime or a regulatory violation. As a drug user, he may have personal problems, but as a U.S. citizen, these disabilities would not naturally include being regulated or subjected to prison.

A Kansan's pursuit of happiness

Consider a marijuana smoker from Kansas who drives to Colorado to buy some "wax" (Colorado hash) for himself or his wife. Because he is an ultimate user acquiring drugs for his own household and because he is not in interstate commerce of controlled substances, he is not subject to the DEA when he returns to his home in Kansas. Because he is also exempt from regulation and criminal prosecution by Kansas' ultimate user provision at Kansas Code 65-4116(c)(3), he may "lawfully possess" this hashish in Kansas, where the Kansas courts have no criminal jurisdiction over people who do others no harm.

Interstate marijuana commerce

Another scenario is of a U.S. citizen who arrives in Indiana from

Colorado with a car full of lawfully acquired weed, with the intent to sell it in Indiana for profit. Under Congress' authority to regulate interstate commerce, as *Gonzales v. Raich* (2005) [432] tells us, the DEA or the Indiana pharmacy board may confiscate the marijuana (and probably the car), and the U.S. or state Attorneys General may administratively enjoin his future attempts at drug dealing. (This is analogous to governments' confiscation of cigarettes without proper tax stamps.)

Having not committed a crime by republican standards, the citizen is not subject to arrest. Under administrative law, the DEA or the Indiana pharmacy board, as the case may be, inventories the marijuana that it confiscates, hands the disappointed drug dealer a list of property taken, and promptly files the list with a judicial clerk to initiate forfeiture proceedings against the property.

The drug dealer is not happy about the loss of his property (the marijuana, future profit and his car), but he goes home to sleep in his own bed and he gets to keep the marijuana that the DEA agents found in his pocket during their consented-to search for weapons. His possession of drugs in his pocket was a personal and non-commercial exercise of a natural right in the natural law jurisdiction of Indiana, as secured by the above state and federal ultimate user statutes.

Ultimately, as we learned earlier, the DEA has only the authority to regulate – and not criminally prohibit – the interstate commerce of marijuana by this U.S. citizen. Within the state republics, each republic through which he drove imposes criminal penalties upon him only for real crime, as the natural law meaning of their republican constitutions define.

A natural born citizen visits Washington, D.C.

Imagine a natural born citizen who gets caught by metal detectors with a resin-coated metal marijuana pipe as he enters a federal building in Washington, D.C. Given the criminal exemption of ultimate users, as recognized at 21 USC 844(a), 21 USC 822(c) and 21 USC 802(27), this knowledgeable Congressional subject successfully asserts this defense. Reluctantly officials release him, and hand back his stinky resinated pipe.

Motorboaters beware

The same fate as in the example above faces a natural born citizen who gets caught with a small amount of cocaine by DEA agents on his speed boat on the Ohio River, which is defined at 18 USC 7 to be within the federal areas.

Because he is criminally exempt from drug possession charges by 21 USC 844(a), 21 USC 822(c) and 21 USC 807(27), he should not be criminally charged for drug possession, and he should be able to keep his cocaine. However, because he is a licensed boater, the evidence of his cocaine possession might be used by federal or state regulators to suspend, revoke or not renew his boating license or registration.

On the other hand, if this person is caught trafficking drugs on the Ohio River, then he likely faces federal criminal charges in Article I courts for possessing drugs in the federal areas with intent to distribute. If, as the Supreme Court asserts, Congress can legislate over the federal areas as a non-republic – and to define the meaning of crime there, irrespective of natural law and the case or controversy requirement – then this person faces horrendous federal criminal charges under 21 USC 841 – 843.

Note: the U.S. non-republic also has similar criminal jurisdiction over drug commerce on ships and aircraft registered to the U.S. [433]

Lessons

To sum up this chapter of examples, none of the above drug or gun scenarios present evidence of real crimes in America's republics over which the DEA or BATFE have anything but the power to regulate within the states. Congress – at most – has the power to criminally prohibit drugs or guns only in federal areas. Other than the last example involving a motorboat on the Ohio River, the above scenarios at most provide evidence of interstate regulatory violations which both of these agencies (and their state counterparts) may only administratively, non-criminally sanction.

This is all to say that no persons may sell, for example, drugs, guns and alcohol within the fifty states without governments' permission, but also that it is not criminal for U.S. citizens to do so. Criminal prohibitions against guns, drugs and alcohol do not apply to people except in the federal areas, where the U.S. criminal code predominantly applies.

Outside of those areas, with only a few exceptions, 1) U.S. citizens may be incarcerated only in the law jurisdiction of state courts for injuring others, 2) U.S. citizens are subject only to a handful of crimes within the states relating to federal powers, and 3) U.S. citizens are not naturally subject to the U.S. non-republic's Article I courts, whose criminal jurisdiction is foreign to their state republican governments.

Short of a constitutional amendment which places such *malum prohibita* into the law jurisdiction of state and Article III judicial courts, then mere commerce in drugs, guns and alcohol within the states by individuals is never subject to criminal law. Again, because natural persons are always entitled to a republican government except perhaps in the federal areas, then they are always entitled to their liberty until they commit real crimes as defined by natural law in the law jurisdiction of state and federal judicial courts. As well, if they enter commerce, then they are subject to state and/or federal regulators in the executive branch, but their enterprise is not primarily subject to judicial courts or the penal system.

The facts are that guns, drugs and alcohol are legal in America's republics, and that the interstate commerce in guns, drugs and alcohol is subject only to regulation in Congress' republican capacity. Acting as a republic among the states, Congress' regulatory authority under equity includes the power to enjoin any unauthorized commerce in guns, drugs and alcohol, and to confiscate its fruits.

However, legislating as a republic among the states, Congress does not have authority to criminally prohibit this commerce. Within the states, people have substantive rights not to be arrested or enslaved except for real crime. Only in its federal areas may Congress treat U.S. citizens like subjects, which it achieves by defining cases and crimes in Article I courts to be whatever it wants them to be.

As we have seen, the commerce of guns, drugs and alcohol, for example, may be placed into Congress' criminal jurisdictions in two manners.

First, Congress – acting as a non-republic over the federal areas – may criminally prohibit the possession or commerce of any property in those areas, and to subject them to the U.S. non-republic's plenary criminal jurisdiction.

Second, Congress may initiate an amendment to the U.S. constitution to allow it and the states to criminally prohibit such commerce within the states, which commerce is already subject to its authority to regulate.

Thus Congress may criminally prohibit guns, drugs and alcohol: 1) when their possession or commerce occur in a federal area, or 2) when such commerce is placed into the law jurisdiction of the U.S. republic by constitutional amendment and when the amendment expressly shares criminal authority between the state and federal governments, as occurred with the 18th Amendment prohibiting alcohol commerce. Governments may likely also prohibit possession of guns as a penalty for the conviction of certain crimes, as crimes are defined by constitutions.

The 18th Amendment expressly granted "Congress and the several States" with "concurrent power to enforce" the article with appropriate legislation. Otherwise, Congress would have had no authority to enforce any kind of prohibition of commerce within a state, where it has no criminal jurisdiction except over federal enumerated powers, over offenses against the United States and over its federal areas.

The prohibition of any commerce violates natural law, and is anti-republican, which is why the 18th Amendment was required to deviate from the rule. Alcohol commerce would naturally not be subject to the law jurisdiction, which has authority only over injury caused by natural persons. Instead, commerce is not naturally prohibited and is regulated in equity by the executive branch of America's republics, which exercises no criminal authority.

It is because America's drug statutes do not violate people's individual rights of possession, but only regulate drug commerce, that they are constitutional, moral and good. With regard to drugs, the positive law jurisdiction of the legislature literally does not invade the natural law jurisdiction of individual freedom, but instead secures it. The positive law jurisdiction may tax and regulate commerce and define punishment for crime, but it does not (because it may not) invade the natural law jurisdiction of individuals where the right of drug possession exists and where crime is defined by Nature.

This is what the natural law says. It is what America's constitutions say. It is what the drug statutes say. It is what case law says. If you think otherwise, you are practicing religion, or you are on some kind of dope.

Other than with the prohibition of slavery, the law of subject matter jurisdiction and the separation of powers has not substantially changed since Indiana or the United States were created. In the case of controlled substances, the law is merely being violated in spades by government officials, acting under false color, with the help of America's defense attorneys.

Unfortunately, because the drug laws are not followed by government officials, their power is exercised extra-constitutionally, immorally and for special interests. Governments are good if they can stay within their constitutional limits, and they are bad if they cannot.

In the case of legitimate drug regulation, the government has not even remotely stayed within its constitutional or statutory bounds. Almost all of its "criminal" cases for drug possession and commerce have been rogue, illegitimate and indeed illegal.

In conclusion, we have come a long way conceptually so far. We have seen the enforcement of drug laws in a whole new light. We now see how they apply within America's republics only 1) to real drug crimes, such as fraud, and 2) to the manufacture, distribution and dispensing of drugs, which are to be regulated. We see how this commerce is to be controlled – through investigation, inspection, confiscation and injunction – not through criminal enslavement.

We see that neither administrative law courts nor judicial courts have subject matter jurisdiction over drug possession. We see how drug possession is not only unregulated by the state, but is explicitly exempted from regulation and prosecution by the drug statutes themselves. We see that these rights apply throughout the United States, and only may not apply in the federal areas. We were once blind, but now we see.

25
A look at some U.S. indictments

In the previous chapter we looked at several hypothetical situations to determine their legal outcomes. In this chapter we will look at actual federal criminal drug indictments or complaints that I have randomly found on the Internet, and we will analyze them with the knowledge about jurisdiction provided in this book.

I have no idea about the outcome of these matters. In this chapter I analyze only the (mostly faulty) charging instruments. I presume that many people falsely went, or are in the false process of going, to jail. As we will see from these dozen examples, only in select drug cases are defendants subject to federal criminal subject matter jurisdiction. [434]

U.S. v. Villareal (2011)

In the arrest warrant in *U.S. v. Villareal* (2011), [435] two Massachusetts defendants were accused:

- of obtaining controlled substances by fraud or forgery under 21 USC 843(a)(3),
- of possessing controlled substances with the intent to distribute under 21 USC 841(a)(1), and
- of conspiring to distribute controlled substances under 21 USC 846 by conspiring to write fraudulent or forged prescriptions.

The charges for obtaining a controlled substance by fraud or forgery under 21 USC 843(a)(3) were indeed criminal charges. That Villareal was criminally charged was proper because he allegedly wrote fraudulent or forged prescriptions for various controlled substances under the authority of another doctor. However, the use of fraud or forgery to obtain controlled substances is a state crime in Massachusetts. Part I, Title XV, Chapter 94C (the Controlled Substances Act), Section 33(b) reads in pertinent part:

"No person shall utter a false prescription for a controlled substance, nor knowingly or intentionally acquire or obtain possession of a controlled substance by means of forgery, fraud, deception or subterfuge, including but not limited to the forgery or falsification of a prescription or the nondisclosure of a material fact in order to obtain a controlled substance from a practitioner."

Because 1) the possession and distribution of controlled substances is not among the crimes related to Congress' enumerated powers, 2) because the use of fraud or forgery to obtain controlled substances is a state crime in Massachusetts and 3) because Villareal's drug distribution and conspiracy operated wholly outside of the federal areas, then pursuant to *United States v. Fox* (1878) [436] and *Bond v. United States* (2014), [437] Villareal's fraud or forgery is subject to state prosecution, not federal prosecution.

This analysis is consistent with 21 USC 903 from the U.S. Controlled Substances Act which reads:

"No provision of this subchapter shall be construed as indicating an intent on the part of the Congress to occupy the field in which that provision operates, including criminal penalties, to the exclusion of any State law on the same subject matter which would otherwise be within the authority of the State, unless there is a positive conflict between that provision of this subchapter and that State law so that the two cannot consistently stand together."

Because there are no conflicts between state and federal provisions regarding the use of fraud or forgery to obtain drugs, then it is the intent of Congress to not occupy the same field as the state, on the same subject matter, and it is the intent of Congress to defer to state criminal authority. (The U.S. constitution requires this of Congress because the constitution has already carved out state and federal criminal jurisdiction.)

Because the Commonwealth of Massachusetts has criminal jurisdiction over this fraud or forgery, then we can conclude that 21 USC 843(a)(3) does not apply to the fraud or forgery in this case and that it applies only in the federal areas. This means 1) that Article III courts operating within the states have no subject matter jurisdiction over 21 USC 843(a)(3); 2) that the complaint has been brought in the wrong court; and 3) that this federal criminal case is subject to dismissal. If the accusations against Villareal are true, then he is a state criminal and is not subject to federal criminal prosecution. Likewise, Villareal's conspiracy to commit fraud violates state law and would also be a state crime.

With regard to the charge that Villareal violated 21 USC 841(a)(1) by possessing controlled substances with the intent to distribute them, I would merely point out that within America's republics the U.S. Attorney General regulates the distribution of controlled substances at 21 USC 822(a). This would mean that for distributing controlled substances in Massachusetts, Villareal is subject to regulation by the Massachusetts Board of Registration in Pharmacy or by the U.S. Attorney General, but is not subject to criminal prosecution. This would serve to reiterate that as a criminal provision 21 USC 841(a)(1) does not apply within the states, but only within the federal areas.

U.S. v. FedEx (2014)

In the indictment in *U.S. v. FedEx Corporation, FedEx Express, Inc., and FedEx Corporate Services, Inc.* (2014), [438] these commercial carriers are charged with various criminal counts for distributing controlled substances on behalf of online pharmacies. In particular the carriers were charged:

- with conspiracy to distribute controlled substances under 21 USC 846,
- with possession of controlled substances with intent to distribute under 21 USC 841(a)(1),
- with conspiracy to distribute misbranded drugs under 18 USC 371,
- with misbranding drugs under 21 USC 331, 333 and 353, and
- with forfeiture of certain assets under 18 USC 982, 21 USC 853 and 28 USC 2461.

What is of initial interest in this matter is the fact that FedEx is charged with crimes, as the CR on the indictment indicates. As we have seen, this process would be improper because corporations cannot be charged with crimes within an American republic, such as California. This is 1) because crime is adjudicated at law, 2) because corporations operate in equity, which is a non-criminal jurisdiction, and 3) because corporations may not be physically incarcerated.

Only corporate officers may be incarcerated for their *malum in se* against corporate victims, but none are indicted in this matter. Because the law jurisdiction of judicial courts may both fine and incarcerate natural criminals for their crimes, prosecutors falsely bring criminal charges against artificial persons in the law jurisdiction in order to falsely fine them.

Because this case both seeks to levy fines (which is a law remedy) and to enforce forfeiture (which is an equitable remedy), then the U.S. District Attorney is trying to operate in both law and equity, only one jurisdiction of which has actual authority. As we shall see, this case is to operate solely in non-criminal equity.

All legitimate criminal trials in America's republics operate in the law jurisdiction of judicial courts. All criminal trials outside of the federal areas involve natural persons. There are no recognized natural persons in the federal areas, except for natural born citizen Presidents and Vice Presidents. This is because everyone else there is a subject of Congress as the U.S. non-republic.

Republics may only use their criminal processes against natural persons, such as corporate officers. "Corporations can only commit crimes through flesh-and-blood people," stated U.S. Deputy Attorney General Sally Q. Yates in September, 2015. [439] However, there are no named natural corporate defendants in this FedEx matter; which is further proof that this false criminal indictment operates in non-criminal equity.

That the companies are charged with distributing drugs within America's republics is sufficient proof that they are subject to the regulatory authority of the U.S. Attorney General – not to the criminal authority of a U.S. District Attorney. According to 21 USC 822(a) all interstate distributors of drugs are required to seek a "registration" from the Attorney General. This is because drug distribution is regulated except in the federal areas, where it is prohibited. These rules subject all non-registrants – such as FexEx – to the government's regulatory process and its equitable remedies.

Again, U.S. officials are misrepresenting American law – perhaps unwittingly – by mixing and blurring the law and equity jurisdictions. Because drugs are regulated in American republics, the criminal penalties at 21 USC 841 and 846 relate only to distributing (and conspiring to distribute) drugs within the federal areas. To conspire to distribute drugs within America's republics is to conspire to enter government's equity jurisdiction, which is not criminal and which is to be regulated.

The District Attorney's third charge is that FedEx conspired to distribute misbranded drugs under 18 USC 371. This statute reads:

> "If two or more persons conspire either to commit any offense against the United States, or to defraud the United States, or any agency thereof in any manner or for any purpose, and one or more of such persons do any act to effect the object of the conspiracy, each shall be fined under this title or imprisoned not more than five years, or both.

If, however, the offense, the commission of which is the object of the conspiracy, is a misdemeanor only, the punishment for such conspiracy shall not exceed the maximum punishment provided for such misdemeanor."

This charge is false because the fines and imprisonment authorized by 18 USC 371 apply only in the federal areas. As we saw in chapters 8 and 9, with few exceptions, the U.S. criminal code operates in its territorial sense. With the exception of federal functions and offenses against the United States, U.S. criminal jurisdiction extends only to the federal areas.

To misbrand is to fail to meet the labeling standards of, for example, the Food and Drug Administration. Outside the federal areas – that is, within the states – misbranding is not a criminal, but instead a regulatory matter. Therefore, a conspiracy to misbrand within the states would be to conspire to violate a republic's regulatory authority, which is not criminal.

The imposition of labeling duties upon drug distributors operates in equity, not at law. Because fines and incarceration are remedies at law, thus the fines and incarceration imposed for conspiring to misbrand at 18 USC 371 could only operate within the federal areas where Congress can likely fine and incarcerate anyone for anything. (The criminal charges under 18 USC 371 would be applicable to FedEx only if it manufactures or distributes drugs within the federal areas, which crucial fact is not averred in the indictment.)

That the criminal penalties of 18 USC 371 are applicable only in the federal areas is evidenced by statute's use of the word prohibited. As we have seen, criminal prohibition operates only 1) in the federal areas according to the will of Congress, 2) against *malum in se* within the state republics and 3) against *malum prohibita* placed into the law jurisdiction of a republic by a constitutional amendment. In the absence of a constitutional amendment, for a U.S. statute to claim that it prohibits anything means that it operates only in the federal areas.

That the criminal penalties of 18 USC 371 are applicable only in the federal areas is also evidenced by the indictment's fourth charge of misbranding drugs under 21 USC 331, 333 and 353, whose criminal provisions are also only applicable in the federal areas. This is evidenced by 21 USC 332 which grants both Article III and Article I courts the power to enjoin misbranding violations.

Whereas Article I courts can be granted by Congress with powers to both criminally punish and enjoin unwanted activity, i.e., to simultaneously operate at law and in equity, Article III courts cannot mix and match these jurisdictions. In a republic, misbranding operates in equity and not at criminal law.

Thus, the power of Article III courts to enjoin misbranding – at 21 USC 332, which goes unmentioned in the indictment – is the courts' ultimate authority over misbranding within a republic. This is analogous to a judicial court's ultimate authority over drug dealing, which is to enjoin it.

That 21 USC 331, 332, 333 and 353 have both 1) republican provisions that regulate commerce within the states and 2) plenary provisions that both enjoin and criminally sanction unwanted commercial activity within the federal areas, is demonstrated by the provisions themselves. For example, 21 USC 331(a) – (d) prohibits certain misbranding in interstate commerce. These provisions operate within the states in equity by which Congress regulates interstate commerce.

Contrast this with 21 USC 331(g) which applies only to misbranding in the federal areas, i.e., "within any Territory." Misbranding is regulated in America's republics. It is criminal only within the federal areas.

That misbranding operates in equity within the states is evidenced by state statutes about misbranding. Given that the FedEx case was brought in a U.S. District Court in California, let's take a look at California's mislabeling laws.

Recall, that because of the Supremacy Clause at Article VI, Section 2 of the U.S. constitution, Congress' authority to regulate interstate commerce trumps California's concurrent authority to regulate intrastate commerce. Nonetheless, if the U.S. Attorney General fails to properly regulate misbranding within California, then the California legislature claims the equitable authority to do this. Section 111440 of the California Code regulates various types of misbranding. That these requirements operate under regulation in non-criminal equity is evidenced by the statute itself, which reads:

> "A drug or device is deemed misbranded under the laws of this state if it is subject to regulations issued by the United States Food and Drug Administration relating to tamper-resistant packaging, as set forth in Parts 200, 211, 314, and 800 of part 21 of the Code of Federal Regulations, as amended, but is not in compliance therewith."

Within a republic FedEx's misbranding cannot be both equitable and criminal. Because misbranding involves commerce by an artificial enterprise, it is subject to republics' equity jurisdiction, not their criminal jurisdiction. Thus, ironically, the indictment for mislabeling is mislabeled as a criminal matter. To designate this matter as criminal, or to act as if this matter is criminal, is a misrepresentation to the court and to the public.

Last, the indictment calls for FedEx's payment of fines under 18 USC 3571(d) Alternative Fine Based On Gain or Loss, which reads:

> "If any person derives pecuniary gain from the offense, or if the offense results in pecuniary loss to a person other than the defendant, the defendant may be fined not more than the greater of twice the gross gain or twice the gross loss, unless imposition of a fine under this subsection would unduly complicate or prolong the sentencing process."

Such a fine would be a remedy at law, not in equity. U.S. officials falsely bring this criminal indictment against a corporation in order to shake it down for money. This process is false on its face 1) because within America's republics, fines are remedies at law and not in equity, 2) because FedEx is an artificial entity that is subject to equity, not law, and 3) because fines are applicable to natural persons, which corporations are not.

Both *Bouvier's Law Dictionary* and *Black's Law Dictionary* define the word fine as used at 18 USC 371. A fine is a "(p)ecuniary punishment that is imposed by a lawful tribunal upon a person convicted of crime or misdemeanor." (Note: Bouvier defines two other uses of the word fine, which are unrelated to the use of fine at 18 USC 371.)

Such a "lawful tribunal" is a court of law – or criminal law – instead of a court of equity. The definition refers to "a person convicted of crime or misdemeanor," which excludes artificial persons, which are not subject to the law jurisdiction and which cannot be criminally convicted.

That such a fine is inapplicable to Federal Express is because fines are levied in the law jurisdiction, but the U.S. District Court is operating in equity. That fines are a remedy at law – and in criminal law – is evidenced by both the definitions above and by the 8th Amendment to the U.S. constitution, which says that "excessive bail shall not be required, nor excessive fines imposed, nor cruel and unusual punishments inflicted." In that the indictment seeks the law remedy of fines and the equitable remedy of forfeiture demonstrates that the U.S. District Attorney has falsely mixed and matched the law and equity jurisdictions to suit her objectives and her subjective, religious and unprovable opinions about jurisdiction.

For this and all the above reasons, the FedEx indictment has no jurisdiction in the United States District Court for the Northern District of California. Instead, the U.S. Attorney General – in the office's regulatory capacity – may use 21 USC 332 to enjoin FedEx's misbranding of controlled substance and may use 21 USC 882 to enjoin its future distribution of controlled substances. However, the criminal provisions of 21 USC 841 and 846 operate only in the federal areas and are inapplicable to FedEx's officers, unless the company delivers drugs there. The U.S. District Attorney's charge against FedEx for distributing controlled substances is her admission that FedEx is to be regulated by the U.S. Attorney General, who regulates the interstate distribution of drugs.

(Postscript to the 1st edition: 18 USC 7 says that the federal areas include FexEx's airplanes. These airplanes' crews operate under Congress' non-republican law. Presumably they could personally be charged with drug crimes under 21 USC 841 – 843, which operate only in the federal areas. To avoid forfeiture of its airplanes, FedEx could transport all drugs in trucks, which are not subject to Congress' non-republican jurisdiction and its criminal drug prohibitions.)

U.S. v. Licciardi (2014)

In the case of *U.S. v. Licciardi* (2014), [440] the two Louisiana defendants were either singularly or together charged:

- with corruptly persuading a witness to provide false information or withhold testimony, in violation of 18 USC 1512(b)(2)(A)
- with attempting to corrupt, influence or impede an official proceeding, in violation of 18 USC 1512(c)(2)
- with distributing a date-rape drug with the intent to rape, in violation of 21 USC 841(a)(1), 21 USC 841(b)(1)(d), 21 USC 841(b)(1)(E)(7)(B) and 18 USC 2
- with criminal forfeiture under 18 USC 982, and
- with conspiracy to distribute controlled substances, contrary to 21 USC 846.

The first thing that should be noted is that this is an actual criminal case. Unlike with the *FedEx* regulatory matters above, this felony indictment is for actual crimes, i.e., witness tampering and distributing drugs with the intent to rape.

However, as we shall see below, 1) this case is being brought under the false authority of the United States against persons who are not offenders of the United States, 2) the U.S. District Court has no subject matter jurisdiction over criminal cases that do not involve Congress' enumerated powers, and 3) that distributing drugs with the intent to rape and tampering with witnesses are state crimes in Louisiana, over which Congress has no legislative jurisdiction and over which Article III courts have no subject matter jurisdiction.

The first issue that I see with this indictment is that distributing drugs with the intent to rape is not an offense against the United States, as the U.S. is referred to at 18 USC 2. As both 18 USC 5 and 18 USC 7 indicate, most offenses against the United States are committed within Congress' plenary territorial jurisdiction, referred to as the federal areas. As the U.S. Supreme Court recently told us in *Bond v. United States* (2014), [441] quoting *United States v. Fox* (1878) [442] :

> "A criminal act committed wholly within a State 'cannot be made an offence against the United States, unless it have some relation to the execution of a power of Congress, or to some matter within the jurisdiction of the United States.'"

In other words, state crimes are actions not related to federal enumerated powers, or actions that are not committed "within the jurisdiction of the United States," which refers to the federal areas. A criminal act wholly committed within Louisiana, wholly committed outside of the federal areas, and wholly unrelated to a federal function is not an offense against the United States.

Given that drug distribution is a federal regulatory matter, given that to conspire to distribute drugs is a federal regulatory matter, and given that distributing date-rape drugs with the intent to rape is not among Congress' enumerated powers, thus such alleged crime is not a offense against the United States, unless it was performed in the federal areas where most of the U.S. criminal code (at Title 18 United States Code) is applicable.

Second, because distributing drugs with intent to rape is not a crime related to Congress' enumerated powers, Article III courts have no subject matter jurisdiction over it. Likewise, because neither distributing drugs nor conspiring to distribute drugs occurred in the federal areas in this matter, Article I courts likewise had no subject matter jurisdiction over the matters mentioned in the indictment.

Third, Louisiana has criminal jurisdiction in this matter. The state has criminal statutes that directly apply to the alleged criminal behavior. Its statute against forcible rape at La. Rev. Stat. Ann. § 14:42.1 criminally punishes sex when "the victim is prevented from resisting or understanding the nature of the act due to a narcotic or other controlled substance administered by the defendant without the victim's knowledge."

Likewise, the defendant's alleged crime of witness tampering is codified by Louisiana statutory law. Section A(2)(a) of § 14:130.1, entitled Obstruction of justice, makes it a crime to use or threaten force toward a witness to influence the testimony of that person in a criminal proceeding.

In short, the U.S. District Court for the Eastern District of Louisiana lacks subject matter jurisdiction in this case. Not only is distributing and conspiring to distribute date-rape drugs not within Congress' enumerated powers, but such behavior is otherwise not an offense against the United States. Louisiana wholly has criminal jurisdiction over this *malum in se* within its borders.

United States v. Tyler (2014)

In the indictment of *United States v. Tyler* (2014), [443] two Louisiana defendants are criminally charged separately or together:

- with distributing controlled substances under 21 USC 841(a)(1) and 21 USC 841(b)(1)(B) and (C)
- with conspiring to distribute controlled substances under 21 USC 846, and
- with possession of numerous firearms in furtherance of the drug trafficking crime under 21 USC 841(a)(1) and 18 USC 924(c)(1)

As we have seen, distributing controlled substances is a non-judicial / non-criminal regulatory matter within America's republics. Thus, these defendants' alleged distribution of heroin is subject to the regulation of the U.S. Attorney General, including his attempts to enjoin their future drug dealing. However, their alleged distribution of heroin is not subject to an Article III court. Their alleged distribution of heroin would only be a crime if performed in the federal areas, subject to an Article I court.

This invalidates the charges for possessing guns in furtherance of a drug trafficking crime under 18 USC 924(c)(1). This is because drug trafficking is a crime only in the federal areas. Within and among the states, drug trafficking is not a crime but is a regulated commercial activity. This means that the defendant's possession of guns was not in furtherance of a "drug trafficking crime."

His possession of guns was, at worse, in furtherance of regulated activity. His possession of guns would be analogous to that of the security staff of a large pharmaceutical company or of personnel in charge of armored cars.

The point is that possession of guns is not a crime within a republic when accompanying only citizens' regulatory violations. Possession of guns is a crime when committing real crimes with them, or likely in most states when possession is by a convicted felon. (Theoretically, persons convicted of only phony drug "felonies" should be able to regain their right to possess guns.)

In conclusion, distributing controlled substances is not a crime because it is activity to be regulated by the U.S. Attorney General or by a state agency. That distributing drugs is licensed activity for favored drug dealers is proof that it is not criminal. Distributing controlled substances operates in equity, which is a completely separate judicial jurisdiction than criminal law.

Likewise, conspiring to distribute controlled substances is to conspire to violate the equity jurisdiction, which has no criminal sanctioning power. It is to conspire to commit a non-crime, which by definition would not be a criminal conspiracy.

Because distributing drugs is not criminal within republics, 18 USC 924(c)(1) is applicable only in the federal areas and only in "courts of the United States," where 18 USC 5 defines the United States in its territorial sense. I would add, however, that the guns are likely subject to confiscation by the DEA under 21 USC 778 – 780 and to forfeiture under 21 USC 881, which are within the agency's regulatory powers.

United States v. Acevedo (circa 2011)

In the indictment in *United States v. Acevedo* (circa 2011), [444] the Pennsylvania defendant was charged:

- with distributing controlled substances in violation of 21 USC 841(a)(1) and 21 USC 841(b)(1)(B), and
- with possessing a gun as a felon in violation of 18 USC 922(g)(1).

As in the *Villareal, FedEx, Licciardi* and *Tyler* regulatory matters above, the defendant in this case is committing no crime by distributing crack cocaine. The defendant is only committing a regulatory violation under both U.S. and Pennsylvania law. He is subject to both the U.S. Attorney General in his regulatory capacity and to the Pennsylvania Drug, Device and Cosmetics Board. This means 1) that his commercial property, including his drugs and his gun, is subject to be confiscated and forfeited to the regulators under their equitable powers, and b) that his unwanted drug business is subject to being both administratively and judicially enjoined.

This being said, the defendant's federal gun charge should be dismissed 1) because 18 USC 922(g)(1) is applicable only in the federal areas, 2) because gun possession is not within the purview of Congress' enumerated powers, and 3) because gun possession in Pennsylvania by a felon is within the legislative jurisdiction of the Pennsylvania legislature, not Congress. The defendant's possession of a gun as a felon is a Pennsylvania state crime at 18 Pa.C.S. 6105, subject to state prosecution. The Commonwealth of Pennsylvania has jurisdiction over the defendant's gun possession, not the United States.

United States v. Brenes (2014)

In the indictment of the *United States v. Brenes* (2014), [445] Florida defendants were charged:

- with distributing controlled substances in contravention of 21 USC 841(a)(1) and 21 USC 841(b)(1)(C)
- with conspiring to distribute controlled substances in violation of 21 USC 846, and
- with criminal forfeiture of the proceeds of their drug business under 21 USC 853.

As in the *Villareal, FedEx, Licciardi, Tyler* and *Acevedo* regulatory matters above, the charges of distributing controlled substances are admissions by the District Attorney 1) that the charges are not criminal in nature, and 2) that the defendants are subject instead to the regulatory authority of the U.S. Attorney General, who non-criminally regulates drug distribution among the states at 21 USC 822.

Likewise, because drug distribution is not a crime except within the federal areas, where 21 USC 841 is applicable, the criminal forfeiture provisions at 21 USC 853 are inapplicable to these defendants. Because drug dealing is criminally prohibited only in the federal areas, then the criminal forfeiture provisions at 21 USC 853 are also only applicable there. Instead, within Florida where the alleged drug dealing occurred, the civil forfeiture powers of the DEA under 21 USC 881 are instead available to the United States republic.

United States v. Barba (2008)

In the indictment in *United States v. Barba* (2008), [446] various Tennessee defendants were charged:

- with distributing controlled substances under 21 USC 841(a)(1),
- with conspiring to distribute controlled substances under 21 USC 846,
- with criminal forfeiture of property under 21 USC 853, 18 USC 982 and 18 USC 1956, and
- with regard only to Alfredo Barba, with immigration violations pursuant to 8 USC 1326 and 6 USC 202 and 557.

With regard to the charges under 21 USC 841 (distribution), 21 USC 846 (conspiracy) and 21 USC 853 (criminal forfeiture), the names have changed but the story is the same as in the *Villareal, FedEx, Licciardi, Tyler, Acevedo* and *Brenes* matters. Drug distribution is not a crime within America's republics, and the defendants' profits are not subject to criminal forfeiture.

This is not to say that defendants' alleged drug dealing is not subject to the U.S. Attorney General regulatory authority, including civil forfeiture of property seized under 21 USC 878 – 880 and including the office's power to enjoin regulatory violations at 21 USC 882.

Last, while Congress' plenary criminal power is limited to the federal areas, and while its interstate criminal powers are limited to its enumerated functions, as we saw in chapter 9, Congress has plenary power over aliens within the fifty states. Because of this, immigration proceedings against Alfredo Barba are likely proper. Because his presence in the U.S. is at the permission of Congress, he is subject to deportation regardless of the above false drug charges.

United States v. Melendrez (2012)

In the indictment in *United States v. Melendrez* (2012), [447] the defendant was charged:

- with two counts of distributing cocaine in violation of 21 USC 841(a)(1) and 21 USC 841(b)(1)(C), and
- with criminal forfeiture at 21 USC 853.

As in the *Licciardi* case above, these alleged crimes are noted as "offenses against the United States" under 18 USC 2. As we saw in my analysis of the *Licciardi* indictment above, and as the U.S. Supreme Court recently told us in *Bond v. United States* (2014), distributing drugs within the fifty states is not an "offense against the United States" unless it has "some relation to the execution of a power of Congress, or to some matter within the jurisdiction of the United States.'" [448]

Because distributing drugs has no relation to the execution of an enumerated criminal power of Congress and because the alleged drug dealing in this matter occurred in Texas, outside of the territorial plenary criminal jurisdiction of Congress, then such distributing of controlled substances is not prohibited, and is not subject to criminal forfeiture under 21 USC 853. Instead, as in the *Villareal, FedEx, Licciardi, Tyler, Acevedo, Brenes* and *Barba* matters (above), distributing controlled substances is commercial activity that is subject to both intrastate and interstate regulation. As well, because regulatory violations are not criminal cases, this matter is subject to civil forfeiture instead of criminal forfeiture.

United States v. Herndon et al. (2014)

In the criminal complaint in *United States v. Herndon et al.* (2014), [449] multiple Illinois defendants are charged:

- with separate counts of distributing controlled substances under 21 USC 841(a)(1),
- with conspiring with one another to distribute controlled substances under 21 USC 846, and one defendant is charged
- with gun possession as a convicted felon under 18 USC 922(g)(1).

This scenario is similar on multiple counts with the *Acevedo* case above, where the defendant was charged within a state with criminal prohibitions (at 21 USC 841 and 846) that are applicable only in the federal areas, and where the state – and not the federal government – had subject matter jurisdiction over his gun possession as a convicted felon.

As in the *Acevedo* matter, the proper application of government power would be 1) for the U.S. Attorney General or the Illinois Department of Professional Regulation to enjoin future drug dealing by the defendants, and 2) for the state of Illinois to prosecute the one defendant charged with gun possession as a convicted felon (under Illinois statute 720 ILCS 5/24-1.1).

United States v. Gandara (2008)

In the indictment of *United States v. Gandara* (2008), [450] the Texas defendant was charged in pertinent part:

- with importing controlled substances under 21 USC 952(a)
- with possession of controlled substances with intent to distribute under 21 USC 841(a)(1)
- with carrying a firearm during the commission of a drug trafficking crime under 18 USC 924(c).

As we have seen in some of the above matters, the defendant's charges under 21 USC 841 for possession of controlled substances with intent to distribute should be dismissed because this penal statute operates only in the federal areas, and not in Texas. Distribution of controlled substances within Texas is not illegal because both the state of Texas and the U.S. Attorney General license the distribution of controlled substances.

Because such offices cannot license crime within America's republics, we know that possessing drugs with the intent to distribute them is not criminal. Instead, as this book thoroughly shows, it is commercial activity to be regulated.

The dropping of the 841 charges is good news for the defendant, but it is likely his only good news in this case. Otherwise, he's in a heap of trouble for his drug dealing. The reason for this is that he violated the rules of the wrong, most ruthless U.S. sovereign.

His drug dealing is regulated in state republics like Texas, but his importation of drugs invokes the power and the wrath of the U.S. non-republic. His importation of cocaine and methamphetamine from Mexico breached the "customs territory" [451] of the U.S. non-republic, where Congress can criminally prohibit any kind of personal or commercial activity.

We know that the customs territory is under Congress' plenary power, as are the coastal waterways under 18 USC 7, because 21 USC 952 (under which the defendant in this case is being charged for importing drugs) grants the U.S. Attorney General with authority to authorize the importation of various controlled substances, all the while prosecuting defendants for doing the same.

This exercise of arbitrary power is legitimate only in a non-republic, where a king may do what his subjects may not. In the U.S. republic, the Attorney General may not license crime, which is defined by Nature. However, under the authority of the U.S. non-republic – in its federal areas and its tariff zones where Congress dictates what is criminal – then the Attorney General apparently may license what Congress otherwise makes criminal.

That is why it essential to know with which U.S. sovereign one is dealing. The U.S. republic is required to be much more respectful of free enterprise than is the U.S. non-republic.

This is my long way of saying that importing drugs is in fact "an offense against the United States," punishable by imprisonment, whereas drug dealing within America's republics is not. Importing drugs is a crime because it offends the legislative jurisdiction of the U.S. non-republic, which drug dealing within the states does not. This is because the U.S. non-republic does not operate within the states, which instead deal with Congress as the U.S. republic.

Thus, because importing drugs is an actual crime (as defined by the U.S. non-republic) within the federal areas and customs territories, then the charge against the defendant for carrying a firearm during the commission of a drug trafficking crime under 18 USC 924(c) should also be enforceable. This is in contrast to drug dealing within an American republic, such as in the above *United States v. Tyler* (2014) matter, which is at most a regulatory violation, to which 18 USC 924(c) would not be applicable.

United States v. Avila et al. (2011)

In *United States v. Avila et al.* (2011), [452] multiple Arizona defendants were charged in pertinent part:

- with dealing in firearms without a license under 18 USC 922(a)(1)(A)
- with making false statements in connection with the acquisition of firearms under 18 USC 924(a)(1)(A)
- with possession of controlled substances with intent to distribute under 21 USC 841(a)(1), and
- with conspiracy to possess controlled substances with intent to distribute under 21 USC 846.

(I have excluded other conspiracy, weapons, money laundering, smuggling and forfeiture counts which are beyond the scope of this chapter.)

With regard to the first charge (above) about dealing in firearms without a license, this is a regulatory violation in a republic. Because the U.S. Attorney General may not license people to commit crimes within

America's republics, then selling guns (which is a licensed activity) is not criminal. Instead, selling guns is regulated, and the unlicensed distribution of guns is dealt with in non-criminal equity.

Likewise, with regard to the charges under 21 USC 841(a)(1) for possession of drugs with intent to distribute them and under 21 USC 846 for conspiracy to distribute, neither of these criminal charges apply to this case's defendants in Arizona. Their drug commerce is instead regulated by the U.S. Attorney General or by the Arizona state board of pharmacy. As with gun prohibition, the criminal provisions of Section 841 and 846 operate only in the federal areas, and are inapplicable to drug makers and distributors within the state republics.

With regard to making false statements in connection with acquiring firearms, the charges under 18 USC 924(a)(1)(A) should stick. Similar to signing an income tax form under penalty of perjury, one's willful misrepresentations to the United States are subject to criminal penalty. This is because they are offenses against the United States, as is required for federal criminal jurisdiction.

United States v. Church et al. (2014)

In the indictments in *United States v. Mosley et al.*,[453] in *United States v. Mills et al.* (2014),[454] in *United States v. Church et al.* (2014), [455] and in *United States v. Potter* (2014), [456] various Pennsylvania defendants are charged:

- with conspiracy to distribute controlled substances under 21 USC 846,
- with maintaining a communication facility under 21 USC 843(b), and
- with aiding and abetting the commission of crime under 18 USC 2.

As we have seen, these various defendants' conspiracy to distribute drugs within Pennsylvania was really an agreement to enter the regulatory regime of the U.S. Attorney General. According to 21 USC 822(a) their intention to sell drugs required them to seek a "registration" from the Attorney General.

For failing to acquire such a license, the Attorney General could shut down their enterprises, could get their property forfeited and could enjoin the defendants from future drug dealing. That is what should have happened in these matters, considering that the criminal prohibitions of 21

USC 846 apply only within the federal areas, as does possession of drugs with intent to distribute under 21 USC 841(a)(1).

With regard to maintaining a communication facility under 21 USC 843(b), which in the indictments amounted to commercially using the telephone and making text messages, this count suffers the same ill fate as the above conspiracy charges. Both sorts of charges apply only in the federal areas where the U.S. non-republic defines crime. In a republic it is not a crime to use a telephone to violate the authority of regulators, who operate in equity.

With regard to invoking 18 USC 2, we have already seen in the *Licciardi* and *Melendez* cases that, because drug commerce is not a crime related to an enumerated power of Congress, then violations of 21 USC 841 – 844A are "offenses against the United States" only if they are committed within the federal areas or otherwise harm the United States, such as by bombing it or defrauding it. Given that all the acts in the above matters were committed in Pennsylvania, the defendants' agreements to deal in drugs, their acts in furtherance of their agreements, and their use of communication facilities were at most regulatory violations.

In the republic called the Commonwealth of Pennsylvania, the U.S. Attorney General may enjoin defendants' future violations of U.S. equity authority, but U.S. District Attorneys may not prosecute these regulatory violations as federal crimes. To do so would be to confuse equity for law and the sovereign authority of the U.S. non-republic for that of the U.S. republic, which has in fact occurred.

26
The crime of the (previous) century

No room for guessers

Stand up and take a bow. I mean it. You deserve it. For the first time in your life, you now know what the drug laws really say and how they work. Plus you know why they say what they say.

They say what they say because they are republican in nature. However, America's governments operate as a *de facto* non-republics. Their illegal war on drugs exists only because government officials do not follow America's drug laws which are written to secure Americans' rights.

You are now empowered by knowledge that you never had before. All the contradictory crap that you have heard, read, digested and absorbed in the past about the prohibition of drugs and the glory of government has all been false.

What we thought was true is not. What we have believed is nothing other than propaganda for the preservation and propagation of those working in government and other special interest groups. The war on drugs, from start to finish and top to bottom, is layer-upon-layer of self-serving falsity through which we can now clearly see – not to mention a full employment syndicate for public safety personnel and attorneys.

Aren't you glad that you cannot be lied to about the war on drugs in the United States ever again? (You even now know what the United States are. They are republican states with the guarantee of a republican form of government from Congress.)

Government officials have violated the rights of millions of people in America over the past fifty years based on nothing but a misrepresentation of their authority. These officials who took oaths to uphold the Indiana and U.S. constitutions have been shown to routinely violate their oaths.

This betrayal of law is either tortious or criminal. It is either negligent or intentionally evil. There is really no denying that enslaving people under false color of law, in reckless or willful disregard of our statutes and constitutions, is at best a woeful neglect of official duty.

Officials are personally liable because it is their primary duty to know and execute the law – not to violate it. It is a duty for them to read and understand the law, or to get the hell out of Dodge.

False law enforcement exists because the rest of us have exhibited very low standards for ourselves and our officials with regard to truth and veracity. As a species, we are pretty lazy and gullible. Instead of going to the primary source of law, as all law schools teach, or instead of not tolerating people who say false things to us (remember all the anomalies that motivated me to look into the subject?), we have been getting all our information third- and fourth-hand from non-republicans in government whose self-interests and lack of education are inimical to our public interests.

"In religion and politics people's beliefs and convictions are in almost every case gotten at second-hand, and without examination, from authorities who have not themselves examined the questions at issue but have taken them at second-hand from other non-examiners, whose opinions about them were not worth a brass farthing," Mark Twain wrote in his autobiography.

In the case of the war on drugs, we have been getting our information umpteenth-hand, not even second-hand. You are getting this information right now second-hand from me. Hopefully you will hear this information again and again, ninth- and tenth-hand.

Better yet, if you are a defense attorney, hopefully you will confirm the information in this book first-hand by researching the law in your own state. This should not be hard because I have provided you a good outline.

The irony is that, at the very moment I write this, I am presumably one of the few who knows the criminal and administrative law regarding drugs first-hand, other than those in government who are knowingly violating it. This is because anyone who knows the law first-hand would know and enforce it as this book accurately portrays it.

This means that there may be no government attorneys who will admit to knowing the information in this book before its publication, or they will expose themselves as knowingly and intentionally acting criminally. As I have said, the war on drugs is based on a degree of either criminal intent or negligence. It is either willful or wanton.

This situation is as if the Peter Principle ruled government, to wit that everyone enforcing our drug laws has been promoted beyond the level of their ability to understand and properly enforce them – such that people are now in positions where they can neither read and comprehend statutes, nor discern real from unreal and right from wrong. Seriously.

It is as if everyone who falsely enforces our drug laws brought baseball bats to Little League Baseball games, but did not know the proper scope of swinging them. Swinging a bat is proper on the playing field to hit a baseball, but it is not proper to swing bats in the grandstands. The war on drugs is as if public officials were swinging their bats in the grandstands, misusing their rightful power over crime to harm innocent non-criminals.

The drug war is as if Stanley Milgram's obedience experiments were actually happening, where he could get law enforcers, prosecutors and even judges to do wrongful and hurtful things merely by encouraging them to be mean.

The war on drugs is like the rhesus monkey experiments of G.R. Stephenson (1967), [457] where five monkeys were hosed with water when any one of them went for some hanging bananas. When new monkeys replaced veterans in the pen and naturally went for the bananas, the other monkeys beat them so that all the monkeys would not be hosed. These new monkeys learned not to go for the bananas from the beatings by other monkeys – not from the hosings by monkey trainers.

Eventually when all the veteran monkeys were replaced with new ones, all the new ones stayed away from the bananas, but without knowing the original reason why, i.e., that all of them got hosed with water when merely one of them went for the bananas. Perhaps this describes why legal efforts against the drug war have been so futile. When one monkey jumps out of line, the others beat him without knowing why. Lacking comprehension, we have all been hosed.

The war on drugs is also an example of what Kurt Vonnegut Jr. claimed in his last book *A Man Without A Country* (2004). It is an example of a world run by a cabal of guessers who are too lazy, disinterested, arrogant or self-serving to know the real answers. In his novel *Mother Night* (1961) he wrote: "We are what we pretend to be, so we must be careful about what we pretend to be."

If we and government officials pretend that "crimes" are crimes, that judicial courts have jurisdiction over anything a legislature says, that the AOPA (or APA) does not apply to infractions and to drug commerce, that the CSAs criminally prohibit the possession of drugs, that individuals may be criminally liable for property possession, that drug control is judicial instead of regulatory, and that the state's remedies against drugs are at law instead of in equity, for example, then we have been more than guessing. Based on all this pretending, America's legal system has been way off in some la-la land, incapable of objective jurisprudence.

To be so blind to our own law is tantamount to being unconscious to the contradictions inherent in its false enforcement. It is to substitute supernatural powers and subjective fibs of legislatures for objective judicial standards. It is to divorce ourselves from the natural reality of republican criminal law, which is based on injury and which is not subject to religion.

To be so blind is to never know or to completely forget what makes America's constitutional system so exceptional. It is to run our legal system stupidly and immorally – because it is stupid or immoral to wish a non-republican form of government upon anyone, especially ourselves.

The war on drugs is a public policy upon which we have misspent billions of dollars incarcerating innocent people, in which we have misused our most sacrosanct public institutions, in which we have imposed slanderous labels on disfavored people, and where – based on nothing but umpteenth-hand misrepresentations, trumpeted by a lap-dog propaganda machine – we have emasculated and disenfranchised the rights of U.S. citizens with force and fraud to make them bow to government officials, instead of the other way around.

For these reasons alone, the nature and scope of the scam is really quite extraordinary. We U.S. citizens have really let down our guards.

The war has not only wasted half of all our judicial resources earmarked to fight real crime, but it has turned our judicial system into a criminal enterprise, void of legitimate authority and based on nothing but ignorance, lies, religious fervor and terror. In essence, it is to use violence to force one's subjective and supernatural religion onto others, which actions by definition are non-republican and against the 1st Amendment. Regrettably, this is the state of America's criminal justice system.

This situation is to have turned our American republics into non-republics, which do not respect the natural law jurisdiction over which individuals are sovereign. It is to have literally ended, ruined or diminished millions of Americans' lives in the process.

> In December, 2014 my neighbor and I had our late-model vehicles Molotov cocktail'd by a heroin dealer across the street who thought we were snitching on him. *Moi?* Our vehicles were totaled, and the losses came directly out of our pockets. Unquestionably, as with millions of others, my neighbors and I are victims of the drug war, which hasn't done our neighborhoods any favors.

Delusions about the law and ourselves is why we have a war on drugs that abuses innocent people on behalf of the powerful, while misusing the judicial branch, which branch is not to tolerate any false third- and fourth-hand information from guessers. The criminal law jurisdiction of judicial courts is to be based on objective criteria, not subjectivity or guessing.

In an American republic, there can be no guessing what crimes and natural born citizens are. They are self-evident facts of Nature. Both literally and figuratively, because Americans and their officials are so out of touch with not only Nature, but their own nature, they have lost their republican form of government.

These officials have been unable to secure the proverbial lines in the sand because they have been subjectively guessing where the lines are drawn and what they mean. In doing so, whether intentionally or unconsciously, they have moved the lines of legal right and wrong – the goalposts so-to-speak – on a *de facto* basis, without changing our constitutions.

To do this unconsciously is the norm. To do this consciously is treasonous. To not undo the perversion is to be non-republican.

Few people in Indiana have been as vigilant with their rights and privileges, or the rights and privileges of their legal clients, enough to have read and understood the Controlled Substances Act, the Administrative Order and Procedures Act and the U.S. and Indiana constitutions sufficiently to see the proper lines drawn in the sand. These lines secure the separation of government powers with regard to controlled substances, and show how governments are supposed to treat drugs under all circumstances. The lines between a republic's criminal law jurisdiction and its administrative law jurisdiction are predictably placed. This is so that they can be easily discerned by simple people like me.

Never is the state of Indiana to treat mere drug possession or drug dealing as criminal. No constitutional amendment has ever been passed or ratified that places drug possession or drug commerce into the criminal law jurisdiction.

Most Americans believe in the war on drugs because the drug laws, including the Controlled Substances Acts, have been misrepresented to them. Predominantly, if not also completely, the laws have been misrepresented to the public by people who have never read them. These people should be disqualified from talking about and ruling upon any laws until they read and understand them.

That goes especially for prosecutors. Until they understand the CSAs, and how administrative law applies to drug commerce, then their misrepresentations of law are not even deniable. In the next section, I list many of the misconceptions that routinely consume them. This is to say that their subjective misconceptions – and not the law – rule their behavior. This means that they do not practice law with regard to drugs, but they instead practice religion.

Any "law" school 1) that does not teach natural law (which is one of the two jurisdictions in republican constitutions and is the only check upon positive law), and 2) that teaches only positive law, is teaching only the subjective and supernatural religion of a non-republic. For this reason such "law" school, for example the one I attended, is really a school of state religion. If the education is not based on natural law, then it is based on unnatural or supernatural law, which is religious.

The subjective and supernatural basis of such religion is 1) that legislatures are more powerful than the constitutions that created them, 2) that legislatures are more powerful than Nature (or human nature) upon which republican criminal law is based, and 3) that legislatures can legitimately declare certain behavior to be criminal and certain people to be *natural born citizens* that natural law does not. These are the delusions of misinformed non-republicans within America's republics who wrongly monopolize the justice system. Their just-us system is void of natural law, its jurisprudence and its objective standards of criminality and citizenship.

Prosecutors' misrepresentations of law are to present things as true that are not true. A misrepresentation is "(a)ny manifestation by words or other conduct by one person to another that, under the circumstances, amounts to an assertion not in accordance with the facts. An untrue statement of fact. An incorrect or false representation." [458] Thus, any false representation, whether intended to be false or not, is a misrepresentation.

The most culpable and purposeful form of misrepresentation is intentional misrepresentation, which is an element of fraud. Fraud is "an intentional perversion of truth for the purpose of inducing another in reliance upon it to part with some valuable thing belonging to him or to surrender a legal right." [459] Being intentional, it is perpetrated with "conscious object to" [460] deprive another of a legal right or valuable thing.

The main difference between misrepresentation and fraud is intent. Fraud includes a *mens rea* or state of mind to knowingly and intentionally misstate the truth in order to harm others, while mere misrepresentation of law, such as misstating it, does not necessarily include such *mal* intent.

For example, misstating and falsely enforcing drug laws by government officials may be the result of their gullibility, instead of their evil desires to deprive others of their rights. But, of course, only government officials would know their own motives to violate statutory and constitutional law. In any event, they can hardly be described as innocent.

This book is written so that these government officials can no longer lie to us or themselves about the drug laws that are supposed to govern their behavior. We will see that each branch of Indiana government participates in this misrepresentation to the harm of thousands of people. We will also see who began the fraud and who is responsible for its perpetuation.

Previously noted misrepresentations in the enforcement of the law.

The following numerous examples are the misrepresentations in word or deed by government officials that I have already noted in this book with relevance to Indiana's drug laws. (There are many more misrepresentations that I will discuss in the pages that follow this list.) The following are all major misrepresentations of law, layer-upon-layer of which current government Indiana officials are responsible. As misrepresentations, the following facts are all untrue yet are misrepresented to us by our government officials as true.

- That Indiana law enforcers have constitutional authority to arrest and prosecute people for behavior that does amount to crime, as the definition of crime is secured by the U.S. constitution.

- That prosecutors have express statutory authority to prosecute drug matters in judicial courts, which statutory authority would be similar to that granted to prosecute forfeiture proceedings at IC 34-24-1.

- That prosecutors have constitutional authority, in the form of standing and justiciability, to bring non-injurious drug matters into judicial courts.

- That the words "case," "crime," "offense," "felony" and "misdemeanor" used in the Controlled Substances Act have the same requisite meaning as case, crime, offense, felony and misdemeanor used in our constitutions.

- That the Indiana legislature can define crime to not include injury.

- That judicial courts have criminal jurisdiction over subject matter besides injury, including non-injurious infractions, "misdemeanors" and "felonies."

- That judicial courts may lawfully enforce *malum prohibita* against natural persons in the criminal law jurisdiction.

- That the regulatory provisions of the AOPA and the CSA apply only to pharmaceutical company officials, but not to disfavored drug makers and dealers, to which criminal law instead applies.

- That the Indiana legislature may grant criminal immunity to pharmaceutical company officials.

- That IC 33-28-1-2 and IC 33-29-1-1.5 grant Indiana's judicial courts subject matter jurisdiction over non-cases, such as infractions.

- That other Indiana statutes – other than those immediately above – grant subject matter jurisdiction to Indiana's judicial courts.

- That one can lawfully obtain certain drugs only through a medical practitioner.

- That one can unlawfully use drugs and other property in any manner other than to commit real crimes with them.

- That the executive branch has the discretion to treat the same activity, such as drug dealing, as either a crime subject to criminal prosecution or as an activity that may be regulated.

- That the U.S. Attorney General has authority to represent two sovereigns, i.e., the U.S. non-republic and the U.S. republic, over the same subject matter, such as interstate drug commerce.

- That the U.S. Attorney General has authority to apply the rules of one U.S. sovereign Congress to the subject matter of the other.

- That regulation means, or may primarily include a form of, criminal incarceration.

- That Article III courts may be used to prosecute U.S. drug prohibition, which operates at best only in the federal areas and in Article I courts.

- That the violation of a privilege to operate in interstate drug commerce is the subject matter of Article III courts.

- That the case or controversy requirement at Article III of the U.S. constitution is not applicable in criminal trials.

- That state legislatures and Congress can impose civil or criminal duties upon natural persons that exceed those that already exist naturally, the latter which have been enforceable in the law jurisdiction of our courts since the beginning of the United States.

- That the natural rights mentioned in state constitutions are not real, do not exist and are to be overlooked.

- That drug users and dealers can contract into or consent to the criminal jurisdiction of republican judicial courts.

- That a republican government may jail people for failing to keep records, and for other regulatory violations.

- That drug commerce and drug enterprises are subject to the criminal law jurisdiction, instead of to equity.

All of the above statements are untrue. As we have seen, America's war on drugs is based on all of the above false statements, and more, to which the knowledge provided in this book about the real republican law is the only answer.

Culpability for this misrepresentation

There should by now be no question that government officials have been wrongly enforcing the Controlled Substances Acts at the expense of millions of honest and nonviolent drug users and business people seeking better lives and happiness. The above misrepresentations of law have caused terrible consequences to individuals, their families and the American society as a whole. The war on drugs has not been waged in a vacuum.

Given this, our attention now turns to who is responsible for these misrepresentations and then to what degree our current government officials are culpable for them. We know that current officials are responsible for the current false enforcement of our drug laws, but we do not know the degree of their culpability.

Culpability means blameworthiness "involving the breach of a legal duty or the commission of a fault." [461] Our inquiry will lead to accountability for fault all-the-while explaining why our drug laws have been falsely enforced.

Because, as we have seen, the Controlled Substances Acts themselves misrepresent the law with regard to controlled substances, the people who authored the CSAs are blameworthy for the writing. So are the legislators who passed the CSAs, and who likely did not read it. This is culpability from the past.

However, there is culpability of government officials in the present, as well. Their degree of present blameworthiness depends upon whether they have acted purposely, knowingly, recklessly or negligently to misrepresent the law and their authority to bust and criminally prosecute drug users and dealers.

To determine their culpability, we will use Indiana's statutory definitions of criminal culpability at IC 35-41-2-2, which says:

> "(a) A person engages in conduct "intentionally" if, when he engages in the conduct, it is his conscious objective to do so.
> (b) A person engages in conduct "knowingly" if, when he engages in the conduct, he is aware of a high probability that he is doing so.
> (c) A person engages in conduct "recklessly" if he engages in the conduct in plain, conscious, and unjustifiable disregard of harm that might result and the disregard involves a substantial deviation from acceptable standards of conduct."

To these degrees of criminal culpability for injuring others, we add a civil standard based on negligence, or neglect of duty.

> A person engages in conduct "negligently" if he neglects or violates a duty to another person that causes injury, about which duty he knew or should have known.

Given that government officials are improperly waging a war on drugs in contradiction to the Controlled Substances Acts and America's constitutions, and given the parameters of culpability above, the essential issue for us comes down to this:

Whether government officials have willfully or wantonly violated our statutory and constitutional law to harm drug users and dealers? I am inclined to claim that they are wanton.

To knowingly and intentionally enforce the Controlled Substances Act falsely is more culpable and blameworthy than to recklessly or negligently do so, although the amount of harm inflicted is the same. It is more culpable to purposefully misapply the law in violation of our constitutions than to do so out of not being competent in the law. The distinction between being negligent with the law or reckless with the law relates to how substantial the deviation is from acceptable standards of conduct.

Given that the legal standard for acceptable conduct is contained in the law that I describe in this book, the reader is qualified to judge the degree of deviation by government officials from legally acceptable behavior. Given that millions of people's lives have been damaged or burdened by the war on drugs; given that the war could have been avoided fifty years ago if someone had just studied the CSAs and constitutions as I have done; given that prosecutors have ventured into courts without standing or justiciable cases, which violates rudimentary law; given that the state of Indiana has no judicial or regulatory jurisdiction over drug possession, which is a natural right; given that the state has fulfilled its "minimum procedural duties" under the AOPA only to favored drug dealers; given that U.S. Attorneys General have misrepresented the U.S. non-republic as the U.S. republic, and given that the law discussed in this book has been available for all to discover for nearly fifty years, for example, I'd say this deviation "from acceptable standards of conduct" and government officials' blameworthiness are quite substantial – willful or not.

If I had to assign blame, it would go to those most responsible for failing to uphold the separation of powers in our constitutions and failing to know the subject matter jurisdiction of their own courts: the judiciary. Next in the pecking order would be Attorneys General, who also should know the proper separation of governmental powers.

The third tier of blameworthiness would go to prosecutors, to defense attorneys and to members of the regulatory boards that are responsible for properly enforcing the drug laws. Prosecutors exceed their authority by bringing non-cases and non-crimes into courts without jurisdiction, while regulators shirk their duty to regulate undesirable drug dealers. Defense attorneys are to know this, but haven't.

Legal educators share much of the blame as well.

Last in culpability are police officers, who take orders from prosecutors, Attorneys General and judges, whose claims of having superior knowledge of drug laws have been shown here to be unfounded.

In any event, regardless who does the wrong, it is out of either purposefulness or legal neglect that the Controlled Substances Act has been so grossly misapplied and misrepresented by government officials. Either government officials have been just plain wrong and really misguided about their so-called drug prohibition, or they have been downright evil about it. There is no in-between.

Causation

There are two kinds of legal causation: cause-in-fact and proximate cause. A cause in fact is "that particular cause which produces an event and without which the event would not have occurred." [462] Proximate cause is that which is nearest in the order of responsible causation. It is "that which stands next in causation to the effect, not necessarily in time or space but in causal relation." [463]

The authors of the Controlled Substance Acts, and officials who adopted the Uniform act for state legislatures, are the cause-in-fact of America's pathetic and illegally waged drug war. Without their devious and criminal handiwork, the CSAs would not have taken the form that they do and would not be misapplied.

In contrast, today's law enforcers and officers of the courts are the proximate cause of the drug war's illegality. Such people are solely responsible for the CSAs' false enforcement, not its authors. This more proximate responsibility for harm is appropriate because every day is a new day for them to read and understand America's drug laws.

Suffice to say, there is plenty of culpability to go around for the drug war. Each branch of government shares in the blame for either the make-up or the false enforcement of drug laws.

In the next two chapters, we will discuss the executive branch's culpability for writing the CSAs and the legislative branch's culpability for enacting them. As well, we will further discuss the executive and judicial branches' current culpability for falsely enforcing the CSAs.

27

The fraud exposed

Culpability for writing the CSA

In 1969 President Richard Nixon announced that his Attorney General John Mitchell, head of the U.S. Department of Justice, was preparing comprehensive new measures to address narcotics and dangerous drug problems in America. This work resulted in the U.S. Controlled Substances Act.

Simultaneously, the Uniform Controlled Substances Act was drafted and promulgated by the U.S. Department of Justice in conjunction with the National Conference of Commissioners on Uniform State Laws, herein also referred to as the Uniform Law Commission. According to Wikipedia, forty-six states have adopted the Commission's Uniform CSA of 1970. This replaced the Uniform Narcotic Drug Act, promulgated in 1934.

Thus, the U.S. Department of Justice and the Uniform Law Commission were responsible for the writing and promulgation of the various CSAs. If the acts themselves or their promulgation were fraudulent, which this and the next chapter show them to be, then the fraud stems from said Department and Commission.

Both the state and federal versions of the CSAs are smarmy, deceptively written pieces of legislation that are intended to be constitutional yet to be so incredibly hard to understand so as to be improperly enforced. The authors of the CSAs never intended for government officials to understand the acts sufficiently enough to enforce them properly. Or at least, that was their hope.

I would defy anyone to read either a state or U.S. CSA, particularly without help from this book, and to come to a different conclusion. The only proper conclusion from thoroughly reading and understanding the CSAs and other drug laws is that their authors wrote them to obscure the law. This was done to defraud millions of natural people within the states of their substantive rights to property and to not be arrested except for the commission of real crime.

As we have seen, the state and federal CSAs are constitutional 1) because they secure natural persons' natural rights to possess drugs in republics, 2) because they responsibly assign real drug crimes to the judicial branch of republics, 3) because they properly assign the regulation of drug commerce to the executive branch of republics, 4) because they prohibit drug commerce only in the federal areas, and 5) because they prohibit nothing within the state republics that is not already criminal, or *malum in se*.

To criminally prohibit a lawful activity, and to place it in the criminal law jurisdiction of judicial courts, can only be achieved in a republic by a constitutional amendment. Perhaps not all, but for sure at least some, of the authors of the U.S. and Uniform CSAs were well aware of this and the other legal principles defined in this book.

For example, at least some were well aware of the natural law jurisdiction of the constitution, of the criminal law jurisdiction of our judicial courts over injury, of the regulatory jurisdiction of our executive branch over commerce, of the natural sovereignty of individuals, of Congress' non-republican governance in the federal areas, and of the Attorney General's republican duties toward the fifty state republics. This awareness is self-evident from the CSAs themselves.

Also self-evident is the authors' awareness of America's four categories of sovereigns. On their face, the CSAs respect each of these sovereigns jurisdictional boundaries. The acts reflect the proper separation of powers between the executive and judicial branches, between the natural and positive law jurisdictions, between the law and equity jurisdictions, between administrative and judicial courts, between the U.S. non-republic and the U.S. republic, and between the individual and the state.

For example, the acts do not regulate – let alone prohibit – drug possession within America's republics because such a provision would impose positive law into the natural law jurisdiction. Republican governments can only impose positive law onto that which is in equity, which excludes natural persons operating in their natural capacities, with rights to property possession and intoxication.

More specifically, the CSAs respect the natural sovereignty of individuals and the law jurisdiction of judicial courts by not regulating the possession of drugs, and by waiving legal liability for it. As well, they properly assign primary jurisdiction over drug commerce to administrative agencies in the executive branch, and properly limit this regulatory authority in equity to breaking up and enjoining the unwanted manufacture, distribution and dispensing of drugs.

This limited statutory grant over commerce within the state republics should alone be sufficient to keep the actions of law enforcers limited to regulating drug commerce in the executive branch, instead of venturing into the criminal jurisdiction of judicial courts, as they wrongly have done with regard to drug possession and commerce.

However, as if the limited grant of power to regulate drug commerce would not be sufficient to keep the executive branch from also illegally cracking down on drug possession criminally, which unfortunately has been the case, the authors of the CSAs included the ultimate user provisions at IC 35-48-3-3(e)(3) and 21 U.S.C. 822(c), which recognize the natural right of natural persons to possess drugs for their own use within America's republics.

Given that people had these natural rights to possess property before the U.S. constitution was established and before the CSAs were enacted, the ultimate user provision is merely declaratory of preexisting natural rights, which are also secured by the 9th Amendment. The authors included the ultimate user provision to specifically prevent the denial of these preexisting natural rights to drug use and possession by people who do not understand the U.S. and their state constitutions. They also provided an affirmative defense for drug possession in the federal areas at 21 USC 844(a).

Thus, even though the authors of the CSAs were completely devious about falsely portraying delegated authority under the acts, they nonetheless gave drug users an affirmative defense against prosecutions for drug possession. By providing a way to escape their deviousness, then perhaps they could argue that their actions were not only constitutional (which I claim), but also moral (which I deny).

Together Indiana's CSA and its AOPA statutorily guarantee administrative (non-judicial) adjudication of the privileges to make, distribute or dispense drugs. This means that the CSA is constitutional because 1) it regulates that which is to be regulated, i.e. drug commerce; 2) it criminally punishes that which is criminal, i.e., real crime, and 3) it respects the separation of powers doctrine of our constitutions a) by assigning primary power over drug commerce to the executive branch of government and b) by respecting the sovereignty of individuals to exercise their natural rights.

However, despite this constitutionality, the CSAs' authors intentionally wrote the acts to misrepresent the law to the public and to legal practitioners, the latter:

- who in general were taught nothing in school about the natural law jurisdiction in American constitutions,

- who were not sufficiently taught the differences between the (natural, common, criminal) law jurisdiction and the equity jurisdiction of republican judicial courts,
- who therefore do not know where rights come from or where they are secured,
- who have not been able to distinguish the proper roles of judicial authority and regulatory authority,
- who do not know what real cases, crimes, offenses, felonies and misdemeanors are,
- who do not know the meaning of republics, and how they are secured from becoming non-republics,
- who have not known on whose behalf American republics exist, i.e., U.S. citizens,
- who do not know the meaning and source of natural born citizens,
- who have not realized that judicial and criminal subject matter jurisdiction in republics is only over injury,
- who have not been willing to put in the effort that it takes to find, read and understand our drugs laws, and
- who will likely deny and make up excuses to avoid accountability for all these personal and professional failings.

As we have seen to some extent and shall see further below, the authors of the CSAs (and those in state legislative services agencies who adopted the Uniform CSA for each state) took advantage of this lack of legal knowledge and intellectual integrity of government officials:

- by writing the acts so that they would be very difficult to read and to understand,
- by scattering the drug laws so that they are hard to find,
- by not cross-referencing relevant provisions,
- by combining executive and judicial functions and powers into single statutes so as to obscure their distinctions,
- by including misleading statutory provisions that are meant to deceive,
- by co-opting constitutional words with new ones created by the legislatures,
- by including criminal penalty provisions that are not enforceable by the criminal law jurisdiction of judicial courts, and
- by including draconian penalty provisions that are not enforceable

within the fifty states by U.S. District Attorneys under their republican authority, but which they falsely enforce there anyway.

These categories of transgressions are in addition to the numerous individual instances of misrepresentation that we summarized nearer the beginning of this chapter. Below and in the next chapter we will address in detail each of these <u>categories</u> of criminal fraud embodied in the Controlled Substance Acts and other drug laws.

Statutory encryption

The cleanest criminal fingerprint on the CSAs is the cryptic nature in which they are written. Let us call this encryption. The acts were intentionally written to be difficult to read and understand so that attorneys would rarely read them, would scarcely understand them, and would instead accept the summary or cartoon version of the acts, as offered by their proponents in the U.S. Department of Justice and the Uniform Law Commission.

To make the encrypted information readable again is referred to as decryption (i.e., to make it unencrypted). I have decrypted the Indiana and U.S. CSA in chapters 16 – 22 so that others can understand them. During this process we learned that the state versions of the CSA are mostly regulatory statutes, with a handful of real drug crimes thrown in that are enforceable in the law jurisdiction of state judicial courts. The U.S. CSA is both a regulatory instrument with regard to the states – without any criminal authority – and it is criminal legislation with regard to the federal areas, where Congress' drug prohibitions are likely enforceable.

Truly the best and perhaps only way to grasp the incomprehensibility of the CSAs is to try to read the ugly things oneself. From such acts of futility one learns that encrypted, nearly incomprehensible statutes happen for a deliberately criminal reason. All intentionally difficult-to-read statutes are *malum in se*, or evil in themselves. They are themselves criminal.

This is because they are inherently written to deceive readers, and because there is no legitimate reason 1) for them to be written as incomprehensibly as they are, or 2) for them to try to deceive readers. That is, there is no legitimate reason for statutes to be anything but plainly written, readable and understandable.

Logic tells us that all such cryptic, hard-to-read statutes serve to deliberately obscure something, or they would not be written that way. To obscure the truth of our law is inherently bad and evil. It is naturally wrong.

Conversely, to conclude that the CSAs were written to be properly understood would be to think that some of our governments' best attorneys cannot write more clearly and succinctly, and really cannot organize their thoughts any better, than children.

Yet from the authors' positions of power, from their expertise in law and from the nearly incomprehensible way they wrote the CSAs, we can infer their bad, criminal intent to deceive other government officials, legal professionals, the media and the public about the meaning of the state and U.S. CSAs. Again, one cannot read the CSAs without smelling the rotten fish that they were made to wrap.

Because we have seen that government officials in every branch are incapable and cannot be trusted to read, comprehend and know the laws with which they are charged to enforce – which is ultimately America's constitutions – at best they can be trusted to enforce only second- or third-hand summaries of the law.

The criminals who wrote the CSAs knew this dynamic. They figured correctly that they could write the drug laws so that no one would read or understand them, and that they could defraud all the states' law enforcers (including drug enforcers, police officers, prosecutors and state Attorneys General), as well as state judicial officers, by the use of false summaries.

This is obvious as a result of reading and comprehending what the CSAs really say and by comparing this with the false narrative that the three branches of Indiana government go by today, as in the past. Indiana officials have been following false summaries of the law promulgated by the U.S. Department of Justice and the Uniform Law Commission – to wit that criminal prosecutors can use republican judicial trial courts to criminally punish individuals for the exercise of their natural rights and commercial privileges. Until now, scarcely anyone has ever examined or challenged this completely fallacious and superficial view of the law, which harms innocent people, constipates our criminal justice system, and has robbed Americans of their republics.

If law enforcers and judicial officers are unable to read and comprehend our drug statutes, then at least they should follow the correct summary of the law, which this book provides. If these officials are capable only of enforcing the law on a superficial cartoon basis, which they have demonstrated of themselves, then they should at least use the correct summary of the law that I provide – not the fraudulent "criminal" one that was perpetrated by the U.S. Department of Justice and the Uniform Law Commission.

By the way, the following is the correct summary of America's drug laws, and an example how simply statutes could be written or outlined for public consumption:

1. Real *malum in se* crimes that involve drugs are criminally prohibited – that is, proscribed by Nature – everywhere within the fifty states and federal areas.
2. Drug possession is lawful in America's republics because it is the exercise of a natural right.
3. Drug possession is legal in the federal areas because Congress makes this privilege applicable there.
4. Drug dealing is regulated in America's republics because it is the exercise of a commercial privilege in equity.
5. Drug dealing is likely subject to criminal penalties in the federal areas.

However, the points that I am making here are 1) that no one should have to rely on a summary of the law in order to understand and enforce it, 2) that all laws should be readable and understandable to those who enforce them, and 3) that it is incumbent upon law enforcers and judges to read and understand our laws – not just cartoon versions of them – in order to uphold their oaths to the state and federal constitutions.

It is a completely ludicrous fallacy that law enforcers and judicial officers can properly enforce laws that they cannot comprehend, or that they can properly uphold constitutions which they have not read or have been taught to know and enforce only superficially. Ultimately, if government officials cannot read and comprehend the constitutions and statutes that make up American law, then they cannot properly enforce the law. Until they are able and willing to do this, they are susceptible to false cartoon summaries of law provided by traitorous people with greater power and evil motives to violate our constitutions and the rights of Americans.

Because government officials have not been diligent to read and follow the law, we have been living in a lawless society where they, as tortfeasors or criminals, have been misusing the law to harm or terrorize undesirables. As a society we should not tolerate statutes that few can read and understand. And we should not tolerate government officials and legal professionals who either do not read or cannot properly comprehend statutes, regardless how cryptically that they are written.

Again, proper statutory reading derives from knowing *a priori* the subject matter jurisdiction of America's four categories of sovereigns. People who do not have this framework in mind cannot read American criminal statutes properly because such statutes are intentionally (and criminally) written to obscure these sovereigns and their respective powers.

There is absolutely no reason for the authors to have written the Controlled Substances Acts as they did except to confuse, obscure and misrepresent the law that the executive branch seeks to circumvent. As we will see further below, fraud is exactly what the authors of the Controlled Substances Act used to exploit the weaknesses of other government officials, their education, and their subjective understanding of their oaths of office. Criminals wrote the legislation so that the law would not be understood and so that legal precedent, as cited in this book, as well as the separation of powers doctrine, would be forgotten or disregarded.

That they thought they could get away with this fraud, and yet that they almost did, defies all probabilities, if not also comprehension.

Difficult codification and poor cross-referencing

Indiana's drug laws are not only cryptically written, but are unnecessarily strewn over various separate titles of the Indiana Code. This necessitates that one first hunts to find these provisions in the statute books, which are often not cross-referenced, and that one pieces them altogether to come up with statutory meaning. That is what I had to do to write this book.

For example, to discover the arrest powers of law enforcers with regard to controlled substances, I had to first find relevant statutory provisions in three separate titles of the Indiana Code: Titles 16, 31 and 35. Because cross-referencing is inadequate, I found them only by pouring over the table of contents of each of Indiana Code thirty-six titles.

With regard to law enforcers' arrest powers, IC 16-42-20-1 in Title 16 grants law enforcers with authority to make arrests for "offenses relating to controlled substances." "Offenses relating to controlled substances" is defined in Title 35 at IC 35-31.5-2-217. Because neither IC 16-42-20-1 nor IC 35-31.5-2-217 cross-reference each other, and because neither of them cross-reference IC 35-48-4 of the Controlled Substances Act, where all the "offenses relating to controlled substances" are penalized, a reader must literally find all of these statutes in the code-haystack, piece together their connections by reading each carefully, and then make a logical conclusion divorced from third-hand opinion about law enforcers' arrest powers over drug matters. This is no easy task.

This perverted process artificially increases both human and financial costs of justice, and thus is counterproductive to justice. Although this legislative obstacle course is not unbeatable, as this book proves, it was invented by criminals to deter legal understanding, to misuse the judicial system, to violate the separation of powers doctrine, and to violate people's individual rights. If defies further explanation. That certain of the CSAs authors were criminals, but perhaps not all, defies further description.

As well, there is no defense for it. There is no legitimate reason for law to be hard to find or to understand by the public or legal professionals. Once one finds and reads the CSA and other drug statutes strewn throughout code books, one realizes that there has been a deliberate and concerted effort to divorce truth seekers of the law from finding, understanding and acting upon it.

For a society based on the rule of law, this is intolerable. This is legislative malfeasance *per se*. It is *malum in se* – that is, it is criminal – to misrepresent the law in order to harm other people, or to acquire their power. There is no other legislative motive that is discernible from the chaotic presentation of drug laws in the Indiana Code.

Intentionally misleading use or placement of words

As we saw earlier, the authors of the Controlled Substances Acts also used misleading words to misrepresent statutory meaning except to the most discerning of readers.

At 21 USC 844(a) of the U.S. CSA, which incorporates by reference the ultimate user provision at 21 USC 822(c), authors suggest to superficial readers that drug possession requires medical approval. However, our more careful reading of the statutes showed that drug users can lawfully acquire drugs other than from government licensed practitioners, even in the federal areas.

As we also saw, the authors misrepresented the meaning of: to "unlawfully use controlled substances" at IC 35-48-4-13. After some thought, we concluded that to unlawfully use any property is to use it to hurt someone else. For example, the lawful use of a baseball bat is to hit baseballs, not to batter people. The lawful use of drugs is for them to be ingested.

The only unlawful use of drugs, as with any property, is to forcefully or fraudulently hurt other people with it, or to steal it from them. Thus, to ingest drugs is not to unlawfully use them, as the CSAs' authors intended to misrepresent.

As well, the authors misrepresented the term "court of record" in the Indiana CSA by ill-defining it. For example, IC 16-42-20-3 says that: "Any court of record has jurisdiction to restrain or enjoin violations of law relating to controlled substances." Any court of record? How 'bout a tax court? All judicial and administrative courts are courts of record in that they record their proceedings. However, only one of these types of courts has jurisdiction over drugs at any given time.

Long story short: it took me three hours to finally conclude with certainty that this "court of record" primarily referred to an administrative law court of the Indiana State Board of Pharmacy, and not to a court of record in the judicial branch. Later I learned that both kinds of courts may enjoin unwanted drug dealing at different times in the administrative law process. This long discovery process was necessary because the authors of the act intentionally sought to confuse me as a reader.

They could have easily qualified this court by writing: "a court of record of the pharmacy board," but they wanted readers to falsely think that judicial courts have primary jurisdiction over drugs, although they do not. Ultimately my comprehension skills won out over their criminal skills to intentionally obscure or misrepresent the law by ill-defining the administrative law courts with primary, subject matter jurisdiction over drugs.

The co-option of constitutional terms

The single most fraudulent thing that the authors of the Indiana Controlled Substances Act did was to intentionally misrepresent the meaning of certain constitutional words, in order to give color of authority to the state CSAs' phony "criminal" provisions. The authors sought to misappropriate and misrepresent the meaning of words such as case, crime, offense, felony, and misdemeanor, which are used in America's constitutions and whose meanings even predate the constitutions. They did this to fraudulently and thus illegally expand the subject matter jurisdiction of judicial courts to include non-injurious "cases" and "crimes" over which the courts have no constitutional authority.

By misappropriating the words and by misrepresenting their meanings, which subordinated their constitutional meanings to inconsistent legislative meanings, the authors used fraud to circumvent the U.S. constitution and to falsely ensnare non-criminals and non-tortfeasors into their false "criminal" jurisdiction over non-injury.

It is upon this misappropriation, co-opting and criminal conversion of constitutional terms that the fraud called the war on drugs is still particularly dependent. Only by falsely equating fake "crimes" with real crimes do we realize that the subject matter jurisdiction of judicial courts has been purposely perverted to circumvent our constitutions, which officials took oaths to protect.

In contrast, when Congress legislates for the federal areas, it does not need to misappropriate the constitutional words crime, offense, felony or misdemeanor, which are defined under natural law within America's republics. Instead, because natural law is likely not recognized in the federal areas, Congress in the U.S. CSA refers to drug possession and drug commerce as "violations" [464] instead of as "crime," "offenses," "felonies" and "misdemeanors," the latter which have a natural law meaning.

As well, because Congress as the U.S. non-republic can criminally prohibit behavior that is lawful in republics, its use of the word prohibition (in the statutes' titles) to describe the criminal penalty provisions at 21 USC 841 – 843 is proper. In contrast, republics may not prohibit any kind of property or commerce without a constitutional amendment, and for this reason, the words prohibit or prohibition are not used in Indiana's CSA.

For example, the Indiana CSA does not prohibit anything, and does not call any behavior unlawful, as does 21 USC 841 – 843. Instead, it merely designates drug possession and dealing as "misdemeanors" and "felonies." Thus, judges have inherent reason to question whether drug possession and dealing are prohibited and unlawful within the states, which they are not.

Indeed, drug commerce is not prohibited under natural law, but is strictly a violation of the edicts of the king, named Congress, within the federal areas. Using the word violations in 21 USC 841 – 843 is an admission by Congress that these violations do not amount to crimes outside the areas under its exclusive legislative jurisdiction. Likewise, Congress' proper use of the word prohibition, which does not operate within the states without a constitutional amendment, shows exactly where Congress' drug prohibitions are to operate.

Within the territorial jurisdiction of Congress as a non-republic, Congress is the author of cases and crimes, which means it determines the subject matter jurisdiction of its Article I courts. By comparison, in the U.S. republic which operates within and among the fifty states, the subject matter jurisdiction of Article III judicial courts is determined by the U.S. constitution – not by Congress. Among the states where the U.S. republic operates, the subject matter jurisdiction of Article III courts is always over injury-in-fact.

Because in a non-republic, courts' subject matter jurisdiction is strictly defined by a legislature or king, theoretically all of Congress' Article I criminal courts operate under Congress' plenary authority – not under the law and equity jurisdictions. The law jurisdiction does not likely exist in the federal areas because – by definition – natural persons, natural rights and natural law are not recognized by the U.S. non-republic.

Says the Supreme Court, all rights are artificial in the federal areas. All rights exist in the federal areas to the extent that Congress makes them applicable. [465]

This essentially means three significant things in those federal areas that are subject only to Congress: 1) that Article I courts have no judicial law jurisdiction where natural rights are respected; 2) that there is no real separation between judicial and administrative functions because everyone is treated as an artificial person, with artificial positive law (legal) privileges which are granted by Congress; and 3) that the ultimate user provision at 21 USC 822(c), 21 USC 802(27) and at 21 USC 844(a) is where Congress recognizes and makes applicable its subjects' legal right of drug possession.

In contrast, in the U.S. republic which operates among the states, 1) all Article III judicial courts have a law jurisdiction; 2) there is a clear separation of powers between the judicial and administrative branches; 3) statutes secure the natural right of drug users; and 4) drug commerce is regulated in equity – and is not criminally prohibited.

The CSAs' writers knew that if the U.S. Department of Justice could defraud the republics into believing that Congress' criminal prohibitions at 21 USC 841 – 844A, which were legislated for the federal areas, also applied to them, then Congress could expand its *de jure* non-republic – that was operating in the federal areas – into a *de facto* non-republic within the states. [466]

Only such crooks, who understood all the jurisdictions operating within the U.S. constitution, and who knew that there were two United States – one a republic, the other a non-republic – could have pulled off this fraud. They not only finessed the element of injury out of the definition of crime on a national basis, but also passed-off Congress' plenary powers over the federal areas for those of the People's republican government. Again, this was possible only because few attorneys understood legislative and subject matter jurisdiction, and the proper separation of these powers.

Combining powers to fudge their distinctions

Another self-evident technique in the CSA authors' trick bag of fraud was to combine governments' powers into one statute in order to fudge the proper separation of powers between the branches' respective jurisdictions.

For example, as we have seen, IC 16-42-20-1(b) combines powers and fudges the distinctions between drug enforcers' judicial authority (with its power to arrest) and their administrative authority (with its power to regulate). The authors lump all of law enforcers' powers together so that readers will not realize that law enforcers have two separate police powers, i.e., judicial and regulatory, that they function in two separate capacities, representing authority of two separate branches of government and of two separate judicial jurisdictions in American constitutions.

This grouping of powers to misrepresent the law is also apparent in the drug penalty provisions of the Indiana CSA. For example, by listing cocaine possession as a "felony" at IC 35-48-4-6, along with the nine real crimes listed at IC 35-48-4, the authors tried to mislead readers to think that all "felonies" and "misdemeanors" at IC 35-48-4 were real crimes or offenses, subject to arrest and prosecution.

By combining regulatory and judicial enforcement powers into one statute and by fudging the distinction between "crimes" and real crimes, the authors were able to falsely suggest to undiscerning readers, e.g., those working in police departments, prosecutors' offices and court rooms, that law enforcers could arrest and prosecute people 1) for exercises of their natural rights and 2) for regulatory violations. Likewise, by fudging the two legislative jurisdictions of Congress, the *de facto* non-republic has falsely criminalized regulatory violations using courts of the *de jure* U.S. republic.

This fraud was easy to perpetrate upon law enforcers, other government officials, legal practitioners and the public who were not familiar with the distinctions between judicial and regulatory police powers, between Congress' authority as a republic and its powers as a non-republic; and between the criminal law jurisdiction and equity. It was easy to perpetrate upon those who knew nothing about the natural law jurisdiction of the U.S. and Indiana constitutions, which is the only check upon authoritarian positive law, and upon those who were unwilling to read and study the CSA, as was required.

Again, because I did not learn in law school that law enforcers have both judicial and regulatory powers, it was in fact my reading and re-reading of the CSA (and other Indiana pharmaceutical statutes) that taught me this lesson. This lesson is essential to understanding our drug laws. In order to teach me this lesson by means of their words, the authors of these statutes had to already know this information *a priori* before me.

These authors created IC 35-48-4, which combines fake "crimes" with real crimes into single statutes, and IC 16-42-20-1(b), which combines administrative and judicial law enforcement powers into one statute, to obscure the differences between law enforcers' administrative and judicial powers, between real crimes and phony "crimes," between courts' law and equitable powers, between natural rights and commercial privileges, and between positive and natural law. This technique, combined with others, has sufficiently prevented the proper understanding of judicial and administrative subject matter jurisdiction as well as the lawful enforcement of drug statutes.

One can properly read the Indiana CSA only by knowing *a priori* the difference between judicial and regulatory authorities. Otherwise one is likely to mistake *malum prohibita* "crimes" created by the legislature for *malum in se* crimes as defined in Nature, only the latter which is within the subject matter jurisdiction of criminal law.

As well, one can properly read the federal CSA only by knowing *a priori* the difference between Congress' republican and non-republican sovereignties, which the reader now does. Otherwise one is likely to mistake the U.S. non-republic's municipal authority in the federal areas for its republican interstate regulatory authority that applies to activity within the states, which the act does not expressly differentiate.

The national war on drugs is achieved by the U.S. Department of Justice stealthily masquerading the powers of one United States, i.e., the U.S. non-republic, for the other, i.e., the U.S. republic, on criminal charging documents, which are primary evidence of either misrepresentation or fraud upon U.S. courts. This results in a total breakdown in the separation of powers doctrine and the duality of sovereigns due to the misapplication of subject matter jurisdiction.

At the federal level, the U.S. CSA is improperly enforced because government officials likely do not know the differences between Congress' republican and non-republican authorities, and what a republic may and may not do. On the state level, the drug war is the result of knowing neither that a republic secures the natural rights of natural persons in its law jurisdiction, nor that all commerce (except slavery) is subject to regulation in the executive branch of republican governments under non-criminal equity.

The authors of the CSAs took a calculated gamble that most attorneys in America would know little or nothing about Congress' exclusive legislative authority over federal areas, at least sufficiently to spot this power being falsely exercised against society's undesirable interstate business people. They also gambled that other attorneys would not know judicial subject matter jurisdiction sufficiently to invoke the law jurisdiction's protections of natural rights in judicial courts. Otherwise these authors might have earlier been caught in their fraud, have been tried for their treason and have died in prison, which should have been these traitors' justice.

Obvious means overlooked

Another type of misrepresentation that I would like to point out is what I call "obvious means overlooked." [467] I use the term to describe statutory provisions that are so clear, and so legally correct, that they are overlooked and not believed – because they couldn't possibly mean what they say.

The best example of this is the ultimate user provision in the Indiana Controlled Substances Act at IC 35-48-3-3(e)(3), with an ultimate user defined at IC 35-48-1-27. As we have seen, taken together these statutes literally say that an ultimate user of controlled substances may lawfully possess controlled substances for his / her own use and the use of his / her household. There is nothing ambiguous about these provisions.

The federal ultimate user provisions at 21 USC 822(c), 21 USC 802 (27) and 21 USC 844(a) are a little trickier to read, but they ultimately say the same thing as Indiana's provisions, i.e., that drug possession is legal for end users of drugs.

Besides not knowing about the ultimate user provision because it is rather buried in the CSAs, its meaning has been overlooked by American attorneys likely because they deny what the statute clearly says. They deny the obvious.

"Obviously, to lawfully possess Oxycontin must mean only to acquire it through a medical practitioner or at a pharmacy," they wrongly say to themselves. "Obviously," they say, "this statute cannot mean what it literally says, or the war on drugs would be illegal."

This would be their minds playing tricks on them, at the expense of the rights of defendants. It would be an example of cognitive dissonance, which is that weakened mental condition – torn between loyalties – that allows a false narrative to overcome an obviously true one.

Cognitive dissonance is where minds conditionally accept falsity, for example that drugs are illegal, until the conflict between falsity and the truth becomes emotionally unbearable. The purpose of the ultimate user provision is to make its conclusions so obvious as to induce defense attorneys and judges to deny them. It is sad, but understandable, that people vested for many years in a law's false enforcement would deny the obviousness of the ultimate user provision as a Rule 8 defense.

This occurred in the matter of *State of Indiana v. Wann* (2012), [468] where Andrew Wann was likely the first person in Indiana to assert the ultimate user defense against a charge for marijuana possession. Wann did this by taking the witness stand, and by testifying to be an ultimate marijuana user. (Recall that affirmative defenses must be asserted in responsive pleadings, or they are likely waived.)

This defense was denied by the initial trial judge in the matter, and ultimately Wann spent ninety days in jail for possession of small amounts of dried plant parts. (His attorney appealed other matters that were unrelated to the assertion of Wann's ultimate user defense.)

> Parenthetically, ten of these ninety days of incarceration were paid by Andrew Wann when he should have been paid by me. Andy is a master workman who did most of the plumbing, electrical, drywall, ceramic tile, cabinetry and flooring installation, foundation, HAC, drainage and utility installation work on a house that I owned. He is also a really nice guy.
>
> The fulfillment of Andy's ninety-day sentence pushed my rehab project back at least two weeks. His sentence was a quantum waste of both Andy's valuable time and the resources of Indiana's criminal justice system. As I wrote earlier, the grotesque drug war does not happen in a vacuum. It affects everyone. That Andy is not a criminal, and that he was falsely prosecuted and illegally enslaved in contradiction of the 13th Amendment and the ultimate user provision, now goes without saying.

Another "obvious means overlooked" provision is 21 USC 883 in the U.S. CSA, which is about criminal referral conferences. This provision says that a DEA manager may grant a conference to a drug-law violator to help determine whether to refer the matter to a criminal prosecutor in the same U.S. Department of Justice.

What this provision obviously means is that not all drug-law violators are criminals, and that at least some violations are regulatory. If all drug-law violators were criminal, then all would be referred to prosecutors for prosecution, and there would be no need for referral conferences. Thus, defense attorneys should be mindful that some U.S. CSA violators are criminals, but most others are not.

Another "obvious means overlooked" admission that drugs are legal in America's republics is the statutory distinction between manufacture and production. The words obviously mean separate things because they have separate definitions and code sections. In fact, as we learned earlier, they also operate in separate jurisdictions.

Production operates under law. Manufacturing operates under equity. To produce is a natural right. To manufacture is a bestowed legal privilege by a sovereign with power to regulate it. To secure the natural right of production is the law jurisdiction's role.

This is obvious to anyone who knows the difference between the law and equity jurisdictions. It is overlooked by anyone who does not.

Thus, in each of these examples, the obvious often gets overlooked, and if pointed out, it often gets denied. The above are obvious statutory examples that drugs are generally lawful, and that they always have been.

These examples stand for the idea that we not only have permission to read statutes literally, but that we really are supposed to. In particular, criminal statutes are to be strictly construed. And the obvious is not to be overlooked.

28
Discovering the fraud

The inclusion of unenforceable penalty provisions

To complete the fraud that republican judicial courts have subject matter jurisdiction over honest and nonviolent drug matters, the authors of the Indiana Controlled Substances Act included "criminal" penalty provisions at IC 35-48-4: 1) that appear to criminalize all sorts of natural rights that are not subject to positive law, 2) that appear to criminalize commercial privileges that are subject to positive law but are only to be regulated in republics, and 3) that appear to criminalize regulatory omissions, such as the failure to keep commercial records.

Each of these examples is an attempt to criminalize an artificial duty imposed by the Indiana legislature. Such attempts are misrepresentations of law in a republic where all crimes are violations of natural duties that we owe to other people – and are not violations of duties that we owe to legislatures.

These attempts are in fact fraudulent because the CSAs' authors knew that they could not criminally sanction either 1) exercises of natural rights, such as drug possession, which are not subject to any court, or 2) exercises of commercial rights, which are subject to regulation under equity. IC 35-48-3-3(a) and (b) and 21 USC 822(a) which regulate drug commerce, and the ultimate user provisions at IC 35-48-3-3(e) and 21 USC 822(c), serve as proof that the authors very well knew that drug possession is lawful and drug dealing is only regulated within America's republics.

Likewise, legislative grants of forfeiture powers to Indiana prosecutors at IC 34-24-1-3(a) and grants of injunctive powers to Indiana's Attorney General at IC 35-48-3-3(i) are evidence that the Indiana CSA's authors knew that such equitable, non-criminal powers are the extent of the state's power over drug dealing. In fact, IC 35-48-3-3(i) went into effect only in 2014, so we can assume that both the near-past Indiana Attorney General Gregory Zoeller and the authors of the 2014 provision know – when the law was changed – that the state's only and ultimate powers against drug commerce are equitable. Despite this actual or constructive knowledge, Mr. Zoeller allowed and defended (against my accusations) the use of criminal courts to wage the war on drugs, including the state's war on infractions.

In the Indiana CSA at IC 35-48-4, we know that most of these "criminal" provisions are fraudulent, and exist for no other reason than to misrepresent the law to those government officials who can be persuaded by umpteenth-hand information that the positive law authority of the Indiana legislature is sovereign in the criminal law jurisdiction of the state's judicial courts. We know this because judicial courts have no criminal subject matter jurisdiction over non-injury and because the executive agency charged in Indiana with enforcing the drug laws (and these penalties) has no criminal enforcement authority.

The unenforceable penalty provisions exist to be misapplied by state officials who do not recognize the natural law jurisdiction in our constitutions and the boundaries of the criminal law jurisdiction as determined by injury. Because there is no legitimate reason to include unenforceable penalty provisions in the CSA, the only reasons that they exist are illegitimate – i.e., to intentionally misrepresent the criminal jurisdiction of judicial courts. We can infer from the inclusion of these provisions the authors' intent for government officials to give these false, misleading and unenforceable statutes constitutional effect.

This was fraud on its face because the authors knowingly and intentionally assigned criminal penalties to behavior over which they knew prosecutors had no authority to legitimately enforce in the criminal law jurisdiction of Indiana's judicial courts. This was fraud on its face because they knew that drug commerce – in fact all commerce except slavery – is subject to the equity jurisdiction, and not to criminal law. (Most attorneys have not known this information because they have not been taught it. I learned it only by studying the Indiana and U.S. CSAs.)

It was clear that the authors knew these were misrepresentations of crime 1) because they codified real crimes involving drugs side-by-side with the phony "crimes" in both the Indiana and U.S. CSAs, 2) because they included the ultimate user provisions at IC 35-48-3-3(e) and 21 USC 822(c), which both codify the natural right of drug possession and which thus negate the enforceability of most of the phony "criminal" provisions, and 3) because Indiana's authors created separate statutes at 16-42-20-1(b)(3) and IC 35-31.5-2-217 (that we discussed in chapter 22) to grant false arrest powers to law enforcers. These statutes purposefully excluded real drug crimes from the phony "offenses relating to controlled substances." [469]

Along with all the obscuring, fudging and co-opting that we discussed in the previous chapter, the CSA is a self-evident scheme to undermine the law jurisdiction and to circumvent its natural law. That the authors knowingly and intentionally attempted to violate the U.S. constitution is *res ipsa loquitur* .

Res ipsa loquitur, which in Latin means "the thing speaks for itself," is a legal doctrine in Tort (and thus, criminal) law. It creates a rebuttable presumption of culpability for an injury caused by an instrumentality under defendants' exclusive control, and for an injury that would not have occurred in the absence of defendants' actions.

That is, it attaches culpability to persons who are uniquely situated to exclusively commit certain acts that cause other people harm. In the case of the fraudulent war on drugs, the doctrine creates a rebuttable presumption or inference that the false enforcement of the CSAs is the result of how the U.S. Department of Justice and the Uniform Law Commission wrote and promulgated the acts. The false reading and false enforcement of the CSAs would not have occurred otherwise.

Res ipsa loquitur is demonstrated by "scalpel left behind" cases. X-rays that show a scalpel in the abdomen of an appendectomy patient require no further explanation than the surgeon who removed the appendix was negligent. The surgeon's negligence can be inferred from the very nature of the patient's condition.

Likewise, the fraud on the part of the CSAs' authors can be inferred as a matter of *res ipsa loquitur* because the instrumentality or agency that caused the crime, i.e., the fraudulent manner in which the CSAs were written and promulgated, was under the exclusive control of the Department of Justice and Uniform Law Commission.

This creates a rebuttable presumption or inference that these organizations intended (or were negligent) to misrepresent the law. The fraudulent writing of the CSAs was under their exclusive control, and the states' and U.S. Attorneys' false enforcement would not have happened without their direction. That the authors intended to defraud the public and its public servants, and to violate the republican relationship between Congress and the states, is *res ipsa loquitur*. Their crime speaks for itself.

Superior knowledge of law and Intent to defraud logically inferred

The elements of criminal fraud are 1) the intent to misrepresent a material fact in order to induce someone's reliance on the misrepresentation, 2) the actual misrepresentation of a material fact that induces someone's reliance on the misrepresentation, and 3) the harm that results from making such intentionally false representations.

We can infer the authors' intent to defraud readers of the CSA from their writing alone. There is absolutely no reason to write the CSAs as their authors did except to misrepresent the law to its readers. The authors wrote the acts with the intent that they would be rarely read, that they would be extremely difficult to understand, that they would be misread, and that they would be improperly enforced.

Their objective was to circumvent the U.S. and state constitutions in order to incarcerate non-criminals as undesirables. No other intent can possibly be inferred given their superior knowledge of law and their means to misinform the legal community about their legislation.

This national fraud was pretty ingenious given that its perpetrators never really defined the police powers that were legislated. As we have seen, police powers take only two forms: judicial prohibition and administrative regulation, which distinctions the drug war fudges and the CSAs teach us.

With regard to drugs, U.S. police powers are two-fold: 1) that the U.S. government prohibits drug dealing in the federal areas, and 2) that the U.S. government regulates drug dealing within the states. The police power as applied to interstate business activities, such as drug commerce, is the power to regulate those activities, wrote the U.S. Supreme Court in *Ohio v. Helvering* (1934). [470] The authors' intent was to pass-off regulatory provisions as criminal provisions, and to pass-off provisions applicable only in the federal areas as provisions applicable within the states.

To pull-off this fraud certain authors of the CSAs had to have superior knowledge of the law. They literally had to know all the jurisdictional distinctions between natural law and positive law; between law, equity and Congress' plenary power; between the U.S. republic and U.S. non-republic; and between the judicial and executive branches that are discussed in this book both 1) to make the CSAs constitutional and 2) to write them in a fashion to misrepresent the law to law enforcers and attorneys with less knowledge of America's constitutions.

The authors' superior knowledge of the law can also be inferred from what the CSAs teach discerning readers about the law. For example, before reading Indiana's drug statutes, I personally did not know that law enforcers exercised two kinds of police power, i.e., regulatory and prohibitory.

Not having been a criminal attorney, I never really had thought about this issue beforehand. I also did not know that to investigate, confiscate and enjoin was the limit of regulatory power. I did not know either of these lessons until the authors of the CSA taught them to me, however cryptically.

The authors' superior knowledge of the law was evident in my numerous "ah ha" moments as I read and studied state and federal drug statutes, when I literally said to myself, "Okay, now I see!" All of these "ah ha" moments are chronicled in the endnotes of this book.

As I mentioned, my first "ah ha" moment happened nearly a decade ago when I was first shown the ultimate user provision by Johnny Appleseed in Pennsylvania. Another moment occurred on September 11, 2012 – the day of the attack of the U.S. consulate in Benghazi, Libya, when I realized that the state of Indiana had statutory power to enjoin unwanted drug commerce, but no power to prosecute it as crime.

Another occasion occurred on December 20, 2012 when I realized that law enforcers exercise both regulatory and judicial powers, and that their exercise of judicial power applies only to serving judicial process and to arresting people for real crimes and cases of judicial contempt. It was that particular day that I realized that their arrest authority did not extend to the non-injurious exercise of natural rights or to regulatory violations.

Yet another "ah ha" moment happened almost a year later on November 14, 2013, over a year after I started this book, when I realized that the U.S. Attorney General had authority to regulate the commerce of drugs within the fifty states, but no authority to criminally prohibit it there.

Similarly on February 15, 2014, I realized that U.S. Attorneys General were fraudulently enforcing the law of the U.S. non-republic against inter-state business people. This is how they have been able to regulate (in their republican capacity) favored drug dealers, such as pharmaceutical companies, all-the-while prosecuting (using Congress' non-republican law) disfavored interstate drug dealers.

One of the latest revelations that the authors taught me was fundamental to almost all others. As late as November 25, 2014, I realized 1) that all commerce (except slavery) operates under equity, which has no criminal power, and 2) that because drug commerce operates under equity, it logically cannot be subject to a republic's criminal authority.

In other words, 1) other than real *malum in se* drug crimes proscribed by Nature and listed in state CSAs, and 2) other than drug crimes proscribed by Congress for the federal areas, ALL other provisions in the state and U.S. CSAs are regulatory and operate in non-criminal equity. To know this simple jurisdictional truth is to know that the criminal prosecution of drug possessors and dealers within America's republics is unlawful.

It was only by reading and pondering the Indiana and U.S. CSAs over-and-over again that the meaning and significance of the above revelations came to me. Thus, I have no one else to thank besides the authors of the CSAs for leading me to ALL of these extremely important realizations of law, which I (and apparently most criminal attorneys) escaped law school without learning. These discoveries are major, major pillars of legal knowledge and statutory insight that no law students should be allowed to graduate from law school without knowing.

The same thing can be said for knowing the meaning and origin of crime and natural born citizen. It goes without saying that one can hardly take an oath to uphold the Indiana and U.S. republics when those in charge of legal education do not teach, and likely do not know, the meaning and elements of a republic. The reason that law students routinely graduate law school without knowing the major lessons taught to me by the criminal authors of the CSA, or without knowing the meaning of crime and natural born citizen, is that the information does not benefit America's *de facto* non-republics and the special interest groups that they serve.

Only when one thoroughly reads and studies the entire Indiana CSA does one see the separation of judicial and executive functions and the lines of distinction between criminal and administrative law that current government officials have been missing. Only by knowing the distinctions between Congress' powers at Article I, Section 8, Clause 3 and its powers at Article I, Section 8, Clause 17 and at Article IV, Section 3, Clause 2, can one see these distinctions played out in the U.S. CSA. Because the U.S. and Indiana CSAs solely and exclusively taught me these lessons, I can surmise that at least some of its authors knew the lessons in order to teach them to me.

As with the doctrine of *res ipsa loquitur*, the instrumentality of my learning was strictly in their hands. I can infer that the authors knew everything that they taught me. Thus, the authors of the CSAs taught me the law – "the definition and limitation of power" [471] – and they could not have done this without first knowing the real law, i.e., the state and U.S. constitutions, very, very well.

Had I not learned these important lessons from them, I could not have accurately written this book. Had I not been required to piece together the law because of their deviousness, then I would not have found the above missing puzzle pieces to my prior misconceptions.

So, ironically, I owe the criminal authors of the CSAs a large thanks for teaching me important components of law which I graduated from law school without knowing, and without which I could not have accurately written this book. I thank the authors for showing me that statutory law actually does follow our constitutions, but that – by the authors' devious design – modern officials in the executive and judicial branches do not follow the statutory criminal law.

The authors also taught me how to think and act like a non-republican, which in a republic is to be criminal. Learning the law by reading the CSAs is like going to prison to learn how to be criminal by the real experts.

The CSAs are examples how to write legislation in order to circumvent the republic, which methodology has been outlined in this and the previous chapter. The methodology is to deliberately misrepresent the law in various ways. But law and lies mix like water and oil, and that's why we can eventually discern their differences.

Although a constitutional amendment is required to deny Americans a republican form of government, the CSAs' authors show that a *de facto* non-republic is achievable merely if it masquerades as a republic. This masquerade is achieved by fraudulently co-opting constitutional words like crime and offense, by trying drug defendants in false jurisdictions, by enforcing *malum prohibita* as real crimes, by ignoring affirmative criminal defenses, by ignoring commercial defendants' legal rights to administrative due process, and by misrepresenting non-republican U.S. criminal statutes as republican.

Essentially the fraud is achieved in states like Indiana by granting law enforcers both regulatory and judicial authority, but by not telling them 1) that their power to arrest and to prosecute is strictly judicial, 2) that it is enforced in the law jurisdiction of judicial courts (over violations of natural law), and 3) that it is based strictly on the commission of a real crime, as referred to by the 13th Amendment. Somehow police officers and prosecutors get through their respective training schools without learning any of these basic principles.

The fraud is achieved federally by not telling DEA agents and U.S. District Attorneys that Congress' criminal penalties against drug commerce have authority only in the federal areas, where Congress may legislate in its role as a non-republic, impervious to natural law. Elsewhere within the United States, Congress must legislate in its republican capacity. This is to be respectful of natural rights, as enforced by adherence to judicial subject matter jurisdiction over injury, and to enforce regulatory instead of prohibitory remedies for unwanted drug commerce.

Means and capability.

Not only did the authors' actions display their intent to defraud the public, the courts and the legal profession, the authors in the U.S. Department of Justice and the Uniform Law Commission were likely the only persons in the country with the means and capability of pulling off the fraud. They not only wrote the CSAs, but they also misrepresented them to government officials throughout the United States.

These recipients likely preferred to get the information second- and third-hand rather than to spend day-after-day, as I did, trying to decrypt and piece together the CSAs' true meaning, i.e., that drug possession is a natural right and that drug dealing is regulated.

The fraud was able to be carried out because of the disparity of knowledge between attorneys in the U.S. Justice Department and the Uniform Law Commission on one hand, and between state Attorneys General, prosecutors and all other criminal attorneys in the United States.

As supporters of a non-republican government, the CSAs' authors had no interest in securing the rights of defendants. From their positions of power, they had the means to both write the fraud and promulgate it as legitimate. Because the CSAs were nearly impossible to quickly comprehend, the legal community was ripe for second- and third-hand information, which the department and commissioners spoon fed as the act's leading authorities.

Through this process that I watched on television in the early 1970s as a highschooler, the authors of the CSAs misrepresented what Wikipedia calls "expanded police powers." Because *malum in se* drug crimes were already subject to America's republican police powers, the CSAs provided law enforcers with two additional police powers: 1) additional regulatory powers to investigate, confiscate, forfeit and enjoin either intrastate or interstate drug commerce, and 2) additional criminal police powers in the federal areas.

Thus, these "expanded police powers" within the states were strictly expanded regulatory powers, 1) that had no criminal sanctions outside the federal areas, 2) whose equitable subject matter was already well within the authority of state legislatures to define, and 3) which did not affect the liberty of natural persons. However, these expanded regulatory (executive branch) powers within the states were misrepresented as expanded criminal (judicial branch) powers.

To represent the CSAs as expanding police power within the Indiana republic to include the power to arrest and prosecute non-criminals could only have been misrepresented by second- and third-hand information handed down from the Justice Department and the Uniform Law Commission. This is because such knowledge does not derive from the CSAs themselves, which only regulate drug commerce within America's republics.

Thus, the U.S. Department of Justice and the Uniform Law Commission not only authored the CSAs to misrepresent the law, which has led to the war on drugs. These organizations also promulgated false secondary information about the CSAs which misguided and led astray all those law enforcers and judges who ever tried to superficially read it.

The ability and means of such powerful criminal organizations to perpetrate this fraud is fundamentally described by criminologist Harold E. Pepinsky in his book *The Geometry of Violence and Democracy* (1991). Pepinsky suggests that the concepts of power, control and dominance are central to the continuation, if not proliferation, of violence in our society – and of course, vice versa.

Democracy has degenerated into Weberian patterns of authority, he suggests, which "entail the belief that one person is qualified to make decisions for others." [472] This is the core belief of all non-republicans and authoritarians.

These authority patterns are maintained by "political sleight of hand" where society's most powerful institutions and individuals conveniently relieve themselves of responsibility for the disorder. [473] Yet, "unless we reject a broad range of conventional criminological theory," Pepinsky writes, "it is more plausible to presume that people punish those they can punish to draw attention away from their own crookedness." [474]

Pepinsky's thesis is "that power over others is the major cause of crime and violence, for example the war on drugs, and that those who victimize more often and more seriously are those who are less closely supervised, who command greater resources, and who have greater capacity to resist detection and punishment." [475] By the very nature of "control theory, opportunity theory, and deterrence theory, taken together. . .," [476] he writes, "those who have the power to punish offenders are likely to be greater offenders than those they punish." [477]

This perfectly describes the means and methods of the CSAs' authors in the U.S. Department of Justice and the Uniform Law Commission. They established the idea on a national basis that crime is to be politically partisan – a matter of who defines the situation. However, as we have seen, politics is not to define the criminal law jurisdiction in a republic. Political control of the meaning of crime is the mark of a non-republic.

This blurring of distinctions between crime and liberty, natural law and positive law, the law jurisdiction and equity, judicial power and regulatory power, the individual and state, republics and non-republics, and law and politics is clearly what the relativist authors of the CSAs intended. They knowingly sought to misrepresent the constitutional meaning of crime as something within the power of republican legislatures to define, although they knew that it was not. Their inclusions of the ultimate user provision and of the distinctions between production and manufacturing are two of their several statutory admissions of this fact.

As we now know, republican governments' political branches cannot prescribe crime inconsistently with natural law or with republican consti- tutions, which define all crime to be violations of natural rights that cause injury. In a republic, the reasons that people go to jail are not to be subject to politics or political partisanship, as they are in non-republics.

Agents of the U.S. Department of Justice and the Uniform Law Commission clearly defrauded the entire legal community and the public through these intentional misrepresentations because never did they cor- rect the legal community's false reliance on their second- and third-hand information. The authors wrote the CSAs in the form that they did because they knew legal professionals were ill-equipped to discover the fraud behind them, were ill-equipped to come to understand them thoroughly, and could ill afford the time to figure them out. (I took the time.) Even fewer people might take the time to explain this fraud to others, as I have.

They also knew that their politically-chosen judiciary – likely out of the same ignorance and gullibility – would rubber-stamp their co-opting of constitutional terms, their inclusion of penalty provisions for phony "crimes," and their stripping of jurisdictional distinctions, if they were merely encouraged to do so.

They also figured that they could install and maintain this false regime through the legal education and certification system. Perhaps it is ironic that Indiana adopted its first system to certify and control the standards of attorneys around the same time that it passed the CSA.

Non-republicans such as the authors of the CSA would increase if not ensure their chances of never being caught by teaching and certifying only the positive law authority of non-republics, i.e. that the judicial branch serves the will of the legislature, as if the legislature had no natural limita- tions imposed by the (natural) law jurisdiction.

By the time I reached law school in 1983, there was no mention of the natural law basis of the U.S. constitution, and scarcely any mention of the Indiana constitution in my law school's curriculum. There was no discussion about the differences between republics and non-republics, which we now know is essential to understand America's constitutional exceptionalism, not to mention to properly read criminal statutes.

What the CSAs' authors did not know, but only hoped and depended upon, was that their knowledge of the natural law jurisdiction in the U.S.

and various state constitutions, and their knowledge of the law and equity jurisdiction of judicial courts, was not shared by others, or at least by a sufficient number of others, to prevent their fraud from working. As in the experiments by G.R. Stephenson (1967) about socially acquired monkey behavior [478], their strategy was to train attorneys so that none of us knew why nor would ask why the proverbial bananas were off limits.

I took Constitutional Law for an entire academic year in law school. It never addressed the differences between republics and non-republics, nor the territoriality of criminal jurisdiction, nor that Congress acts as a sovereign non-republic in the federal areas, nor that Congress must legislate as a republic toward the states, nor that a key feature of an American republic is the securing of natural persons' natural rights in the law juris-diction of its judicial courts, nor the meaning of crime and natural born citizen.

In a legal educational system that teaches only the positive law authority of a non-republic, more than just bananas are apparently off-limits by the animal keepers. Welcome to the monkey house. [479]

But what the experimenters hoped would never happen has happened. One of the monkeys finally caught-on to their banana trick and is explaining the scam to all the other monkeys. In his funny monkey lan-guage, as he jumps up-and-down, screeching, and pointing toward the District of Columbia, he is telling the other monkeys that the King of England has returned to the shores of America, and has stolen our republics with little more than phony words and water hoses.

29

The drug war's *corpus delicti*

Evidence of the fraud

Crimes do not occur in vacuums. By definition, crimes are crimes because they victimize people. They leave behind a *corpus delicti*, which is "the body (material substance) upon which a crime has been committed." [480] In the case of the war on drugs, the *corpus delicti* of the crime are the million-plus Americans who are falsely ticketed or arrested and incarcerated each year for drug possession and commerce.

More than just offering a few examples, we noted in the previous chapters at least eight separate <u>categories</u> of behavior that were each meant to misrepresent the law to unsuspecting government officials, defense attorneys and the public. Combined, these categories are evidence of a grand scheme – or a pattern and practice – to defraud politically-incorrect drug users and dealers of their right of liberty, their right of property possession, and their substantive right to a law jurisdiction wherein their natural rights are to be secured.

The criminal authors could have truthfully represented our drug laws as I do, but instead they chose to misrepresent them. Their misrepresent-ations chronicle their crime.

If the authors had written the CSAs properly, then there would be no anomalies between governments' propaganda and the way that officials are required to enforce drug laws. Likewise, if the authors had written the CSAs properly, then they would have been enforced properly, and thus there would be no evidence of their wrongdoing or their intent to do wrong, as there is.

For example, if the authors were going to try to misrepresent the meaning of lawful possession (which they did), then there would be (and is) evidence of their deliberate attempt to misrepresent the term. They could have told readers the real law, i.e., that to lawfully possess drugs is to acquire them without force, threat or fraud. Instead they tried to make readers believe that lawful possession of drugs necessarily comes from a relationship with licensed medical practitioners or with pharmaceutical companies.

They did not have to try to misrepresent the meaning of lawful possession. Plus, there is no legitimate reason to do so. Thus, their attempt demonstrates the deliberateness of their misrepresentations. This deliberateness makes all their misrepresentations of law fraudulent.

The authors literally tried to confuse readers by blurring the distinctions between natural and positive law, and by getting readers to think that they cannot exercise their natural rights to property possession without permission from positive law authorities. (As we have seen, the federal CSA makes this misrepresentation at 21 USC 844(a) to a greater degree than the state CSAs.) By deliberately (and snarkily) making the law hard to read, these authors give evidence of their criminal wrongdoing.

Pointing out this misrepresentation allows us to more clearly understand the law, which says that lawful possession is not and never has been a creature of the legislature, but that it is a natural right defined by Nature and enforced in the law jurisdiction of judicial courts. This natural right is secured by Article I, Section 1 of the Indiana constitution (1816), which recognizes that "all men are born equally free and independent, and have certain natural, inherent, and unalienable rights" which include "acquiring, possessing, and protecting property..."

It is also secured by Article I, Section 37 of the Indiana constitution (1851) and by the 13th Amendment, which guarantee the substantive right to be arrested and tried in the law jurisdiction only for real crime – not for just one's possession of disfavored personal property.

The drug war exists by the authors blurring the lines between Nature and man, law and equity, the judicial and regulatory branches, and the U.S. republic and the U.S. non-republic. It exists because the law of jurisdiction has been lost and the separation of powers doctrine has been terribly violated.

It exists only because a handful of criminal minds put together a short legislative act that is nearly incomprehensible, but which after much thought, ironically reveals the true law from the fake one and real crimes from phony ones – all of which it contains.

One risk of defrauding people is that eventually one may get caught in the fraud. After fifty years of harming others, this is what finally has happened to those despicable authors of the state and federal CSAs who knowingly sought to circumvent the U.S. constitution and to deprive then hippy and minority drug users of their substantive rights. This goes also for the authors of the latest changes to the Indiana CSA, effective 2014, who show that the state's remedies against unwanted commerce are equitable.

Culpability for modern enforcement

The above discussion shows why the authors of the CSAs were (are) responsible for the illegal war on drugs. But for the national fraud perpetrated by these criminals, and the susceptibility of the legal profession for bad third- and fourth-hand information, there would not have been a war on drugs.

However, that was nearly fifty years ago. Since then Indiana's prosecutors, judges, members of the Indiana State Board of Pharmacy and other law enforcers have been maintaining this fraud to the injury of thousands of innocent Hoosiers. What is their culpability for carrying on the fraud started by the U.S. Department of Justice and the Uniform Law Commission?

Whereas we can infer malice towards Americans and their constitutions from the fraudulent writing of the CSAs, and from their false promulgation, such malice cannot necessarily be inferred in the act's false enforcement by today's officials. I know some of them. These are mostly honorable people. More than likely their false enforcement of Indiana's drug laws has been out of gross ignorance of these laws.

One of the most quoted legal maxims is that ignorance of the law is no excuse. The actual maxim reads: *Ignorantia facti excusat, ignorantia juris non excusat. Ignorance of facts excuses; ignorance of law does not excuse.* The war on drugs is one BIG mistake (or ignorance) of law.

As other maxims show, lawyers and judges have clearly never been exempt from being ignorant. *Ignorantia judicis est calamitas innocentis,* reads a maxim. *The ignorance of the judge is the misfortune of the innocent.*

Imperitia culpae annumeratur, reads another. *Ignorance, or want of skill, is considered a negligence, for which one who professes skill is responsible.*

These maxims are accurate, but they do not capture the essence of America's legal problem with regard to the war on drugs. This legal problem is that government officials have not been following the law. We can definitively say this because *non est certandum de regulis juris. There is no disputing about rules of law.*

Ignorance of our drug laws is no excuse because there is no disputing what they really say. Ignorance of drug law is only forgivable because the writers and promulgators of the CSAs defrauded everyone about the law, and because few people have sufficiently read the acts. These authors deliberately misrepresented the law to fellow attorneys so that the latter would neglect the real law in their practices. These authors deliberately misrepresented the law to government officials so that they would misuse the power of the judicial branch against undesirables.

Does this let current practitioners off the moral hook? Not really. Just because everyone has been falsely enforcing the CSAs does not make the practice right. *Multitudo errantium non parit errori patrocinium. The multitude of those who err is no excuse for error.*

If there is a duty to know the law, this duty falls first on legal practitioners, particularly in government. *Idem est scire aut scire debet aut potuisse. To be able to know is the same as to know.*

Through neglect, legal practitioners have ratified the false enforcement of the glorified Controlled Substances Act for nearly half a century. *In maleficio ratihabitio mandato comparatur. He who ratifies a bad action is considered as having ordered it.*

Multitudo imperitorum perdit curiam, reads another maxim. *A multitude of ignorant practitioners destroys a court.* Indeed.

Unfortunately, for all the victims of the illegal drug war, the past fifty years of injury is not legally actionable. Government officials acting in their sovereign immunity and their zone of ignorance are immune from liability. Being ignorant of their wrong negates their intent to harm.

For all the cops who have falsely incarcerated drug users, for all the prosecutors who have falsely prosecuted business people, and for all the judicial officials who have participated in this scam, the ignorant bliss is over. These people are left with the cold reality of not only the harm they have caused others, but a fully revealed constitutional and statutory scheme upon which they have remorselessly been crapping.

This book puts all government officials on notice that they have been ignorantly and therefore arrogantly misenforcing drug laws to the harm of millions of people, and that they have a duty to stop. Given these officials' oaths to follow the law, any future harm from their knowing and willful failure to do so, and to uphold the U.S. and Indiana constitutions hereafter, becomes actionable for their victims.

In the light of day, the fraud is exposed, and so is the lack of judicial subject matter jurisdiction over drug possession and dealing. This squares with the legal maxim: *Ex dolo malo non oritur action. Out of fraud no action arises.* Now that the fraudulent nature of the drug war is exposed, false prosecutions should end.

Because ignorance of the law is now vanquished, officials can no longer hide behind theirs. *Non decipitur qui scit se decipi. He is not deceived who knows himself to be deceived.*

From now on, given that we all know what the drug laws say, and what crimes are, then future victims of the drug war can hold these officials accountable to the proper execution of the CSAs and to America's constitutions. Under the new regime, government officials must leave drug users alone and must deal with unwanted drug makers and dealers through remedies available in equity, not the criminal justice system. Otherwise they must personally pay the price for not doing so.

That Indiana's top lawyers know that drug commerce operates in non-criminal equity is self-evident from the a 2013 amendment to the Indiana CSA, which took effect on January 1, 2014. The new IC 35-48-3-3(i) granted the Indiana Attorney General the authority to enjoin violations of the Controlled Substances Act.

From this enactment, there can be no doubt that Indiana's Attorney General at the time, Greg Zoeller, as the state's supreme law enforcement authority and as the sole officer granted authority to seek judicial injunctions against drug law violators, had notice 1) that the state's most powerful remedy against drug dealing is to enjoin it (and not to criminally prosecute it), and 2) that the state's ultimate powers against disfavored drug dealing are equitable (and do not operate at criminal law). This constructive knowledge bespeaks the falsity of the war on drugs that he, his predecessors and his successor have waged.

In conclusion, the authors of the CSAs have been exposed as the cause-in-fact of the unlawful and criminal war on drugs. Current government officials are the proximate cause of this travesty. Their cat is now out of their hat. Whether their actions are corrupt or just inept is the only real question.

America's judiciary has had a fifty-year carnal affair with the political branches, while also doing their mistresses' dirty bidding of putting undesirable non-criminals in jail. The branches have not only been sleeping together, in violation of the separation of powers doctrine. They have also contaminated each other with a germ of unadulterated falsity, religiosity and evil spawned in Washington, D.C. To rid them of this germ requires a thorough house cleaning, if not also a good monkey hosing.

As well, this germ has contaminated the pages of legal professionalism and scholarship. The war on drugs exists because the law has been hijacked by a false, subjective and inbred viewpoint that is divorced from natural law, jurisprudence and therefore America's republican form of government.

The war on drugs and the demise of America's republics is strictly the result of how attorneys are trained to falsely think. They are trained to believe that there is only one sovereign in America's republics – the legislative branch. They are taught to not know natural law's check upon positive law. This false thinking, which is based upon the forgotten natural law jurisdiction and upon the disregard for the sovereignty of individuals, is the cause of America's despotic dis/ease.

Untempered by the objective standards of natural law and juris-prudence, it is the false belief in the plenary authority of legislative sovereigns that puts America under a state religion. Such a false republican belief allows infidels to be enslaved for violating the emperor's religion, instead of for violating the natural criminal standards of a republic.

But we can now rejoice throughout the kingdom because this ignorant emperor may soon be dead. He has been exposed as not only naked, but also syphilitic.

30
Why I wrote this book

My own private Indiana

As I mentioned in the Preface, what inspired this book was an appeal of a speeding-infraction conviction, which I took to the U.S. Supreme Court.

In this appeal I contended that the Commissioner of the Indiana Bureau of Motor Vehicles in the executive branch has primary, subject matter jurisdiction over speeding infractions in Indiana – and not the trial courts in the state's judicial branch, where I was falsely summoned and tried. As we saw from the example of that family from Ohio, this regulatory power over operating a motor vehicle is analogous to the primary subject matter jurisdiction of the Indiana State Board of Pharmacy to regulate drug dealing.

This speeding-infraction appeal is relevant to this book because it was to be a test case for a future challenge against the legality of the war on drugs. This is because both traffic infractions and commercial drug transactions are regulatory, and thus falsely enforced in judicial courts.

Therefore, similar arguments to successfully challenge the false judicial enforcement of traffic infractions could be used to challenge the false judicial enforcement of the phony "misdemeanors" and "felonies" upon which the war on drugs is based. Consequently, to challenge a speeding ticket *pro se* was a perfect way for me to test the enforcement mechanism of the war on drugs without my having to get busted for drug possession.

But why *pro* se? Why did I represent myself in this matter? Do not attorneys make the worst clients? (Not really. I am probably the best client I ever had.)

First, I represented myself because I was qualified to do so, and because no client could pay me what it was worth to devote a year or more of my life to fight a traffic infraction for them as a fiduciary. Second, going *pro se* presents no moral issue of encouraging a client to pursue a losing battle or cause. Third, going *pro se* offers easier access to the U.S. Supreme Court, otherwise which highly qualifies those attorneys that practice before it on behalf of clients.

As an individual sovereign with substantive legal rights in America's republics (a topic in chapters 2 and 3), I exercised my right of direct access to the Supreme Court. The only middlemen between me and the justices were their clerks.

I have such direct access to the U.S. Supreme Court not because I have a law degree, or not because I am privileged, or even because I am a natural born citizen, which is the highest political status on Earth. I have such access to the Court because I am an ordinary natural person with substantive rights under the U.S. constitution. Because of America's beautiful legal structure – which is not to say the people running it – we each have direct access to the highest court in the land, although most matters are presented by attorneys.

Cool, huh? You bet it is. American law reminds us over and over again what the U.S. Supreme Court told us in *Yick Wo v. Hopkins* (1886): that individual sovereigns are not subject to positive law, but are instead its authors. [481] Statutes and court rules are generally written just the way we should want them to be. Unfortunately, this wonderful law is not always followed.

In any event, my briefs in the traffic infraction appeal respectfully told each of the courts that my due process rights were being violated by state officials, acting under color of law, who falsely summoned me to the wrong court, in the wrong branch of government, in contradiction to the Motor Vehicle Code and the Indiana constitution. These are very similar to my contentions in this book about the false enforcement of Indiana and U.S. drug laws.

Mine was an appeal of first impression. This means that there is no Indiana case law on the jurisdictional issues that I raised. As I will soon explain, even after the case was concluded, there is still no Indiana case law on the issues.

My briefs showed 1) that Indiana Code 9-30-3-8, which is cited on traffic tickets to establish the subject matter of judicial courts, refers instead to courts under authority of the Commissioner of the BMV – and not to courts in the judicial branch, 2) that the Indiana constitution and statutes require an injury – not just an infraction – for a party to enter a judicial court for a remedy, and 3) that regulated drivers have legal rights to administrative due process in Indiana's executive branch, before having to face a judicial court. The Court of Appeals upheld the denial of my motion to dismiss without addressing any of these three issues. As I told the U.S. Supreme Court, that omission was itself a violation of my due process.

At www.drugsarelegal.com/appealdocs.html you can read the Court of Appeals' memorandum decision, the state of Indiana's only response to my four appellate briefs, and my Indiana and U.S. Supreme Court briefs, neither of which the Indiana Attorney General's office ever addressed. [482]

As this record shows, the Indiana Court of Appeals' memorandum decision, 1) failed to address any of the issues that I raised, 2) rendered a decision on the merits without addressing the Court's lack of authority to do so, which was the main issue in the matter, 3) cited insufficient law, 4) libeled my legal work as "without merit," and 5) imposed neither a *stare decisis* nor *res judicata* ruling upon me or anyone else.

In other words, no one – including the state of Indiana – can cite the memorandum decision as being a precedent in someone's future challenge to a judicial court's jurisdiction over infractions. Nor can the case be used to prevent me from raising the same subject matter jurisdiction issue again in another court, over another infraction. The Court's memorandum decision was very, very unusual to me 1) because it did not address the issues I raised, and 2) because the decision applied to me and no one else. Hmmmmm.

> When I went to law school, no one told me that appellate courts could render private justice, but apparently they do. [483] What is private justice?
>
> It is when a branch of government makes up rules only for one private person, such as the Court's memorandum decision did for me. Because this short decision has no *res judicata* effect on me or any *stare decisis* effect on me or anyone else, it essentially says: "These are the rules only for Kurt St. Angelo in this instance. They are good enough for him, but are not good enough for anyone else."
>
> Clearly, this is the effect of the Court's memorandum decision in my infraction matter. This would be like the IRS arbitrarily charging each of us different tax rates. Everyone will have to litigate this issue just as I did, and no one is guaranteed better justice than I received, or even on the same grounds.
>
> Of course, this dispensing of private justice is reprehensible in and inimical to the republican form of government. If the law isn't good enough for everyone, then it is not good enough to be written down for anyone, eh? As a litigant, I have a substantive right to equal protection, which subsumes that judicial decisions will apply not only to me, but to everyone else in my commercial class.

As this book shows, courts may not dispense private justice toward individuals, and yet call themselves judicial or republican. In the absence of a better description, and to be generous, we have called such courts non-republican. They are non-republican because they do not respect the republican form of government's separation of powers, wherein the executive branch regulates commerce.

Quite obviously, such faulty governance does not respect anything in the law – its premises, its divisions of power, its logic, its purposes. Not only the trying of my infraction in a judicial court, but also the memorandum decision in my appeal, shows just how unaccountable that Indiana's courts have become, and how far they have strayed from their proper roles.

The proper roles and jurisdiction of Indiana's Circuit and Superior courts are prescribed at IC 33-28-1-2 and IC 33-29-1-1.5. These functions are 1) to adjudicate civil and criminal cases and 2) to serve as an appellate court for lesser courts, such as the administrative law courts of the Commissioner of the BMV. This does not include the power to try infractions, which are not cases, or to do the Commissioner's work, which is regulatory.

The memorandum decision in my infraction appeal is also the result of secret justice. For example, it does not reveal its false premise, i.e., that the Indiana legislature defines the subject matter jurisdiction of Indiana's judicial courts. As well, it does not address its glaring contradiction to the Indiana Supreme Court in *Gallup v. Schmidt* (1900), which wrote that "The courts are open to those only who are injured." [484] The Court's reasoning is secret.

The Indiana Court of Appeals owed me a duty to address the merits of my challenges to its jurisdiction before it did anything else, as I twice told it. "It is the duty of a court, including this court," wrote the Indiana Court of Appeals in *Dailey Oil, Inc. v. Jet Star, Inc.* (1995), "to determine whether it has jurisdiction before it proceeds to determine the rights of the parties on the merits." [485]

Procedurally, after the Court of Appeals issued its memorandum decision, I asked it to reconsider this ruling. When it denied this request, I appealed to the Indiana Supreme Court and then to the U.S. Supreme Court, both courts which declined to exercise their discretionary appellate jurisdiction over the matter.

Thus, it was the Court of Appeals' memorandum decision that I appealed to the Indiana and U.S. Supreme Courts, and it was the refusal of the Court of Appeals and of the Indiana Attorney General's office to address the constitutional and statutory issues that I raised in my briefs that caused me to write this book. These issues were strictly about the misuse of prosecutorial and judicial power. Such significant issues required a public ruling, and one on the merits – not a private ruling that perversely, superficially and secretly litigated only my legal rights.

Not only did none of the courts address my arguments, but the Indiana Attorney General did not even respond to, or try to refute, the last three briefs that I wrote, respectively to the Indiana Court of Appeals, the Indiana Supreme Court and the U.S. Supreme Court. Can you imagine a state Attorney General not responding to a 3-part argument, made to the highest court in the land, that said his office was falsely enforcing the state's traffic laws, which was tantamount to defrauding traffic defendants into the wrong courts that had no subject matter jurisdiction and that violated defendants' right to substantive due process?

Needless to say, according to Rule 1.2 of the Indiana Rules of Professional Conduct (for attorneys), the Attorney General "shall not counsel a client to engage, or assist a client, in conduct that the lawyer knows is criminal or fraudulent..." My numerous briefs put Indiana Attorney General Greg Zoeller on notice that the state of Indiana is committing a fraud by knowingly misrepresenting judicial courts as those courts referred to by the citation of 9-30-3-8 on Indiana traffic tickets. Instead, this citation refers to administrative law courts under authority of the Commissioner of the BMV in the executive branch. It is this misrepresentation by the state's executive branch that induces Indiana motorists into the wrong courts.

Equally, with regard to the war on drugs, the Indiana Attorney General has at least constructive knowledge that his power to enjoin violations of the Controlled Substances Act at IC 35-48-3-3(i) is the state's ultimate remedy (power) against unwanted drug dealing. [486] Thus, he knows or should know that his directing of Indiana prosecutors to falsely prosecute drug possession and dealing matters in judicial courts is to exceed his client's authority under equity, and to misrepresent the law to judicial courts.

Equally, to knowingly regulate favored drug dealers in equity while prosecuting disfavored drug dealers as criminals is to misrepresent and falsely apply the Indiana Controlled Substances Act, and to violate disfavored drug dealers' rights to administrative due process and equal protection.

The Attorney General should know this. I outlined the state's improprieties in the enforcement of both drug and traffic laws in a letter to him and Governor Mitch Daniels in 2011, which neither answered. (You can read the letter at: www.drugsarelegal.com/appealdocs.html. To me, it is remarkable how correct this letter was, despite that I wrote it with only about a twentieth of the knowledge on the subject that I now possess.)

Not ironically, prior to running for office, Governor Daniels headed up the legal department of the Eli Lilly pharmaceutical company. (He was also busted for a marijuana "offense" in college.) If anyone knows the U.S. and Indiana Controlled Substances Acts, it would be Eli Lilly's attorneys. Likely above all other attorneys in the state of Indiana who have read the act, they would 1) know how drug dealing is regulated and 2) know that drug dealing is not criminal.

Otherwise, the company's legal department would have to maintain an active criminal defense section. As we saw in the discussion of the *United States v. Federal Express* (2014) indictment in chapter 25, corporations like Eli Lilly are not subject to criminal law because they operate in equity. If they do things that the state does not like, then these activities or the company can be enjoined.

Corporate officers and employees are subject to criminal law within America's republics (because natural persons are subject to the law jurisdiction), but their commercial enterprises are not. Instead, commercial businesses operate under the non-criminal rules of equity, whose sovereign is either Congress or a state legislature, and whose sovereign's remedies are equitable.

Thus, it is almost incomprehensible that neither former Governor Daniels nor former Attorney General Greg Zoeller would not know 1) that commerce – including unwanted drug commerce – operates under non-criminal equity, 2) that the state's police power with regard to commerce is regulatory – not judicial, and 3) that to enjoin unwanted commercial behavior, such as drug dealing or fast driving, is the Attorney General's and the state's greatest power against such.

Yet somehow both the Attorney General and the former Governor never drew the right conclusions from these premises, or never would admit to them – to wit that both drug dealing and driving are to be regulated in the executive branch. Nonetheless these state officers are presumed to know this. This is not just because I informed them of it. This is because – as this book serves to explain – it is the law.

State officials have a duty to know and enforce the law. Given their roles, this is a self-evident natural duty. It does not need to be written down, and its willful breach is *malum in se* and subject to criminal sanction.

Ignoring the big bump under the rug

Essentially, by rendering a private ruling that applied only to me, the Indiana Court of Appeals merely – and with great cowardice – put off the inevitable. Metaphorically, its failure to address the legal issues in my appeal was like irresponsibly kicking a can down the road for someone else to pick up.

It is like sweeping an elephant under the rug and hoping a higher court would not make note of the big bump. Yet literally, this false process robbed me of justice and robbed the public of a right to know how they are to be treated in traffic infraction matters.

This is not to ignore that all of the courts' decisions in this appeal also allowed the above-cited misrepresentation or fraud to continue. When it was reported to them, every government official who was intimate with this matter – i.e., an Indiana State Police officer, a county prosecutor, a Circuit Court trial judge, the Indiana Attorney General, a Deputy Attorney General and members of Indiana's two highest courts – had a duty to stop the state's misrepresentations (or to look into them). Each of these govern-ment officials failed this duty and allowed these misrepresentations to continue. (Crime is okay if government does it.)

This driving infraction matter was the only, the proper and the per-fect opportunity for them all to address the issues that I raised and to put an end to the fraud, but none of them did. Sometimes opportunities like my challenge happen only once, and officials must not only do their jobs, but seize the day to squarely address them. Instead, they each abdicated their duties, likely out of fear of shaking up the political status quo, which was not supposed to be one of their judicial considerations.

In other words, I wrote this book because every level of the justice system in Indiana completely broke down. By bringing my issues all the way to the U.S. Supreme Court, at considerable personal expense, I gave state officials every good faith opportunity to discuss the big bump under the carpet on its merits, which every single one of them chose not to do.

I pointed out these repeated refusals to them in my briefs along the way because ignoring significant issues is not how the adversarial legal system is supposed to operate. I think I paid $250 for the right to petition the Court of Appeals, and all I got was a false and frivolous decision that would fit on a lousy t-shirt.

Given this, I imagine that the judicial system will break down again if I would bring an even bigger elephant into the room, i.e., the impropriety of using judicial courts to wage the fraudulent war on drugs. With regard to misusing courts to falsely prosecute drug dealers, this bump would be even bigger and more obvious than that from the state's false enforcement of traffic infractions.

This is because the consequences of governments' abusive process toward drug use and dealing have been far more devastating than those of its false process against driving too fast. Not only in drug matters are judicial courts misused, but worse, they are misused to enslave and libel people, instead of just to commit highway robbery.

When the judiciary subjectively defines judicial jurisdiction, instead of by using constitutional, statutory and natural criteria, i.e., injury, then it automatically violates the 13th Amendment and defendants' substantive due process by indenturing people with compulsory process based on arbitrary standards. As well, when courts are consumed in raising state revenue by falsely enforcing traffic infractions, it should go without saying that someone is steering them wrong.

The person steering Indiana prosecutors to wrongly prosecute infractions and false drug "crimes" in judicial courts is the Indiana Attorney General. The persons responsible for the misuse of the judicial branch to adjudicate infractions and other *malum prohibita* are prosecutors, judges and justices, who are presumed to know their courts' jurisdiction. These officials are also trained to know fraud, and are ultimately responsible for protecting Hoosiers from it, which they also have failed to do. In fact, they are all participants in the fraud.

All relevant Indiana law that we have looked at – its constitutional law, its statutory law, and its case law – leads to the same logical conclusions, to wit 1) that both traffic infractions and drug dealing "offenses" are under the authority of Indiana's executive branch, not its judicial branch, and 2) that both driving and drug dealing are subject to the equity jurisdiction of the Indiana republic, not to the state's law jurisdiction – which is to say, not to the state's criminal law jurisdiction. The public relies on law enforcers, Attorneys General, prosecutors, judges and justices to know this information which, despite my numerous attempts to inform them – in the most formal, firmest but gentlest of ways – they have refused to believe is true, and yet with nothing to show for their false and religious beliefs.

This denial is the result of their state religion, which is an element of all non-republican forms of government. All non-republics are based on artificial, false and unprovable premises, such as the divine right of kings. Republics are based on natural and objective criteria, which are to be used to identify crimes, determine jurisdictions and verify the eligibility of people to certain leadership roles.

Officials' false criminal processes, their false jurisdictions and their false "Presidents" are religious in nature because they cannot be proven by either natural evidence or by positive law authority. That is, there is neither natural nor positive law authority for false "crimes," false "jurisdictions" and false "Presidents" within America's republics.

For example, the three statutes in the memorandum decision that the Indiana Court of Appeals uses to substantiate judicial courts' subject matter jurisdiction over infractions, i.e., IC 33-33-51-1(b), IC 33-28-3-2(b), and IC 33-28-3-8(a), do not even mention primary or subject matter jurisdiction, and thus cannot grant such power.

The latter statute states that "(t)he minor offenses and violations docket has jurisdiction over . . . All infraction cases." This statute actually refers to an Indiana Circuit Court's appellate jurisdiction under IC 33-28-1-2. To claim that these three statutes, [487] which do not mention subject matter jurisdiction, can confer subject matter jurisdiction is logically unprovable.

Likewise unprovable is Barack Obama's natural right as a natural born citizen to occupy the office of U.S. President. This right would be objectively provable only if he has the DNA of a U.S. citizen father. As with crime, being a natural born citizen is a provable fact of Nature.

To convince government officials of these proofs would be to confront the unnatural and irrational basis of their false religious beliefs, to wit, 1) that there is no natural law basis for the definition of crime, criminal jurisdiction, marriage and U.S. Presidents in America, 2) that republican legislatures (or Supreme Court justices) define crime, criminal jurisdiction, marriage, production, lawful possession and natural born citizens instead of Nature, and 3) that republican legislatures can determine the jurisdiction of judicial courts in a manner contrary to how constitutions established both the courts' and legislatures' jurisdictions, and in a manner contrary to the separation of powers doctrine.

This is the religion of non-republicans. By definition, as we saw in chapters 5-7, non-republicans do not believe in the separation of powers (or in judicial review). Non-republics require a judiciary which is subservient to or in tandem with a monarch or a legislature, which defines their courts' jurisdiction. America's de facto non-republican courts falsely listen to legislatures, ignore the separation of powers doctrine, and offer faulty proof of their power.

This religion is steeped in the subjective and is void of natural law because it is void of logic and reason. Such irrationality can only serve as a basis for a non-republican form of government. Likewise the war on drugs can be rationalized only with such irrationality.

It can be justified only by violating the Supremacy Clause of republican constitutions and by disregarding the natural meaning of the words they use. This can only occur as a result of listening to the voice of the wrong, unnatural sovereign, i.e., the legislature (which is sovereign over equity), instead of to Nature, which is the true sovereign over criminal law.

As we have seen, the rule of law in America's republics separates authority over all activity between four categories of sovereigns. Within America's republics, three of these sovereigns revolve around the fourth, which created them. When individual sovereigns cut off their support of the other sovereigns, particularly in the form of civil disobedience, then the other sovereigns can fail.

The fraudulent war on drugs has failed because drug users have not consented to government officials' violation of their inherent natural law jurisdiction, which the judicial branch denies to them. People inherently know that they have a natural right to exchange the value of their labor for whatever property they want, even though government officials misrepresent the law to say that these people do not. This misrepresentation of law is tortious or criminals, and must stop.

Again, America's sovereigns and their positive laws are generally legit. For most intents and purposes, these sovereigns have legislated their positive law properly. However, the problem is that the agents of these legitimate sovereigns do not follow their sovereigns' good laws. As non-republicans, the rogue agents of legitimate American republics are bound to say and do anything to establish or maintain their *de facto* non-republics.

For example in *Beebe v. State* (1855), the rogue agents of the state of Indiana flagrantly and falsely argued that people in Indiana do not have natural rights, for example the natural right to possess alcohol. As pointed out by the state Supreme Court in that case, this absurd assertion is in direct conflict with the Indiana constitution, which says that people clearly do have this right.

Again, a non-republican form of government, which officials (perhaps unwittingly) wish for the state of Indiana, cannot live in a climate where people's natural rights are respected. Thus, rogue state agents must deny people's natural rights – and currently do – in order to wage their illegal war on drugs, which is in contradiction to the Indiana constitution.

For judicial courts, whose jurisdiction is over injury, to claim authority over the non-injurious exercise of natural and commercial rights is very unnatural. Making such a misrepresentation of republican law is like claiming to be at the center of the solar system, without any natural or positive law authority on which to base such a false claim.

Making and upholding the memorandum decision in my infraction appeal was merely the courts' way of claiming that the rule of law revolves around them instead of the Indiana and U.S. constitutions. The Court of Appeals' usurpation of the Indiana constitution was so complete that – without any jurisdiction – it established private law just for me in my own private Indiana.

This perfectly exemplifies the unnatural law of the ruler as opposed to the natural rule of law, which objectively required the Court to address my issues on their merits, and which such duty the Court undeniably shirked in violation of the positive law rights of all motor vehicle drivers.

One would have to ignore all the various law that I cite in this book (as government officials do) and all the law that I cited in my briefs (as officials did) to conclude that legislatures and courts do not answer to state and federal constitutions. One would have to ignore all the natural, constitutional, statutory and judicial case law cited herein, and to adopt an unnatural, religious and non-republican point of view, so as to believe that judicial courts have subject matter over *malum prohibita* within America's republics, and other unprovable concepts.

For example, we would have to adopt the artificial religion of government to believe that it is the source of our authority instead of We being the natural source of its authority. We would have to adopt an artificial religion to believe that God ordained the legislature with authority to invade our personal lives and violate our personal rights.

Likewise, we would have to adopt an artificial religion to equate natural born citizens with naturalized ones. And we would have to adopt an artificial religion to believe that we naturally owe government anything, when in fact we naturally owe duties only to other natural people. The adoption of these false and religious viewpoints would make us non-republican – instead of being free from such subjectivity and stupidity.

I certainly understand why state officials felt the need to ignore the legal issues in my infraction appeal, and to hide them under the rug. I was attempting to take out the pillars of the executive branch's entire scam to falsely enforce regulatory matters – such as driving and drug dealing – by its misuse of the state's sacrosanct judicial courts. (I never imagined that the courts would help prosecutors continue this scam.)

The judges avoided my arguments because I was directly challenging the *de facto* non-republic or dictatorship that their predecessors had falsely established in Indiana, which they innocently inherited and by which they were trained. When these judges sought to address the arguments in my briefs, they were confronted by the fact that the use of Indiana's courts to adjudicate traffic infractions is not based on any objective positive law that they could legitimately cite.

None. This why the Court of Appeals did not cite any statute that mentioned a judicial court's primary or subject matter jurisdiction over infractions, which was the matter's only issue.

Far from granting judicial subject matter jurisdiction over traffic infractions, the Indiana motor vehicle statutes are written to secure drivers' legal rights to administrative due process in the executive branch, which the judicial branch denies. As I wrote in the introduction to this book, judicial authority over infractions exists only in judges' heads because it does not exist on paper – in the positive law. Thus, judicial authority over infractions and drug matters is based on pure religion – void of Nature, logic and even positive law authority.

Believing in such unnatural powers of government, as with a belief in Santa Claus, are just symptoms of the state religion under which most American attorneys have been falsely raised. As I mentioned much earlier, criminal attorneys practice either real law (based on natural objective criteria, such as injury) or they practice religion (based on subjectivity and beliefs in supernatural powers of legislatures).

If the Court of Appeals had had good law on its side, as my side of the legal matter did, then it would not have rendered a memorandum decision, which had no *stare decisis* or *res judicata* value. The Court would have also offered more substantial justification for the trial court's subject matter jurisdiction than three irrelevant statutes.

As well, it would have answered the issues that I raised: 1) whether the court referred to at IC 9-30-3-8 (on the traffic ticket) is an administrative law court or a judicial court, 2) whether injury is still required to invoke a judicial court's subject matter jurisdiction, and 3) whether I was owed administrative due process over my speeding infraction. These are very simple questions that have very simple and obvious answers, but they are not the answers to which Indiana officials, who are working for a *de facto* non-republic, wanted to admit.

Ultimately the courts ignored that subject matter jurisdiction is con-ferred upon Indiana's judicial courts exclusively at IC 33-28-1-2 and IC 33-

29-1-1.5, which does not mention infractions. More fundamentally, the courts ignored that their subject matter jurisdiction is determined by the state constitution, which also does not mention infractions.

The false enforcement of traffic and drug laws has served the political status quo, but it has not served the written or natural constitutional law. As we have seen, this status quo is the process of defrauding defendants into false courts and shaking them down without subject matter jurisdiction and due process.

Whether in traffic or drug matters, to admit to have operated outside the law for tens of years would be quite embarrassing to those responsible for the law's proper enforcement. (In hindsight, it would have been less embarrassing for government officials to have dealt with these issues in the proper, judicial forum than in this public forum.) And to say the least, to actually follow the law will be very consequential to a state government that is presently doing it wrongly with regard to controlled substances and traffic infractions (and likely prostitution and guns as well).

Face the music. Don't deface the music.

Given that the drug war is exposed as a fraud, then if I was a government official, I would want to be on the right side of this issue immediately, particularly before the first court agrees with the conclusions in this book. In America's republics, these conclusions are: 1) that individuals have a natural and statutory right to lawfully possess drugs, 2) that drug commerce is regulated, not criminally prohibited and 3) that future victims of false arrest and enforcement have causes of action for the injury done to them. Points 1 and 2 above were two of the holdings of *Beebe v. State* (1855). [488] Without a change to the Indiana constitution, this case exposes the state's current practices as lawless and civilly actionable.

Both the false enforcement of the Indiana motor vehicle code and of the state's drug laws involve unlawfully using Indiana's judicial courts to perform administrative law functions against drivers and drug dealers, who are instead to be regulated by the executive branch. Because regulation is primarily non-judicial, this false practice violates not only the motor vehicle and drug codes, but also the state constitution's separation of powers doctrine and defendants' right to administrative due process.

This false process has effectively eliminated one whole legal step that the state of Indiana owes to all drug dealers and traffic violators, i.e., administrative due process in the executive branch. It also defrauds them prematurely into a judicial court, where they have been falsely fined or imprisoned for a non-criminal equitable matter, before the state exhausts its equitable administrative remedies.

Ultimately, drug dealing and driving too fast are regulatory violations that operate in a separate judicial jurisdiction from criminal law. Because equity has no criminal authority, then it is quite egregious for drug dealers and other regulation violators to be enslaved and / or fined instead of just being regulated.

The war on drugs is egregious because it is modern slavery. It causes people to be enslaved without the commission of crime, as is required by the 13th Amendment. Because of its now-obvious illegality and egregiousness, executive branch officials should immediately end the state's false practices. This would be to mitigate damages that their false enforcement of the law has inflicted upon their past victims. Because of the now-obviousness of the state's regulatory structure, no judicial litigation should be necessary to accomplish the drug war's end.

Based on the false treatment that I received in my infraction appeal, I chose not to use the judicial system to single-handedly try to stop the state's false enforcement of its drug laws, as I tried to do with traffic laws. Instead, 1) I will rely on government officials to correct their own behavior by freeing all non-criminals and by administratively enforcing all traffic and drug controls in the future, 2) I will rely on criminal defense attorneys to assert the ultimate user defense, to challenge subject matter jurisdiction of judicial courts in drug matters, and to get drug clients out of jail, 3) I will rely on malpractice attorneys to pressure recalcitrant defense attorneys to face the music, and 4) I will rely on civil rights attorneys to seek damages for arrogant and stubborn state actors who are now – based on the information in this book – put on notice that they are knowingly and unlawfully acting under false color of law.

No longer may these actors hide behind their ignorance. *Idem est scire aut scire debet aut* potuisse, repeats a legal maxim. *To be able to know is the same as to know.* State officials have always had the duty to properly enforce the drug laws. Now they have the knowledge to do this.

In a republican judicial system a) that works properly, b) that leaves political questions to the political branches, c) that adjudicates cases instead of *malum prohibita*, d) that uses logic, objectivity and reasoning instead of religion to determine judicial subject matter jurisdiction and U.S. Presidents; and e) that does not render private and secretly reasoned justice without public effect – then a well honed salvo by one person, such as me, should have been enough to bring down this fraudulent non-republican Goliath. I wrote this book because my salvo did not.

But why did it not?

It is because the state's judiciary did not require the state's giant motor-vehicle fraud to show up for battle, but instead hid it under the rug. This was to allow the fraud to continue so as to not shake up the state's political status quo and money train. This was to serve politics instead of to serve the law, i.e., the Indiana and U.S. constitutions, to which everyone involved in the matter had sworn to uphold.

This usurpation and faulty justice caused me write this book. This process caused me to study and learn law as I never had before, which has been very rewarding. In retrospect, because of this knowledge and for the motivation that they provided me to complete this book, I am now very grateful to all the law's usurpers and non-defenders. Their bad made good.

All is well that will end well. Although the Philistines claimed a temporary victory – figuratively saying that my accurate salvo could not hit the broad side of a barn – this book is ultimately a more powerful weapon against their misuse of government than my old trusty sling.

31
A few concluding and parting thoughts

Ben Franklin, your republic is gone

In the notes of Dr. James McHenry, one of Maryland's delegates to the Constitutional Convention in 1787, the author includes a famous anecdote about Benjamin Franklin on the closing day of the convention.

"A lady asked Dr. Franklin, Well Doctor what have we got a republic or a monarchy. A republic replied the Doctor if you can keep it." [489]

In retrospect, Benjamin Franklin might have been more accurate. On one hand, he could have said "... a republic, if you don't forget what one is...," which essentially is what has happened. On the other hand, if Franklin believed at the time that Congress need not be republican in the federal areas, then he might have answered, "Both. You have gotten both a republic and a monarchy, if you can keep them separate."

Nonetheless, Franklin's real answer (and the ones I make up for him) can <u>only</u> be understood in terms of the duality of natural and positive law in America's constitutions. Without knowing about this duality, about the existence of the natural law jurisdiction and about its operation in defining crime and citizenship, then political scientists and lawyers have been merely guessing at what Franklin's statement actually meant.

They have been guessing because they have not known what republics are. That a war on drugs is waged in the United States is self-proof that at least its officials do not know the meaning of a republican form of government, which maintains a law jurisdiction that secures people's rights.

Franklin was saying that the constitutional convention gave us a republic as long as we could keep the positive law of kings and congresses out of the natural law jurisdiction of individuals, and out of the law jurisdiction of judicial courts. This includes securing the natural political rights of natural born citizens, for whom the republic exists.

That is the only thing that his statement could have meant. It was strictly the result of his knowing the difference between a republic and a monarchy, of knowing the separate roles of natural law and positive law, and of his knowing the differences between the criminal law jurisdiction of republics and either a) the equity jurisdiction of republican governments or b) the plenary criminal jurisdiction of the U.S. non-republic. Franklin's statement was essentially jurisdictional, as is the argument in this book – that we could keep the republic if we could keep the powers of monarchs out of the republican form of government, which Americans sadly have not.

As I wrote in previous chapters, it is solely the law jurisdiction of our judicial courts that judicially secures (or does not secure) America's republics from being non-republics. To prevent a non-republic from invading the jurisdiction of individuals, the law jurisdiction has judicial authority only over injury to people and their rights, including their natural right of citizenship. This objective standard exists so that rulers cannot dictate what crimes are or what Presidents are, and so government will install only real Presidents and enslave only real criminals who harm other people.

Based on this substantive principle, the law jurisdiction is not subject to a king's whimsical definitions or *malum prohibita*. Likewise, to prevent the U.S. presidency from being occupied by a foreign king, and to cause it to be representative of the nation's organic citizens, the U.S. is to elect its Presidents from the ranks of natural born citizens. Further, titles of nobility and the establishment of a state religion are constitutionally prohibited to also prevent a non-republican form of government. [490]

Securing the natural law jurisdiction's preeminence in our constitutions in these manners was the Founders' brilliant way to deny both the preeminence of a king's dictatorial power and a means for a non-republican government to invade the U.S. republic. Their brilliance can be recognized and extolled only by acknowledging the duality between natural and positive law that they built into the U.S. constitution, and the role that natural law plays as a check upon positive law. This form of check and balance was largely forgotten and stripped from the operation of law before most of us were born.

Without knowing about these two jurisdictions, no one can really say what is so special about the U.S. and most state constitutions. Without recognizing these two jurisdictions, there is no basis to discuss America's constitutional exceptionalism, or to even have a constitutional discussion.

All so-called republican governments in the United States that do not recognize the natural law jurisdiction of individuals are by definition non-republican. Recognition of the natural law in the law jurisdiction is what separates America's exalted justice from most other forms.

It is the recognition of the natural law jurisdiction, the establishment of the law jurisdiction in judicial courts to secure it, and the securing of natural physical and political rights of U.S. citizens that makes the U.S. constitution unusual and revolutionary. This significance is dethroned by non-republicans who deny the constitutional and natural law definitions of tort, crime, victim, natural born citizen, ultimate users, marriage, production and lawful possession – all and only which secure people's natural God-given rights under a republican form of government.

A big part of keeping the republic, so to speak, is to keep each branch of government within the separation of powers established by America's constitutions. This separation of powers requires not only that the branches of government keep their subject matter jurisdiction separate from each other, and from individual sovereigns, but that the judicial branch keep its natural law (law) and positive law (equity) jurisdictions separate. This is so that positive law statutes under equity do not get imposed upon natural persons operating outside of commerce in their own natural capacities.

The central idea of American law is this: that as long as people do not enter commerce or harm others, then they are to be free and sovereign in their own natural law jurisdiction, which is to be free from the positive law of legislatures. The judicial branch is to know, recognize and protect this individual jurisdiction by the enforcement of the previously discussed substantive rights.

These are rights that must be secured <u>from</u> kings and legislatures for the exercise and fulfillment of U.S. citizens' natural rights to life, to liberty, to property, to the pursuit of happiness and to a representative government led by natural born citizens. Only in this manner can America's constitutional republics be preserved.

Government officials who refuse to secure the law jurisdiction for the nation's individual sovereigns are by definition non-republican. These are deniers of natural law. That they have not known this until the publication of this book shows how effective the *de facto* non-republic has been at lying to all of us, or keeping all of us in the dark, about the meaning of a republican form of government. For most attorneys, like me, the topic was hardly discussed in our law schools.

You can keep the republic, Franklin told us, if you can keep the Laws of Nature and the positive law of monarchs separate, and if you can keep the branches of government from sleeping with each other in violation of the sovereignty of U.S. citizens. If you cannot, Franklin was saying, and if your courts allow the legislature and executive branch to encroach into that area reserved for natural persons, i.e., the natural law jurisdiction, whose power in that jurisdiction is to be sovereign and equal to kings, then you convert citizens into subjects and the republics into monarchies. As well, Franklin might have told us, you can keep the republic only if you can secure the superior natural political rights of natural born citizens, including their right to have a President who is a natural born citizen.

Ben Franklin warned us to keep the republic, but the lady in James McHenry's anecdote failed to follow up with the logical question: "But Mr. Franklin, can you succinctly tell us how to keep the republic?"

"Yes," Franklin might have said, "by keeping the positive law of legislatures out of the criminal law jurisdiction of judicial courts, thereby securing the natural rights of citizens from the whims of American legislatures."

Just a little more information from Ben Franklin, based on a slightly deeper inquiry, might have changed the story and saved the U.S. republic from its current non-republican takeover.

On second thought, naaaaaaah. Only better information than Franklin's pompous and hurried lesson – and a lot more civic consciousness – can restore America's republican form of government, and give the United States any chance of reclaiming their former greatness.

Try disputing these conclusions

In the previous chapters, using the law of Indiana as an example, we have drawn the following conclusions:

- that drug possession is lawful in America's republics because people have a natural unalienable right of acquiring, possessing and defending property (see Article I, Section 1 of the Indiana constitution (1816)), as well as a natural unalienable right of intoxication (see the 9th Amendment to the U.S. constitution);

- that drug possession is legal because drug users are not required to register with the Indiana State Board of Pharmacy (see IC 35-48-3-3(a)) or with the U.S. Attorney General (see 21 USC 822(a)), and they have a statutory, legal right to "lawfully possess" drugs for their own use and that of the households (see IC 35-46-3-3(e)(3) and 21 USC 822(c));

- that drug possession and dealing are lawful because the law jurisdiction of Indiana's judicial courts, which is the only criminal jurisdiction in Indiana, has authority only over injury to one's person, property or reputation (see Article I, Section 12 of the Indiana constitution (1851));

- that crimes are torts as defined by natural law to include a victim (see Article I, Section 13 of the Indiana constitution (1851))

- that drug dealers have a statutory legal right to administrative due process regarding their manufacture, distribution and dispensing of drugs (see IC 4-21.5-3 and IC 35-48-3)

- that Indiana's drug enforcers have authority to shut down and confiscate the fruits of unwanted drug-dealing operations (see IC 16-42-20-1), but no power to incarcerate people merely for being in the business or commerce of drugs (see the 18th and 21st Amendments and *Beebe v. State* (1855) [491],

- that Indiana prosecutors have authority to move for drug contraband to be judicially forfeited (see IC 34-24-1-3(a)) and the state Attorney General has authority to move to enjoin unwanted drug dealing (see IC 35-48-3-3(i)), but neither office has power to criminally prosecute people merely for being in the business of drugs (see the 18th and 21st Amendments and *Beebe v. State* (1855) [492]).

- that because of the Supremacy Clause at Article VI of the U.S. constitution and at Article I, Section 25 of the Indiana constitution (1851), that because IC 1-1-2-1 says that the Indiana legislature must legislate consistently with the Indiana and U.S. constitutions, and that because IC 33-28-1-5(2) says that Indiana courts must rule consistently with the constitutions, the words "case," "criminal case," "crime," "offense," "felony" and "misdemeanor" as used in the Indiana Code, must match the meaning of the same words case, criminal case, crime, offense, felony and misdemeanor as used in the Indiana and / or U.S. constitutions.

- that because the Indiana constitution created the subject matter jurisdiction of the Indiana judicial courts, then the state legislature may not change or enlarge the subject matter jurisdiction of state judicial courts, by redefining the meaning of case, criminal case, crime, offense, felony and misdemeanor, without a constitutional amendment,

- that, in any regard, a constitutional amendment is required to change the subject matter jurisdiction of the state's republican judicial courts in order to criminalize any business within Indiana (see the 13th, 18th and 21st Amendments to the U.S. Constitution and *Beebe v. State* (1855); [493] and

- that enslaving people for non-criminal behavior – as crime is referred to by the 13th Amendment to the U.S. constitution and at Article I, Section 37 of the Indiana constitution (1851) – amounts to illegal slavery.

As well, we have learned the following facts about federal law:

- that the United States' criminal jurisdiction is largely territorial, that Congress has criminal jurisdiction within the states only over crimes related to its enumerated powers, and that Congress criminally prohibits drug dealing only within the federal areas;

- that Article III courts have subject matter jurisdiction only over injury, which excludes jurisdiction over the exercise of natural rights within America's republics, such as drug possession, and over the criminalization of non-injurious business practices within the republics, such as drug dealing, the latter which are subject to non-criminal regulation under equity;

- that a constitutional amendment is required to change the subject matter jurisdiction of Article III courts in order to criminalize any business within the state republics (see the 13th, 18th and 21st Amendments to the U.S. Constitution);

- that, at most, only plenary Article I courts have criminal jurisdiction over non-injury and non-injurious business practices, and which occur within the federal areas, as proscribed by Congress;

- that drug dealing is not a crime related to an enumerated Congressional power under Article I, Section 8 of the U.S. constitution, but is instead a business activity subject to regulation under Congress'

Interstate Commerce Clause (see Article I, Section 8, Clause 3 of the U.S. Constitution); and

- that the U.S. republic is to treat all interstate commerce (except for the commerce in slaves, which is a state crime) as regulated – non-criminal – activity, subject to the non-criminal equity jurisdiction of its republican administrative law courts, whose remedies must first be exhausted before judicial authority is invoked.

These statements lead to the inevitable conclusions that drug possession is a natural right, that drug dealing is a regulated activity, and that to lawfully treat either a natural right or a business as a crime within the Indiana republic requires an amendment to the state's constitution, just as the 18th Amendment was required to criminalize the commerce of alcohol nationwide.

Indiana officials can point to no changes in the Indiana or U.S. constitutions which authorize their arrest, prosecution, conviction or incarceration of unwanted drug users and dealers in Indiana, except those drug dealers who injure others or who violate judicial injunctions not to deal drugs. This is to say that to criminalize non-crimes on a *de facto* basis, with absolutely no positive law authority, is for officials themselves to commit torts or crimes on behalf of their state religion, just as the agents of King George III did prior to the nation's independence.

Busted: the war on drugs is the epitome of meritlessness

As we have seen, there is nothing more frivolous than the legal and social justifications for the war on drugs, which necessarily violates not only state and federal constitutions, but republican statutory law as well. The drug war exists – not because republican law mandates or allows it – but because government officials do not follow republican law. This makes their drug war undeniably lawless.

Not only will officials' justifications be scant, but their legal justifications will literally have no weight compared to the force and effect of the primary law that we have read in this book. For example, Indiana officials will point to IC 35-48-4 to say that cocaine possession and dealing are "felonies," and are thus subject to years of incarceration. However, this subjective, religious and insubstantial opinion will necessarily ignore:

1. that property possession is an unalienable natural right in

Indiana (see Article I, Section 1 of the Indiana constitution (1816), the 9th Amendment to the U.S. constitution, and *Beebe v. State* (1855), [494]

2. that drug users have a statutory, legal right to "lawfully possess" drugs for their own use and the use of their households (see IC 35-48-3-3(e) and 21 USC 822(c)),

3. that the Indiana State Board of Pharmacy has primary jurisdiction over the manufacture, distribution and dispensing of drugs in Indiana, but not over drug possession (see IC 35-48-3-3),

4. that Indiana's judicial courts have subject matter jurisdiction over injury, but not over drug possession or drug commerce, which cause no injury (see Article I, Section 12 of the Indiana constitution (1851)),

5. that Indiana judicial courts also have appellate jurisdiction over decisions made by administrative law courts and administrative agents concerning commercial *malum prohibita* (see IC 4-21.5-5),

6. that this is to ensure that commercial persons are accorded administrative due process by the executive branch (see IC 4-21.5-3), which is to exhaust all its administrative remedies before invoking judicial power,

7. that people may be enslaved only for the commission of crime (see the 13th Amendment and Article I, Section 37 of the Indiana constitution (1851)),

8. that crime is defined by (natural) law to involve victims of injury (see Article I, Section 13 of the Indiana constitution (1851)),

9. that the words case, crime, offense, felony and misdemeanor are used in the U.S. constitution and are given meaning there,

10. that the Supremacy Clauses of the U.S. and Indiana

constitutions say that the meaning of these words will be defined by constitutions, not by inconsistent legislatures (see Article VI of the U.S. Constitution and Article I, Section 25 of the Indiana constitution (1851),

11. that legislatures must legislate consistently with constitutions and the common law (see IC 1-1-2-1),

12. that judicial courts must rule consistently with constitutions (see IC 33-28-1-5(2)),

13. that because of the separation of powers doctrine and the fact that the Indiana constitution created the jurisdiction of both the Indiana legislative and judicial branches, the Indiana legislature may not on its own authority change the subject matter jurisdiction of Indiana's judicial courts, whose jurisdiction over injury is established in the Indiana constitution, and can only be changed by a constitutional amendment, and

14. that Indiana's only rightful power is over drug commerce, that such authority is enforced in the equity jurisdiction – not the criminal law jurisdiction, and that such power is limited to getting the property of unauthorized drug operations forfeited and to enjoining unwanted drug dealing, which such powers accrue only after the state exhausts it administrative remedies.

Therefore to claim, as Indiana executive and judicial officers likely will, that a sentence in a statute book – a) which does not apply to natural persons in the law jurisdiction, b) which does not mention the word prohibit or unlawful, and c) which in fact fraudulently co-opts the constitutional word felony – is to be given judicial effect in a republic, in contradiction to the voluminous, contrary and superior law that we have herein read, is untenable and ludicrous, if not intentionally meant to misrepresent the law.

America has a *de facto* non-republic because the U.S. and state governments train and certify all officials to blindly be non-republicans, and thus to enforce and defend the wrong form of government with their monopoly over justice. That these officials are traitors to the republican form of government is not their fault, but is instead the consequence of their (and my) false education to ignore or deny the role of natural law, which is the only check upon non-republicans.

The authors and promulgators of the Controlled Substances Acts – perhaps America's greatest criminal minds of all time – knew this. Their genius as crooks was 1) to deviously write the CSAs to be both constitutional and misunderstood, and 2) to deviously misrepresent the law on controlled substances to just the right people, for example gullible state Attorneys General and prosecutors, who would then falsely enforce it in perpetuity, yet who would think that they were doing it right.

Then this monopoly on justice would unanimously defend its false enforcement of a law that few of its members had ever read or could understand (because they did not know *a priori* the laws of legislative and subject matter jurisdiction). This ignorance would only compound over time. Forty-five years later, it would culminate in the most reluctant of persons writing a book about how – as a result of this ignorance – that the republican form of government and its system of justice have broken down.

As I tried to model in my traffic infraction appeal, I would prefer to show readers how to be self-responsible. To be legally self-responsible in this day-and-age is to get a legal education – and then to never stop learning about law – merely to defend oneself against government officials' false assertions of power and other now criminal misrepresentations of law.

Confessions of an outlawyer

As I mentioned in chapter 2, I have never really practiced law. My entire "law" practice was really in equity. My whole practice, as is most attorneys', operated in a different judicial jurisdiction than law.

Consequently, I mostly attended an equity school, not a law school. I earlier referred to "law" schools as religious schools because they do not teach natural law, where Nature is sovereign over the law jurisdiction of judicial courts. Instead, they predominantly teach equity, whose sovereign is the legislature. Legislatures enact cryptic legislation mostly to not publicly acknowledge that there is a sovereign besides themselves – and a natural one at that – which reigns over their criminal law.

Today's "law" schools teach very little law, which is based on natural law. They co-opt the word law to convey some natural legitimacy, but they rarely if ever discuss the natural law basis of republican constitutions.

But "law" schools that do not teach natural law cannot by definition teach real law, which operates in the law jurisdiction. In other words, unless they teach natural law, they cannot be real law schools. They are really just equity schools, teaching the religion of the legislature, i.e., that it is sovereign over both the equity and law jurisdictions of the judicial branch.

Given this, if you ask most "criminal" attorneys in America where they got their law degrees, their universal answer should be: "from a Cracker Jack box." A diploma from one of these equity schools certifies that students are taught little or nothing:

- about the natural law basis of the U.S. constitution,
- about the territoriality of legislative (and thus criminal) jurisdiction (and its handful of exceptions),
- about the existence and distinctions between the U.S. republic (operating among the states) and the U.S. non-republic (operating in the federal areas),
- about the meaning of a republican form of government,
- about the natural law basis of crime, marriage and citizens,
- about the distinctions between foreigners and U.S citizens,
- about the distinctions between natural born citizens and citizens of the United States,
- about the distinctions between the law and equity jurisdictions,
- about the distinctions between natural persons and artificial persons,
- about the roles and jurisdictions of administrative and criminal law,
- about how almost all subject matter is subject to only one sovereign at a time, and
- about America's four sovereigns, as recognized in its constitutions and statutes.

These educational omissions – which are essentially over the roles of the natural and positive law jurisdictions – result in attorneys unconsciously upholding America's *de facto* non-republics, which are void of natural law and the separation of powers. These omissions in fact certify attorneys' incompetence to practice criminal defense law in America's republics. They ensure attorneys' inability to protect the substantive rights of their law and legal clients against such things as the fraudulent war on drugs.

Attorneys would first have to see the war on drugs as a fraud, as this book demonstrates it to be from every angle, in order to protect their clients from it. This would be almost impossible unless one studied federal criminal jurisdiction, which was not taught in the religious school that I attended. (Chapters 8 and 9 herein are a crash course in federal legislative and subject matter jurisdiction.)

In other words, if I had ever practiced criminal defense law, which I never have, then I would have been certified by the religious equity school that I attended to do it wrong. This is because, without knowing about the natural law jurisdiction of the Indiana and U.S. constitutions, then there is no defense – even with an understanding of the ultimate user provision as an affirmative defense – against the false enforcement in judicial courts of *malum prohibita*.

The only check upon the positive law authority of a legislature is the natural law jurisdiction of the individual, as secured by the law jurisdiction under republican constitutions. If individual sovereignty is not recognized by the law jurisdiction, or if it is not known by legal practitioners, then there is no basis for the protection of natural rights or for a republican form of government. These rights must be invoked by people with knowledge of them, which this book provides.

The ridding of non-republican wrongdoing and the restoration of America's republics should be Americans' chief legal and political priorities. The battle between *de jure* republican governments and their officials' unofficial non-republics is one between good and evil, right and wrong, transparency and lies, freedom and slavery, and wisdom and stupidity.

Can we all agree that it is stupid to wish a monarchy or a dictatorship upon ourselves? And should we not act to invalidate all republican imposters, starting today?

The ultimate demurrer and defense to drug "crimes"

As I was writing the above section, thinking that it might be the last in this book, it dawned on me that I had not really given you readers the real punchline to all the information that you have been absorbing. Similar to a logline of a screenplay, this punchline is something that you can easily remember that will sum up all the lessons you learned in this book about subject matter jurisdiction, about the separation of powers doctrine, and about individual sovereignty, for example.

Suppose I was arrested and charged with drug possession within a state republic, such as Indiana. Certainly I (or my attorney) could invoke a Rule 8 affirmative defense that is provided by the ultimate user provision at IC 35-48-3-3(e) and 22 USC 822(c), which we discussed in chapter 21. We could also move to dismiss the matter for want of subject matter jurisdiction, which would likely cause us to make all the laborious arguments in this book. In Indiana, we would also challenge the constitutionality of law enforcers' arrest powers granted at IC 16-42-20-1(b) and IC 35-31.5-2-217.

However, the highest form of defense is a simple sentence: "Your Honor, I move for dismissal because my client is a U.S. citizen." Or more specifically in my case: "Your Honor, I move for dismissal because my client is a natural born citizen," which is the strongest demurrer in the entire world of civilized law.

Whichever line is appropriate, it should be sufficient to stop any republican judge in his or her tracks from exercising judicial power over a drug possession or a drug dealing matter. If it is not sufficient, then some further explanation may be necessary, as follows.

"Your Honor, I move for dismissal because my client is a natural born citizen. As such, he is entitled to a republican form of government that respects his liberty and sovereignty, including his natural right to possess property. His assertion of citizenship is the highest expression of his substantive, natural and legal rights.

Because he has a natural and statutory right to possess drugs for his own use, this court has no criminal jurisdiction over his alleged drug possession. Because he is not a foreigner, then he is not naturally subject to any plenary power of Congress. Because his alleged drug possession was not commercial, he is not subject to this court's non-criminal, equitable appellate jurisdiction.

Under such a republican government – not only as a U.S. citizen, but also merely as a natural person – he is entitled to be charged for crimes only in the law jurisdiction of judicial courts, which is the state's only criminal jurisdiction. Further, he is entitled to be enslaved by the state only for crimes, as crimes are defined by injury in the Indiana and U.S. constitutions.

According to Article I, Sections 1, 12, 13 and 37 of the Indiana constitution, in the absence of an injury and a criminal victim, this court may not alienate my client from his liberty or sovereignty, or from his natural right to acquire, possess and defend personal property. Only if he is a foreigner is he naturally subject to America's equity jurisdiction. Only if he is in commerce is his commercial enterprise and property subject to the state's *malum prohibita* under equity.

Based on these grounds, I move to dismiss this matter for want of subject matter jurisdiction. Unless my client has hurt someone, then he is not subject to the (natural and criminal) law jurisdiction of this Court. Plus, I move to have his drugs, which were lawfully acquired in his non-commercial capacity and which were unlawfully taken by state agents, be returned to his lawful possession. My client is grateful to this Court and to its natural sovereign for these rights and defenses."

That the above paragraphs are subsumed in the simple demurrer "My client is a U.S. Citizen" would be lost on government officials who do not know about the meaning and types of U.S. citizenship, about the jurisdiction of republican judicial courts over injury, about the differences between the law and equity jurisdictions, about the separate roles of the judicial and executive branches, about people's natural rights to liberty and to property possession, about the differences between U.S. citizens and foreigners, about natural born citizens' sovereignty from positive law, or about the meaning of a republican form of government, based on natural law. It would be lost on officials who falsely see other people as royal subjects instead of as sovereign individuals.

This describes almost all officials in all three branches of America's governments at the time of this book's first publication. Their war on drugs and their natural born foreign "President" bespoke their lack of knowledge of republican law, which is to revolve around the sovereignty of America's citizens, particularly its natural ones.

I have written this book for the education of government officials and U.S. citizens so that its lessons about the natural law basis of crime, citizenship, and our substantive rights need never again be overlooked or forgotten. The republican form of government in America is clearly at its flashpoint. If I did not write this book, then most of the issues in it would never be addressed, or would likely not ever be seriously raised.

That the natural law basis of crime and citizenship has been forgotten or overlooked by current government officials does not mean that this situation cannot be corrected. Most easily, as this book has shown, America's republics – along with the sanity of their natural and objective standards – can be restored if government officials merely learn to properly enforce the republics' laws that are already on the books. This is generally accomplished by not exceeding statutes' delegated powers.

The true irony of the war on drugs is that it would not exist if government officials understood and followed their own statutes, instead of their subjective religion based on their belief in supernatural legislatures. In spite that drug statutes are intentionally written to turn jurisdictional distinctions into mush, these statutes nonetheless sufficiently convey to discerning readers the proper separation of powers between governments' branches and sovereign individuals, as herein described.

In a nutshell, the separation of powers within America's republics breaks down as follows with regard to drugs: Individuals have jurisdiction over drug possession. The executive branch has authority to regulate drug commerce, including the power to enjoin it.

The judicial branch has authority to adjudicate real drug crimes and to review or enforce administrative actions by regulators. Congress likely has constitutional authority to prohibit both drug possession and dealing in the federal areas. Nonetheless, absent a constitutional amendment, no American republican judicial court has criminal subject matter jurisdiction over drug possession or drug commerce, which amount to neither crimes nor even cases.

Thus, republics' police power to regulate is separate and apart from their police power to judicially prohibit. As we have seen, 1) such powers operate in separate judicial jurisdictions, over separate kinds of persons and subject matters, and 2) the power to regulate does not include the power to criminally incarcerate.

Absent a constitutional amendment, all commerce except slavery is regulated in non-criminal equity – and is not prohibited in the criminal law jurisdiction of America's republics. As reflected by the 13th Amendment, the enslavement of people for non-cases and non-crimes – as routinely occurs in America's drug war – amounts to illegal slavery.

Index

Indiana Constitution

Indiana Code

Louisiana Code

Cases

Endnotes

1 Author Kurt St. Angelo is an alumnus of the University of Sweden, 1977 (Lund, Sweden), Pomona College, 1978 (Claremont, CA), the Robert H. McKinney School of Law – Indiana University, 1986 (Indianapolis, IN), Toastmasters International, and Nicotine Anonymous. During the past thirty years, Kurt has practiced appellate law, been an entrepreneur, been active in the Libertarian Party, and written or co-written a dozen screenplays.

2 This is an endnote about the following endnotes. As you will see, my style is fairly simple. I generally write out stand-alone references, and then use *id.* (short for *idem*) to refer to the citation that is immediately above the *id.*

3 Exposé, The Free Dictionary, http://www.thefreedictionary.com/expos%C3%A9

4 *St. Angelo v. State of Indiana*, 952 N.E.2d 885 (2011), trans denied 963 N.E.2d 1116 (2012), certiorari denied 567 U.S. ___, 132 S.Ct. 2747, re: No. 11-1214 (Order List: June 11, 2012) http://www.supremecourt.gov/orders/courtorders/061112zor.pdf

5 I realized this on November 14, 2013. Before this date, I did not know what a republic is.

6 I realized this on February 15, 2014.

7 This is the teaching approach of a favorite teacher of mine: 9th grade world history teacher Jack Foster at Northview Junior High School (now Middle School), Indianapolis. Indiana 1970-1971

8 I would like to thank the library staff of my alma mater The Robert H. McKinney School of Law, Indiana University, Indianapolis, who have always been very helpful.

9 Sovereign, *Black's Law Dictionary, 5th Edition*, p. 1252

10 *Yick Wo v. Hopkins*, 118 U.S. 356, 370 (1886)

11 *Extraterritorial Application of American Criminal Law* by Charles Doyle, Congressional Research Service, 7-5700, www.crs.gov, 94-166, February 15, 2012, p. 1

12 See 18 USC 7

13 Tort, *Black's Law Dictionary, 5th Edition*, p. 1335

14 Indiana Code (IC) 35-48-3-3(i)

15 I realized this on September 11, 2012.

16 I realized this on November 25, 2014.

17 I realized this on December 20, 2012.

18 I conceived and began to write this book on August 16, 2012.

19 Republican government, *A Law Dictionary* by John Bouvier, Revised 6th Edition, 1856

20 Republic, *Black's Law Dictionary, 5th Edition*, p. 1171

21 Republican government, *A Law Dictionary* by John Bouvier, Revised 6th Edition, 1856

22 See *In re Duncan*, 139 U.S. 449, 461 (1891)

23 *Gallup v. Schmidt*, 56 N.E. 443, 445 (Ind. 1900), *aff'd*, 183 U.S. 300 (1902)

24 I realized this on December 1, 2014.

25 *Beebe v. State*, 6 Ind. 501, 510 (1855)

26 Equity, *Black's Law Dictionary, 5th Edition*, p. 484

27 Sir William Blackstone, *Commentaries on the Laws of England* (1752) ed. George Sharswood (Philadelphia: J.B. Lippincott, 1893), Volume 1, Book 1, p. 40, http://oll.libertyfund.org/titles/blackstone-commentaries-on-the-laws-of-england-in-four-books-vol-1

28 See IC 1-1-2-1

29 *Malum in se, Black's Law Dictionary, 5th Edition*, p. 865

30 *id.*

31 *Hilton v. Guyot,* 159 U.S. 113, 163 (1895)

32 See Article I, Section 12 Indiana constitution (1851)

33 Thomas Jefferson: Reply to the Citizens of Wilmington, 1809. ME 16:336

34 Article IV, Section 4 U.S. constitution

35 John F. Finerty "*State Rights under the Federal Prohibition Law,*" 8 Notre Dame Law Review, Issue 1, Article 2, p. 15, 16 (1932)

Endnotes

36 *id.*

37 *Brown v. Texas*, 443 U.S. 47 (1979)

38 My friend is Paul Guthrie, who is a leading authority on natural law. In August 2015 he published a book about natural law, called *DEMONIC POSITIVISM Versus The Science of "natural born citizen"* (ISBN 9781511911818), which I look forward to reading. The basis of the information herein about natural born citizens is from discussions with Paul.

39 Thomas Jefferson to Isaac H. Tiffany, 1819

40 *Beebe v. State*, 6 Ind. 501, 512 (1855)

41 *McIlvaine v. Coxe's Lessee*, 6 U.S. 280, 325 (1805)

42 *Brown v. Texas*, 443 U.S. 47 (1979)

43 *Illinois v. Wardlow*, 528 U.S. 119, 125 (2000)

44 *Florida v. Royer*, 460 U.S. 491, 497-498 (1983)

45 *In re Todd*, 193 N.E. 865, 873 (Ind. 1935)

46 IC 33-28-1-2, IC 33-29-1-1.5

47 *Board of Trustees of the Town (Now City) of New Haven v. City of Fort Wayne*, 375 N.E.2d 1112, 1117 (Ind. 1978)

48 *Brewington v. Lowe*, 1 Ind. 21, 23-24 (Ind. 1848)

49 IC 33-28-1-2, IC 33-29-1-1.5

50 *Gallup v. Schmidt* , 56 N.E. 443, 445 (Ind. 1900) *aff'd*, 183 U.S. 300 (1902)

51 *Whitmore v. Arkansas*, 495 U.S. 149, 155 (1990)

52 *Summers v. Earth Island Institute*, 555 U.S. 488, 497 (2009)

53 Quoting U.S. Supreme Court Justice Stephen Breyer on Fox News' Greta, September 17, 2015

54 *Aetna Life Ins. Co. v. Haworth*, 300 U.S. 227, 239 (1937)

55 *id.*

56 See IC 33-28-1-2 and IC 33-29-1-1.5 and Article I, Sections 19 and 20 of the Indiana constitution (1851)

57 Standing, *Black's Law Dictionary, 5th Edition*, p. 1260

58 *Horne v. Flores*, 129 S.Ct. 2579, 2592 (2009)

59 *Valley Forge Christian College v. Americans United for Separation of Church and State, Inc.*, 454 U.S. 464, 475-476 (1982)

60 *State ex rel. Cittadine v. Indiana Dep't of Transp.*, 790 N.E.2d 978, 979 (Ind. 2003)

61 *Baker v. Carr* , 369 U.S. 186, 198 (1962)

62 *id.*

63 *id.* at 199

64 Crime, *Black's Law Dictionary, 5th Edition*, p. 334

65 *id.*

66 *Baker v. Carr* , 369 U.S. 186, 198 (1962)

67 *State v. Sproles*, 672 N.E.2d 1353, 1356 (Ind. 1996)

68 *Herman v. State*, 272 Ind. 361, 363, 397 N.E.2d 978, 979 (1979) citing *Nichols v. State*, 127 Ind. 406, 413, 26 N.E. 839, 840 (1890)

69 Lysander Spooner (with Introduction by George H. Smith), *The Lysander Spooner Reader* (San Francisco: Fox & Wilkes, 1992) p. 23

70 *id.*

71 Thomas Jefferson to William Johnson, 1823, ME15-441

72 West's *Indiana Law Encyclopedia*, Alcoholic Beverages, § 1, citing *State ex rel Pollard v. Superior Cour of Marion County, Room 3*, 233 Ind 667, 122 N. E.2d 612 (1954)

73 Article I, Section 12 Indiana constitution (1851)

74 Article I, Section 13 Indiana constitution (1851)

Endnotes

75 Sir William Blackstone, *Commentaries on the Laws of England* (1752) ed. George
Sharswood (Philadelphia: J.B. Lippincott, 1893), Volume 2, Book IV, p. 5

76 *State ex rel. Johnson v. White Circuit Court*, 77 N.E.2d 298, 300-301 (Ind. 1948)

77 *id.*

78 *id.*

79 21 Am Jur 2d Criminal Law § 1 (2008)

80 Sir William Blackstone, *Commentaries on the Laws of England* (1752) ed. George
Sharswood (Philadelphia: J.B. Lippincott, 1893), Volume 2, Book IV, p. 5

81 *District of Columbia v. Clawans*, 300 U.S. 617, 625 (1937)

82 *District of Columbia v. Colts*, 282 U.S. 63, 72-73 (1930)

83 *id.*

84 *Board of Trustees of the Town (Now City) of New Haven v. City of Fort Wayne*, 375
N.E.2d 1112, 1116 (Ind. 1978)

85 *Allen v. Wright*, 468 U.S. 737, 752 (1984)

86 *District of Columbia v. Colts,* 282 U.S. 63, 72-73 (1930)

87 Sir William Blackstone, *Commentaries on the Laws of England* (1752) ed. George
Sharswood (Philadelphia: J.B. Lippincott, 1893), Volume 2, Book III, p. 5

88 *id.* Volume 2, Book IV, p. 5

89 *id.* Volume 2, Book III, p. 5

90 *id.*

91 *Schick v. United States* 195 U.S. 65, 67-68 (1904)

92 *id.*

93 See *Marbury v. Madison*, 5 U.S. 137, 1 Cranch 137 (1803) and *Beebe v. State*, 6 Ind 501,
508 (1855)

94 *Beebe v. State*, 6 Ind. 501, 513 (1855)

95 *Parham v. Cortese*, 407 U.S. 67, 92 S.Ct. 1983 (1994)

96 *Babineaux v. Judiciary Commission*, 341 So.2d 396, 400 (Louisiana, 1976)

97 *Osborn v. Review Bd. of Indiana Employment Sec. Division*, 381 N.E.2d 495, 500
(Ind.App. 1978) quoting *Miedreich v. Lauenstein*, 232 U.S. 236, 246 (1913)

98 *State ex rel. Benjamin v. Criminal Court of Marion County, Division No. III*, 341 N.E.2d
495, 497 (Ind. 1976)

99 *State ex rel. Hurd v. Davis*, 82 N.E.2d 82, 86 (Ind. 1948) citing *Arrowsmith v.
Harmouning, Admix. et al.*, 118 U.S. 194, 195 (1885)

100 *id.*

101 *id.*

102 *Osborn v. Review Bd. of Indiana Employment Sec. Division,* 381 N.E.2d 495, 500
(Ind.App. 1978) quoting *Miedreich v. Lauenstein,* 232 U.S. 236, 246 (1913)

103 *State ex rel. Hurd v. Davis,* 82 N.E.2d 82, 86 (Ind. 1948) citing *Arrowsmith v.
Harmouning, Admix. et al.,* 118 U.S. 194, 195 (1885)

104 *Hall v State of Indiana*, 403 N.E.2d 1382 (1980)

105 I realized this on November 24, 2014.

106 *Yick Wo v. Hopkins*, 118 U.S. 356, 370 (1886)

107 Declaration of Independence

108 *Yick Wo v. Hopkins,* 118 U.S. 356, 370 (1886)

109 Sir William Blackstone, *Commentaries on the Laws of England* (1752) ed.
George Sharswood (Philadelphia: J.B. Lippincott, 1893), Volume 1, Book I, p.
42

110 *id.* at 41

111 *id.* at 43

112 *id.* at 40

Endnotes

113 *Yick Wo v. Hopkins,* 118 U.S. 356, 370 (1886)

114 *McIlvaine v. Coxe's Lessee* , 6 U.S. 280, 323 (1805)

115 *Yick Wo v. Hopkins,* 118 U.S. 356, 370 (1886)

116 *Beebe v. State,* 6 Ind. 501, 506 (1855)

117 *Yick Wo v. Hopkins,* 118 U.S. 356, 370 (1886)

118 *id.*

119 *Beebe v. State,* 6 Ind. 501, 510 (1855)

120 *Yick Wo v. Hopkins,* 118 U.S. 356, 370 (1886)

121 *id.*

122 *id.*

123 See *Brown v. Texas,* 443 U.S. 47 (1979), *Florida v. Royer,* 460 U.S. 491, 497-498 (1983), *Illinois v. Wardlow,* 528 U.S. 119, 125 (2000)

124 Allodial, *Black's Law Dictionary, 5th Edition,* p. 70

125 IC 35-48-3-3(e)(3) and 21 USC 822(c)

126 Article I, Section1 of the Indiana constitution (1816)

127 See IC 35-48-3-3(e) and 21 USC 822(c)

128 *Beebe v. State,* 6 Ind. 501, 511 (1855)

129 See 13th Amendment and Article I, Section 37 Indiana constitution (1851)

130 Plenary, *Black's Law Dictionary, 5th Edition,* p. 1038

131 *id.*

132 Plenary, *Black's Law Dictionary, 5th Edition,* p. 1038

133 *id.*

134 *Palmore v. United States,* 411 U.S. 389, 412 (1973), Douglas dissenting

135 *Ostrow v. Samuel Brilliant Co.,* 66 F. Supp. 593, ___ (D.C. Mass. 1946)

136 *Hill v. Dorsey,* 22 F.2d 1003, 1004 (D.C. Cir. 1927)

137 *id.* citing *Keller v. Potomac Elec. Co.,* 261 U.S. 428, 443 (1922)

138 *id.*

139 *Palmore v. United States,* 411 U.S. 389, 393 (1973) quoting *Palmore v. United States,* 290 A.2d 573, 576-577 (1972)

140 *id.* at 407

141 *Kendall v. United States,* 37 U.S. 524, 526 (1838)

142 *LaForest v. Board of Commissioner of District of Columbia,* 92 F.2d 547, 67 App. D.C. 396, certiorari denied 302 U.S. 760 (1937)

143 *Palmore v. United States,* 411 U.S. 389, 412 (1973), Douglas dissent citing *District of Columbia v. Thompson,* 346 U.S. 100, 104-110 (____)

144 *Hooven & Allison Co. v. Evatt,* 324 U.S. 652, 674 (1945)

145 *id.*

146 *id.*

147 *Palmore v. United States,* 411 U.S. 389, 397-398, citing *Gibbons v. District of Columbia,* 116 U.S. 404, 408 (1886)

148 *id.*

149 *Palmore v. United States,* 411 U.S. 389, 393 (1973) quoting *Palmore v. United States,* 290 A.2d 573, 576-577 (1972)

150 21 USC 822(a)(1)

151 *id.*

152 LexusNexus® headnote in *Bevans v. United States,* 16 U.S. 336 (1818), p. 3 of 22 on LexusNexus®

153 *Palmore v. United States,* 411 U.S. 389, 393 (1973) quoting *Palmore v. United States,* 290 A.2d 573, 576-577 (1972)

154 *id.*

155 See Article II, Section 2 of the U.S. Constitution

Endnotes

156 *National Bank v. County of Yankton*, 101 U.S. 129, 133 (1879)
157 *Jurisdiction Over Federal Areas Within The States, Report of the Interdepartmental Committee for the Study of Jurisdiction Over Federal Areas Within the States*, April 1956, Part I, p. 13-14
158 *id.* Part II, p. 105, citing *Bowen v. Johnston*, 306 U.S. 19 (1939); *United States v. Unzeuta*, 281 U.S. 138 (1930); *United States v. Watkins*, 22 F. 2d 437 (N.D. Cal., 1927)
159 *id.* Part I, p. 9
160 *id.* Part II, p. 106, citing *In re Ladd*, 74 Fed. 31, 40 (C.C.N.D. Neb., 1896)
161 *Jurisdiction Over Federal Areas Within The States, Report of the Interdepartmental Committee for the Study of Jurisdiction Over Federal Areas Within the States*, April 1956, Part II, p. 106
162 *id.* at Part I, p. 45-46
163 *id.* at Part I, p. 45
164 *Caha v. United States*, 152 U.S. 211, 215 (1894)
165 *id.*
166 *Cohens v. Virginia*, 19 U.S. 264, 429, 6 Wheat. 264 (1821)
167 *Jurisdiction Over Federal Areas Within The States, Report of the Interdepartmental Committee for the Study of Jurisdiction Over Federal Areas Within the States*, April 1956, Part II, p. 107
168 18 USC 5
169 18 USC 7
170 18 USC 5
171 *U.S. v. Fox*, 95 U.S. 670, 672 (1877)
172 *id.*
173 *Bond v. United States*, 134 S. Ct. 2077, 2086, 189 L. Ed. 2d 1 (2014) [2014 BL 151637]
174 *Ohio v. Helvering*, 292 U.S. 360, 369 (1934) citing *Rippe v. Becker*, 56 Minn. 100, 111, 57 N.W. 331 (1894)
175 *Jurisdiction Over Federal Areas Within The States, Report of the Interdepartmental Committee for the Study of Jurisdiction Over Federal Areas Within the States*, April 1956, Part I, p. 45-46
176 *United States v. Lopez*, 514 U.S. 549 (1995)
177 *id.* at 554
178 See *Behlert v. James Foundation of N.Y.*, 60 F.Supp 706 (S.D.N.Y 1945), *Ostrow v. Samuel Brilliant Co.*, 66 F. Supp. 593 (D.C. Mass. 1946) and *Wilson v. Guggenheim*, 70 F.Supp. 417 (D.C.S.C. 1947)
179 *Jurisdiction Over Federal Areas Within The States, Report of the Interdepartmental Committee for the Study of Jurisdiction Over Federal Areas Within the States*, April 1956, Part II, p. 107
180 *id.*
181 *U.S. v. Fox*, 95 U.S. 670, 672 (1877)
182 *Wong Wing v. United States*, 263 U.S. 228 (1896)
183 28 USC 1251(b)(1)
184 See 21 USC 822(a)
185 8 Code of Federal Regulations Section 1003.1
186 *id.*
187 See *Personal Responsibility and Work Opportunity Reconciliation Act of 1996*, Public
    Law 104-193, August 22, 1996, 110 Stat. 2105
188 *State ex rel. Camden v. Gibson Circuit Court*, 640 N.E.2d 696, 697 (Ind. 1994)

Endnotes

189 *Utley v. State*, 281 N.E.2d 888, 889 (Ind. 1972)

190 *State ex rel. Camden v. Gibson Circuit Court,* 640 N.E.2d 696, 697 (Ind. 1994)

191 *Utley v. State,* 281 N.E.2d 888, 889 (Ind. 1972)

192 *See* IC 33-28-1-2 and IC 33-29-1-1.5 and Article I, Sections 19 and 20 of the Indiana constitution (1851)

193 *State ex rel. Camden v. Gibson Circuit Court,* 640 N.E.2d 696, 697 (Ind. 1994)

194 *Utley v. State,* 281 N.E.2d 888, 889 (Ind. 1972)

195 *State ex rel. Camden v. Gibson Circuit Court,* 640 N.E.2d 696, 697 (Ind. 1994)

196 *Utley v. State,* 281 N.E.2d 888, 889 (Ind. 1972)

197 *Payne v. Tennessee*, 501 U.S. 808, 824 (1991)

198 *Millers Nat. Ins. Co. v. American State Bank of East Chicago*, 190 N.E. 433, 435 (1939)

199 *State ex rel. Camden v. Gibson Circuit Court,* 640 N.E.2d 696, 697 (Ind. 1994)

200 *Utley v. State,* 281 N.E.2d 888, 889 (Ind. 1972)

201 *State ex rel. Camden v. Gibson Circuit Court*, 640 N.E.2d 696, 697 (Ind. 1994)

202 See IC 16-42-20-4(a)(4)

203 Tort, *Black's Law Dictionary, 5th Edition*, p. 1335

204 See IC 33-28-1-2 and IC 33-29-1-1.5

205 Article VII, Section 1 Indiana constitution

206 Prescribe, *Black's Law Dictionary, 5th Edition*, p. 1065

207 *McCulloch v. Maryland*, 4 Wheat 418, 429 (1819)

208 *id.*

209 *Hook v. State*, 775 N.E.2d 1125, 1127 (Ind.App. 2002), *trans. denied* 783 N.E.2d 704 (2002)

210 Original jurisdiction, *Black's Law Dictionary, 5th Edition*, p. 991

211 *St. Angelo v. State of Indiana,* In the Court of Appeals of Indiana, re: 51A01-1105-IF-00189, http://www.ai.org/judiciary/opinions/pdf/08161112jsk.pdf

212 Article I, Section 1 Indiana constitution (1816)

213 Article I, Section 37 Indiana constitution (1851)

214 Article I, Section 1 Indiana constitution (1816)

215 *constitutional vandalism* used by George Will, Special Report, Fox News, August 4, 2015

216 Emmerich de Vattel, *The Law of Nations, or The Principles of the Law of Nature Applied to Nations and Sovereigns*, Book 1, Chapter IXX, Section 212, HTML version, Constitution Society http://www.constitution.org/vattel/vattel.htm

217 *id.*

218 *id.*

219 *id.* at Book 1, Chapter IXX, Section 214

220 Naturalization, *A Law Dictionary* by John Bouvier, Revised 6th Edition, 1856, Constitution Society http://www.constitution.org/bouv/bouvier.htm

221 Naturalized citizen, *A Law Dictionary* by John Bouvier, Revised 6th Edition, 1856, Constitution Society http://www.constitution.org/bouv/bouvier.htm

222 *Minor v. Happersett*, 88 U.S. 162 (1875)

223 *id.* at 170

224 *id.* at 167

225 *id.*

226 Naturalized citizen, *A Law Dictionary* by John Bouvier, *Revised 6th Edition, 1856, Constitution Society http://www.constitution.org/bouv/bouvier.htm*

227 Emmerich de Vattel, *The Law of Nations, or The Principles of the Law of Nature Applied to Nations and Sovereigns*, Book 1, Chapter IXX, Section 212, HTML version, Constitution Society http://www.constitution.org/vattel/vattel.htm

Endnotes

228 *id.*

229 8 USC 1409(a)

230 http://en.wikipedia.org/wiki/Birth_registration_in_Ancient_Rome

231 *Tuan Anh Nguyen and Joseph Boulais v. INS*, 533 U.S. 53 (2001)

232 *id.* at 60

233 *id.* at 58-59

234 *id.* at 64

235 *id.* at 73

236 *id.*

237 *Yick Wo v. Hopkins*, 118 U.S. 356, 370 (1886)

238 Oyez / Scholars, Chicago Kent College of Law at Illinois Tech,
     http://www.oyez.org/cases/2000-2009/2000/2000_99_2071

239 Article II, Section 1 U.S. constitution

240 See http://www.us-immigration.com/certificate-of-citizenship-N-600.jsp,
     http://www.uscis.gov/sites/default/files/files/form/n-600instr.pdf

241 Paul Guthrie is author of *DEMONIC POSITIVISM Versus The Science of "natural born
     citizen"* (ISBN 9781511911818)

242 *Obergefell v. Hodges, Director, Ohio Department of Health* (2015)
     http://www.supremecourt.gov/opinions/14pdf/14-556_3204.pdf

243 I realized this on February 28, 2015.

244 Emmerich de Vattel, *The Law of Nations, or The Principles of the Law of Nature
     Applied to Nations and Sovereigns*, Book 1, Chapter IXX, Section 215, HTML version,
     Constitution Society http://www.constitution.org/vattel/vattel.htm

245 Article II, Section 1, Clause 5 U.S. constitution

246 Article I, Section 9, Clause 8 U.S. constitution

247 Jurisprudence, *Black's Law Dictionary, 5th Edition*, p. 787

248 *id.*

249 *Obergefell v. Hodges, Director, Ohio Department of Health* (2015)
     http://www.supremecourt.gov/opinions/14pdf/14-556_3204.pdf

250 Article I, Section 9, Clause 8 U.S. constitution

251 Citizenship was first explained to me by Paul Guthrie, author of *Demonic Positivism
     Versus The Science of "natural born citizen"* (ISBN 9781511911818)

252 *Steinkauler's Case*, 15 Op.Atty.Gen 15 (circa 1875)

253 *Perkins v. Elg* 307 U.S. 325 (1939)

254 *id.* at *330*

255 *id.* citing *Steinkauler's Case*, 15 Op.Atty.Gen 15 (circa 1875)

256 *id.* at 339-340

257 See the preamble of 22 USC 7101

258 13th Amendment U.S. constitution

259 *id.*

260 Jane Hedeen, *The Road to Prohibition in Indiana*, Indiana Historical Society, 2011
     http://www.indianahistory.org/teachers-students/plan-a-field-trip/Prohibition%20Essay

261 *Beebe v. State*, 6 Indiana 501 (1855)

262 *id.* at 503-504

263 *id.* at 523

264 *Beebe v. State*, 6 Indiana 501, 519 (1855)

265 *Maybury v. Madison*, 1 Cranch 137, 5 U.S. 137 (1803)

266 *O'Daily v. State*, 9 Ind 494 (1857)

267 *Connell v. State*, 11 Ind. 491 (1858)

268 *Beebe v. State*, 6 Indiana 501, 505 (1855)

269 *id.*

Endnotes

270 *id.* at 519

271 *Andrews v. Russell,* 7 Blackf. 474, 477 (1845)

272 *Beebe v. State,* 6 Indiana 501, 508-509 (1855)

273 *id.* at 512

274 *id.* at 516

275 *id.* at 519

276 *id.* at 501-502

277 *id.* at 521

278 *id.* at 510

279 *id.* at 514

280 *Maybury v. Madison,* 1 Cranch 137, 5 U.S. 137 (1803)

281 *Beebe v. State,* 6 Indiana 501, 516 (1855)

282 *id.* at 517

283 Jane Hedeen, *The Road to Prohibition in Indiana,* Indiana Historical Society, 2011
http://www.indianahistory.org/teachers-students/plan-a-field-trip/Prohibition%20Essay

284 *id.* at p. 4

285 *id.*

286 *Beebe v. State,* 6 Indiana 501, 518 (1855)

287 *Schick v. United States* 195 U.S. 65 (1904)

288 *District of Columbia v. Colts,* 282 U.S. 63 (1930)

289 *District of Columbia v. Clawans,* 300 U.S. 617 (1937)

290 *Morrison v. Sadler* , 821 N.E.2d 15, Footnote 15 (Ind.Ct.App. 2005), citing *Schmitt v. F.W. Cook Brewing Co.,* 187 Ind. 623, 120 N.E. 19 (1918)

291 Ian Frazier, *Family* (New York: Farrar Straus Giroux, 1994) p. 188 - 189

292 *id.*

293 See IC 16-42-20-4(a)(4)

294 See IC 16-42-20-3, 21 USC 882(a)

295 See IC 35-48-3-3(i), 21 USC 882(b)

296 Politics, *Black's Law Dictionary, 5th Edition,* p. 1043

297 Jurisprudence, *Black's Law Dictionary, 5th Edition,* p. 767

298 *McCulloch v. Maryland,* 4 Wheat 418, 429 (1819)

299 Preamble to 22 U.S.C. 7101

300 *Yick Wo v. Hopkins,* 118 U.S. 356, 370 (1886)

301 *id.*

302 Politics, *Black's Law Dictionary, 5th Edition,* p. 1043

303 See IC 35-48-3-3(e)(3) with IC 35-48-1-27 and 21 USC 822(c) with 21 USC 802(27); see also 21 USC 841(a)

304 *Hooven & Allison Co. v. Evatt,* 324 U.S. 652 (1945) and *Palmore v. United States* 411 U.S. 389 (1973)

305 *Yick Wo v. Hopkins,* 118 U.S. 356, 370 (1886)

306 21 USC 841 – 844A

307 See IC 35-48-3-3(e)(3), 21 USC 822(c) and 21 USC 844(a)

308 *Texas Legislative Council Drafting Manual* (Austin, Texas: Texas Legislative Council, August 2014) p. 15, http://www.tlc.state.tx.us/legal/dm/draftingmanual.pdf

309 *id.*

310 *id.*

311 *id.*

312 I say "mostly" because I continue to have epiphanies in understanding the law. One came on November 14, 2013, when I realized that the executive branch of the U.S. government was falsely enforcing criminal power within the states, which Congress had

legislated for the federal areas.

313 It was not until November 30, 2014 that I realized that, other than roughly eleven criminal law provisions in the Indiana CSA, the entire rest of the act operates in non-criminal equity.

314 *Beebe v. State,* 6 Ind. 501 (1855)

315 Article I, Section 11 Indiana constitution (1816), Article I, Section 12 Indiana constitution (1851)

316 *Hook v. State,* 775 N.E.2d 1125, 1127 (Ind.App. 2002), *trans. denied* 783 N.E.2d 704 (2002)

317 Ironically, my former sister-in-law Sara New St. Angelo was on the Indiana State Board of Pharmacy for many years, twice presiding as President. Because Sara passed away in late 2014, I was unable to share the information in this book with her.

318 21 USC 822

319 See IC 16-42-20-5, IC 34-24-1-3(a) and IC 35-48-3-3(i)

320 IC 33-28-1-2 and IC 33-29-1-1.5

321 21 USC 853

322 See 21 USC 841-844A

323 See 21 USC 881

324 IC 35-48-1-20, 21 USC Section 802(17).

325 IC 35-48-1-26

326 See IC 35-48-3-3(e) and 21 USC 822(c)

327 Article I, Section 1 Indiana constitution (1816)

328 See IC 16-42-20-2(a) and IC 16-18-2-78

329 IC 16-42-20-1(a)

330 16-42-20-5

331 Probable cause, *Black's Law Dictionary, 5th Edition,* p. 1081

332 See IC 16-42-20-2(a) and IC 16-18-2-78

333 IC 16-42-2-2(b)(4)(E)

334 IC 16 42-20-2(c)(2)

335 IC 16-42-20-2(b)(6)

336 IC 34-24-1-3

337 IC 4-21.5-3-5

338 IC 4-21.5-3-7

339 IC 35-48-3-3(i)

340 I realized this on September 11, 2012.

341 *Gonzales v. Raich,* 545 U.S. 1, __ (2005)

342 *LHT Capital, LLC v. Indiana Horse Racing Comm'n,* 891 N.E.2d 646, 652 (Ind. App. 2008) citing *Johnson v. Celebration Fireworks, Inc.,* 829 N.E.2d 979, 984 (Ind. 2005)

343 *Sun Life Assurance Company of Canada v. Indiana Comprehensive Health Insurance,* 827 N.E.2d 1206, 1208 (Ind. App. 2005) citing *M-Plan, Inc. v. Indiana Comprehensive Health Insurance Association,* 809 N.E.2d 834, 837 (Ind. 2004); trans den *Sun Life Assurance Company of Canada v. Indiana Comprehensive Health Insurance Association,* 841 N.E.2d 186 (Ind. 2005)

344 *id.* citing *Save the Valley, Inc. v. Indiana Department of Environmental Management,* 724 N.E.2d 665, 668 (2000)

345 *Austin Lakes Joint Venture v. Avon Utilities, Inc.,* 648 N.E.2d 641, 645 (Ind. 1995)

346 *Title Service, LLC v. Womacks,* 848 N.E.2d 1151, 1155 (Ind. App. 2006)

347 *id.* citing *Romine v. Gagle,* 782 N.E.2d 369, 379 (Ind. App. 2003)

348 IC 4-21.5-2-1

349 IC 4-21.5-2-2

350 IC 4-21.5-5-4

Endnotes

351 See IC 4-21.5-2-1 and -2

352 *LHT Capital, LLC v. Indiana Horse Racing Comm'n,* 891 N.E.2d 646, 652 (Ind. App. 2008)

353 *Title Service, LLC v. Womacks,* 848 N.E.2d 1151, 1155 (Ind. App. 2006)

354 IC 35-48-3-3(e) and 21 USC 822(c)

355 Todd Garvey, *Medical Marijuana: The Supremacy Clause, Federalism, and the Interplay Between State and Federal Laws* (Washington, D.C.: Congressional Research Service, November 9, 2012), 7-5700, R42398
https://www.fas.org/sgp/crs/misc/R42398.pdf

356 *id.* Summary page

357 *id.*

358 *id.*

359 *Gonzales v. Raich,* 545 U.S. 1 (2005)

360 *Todd Garvey, Medical Marijuana: The Supremacy Clause, Federalism, and the Interplay Between State and Federal Laws* (Washington, D.C.: Congressional Research Service, November 9, 2012)*, 7-5700, R42398,* page 1,
https://www.fas.org/sgp/crs/misc/R42398.pdf

361 IC 35-48-3-3(e) and 21 USC 822(c)

362 Oyez / Scholars, IIT Chicago-Kent School of Law, http://www.oyez.org/cases/2000-2009/2004/2004_03_1454/

363 *id.*

364 *Ohio v. Helvering,* 292 U.S. 360, 369 (1934) citing *Rippe v. Becker,* 56 Minn. 100, 111, 57 N.W. 331 (1894)

365 *Champion v. Ames (Lottery Case),* 188 U.S. 321 (1903)

366 *id.* at 354

367 *id.* at 353

368 *id.* at 359

369 Article 1, Section 1 Indiana constitution (1816)

370 *Schick v. United States* 195 U.S. 65 (1904)

371 *Champion v. Ames (Lottery Case),* 188 U.S. 321 (1903)

372 *Bond v. United States,* 134 S.Ct. 2077, 2086; 189 L.Ed.2d 1 (2014) quoting *U.S. v. Fox,* 95 U.S. 670, 672 (1877)

373 *Ohio v. Helvering,* 292 U.S. 360, 369 (1934) citing *Rippe v. Becker,* 56 Minn. 100, 111, 57 N.W. 331 (1894)

374 *Champion v. Ames (Lottery Case),* 188 U.S. 321, 359 (1903)

375 *id.* at 364-365

376 *id.* at 365

377 *License Cases.* 5 Jpw/ 504, 46 U.S. 600 (1847)

378 *United States v. E. C. Knight Company,* 156 U. S. 1, 13 (1894)

379 *Champion v. Ames (Lottery Case),* 188 U.S. 321, 366 (1903)

380 Act of Congress of March 2, 1895, c. 191 at 28 Stat. 963., Section 1

381 *Champion v. Ames (Lottery Case),* 188 U.S. 321, 359 (1903)

382 See IC 4-21.5-5, IC 4-21.5-6, and 21 USC 877

383 IC 4-21.5-3-4

384 Michael J. Lewis, *DEA Update on Regulations and Enforcement,* Diversion Program Manager, Los Angeles Field Division, U.S. Department of Justice, Drug Enforcement Administration, Office of Diversion Control, page 41;
http://www.nabp.net/events/assets/Lewis.pdf

385 *id.*

386 See Article I, Section 12 Indiana constitution (1851)

Endnotes

387 IC 16-42-20-4, 21 USC 873(a)

388 *Beebe v. State,* 6 Ind. 501, 508-509 (1855)

389 *Beebe v. State,* 6 Ind. 501, 512 (1855) quoting *Arrowsmith v. Burlingim,* 4 McLean 489, 1 Amer. Law J.(N.S.) 448 (Circuit Court, D. Illinois, 1848)

390 *id.*

391 IC 35-48-3-3(e)

392 *Hooven & Allison Co. v. Evatt,* 324 U.S. 652, 674 (1945)

393 I came to this conclusion on April 2, 2015.

394 *Palmore v. United States* 411 U.S. 389, 416 (1973) citing *O'Donoghue v. United States,* 289 U.S. 516, 546 (1933)

395 *Schick v. United States,* 195 U.S. 65, 67-68 (1904)

396 *District of Columbia v. Colts,* 282 U.S. 63, 72-73 (1930)

397 *District of Columbia v. Clawans,* 300 U.S. 617, 625 (1937)

398 Article I, Section 1 Indiana constitution (1816)

399 IC 35-48-3-3(e), IC 35-48-1-27, 21 USC 822(c), 21 USC 902(27) and 21 USC 844(a)

400 *Gonzales v. Raich,* 545 U.S. 1 (2005)

401 *id.* at 17 citing *Perez v. United States,* 402 U.S. 146, 151 (1971)

402 *id.* quoting *Wickard v. Filburn,* 317 U.S. 111, 128-129 (1942)

403 *id.* citing *Perez v. United States,* 402 U.S. 146, 154-155 (1971)

404 Sir William Blackstone, *Commentaries on the Laws of England* (1752) ed. George Sharswood (Philadelphia: J.B. Lippincott, 1893), part 1, Book I, p. 40-42

405 *Schick v. United States,* 195 U.S. 65, 67-68 (1904)

406 *District of Columbia v. Colts,* 282 U.S. 63, 72-73 (1930)

407 *District of Columbia v. Clawans,* 300 U.S. 617, 625 (1937)

408 *Palmore v. United States, 411 U.S. 389, 393 (1973)* quoting *Palmore v. United States,* 290 A.2d 573, 576-577 (1972)

409 *Ohio v. Helvering,* 292 U.S. 360, 369 (1934) citing *Rippe v. Becker,* 56 Minn. 100, 111, 57 N.W. 331 (1894)

410 IC 35-31.5-2-217

411 *Gonzales v. Raich,* 545 U.S. 1 (2005)

412 See, for example, 21 USC 824(f), 853, 863, 881 and 888

413 *Gonzales v. Raich,* 545 U.S. 1, 17 (2005)

414 *id.* citing *Wickard v. Filburn,* 317 U.S. 111, 127-128 (1942)

415 Article I, Section 8, Clause 3 U.S. constitution

416 *Geofroy v. Riggs* 133 U.S. 258, 267 (1890)

417 *id.*

418 *Holden v. Joy,* 84 U.S. (17 Wall.) 211, 242 (1872)

419 *id.*

420 *Mayor of New Orleans v. United States,* 35 U.S. (10 Pet.) 662, 736 (1836)

421 *Gonzales v. Raich,* 545 U.S. 1, 17 (2005) citing *Perez v. United States,* 402 U.S. 146, 154 – 155 (1971)

422 *id.*

423 *Truax v. Corrigan,* 257 US 312, 336 (1921)

424 *Corpus Juris Secundum,* Constitutional Law ¶ 890

425 *id.*

426 *Ohio v. Helvering,* 292 U.S. 360, 369 (1934) citing *Rippe v. Becker,* 56 Minn. 100, 111, 57 N.W. 331 (1894)

427 *Bond v. United States* 134 S.Ct. 2077, 2086, 189 L.Ed.2d (2014)

428 See the 5th and 14th Amendments

429 21 USC 822(a)

430 *Jurisdiction Over Federal Areas Within The States, Report of the Interdepartmental*

Endnotes

Committee for the Study of Jurisdiction Over Federal Areas Within the States, April 1956, Part I, p. 45-46

431 21 USC 873

432 *Gonzales v. Raich*, 545 U.S. 1 (2005)

433 See 18 USC 7

434 This is the last substantive task I did for this book, between March 3 - 6, 2015.

435 Arrest Warrant, *U.S. v. Robert Villareal*, 1:11MJ170A, U.S. District Court for the District of Rhode Island, August 3, 2011 https://wrnihealthcareblog.files.wordpress.com/2011/08/villarreal-menissian-affidavit.pdf

436 *United States v. Fox*, 95 U.S. 670, 672 (1878)

437 *Bond v. United States* 134 S.Ct. 2077, 2086, 189 L.Ed.2d 1 (2014)

438 Indictment, *U.S. v. FedEx Corp., et al.*, CR 14 380, United States District Court for the Northern District of California, July 17, 2014, http://www.justice.gov/sites/default/files/usao-ndca/legacy/2014/07/17/FedEx %20Indictment%20-%20July%2017,%202014.pdf

439 Matt Apuzzo and Ben Protess, "Justice Department Sets Sights on Wall Street Executives," New York Times online, September 9, 2015 http://www.nytimes.com/2015/09/10/us/politics/new-justice-dept-rules-aimed-at-prosecuting-corporate-executives.html

440 Indictment, *U.S. v. Licciardi*, U.S. District Court for the Eastern District of Louisiana, 2014, http://www.justice.gov/sites/default/files/usao-edla/press-releases/attachments/2014/12/12/sharper_darren_liccardi_brandon_ind.pdf

441 *Bond v. United States* 134 S.Ct. 2077, 2086, 189 L.Ed.2d 1 (2014)

442 *U.S. v. Fox*, 95 U.S. 670, 672 (1877)

443 Indictment, *United States v. Tyler*, U.S. District Court for the Eastern District of Louisiana, 2014, http://www.justice.gov/sites/default/files/usao-edla/legacy/2013/05/17/indictment_Tyler_%26_Stevenson.pdf

444 Indictment, *United States v. Acevedo*, U.S. District Court for the Eastern District of Pennsylvania, circa 2011, http://www.justice.gov/archive/usao/pae/News/2010/Jun/acevedo,j_indictment.pdf

445 Indictment, *United States v. Brenes*, Case 14-20551, U.S. District Court for the Southern District of Florida, 2014, http://www.dea.gov/divisions/mia/2014/mia080514-brenes-indictment.pdf

446 Superseding Indictment, *United States v. Barba*, 3:08-cr-46, U.S. District Court of the Eastern District of Tennessee, September 26, 2008, http://media.graytvinc.com/documents/Indictment+1.pdf

447 Indictment, *United States v. Melendrez*, A12CR 101 SS, U.S. District Court of the Western District of Texas, March 20, 2012, http://content.austin.ynn.com/auscontent/DTclubs.pdf

448 *Bond v. United States 134 S.Ct. 2077, 2086, 189 L.Ed.2d 1 (2014)* quoting *U.S. v. Fox*, 95 U.S. 670, 672 (1877)

449 Criminal Complaint, *United States v. Herndon et al.* U.S. District Court in the Northern District of Illinois, Eastern Division, August 6, 2014, http://dig.abclocal.go.com/wls/documents/Herndon%20Complaint.pdf

450 Indictment, *United States v. Gandara*, EP08CR3355, U.S. District Court for the Western District of Texas, El Paso Division, 2008, https://www.vpc.org/texas/TXGandaraIndictment081210.pdf

451 See 21 USC 952

452 Indictment, *United States v. Avila et al.*, CR'11 – 126 PHX JAT (LOA), U.S. District Court for the District of Arizona, January 19, 2011

453 Indictment, *United States v. Mosley et. al.*, U.S. District Court for the Eastern District of

Endnotes

Pennsylvania, October 22, 2014, http://www.justice.gov/sites/default/files/usao-edpa/legacy/2014/10/22/Indictment%20-%20Church,Mosley.pdf

454 Indictment, *United States v. Mills et al.*, U.S. District Court for the Eastern District of Pennsylvania, October 22, 2014, http://www.justice.gov/sites/default/files/usao-edpa/legacy/2014/10/22/Indictment%20-%20Church,Millsetal.pdf

455 Indictment, *United States v. Church et al.*, U.S. District Court for the Eastern District of Pennsylvania, October 22, 2014, http://www.justice.gov/sites/default/files/usao-edpa/legacy/2014/10/22/Indictment%20-%20Church,Womack.pdf

456 Indictment, *United States v. Potter et al.*, U.S. District Court for the Eastern District of Pennsylvania, October 22, 2014, http://www.justice.gov/sites/default/files/usao-edpa/legacy/2014/10/22/Indictment%20-%20Church,Potter.pdf

457 Stephenson, G. R. (1967). *Cultural acquisition of a specific learned response among rhesus monkeys*. In: Starek, D., Schneider, R., and Kuhn, H. J. (eds.), *Progress in Primatology*, Stuttgart: Fischer, pp. 279-288.

458 Misrepresentation, *Black's Law Dictionary, 5th Edition*, p. 903

459 Fraud, *Black's Law Dictionary, 5th Edition*, p. 594

460 IC 35-41-2-2

461 Culpability, *Black's Law Dictionary, 5th Edition*, p. 341

462 Cause in fact, *Black's Law Dictionary, 5th Edition*, p. 201

463 Proximate cause, *Black's Law Dictionary, 5th Edition*, p. 1103

464 21 USC 841 – 843

465 *Hooven & Allison Co. v. Evatt,* 324 U.S. 652, 674 (1945)

466 I realized this on November 14, 2013

467 This is an expression made known by libertarian activist Michael Cloud

468 *State of Indiana v. Wann*, Hendrick's Superior Court, 32D04-0905-CM-228 (2012), see also *Wann v. State of Indiana*, 32A01-1303-CR-123 (2013), http://www.in.gov/judiciary/opinions/pdf/11051301.lmb.pdf

469 IC 35-31.5-2-217

470 *Ohio v. Helvering,* 292 U.S. 360, 369 (1934) citing *Rippe v. Becker,* 56 Minn. 100, 111, 57 N.W. 331 (1894)

471 *Yick Wo v. Hopkins,* 118 U.S. 356, 370 (1886)

472 Harold E. Pepinsky, *The Geometry of Violence and Democracy* (Bloomington, Indiana: Indiana University Press, 1991) p. 28

473 *id.*, p. 15

474 *id.*, p. 9

475 *id.*, p. 8

476 *id.*, p. 8

477 *id.*, p. 9

478 Stephenson, G. R. (1967). *Cultural acquisition of a specific learned response among rhesus monkeys*. In: Starek, D., Schneider, R., and Kuhn, H. J. (eds.), *Progress in Primatology*, Stuttgart: Fischer, pp. 279-288

479 *Welcome to the Monkey House* by Kurt Vonnegut, Jr. (1968)

480 Corpus delicti, *Black's Law Dictionary, 5th Edition*, p. 310

481 *Yick Wo v. Hopkins,* 118 U.S. 356, 370 (1886)

482 My Supreme Court brief in *St. Angelo v. State of Indiana* (2012) is also available to read at http://cocklelegalbriefs.com/wp-content/uploads/2012/04/26255-pdf-St.-Angelo.pdf

483 I realized this on March 16, 2015.

484 *Gallup v. Schmidt,* 56 N.E. 443, 445 (Ind. 1900), *aff'd,* 183 U.S. 300 (1902)

485 *Dailey Oil, Inc. v. Jet Star, Inc.,* 650 N.E.2d 345, 346 (Ind.App. 1995)

486 IC 35-48-3-3(i)

Endnotes

487 IC 33-33-51-1(b), IC 33-28-3-2(b), and IC 33-28-3-8(a)

488 *Beebe v. State,* 6 Ind. 501 (1855)

489 *The American Historical Review,* vol. 11, 1906, p. 618 and *The Records of the Federal Convention of 1787,* ed. Max Farrand, vol. 3, appendix A, p. 85 (1911, reprinted 1934)

490 Article I, Section 9, Clause 8 U.S. constitution

491 *Beebe v. State,* 6 Ind. 501 (1855)

492 *id.*

493 *id.*

494 *id.*

www.ingramcontent.com/pod-product-compliance
Lightning Source LLC
Chambersburg PA
CBHW061126210326
41518CB00034B/2502